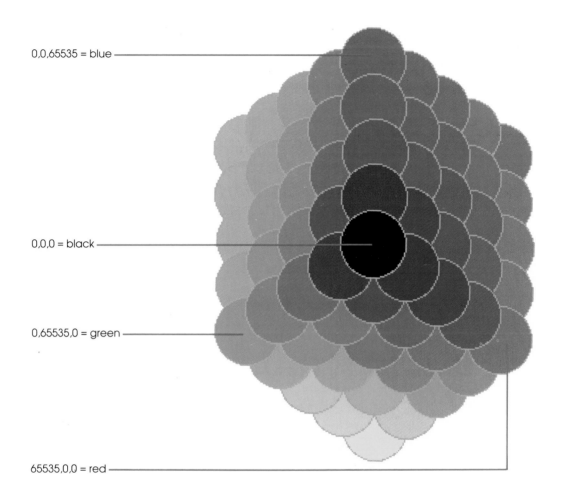

0,0,65535 = blue

0,0,0 = black

0,65535,0 = green

65535,0,0 = red

65535,65535,65535 = white

RGB Color Cube (see page V-43)

Color art was created on a Macintosh II computer and an AppleColor™ high-resolution RGB monitor using Modern Artist™ software by Computer Friends, Inc. Final color prints were produced by ColorSet™ from ImageSet™ Corporation.

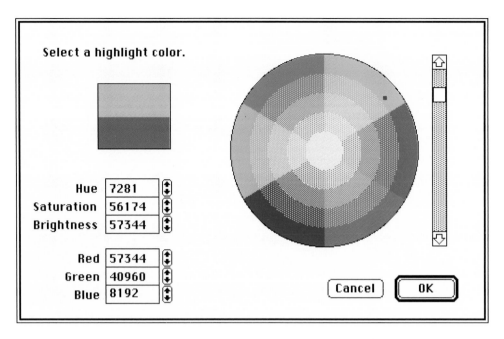

Color Picker Dialog Box (see page V-173)

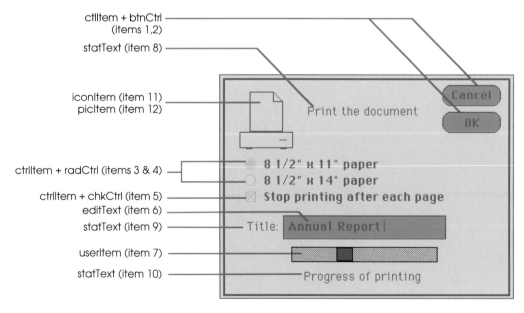

ctlItem + btnCtrl
(items 1,2)

statText (item 8)

iconItem (item 11)
picItem (item 12)

ctrlItem + radCtrl (items 3 & 4)

ctrlItem + chkCtrl (item 5)
editText (item 6)
statText (item 9)

userItem (item 7)

statText (item 10)

Sample Dialog with Color Dialog Items (see page V-282)

Inside Macintosh™
Volume V

Addison-Wesley Publishing Company, Inc.

Reading, Massachusetts Menlo Park, California Don Mills, Ontario Wokingham, England
Amsterdam Sydney Singapore Tokyo Madrid Bogotá Santiago San Juan

ISBN 0-201-17719-6
CDEFGHIJ-MU-898
Third Printing, May 1988

Inside Macintosh
Volume V

PREFACE

Reader's guide: Read this preface first, before you go on to the rest of the book. It contains important general information that will save you time and help you understand the material that follows.

ABOUT INSIDE MACINTOSH VOLUME V

The first three volumes of *Inside Macintosh* provided information that everyone needs to write software for any of the Apple® Macintosh™ family of computers. Volume IV provided additional information specific to the Macintosh Plus and Macintosh 512K enhanced models. This book, Volume V, presents new material specific to the Macintosh SE and Macintosh II computers. Familiarity with the material presented in the first four volumes is assumed, since most of the information presented in Volume V consists of changes and additions to that original material.

As in Volume IV, many of the chapters in the first three volumes have a corresponding chapter in Volume V describing new routines, modified data structures, additional error codes, and so on. Other chapters describe entirely new parts of the Macintosh toolbox and operating system.

This volume introduces **reader's guides.** They are notes that stand out from the text, usually placed at the beginning of a chapter or section. Reader's guides help you decide whether you need to understand the succeeding material. There is one at the beginning of this preface.

WHAT'S NEW?

The Macintosh II and Macintosh SE computers both contain new capabilities not present in earlier Macintosh models. They include:

- Sophisticated sound. Your application can now generate sophisticated music and sound effects, using special resource types.

- Enhanced menus. The Macintosh Toolbox now supports hierarchical, scrolling, and pop-up menus.

- More flexible text. Your application can now determine the font, size, style, and color of text on a character-by-character basis.

- More powerful AppleTalk® networking system. A number of new features give AppleTalk added capabilities as a network interface.

- International localization. Your application can now write and edit scripts such as Japanese and Arabic, as well as handle accented characters and European date and time formats.

- New keyboards. The Macintosh SE and Macintosh II accept a variety of plug-in keyboards and let your application determine their key assignments.

- Custom control panel. Your application can now customize the Macintosh control panel.

In addition, the Macintosh II alone supports these new features:

- Color. Your application can determine whether or not the Macintosh II user has a video card and screen that displays in color. If the required equipment is present, your application can add color to menus, windows, controls, dialogs, text, and graphic objects.

- Slot cards. The Macintosh II accepts plug-in cards that can support peripherals such as video displays, data storage devices, communication equipment, and additional processors.

- Multiple displays. With the Macintosh II, multiple monitors may now display different parts of the QuickDraw drawing space.

- Different addressing modes. The Macintosh II supports both 24-bit and 32-bit addressing modes.

THE MATERIAL IN THIS VOLUME

Most programmers will never need to read all the material in this book. While some chapters are of general interest, others are written only for programmers who are doing specialized tasks. Many chapters begin with reader's guides, which help you determine in advance whether you need to read them.

The following is a summary of the contents of this volume, broken down by areas of interest.

New Features of General Interest

The following chapters cover new Macintosh features that most programmers will need to understand.

- Chapter 1, "Compatibility Guidelines", provides an overview of the new machines with an eye to the past and future. It tells how to write code that can determine what features are available on a given machine, gives guidelines for writing software that will run on the entire Macintosh family, and provides tips for writing software that can be easily modified for use in other countries.

- Chapter 2, "The Macintosh User Interface Guidelines", extends the philosophy set forth in Volumes I and IV. With the introduction of color graphics and slot devices, it's especially important that applications present the user with a consistent and reasoned interface.

- Chapter 3, "The Resource Manager", describes several new system resources available for your use.

- Chapter 4, "Color QuickDraw", tells you how to make QuickDraw calls in color. Unless your application uses color in a sophisticated way (for example, as a color drawing program), this chapter gives you all you need to know about adding color to the content area of the desktop.

- Chapter 11, "The Window Manager", tells you how to add color to windows.

- Chapter 12, "The Control Manager", explains how to specify colored controls.

- Chapter 13, "The Menu Manager", discusses the new hierarchical, scrolling, and pop-up menus, as well as describing how to add color to menus.

- Chapter 14, "TextEdit", describes how you can now determine the font, size, style, and color of text on a character-by-character basis.

- Chapter 15, "The Dialog Manager", tells you how to display dialog boxes in color.

Extensions and Enhancements

The following chapters list ways that features described in Volumes I, II, III, and IV have been extended or improved.

- Chapter 9, "The Font Manager", discusses new font handling features and clarifies some old features.

- Chapter 22, "The Printing Manager", lists new low-level printer controls.

- Chapter 26, "The Disk Driver", describes some new advanced control calls.

- Chapter 28, "The AppleTalk Manager", discusses many new enhancements to the AppleTalk network interface.

- Chapter 30, "The System Error Handler", lists new system error codes.

- Chapter 31, "The SCSI Manager", tells you how the SCSI Manager has been improved.

- Chapter 34, "The Floating-Point Arithmetic and Transcendental Functions Packages", describes briefly the role of the new MC68881 coprocessor in mathematical calculations.

Sophisticated Color Management

Two chapters give you basic information about using color.

- Chapter 4, "Color QuickDraw", gives you fundamental color theory and tells you how to add color information to QuickDraw calls.

- Chapter 7, "The Palette Manager", explains the facilities that help your application establish a working color environment.

If you are using color in a precise or sophisticated way, rather than as a simple enhancement for your application, you may need some of the information in two other chapters:

■ Chapter 6, "The Color Manager", lists the low-level calls that QuickDraw uses to manage the color responses of Macintosh II video cards. Applications seldom use these calls.

■ Chapter 8, "The Color Picker Package", describes the new standard interface for color selection by the user.

Using Multiple Displays

Two chapters in this volume discuss new facilities that allow an application to use more than one display screen.

■ Chapter 5, "Graphics Devices", tells you how to manage more than one output display.

■ Chapter 29, "The Vertical Retrace Manager", describes how vertical retrace tasks can be allocated among multiple display screens.

Slot Card Management

Three chapters in this volume describe the tools that manage plug-in cards in the NuBus slots of the Macintosh II. The Macintosh system normally handles all slot card management; hence most applications do not need to use these tools. The following chapters are of interest if your application needs to interrogate a slot card directly or change its operating mode.

■ Chapter 23, "The Device Manager", tells you how slot devices are installed and opened, as well as how corresponding changes to the Chooser are made.

■ Chapter 24, "The Slot Manager", explains how the system keeps track of slot resources.

■ Chapter 25, "The Deferred Task Manager", describes how tasks initiated by slot cards may be deferred until other tasks are completed.

In addition to this material, slot cards are thoroughly discussed in the separate Apple book *Designing Cards and Drivers for Macintosh II and Macintosh SE*.

International Localization

Two chapters in this volume help you write applications for use in foreign countries.

■ Chapter 16, "The International Utilities Package", describes new facilities for handling accented characters and European date and time formats.

■ Chapter 17, "The Script Manager", explains how applications can now handle text in such languages as Japanese and Arabic.

Sound Creation

Chapter 27, "The Sound Manager", discusses new facilities for creating music and other complex sound effects with the Macintosh.

Using Different Keyboards

Chapter 10, "The Toolbox Event Manager", describes new keyboards available for the Macintosh (including multiple keyboard configurations) and discusses how key layouts can be changed.

Calling the Operating System

The following chapters are addressed to programmers who need to write code that calls parts of the Macintosh operating system directly.

- Chapter 18, "The Control Panel", tells you how to customize the Control Panel.
- Chapter 19, "The Start Manager", describes how the Macintosh II and Macintosh SE start up.
- Chapter 20, "The Apple Desktop Bus", discusses the operation of the bus that connects the system to user input devices such as keyboards and the mouse.
- Chapter 21, "File Manager Extensions in a Shared Environment", explains the new routines that support file access in a shared environment.
- Chapter 32, "The Shutdown Manager", describes how the Macintosh II and Macintosh SE shut down.
- Chapter 33, "The Operating System Utilities", explains how to switch the Macintosh II between 24-bit and 32-bit addressing modes.

THE LANGUAGES

The routines described in this book are written in assembly language, but (with a few exceptions) they're also accessible from higher-level languages. The first four volumes of *Inside Macintosh* document the interfaces to these routines on the Lisa Workshop development system. A powerful new development system, the Macintosh Programmers Workshop (MPW), is now available. Volume V documents the MPW Pascal interfaces to the routines and the symbolic identifiers defined for assembly-language programmers using MPW. These identifiers are usually identical to their Lisa Workshop counterparts. If you're using a different development system, its documentation should tell you how to apply the information presented here to that system.

Inside Macintosh is intended to serve the needs of both high-level language and assembly-language programmers. Every routine is shown in its Pascal form (if it has one), but assembly-language programmers are told how they can access the routines. Information of interest only to assembly-language programmers is set apart and labeled so that other programmers can conveniently skip it.

Familiarity with MPW Pascal (or a similar high-level language) is recommended for all readers, since it's used for most examples. MPW Pascal is described in the documentation for the Macintosh Programmer's Workshop.

VERSION NUMBERS

This edition of *Inside Macintosh Volume V* describes the following version of the software:

- version 118 ($76) of the ROM in the Macintosh SE
- version 120 ($78) of the ROM in the Macintosh II
- version 2.0 of the MPW Pascal interfaces and the assembly-language definitions

Some of the RAM-based software is read from the file named System (usually kept in the System Folder). This manual describes the software in the System file version 4.1. In certain cases, a feature can be found in earlier versions of the System file; these cases are noted in the text.

CONVENTIONS

The following notations are used in Volume V to draw your attention to particular items of information:

Reader's guide: Advice to you, the reader, that will help you decide whether or not you need to understand the material in a specific chapter or section.

Note: An item of technical information that you may find interesting or useful.

Warning: A point you need to be cautious about.

Assembly-language note: Information of interest to assembly-language programmers only. For a discussion of Macintosh assembly-language programming, see the chapter "Using Assembly Language" in Volume I.

[Not in ROM]

Routines marked with the notation [Not in ROM] are not part of the Macintosh ROM. Depending on which System file the user has and on how complete the interfaces are in the development system you're using, these routines may or may not be available. They're available with Version 4.1 and later of the Macintosh System file and in programs developed with the Macintosh Programmer's Workshop.

[Macintosh II]

Routines marked with the name or names of specific models work only on those machines.

1   COMPATIBILITY GUIDELINES

ABOUT THIS CHAPTER

Compatibility is a concern for anyone writing software. For some programmers, it's a concern because they want to write software that will run, with little or no modification, on all versions of the Macintosh. Other programmers want to take advantage of particular software and hardware features; they need to know where and when these features are available.

This chapter gives guidelines for making it more likely that your program will run on different versions, present and future, of the Macintosh. It also gives tips for writing software that can be easily modified for use in other countries. Finally, it explains how to determine what features are available on a given machine.

COMPATIBILITY

The key to compatibility is not to depend on things that may change. *Inside Macintosh* contains hundreds of warnings where information is likely to change; all of these warnings can be summarized by a single rule: use global variable names and system calls, rather than addresses and numeric values.

At the most basic level, all of the software and hardware components of the Macintosh—each line of ROM code, each RAM memory location, each hardware device—are represented by numbers. Symbolic names have been defined for virtually every routine, variable, data structure, memory location, and hardware device that your application will need to use. Use of these names instead of the actual numbers will simplify the process of updating your application when the numbers change.

General Guidelines

Any field that's marked in *Inside Macintosh* as "not used" should be considered "reserved by Apple" and usually be left 0.

While *Inside Macintosh* gives the structure of low-level data structures (for instance, file control blocks, volume control blocks, and system queues), it's best not to access or manipulate these structures directly; whenever possible, use the routines provided for doing this.

You shouldn't rely on system resources being in RAM; on the Macintosh Plus, Macintosh SE, and Macintosh II, certain system resources are in ROM. Don't assume, for example, that you can regain RAM space by releasing system resources.

A variety of different keyboards are available for the Macintosh; you should always read ASCII codes rather than key codes.

Don't count on the alternate (page 2) sound or video buffers. On the Macintosh II, you can determine the number of video pages and switch between them; for details, see the Video Drivers chapter in this volume.

To be compatible with printers connected directly to the Macintosh or via AppleTalk, use either the Printing Manager or the Printer Driver's control calls for text-streaming and bitmap-printing (as documented in *Inside Macintosh*). Don't send ASCII codes directly to the Printer Driver. In general, you should avoid using printer-specific features and should not access the fields of the print record directly.

Memory

You shouldn't depend on either the system or application heap zones starting at certain addresses. Use the global variable ApplZone to find the application heap and the variable SysZone to locate the system heap. You should not count on the application heap zone starting at an address less than 65536; in other words, don't expect a system heap that's smaller than 64K in size.

Space in the system heap is extremely limited. In general, avoid using the system heap; if you must, allocate only very small objects (about 32 bytes or less). If you need memory that won't be reinitialized when your application ends, allocate it with an 'INIT' resource; for details, see the System Resource File chapter in Volume IV.

The high-order byte of a master pointer contains flags used by the Memory Manager. In the future, all 32 bits of the pointer may be needed, in which case the flags byte will have to be moved elsewhere. For this reason, you should never set or clear these flags directly but should instead use the Memory Manager routines HPurge, HNoPurge, HLock, HUnlock, HSetRBit, HClrRBit, HGetState, and HSetState.

You should allow for a variety of RAM memory sizes. While 128K, 512K, 1 MB, and 2 MB are standard sizes, many other RAM configurations are possible.

NIL handles (handles whose value is zero) are common bugs; they typically come from unsuccessful GetResource calls and often result (eventually) in address errors. The 68020 does not give address errors when accessing data, so be sure to test your code for NIL handles and null pointers.

Assembly Language

In general, you shouldn't use 68000 instructions that depend on supervisor mode; these include instructions that modify the contents of the Status Register (SR). Programmers typically modify the SR only as a means of changing the Condition Code Register (CCR) half of the register; an instruction that addresses the CCR directly will work fine instead. You should also not use the User Stack Pointer or turn interrupts on and off.

Timing loops that depend on the clock speed of a particular processor will fail when faster processors are introduced. You can use the Operating System Utility procedure Delay for timing, or you can check the contents of the global variable Ticks. For more precise timings, you can use the Time Manager (taking advantage of the VIA timers). Several global variables also contain useful timing information; they're described in the Start Manager chapter.

If you wish to handle your own exceptions (thereby relying on the position of data in the exception's local stack frame), be aware that exception stack frames vary within the 68000 family.

In particular, don't use the TRAP instruction. Also, the TAS instruction, which uses a special read-modify-write memory cycle, is not supported by the Macintosh SE and Macintosh II hardware.

A memory management unit in the Macintosh II may prevent code from writing to addresses within code segments. Also, the 68020 caches code as it's encountered. Your data blocks should be allocated on the stack or in heap blocks separate from the code, and your code should not modify itself.

> **Note:** You can determine which microprocessor is installed by calling the SysEnvirons function; it's described below.

The Floating-Point Arithmetic and Transcendental Functions Packages have been extended to take advantage of the MC68881 numerics coprocessor; using the routines in these packages will ensure compatibility on all current and future versions of the Macintosh. (For details on these packages, see the Floating-Point Arithmetic and Transcendental Functions Packages chapter in this volume.)

Memory locations below the system heap that aren't documented may not be available for use in future systems. Also, microprocessors in the 68000 family use the exception vectors in locations $0 through $FF in different ways. In general, don't depend on any global variable that isn't documented in *Inside Macintosh*.

Don't store information in the application parameters area (the 32 bytes between the application globals and the jump table); this space is reserved for use by Apple.

Don't depend on the format of the trap dispatch table. Use the Operating System Utility routines GetTrapAddress and SetTrapAddress to access the trap dispatch table. You should also not use unassigned entries in the trap table, or any other unused low memory location.

Inside Macintosh documents the values returned by register-based routines; don't depend on return values that aren't documented here.

Hardware

As a general rule, you should never address hardware directly; whenever possible, use the routines provided by the various device drivers. The addresses of memory-mapped hardware (like the VIA1, VIA2, SCC, and IWM) are always subject to change, and direct access to such hardware may not be possible. For instance, the Macintosh II memory-management unit may prevent access to memory-mapped hardware. If you must access the hardware directly, get the base address of the device from the appropriate global variable; see the *Macintosh Family Hardware Reference Manual* for details.

> **Warning**: Although there's a global variable that contains the SCSI base address, you should use the SCSI Manager; this is especially important with regard to asynchronous operation.

> **Note**: Copy-protection schemes that rely on particular hardware characteristics are subject to failure when the hardware changes.

You should avoid writing directly to the screen; use QuickDraw whenever possible. If you must write directly to the screen, don't "hard code" the screen size and location. The global variable ScreenBits contains a bit map corresponding to the screen being used. ScreenBits.bounds is the size of the screen, ScreenBits.baseAddr is the start of the screen, and ScreenBits.rowBytes gives the offset between rows.

> **Warning**: The screen size can exceed 32K; use long word values in screen calculations. Also, the screen may be more than one pixel in depth; see the QuickDraw chapter for details.

There are many sizes of disks for the Macintosh from Apple, and more from third-party vendors. Use the Standard File Package and File Manager calls to determine the number and size of disk drives.

DETERMINING THE FEATURES OF A MACHINE

As the Macintosh family grows, applications need a reliable and comprehensive way of determining what software and hardware features are available on a given machine. Although the Operating System Utilities routine Environs indicates the type of machine and ROM version running, it provides no help in distinguishing between the plethora of different software feature sets and hardware configurations that an application may encounter.

A new function, SysEnvirons, provides detailed information about what software functionality (Color QuickDraw, as an example) is available, as well as what hardware devices (processors, peripherals, and so on) are installed or connected.

All of the Toolbox Managers must be initialized before calling SysEnvirons. In addition, the AppleTalk Manager routine MPPOpen must be called if the driver version information in atDrvrVersNum is desired. SysEnvirons is not intended for use by device drivers, but can be called from desk accessories. (It does not assume that register A5 has been properly set up.)

```
FUNCTION SysEnvirons (versReqested: INTEGER; VAR theWorld:
        SysEnvRecPtr) : OSErr;   [Not in ROM]
```

Trap macro	_SysEnvirons
On entry	A0: sysEnvRecPtr (pointer)
	D0: versReqested (word)
On exit	A0: sysEnvRecPtr (pointer)
	D0: result code (word)

Result codes	noErr	No error
	envNotPresent	SysEnvirons trap not present
	envBadVers	Nonpositive version number passed
	envVersTooBig	Requested version of SysEnvirons call not available

In theWorld, SysEnvirons returns a pointer to a **system environment record** describing the features of the machine. Designed to be extendible, SysEnvirons will be updated as new features are added, and the system environment record that's returned will be expanded. System File 4.1 contains version 1 of SysEnvirons; subsequent versions will be incremented by 1.

The system environment record for version 1 of SysEnvirons contains the following fields:

```
TYPE  SysEnvRec = RECORD
                environsVersion:  INTEGER;
                machineType:      INTEGER;
                systemVersion:    INTEGER;
                processor:        INTEGER;
                hasFPU:           BOOLEAN;
                hasColorQD:       BOOLEAN;
                keyBoardType:     INTEGER;
                atDrvrVersNum:    INTEGER;
                sysVRefNum:       INTEGER
            END;

      SysEnvPtr =    ^SysEnvRec;
```

New versions of the call will add fields to this record. To distinguish between different versions of the call, and thereby between the different sizes of records they return, SysEnvirons returns its version number in the environsVersion field. If you request version 2, for instance, but only version 1 is available, the environsVersion field will contain the value 1, and the result code envVersTooBig will be returned. This tells you that only the information for version 1 has been returned in SysEnvRec.

The MPW 2.0 interface files contain code, or "glue", for System file versions earlier than 4.1, as well as for the 64K and the Macintosh XL ROMs. The glue checks for the existence of the trap at runtime; if the call does not exist, the glue fills in all fields of the record except systemVersion and returns the result code envNotPresent.

Assembly-language note: As with the MoveHHi procedure, assembly-language programmers using MPW should link with the glue and execute

```
JSR SysEnvirons
```

If you're using another development system, refer to its documentation for details.

The machineType field returns one of the following constants:

```
CONST envMachUnknown = 0;   {new version of Macintosh--not covered }
                            { by this version of SysEnvirons}
      env512KE       = 1;   {Macintosh 512K enhanced}
      envMacPlus     = 2;   {Macintosh Plus}
      envSE          = 3;   {Macintosh SE}
      envMacII       = 4;   {Macintosh II}
```

In addition to these, the glue for SysEnvirons may return one of the following:

```
CONST envMac = -1; {Macintosh with 64K ROM}
      envXL  = -2; {Macintosh XL}
```

The systemVersion field returns the version number of the System file represented as two byte-long numbers, separated by a period. (It is *not* a fixed point number.) For instance, System 4.1 returns $0410 or 04.10 in this field. (Applications can use this for compare operations.) If SysEnvirons is called while a system earlier than System 4.1 is running, the glue will return a $0 in this field, and the result code envNotPresent will be returned.

The processor field returns one of the following constants:

```
CONST envCPUUnknown = 0;   {new processor--not yet covered by this }
                           { version of SysEnvirons}
      env68000      = 1;   {MC68000 processor}
      env68010      = 2;   {MC68010 processor}
      env68020      = 3;   {MC68020 processor}
```

The hasFPU field tells whether or not a Motorola MC68881 floating-point coprocessor unit is present. (This field does not apply to third-party memory-mapped coprocessor add-ons.)

The hasColorQD field tells whether or not Color QuickDraw is present. It does not indicate whether or not a color screen is present (high-level QuickDraw calls provide this information).

The keyboardType field returns one of the following constants:

```
CONST envUnknownKbd = 0;   {Macintosh Plus keyboard with keypad}
      envMacKbd     = 1;   {Macintosh keyboard}
      envMacAndPad  = 2;   {Macintosh keyboard and keypad}
      envMacPlusKbd = 3;   {Macintosh Plus keyboard}
      envAExtendKbd = 4;   {Apple extended keyboard}
      envStandADBKbd = 5;  {standard Apple Desktop Bus keyboard}
```

If the Apple Desktop Bus™ is in use, this field returns the keyboard type of the keyboard on which a keystroke was last made.

ATDrvrVersNum returns the version number of AppleTalk, if it's been loaded (that is, if MPPOpen has been called); otherwise, 0 is returned in this field.

SysVRefNum returns the working directory reference number (or volume reference number) of the directory that contains the currently open System file.

LOCALIZATION

Localization is the process of adapting an application to a specific language and country. By making localization relatively painless, you ensure that international markets are available for your product in the future. You also allow English-speaking users in other countries to buy the U.S. English version of your software and use it with their native languages.

The key to easy localization is to store the country-dependent information used by your application as resources (rather than within the application's code). This means that text seen by the user can be translated without modifying the code. In addition, storing this information in resources means that your application can be adapted for a different country simply by substituting the appropriate resources.

¿Pero, Se Habla Español?

Not all languages have the same rules for punctuation, word order, and alphabetizing. In Spanish, questions begin with an upside-down question mark. The roles of commas and periods in numbers are sometimes the reverse of what you may be used to; in many countries, for instance, the number 3,546.98 is rendered 3.546,98.

Laws and customs vary between countries. The elements of addresses don't always appear in the same order. In some countries, the postal zone code precedes the name of the city, while in other countries the reverse is true. Postal zone codes vary in length and can contain letters as well as numbers. The rules for amortizing mortgages and calculating interest rates vary from country to country—even between Canada and the United States.

Units of measure and standard formats for time and date differ from country to country. For example, "lines per inch" is meaningless in the metric world—that is, almost everywhere. In some countries, the 24-hour clock prevails.

Words aren't the only things that change from country to country. Telephones and mailboxes, to name just two examples often used in telecommunications programs, don't look the same in all parts of the world. Either make your graphics culturally neutral, or be prepared to create alternate graphics for various cultures.

Mnemonic shortcuts (such as Command-key equivalents for menu items) that are valid in one language may not be valid in others; be sure all such shortcuts are stored as resources.

Keyboards vary from country to country. Keystrokes that are easily performed with one hand in your own country may require two hands in another. In France and Italy, for instance, typing numerals requires pressing the Shift key.

If you rely on properties of the ASCII code table or use data compression codes that assume a certain number of letters in the alphabet, remember that not all alphabets have the same numbers of characters. Don't rely on strings having a particular length; translation will make most strings longer. (As an example, the length of Apple manuals has been known to increase as much as 30% in translation.) Also, some languages require two bytes instead of one to store characters.

Non-Roman Writing Systems

The Script Manager contains routines that allow an application to function correctly with non-Roman scripts (or writing systems). It also contains utility routines for text processing and parsing, which are useful for applications that do a lot of text manipulation. General applications don't need to call Script Manager routines directly, but can be localized for non-Roman alphabets through such script interface systems as Apple's Kanji Interface System and Arabic Interface System. (Scripts and script interface systems are described in the Script Manager chapter in this volume.)

The International Utilities Package provides routines for sorting, comparing strings, and specifying currency, measurements, dates, and time. It's better to use the routines in this package instead of the Operating System Utility routines (which aren't as accurate and can't be localized).

You should neither change nor depend upon the system font and system font size. Some non-Roman characters demand higher resolution than Roman characters. On Japanese versions of the Macintosh, for instance, the system font must allow for 16-by-16 pixel characters. You can use the global variables SysFontFam and SysFontSize for determining the system font and system font size.

The Menu Manager uses the system font and the system font size in setting up the height of the menu bar and menu items. Because the system font size can vary, the height of the menu bar can also vary. When determining window placement on the screen, don't assume that the menu bar height is 20 pixels. Use the global variable MBarHeight for determining the height of the menu bar.

Avoid using too many menus; translation into other languages almost always widens menu titles, forcing some far to the right (possibly conflicting with Switcher™) or even off the screen.

Most Roman fonts for the Macintosh have space above all the letters to allow for diacritical marks as with Ä or Ñ. If text is drawn using a standard font immediately below a dark line, for example, it will appear to be separated from the line by at least one row of blank pixels (for all but a few exceptional characters). Pixels in some non-Roman fonts, on the other hand, extend to the top of the font rectangle, and appear to merge with the preceding line. To avoid character display overlap, applications should leave blank space around text (as in dialog editText or statText items), or add space between lines of text, as well as before the first line and after the last line of text.

The choice of script (Roman, Japanese, Arabic, and so on) is determined by the fonts selected by the user. If an application doesn't allow the user to change fonts, or allows the user to select only a global font for the whole document, the user is restricted in the choice and mix of scripts.

If text must be displayed in either uppercase or lowercase, you should call the Script Manager Transliterate routine rather than the UprString routine (which doesn't handle diacritical marks or non-Roman scripts correctly).

APPLICATIONS IN A SHARED ENVIRONMENT

A number of new products create environments in which users can share information. Network file servers (like AppleShare™), for instance, make it possible for users to share data, applications, and disk storage space. Multitasking operating systems and programs like Switcher can also be considered shared environments, allowing data to be shared between applications.

To operate smoothly in a shared environment, you'll need to be sensitive to issues like multiple file access, access privileges, and multiple launches. For a complete discussion of how to operate in shared environments, see the File Manager Extensions in a Shared Environment chapter in this volume.

SUMMARY OF COMPATIBILITY GUIDELINES

Data Type

```
TYPE SysEnvRec = RECORD
                environsVersion:   INTEGER;
                machineType:       INTEGER;
                systemVersion:     INTEGER;
                processor:         INTEGER;
                hasFPU:            BOOLEAN;
                hasColorQD:        BOOLEAN;
                keyBoardType:      INTEGER;
                atDrvrVersNum:     INTEGER;
                sysVRefNum:        INTEGER
              END;

    SysEnvPtr = ^SysEnvRec;
```

Routine

```
FUNCTION SysEnvirons (versionRequested: INTEGER; VAR theWorld:
                SysEnvRec) : OSErr;   [Not in ROM]
```

Result Codes

Name	Value	Meaning
noErr	0	No error
envNotPresent	−5500	SysEnvirons trap not present (System File earlier than version 4.1); glue returns values for all fields except systemVersion
envBadVers	−5501	A nonpositive version number was passed—no information is returned
envVersTooBig	−5502	Requested version of SysEnvirons call was not available

Assembly-Language Information

Structure of System Environment Record

environsVersion	(word)
machineType	(word)
systemVersion	(word)
processor	(word)
hasFPU	(byte)
hasColorQD	(byte)
keyBoardType	(word)
atDrvrVersNum	(word)
sysVRefNum	(word)
sysEnvRecSize	Size of system environment record

Routine

Trap macro	On entry	On exit
_SysEnvirons	A0: sysEnvRecPtr (ptr) D0: versRequested (word)	A0: sysEnvRecPtr (ptr) D0: result code (word)

Variables

ApplZone	Address of application heap zone
MBarHeight	Height of menu bar (word)
MemTop	Address of end of RAM
ScreenBits	Bit map of screen in use (bitMapRec bytes)
SysZone	Address of system heap zone
Ticks	Current number of ticks since system startup (long)

2 THE MACINTOSH USER INTERFACE GUIDELINES

ABOUT THIS CHAPTER

This chapter describes the following new features of the Macintosh user interface:

- color
- sound
- new keyboard keys
- new menu features—hierarchical and pop-up menus and a scrolling menu indicator.

The chapter concludes with some suggestions for user testing.

For more complete information about the Macintosh user interface, see *Human Interface Guidelines: The Apple Desktop Interface* (available through APDA). These guidelines are significantly extended from the guidelines chapter in the original *Inside Macintosh;* they include the principles behind the desktop interface used by both the Macintosh and Apple IIGS™, as well as specific guidelines for how interface elements should be used.

For more information about color, see the Color Manager and Color Picker Package chapters. Some reference works on color in the computer/user interface are listed at the end of this chapter. For more information about sound and menus, see the Sound and Menu Manager chapters, respectively.

COLOR

Apple's goal in adding color to the desktop user interface is to add meaning, not just to color things so they "look good". Color can be a valuable additional channel of information to the user, but must be used carefully; otherwise, it can have the opposite of the effect you were trying for, and can be overwhelming visually (or look game-like).

Color is ultimately the domain of the user, who should be able to modify or remove any coloring imposed by the application. Unless you are implementing a color application such as a paint or draw program, you should consider color only for the data, not the interface.

In order to successfully implement color in an application, you should understand some of the complex issues surrounding its use. Many major theories on the proper use of color are not complete or well defined. The way in which the human eye sees color is not fully understood, nor are color's subjective effects.

Standard Uses of Color

In traditional user interface design, color is used to associate or separate objects and information in the following ways:

- discriminate between different areas
- show which things are functionally related
- show relationships between things
- identify crucial features

Color Coding

Different colors have standard associations in different cultures. "Meanings" of colors usually have nothing to do with the wavelength of the color, but are learned through conditioning within a particular culture. Some of the more universal meanings for colors are

- Red: stop, error, or failure. (For disk drives, red also means disk access in progress; don't remove the disk or turn it off.).
- Yellow: warning, caution, or delay.
- Green: go, ready, or power on.
- Warm versus cold: reds, oranges, and yellows are perceived as hot or exciting colors; blues and greens are cool, calm colors.

Colors often have additional standard meanings within a particular discipline: in the financial world, red means loss and black means gain. To a mapmaker, green means wooded areas, blue means water, yellow means deserts. In an application for a specific field, you can take advantage of these meanings; in a general application, you should allow users to change the colors and to turn off any color-coding that you use as a default.

For attracting the user's attention, orange and red are more effective than other colors, but usually connote "warning" or "danger". (Be aware, though, that in some cases, attracting the eye might not be what you want to do; for example, if "dangerous" menu items are colored red, the user's eye will be attracted to the red items, and the user might be more likely to select the items by mistake.)

Although the screen may be able to display 256 or more colors, the human eye can discriminate only around 128 pure hues. Furthermore, when colors are used to signify information, studies have shown that the mind can only effectively follow four to seven color assignments on a screen at once.

General Principles of Color Design

Two principles should guide the design of your application: begin the design in black and white, and limit the use of color, especially in the application's use of the standard interface.

Design in Black and White

You should design your application first in black and white. Color should be *supplementary,* providing extra information for those users who have color. Color shouldn't be the only thing that distinguishes two objects; there should always be other cues, such as shape, location, pattern, or sound. There are several reasons for this:

- Monitors: Most of your users won't have color. The majority of Macintosh computers that Apple ships are black and white, and will continue to be so for some time.

- Printing: Currently, color printing is not very accurate, and even when high-quality color printing becomes available, there is usually a significant change in colors between media.

- Colorblindness: A significant percentage of the population is colorblind to some degree. (In Europe and America, about 8% of males and 0.5% of females have some sort of defective color vision.) The most common form of colorblindness is a loss of ability to distinguish red and green from gray. In another form, yellow, blue, and gray are indistinguishable.

- Lighting: Under dim lighting conditions, colors tend to wash out and become difficult for the eye to distinguish—the differences between colors must be greater, and the number of colors fewer, for them to be discernable. You can't know the conditions under which your application may be used.

Limit Color Use

In the *standard interface* part of applications (menus, window frames, etc.), color should be used mimimally or not at all; the Macintosh interface is very succesful in black and white. You want the user's attention focused on the content of the application, rather than distracted by color in the menus or scroll bars. Availability of color in the *content area* of your application depends on the sort of application:

- *Graphics applications,* which are concerned with the image itself, should take full advantage of the color capabilities of Color QuickDraw, letting the user choose from and modify as many colors as are available.

- *Other applications,* which deal with the organization of information, should limit the use of color much more than this. Color-coding should be allowed or provided to make the information clearer. Providing the user with a small initial selection of distinct colors—four to seven at most—with the capability of changing those or adding more, is the best solution to this.

Contrast and Discrimination

Color adds another dimension to the array of possible contrasts, and care must be given to maintain good readability and discernment.

Colors on Grays

Colors look best against a background of neutral gray, like the desktop. Colors within your application will stand out more if the background and surrounding areas (such as the window frame and menus) are black and white or gray.

Colored Text

Reading and legibility studies in the print (paper) world show that colored text is harder to read than black text on a white background. This also appears to be true in the limited studies that have been done in the computer domain, although almost all these studies have looked at colors on a black background, not the white background used in the Macintosh.

Beware of Blue

The most illegible color is light blue, which should be avoided for text, thin lines, and small shapes. Adjacent colors that differ only in the amount of blue should also be avoided. However, for things that you want to go unnoticed, like grid lines, blue is the perfect color (think of graph paper or lined paper).

Small Objects

People cannot easily discriminate between small areas of color—to be able to tell what color something is, you have to have enough of it. Changes in the color of small objects must be obvious, not subtle.

Specific Recommendations

Remember that color should never be the only thing that distinguishes objects. Other cues such as shape, location, pattern, or sound, should always be used in addition to color, for the reasons discussed above.

Color the Black Bits Only

Generally, all interface elements should maintain a white background, using color to replace black pixels as appropriate. Maintaining the white background and only coloring what is already black (if something needs to be colored at all) helps to maintain the clarity and the "look and feel" of the Macintosh interface.

Leave Outlines Black

Outlines of menus, windows, and alert and dialog boxes should remain in black. Edges formed by color differences alone are hard for the eye to focus on, and these objects may appear against a colored desktop or window.

Highlighting and Selection

Most things—menu items, icons, buttons, and so forth—should highlight by reversing the white background with the colored or black bits when selected. (For example, if the item is red on a white background, it should highlight to white on a red background.) However, if multiple colors of *text* appear together, Color TextEdit allows the user to set the highlighting bar color to something other than black to highlight the text better. The default for the bar color is always black.

Menus

In general, the only use of color in menus should be in menus used to choose colors. However, color could also be useful for directing the user's choices in training and tutorial materials: one color can lead the user through a lesson.

Windows

Since the focus of attention is on the content region of the window, color should be used only in that area. Using color in the scroll bars or title bar can simply distract the user. (A possible exception would be coloring part of a window to match the color of the icon from which it came.)

Dialogs and Alerts

Except for dialog boxes used to select colors, there's no reason to color dialog boxes; they should be designed and laid out clearly enough that color isn't necessary to separate different sections or items. Alert boxes must be as clear as possible; color can add confusion instead of clarity. For example, if you tried to make things clearer by using red to mean "dangerous" and green to mean "safe" in the Erase Disk alert, the OK button ("go") would be *red* and the Cancel ("stop") button would be *green*. Don't do this.

Pointers

Most of the time, when the pointer is being used for selecting and pointing, it should remain black—color might not be visible over potentially different colored backgrounds, and wouldn't give the user any extra information. However, when the user is drawing or typing in color, the drawing or text-insertion pointer should appear in the color that is being used. Except for multicolored paintbrush pointers, the pointer shouldn't contain more than one color at once—it's hard for the eye to discriminate small areas of color.

SOUND

The high-quality sound capabilities of the Macintosh let sound be integrated into the human interface to give users additional information. This section refers to sound as a part of the interface in standard applications, not to the way sound is used in an application that uses the sound itself as data, such as a music composition application.

When to Use Sound

There are two general ways that sound can be used in the interface:

- It can be integrated throughout the standard interface to help make the user aware of the state of the computer or application.
- It can be used to alert the user when something happens unexpectedly, in the background, or when the user is not looking at the screen.

In general, when you put an indicator on the screen to tell the user something—for example, to tell the user that mail has come in, or to show a particular state—it's also appropriate to use a sound.

Getting Attention

If the computer is doing something time-consuming, and the user may have turned away from the screen, sound is a good way to let the user know that the process is finished, or it needs attention. (There should also be an indication on the screen, of course.)

Alerts

Common alerts can use sounds other than the SysBeep for their first stage or two before bringing up an alert box. For example, when users try to paste when there's nothing in the Clipboard, or try to backspace past the top of a field, different sounds could alert them.

Modes

If your application has different states or modes, each one can have a particular sound when the user enters or leaves. This can emphasize the current mode, and prevent confusion.

General Guidelines

Although the use of sound in the Desktop Interface hasn't been investigated thoroughly, these are some general guidelines to keep in mind.

Don't Go Overboard

Be thoughtful about where and how you use sound in an application. If you overuse sound, it won't add any meaning to the interface, and will probably be annoying.

Use Redundancy

Sound should never be the only indication that something has happened; there should always be a visible indication on the screen, too, especially when the user needs to know what happened. The user may have all sound turned off, may have been out of hearing range of the computer, or may have a hearing impairment.

Natural and Unobtrusive

Most sounds can be quite subtle and still getting their meaning across. Loud, harsh sounds can be offensive or intimidating. You should always use the sound yourself and test it on users for a significant period of time (a week or two, not twenty minutes) before including it in your application—if you turn it off after a day, chances are other people will, too. You should also avoid using tunes or jingles—more than two or three notes of a tune may become annoying or sound silly if heard very often.

Significant Differences

Users can learn to recognize and discriminate between sounds, but different sounds should be significantly different. Nonmusicians often can't tell the difference between two similar notes or chords, especially when the sounds are separated by a space of time.

User Control

The user can change the volume of sounds, or turn sound off altogether, using the Control Panel desk accessory. Never override this capability.

Resources

Always store sounds as resources, so users can change sounds and add additional sounds.

NEW KEYBOARD KEYS

The standard keyboard for the Macintosh SE and Macintosh II includes a Control key and an Escape key. The optional extended keyboard has in addition 6 dedicated function keys, 15 function keys that are user-definable, and 3 LED indicators for key lock conditions. The Apple Extended Keyboard is shown in Figure 1.

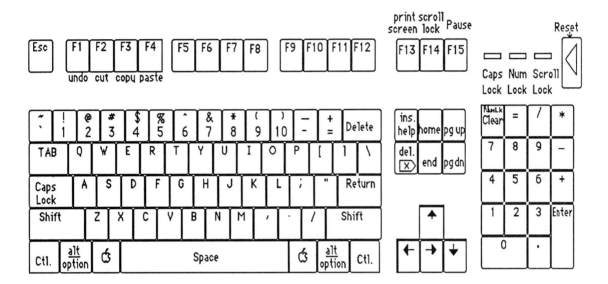

Figure 1. The Apple Extended Keyboard

Control and Escape Keys

The Control and Esc (Escape) keys should be used for their standard meanings; neither should be used as an additional command-key modifier. Since not all keyboards may have a Control or Esc key, neither should be depended upon.

The main use of the Control key is to generate control characters for terminal emulation programs. (The Command key is used for this purpose on terminals lacking a Control key.) A secondary use that also derives from past practice is calling user-defined functions, or macros. The varying placement of the Control key on different keyboards means that it should not be used for routine entry, as touch-typists may find its position inconvenient.

The Esc key has the general meaning "let me out of here". In certain contexts its meaning is specific:

■ The user can press Esc as a quick way to indicate Cancel in a dialog box.

■ The user can press Esc to stop an operation in progress, such as printing. (Using Esc this way is like pressing Command-period.)

■ If an application absolutely requires a series of dialog boxes (a fresh look at program design usually eliminates such sequences), the user should be able to use Esc to move backward through the boxes.

Pressing Esc should never cause the user to back out of an operation that would require extensive time or work to reenter, and it should never cause the user to lose valuable information. When the user presses Esc during a lengthy operation, the application should display a confirmation dialog box to be sure Esc wasn't pressed accidentally.

Function Keys

There are two types of function keys: dedicated and user-definable. The user-definable keys—labeled F1 through F15—are not to be defined by an application. F1 through F4 represent Undo, Cut, Copy, and Paste, respectively, in any applications that use these commands.

The six dedicated function keys are labeled Help, Del, Home, End, Page Up, and Page Down. These keys are used as follows:

■ **Help:** Pressing the Help key should produce help (it's equivalent to pressing Command-?). The sort of help available varies between applications; if a full, contextual help system is not available, some sort of useful help screen should be provided.

■ **Fwd Del:** Pressing Fwd Del performs a forward delete: the character directly to the right of the insertion point is removed, pulling everything to the right of the removed character toward the insertion point. The effect is that the insertion point remains stable while it "vacuums" everything ahead of it.

   If Fwd Del is pressed when there is a current selection, it has the same effect as pressing Delete (Backspace) or choosing Clear from the Edit menu.

■ **Home:** Pressing the Home key is equivalent to moving the scroll boxes (elevators) all the way to the top of the vertical scroll bar and to the left end of the horizontal scroll bar.

■ **End:** The flip-side of Home: it's equivalent to moving the scroll boxes (elevators) all the way to the bottom of the vertical scroll bar and to the right end of the horizontal scroll bar.

■ **Page Up:** Equivalent to clicking the mouse pointer in the upper gray region of the vertical scroll bar.

■ **Page Down:** Equivalent to clicking the mouse pointer in the lower gray region of the vertical scroll bar.

Notice that the Home, End, Page Up, and Page Down keys *have no effect on the insertion point or on any selected material.* These keys change the screen display only, for three reasons:

■ The analogy to scrolling means that the keys behave as users expect.

■ Users can easily change the insertion point by clicking in the jumped-to window.

- Window-by-window jumping with a moving insertion point can be done by Command–arrow key combinations, as described in Volume IV of *Inside Macintosh*.

Because the keys are visual only, the Page Up and Page Down keys jump relative to the visible window, not relative to the insertion point.

NEW MENU FEATURES

The Menu Manager now supports two new capabilities: hierarchical and pop-up menus. In addition, scrolling menus, introduced with the Macintosh Plus and Macintosh 512K Enhanced, are made visible with a scrolling menu indicator.

Hierarchical Menus

Hierarchical menus are a logical extension of the current menu metaphor: another dimension is added to a menu, so that a menu item can be the title of a submenu. When the user drags the pointer through a hierarchical menu item, a submenu appears after a brief delay.

Hierarchical menu items have an indicator (a small black triangle pointing to the right, to indicate "more") at the edge of the menu, as illustrated in Figure 2.

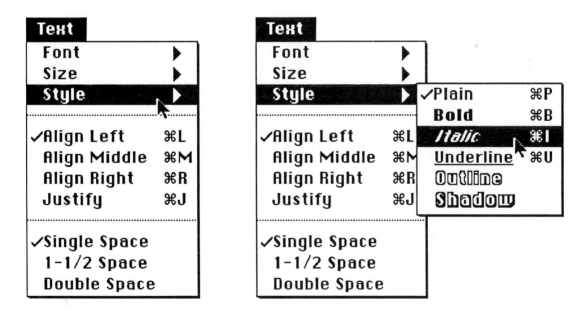

Figure 2. Main Menu Before and After Submenu Appears

One main menu can contain both standard menu items and submenus; both levels can have Command-key equivalents. (The submenu title can't have a Command-key equivalent, of course, because it's not a command. Key combinations aren't used to pull down menus.)

Two delay values enable submenus to function smoothly, without jarring distractions to the user: The **submenu delay** is the length of time before a submenu appears as the user drags the pointer through a hierarchical menu item. It prevents flashing due to rapid appearance–disappearance of submenus. The **drag delay** allows the user to drag diagonally from the submenu title into the submenu, briefly crossing part of the main menu, without the submenu disappearing (which would ordinarily happen when the pointer was dragged into another main menu item). See Figure 3.

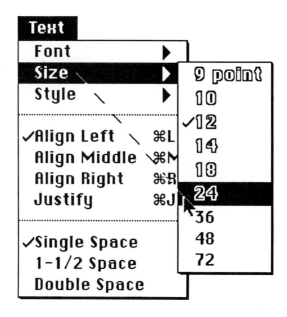

Figure 3. Dragging Diagonally to a Submenu Item

Other aspects of submenus—menu blink for example—behave exactly the same way as in standard menus.

The original Macintosh menus were designed so that the user could drag the mouse across the menu bar and immediately see *all* of the choices currently available. Although developers have found they need more menu space, and hierarchical menus were designed to meet that need, it's important that this original capability be maintained as much as possible. To keep this essential simplicity and clarity, follow these guidelines:

- Hierarchical menus should be used only for *lists of related items*, such as fonts or font sizes (in this case, the title of the submenu clearly tells what the submenu contains).

- *Only one level* of hierarchical menu should be used, although the capability for more is provided. This one extra layer of menus potentially increases by an order of magnitude the number of menu items that can be used; if you need more layers than that, your application is probably more complex than most users can understand, and you should rethink your design.

Pop-Up Menus

A **pop-up menu** is one that isn't in the menu bar, but appears somewhere else on the screen (usually in a dialog) when the user presses in a particular place, as shown in Figure 4.

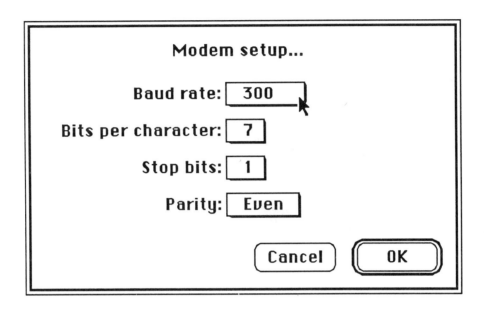

Figure 4. Dialog Box With Pop-Up Menus

Pop-up menus are used for setting values or choosing from lists of related items. The indication that there is a pop-up menu is a box with a one-pixel thick drop shadow, drawn around the current value. When the user presses this box, the pop-up menu appears, with the current value—checked and highlighted—under the pointer, as shown in Figure 5. If the menu has a title, the title is highlighted while the menu is visible.

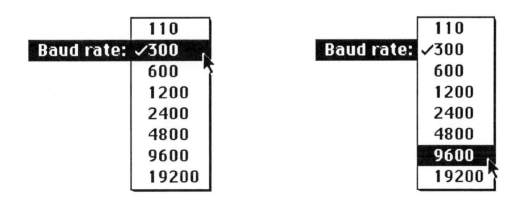

Figure 5. Dragging Through a Pop-up Menu

The pop-up menu acts like other menus: the user can move around in it and choose another item, which then appears in the box, or can move outside it to leave the current value active. If a pop-up menu reaches the top or bottom of the screen, it scrolls like other menus.

When designing an application that uses pop-up menus, keep in mind the following points:

- Pop-up menus should only be used for lists of values or related items (much like hierarchical menus); they should not be used for commands.

- You must draw the shadowed box indicating that there is a pop-up menu, so the user knows that it's there—pop-up menus should never be invisible.

- While the menu is showing, its title should be inverted. If several pop-up menus are near each other, this lessens ambiguity about which one is being used.

- The current value should always appear under the pointer when the menu pops up, so that simply clicking the box doesn't change the item.

- Hierarchical pop-up menus should not be used.

Always consider whether a pop-up menu is the simplest thing to use in each case. For example, rather than have a pop-up menu choose all paper sizes, icons could represent commonly used sizes, with a pop-up menu for non-standard sizes.

Scrolling Menu Indicator

Scrolling menus were introduced with the Macintosh Plus and Macintosh 512K Enhanced, but this feature was invisible. When there were more than eighteen items in a menu (which can happen with fonts on a hard disk), the menu scrolled to show more items as the user moved the pointer past the last item; but users didn't know whether there were any more items in a menu unless they happened to drag past the bottom of it. The scrolling menu feature is now made visible by an indicator (similar to the hierarchical menu indicator), which appears at the bottom of the menu when there are more items, as shown in Figure 6.

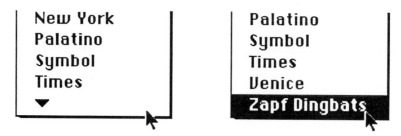

Figure 6. Scrolling Menus: Indicator at Bottom

The indicator area itself doesn't highlight, but the menu scrolls as the user drags over it. When the last item is shown, the indicator disappears.

As soon as the menu starts scrolling, another indicator appears at the top of the menu to show that some items are now hidden in that direction (see Figure 7).

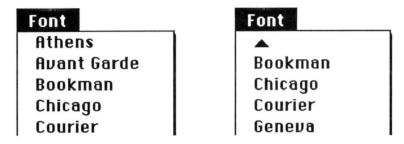

Figure 7. Scrolling Menus: Indicator at Top

If the user drags back up to the top, the menu scrolls back down in the same manner. If the user releases the mouse button or selects another menu, and then selects the menu again, it appears in its original position, with the hidden items and the indicator at the bottom.

USER TESTING

The primary test of the user interface is its success with users: can people understand what to do and can they accomplish the task at hand easily and efficiently? The best way to answer these questions is to put them to the users.

Build User Testing Into the Design Process

Users should be involved early in the design process so that changes in the basic concept of the product can still be made, if necessary. Although there's a natural tendency to wait for a good working prototype before showing the product to anyone, this is too late for the user to have a significant impact on design. In the absence of working code, you can show test subjects alternate designs on paper or storyboards. There are lots of ways that early concepts can be tested on potential users of a product. Then, as the design progresses, the testing can become more refined and can focus on screen designs and specific features of the interface.

Test Subjects

There is no such thing as a "typical user". You should, however, be able to identify some people who are familiar with the *task* your application supports but are unfamiliar with the specific *technology* you are using. These "naive experts" make good subjects because they don't have to be taught what the application is for, they are probably already motivated to use it, and they know what is required to accomplish the task.

You don't need to test a lot of people. The best procedure for formative testing (testing during the design process) is to collect data from a few subjects, analyze the results and apply them as appropriate. Then, identify new questions that arise and questions that still need answers, and begin all over again—it is an iterative process.

Procedures

Planning and carrying out a true experimental test takes time and expert training. But many of the questions you may have about your design do not require such a rigid approach. Furthermore, the computer and application already provide a controlled setting from which objective data can be gathered quite reliably. The major requirements are

- to make *objective* observations
- to record the data *during the user-product interaction*

Objective observations include measures of time, frequencies, error rates, and so forth. The simple and direct recording of what the person does and says while working is also an objective observation, however, and is often very useful to designers. Test subjects can be encouraged to talk as they work, telling what they are doing, trying to do, expect to happen, etc. This record of a person's thinking aloud is called a *protocol* by researchers in the fields of cognition and problem-solving, and is a major source of their data.

The process of testing described here involves the application designer and the test subjects in a regular cycle of feedback and revision. Although the test procedures themselves may be informal, user-testing of the concepts and features of the interface becomes a regular, integral part of the design process.

BIBLIOGRAPHY

The following books are recommended reading for those interested in the effective use of color in the user interface.

Favre, J., and A. November. *Color and Communication*. Zurich, Switzerland: ABC Edition, 1979.

Greenberg, D., A. Marcus, A. Schmidt, and V. Gorter. *The Computer Image*. Menlo Park, California: Addison-Wesley Publishing Co., 1982.

Itten, J. *The Elements of Color,* edited by F. Birren. New York: Van Nostrand Reinhold Co., 1970.

Schneiderman, B. *Designing the User Interface: Strategies for Effective Human-Computer Interaction*. Reading, Massachusetts: Addison-Wesley Publishing Co., 1987.

3 THE RESOURCE MANAGER

3 Resource Manager

ABOUT THIS CHAPTER

This chapter describes new resource types, changes to the Resource Manager, and the contents of the Macintosh SE and Macintosh II ROMs and of System file version 4.1.

THE RESOURCE MANAGER

As described in chapter 3 of Volume IV, in order to use the ROM resources in your calls to the Resource Manager, the ROM map must be inserted in front of the map for the System Resource File prior to making the call. Unless the ROM map is inserted, the GetResource call will not search the ROM resources. Sometimes, however, you'll first want to try to get the resource from any open resource files, and then if it's not found, to get it from ROM. A new routine, RGetResource, lets you do this easily. It searches the chain of open resource files (including the System Resource File) for the given resource; if it's not there, it looks in ROM.

Routine

```
FUNCTION RGetResource (theType: ResType; theID: INTEGER) : Handle;
```

RGetResource is identical in function to GetResource except that it looks through the chain of open resource files for the specified resource, and if it doesn't find it there, it looks in the ROM resources.

> **Note:** With System file version 4.1 or later, RGetResource will also work on the Macintosh Plus.

RESOURCES

The following standard resource types have been defined (System file 4.1 or later). All-uppercase resource types are listed first. Types new with this volume are in boldface.

Resource type	Meaning
'ALRT'	Alert template
'ADBS'	Apple Desktop Bus service routine
'BNDL'	Bundle
'CACH'	RAM cache code
'CDEF'	Control definition function

Resource Meaning
type

Resource type	Meaning
'CNTL'	Control template
'CODE'	Application code segment
'CURS'	Cursor
'DITL'	Item list in a dialog or alert
'DLOG'	Dialog template
'DRVR'	Desk accessory or other device driver
'DSAT'	System startup alert table
'FKEY'	Command-Shift-number routine
'FMTR'	3 1/2-inch disk formatting code
'FOND'	Font family record
'FONT'	Font
'FREF'	File reference
'FRSV'	IDs of fonts reserved for system use
'FWID'	Font widths
'ICN#'	Icon list
'ICON'	Icon
'INIT'	Initialization resource
'INTL'	International resource
'INT#'	List of integers owned by Find File
'KCAP'	Physical layout of keyboard (used by Key Caps desk accessory)
'KCHR'	ASCII mapping (software)
'KMAP'	Keyboard mapping (hardware)
'KSWP'	Keyboard script table
'LDEF'	List definition procedure
'MBAR'	Menu bar
'MBDF'	Default menu definition procedure
'MDEF'	Menu definition procedure
'MENU'	Menu
'MMAP'	Mouse tracking code
'NBPC'	Appletalk bundle
'NFNT'	128K ROM font
'PACK'	Package
'PAT '	Pattern (The space is required.)
'PAT#'	Pattern list
'PDEF'	Printing code
'PICT'	Picture
'PREC'	Print record
'PRER'	Device type for Chooser
'PRES'	Device type for Chooser
'PTCH'	ROM patch code
'RDEV'	Device type for Chooser
'ROvr'	Code for overriding ROM resources
'ROv#'	List of ROM resources to override
'SERD'	RAM Serial Driver
'SICN'	Script symbol
'STR '	String (The space is required.)
'STR#'	String list
'WDEF'	Window definition function

3 Resource Manager

Resource type	Meaning
'WIND'	Window template
'actb'	Alert color table
'atpl'	Internal AppleTalk resource
'bmap'	Bit maps used by the Control Panel
'boot'	Copy of boot blocks
'cctb'	Control color table
'cicn'	Color Macintosh icon
'clst'	Cached icon lists used by Chooser and Control Panel
'clut'	Color look-up table
'crsr'	Color cursor
'ctab'	Used by the Control Panel
'dctb'	Dialog color table
'fctb'	Font color table
'finf'	Font information
'gama'	Color correction table
'ictb'	Color table dialog item
'insc'	Installer script
'itl0'	Date and time formats
'itl1'	Names of days and months
'itl2'	International Utilities Package sort hooks
'itlb'	International Utilities Package script bundles
'itlc'	International configuration for Script Manager
'lmem'	Low memory globals
'mcky'	Mouse tracking
'mctb'	Menu color information table
'mitq'	Internal memory requirements for MakeITable
'mppc'	AppleTalk configuration code
'nrct'	Rectangle positions
'pltt'	Color palette
'ppat'	Pixel pattern
'snd '	Sound (The space is required.)
'snth'	Synthesizer
'wctb'	Window color table

RESOURCES IN ROM

Certain system resources were placed in the 128K ROM for quick access. The Macintosh SE and Macintosh II ROMs include additional resources in ROM; they're outlined below.

The following system resources are stored in the Macintosh SE ROM (the resource IDs are in hexadecimal):

Type	ID	Description
'CDEF'	0	Default button definition procedure
'CDEF'	1	Default scroll bar definition procedure
'CURS'	1	IBeamCursor
'CURS'	2	CrossCursor

Type	ID	Description
'CURS'	3	PlusCursor
'CURS'	4	WatchCursor
'DRVR'	3	Sound Driver (.Sound)
'DRVR'	4	Disk Driver (.Sony)
'DRVR'	9	AppleTalk driver (.MPP)
'DRVR'	A	AppleTalk driver (.ATP)
'DRVR'	28	AppleTalk driver (.XPP)
'FONT'	0	Name of system font
'FONT'	C	System font (Chicago 12)
'FONT'	189	Geneva 9 font
'FONT'	18C	Geneva 12 font
'FONT'	209	Monaco 9 font
'KMAP'	0	Keyboard map for keyboard driver
'MBDF'	0	Default menu bar procedure
'MDEF'	0	Default menu definition procedure
'PACK'	4	Floating-Point Arithmetic Package
'PACK'	5	Transcendental Functions Package
'PACK'	7	Binary-Decimal Conversion Package
'SERD'	0	Serial Driver
'WDEF'	0	Default window definition function (document window)
'WDEF'	1	Default window definition function (rounded window)

The following system resources are stored in the Macintosh II ROM (the resource IDs are in hexadecimal):

Type	ID	Description
'CDEF'	0	Default button definition procedure
'CDEF'	1	Default scroll bar definition procedure
'CURS'	1	IBeamCursor
'CURS'	2	CrossCursor
'CURS'	3	PlusCursor
'CURS'	4	WatchCursor
'DRVR'	3	Sound Driver (.Sound)
'DRVR'	4	Disk Driver (.Sony)
'DRVR'	9	AppleTalk driver (.MPP)
'DRVR'	A	AppleTalk driver (.ATP)
'DRVR'	28	AppleTalk driver (.XPP)
'FONT'	0	Name of system font
'FONT'	C	System font (Chicago 12)
'FONT'	180	Name of Geneva font
'FONT'	189	Geneva 9 font
'FONT'	18C	Geneva 12 font
'FONT'	200	Name of Monaco font
'FONT'	209	Monaco 9 font
'KCHR'	0	ASCII mapping (software)
'KMAP'	0	Keyboard mapping (hardware)
'MBDF'	0	Default menu bar procedure
'MDEF'	0	Default menu definition procedure
'NFNT'	2	Chicago 12 font (4-bit)
'NFNT'	3	Chicago 12 font (8-bit)
'NFNT'	22	Geneva 9 font (4-bit)
'PACK'	4	Floating-Point Arithmetic Package

3 Resource Manager

Type	ID	Description
'PACK'	5	Transcendental Functions Package
'PACK'	7	Binary-Decimal Conversion Package
'SERD'	0	Serial Driver
'WDEF'	0	Default window definition function (document window)
'WDEF'	1	Default window definition function (rounded window)
'cctb'	0	Control color table
'clut'	1	Color look-up table
'clut'	2	Color look-up table
'clut'	4	Color look-up table
'clut'	8	Color look-up table
'clut'	7F	Color look-up table
'gama'	0	Color correction table
'mitq'	0	Internal memory requirements for MakeITable
'snd '	1	Brass horn
'wctb'	0	Window color table

RESOURCES IN THE SYSTEM FILE

The System Resource File contains standard resources that are shared by all applications, and are used by the Macintosh Toolbox and Operating System as well. This file can be modified by the user with the Installer and Font/DA Mover programs.

Warning: Your program should not directly add resources to, or delete resources from, the System Resource File.

Applications should not alter resources in the System file, except for resources owned by the application, as discussed in the Resource Manager chapter of Volume I. With applications that need to install drivers, fonts, or desk accessories, developers should ship an Apple-released copy of the file along with either the Installer and a script (for drivers) or the Font/DA Mover (for fonts and desk accessories).

Note: Some of the resources in the System Resource File are also contained in the 128K and 256K ROMs; they're duplicated in the System Resource File for compatibility with machines in which these resources are not in ROM.

The rest of this section presents an overview of the System Resource File's resources, grouped by function.

Packages

The System Resource File contains the standard Macintosh packages and the resources they use (or own):

- the List Manager Package ('PACK' resource 0), and the standard list definition procedure ('LDEF' resource 0)

- the Disk Initialization Package ('PACK' resource 2), and code (resource type 'FMTR') used in formatting disks

- the Standard File Package ('PACK' resource 3), and resources used to create its alerts and dialogs (resource types 'ALRT', 'DITL', and 'DLOG')

- the Floating-Point Arithmetic Package ('PACK' resource 4)

- the Transcendental Functions Package ('PACK' resource 5)

- the International Utilities Package ('PACK' resource 6)

- the Binary-Decimal Conversion Package ('PACK' resource 7)

- the Color Picker Package ('PACK' resource 12)

Drivers and Desk Accessories

Certain device drivers (including desk accessories) and the resources they use or own are found in the System Resource File; these resources include

- the .PRINT driver ('DRVR' resource 2) that communicates between the Print Manager and the printer.

- the .MPP, .ATP, and .XPP drivers ('DRVR' resources 9, 10, and 28 respectively) used by version 42 of AppleTalk.

- the Control Panel desk accessory ('DRVR' resource 18) and the resources used in displaying its various options. The Control Panel also uses a resource of type 'clst' to list the cached icons of the devices in order to improve performance.

- the Chooser desk accessory, which uses the same class of resources as the Control Panel, including its own 'clst'.

3 Resource Manager

Patches

For each ROM (64K, 128K, 256K) there are two patch resources of type 'PTCH' that provide updates for ROM routines. At startup, the machine's ROM is checked and the appropriate 'PTCH' resources are installed and locked in the system heap. The 'PTCH' resources are:

All ROMS	'PTCH' 0
64K ROM	'PTCH' 105
128K ROM	'PTCH' 117
256K ROM (Macintosh SE)	'PTCH' 630
256K ROM (Macintosh II)	'PTCH' 376

General Resources

Other resources contained in the System Resource File include

- Standard definition procedures for creating windows, menus, controls, and lists.

- System fonts and font families (resource types 'FONT' and 'FOND').

- System icons.

- The screen utility resources 'FKEY' 3 and 4, which execute a MacPaint screen snapshot when Command-Shift-3 is pressed, and print a screen snapshot when Command-Shift-4 is pressed, respectively. Note that Command-Shift-4 only works with the ImageWriter®; it is useful for a quick print, but should not be an application's print strategy.

- Mouse tracking resources: 'mcky' 0 to 4, which provide parameters for various mouse tracking setups; 'MMAP' 0, which provides mouse tracking code for use when it is not in ROM.

- Key mapping resources, which implement keyboard mapping in conjunction with the Apple Desktop Bus: 'ADBS' 2, 'KMAP' 1 and 2, and 'KCHR', which has IDs for each language. Note that 'INIT' resources 1 and 2, which used to handle key translation, now point to the 'ADBS'/'KCHR' system instead.

- Color resources: 'wctb' 0, 'cctb' 0, and 'mitq' 0, which implement color tables, and 'cicn' 0, the color Macintosh icon. See the Color Quickdraw and Color Manager chapters for more information.

SUMMARY OF THE RESOURCE MANAGER

Routine

```
FUNCTION RGetResource (theType: ResType; theID: INTEGER) : Handle;
```

4 COLOR QUICKDRAW

4 · Color QuickDraw

ABOUT THIS CHAPTER

A new version of QuickDraw has been created to take advantage of the capabilities of the Macintosh II. Color QuickDraw is able to use a very large number of colors and can take advantage of systems that have one or more screens of any size. This chapter describes the use of color with one screen. The following chapter, "Graphics Devices", explains what your program should do to support more than one screen.

The features of Color QuickDraw implemented for the Macintosh Plus, the Macintosh SE, and the Macintosh II are

■ Text drawing modes are enhanced, and now include a text mask mode, drawing with multibit fonts, and fractional character positioning.

■ The QuickDraw picture format (PICT) has been enhanced, and includes a number of new opcodes.

Some of the features of Color QuickDraw for the Macintosh II are

■ All drawing operations supported by old QuickDraw can now be performed in color.

■ Color QuickDraw supports the use of as many as 2^{48} colors. In addition, Color QuickDraw's color model is hardware-independent, allowing programs to operate independently of the display device.

■ Color QuickDraw includes several new data types: color tables, color icons, color patterns, and color cursors. These types can be stored as resources that are easily used by your program.

■ A new set of transfer modes has been added. These modes allow colors to be blended with or added to the colors that are already on the screen.

■ Most Toolbox Managers have been enhanced to use color. Thus you can now add color to windows, menus, controls, dialog boxes, and TextEdit text. Refer to the appropriate chapters for more information.

■ The QuickDraw picture format (PICT) has been extended so that Color QuickDraw images can be recorded in pictures.

This chapter introduces the basic concepts, terminology, and data structures underlying the Macintosh II approach to graphics. The material presented here assumes familiarity with the QuickDraw concepts described in Volume I, such as bit maps, graphics ports, patterns, cursors, and transfer modes. You should also be familiar with the use of resources, as presented in the Resource Manager chapter.

4 Color QuickDraw

COLOR REPRESENTATION

The following sections introduce the basic concepts and terminology used in Color QuickDraw. It's important to keep in mind that Color QuickDraw is designed to be device-independent. The range of colors available is the result of the system configuration: the screen resolution, the graphics hardware used to produce color, and the software used to select and store color values. Color QuickDraw provides a consistent way of dealing with color, regardless of the characteristics of the video card or display device.

The original QuickDraw represents each dot on the screen (known as a **pixel**) as a single bit in memory. Each bit can have two values, zero or one. This allows two colors, usually black and white, to be displayed.

To produce color graphics, more than one bit of memory per pixel displayed is needed. If two bits per pixel are available, four colors can be displayed. Four bits per pixel provides a display of 16 colors, and eight bits per pixel provides a display of 256 colors. The bits in a pixel, taken together, form a number known as the **pixel value.**

The number of possible colors is related to the amount of memory used to store each pixel. Since displayed pixels are stored in RAM on the video card, rather than in the RAM in the Macintosh, the quality of the graphics depends on capabilities of the video card used.

RGB Space

Color QuickDraw represents colors in **RGB space.** Each color has a red, a green, and a blue component, hence the name RGB. These components may be visualized as being mapped into a color cube, as shown in Figure 1. (See frontispiece for a color representation of this art.)

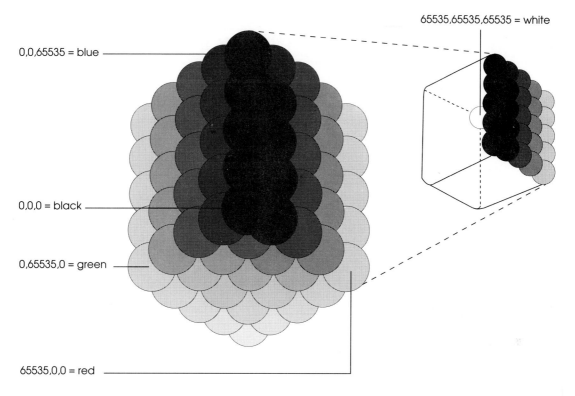

Figure 1. RGB Color Cube

The data structures used within Color Quickdraw express each RGB component as an unsigned integer value. Each R, G, and B can have a value from $0000 to $FFFF (or 0 to 65,535). RGB color is additive; that is, as the value of a component is increased, the amount of that component in the total color increases. An RGB color is black if all three components are set to 0, or white if each component is set to 65,535. Pixel values between these two extremes can be combined to represent all the possible colors. For instance, pixel values that lie along the diagonal between black and white, and for which R = G = B, are all perceived as shades of gray.

Other Color Spaces

In addition to RGB, several other color models are commonly used to represent colors. These other models include HSV (hue, saturation, value), HLS (hue, lightness, saturation), and CMY (cyan, magenta, yellow). If you wish to work in a different color space in your program, you can use the conversion routines provided in the Color Picker Package to convert colors to their RGB equivalents before passing them to Color QuickDraw. Please refer to the Color Picker Package chapter for more details.

USING COLOR ON THE MACINTOSH II

Before you read about the details of how to use Color QuickDraw, it's useful to understand the various components of the color system and how they interact with each other. This section, through a series of rules and examples, attempts to illustrate these interactions.

Rule 1: The user selects the depth of the screen using the Control Panel.

This rule is mentioned first to convey the fundamental need for device independence. Your application shouldn't change the depth of the screen, because it must avoid conflicts with desk accessories or other applications that are using the screen at the same time. Let the user decide how many colors should be displayed.

Rule 2: Work with colors in RGB space, not with the colors on the screen.

Whenever possible, your application should assume that it's drawing to a screen that has 2^{48} colors. Let Color QuickDraw determine what colors to actually display on the screen. This lets your program work better when drawing to devices that support more colors.

The easiest way to follow this rule is for a program to call the Color Picker Package to select colors. The Color Picker returns an RGB value, which can then be used as the current color. When Color QuickDraw draws using that color, it selects the color that best matches the specified RGB.

Rule 3: To ensure good color matching, and to avoid conflict with other applications and desk accessories, use the Palette Manager.

If your program requires a very specific set of colors not found in the default selection of colors, for instance 128 levels of gray, then you should use the Palette Manager. The Palette Manager lets you specify the set of colors that is to be used by a particular window. When that window is brought to the front, its set of colors is switched in (with a minimal amount of impact on the rest of the screen).

You should also use the Palette Manager if your application needs to animate colors (that is, to change the colors of pixels that are already displayed).

The Palette Manager is a powerful tool because it makes sure that your application gets the best selection of colors across multiple screen devices and multiple screen depths. You don't have to worry about interactions with desk accessories or other applications. Please refer to the chapter on the Palette Manager for more information on using the Palette Manager routines.

Rule 4: Be aware that systems may have multiple video devices.

Since the Macintosh II is able to support multiple screen devices, make sure your application takes into account the variable-sized desktop. For instance, a document may have been dragged to an alternate screen on one system, and then copied and used on another system. You should leave the document positioned where it is if it lies within the desktop, but move it to the main screen if it doesn't. Please refer to the Graphics Devices chapter for more details.

Figure 2 helps to illustrate the relationships between the various parts of the color system.

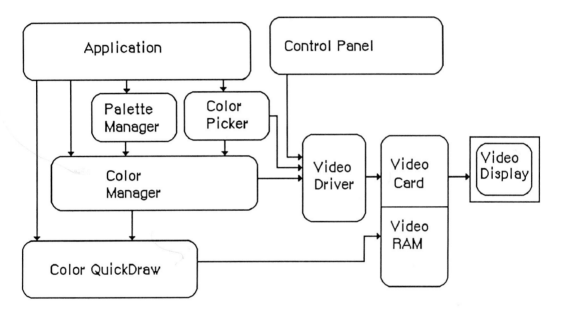

Figure 2. The Macintosh II Color System

From Color to Pixel

To help illustrate the interconnections of the color system, let's examine the steps from the specification of a color to the display of that color on the screen. This is an oversimplified explanation that you should use for conceptual understanding only.

First, you specify the color that you want to display. Color QuickDraw stores the RGB components so that it knows the exact color that you specified. Let's assume that the screen is set to eight bits per pixel. This means that each pixel is able to have 2^8, or 256, different values. Associated with the screen is a structure called a **color table,** which is a list of all the colors that the screen is currently able to display. So in this case the color table has 256 RGB values in it, one for each possible pixel value. The first entry in the color table specifies the color of all pixels that have value 0, the second entry specifies the color of pixels that have value 1, and so on. Thus the color's position in the table determines the pixel value that produces that color.

When you use Color QuickDraw to draw something, it retrieves the stored RGB, and asks the Color Manager to return the pixel value that best represents that color. The Color Manager effectively searches through the color table for the RGB that most closely matches your color. The position in the table of the best match determines the pixel value to be placed on the screen. Color QuickDraw then places that pixel value on the screen.

But how does this pixel cause the assigned color to be displayed? Color QuickDraw has placed this pixel into the RAM on the video card. While your Macintosh II is turned on, the video card is continuously redisplaying every pixel that is stored in its RAM (very, very quickly). Internal to the video card is another color table, the **Color Look-Up Table (CLUT).** It is organized exactly like the first one, but is used the other way around. The video card takes the pixel value and uses it to determine what RGB value that pixel represents. It then uses that RGB to send off three signals (red, green, and blue) to the video monitor, indicating exactly what color the current pixel should be.

Some video cards allow you to change the set of colors displayed at a given time. Although this is normally done transparently through the Palette Manager, it actually happens when both the screen's color table and the one that is internal to the video card are changed to reflect the new set of colors.

A very slight variation of this is used to support the monochrome mode that you can set from the control panel. When you set monochrome mode, the screen's color table doesn't change: from the application's point of view, the same set of colors is still available. Instead, when the video card is told to use monochrome mode, it replaces each entry in the video card's internal color table with a level of gray (R=G=B) that matches the luminance of the color it is replacing. Because of this, the switch between color and monochrome modes has no effect on a running program.

ABOUT COLOR QUICKDRAW

The most fundamental difference between the original QuickDraw and Color QuickDraw is the environment in which drawing takes place. In the original QuickDraw, all drawing is performed in a grafPort, the structure that defines the coordinate system, drawing pattern, background pattern, pen size and location, character font and style, and bit map in which drawing takes place. In Color QuickDraw, drawing takes place in a color grafPort (cGrafPort) instead. As described in later sections, most of the fields in a cGrafPort are the same as fields in a grafPort; however, a few fields have been changed to hold color information.

When you're using a grafPort in your application, you can specify up to eight colors. When drawing to a color screen or printing, these colors will actually be displayed. When drawing to an offscreen bitmap, the colors will be lost (since an offscreen bitmap only has one bit for each pixel).

When you're using a cGrafPort, however, you can specify up to 2^{48} colors. The number of colors that are displayed depends on the setting of the screen, the capability of the printer, or the depth of the offscreen bitmap. There is more information about offscreen bitmaps in the "Drawing to Offscreen Devices" section of the next chapter.

Color grafPorts are used by the system in the same way as grafPorts. They are the same size as grafPorts, and they are the structures upon which a program builds color windows. As with a grafPort, you set thePort to be a cGrafPort using the SetPort command.

You can use all old drawing commands when drawing into a cGrafPort, and you can use all new drawing commands when drawing into a grafPort. However, since new drawing commands that are used in a grafPort don't take advantage of any of the features of Color QuickDraw, it's not recommended.

Drawing Color in a GrafPort

Although the QuickDraw graphics routines were designed mainly for monochrome drawing, they also included some rudimentary color capabilities. A pair of fields in the grafPort record, fgColor and bkColor, allow a foreground and background color to be specified. The color values used in these fields are based on a *planar* model: each bit position corresponds to a different *color plane,* and the value of each bit indicates whether a particular color plane should be activated. (The term color plane refers to a logical plane, rather than a physical plane.) The individual color planes combine to produce the full-color image.

The standard QuickDraw color values consist of one bit for normal monochrome drawing (black on white), one bit for inverted monochrome (white on black), three bits for the additive primary colors (red, green, blue) used in video display, and four bits for the subtractive primary colors (cyan, magenta, yellow, black) used in hardcopy printing. The original QuickDraw interface includes a set of predefined constants for the standard colors:

```
CONST
  blackColor  = 33;
  whiteColor  = 30;
  redColor    = 205;
  greenColor  = 341;
  blueColor   = 409;
  cyanColor   = 273;
  magentaColor = 137;
  yellowColor = 69;
```

These are the only colors available in the original QuickDraw. All programs that draw into grafPorts are limited to these eight colors. When these colors are drawn to the screen on the Macintosh II, Color QuickDraw automatically draws them in color, if the screen is set to a color mode.

Drawing Color in a CGrafPort

Color QuickDraw represents color using the RGBColor record type, which specifies the red, blue, and green components of the color. Three 16-bit unsigned integers give the intensity values for the three additive primary colors:

```
TYPE
  RGBColor = RECORD
              red:    INTEGER;    {red component}
              green:  INTEGER;    {green component}
              blue:   INTEGER     {blue component}
            END;
```

A color of this form is referred to as an **RGB value** and is the form in which an application specifies the colors it needs. The translation from the RGB value to the pixel value is performed at the time the color is drawn. At times the pixel value is stored in the fgColor or bkColor fields. Refer to the Graphics Devices chapter for more details.

When drawing is actually performed, QuickDraw calls the Color Manager to supply the color that most closely matches the requested color for the current device. As described in the Color Manager chapter, you can replace the method used for color matching if necessary. Normally pixel values are handled entirely by Color QuickDraw and the Color Manager; applications only refer to colors as RGB values.

A set of colors is grouped into a structure called a color table:

```
TYPE
  CTabHandle = ^CTabPtr;
  CTabPtr    = ^ColorTable;
  ColorTable = RECORD
                ctSeed:  LONGINT; {unique identifier from table}
                ctFlags: INTEGER; {contains flags describing the }
                                  { specArray; clear for a pixMap}
```

```
ctSize:  INTEGER; {number of entries -1 }
                  { in ctTable}
ctTable: cSpecArray
END;
```

The fields of a color table are fully described in the Color Manager chapter. The ctFlags field contains flags that differentiate between a device color table and an image color table. The ctTable field is composed of a cSpecArray, which contains an array of ColorSpec entries. Notice that each entry in the color table is a ColorSpec, not simply an RGBColor. The type ColorSpec is composed of a value field and an RGB value, as shown below.

```
TYPE
  cSpecArray : ARRAY [0..0] of ColorSpec;
  ColorSpec = RECORD
                value:  INTEGER; {pixel value}
                rgb:    RGBColor {RGB value}
              END;
```

Color tables are used to represent the set of colors that a device is capable of displaying, and they are used to describe the desired colors in an image. If the color table describes an image's colors, then a ColorSpec determines the desired RGB for the pixel value stored in the value field. This is the most common usage, and most of the routines described in this chapter work with a ColorSpec in this manner.

If the color table describes a device's colors, then the value field in a ColorSpec is reserved for use by the Color Manager. In most cases your application won't change the device color table. If you want to know more about the device color table, refer to the Color Manager chapter for more details.

THE COLOR GRAPHICS PORT

As described above, programs designed to take advantage of the more powerful new color facilities available on the Macintosh II must use a new form of graphics port, *the color graphics port* (type cGrafPort). Color grafPorts will generally be created indirectly, as a result of opening a color window with the new routines NewCWindow, GetNewCWindow, and NewCDialog.

In addition, the old routines GetNewWindow, GetNewDialog, Alert, StopAlert, NoteAlert, and CautionAlert will open a color grafPort if certain resources (types 'wctb', 'dctb', or 'actb') are present. Refer to the chapters on the Window and Dialog Managers for more details.

The new cGrafPort structure is the same size as the old-style grafPort and most of its fields are unchanged. The old portBits field, which formerly held a complete 14-byte BitMap record embedded within the grafPort, has been replaced by a 4-byte PixMapHandle (portPixMap), freeing 10 bytes for other uses. (In particular, the new portVersion field, in the position previously occupied by the bit map's rowBytes field, always has its two high bits set; these bits are used to distinguish cGrafPorts from grafPorts, in which the two high bits of rowBytes are always clear. See Figure 3.) Similarly, the old bkPat, pnPat, and fillPat fields, which previously held 8-byte patterns, have been replaced by three 4-byte handles. The resulting 12 bytes of additional space are taken up by two 6-byte RGBColor records.

The structure of the color graphics port is as follows:

```
CGrafPtr  = ^CGrafPort;
CGrafPort = RECORD
                device:        INTEGER;       {device ID for font }
                                              { selection}
                portPixMap:    PixMapHandle;  {port's pixel map}
                portVersion:   INTEGER;       {highest 2 bits always }
                                              { set}
                grafVars:      Handle;        {handle to more fields}
                chExtra:       INTEGER;       {extra characters}
                pnLocHFrac:    INTEGER;       {pen fraction}
                portRect:      Rect;          {port rectangle}
                visRgn:        RgnHandle;     {visible region}
                clipRgn:       RgnHandle;     {clipping region}
                bkPixPat:      PixPatHandle;  {background pattern}
                rgbFgColor:    RGBColor;      {requested foreground }
                                              { color}
                rgbBkColor:    RGBColor;      {requested background }
                                              { color}
                pnLoc:         Point;         {pen location}
                pnSize:        Point;         {pen size}
                pnMode:        INTEGER;       {pen transfer mode}
                pnPixPat:      PixPatHandle;  {pen pattern}
                fillPixPat:    PixPatHandle;  {fill pattern}
                pnVis:         INTEGER;       {pen visibility}
                txFont:        INTEGER;       {font number for text}
                txFace:        Style;         {text's character style}
                txMode:        INTEGER;       {text's transfer mode}
                txSize:        INTEGER;       {font size for text}
                spExtra:       Fixed;         {extra space}
                fgColor:       LONGINT;       {actual foreground color}
                bkColor:       LONGINT;       {actual background color}
                colrBit:       INTEGER;       {plane being drawn}
                patStretch:    INTEGER;       {used internally}
                picSave:       Handle;        {picture being saved}
                rgnSave:       Handle;        {region being saved}
                polySave:      Handle;        {polygon being saved}
                grafProcs:     CQDProcsPtr    {low-level drawing }
                                              { routines}
            END;
```

Field descriptions

portPixMap
: The portPixMap field contains a handle to the port's pixel map. This is the structure that describes the cGrafPort's pixels.

portVersion
: The two high bits of the portVersion field are always set. This allows Color QuickDraw to tell the difference between a grafPort and a cGrafPort. The remainder of the field gives the version number of Color QuickDraw that created this port. (Initial release is version 0.)

grafVars
: The grafVars field contains a handle to additional fields.

chExtra
: The chExtra field is used in proportional spacing. It specifies a fixed point number by which to widen every character, excluding the space character, in a line of text. (The number is in 4.12 fractional notation: four bits of signed integer followed by 12 bits of fraction. This number is multiplied by txSize before it is used.) Default chExtra is 0.

pnLocHFrac
: The pnLocHFrac field contains the fractional horizontal pen position used when drawing text. The initial pen fraction is 1/2.

bkPixPat
: The bkPixPat field contains a handle to the background pixel pattern.

rgbFgColor
: The rgbFgColor field contains the requested foreground color.

rgbBkColor
: The rgbBkColor field contains the requested background color.

pnPixPat
: The pnPixPat field contains a handle to the pixel pattern for pen drawing.

fillPixPat
: The fillPixPat field contains a handle to the pixel pattern for area fill; for internal use only. Notice that this is not in the same location as old fillPat.

fgColor
: The fgColor field contains the pixel value of the foreground color supplied by the Color Manager. This is the best available approximation to rgbFgColor.

bkColor
: The bkColor field contains the pixel value of the background color supplied by the Color Manager. This is the best available approximation to rgbBkColor.

colrBit
: The colrBit field is reserved: not for use by applications.

grafProc
: The grafProc field used with a cGrafPort contains a CQDProcsPtr, instead of the QDProcsPtr used with a grafPort.

All remaining fields have the same meanings as in the old-style grafPort.

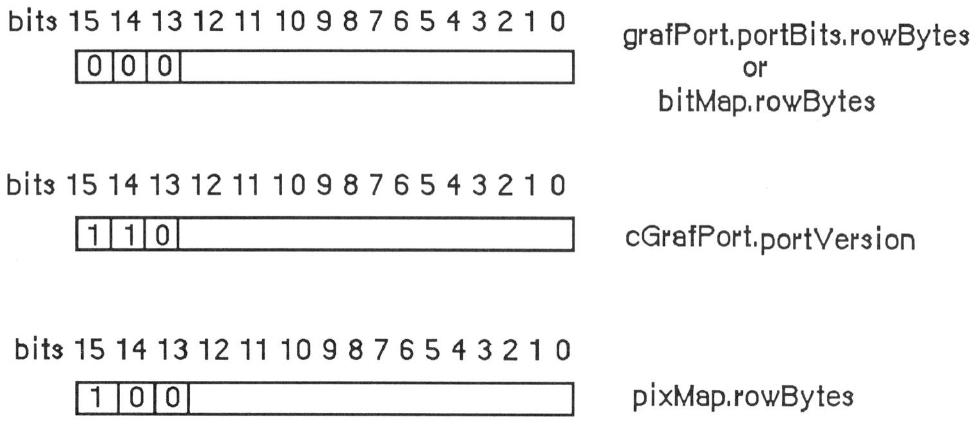

bits 15 14 13 12 11 10 9 8 7 6 5 4 3 2 1 0

| 0 | 0 | 0 | |

grafPort.portBits.rowBytes
or
bitMap.rowBytes

bits 15 14 13 12 11 10 9 8 7 6 5 4 3 2 1 0

| 1 | 1 | 0 | |

cGrafPort.portVersion

bits 15 14 13 12 11 10 9 8 7 6 5 4 3 2 1 0

| 1 | 0 | 0 | |

pixMap.rowBytes

Figure 3. Color QuickDraw Fields

Pixel Images

The representation of a color image in memory is a pixel image, analogous to the bit image used by the original QuickDraw. The number of bits per pixel is called the *depth* of the image; a pixel image one bit deep is equivalent to a bit image. On the Macintosh II, the pixel image that appears on a video screen is normally stored on a graphics card rather than in main memory. To increase speed, your program can build additional images in RAM for rapid transfer to the display device. This technique, called drawing to an offscreen bitmap, is described in the Graphics Devices chapter.

There are several possible arrangements of a pixel image in memory. The size and structure of a pixel image is described by the pixel map data structure; this structure and its various forms are discussed below. See Figure 4 for a representation of a pixel image on a system with screen depth set to eight.

Pixel Maps

Just as the original QuickDraw does all of its drawing in a bit map, Color QuickDraw uses an extended data structure called a pixel map (pixMap). In addition to the dimensions and contents of a pixel image, the pixel map also includes information on the image's storage format, depth, resolution, and color usage:

```
TYPE
 PixMapHandle = ^PixMapPtr;
 PixMapPtr    = ^PixMap;
 PixMap       = RECORD
                   baseAddr:   Ptr;        {pointer to pixMap data}
                   rowBytes:   INTEGER;    {offset to next row}
                   bounds:     Rect;       {boundary rectangle}
```

```
            pmVersion:  INTEGER;      {color QuickDraw version }
                                      { number}
            packType:   INTEGER;      {packing format}
            packSize:   LONGINT;      {size of data in packed }
                                      { state}
            hRes:       Fixed;        {horizontal resolution}
            vRes:       Fixed;        {vertical resolution}
            pixelType:  INTEGER;      {format of pixel image}
            pixelSize:  INTEGER;      {physical bits per pixel}
            cmpCount:   INTEGER;      {logical components per }
                                      { pixel}
            cmpSize:    INTEGER;      {logical bits per component}
            planeBytes: LONGINT;      {offset to next plane}
            pmTable:    CTabHandle;   {absolute colors for this }
                                      { image}
            pmReserved: LONGINT       {reserved for future }
                                      { expansion}
      END;
```

Field descriptions

baseAddr   The baseAddr field contains a pointer to first byte of the pixel image, the same as in a bitMap. For optimal performance this should be a multiple of four.

rowBytes   The rowBytes field contains the offset in bytes from one row of the image to the next, the same as in a bitMap. As before, rowBytes must be even. The high three bits of rowBytes are used as flags. If bit 15 = 1, the data structure is a pixMap; otherwise it is a bitMap. Bits 14 and 13 are not used and must be 0.

bounds   The bounds field is the boundary rectangle, which defines the coordinate system and extent of the pixel map; it's similar to a bitMap. This rectangle is in pixels, so depth has no effect on its values.

pmVersion   The pmVersion is the version number of Color QuickDraw that created this pixel map, which is provided for future compatibility. (Initial release is version 0.)

packType   The packType field identifies the packing algorithm used to compress image data. Color QuickDraw currently supports only packType = 0, which means no packing.

packSize   The packSize field contains the size of the packed image in bytes. When packType = 0, this field should be set to 0.

hRes   The hRes is the horizontal resolution of pixMap data in pixels per inch.

vRes   The vRes is the vertical resolution of pixMap data in pixels per inch. By default, hRes = vRes = 72 pixels per inch.

pixelType   The pixelType field specifies the storage format for a pixel image. 0 = chunky, 1 = chunky/planar, 2 = planar. Only chunky is used in the Macintosh II.

pixelSize   The pixelSize is the physical bits per pixel; it's always a power of 2.

cmpCount   The cmpCount is the number of color components per pixel. For chunky pixel images, this is always 1.

cmpSize   The cmpSize field contains the logical bits per RGBColor component. Note that (cmpCount*cmpSize) doesn't necessarily equal pixelSize. For chunky pixel images, cmpSize = pixelSize.

planeBytes   The planeBytes field is the offset in bytes from one plane to the next. If only one plane is used, as is the case with chunky pixel images, this field is set to 0.

pmTable   The pmTable field is a handle to table of colors used in the pixMap. This may be a device color table or an image color table.

pmReserved   The pmReserved field is reserved for future expansion; it must be set to 0 for future compatibility.

The data in a pixel image can be organized several ways, depending on the characteristics of the device or image. The pixMap data structure supports three pixel image formats: chunky, planar, and chunky/planar.

In a **chunky** pixel image, all of a pixel's bits are stored consecutively in memory, all of a row's pixels are stored consecutively, and rowBytes indicates the offset in memory from one row to the next. This is the only one of the three formats that's supported by this implementation of Color QuickDraw. The pixel depths that are currently supported are 1, 2, 4, and 8 bits per pixel. In a chunky pixMap cmpCount = 1 and cmpSize = pixelSize. Figure 4 shows a chunky pixel image for a system with screen depth set to eight.

A planar pixel image is a pixel image separated into distinct bit images in memory, one for each color plane. Within the bit image, rowBytes indicates the offset in memory from one row to the next. PlaneBytes indicates the offset in memory from one plane to the next. The planar format isn't supported by this implementation of Color QuickDraw.

A chunky/planar pixel image is separated into distinct pixel images in memory, typically one for each color component. Within the pixel image, rowBytes indicates the offset in memory from one row to the next. PlaneBytes indicates the offset in memory from one plane to the next. The chunky/planar format isn't supported by this implementation of Color QuickDraw.

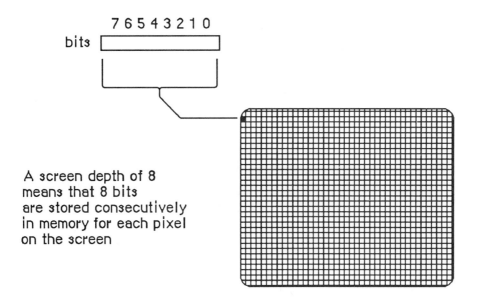

bits
7 6 5 4 3 2 1 0

A screen depth of 8
means that 8 bits
are stored consecutively
in memory for each pixel
on the screen

Figure 4. A Pixel Image

Pixel Patterns

With Color QuickDraw, monochrome patterns are replaced by a new form of pattern
structure, the **pixel pattern,** which offers greater flexibility in the use of color. The three
pattern fields in a grafPort—pnPat, bkPat, and fillPat—have been replaced by the
pnPixPat, bkPixPat, and fillPixPat fields in a cGrafPort. The format for a pixel pattern is
shown below:

```
TYPE
  PixPatHandle = ^PixPatPtr;
  PixPatPtr    = ^PixPat;
  PixPat       = RECORD
                   patType:   INTEGER;       {pattern type}
                   patMap:    PixMapHandle;  {pattern characteristics}
                   patData:   Handle;        {pixel image defining }
                                             { pattern}
                   patXData:  Handle;        {expanded pixel image}
                   patXValid: INTEGER;       {flags for expanded }
                                             { pattern data}
                   patXMap:   Handle;        {handle to expanded }
                                             { pattern data}
                   pat1Data:  Pattern;       {old-style pattern/RGB }
                                             { color}
                 END;
```

4 Color QuickDraw

Field descriptions

patType   The patType field specifies the pattern's type. The possible values
                include: 0 = old-style pattern, 1 = full-color pixel pattern, 2 = RGB
                pattern.

patMap   The patMap field is a handle to the pixel map describing the pattern's
                pixel image.

patData   The patData field is a handle to the pattern's pixel image.

patXData   The patXData field is a handle to an expanded pixel image used
                internally by Color QuickDraw.

patXValid   When the pattern's data or color table change, you can invalidate the
                expanded data by setting the patXValid field to –1.

patXMap   The patXMap field is a handle that is reserved for use by Color
                QuickDraw.

pat1Data   The pat1Data field contains an old-style 8-by-8 pattern to be used
                when this pattern is drawn into old grafPort. NewPixPat sets this
                field to 50% gray.

Old-style patterns are still supported. When used in a cGrafPort, the QuickDraw routines
PenPat and BackPat store the pattern within pnPixPat and bkPixPat, respectively, and set
the patType to 0 to indicate that the structure contains old pattern data. Such patterns are
limited to the original 8-by-8 dimensions and are always drawn using the values in the
cGrafPort's rgbFgColor and rgbBkColor fields. Similarly, filled drawing operations, such
as FillRect, are also supported.

In a pixel pattern (patType = 1), the pattern's dimensions, depth, resolution (only 72 pixels
per inch is supported), set of colors, and other characteristics are defined by a pixel map,
referenced by the patMap handle. Since the pixel map has its own color table, pixel patterns
can consist of any number of colors, and don't usually use the foreground and background
colors. The section on relative patterns, below, describes an exception to this rule.

Furthermore, patType = 1 patterns are not limited to a fixed size: their height and width can
be any power of 2, as specified by the height and width of patMap^^.bounds. (Notice that
a pattern eight bits wide—the original QuickDraw size—has a row width of just one byte,
contrary to the usual rule that the rowBytes field must be even.) This pattern type is
generally read into memory using the GetPixPat routine, or set using the PenPixPat or
BackPixPat routines.

Although the patMap defines the pattern's characteristics, its baseAddr field is ignored; for
a type1 pattern, the actual pixel image defining the pattern is stored in the handle in the
pattern's patData field. The pattern's depth need not match that of the pixel map it's painted
into; the depth will be adjusted automatically when the pattern is drawn. Color QuickDraw
maintains a private copy of the pattern's pixel image, expanded to the current screen depth,
and aligned to the current grafPort or cGrafPort, in the patXData field.

The third pattern type is RGBPat (patType = 2). Using the MakeRGBPat routine, the application can specify the exact color it wants to use. QuickDraw selects a pattern to approximate that color. In this way, an application can effectively increase the color resolution of the screen. Pixel patterns are particularly useful for **dithering:** mixing existing colors together to create the illusion of a third color that's unavailable on a particular device. The MakeRGBPat routine aids in this process by constructing a dithered pattern to approximate a given absolute color. (See the description of MakeRGBPat in the "Color QuickDraw Routines" section for more details.) In the current implementation of ColorQuickDraw, an RGBPat can display 125 different patterns on a 4-bit-deep screen, or 2197 different patterns on an 8-bit-deep screen.

For an RGBPat, the RGB defines the image; there is no image data. An RGBPat has an 8-by-8, 2-bit-deep pattern.

A program that creates a pixMap must initialize the pixMap's color table to describe the pixels. GetCTable could be used to read such a table from a resource file; you could then dispose of the pixMap's color table and replace it with the one returned by GetCTable.

Relative Patterns

Type1 pixel patterns contain color tables that describe the colors they use. Generally such a color table contains one entry for each color used in the pattern. For instance, if your pattern has five colors in it, you would probably create a four-bit-per-pixel pattern that uses pixel values 0–4, and a color table with five entries, numbered 0–4, that contain the RGB specifications for those pixel values.

When the pattern is drawn, each possible pixel value that isn't specified in the color table is assigned a color. The largest unassigned pixel value becomes the foreground color; the smallest unassigned pixel value is assigned the background color. Remaining unassigned pixel values are given colors that are evenly distributed between the foreground and background.

For instance, in the color table mentioned above, pixel values 5–15 are unused. Assume that the foreground color is black and the background color is white. Pixel value 15 is assigned the foreground color, black; pixel value 5 is assigned the background color, white; the nine pixel values between them are assigned evenly distributed shades of gray. If the pixMap's color table is set to NIL, all pixel values are determined by blending the foreground and background colors.

Transfer Modes

A **transfer mode** is a method of placing information on the display devices. It involves an interaction between what your application is drawing (the source) and what's already there (the destination). The original QuickDraw offered eight basic transfer modes:

- completely replacing the destination with the source (Copy), and its inverse (NotCopy)
- combining the destination with the source (Or), and its inverse (NotOr)

4 Color QuickDraw

- selectively clearing the destination with the source (Bic, for "bit clear"), and its inverse (NotBic)

- selectively inverting the destination with the source (Xor), and its inverse (NotXor)

This is how color affects these eight transfer modes when the source pixels are either black (all 1's) or white (all 0's):

Copy   The Copy mode applies the foreground color to the black part of the source (the part containing 1's) and the background color to the white part of the source (the part containing 0's), and replaces the destination with the colored source.

NotCopy   The NotCopy mode applies the foreground color to the white part of the source and the background color to the black part of the source, and replaces the destination with the colored source. It thus has the effect of reversing the foreground and background colors.

Or   The Or mode applies the foreground color to the black part of the source and replaces the destination with the colored source. The white part of the source isn't transferred to the destination. If the foreground is black, the drawing will be faster.

NotOr   The NotOr mode applies the foreground color to the white part of the source and replaces the destination with the colored source. The black part of the source isn't transferred to the destination. If the foreground is black, the drawing will be faster.

Bic   The Bic mode applies the background color to the black part of the source and replaces the destination with the colored source. The white part of the source isn't transferred to the destination.

NotBic   The NotBic mode applies the background color to the white part of the source and replaces the destination with the colored source. The black part of the source isn't transferred to the destination.

Xor   The Xor mode complements the bits in the destination corresponding to the bits equal to 1 in the source. When used on a colored destination, the color of the inverted destination isn't defined.

NotXor   The NotXor mode inverts the bits that are 0 in the source. When used on a colored destination, the color of the inverted destination isn't defined.

Pixels of colors other than black and white aren't all 1's or all 0's, so the application of a foreground color or a background color to the pixel produces an undefined result. For this reason, and because a pixPat already contains color, the foreground and background colors are ignored when your application is drawing with a pixPat. When your program draws a pixMap the foreground and background colors are *not* ignored. Make sure that the foreground is black and the background is white before you call CopyBits or the result will be undefined.

If you intend to draw with pixMaps or pixPats, you will probably want to use the Copy mode or one of the arithmetic modes described in the following section.

To help make color work well on different screen depths, Color QuickDraw does some validity checking of the foreground and background colors. If your application is drawing to a cGrafPort with a depth equal to 1 or 2, and if the RGB values of the foreground and background colors aren't the same, but both of them map to the same pixel value, then the foreground color is inverted. This ensures that, for instance, red text drawn on a green background doesn't map to black on black.

Arithmetic Drawing Modes

Color QuickDraw uses a set of arithmetic drawing modes designed specifically for use with color. These modes change the destination pixels by performing arithmetic operations on the source and destination pixels. These drawing modes are most useful in 8-bit color, but work on 4-bit and 2-bit color as well. If the destination bitmap is one bit deep, the mode reverts to one of the old transfer modes that approximates the arithmetic mode requested.

Each drawing routine converts the source and destination pixels to their RGB components, performs an operation on each pair of components to provide a new RGB value for the destination, and then assigns the destination a pixel value close to the calculated RGB value. The arithmetic modes listed below can be used for all drawing operations; your application can pass them as a parameter to TextMode, PenMode, or CopyBits.

addOver   This mode assigns to the destination pixel the color closest to the sum of the source and destination RGB values. If the sum of any of the RGB components exceeds the maximum allowable value, 65,535, the RGB value wraps around to the value less 65,536. AddOver is slightly faster than addPin. If the destination bitmap is one bit deep, addOver reverts to Xor.

addPin   This mode assigns to the destination pixel the color closest to the sum of the destination RGB values, pinned to a maximum allowable RGB value. For grafPorts, the pin value is always white. For cGrafPorts, the pin value is assigned using OpColor. If the destination bitmap is one bit deep, addPin reverts to Bic.

subOver   This mode assigns to the destination pixel the color closest to the difference of the source and destination RGB values. If the result is less than 0, the RGB value wraps around to 65,536 less the result. SubOver is slightly faster than subPin. If the destination bitmap is one bit deep, subOver reverts to Xor.

subPin   This mode assigns to the destination pixel the color closest to the difference of the sum and the destination RGB values, pinned to a minimum allowable RGB value. For grafPorts, the pin value is always black. In a cGrafPort, the pin value is assigned by using OpColor. If the destination bitmap is one bit deep, subPin reverts to Or.

adMax   (Arithmetic Drawing Max) This mode compares the source and destination pixels, and replaces the destination pixel with the color containing the greater saturation of each of the RGB components. Each RGB component comparison is done independently, so the resulting color isn't necessarily either the source or the destination color. If the destination bitmap is one bit deep, adMax reverts to Bic.

adMin   (Arithmetic Drawing Min) This mode compares the source and destination pixels, and replaces the destination pixel with the color containing the lesser saturation of each of the RGB components. Each RGB component is compared independently, so the resulting color isn't necessarily the source or the destination color. If the destination bitmap is one bit deep, adMin reverts to Or.

blend   This mode replaces the destination pixel with a weighted average of the colors of the source and destination pixels. The formula used to calculate the destination is:

```
dest = source*weight/65,536 + destination*(1-weight/65,536)
```

where weight is an unsigned value between 1 and 65,535. In a grafPort, the weight is set to 50% gray, so that equal weights of the source and destination RGB components are combined to produce the destination color. In a cGrafPort, the weight is an RGBColor that individually specifies the weights of the red, green, and blue components. The weight is assigned using OpColor. If the destination bitmap is one bit deep, blend reverts to Copy.

Because drawing with the arithmetic modes uses the closest matching pixel values, and not necessarily exact matches, these modes might not produce the results you expect. For instance, suppose srcCopy mode is used to paint a green pixel on the screen in 4-bit mode. Of the 16 colors available, the closest green may contain a small amount of red, as in RGB components of 300 red, 65,535 green, and 0 blue. AddOver is then used to paint a red pixel on top of the green pixel, ideally resulting in a yellow pixel. The red pixel's RGB components are 65,535 red, 0 green, and 0 blue. Adding the red components together wraps to 300, since the largest representable value is 65,535. In this case, AddOver would cause no visible change at all. Using AddPin with an opColor of white would produce the desired results.

On the Macintosh II the rules for setting the pen mode and the text mode have been relaxed slightly. It's no longer necessary to specify a pattern mode or a source mode (patCopy as opposed to srcCopy) to perform a particular operation. QuickDraw will choose the correct drawing mode automatically. However, to be compatible with earlier versions of QuickDraw, you application must specify the correct drawing mode. Text and bitmaps should always use a source mode; rectangles, regions, polygons, arcs, ovals, round rectangles, and lines should always use a pattern mode.

The constants used for the arithmetic transfer modes are as follows:

```
CONST
  blend    = 32;
  addPin   = 33;
  addOver  = 34;
  subPin   = 35;
  adMax    = 37;
  subOver  = 38;
  adMin    = 39;
```

*[handwritten annotations: nothing; nothing; Purple → Erase; Nothing; * ; nothing; nothing; 36 Purple → Erase; 50 Nothing]*

Warning: Unlike the rest of QuickDraw, the arithmetic modes don't call the Color Manager when mapping a requested RGB value to a pixel value. If your application replaces the color matching routines, you must either not use these modes, or you must maintain the inverse table using the Color Manager routines.

Replace with Transparency

The transparent mode replaces the destination pixel with the source pixel if the source pixel isn't equal to the background color. This mode is most useful in 8-bit, 4-bit, or 2-bit color modes. To specify a transparent pattern, use the drawing mode transparent+patCopy. If the destination pixMap is one bit deep, the mode is translated to Or. Transparency can be specified as a parameter to TextMode, PenMode, or CopyBits.

Transparent mode is optimized to handle source bitmaps with large transparent holes, as an alternative to specifying an unusual clipping region or mask parameter to CopyMask. Patterns aren't optimized, and may not draw as quickly.

The constant used for transparent mode is

```
CONST
  transparent  = 36;
```

The Hilite Mode

This new method of highlighting exchanges the background color and the highlight color in the destination. This has the visual effect of using a highlighting pen to select the object. For instance, TextEdit uses the hilite mode to select text: if the highlight color is yellow, selected text appears on a yellow background. In general, highlighting should be used in place of inversion when selecting and deselecting objects such as text or graphics.

There are two ways to use hilite mode. The easiest is to call

```
    BitClr (Ptr(HiliteMode,pHiliteBit));
```

just before calling InvertRect, InvertRgn, InvertArc, InvertRoundRct, or InvertPoly or any drawing using srcXor mode. On a one-bit-deep destination, this will work exactly like inversion, and is compatible with all versions of QuickDraw. Color QuickDraw resets the hilite bit after performing each drawing operation, so the hilite bit should be cleared immediately before calling a routine that is to do highlighting. Routines that formerly used

Xor inversion, such as the Invert routines, Paint, Frame, LineTo, text drawing, and CopyBits, will now use hilite mode if the hilite bit is clear.

Assembly language note: You can use

```
BCLR #hiliteBit, hiliteMode
```

Do not alter the other bits in HiliteMode.

The second way to use hilite mode is to pass it directly to TextMode, PenMode, or CopyBits as a parameter.

Hilite mode uses the source or pattern to decide which bits to exchange; only bits that are on in the source or pattern can be highlighted in the destination.

A very small inversion should probably not use hilite mode, because a small selection in the hilite color might be too hard to see. TextEdit, for instance, uses hilite mode to select and deselect text, but not to blink the insertion point.

Hilite mode is optimized to look for consecutive pixels in either the hilite or background colors. For example, if the source is an all black pattern, the highlighting will be especially fast, operating internally on a long word at a time instead of a pixel at a time. Highlighting a large area without such consecutive pixels (a gray pattern, for instance) can be slow.

The global variable HiliteRGB is read from parameter RAM when the machine starts. Old grafPorts use the RGB values in the global HiliteRGB as the highlight color. Color grafPorts default to the global HiliteRGB, but can be overridden by the HiliteColor procedure.

The constants used with hilite mode are listed below:

```
CONST
  hilite     = 50;
  pHiliteBit = 0; {this is the correct value for use when calling }
                  { the BitClear trap. BClr must use the assembly }
                  { language equate hiliteBit}
```

THE COLOR CURSOR

Color QuickDraw supports the use of color cursors. The size of a cursor is still 16-by-16 pixels. The new CCrsr data structure is substantially different from the Cursor data structure used with the original QuickDraw: the CCrsr fields crsr1Data, crsrMask, and crsrHotSpot are the only fields that have counterparts in the Cursor record.

The structure of the color cursor is as follows:

```
TYPE
    CCrsrHandle = ^CCrsrPtr;
    CCrsrPtr    = ^CCrsr;
    CCrsr       = RECORD
                    crsrType:    INTEGER;      {type of cursor}
                    crsrMap:     PixMapHandle; {the cursor's pixmap}
                    crsrData:    Handle;       {cursor's data}
                    crsrXData:   Handle;       {expanded cursor data}
                    crsrXValid:  INTEGER;      {depth of expanded data}
                    crsrXHandle: Handle;       {Reserved for future }
                                               { use}
                    crsr1Data:   Bits16;       {one-bit cursor}
                    crsrMask:    Bits16;       {cursor's mask}
                    crsrHotSpot: Point;        {cursor's hotspot}
                    crsrXTable:  LONGINT;      {private}
                    crsrID:      LONGINT;      {ctSeed for expanded }
                                               { cursor}
                  END;
```

You will not normally need to manipulate the fields of a color cursor. Your application can load in a color cursor using the GetCCursor routine, and display it using the SetCCursor routine. When the application is finished using a color cursor, it should dispose of it using the DisposCCursor routine. These routines are discussed below in the section "Color QuickDraw Routines".

Color cursors are stored in resources of type 'crsr'. The format of the 'crsr' resource is given in the section "Color QuickDraw Resource Formats".

Field descriptions

crsrType
: The crsrType field specifies the type of cursor. Possible values are: $8000 = old cursor, $8001 = new cursor.

crsrMap
: The crsrMap field is a handle to the pixel map defining the cursor's characteristics.

crsrData
: The crsrData field is a handle to the cursor's pixel data.

crsrXData
: The crsrXData field is a handle to the expanded pixel image used internally by Color QuickDraw (private).

crsrXValid
: The crsrXValid field contains the depth of the expanded cursor image. If you change the cursor's data or color table, you should set this field to 0 to cause the cursor to be reexpanded. You should never set it to any other values.

crsrXHandle
: The crsrXHandle field is reserved for future use.

crsr1Data The crsr1Data field contains a 16-by-16 one-bit image to be displayed when the cursor is on 1-bit or 2-bit per pixel screens.

crsrMask The crsrMask field contains the cursor's mask data. The same 1-bit-deep mask is used with crsrData and crsr1Data.

crsrHotSpot The crsrHotSpot field contains the cursor's hot spot.

crsrXTable The crsrXTable field is reserved for future use.

crsrID The crsrID field contains the ctSeed for the cursor.

The first four fields of the CCrsr record are similar to the first four fields of the PixPat record, and are used in the same manner by Color QuickDraw. See the discussion of the patMap field under the section titled "Pixel Patterns" for more information on how the crsrMap is used.

The display of a cursor involves a relationship between a mask, stored in the crsrMask field with the same format used for old cursor masks, and an image. There are two possible sources for a color cursor's image. When the cursor is on a screen whose depth is one or two bits per pixel, the image for the cursor is taken from Crsr1Data, which contains old-style cursor data. In this case, the relationship between data and mask is exactly as before. When the screen depth is greater than two bits per pixel, the image for the cursor is taken from crsrMap and crsrData; the relationship between mask and data is described in the following paragraph.

The data pixels within the mask replace the destination pixels. The data pixels outside the mask are displayed using an XOR with the destination pixels. If data pixels outside the mask are 0 (white), the destination pixels aren't changed. If data pixels outside the mask are all 1's (black), the destination pixels are complemented. All other values outside of the mask cause unpredictable results.

To work properly, a color cursor's image should contain white pixels (R = G = B = $FFFF) for the transparent part of the image, and black pixels (R = G = B = $0000) for the inverting part of the image, in addition to the other colors in the cursor's image. Thus, to define a cursor that contains two colors, it's necessary to use a 2-bit-per-pixel cursor image (that is, a four-color image).

If your application changes the value of your cursor data or its color table, it should set the crsrXValid field to 0 to indicate that the cursor's data needs to be reexpanded, and assign a new unique value to crsrID (unique values can be obtained using the GetCTSeed routine); then it should call SetCCursor to display the changed cursor.

COLOR ICONS

A new data structure, known as CIcon, supports the use of color icons. The structure of the color icon is as follows:

```
TYPE
   CIconHandle = ^CIconPtr;
   CIconPtr    = ^CIcon;
   CIcon       = RECORD
                    iconPMap:   PixMap;     {the icon's pixMap}
                    iconMask:   BitMap;     {the icon's mask bitmap}
                    iconBMap:   BitMap;     {the icon's bitMap}
                    iconData:   Handle;     {the icon's data}
                    iconMaskData: ARRAY[0..0] OF INTEGER;
                                            {icon's mask and bitmap }
                                            { data}
                 END;
```

You won't normally need to manipulate the fields of color icons. Your application can load a color icon into memory using the routine GetCIcon. To draw a color icon that's already in memory, use PlotCIcon. When your application is through with a color icon, it can dispose of it using the DisposCIcon routine. These routines are discussed below in the section "Color QuickDraw Routines".

Color icons are stored in a resource file as resource type 'cicn'. The format of the 'cicn' resource is given in the section "Using Color QuickDraw Resources".

Field descriptions

iconPMap   The iconPMap field contains the pixel map describing the icon. Note that pixMap is inline, not a handle.

iconMask   The iconMask field contains a bit map for the icon's mask.

iconBMap   The iconBMap field contains a bit map for the icon.

iconData   The iconData field contains a handle to the icon's pixel image.

iconMaskData The iconMaskData field is an array containing the icon's mask data followed by the icon's bitmap data. This is only used when the icon is stored as a resource.

You can use color icons in menus in the same way that you could use old icons in menus. The menu definition procedure first tries to load in a 'cicn' with the specified resource ID. If it doesn't find one, then it tries to load in an 'ICON' with that ID. The Dialog Manager will also use a 'cicn' in place of an 'ICON' if there is one with the ID specified in the item list. For more information, see the Menu Manager and Dialog Manager chapters.

USING COLOR QUICKDRAW

This section gives an overview of routines that you will typically call while using Color QuickDraw. All routines are discussed below in the section "Color QuickDraw Routines".

4 Color QuickDraw

Using a color graphics port is much like using an old-style grafPort. The old routines SetPort and GetPort operate on grafPorts or cGrafPorts, and the global variable ThePort points to either to a grafPort or a cGrafPort. Color QuickDraw examines the two high bits of the portBits.rowBytes field (the portVersion field in a cGrafPort). If these bits equal 0, then it is a grafPort; if they are both 1, then it is a cGrafPort. In Pascal, use **type coercion** to convert between GrafPtr and cGrafPtr. For example:

```
VAR myPort: CGrafPtr;
SetPort (GrafPtr(myPort));
```

There's still a graphics pen for line drawing, with a current size, location, pattern, and transfer mode; all of the old line- and shape-drawing operations, such as Move, LineTo, FrameRect, and PaintPoly, still work just as before. However, colors should be set with the new routines RGBForeColor and RGBBackColor (described below) instead of the old ForeColor and BackColor routines. If your application is using the Palette Manager, use the routines PMForeColor and PMBackColor instead.

PenPat and BackPat are still supported, and will construct a pixel pattern equivalent to the specified bit pattern. The patType field of this pattern is set to 0; thus it will always use the port's current foreground and background colors at the time of drawing.

To read a multicolored pattern from a resource file, use the GetPixPat routine. Set these patterns using PenPixPat and BackPixPat, or pass them as parameters to Color QuickDraw's color fill routines (such as FillCRect). These patterns have their own color tables and are generally not affected by the port's foreground and background colors (refer to the earlier discussion of relative patterns).

Most routines that accept bitMaps as parameters also accept pixMaps (not PixMapHandles). Likewise, any new routine that has a pixMap as a parameter will also accept a bitMap. This allows one set of routines to work for all operations on images; the high bit of the rowBytes field distinguishes whether the parameter is a bitMap or a pixMap.

It's worth noting here that resources are used slightly differently by Color QuickDraw than they were used by QuickDraw. For instance, with old QuickDraw, your application could call GetCursor before each SetCursor; the same handle would be passed back to the application each time. With Color QuickDraw, the color cursor is a compound structure, more complex than a simple resource handle. Color QuickDraw reads the requested resource, copies it, and then alters the copy before passing it to the application. Each time your application calls GetCCursor, it gets a new copy of the cursor. This means that your program should only call GetCCursor once, even if it does multiple SetCCursor calls. The new resource types should be marked as purgeable if you are concerned about memory space. This discussion holds true for color cursor, color pattern, color icon, and color table resources.

COLOR QUICKDRAW ROUTINES

Color QuickDraw continues to support all the original QuickDraw calls described in Volume I. The following sections describe in detail the new Color QuickDraw routines, as well as changes to existing routines.

Operations on CGrafPorts

```
PROCEDURE OpenCPort (port: CGrafPtr);
```

The OpenCPort procedure is analogous to OpenPort, except it opens a cGrafPort instead of a grafPort. You will rarely need to use this call, since OpenCPort is called by NewCWindow and GetNewCWindow, as well as by the Dialog Manager when the appropriate color resources are present. OpenCPort allocates storage for all the structures in the cGrafPort, and then calls InitCPort to initialize them. The new structures allocated are the portPixMap, the pnPixPat, the fillPixPat, the bkPixPat, and the grafVars handle. The GrafVars record structure is shown below:

```
TYPE
GrafVars = RECORD
            rgbOpColor:     RGBColor;  {color for addPin, subPin, and }
                                       { blend}
            rgbHiliteColor: RGBColor;  {color for highlighting}
            pmFgColor:      Handle;    {Palette handle for foreground }
                                       { color}
            pmFgIndex:      INTEGER;   {index value for foreground}
            pmBkColor:      Handle;    {Palette handle for background }
                                       { color}
            pmBkIndex:      INTEGER;   {index value for background}
            pmFlags:        INTEGER;   {Flags for Palette Manager}
          END;
```

The rgbOpColor field is initialized as black, and the rgbHiliteColor field is initialized as the default HiliteRGB. All the rest of the GrafVars fields are initially zero.

The portPixMap is not allocated a color table of its own. When InitCPort is called, the handle to the current device's color table is copied into the portPixMap.

```
PROCEDURE InitCPort (port: CGrafPtr);
```

The InitCPort procedure does not allocate any storage. It merely initializes all the fields in the cGrafPort to their default values. All old fields are initialized to the same values as a grafPort's fields. New fields are given the following values:

portPixMap:	copied from theGDevice^^.GDPMap
portVersion:	$C000
grafVars:	opColor initialized to black, rgbHiliteColor initialized as default HiliteRGB. All other fields are initialized as 0.
chExtra:	0
pnLocHFrac:	1/2
bkPixPat:	white
rgbFgColor:	black
rgbBkColor:	white
pnPixPat:	black
fillPixPat:	black

The default portPixMap is set to be the same as the current device's pixMap. This allows you to create an offscreen port that is identical to the screen's grafPort or cGrafPort for drawing offscreen. If you want to use a different set of colors for offscreen drawing, you should create a new gDevice, and set it as the current gDevice before opening the cGrafPort. Refer to the section on offscreen bitMaps in the Graphics Devices chapter for more details.

As mentioned above, InitCPort does not copy the data from the current device's color table to the portPixMap's color table. It simply replaces whatever is in the pmTable field with a copy of the handle to the current device's color table.

If you try to initialize a grafPort using InitCPort, it will simply return without doing anything.

```
PROCEDURE CloseCPort (port: CGrafPtr);
```

CloseCPort releases the memory allocated to the cGrafPort. It disposes of the visRgn, the clipRgn, the bkPixPat, the pnPixPat, the fillPixPat, and the grafVars handle. It also disposes of the portPixMap, but doesn't dispose of the portPixMap's color table (which is really owned by the gDevice). If you have placed your own color table into the portPixMap, either dispose of it *before* calling CloseCPort, or store another reference to it for other uses.

Setting the Foreground and Background Colors

```
PROCEDURE RGBForeColor (color : RGBColor);
PROCEDURE RGBBackColor (color : RGBColor);
```

These two calls set the foreground and background colors to the best available match for the current device. The only drawing operations that aren't affected by these colors are PlotCIcon, and drawing using the new color patterns. Before you call CopyBits with a pixMap as the source, you should set the foreground to black and the background to white.

If the current port is a cGrafPort, the specified RGB is placed in the rgbFgColor or rgbBkColor field (and the pixel value most closely matching that color is placed in the fgColor or bkColor field). If the current port is a grafPort, fgColor or bkColor is set to the old QuickDraw color determined by taking the high bit of each of the R, G, and B components, and using that three-bit number to select one of the eight QuickDraw colors. The ordering of the QuickDraw colors is shown in the GetForeColor description.

```
PROCEDURE GetForeColor (VAR color : RGBColor);
PROCEDURE GetBackColor (VAR color : RGBColor);
```

These two calls return the RGB components of the foreground and background colors set in the current port. The calls work for both grafPorts and cGrafPorts. If the current port is a cGrafPort, the returned value is taken directly from the rgbFgColor or rgbBkColor field. If the current port is a grafPort, then only eight possible RGB values can be returned. These eight values are determined by the values in a global variable named QDColors, which is a pointer to a color table containing the current QuickDraw colors.

The colors are stored in the following order:

Value	Color	Red	Green	Blue
0	black	$0000	$0000	$0000
1	yellow	$FC00	$F37D	$052F
2	magenta	$F2D7	$0856	$84EC
3	red	$DD6B	$08C2	$06A2
4	cyan	$0241	$AB54	$EAFF
5	green	$0000	$8000	$11B0
6	blue	$0000	$0000	$D400
7	white	$FFFF	$FFFF	$FFFF

This is the set of colors that Color QuickDraw uses to determine precisely what colors should be displayed by an old grafPort that is using color. The default set of colors has been adjusted to match the colors produced on the ImageWriter II printer.

Color Drawing Operations

```
PROCEDURE FillCRect (r: Rect; ppat: PixPatHandle);
PROCEDURE FillCOval (r: Rect; ppat: PixPatHandle);
PROCEDURE FillCRoundRect (r: Rect; ovWd,ovHt: INTEGER; ppat:
        PixPatHandle);
PROCEDURE FillCArc (r: Rect; startAngle,arcAngle: INTEGER; ppat:
        PixPatHandle);
PROCEDURE FillCRgn (rgn: RgnHandle; ppat: PixPatHandle);
PROCEDURE FillCPoly (poly: PolyHandle; ppat: PixPatHandle);
```

These calls are analogous to their similarly named counterparts in QuickDraw. They allow a multicolored pattern to be used for filling.

```
PROCEDURE GetCPixel (h,v: INTEGER; VAR cPix: RGBColor);
```

The GetCPixel function returns the RGB of the pixel at the specified position in the current port.

```
PROCEDURE SetCPixel (h,v: INTEGER; cPix: RGBColor);
```

The SetCPixel function sets the pixel at the specified position to the pixel value that most closely matches the specified RGB.

Creating Pixel Maps

```
FUNCTION NewPixMap : PixMapHandle;
```

The NewPixMap function creates a new, initialized pixMap data structure and returns a handle to it. All fields of the pixMap are copied from the current device's pixMap except the color table. A handle to the color table is allocated but not initialized.

```
PROCEDURE DisposPixMap (pm: PixMapHandle);
```

The DisposPixMap procedure releases all storage allocated by NewPixMap. It disposes of the pixMap's color table, and of the pixMap itself. Be careful not to dispose of a pixMap whose color table is the same as the current device's color table.

```
PROCEDURE CopyPixMap (srcPM,dstPM: PixMapHandle);
```

The CopyPixMap routine is used for duplicating the pixMap data structure. CopyPixMap copies the contents of the source pixMap data structure to the destination pixMap data structure. The contents of the color table are copied, so the destination pixMap has its own copy of the color table. Since the baseAddr field of the pixMap is a pointer, the pointer, but not the image itself, is copied.

Operations on Pixel Maps

```
PROCEDURE CopyBits (srcBits,dstBits: BitMap; srcRect, dstRect:
          Rect;  mode: INTEGER; maskRgn: RgnHandle);
```

CopyBits now accepts either bitMaps or pixMaps as parameters. For convenience, just as you could pass the current port^.portBits as a parameter to CopyBits, you can now pass GrafPtr(cPort)^.portBits. (Recall that in a cGrafPort the high two bits of the portVersion field are set. This field, in the same position in the port as portBits.rowBytes, indicates to QuickDraw that it has been passed a portPixMap handle.)

This call transfers an image from one bitMap or pixMap to another bitMap or pixMap. The source and destination may be of different depths, of different sizes, and they may have different color tables. Note, however, that the destination pixMap is assumed to use the same color table as the gDevice. (This is because an inverse table is required for translation to the destination's color table.)

During a CopyBits call, the foreground and background colors are applied to the image. To avoid unwanted coloring of the image, set the foreground to black and the background to white before calling this routine.

```
PROCEDURE CopyMask (srcBits,maskBits,dstBits: BitMap;
        srcRect,maskRect,dstRect: Rect);
```

CopyMask is a new version of the CopyBits procedure, introduced in the Macintosh Plus. It transfers an image from the source to the destination only where the corresponding bit of the mask equals 1. The Macintosh II version will accept either a bitMap or pixMap as the srcBits or dstBits parameters. The maskBits parameter must be a bitMap.

Like the Macintosh Plus version, CopyMask doesn't send any of its drawing commands through grafProc routines; thus CopyMask calls are not recorded in pictures. Unlike the Macintosh Plus version, the Macintosh II version of CopyMask is able to stretch the source and mask to fit the dstRect. The srcRect and maskRect should be the same size. CopyMask uses the same low-level code as CopyBits, so all the same rules regarding depth translation and color table translation apply.

During a CopyMask call, the foreground and background colors are applied to the image. To avoid unwanted coloring, set the foreground to black and the background to white before calling this routine.

```
PROCEDURE SeedCFill  (srcBits, dstBits: BitMap; srcRect, dstRect:
        Rect; seedH, seedV: INTEGER; matchProc: ProcPtr;
        matchData: LONGINT);
```

The SeedCFill procedure generates a mask for use with CopyMask or CopyBits, with bits equal to 1 only in those positions where paint can leak from the starting seed point, like the MacPaint® bucket tool.

Given a rectangle within a source bitMap or pixMap (srcBits), SeedCFill returns a mask (dstBits) that contains 1's in place of all pixels to which paint can leak from the specified seed position (seedH, seedV), expressed in the local coordinate system of the source pixMap. By default, paint can leak to all adjacent pixels whose RGB value exactly match that of the seed. To use this default, set matchProc and matchData to zero.

In generating the mask, SeedCFill performs CopyBits to convert srcBits to a one-bit mask. It installs a default searchProc into the gDevice that returns 0 if the RGB value matches that of the seed; all other RGB values return 1's.

If you want to customize SeedCFill, your application can specify a matchProc that is used instead of the default searchProc. It should return 0's for RGB values that you want to be filled, and 1's for values that shouldn't be filled. When the matchProc is called, the GDRefCon field of the current gDevice contains a pointer to a record having the following structure:

```
MatchRec = RECORD
          red:              INTEGER;
          green:            INTEGER;
          blue:             INTEGER;
          matchData:        LONGINT
       END;
```

In this record the red, green, and blue fields are the RGB of the pixel at the specified seed location. MatchData is simply whatever value you passed to SeedCFill as a parameter. For instance, your application could pass a handle to a color table whose entries should all be filled, and then, in the matchProc, check to see if the specified RGB matches any of the colors in the table.

No automatic scaling is performed: the source and destination rectangles must be the same size. Calls to SeedCFill are not clipped to the current port and are not stored into QuickDraw pictures.

```
PROCEDURE CalcCMask (srcBits, dstBits: BitMap; srcRect, dstRect:
          Rect; seedRGB: RGBColor; matchProc: ProcPtr; matchData:
          LONGINT);
```

This routine generates a mask (dstBits) corresponding to the area in a pixMap (srcBits) to which paint *cannot* leak from outside of the srcRect. The size of srcRect must be the same as the size of dstRect. By default, paint can leak to all adjacent pixels whose RGB values don't match that of the seedRGB. To use this default, set matchProc and matchData to 0.

For instance, if srcBits contains a blue rectangle on a red background, and your application calls CalcCMask with the seedRGB equal to blue, then the returned mask has ones in the positions corresponding to the edges and interior of the rectangle, and zeros outside of the rectangle.

If you want to customize CalcCMask, your application can specify a matchProc that is used instead of the default searchProc. It should return 1's for RGB values that define the edges of the mask, and 0's for values that don't.

When the matchProc is called, the GDRefCon field of the gDevice contains a pointer to a MatchRec record (the structure shown in the SeedCFill description). The red, green, and blue fields are the RGB of the pixel at the specifed seed location. MatchData is simply whatever value your application passed to CalcCMask as a parameter. For instance, your program could pass a handle to a color table whose entries should all be within the mask, and then, in the matchProc, check to see if the specified RGB matches any of the colors in the table.

No automatic scaling is performed: the source and destination rectangles must be the same size. Calls to CalcCMask are not clipped to the current port and are not stored into QuickDraw pictures.

Operations on Pixel Patterns

```
FUNCTION NewPixPat: PixPatHandle;
```

The NewPixPat function creates a new pixPat data structure, and returns a handle to it. It calls NewPixMap to allocate and initialize the pattern's pixMap to the same settings as theGDevice^^.GDPMap, and it sets the type of the pixPat to be a color pattern. The pat1Data field is initialized to a 50% gray pattern. New handles for data, expanded data, expanded map, and color table are allocated but not initialized. Including the pixPat itself, it allocates a total of six handles. You will generally not need to use this routine since the GetPixPat routine can be used to read in a pattern from a resource file.

The sizes of the pixMap and pixPat handles are the size of their respective data structures (see the type declarations in the "Summary" section). The other three handles are initially small in size. Once the pattern is drawn, the size of the expanded data is proportional to the size of the pattern data, but adjusted to the depth of the screen. The color table size is the size of the record structure plus eight bytes times the number of colors in the table.

Creating a PixPat

To create a color pattern, use NewPixPat to allocate a new PixPatHandle. Set the rowBytes, bounds, and pixelSize of the pattern's pixMap to the dimensions of the desired pattern. The rowBytes should be equal to (width of bounds)*pixelSize/8; it need not be even. The width and height of the bounds must be a power of two. Each scanline of the pattern must be at least one byte in length—that is, (width of bounds)*pixelSize must be at least eight. Set the other fields in the pattern's pixMap as described in the section on the pixMap data structure.

Your application can explicitly specify the color corresponding to each pixel value with the color table. The color table for the pattern must be placed in the pmTable in the pixPat's pixMap. Patterns may also contain colors that are relative to the foreground and background at the time that they are drawn. Refer to the section on the pixPat data structure for more information on relative patterns.

```
PROCEDURE DisposPixPat (ppat: PixPatHandle);
```

The DisposPixPat procedure releases all storage allocated by NewPixPat. It disposes of the pixPat's data handle, expanded data handle, and pixMap handle.

```
PROCEDURE CopyPixPat (srcPP,dstPP: PixPatHandle);
```

The CopyPixPat procedure copies the contents of the source pixPat to the destination pixPat. It entirely copies all fields in the source pixPat, including the contents of the data handle, expanded data handle, expanded map, pixMap handle, and color table.

```
FUNCTION GetPixPat (patID: INTEGER): PixPatHandle;
```

The GetPixPat call creates a new pixPat data structure, and then uses the information in the resource of type 'ppat' and the specified ID to initialize the pixPat. The 'ppat' resource format is described in the section "Color QuickDraw Resource Formats". If the resource with the specified ID is not found, then this routine returns a NIL handle.

```
PROCEDURE MakeRGBPat (ppat: PixPatHandle; myColor: RGBColor);
```

The MakeRGBPat procedure is a new call which generates a pixPat that approximates the specified color when drawn. For example, if your application is drawing to a device that has 4 bits per pixel, you will only get 16 colors if you simply set the foreground color and draw. If you use MakeRGBPat to select a pattern, and then draw using that pattern, you will effectively get 125 different colors. More colors are theoretically possible; this implementation opted for a fast pattern selection rather than the best possible pattern selection. If the device has 8 bits per pixel, you will effectively get 2197 colors.

Note that these patterns aren't usually solid; they provide a wide selection of colors by alternating between colors with up to four colors in a pattern. For this reason lines that are one pixel wide may not look good using these patterns. For an RGB pattern, the patMap^^.bounds always contains (0, 0, 8, 8), and the patMap^^.rowbytes equals 2. Figure 5 shows how these colors are arranged.

When MakeRGBPat creates a color table, it only fills in the last colorSpec field: the other colorSpec values are computed at the time the drawing actually takes place, using the current pixel depth for the system.

Value	RGB
0	computed RGB color
1	computed RGB color
2	computed RGB color
3	computed RGB color
4	RGBColor passed to MakeRGBPat routine

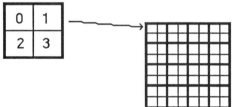

Each component of the 8 x 8 pattern
is made up of the computed colors

Figure 5. RGB Pattern

```
PROCEDURE PenPixPat (ppat: PixPatHandle);
PROCEDURE BackPixPat (ppat: PixPatHandle);
```

The PenPixPat and BackPixPat calls are analogous to PenPat and BackPat, but use multicolor pixel patterns instead of old-style patterns. If you try to use a pixel pattern in a grafPort, the data in the pat1Data field is placed into pnPat, bkPat, or fillPat.

When your application sets a pixel pattern, the handle you provide is actually placed into the grafPort or cGrafPort. In this way, QuickDraw can expand the pattern once (saving it in the patXData field) when the pattern is first set, and won't have to reexpand it each time you set the pattern.

Since your handle is actually stored in the grafPort or cGrafPort, it's considered bad form to dispose of a PixPatHandle that is currently set as the pnPixPat or bkPixPat. (Just in case you forget, QuickDraw will remove all references to your pattern from existing grafPorts or cGrafPorts when you dispose of it.)

Using the old calls PenPat and BackPat, you can still set old-style patterns in a cGrafPort. If necessary, it creates a new pixPatHandle in which to store the pattern (because, as described above, pixPatHandles are owned by the application). As in old grafPorts, old-style patterns are drawn using the foreground and background colors at the time of drawing, not at the time the pattern is set.

Operations on Color Cursors

```
FUNCTION GetCCursor (crsrID: INTEGER): CCrsrHandle;
```

The GetCCursor call creates a new CCrsr data structure, then initializes it using the information in the resource of type 'crsr' with the specified ID. The 'crsr' resource format is described in the section "Color QuickDraw Resource Formats". If the resource with the specified ID isn't found, then this routine returns a NIL handle.

Since GetCCursor creates a new CCrsr data structure each time it is called, your application shouldn't call GetCCursor before each call to SetCCursor (unlike the way GetCursor/SetCursor were normally used). GetCCursor doesn't dispose or detach the resource, so resources of type 'crsr' should typically be purgeable.

```
PROCEDURE  SetCCursor (cCrsr: CCrsrHandle);
```

The SetCCursor procedure allows your application to set a multicolor cursor. At the time the cursor is set, it's expanded to the current screen depth so that it can be drawn rapidly.

If your application has changed the cursor's data or its color table, it must also invalidate the fields crsrXValid and crsrID (described in the section on the Color Cursor data structure), before calling SetCCursor.

```
PROCEDURE DisposCCursor(cCrsr: CCrsrHandle);
```

The DisposCCursor procedure disposes all structures allocated by GetCCursor.

```
PROCEDURE AllocCursor;
```

The AllocCursor procedure reallocates cursor memory. Under normal circumstances, you should never need to use this call, since reallocation of cursor memory is only necessary after the depth of one of the screens has been changed.

Operations on Color Icons

```
FUNCTION GetCIcon(id: INTEGER): CIconHandle;
```

The GetCIcon function allocates a CIcon data structure and initializes it using the information in the resource of type 'cicn' with the specified ID. It returns the handle to the icon's data structure. If the specified resource isn't found, a NIL handle is returned.

The format of the 'cicn' resource is described in the section "Color QuickDraw Resource Formats".

Since GetCIcon creates a new CIcon data structure each time it is called, your application shouldn't call GetCIcon before each call to PlotCIcon. GetCIcon doesn't dispose or detach the resource, so resources of type 'cicn' should typically be purgeable.

```
PROCEDURE DisposCIcon(theIcon: CIconHandle);
```

The DisposCIcon procedure disposes all structures allocated by GetCIcon.

```
PROCEDURE PlotCIcon(theRect: Rect; theIcon: CIconHandle);
```

The PlotCIcon procedure draws the specified icon in the specified rectangle. The iconMask field of the CIcon determines which pixels of the iconPMap are drawn and which are not. Only pixels with 1's in corresponding positions in the iconMask are drawn; all other pixels don't affect the destination. If the screen depth is one or two bits per pixel, the iconBMap is used as the source instead of the iconPMap (unless the rowBytes field of iconBMap is 0, indicating that there is no iconBMap.

When the icon is drawn, the boundsRect of the iconPMap is used as the image's source rectangle. The icon and its mask are both stretched to the destination rectangle. The icon's pixels are remapped to the current depth and color table, if necessary. The bounds fields of the iconPMap, iconBMap, and iconMask are expected to be equal in size.

PlotCIcon is simply a structured call to CopyMask. As such, it doesn't send any of its drawing commands through grafProc routines; thus, PlotCIcon calls are not recorded in pictures.

Operations on CGrafPort Fields

```
PROCEDURE SetPortPix (pm: PixMapHandle);
```

The SetPortPix call is analogous to SetPortBits, and should be used instead of SetPortBits for cGrafPorts. It replaces the portPixMap field of the current cGrafPort with the specified handle. SetPortPix has no effect when used with an old grafPort. If SetPortBits is called when the current port is a cGrafPort, it does nothing.

```
PROCEDURE OpColor (color: RGBColor);
```

If the current port is a cGrafPort, the OpColor procedure sets the red, green, and blue values used by the AddPin, SubPin, and Blend drawing modes. This information is actually stored in the grafVars handle in the cGrafPort, but you should never need to reference it directly. If the current port is a grafPort, OpColor has no effect.

```
PROCEDURE HiliteColor (color:RGBColor);
```

The highlight color is used by all drawing operations that use the highlight transfer mode. When a cGrafPort is created, its highlight color is initialized from the global variable HiliteRGB. The HiliteColor procedure allows you to change the highlighting color used by the current port. This information is actually stored in the grafVars handle in the cGrafPort, but you should never need to reference it directly. If the current port is a grafPort, HiliteColor has no effect.

```
PROCEDURE CharExtra (extra:Fixed);
```

The CharExtra procedure sets the cGrafPort's charExtra field, which specifies the number of pixels by which to widen every character excluding the space character in a line of text. The charExtra field is stored in a compressed format based on the txSize field, so you must set txSize before calling CharExtra. The initial charExtra setting is 0. CharExtra will accept a negative number. CharExtra has no effect on grafPorts.

```
PROCEDURE SetStdCProcs (VAR cProcs: CQDProcs);
```

This procedure sets all the fields of the given CQDProcs record to point to the standard low-level routines. You can then change the ones you wish to point to your own routines. For example, if your procedure that processes picture comments is named MyComments, you will store @MyComments in the commentProc field of the CQD Procs record.

When drawing in a cGrafPort, your application must always use SetStdCProcs instead of SetStdProcs.

Operations on Color Tables

```
FUNCTION GetCTable (ctID: INTEGER): CTabHandle;
```

The GetCTable routine allocates a new color table data structure, and initializes it using the information in the resource of type 'clut' having the specified ID. If the specified resource is not found, a NIL handle is returned.

If you place this handle into a pixMap, you should first dispose of the handle that was already there.

The format of the 'clut' resource is given in the section "Color QuickDraw Resource Formats". Resource ID values 0..127 are reserved for system use. Any 'clut' resources defined by your application should have IDs in the range 128..1023. This value must be in the ctSeed field in the resource, and will be placed in the ctSeed field of the color table (for color table identification). All other possible seed values are used to identify newly created color tables, and color tables that have been modified.

If you modify a color table, you should invalidate it by changing its ctSeed field. You can get a new unique value for ctSeed using the routine GetCTSeed, described in the Color Manager chapter.

```
PROCEDURE DisposCTable(cTable: CTabHandle);
```

The DisposCTable procedure disposes the handle allocated for a color table.

COLOR QUICKDRAW RESOURCE FORMATS

Several new resource types have been defined for use with Color QuickDraw. They are

```
'crsr'    Color cursor resource type
'ppat'    Pixel Pattern resource type
'cicn'    Color Icon resource type
'clut'    Color Look-Up Table resource type
```

The precise formats of resources of these types are given below.

It is important to note that resources are used somewhat differently by Color QuickDraw. For instance, with old QuickDraw, you could do a GetCursor for each SetCursor, and the same handle would be passed back to the application each time. With Color QuickDraw, the color cursor, icon, and pattern are compound structures, more complex than a simple resource handle. Color QuickDraw reads the requested resource, copies it, and then alters the copy before passing it to the application. Each time you call GetCCursor, you get a new copy of the cursor. This means that you should do one GetCCursor call for a cursor, even if you do multiple SetCCursor calls. These new resource types should be marked as purgeable if you are concerned about memory space.

Here are the resource formats of the resources used by Color QuickDraw. All offsets are measured from the beginning of the resource's data.

'crsr' (Color Cursor)

```
CCrsr                    {data structure describing cursor}
    crsrType:        [2 bytes] = $8001
    crsrMap:         [4 bytes] = offset to pixMap structure
    crsrData:        [4 bytes] = offset to pixel data
    crsrXData:       [4 bytes] = 0
    crsrXValid:      [2 bytes] = 0
    crsrXHandle:     [4 bytes] = 0
    crsr1Data:       [32 bytes] = 1 bit image for cursor
```

```
            crsrMask:       [32 bytes] = cursor's mask
            crsrHotSpot:    [4 bytes] = cursor's hotSpot (v,h)
            crsrXTable:     [4 bytes] = 0
            crsrID:         [4 bytes] = 0
       PixMap               {pixMap describing cursor's pixel image}
            baseAddr:       [4 bytes] = 0
            rowBytes:       [2 bytes] = rowBytes of image
            bounds:         [8 bytes] = boundary rectangle of image
            pmVersion:      [2 bytes] = 0
            packType:       [2 bytes] = 0
            packSize:       [4 bytes] = 0
            hRes:           [4 bytes] = $00480000
            vRes:           [4 bytes] = $00480000
            pixelType:      [2 bytes] = 0 = chunky
            pixelSize:      [2 bytes] = bits per pixel in image
            cmpCount:       [2 bytes] = 1
            cmpSize:        [2 bytes] = pixelsize
            planeBytes:     [4 bytes] = 0
            pmTable:        [4 bytes] = offset to color table data
            pmReserved:     [4 bytes] = 0
       pixel data           [see below]              data for cursor
       color table data     [see below]              data for color table
```

The crsrMap field of the CCrsr record contains an offset to the pixMap record from the beginning of the resource data. The crsrData field of the CCrsr record contains an offset to the pixel data from the beginning of the resource data. The pmTable field of the pixMap record contains an offset to the color table data from the beginning of the resource data. The size of the pixelData is calculated by subtracting the offset to the pixel data from the offset to the color table data. The color table data consists of a color table record (ctSeed, ctFlags, ctSize) followed by ctSize+1 color table entries. Each entry in the color table connects a pixel value used in the pixel data to an actual RGB.

'ppat'   (Pixel Pattern)

```
       PixPat record {data structure describing pattern}
            patType         [2 bytes] = 1 (full color pattern)
            patMap          [4 bytes] = offset to pixMap record
            patData         [4 bytes] = offset to pixel data
            patXData        [4 bytes] = 0
            patXValid       [2 bytes] = –1
            patXMap         [4 bytes] = 0
            pat1Data        [8 bytes] = 1 bit pattern data
       PixMap               { pixMap describing pattern's pixel image }
            baseAddr        [4 bytes] = 0
            rowBytes        [2 bytes] = rowBytes of image
            bounds          [8 bytes] = boundary rectangle of image
            pmVersion       [2 bytes] = 0
            packType        [2 bytes] = 0
            packSize        [4 bytes] = 0
            hRes            [4 bytes] = $00480000
            vRes            [4 bytes] = $00480000
```

pixelType	[2 bytes] = 0 = chunky	
pixelSize	[2 bytes] = bits per pixel in image	
cmpCount	[2 bytes] = 1	
cmpSize	[2 bytes] = pixelsize	
planeBytes	[4 bytes] = 0	
pmTable	[4 bytes] = offset to color table data	
pmReserved	[4 bytes] = 0	
pixel data	[see below]	data for pattern
color table data	[see below]	data for color table

The patMap field of the pixPat record contains an offset to the pixMap record from the beginning of the resource data. The patData field of the pixPat record contains an offset to the pixel data from the beginning of the resource data. The pmTable field of the pixMap record contains an offset to the color table data from the beginning of the resource data. The size of the pixelData is calculated by subtracting the offset to the pixel data from the offset to the color table data. The color table data consists of a color table record (ctSeed, ctFlags, ctSize) followed by ctSize+1 color table entries. Each entry in the color table connects a pixel value used in the pixel data to an actual RGB.

'cicn' (Color Icon)

IconPMap	{pixMap describing icon's pixel image}	
baseAddr	[4 bytes] = 0	
rowBytes	[2 bytes] = rowBytes of image	
bounds	[8 bytes] = boundary rectangle of image	
pmVersion	[2 bytes] = 0	
packType	[2 bytes] = 0	
packSize	[4 bytes] = 0	
hRes	[4 bytes] = $00480000	
vRes	[4 bytes] = $00480000	
pixelType	[2 bytes] = 0 = chunky	
pixelSize	[2 bytes] = bits per pixel in image	
cmpCount	[2 bytes] = 1	
cmpSize	[2 bytes] = pixelsize	
planeBytes	[4 bytes] = 0	
pmTable	[4 bytes] = 0	
pmReserved	[4 bytes] = 0	
IconMask	{Mask used when drawing icon}	
baseAddr	[4 bytes] = 0	
rowBytes	[2 bytes] = rowBytes of image	
bounds	[8 bytes] = boundary rectangle of image	
IconBMap	{Image used when drawing to 1 bit screen}	
baseAddr	[4 bytes] = 0	
rowBytes	[2 bytes] = rowBytes of image	
bounds	[8 bytes] = boundary rectangle of image	
IconData	{placeholder for image's handle}	
	[4 bytes] = 0	
MaskData	{the icon's mask data }	
	[n bytes] n = IconMask.rowBytes*height	
BMapData	{the icon's bitMap data }	
	[n bytes] n = IconBMap.rowBytes*height	

PMapCTab	{the icon's color table }
	[n bytes] n = 8+(ColorTable.ctSize+1)*CTEntrySize
PMapData	{the icon's image data }
	[n bytes] n = IconPMap.rowBytes*height

In the calculations above:

height = IconPMap^^.bounds.bottom–IconPMap^^.bounds.top.

IconPMap is the pixMap describing the data in the IconData field. IconMask is the mask that is to be applied to the data when it is drawn. IconBMap is a bitMap to be drawn when the destination is only one or two pixels deep. If the rowbytes field of IconBMap is 0, then no data is loaded in for the IconBMap, and IconPMap is always used when drawing the icon. MaskData is the mask's data. It is immediately followed by the bitMap's data (which may be NIL). Next is the color table describing the IconPMap, as shown below. The final entry in the resource is the pixMap's data.

'clut' (Color Table)

ctSeed	[4 bytes] = 0
ctFlags	[2 bytes] = $0000 if pixMap color table
	= $8000 if device color table
ctSize	[2 bytes] = #entries − 1
table data	[n bytes] n = 8*(ctSize+1)

The 'clut' resource format is an exact duplicate of a color table in memory. Each element in the table data is four integers (eight bytes): a value field followed by red, green, and blue values. If the color table is used to describe a pixMap, then ctFlags should be set to 0, and the value field of each entry contains the pixel value to be associated with the following RGB. If the color table is used to describe a device, then ctFlags should be set to $8000, and the value fields should be set to 0. In this case, the implicit values are based on each entry's position in the table.

There are several default color tables that are in the Macintosh II ROMs. There is one for each of the standard pixel depths. The resource ID for each table is the same as the depth. For example, the default color table used when you switch your system to 8 bits per pixel mode is stored with resource ID = 8.

There is one other default color table. This color table defines the eight QuickDraw colors, the colors displayed by programs using the old QuickDraw model. This color table has ID = 127. Its values are given in the section "Setting the Foreground and Background Colors".

USING TEXT WITH QUICKDRAW

This section explains those QuickDraw features which provide enhanced text handling for the Macintosh Plus, Macintosh SE, and Macintosh II. The drawing mode recommended for all applications is SrcOr, because it uses the least memory and will draw the entire character in all cases. The SrcOr mode will only affect other parts of existing characters if the characters overlap. In srcOr mode the color of the character is determined by the foreground color, although text drawing is fastest when the foreground color is black.

With QuickDraw, characters can kern to the left and to the right. QuickDraw begins drawing a series of characters at the specified pen position plus the kernMax field (part of the Font record), plus any kerning below the baseline caused by italicizing the font. (The kernMax field denotes the kerning allowed by a given font; since its value is normally negative, most fonts kern to the left. Italicizing also normally moves the pen to the left.) QuickDraw then draws through the ending pen position, plus any kerning above the baseline caused by italicizing the font (normally to the right), plus any space required to handle the outlined or shadowed part of the character.

To draw text in any mode, including the kerned part of the leading and trailing characters, it is best to draw the entire line of text at once. If the line must be drawn in pieces, it is best to end each piece with a space character, so that the succeeding piece can harmlessly kern left, and the last character drawn (a space) will not have any right kerning clipped.

> **Macintosh Plus and Macintosh SE Note:** The Macintosh Plus and Macintosh SE versions of QuickDraw clip a leading left-kerning character, and do not take italicizing into account when positioning the pen. Also, it adds a constant of 32 to the width of the character imaging rectangle, causing large italicized fonts to have the rightmost character clipped in drawing modes other than srcOr.

The outline and shadow styles cause the outline and shadow of the character to be drawn in the foreground color. The inside of the character, if drawn at all, is drawn in the background color. The center of shadowed or outlined text is drawn in a grafPort in scrBic mode if the text mode is srcOr, for compatibility with old applications. This allows black text with a white outline on an arbitrary background. If the text mode is srcBic, the center of shadowed or outlined text is drawn in srcOr.

The style underline draws the underline through the entire text line, from the pen starting position through the ending position, plus any offsets from font or italic kerning, as described above. If the underline is outlined or shadowed, the ends aren't capped, that is, consecutively drawn pieces of text should maintain a continuous underline.

> **Macintosh Plus and Macintosh SE Note:** QuickDraw clips the right edge of the underline to the ending pen position, causing outlined or shadowed underlines to match imperfectly when text is drawn in sections.

One of the reasons that SrcOr is recommended is that the maximum stack space required for a text font drawing operation can be considerable. Text drawing uses a minimum amount of stack if the mode is srcOr, the forecolor is black, the visRgn and clipRgn are rectangular (or at least the destination of the text is contained within a rectangular portion of the visRgn), the text is not scaled, and the text does not have to be italicized, boldfaced, outlined, or shadowed by QuickDraw. Otherwise, the amount of stack required to draw all of the text at once depends most on the size and width of the the text and the depth of the destination.

If QuickDraw can't get enough stack space to draw an entire string at once, it will draw the string in pieces. This can produce disconcerting results in modes other than srcOr or srcBic if some of the characters overlap because of kerning or italicizing. If the mode is srcCopy, overlapping characters will be clipped by the last drawn character. If the mode is srcXor, pixels where the characters overlap are not drawn at all. If the mode is one of the arithmetic modes, the arithmetic rules are followed, ignoring that the destination may include part of the string being drawn.

The stack space required for a drawing operation on the Macintosh II is roughly given by this calculation:

(text width) * (text height) * (font depth) / (8 bits per byte) + 3K

Font depth normally equals the screen depth. If the amount of stack space available is small (less than 3.5K), QuickDraw instead uses a font depth of 1, which is slow, but uses less stack space.

On the Macintosh Plus, the required stack space is roughly equal to

(text width) * (text height) / (8 bits per byte) + 2K

Text Mask Mode

For the Macintosh II, the maskConstant may be added to another drawing mode to cause just the character portion of the text to be applied in the current transfer mode to the destination. If the text font contains more than one color, or if the drawing mode is an arithmetic mode or hilite mode, the mask mode causes only the portion of the characters not equal to the background to be drawn.

The arithmetic drawing modes and hilite mode apply the character's background to the destination; this can lead to undesirable results if the text is drawn in pieces. The leftmost part of a text piece is drawn on top of a previous text piece if the font kerns to the left. The maskMode supplied in addition to these modes causes only the foreground part of the character to be drawn. The only reasonable way to kern to the right in text mask mode is to use srcOr, or to add trailing characters. This is because the rightmost kern is clipped.

The constant used with maskMode is

```
CONST
  mask  = 64;
```

Drawing with Multibit Fonts

Multibit fonts may have a specific color. The transfer modes may not produce the desired results with a multibit font. The arithmetic modes, transparent mode, and hilite mode work equally well with single bit and multibit fonts.

Unlike single bit fonts, multibit fonts draw quickly in srcOr only if the foreground is white. Single bit fonts draw quickly in srcOr only if the foreground is black. Grayscale fonts produce a spectrum of colors, rather than just the foreground and background colors.

Inside Macintosh

Fractional Character Positioning

CGrafPorts maintain the fractional horizontal pen position, so that a series of text drawing calls will accumulate the fractional position. The horizontal pen fraction is initially set to 1/2. InitPort, Move, MoveTo, Line and LineTo reset the pen position to 1/2. For an old grafPort, the pen fraction is hard-coded to 1/2.

COLOR PICTURE FORMAT

With the introduction of the Macintosh II, the QuickDraw picture structure has been extended to include new color graphics opcodes. The new version 2 pictures and opcodes solve many of the major problems encountered by developers in using PICT files, and enable future expandability. For example, it is now possible to specify the resolution of bitMap data. Color can also be specified, but only chunky pixels (contiguously stored pixel components) are currently recognized by Color QuickDraw. Your application only needs to generate or recognize the chunky pixel format. This format is indicated by an image or pixMap with a cmpCount = 1.

Most existing applications can use version 2 pictures without modification. On a Macintosh II, version 2 pictures will draw in color (if drawn directly to the screen). Currently, they will print using the old QuickDraw colors. Eventually, new print drivers will be able to take advantage of the new color information.

On a Macintosh 512K enhanced, Macintosh Plus, and Macintosh SE, a patch in the System file beginning with version 4.1 provides QuickDraw with the capability to convert and display version 2 pictures. The original Macintosh and Macintosh 512 can't display version 2 pictures.

Applications that generate pictures in the QuickDraw picture format are free to use any or all available features to support their particular needs. Some will use only the imaging features. You may wish to include comments in the picture that are pertinent to the needs of your application. In general, put a minimal amount of information in your PICT files and avoid redundancy. It's reasonable for receiving applications to ignore picture opcodes that aren't needed.

Differences Between Version 1 and Version 2 Pictures

The major differences between version 1 and version 2 pictures are listed below.

- Version 1 opcodes are a single byte; version 2 opcodes are 2 bytes in length. This means that old opcodes in a version 2 picture take up two bytes, not one.
- Version 1 data may start on byte boundaries; version 2 opcodes and data are always word-aligned.
- In version 2, the high bit of the rowBytes field is used to indicate a pixMap instead of a bitMap; pixData then replaces bitData.

■ All unused version 2 opcodes, as well as the number of data bytes associated with each, have been defined. This was done so that picture parsing code can safely ignore unknown opcodes, enabling future use of these opcodes in a backward-compatible manner.

Drawing With Version 2 Pictures in Old GrafPorts

Enhancements to the DrawPicture routine allow pictures created with Color QuickDraw to be used in either a cGrafPort or an old-style grafPort. You can create a picture using the new drawing commands in a cGrafPort, cut it, and then paste it into an application that draws into an old grafPort. The picture will lose some of its detail when transferred in this way, but should be sufficient for most purposes. The following considerations apply to the use of this technique:

■ The rgbFgColor and rbgBkColor fields are mapped to the old-style Quickdraw constant (one of eight) that most closely approximates that color. For a grafPort with depth greater than one, even old applications will be able to draw color pictures.

■ Patterns created using MakeRGBPat are drawn as old-style patterns having approximately the same luminance as the original pattern.

■ Other new patterns are replaced by the old-style pattern contained in the pat1Data field of the PixPat data structure. This field is initialized to 50% gray by the NewPixPat routine, and is initialized from the resource in a GetPixPat call.

■ PixMaps in the picture are drawn without interpretation. The CopyBits call performs all necessary mapping to the destination screen. If the picture is drawn on a Macintosh Plus or a Macintosh SE, or if the BitsProc routine has been replaced by the application, the pixMap is converted to a bitMap before it's drawn.

■ Changes to the ChExtra and pnLocHFrac fields, and the Hilite color and OpColor, are ignored.

A new standard opcodeProc, SetStdCProc, is called by QuickDraw when it is playing back a color picture and it sees a new opcode that it doesn't recognize. The default routine simply reads and ignores all undefined opcodes.

Picture Representation

The PICT file (defined in Macintosh Technical Note #27) is a data fork file with a 512-byte header, followed by a picture (see Figure 6). This data fork file contains a QuickDraw (and now, Color QuickDraw) data structure within which a graphic application, using standard QuickDraw calls, places drawing opcodes to represent an object or image graphic data. In the QuickDraw picture format, pictures consist of opcodes followed by picture data.

4 Color QuickDraw

```
          ┌─────────────────────────────┐
          │         PICT file           │
          │        (type=PICT)          │
          ├───────────────┬─────────────┤
          │   Data fork   │Resource fork│
          ├───────────────┤             │
          │ 512-byte      │             │
          │ header        │             │
          ├───────────────┤             │
          │ picSize       │             │
          ├───────────────┤             │
          │ picFrame      │             │
          ├───────────────┤             │
          │ opcode        │ This fork is │
          ├───────────────┤             │
          │ picture data  │ empty in    │
          │        •      │             │
          │        •      │ PICT files  │
          │        •      │             │
          ├───────────────┤             │
          │ opcode        │             │
          ├───────────────┤             │
          │ picture data  │             │
          ├───────────────┤             │
          │EndOfPicture   │             │
          └───────────────┴─────────────┘
```

Figure 6. PICT file format.

Picture Parsing

The first 512 bytes of a PICT data file contain application-specific header information. Each QuickDraw (and Color QuickDraw) picture definition consists of a fixed-size header containing information about the size, scaling, and version of the picture, followed by the opcodes and picture data defining the objects drawn between the OpenPicture and ClosePicture calls.

When the OpenPicture routine is called and the port is an old grafPort, a version 1 picture is opened. When the OpenPicture routine is called and the port is a cGrafPort, then a version 2 picture is opened. If any fields in the grafPort are different than the default entries, those fields that are different get recorded in the picture.

Version 4.1 of the Macintosh System file incorporates a patch to QuickDraw that will enable QuickDraw (on machines with 128K or larger ROMs) to parse a version 2 PICT file, read it completely, attempt to convert all Color QuickDraw color opcodes to a suitable black-and-white representation, and draw the picture in an old grafPort. If you are trying to display a version 2 picture on a Macintosh without the system patch, QuickDraw won't be able to draw the picture.

Picture Record Structure

The Pascal record structure of version 1 and version 2 pictures is exactly the same. In both, the picture begins with a picSize, then a picFrame (rect), followed by the picture definition data. Since a picture may include any sequence of drawing commands, its data structure is a variable-length entity. It consists of two fixed-length fields followed by a variable-length field:

```
TYPE Picture = RECORD
               picSize:   INTEGER;   {low order 16 bits of picture }
                                     { size}
               picFrame:  Rect;      {picture frame, used as }
                                     { reference for scaling when }
                                     { the picture is drawn }
               {picture definition data}
           END;
```

To maintain compatibility with the original picture format, the picSize field has not been changed in version 2 pictures. However, the information in this field is only useful if your application supports version 1 pictures not exceeding 32K bytes in size. Because pictures can be much larger than the 32K limit imposed by the 2-byte picSize field, use the GetHandleSize call to determine picture size if the picture is in memory or the file size returned in pBFGetInfo if the picture resides in a file.

The picFrame field is the picture frame that surrounds the picture and gives a frame of reference for scaling when the picture is played back. The rest of the structure contains a compact representation of the image defined by the opcodes. The picture definition data consists of a sequence of the opcodes listed in Table 3 in the Pict Opcodes section, each followed by zero or more bytes of data. Every opcode has an implicit or explicit size associated with it that indicates the number of data bytes following that opcode, ranging from 2 to 2^{32} bytes (this maximum number of bytes applies to version 2 pictures only).

Picture Spooling

In the past, images rarely exceeded the 32K practical limit placed on resources. Today, with the advent of scanners and other image input products, images may easily exceed this size. This increase in image size necessitates a means for handling pictures that are too large to reside entirely in memory. One solution is to place the picture in the data fork of a PICT file, and spool it in as needed. To read the file, an application can simply replace the QuickDraw default getPicProc routine with a procedure (getPICTData) that reads the picture data from a disk file; the disk access would be transparent. Note that this technique applies equally to version 1 (byte-opcode) and version 2 (word-opcode) pictures.

Spooling a Picture From Disk

In order to display pictures of arbitrary size, an application must be able to import a QuickDraw picture from a file of type PICT. (This is the file type produced by a Save As command from MacDraw® with the PICT option selected.) What follows is a small program fragment that demonstrates how to spool in a picture from the data fork of a PICT file. The picture can be larger than the historical 32K resource size limitation.

```
{ The following variable and procedure must be at the }
{ main level of the program }
    VAR
        globalRef: INTEGER;

    PROCEDURE GetPICTData(dataPtr: Ptr; byteCount: INTEGER);
    {replacement for getPicProc routine}

        VAR
            err : INTEGER;
            longCount: LONGINT;

        BEGIN
            longCount := byteCount;
            {longCount is a Pascal VAR parameter and must be a LONGINT}
            err := FSRead(globalRef,longCount,dataPtr);
            {ignore errors here since it is unclear how to handle them}
        END;

    PROCEDURE GetandDrawPICTFile;
    {procedure to draw in a picture from a PICT file selected by the user}

        VAR
            wher: Point; {where to display dialog}
            reply: SFReply; {reply record}
            myFileTypes: SFTypeList; {more of the Standard File goodies}
            NumFileTypes: INTEGER;
            err: OSErr;
            myProcs: QDProcs; {use CQDProcs for a CGrafPort (a color }
                             { window)}
            PICTHand: PicHandle; {we need a picture handle for DrawPicture}
            longCount: LONGINT;
            myPB: ParamBlockRec;

        BEGIN
            wher.h := 20;
            wher.v := 20;
            NumFileTypes := 1; {Display PICT files}
            myFileTypes[0] := 'PICT';
            SFGetFile(wher,'',NIL,NumFileTypes,myFileTypes,NIL,reply);
            IF reply.good THEN BEGIN
                err := FSOpen(reply.fname,reply.vrefnum,globalRef);

                SetStdProcs(myProcs); {use SetStdCProcs for a CGrafPort}
                myWindow^.grafProcs := @myProcs;
                myProcs.getPicProc := @GetPICTData;

                PICTHand := PicHandle(NewHandle(SizeOf(Picture)));
                {get one the size of (size word + frame rectangle)}

                {skip (so to speak) the MacDraw header block}
                err := SetFPos(globalRef,fsFromStart,512);
                longCount := SizeOf(Picture);
                {read in the (obsolete) size word and the picture frame}
                err := FSRead(globalRef,longCount,Ptr(PICTHand^));
```

```
DrawPicture(PICTHand,PICTHand^^.picFrame);
{inside of DrawPicture, QD makes repeated calls to }
{ getPicProc to get actual picture opcodes and data. Since ]
{ we have intercepted GetPicProc, QD will call myProcs to }
{ get getPicProc, instead of calling the default procedure}

err := FSClose(globalRef);

myWindow^.grafProcs := NIL;
DisposHandle(Handle(PICTHand));

        END; {IF reply.good}
    END;
```

Spooling a Picture to a File

Spooling a picture out to a file is equally straightforward. By replacing the standard putPicProc with your own procedure, you can create a PICT file and spool the picture data out to the file.

Here is a sample of code to use as a guide:

```
{these variables and PutPICTData must be at the main program level}
VAR  PICTcount: LONGINT; {the current size of the picture}
     globalRef: INTEGER; {the file system reference number}
     newPICThand: PicHandle;
  {this is the replacement for the StdPutPic routine}
PROCEDURE PutPICTData(dataPtr: Ptr; byteCount: INTEGER);
  VAR  longCount: LONGINT;
       err: INTEGER;
  BEGIN {unfortunately, we don't know what to do with errors}
    longCount := byteCount;
    PICTCount := PICTCount + byteCount;
    err := FSWrite(globalRef, longCount, dataPtr); {ignore error…}
    IF newPICTHand <> NIL THEN newPICTHand^^.picSize := PICTCount;
{update so QD can track the size for oddness and pad out to full words}
  END;
{Note that this assumes the picture is entirely in memory which wouldn't }
{ always be the case. You could (in effect) be feeding the StdGetPic }
{ procedure at the same time, or simply spooling while drawing.}
PROCEDURE SpoolOutPICTFile(PICTHand: PicHandle {the picture to spool});
  VAR  err: OSErr;
       i: INTEGER;
       wher: Point; { where to display dialog }
       longCount, longZero: LONGINT;
       pframe: Rect;
       reply: SFReply; { reply record }
       myProcs: QDProcs; {use CQDProcs for a CGrafPort (a color window)}
  BEGIN
    wher.h := 20;
    wher.v := 20;
    {get a file to output to}
    SFPutFile(wher, 'Save the PICT as:', 'untitled', NIL, reply);
    IF reply.good THEN
```

```
    BEGIN
      err := Create(reply.fname, reply.vrefnum, '????', 'PICT');
      IF (err = noerr) | (err = dupfnerr) THEN
        BEGIN
          {now open the target file and prepare to spool to it}
          signal(FSOpen(reply.fname, reply.vrefnum, globalRef));
          SetStdProcs(myProcs); {use SetStdCProcs for a CGrafPort}
          myWindow^.grafProcs := @myProcs;
          myProcs.putPicProc := @putPICTdata;
          longZero := 0;
          longCount := 4;
          PICTCount := SizeOf(Picture);
   {now write out the 512 byte header and zero (initially) the }
   { Picture structure}
          FOR i := 1 TO 512 DIV 4 + SizeOf(Picture) DO
            Signal(FSWrite(globalRef, longCount, @longZero));
   {open a new picture and draw the old one to it; this will convert }
   { the old picture to fit the type of GrafPort to which we are }
   { currently set}
          pFrame := PICThand^^.picFrame;
          newPICTHand := NIL;
          newPICTHand := OpenPicture(pFrame);
          DrawPicture(PICTHand, pFrame); {draw the picture so the
  bottleneck will be used. In real life you could be spooling while
  doing drawing commands (you might not use DrawPicture)}
          ClosePicture;
          Signal(SetFPos(globalRef, fsFromStart, 512));
   {skip the MacDraw header}
          longCount := SizeOf(Picture);
   {write out the correct (low word of the) size and the frame at }
   { the beginning}
          Signal(FSWrite(globalRef, longCount, Ptr(newPICTHand^)));
          Signal(FSClose(globalRef));
          myWindow^.grafProcs := NIL;
          KillPicture(newPICTHand);
        END
      ELSE
        Signal(err);
    END; {IF reply.good}
  END; {OutPICT}
```

Drawing to an Offscreen Pixel Map

With the advent of high resolution output devices such as laser printers, it has become necessary to support bitmap images at resolutions higher than those supported by the screen. To speed up the interactive manipulation of high-resolution pixel map images, developers may want to first draw them into an off screen pixel map at screen resolution and retain this screen version as long as the document is open.

Note: You can use the formula shown in the section "Sample PICT file" to calculate the resolution of the source data. How to draw into an offscreen pixmap is described in Macintosh Technical Note #120; the Graphics Devices chapter also contains a section describing how to draw to an offscreen device.

New GrafProcs Record

The entire opcode space has been defined or reserved, as shown in the PICT Opcodes section in Table 3, and a new set of routines has been added to the grafProcs record. These changes provide support for anticipated future enhancements in a way that won't cause old applications to crash. It works like this: when Color QuickDraw encounters an unused opcode, it calls the new opcodeProc routine to parse the opcode data. By default, this routine simply ignores the data, since no new opcodes are defined (other than HeaderOp, which is also ignored).

Color QuickDraw has replaced the QDProcs record with a CQDProcs record. In a new grafPort, you should never use the SetStdProcs routine. If you do, it will return the old QDProcs record, which won't contain an entry for the stdOpcodeProc. If you don't use the new SetStdCProcs routine, the first color picture that you try to display may crash your system.

The CQDProcs record structure is shown below. Only the last seven fields are new; the rest of the fields are the same as those in the QDProcs record.

```
CQDProcsPtr = ^CQDProcs
CQDProcs    = RECORD
                textProc:       Ptr;
                lineProc:       Ptr;
                rectProc:       Ptr;
                rRectProc:      Ptr;
                ovalProc:       Ptr;
                arcProc:        Ptr;
                polyProc:       Ptr;
                rgnProc:        Ptr;
                bitsProc:       Ptr;
                commentProc:    Ptr;
                txMeasProc:     Ptr;
                getPicProc:     Ptr;
                putPicProc:     Ptr;
                opcodeProc:     Ptr;    {fields added to QDProcs}
                newProc1:       Ptr;    {reserved for future use}
                newProc2:       Ptr;    {reserved for future use}
                newProc3:       Ptr;    {reserved for future use}
                newProc4:       Ptr;    {reserved for future use}
                newProc5:       Ptr;    {reserved for future use}
                newProc6:       Ptr;    {reserved for future use}
            END;
```

Picture Compatibility

Many applications already support PICT resources larger than 32K. The 128K ROMs (and later) allow pictures as large as memory (or spooling) will accommodate. This was made possible by having QuickDraw ignore the size word and simply read the picture until the end-of-picture opcode is reached.

> **Note:** For maximum safety and convenience, let QuickDraw generate and interpret your pictures.

While the PICT data formats described in this section allow you to read or write picture data directly, it's best to let DrawPicture or OpenPicture and ClosePicture process the opcodes.

One reason to read a picture directly by scanning the opcodes is to disassemble it; for example, extracting a Color QuickDraw pixel map to store in a private data structure. This shouldn't normally be necessary, unless your application is running on a CPU other than the Macintosh. You wouldn't need to do it, of course, if you were using Color QuickDraw.

If your application does use the picture data, be sure it checks the version information. You may want to include an alert box in your application, indicating to users whether a picture was created using a later version of the picture format than is currently recognized by your application, and letting them know that some elements of the picture can't be displayed. If the version information indicates a QuickDraw picture version later than the one recognized by your application, your program should skip over the new opcodes and only attempt to parse the opcodes it knows.

As with reading picture data directly, it's best to use QuickDraw to create data in the PICT format. If you need to create PICT format data directly, it's essential that you understand and follow the format presented in Table 3 and thoroughly test the data produced on both color and black and white Macintosh machines.

Picture Format

This section describes the internal structure of the QuickDraw picture, consisting of a fixed-length header (which is different for version 1 and version 2 pictures), followed by variable-sized picture data. Your picture structure must follow the order shown in the examples below.

The two fixed-length fields, picSize and picFrame, are the same for version 1 and version 2 pictures.

```
picSize:        INTEGER;  {low-order 16 bits of picture size}
picFrame:       RECT;     {picture frame, used as scaling reference}
```

Following these fields is a variable amount of opcode-driven data. Opcodes represent drawing commands and parameters that affect those drawing commands in the picture. The first opcode in any picture must be the version opcode, followed by the version number of the picture.

Picture Definition: Version 1

In a version 1 picture, the version opcode is $11, which is followed by version number $01. When parsing a version 1 picture, Color QuickDraw (or a patched QuickDraw) assumes it's reading an old picture, fetching a byte at a time as opcodes. An end-of-picture byte ($FF) after the last opcode or data byte in the file signals the end of the data stream.

Picture Header (fixed size of 2 bytes):

```
$11        BYTE      {version opcode}
$01        BYTE      {version number of picture}
```

Picture Definition Data   (variable sized):

```
opcode BYTE     {one drawing command}
data . . .
opcode BYTE     {one drawing command}
data . . .

$FF             {end-of-picture opcode}
```

Picture Definition: Version 2

In a version 2 picture, the first opcode is a two-byte version opcode ($0011). This is followed by a two-byte version number ($02FF). On machines without the 4.1 System file, the first $00 byte is skipped, then the $11 is interpreted as a version opcode. On a Macintosh II (or a Macintosh with System file 4.1 or later), this field identifies the picture as a version 2 picture, and all subsequent opcodes are read as words (which are word-aligned within the picture). On a Macintosh without the 4.1 System patch, the $02 is read as the version number, then the $FF is read and interpreted as the end-of-picture opcode. For this reason, DrawPicture terminates without drawing anything.

Picture Header (fixed size of 30 bytes):

```
$0011         WORD      {version opcode}
$02FF         WORD      {version number of new picture}

$0C00         WORD      {reserved header opcode}
24 bytes of data        {reserved for future Apple use}
```

Picture Definition Data (variable sized):

```
opcode WORD     {one drawing command}
data . . .
opcode WORD     {one drawing command}
data . . .

$00FF WORD      {end-of-picture opcode}
```

For future expandibility, the second opcode in every version 2 picture must be a reserved header opcode, followed by 24 bytes of data that aren't used by your application.

PicComments

If your application requires capability beyond that provided by the picture opcodes, the picComment opcode allows data or commands to be passed directly to the output device. PicComments enable MacDraw, for example, to reconstruct graphics primitives not found in QuickDraw (such as rotated text) that are received either from the Clipboard or from another application. PicComments are also used as a means of communicating more effectively with the LaserWriter and with other applications via the scrap or the PICT data file.

Because some operations (like splines and rotated text) can be implemented more efficiently by the LaserWriter, some of the picture comments are designed to be issued along with QuickDraw commands that simulate the commented commands on the Macintosh screen. If the printer you are using has not implemented the comment commands, it ignores them and simulates the operations using the accompanying QuickDraw commands. Otherwise, it uses the comments to implement the desired effect and ignores the appropriate QuickDraw-simulated commands.

> **Note:** The picture comments used by MacDraw are listed and described in Macintosh Technical Note #27.

If you are going to produce or modify your own picture, the structure and use of these comments must be precise. The comments and the embedded QuickDraw commands must come in the correct sequence in order to work properly.

> **Note:** Apple is currently investigating a method to register picComments. If you intend to use new picComments in your application, you must contact Apple's Developer Technical Support to avoid conflict with picComment numbers used by other developers.

Sample PICT File

An example of a version 2 picture data file that can display a single image is shown in Table 1. Applications that generate picture data should set the resolution of the image source data in the hRes and vRes fields of the PICT file. It's recommended, however, that you calculate the image resolution anyway, using the values for srcRect and dstRect according to the following formulas:

$$\text{horizontal resolution (hRes)} = \frac{\text{width of srcRect}}{\text{width of dstRect}} \times 72$$

$$\text{vertical resolution (vRes)} = \frac{\text{height of srcRect}}{\text{height of dstRect}} \times 72$$

Table 1. PICT file example

Size (in bytes)	Name	Description
2	picSize	low word of picture size
8	picFrame	rectangular bounding box of picture, at 72 dpi

Picture Definition Data:

Size	Name	Description
2	version op	version opcode = $0011
2	version	version number = $02FF
2	Header op	header opcode = $0C00
4	size	total size of picture in bytes (–1 for version 2 pictures)
16	fBBox	fixed-point bounding box (–1 for version 2 pictures)
4	reserved	reserved for future Apple use (–1 for version 2 pictures)
2	opbitsRect	bitMap opcode = $0090
2	rowBytes	integer, must have high bit set to signal pixMap
8	bounds	rectangle, bounding rectangle at source resolution
2	pmVersion	integer, pixMap version number
2	packType	integer, defines packing format
4	packSize	LongInt, length of pixel data
4	hRes	fixed, horizontal resolution (dpi) of source data
4	vRes	fixed, vertical resolution (dpi) of source data
2	pixelType	integer, defines pixel type
2	pixelSize	integer, number of bits in pixel
2	cmpCount	integer, number of components in pixel
2	cmpSize	integer, number of bits per component

4 Color QuickDraw

Table 1. PICT file example (Continued)

Size (in bytes)	Name	Description
4	planeBytes	LongInt, offset to next plane
	pmTable	color table = 0
	pmReserved	reserved = 0
4	ctSeed	LongInt, color table seed
2	ctFlags	integer, flags for color table
2	ctSize	integer, number of entries in ctTable –1
(ctSize+1) * 8	ctTable	color lookup table data
8	srcRect	rectangle, source rectangle at source resolution
8	dstRect	rectangle, destination rectangle at 72 dpi resolution
2	mode	integer, transfer mode
see Table 5	pixData	pixel data
2	endPICT op	end-of-picture opcode = $00FF

Color Picture Routines

```
FUNCTION OpenPicture (picFrame: Rect) : PicHandle;
```

The OpenPicture routine has been modified to take advantage of QuickDraw's new color capabilities. If the current port is a cGrafPort, then OpenPicture automatically opens a version 2 picture, as described in the previous section. As before, you close the picture using ClosePicture and draw the picture using DrawPicture.

PICT OPCODES

The opcode information in Table 3 is provided for the purpose of debugging application-generated PICT files. Your application should generate and read PICT files only by using standard QuickDraw or Color QuickDraw routines (OpenPicture, ClosePicture).

The data types listed in Table 2 are used in the Table 3 opcode definitions. Data formats are described in Volume I.

Table 2. Data types

Type	Size
v1 opcode	1 byte
v2 opcode	2 bytes
integer	2 bytes
long integer	4 bytes
mode	2 bytes
point	4 bytes
0..255	1 byte
−128..127	1 byte (signed)
rect	8 bytes (top, left, bottom, right: integer)
poly	10+ bytes
region	10+ bytes
fixed-point number	4 bytes
pattern	8 bytes
rowbytes	2 bytes (always an even quantity)

Valid picture opcodes are listed in Table 3. New opcodes or those altered for version 2 picture files are indicated by a leading asterisk (*). The unused opcodes found throughout the table are reserved for Apple use. The length of the data that follows these opcodes is pre-defined, so if they are encountered in pictures, they can simply be skipped. By default, Color QuickDraw reads and then ignores these opcodes.

Table 3. PICT opcodes

Opcode	Name	Description	Data Size (in bytes)
$0000	NOP	nop	0
$0001	Clip	clip	region size
$0002	BkPat	background pattern	8
$0003	TxFont	text font (word)	2
$0004	TxFace	text face (byte)	1
$0005	TxMode	text mode (word)	2
$0006	SpExtra	space extra (fixed point)	4
$0007	PnSize	pen size (point)	4
$0008	PnMode	pen mode (word)	2
$0009	PnPat	pen pattern	8
$000A	FillPat	fill pattern	8
$000B	OvSize	oval size (point)	4
$000C	Origin	dh, dv (word)	4
$000D	TxSize	text size (word)	2
$000E	FgColor	foreground color (long)	4
$000F	BkColor	background color (long)	4
$0010	TxRatio	numer (point), denom (point)	8
$0011	Version	version (byte)	1
$0012	*BkPixPat	color background pattern	variable: see Table 4

Table 3. PICT opcodes (Continued)

Opcode	Name	Description	Data Size (in bytes)
$0013	*PnPixPat	color pen pattern	variable: see Table 4
$0014	*FillPixPat	color fill pattern	variable: see Table 4
$0015	*PnLocHFrac	fractional pen position	2
$0016	*ChExtra	extra for each character	2
$0017	*reserved for Apple use	opcode	0
$0018	*reserved for Apple use	opcode	0
$0019	*reserved for Apple use	opcode	0
$001A	*RGBFgCol	RGB foreColor	variable: see Table 4
$001B	*RGBBkCol	RGB backColor	variable: see Table 4
$001C	*HiliteMode	hilite mode flag	0
$001D	*HiliteColor	RGB hilite color	variable: see Table 4
$001E	*DefHilite	Use default hilite color	0
$001F	*OpColor	RGB OpColor for arithmetic modes	variable: see Table 4
$0020	Line	pnLoc (point), newPt (point)	8
$0021	LineFrom	newPt (point)	4
$0022	ShortLine	pnLoc (point, dh, dv (-128..127)	6
$0023	ShortLineFrom	dh, dv (-128..127)	2
$0024	*reserved for Apple use	opcode + 2 bytes data length + data	2+ data length
$0025	*reserved for Apple use	opcode + 2 bytes data length + data	2+ data length
$0026	*reserved for Apple use	opcode + 2 bytes data length + data	2+ data length
$0027	*reserved for Apple use	opcode + 2 bytes data length + data	2+ data length
$0028	LongText	txLoc (point), count (0..255), text	5 + text
$0029	DHText	dh (0..255), count (0..255), text	2 + text
$002A	DVText	dv (0..255), count (0..255), text	2 + text
$002B	DHDVText	dh, dv (0..255), count (0..255), text	3 + text
$002C	*reserved for Apple use	opcode + 2 bytes data length + data	2+ data length
$002D	*reserved for Apple use	opcode + 2 bytes data length + data	2+ data length
$002E	*reserved for Apple use	opcode + 2 bytes data length + data	2+ data length
$002F	*reserved for Apple use	opcode + 2 bytes data length + data	2+ data length
$0030	frameRect	rect	8
$0031	paintRect	rect	8

Table 3. PICT opcodes (Continued)

Opcode	Name	Description	Data Size (in bytes)
$0032	eraseRect	rect	8
$0033	invertRect	rect	8
$0034	fillRect	rect	8
$0035	*reserved for Apple use	opcode + 8 bytes data	8
$0036	*reserved for Apple use	opcode + 8 bytes data	8
$0037	*reserved for Apple use	opcode + 8 bytes data	8
$0038	frameSameRect	rect	0
$0039	paintSameRect	rect	0
$003A	eraseSameRect	rect	0
$003B	invertSameRect	rect	0
$003C	fillSameRect	rectangle	0
$003D	*reserved for Apple use	opcode	0
$003E	*reserved for Apple use	opcode	0
$003F	*reserved for Apple use	opcode	0
$0040	frameRRect	rect (see Note # 5)	8
$0041	paintRRect	rect (see Note # 5)	8
$0042	eraseRRect	rect (see Note # 5)	8
$0043	invertRRect	rect (see Note # 5)	8
$0044	fillRRect	rect (see Note # 5)	8
$0045	*reserved for Apple use	opcode + 8 bytes data	8
$0046	*reserved for Apple use	opcode + 8 bytes data	8
$0047	*reserved for Apple use	opcode + 8 bytes data	8
$0048	frameSameRRect	rect	0
$0049	paintSameRRect	rect	0
$004A	eraseSameRRect	rect	0
$004B	invertSameRRect	rect	0
$004C	fillSameRRect	rect	0
$004D	*reserved for Apple use	opcode	0
$004E	*reserved for Apple use	opcode	0
$004F	*reserved for Apple use	opcode	0
$0050	frameOval	rect	8
$0051	paintOval	rect	8
$0052	eraseOval	rect	8
$0053	invertOval	rect	8
$0054	fillOval	rect	8
$0055	*reserved for Apple use	opcode + 8 bytes data	8
$0056	*reserved for Apple use	opcode + 8 bytes data	8
$0057	*reserved for Apple use	opcode + 8 bytes data	8
$0058	frameSameOval	rect	0
$0059	paintSameOval	rect	0
$005A	eraseSameOval	rect	0
$005B	invertSameOval	rect	0
$005C	fillSameOval	rect	0
$005D	*reserved for Apple use	opcode	0
$005E	*reserved for Apple use	opcode	0
$005F	*reserved for Apple use	opcode	0
$0060	frameArc	rect, startAngle, arcAngle	12
$0061	paintArc	rect, startAngle, arcAngle	12
$0062	eraseArc	rect, startAngle, arcAngle	12
$0063	invertArc	rect, startAngle, arcAngle	12

Table 3. PICT opcodes (Continued)

Opcode	Name	Description	Data Size (in bytes)
$0064	fillArc	rect, startAngle, arcAngle	12
$0065	*reserved for Apple use	opcode + 12 bytes	12
$0066	*reserved for Apple use	opcode + 12 bytes	12
$0067	*reserved for Apple use	opcode + 12 bytes	12
$0068	frameSameArc	rect	4
$0069	paintSameArc	rect	4
$006A	eraseSameArc	rect	4
$006B	invertSameArc	rect	4
$006C	fillSameArc	rect	4
$006D	*reserved for Apple use	opcode + 4 bytes	4
$006E	*reserved for Apple use	opcode + 4 bytes	4
$006F	*reserved for Apple use	opcode + 4 bytes	4
$0070	framePoly	poly	polygon size
$0071	paintPoly	poly	polygon size
$0072	erasePoly	poly	polygon size
$0073	invertPoly	poly	polygon size
$0074	fillPoly	poly	polygon size
$0075	*reserved for Apple use	opcode + poly	
$0076	*reserved for Apple use	opcode + poly	
$0077	*reserved for Apple use	opcode word + poly	
$0078	frameSamePoly	(not yet implemented: same as 70, etc)	0
$0079	paintSamePoly	(not yet implemented)	0
$007A	eraseSamePoly	(not yet implemented)	0
$007B	invertSamePoly	(not yet implemented)	0
$007C	fillSamePoly	(not yet implemented)	0
$007D	*reserved for Apple use	opcode	0
$007E	*reserved for Apple use	opcode	0
$007F	*reserved for Apple use	opcode	0
$0080	frameRgn	rgn	region size
$0081	paintRgn	rgn	region size
$0082	eraseRgn	rgn	region size
$0083	invertRgn	rgn	region size
$0084	fillRgn	rgn	region size
$0085	*reserved for Apple use	opcode + rgn	region size
$0086	*reserved for Apple use	opcode + rgn	region size
$0087	*reserved for Apple use	opcode + rgn	region size
$0088	frameSameRgn	(not yet implemented-- same as 80, etc.)	0
$0089	paintSameRgn	(not yet implemented)	0
$008A	eraseSameRgn	(not yet implemented)	0
$008B	invertSameRgn	(not yet implemented)	0
$008C	fillSameRgn	(not yet implemented)	0

Table 3. PICT opcodes (Continued)

Opcode	Name	Description	Data Size (in bytes)
$008D	*reserved for Apple use	opcode	0
$008E	*reserved for Apple use	opcode	0
$008F	*reserved for Apple use	opcode	0
$0090	*BitsRect	copybits, rect clipped	variable: see Table 4
$0091	*BitsRgn	copybits, rgn clipped	variable: see Table 4
$0092	*reserved for Apple use	opcode + 2 bytes data length + data	2+ data length
$0093	*reserved for Apple use	opcode + 2 bytes data length + data	2+ data length
$0094	*reserved for Apple use	opcode + 2 bytes data length + data	2+ data length
$0095	*reserved for Apple use	opcode + 2 bytes data length + data	2+ data length
$0096	*reserved for Apple use	opcode + 2 bytes data length + data	2+ data length
$0097	*reserved for Apple use	opcode word + 2 bytes data length + data	2+ data length
$0098	*PackBitsRect	packed copybits, rect clipped	variable: see Table 4
$0099	*PackBitsRgn	packed copybits, rgn clipped	variable: see Table 4
$009A	*reserved for Apple use	opcode + 2 bytes data length + data	2+ data length
$009B	*reserved for Apple use	opcode + 2 bytes data length + data	2+ data length
$009C	*reserved for Apple use	opcode + 2 bytes data length + data	2+ data length
$009D	*reserved for Apple use	opcode + 2 bytes data length + data	2+ data length
$009E	*reserved for Apple use	opcode + 2 bytes data length + data	2+ data length
$009F	*reserved for Apple use	opcode + 2 bytes data length + data	2+ data length
$00A0	ShortComment	kind (word)	2
$00A1	LongComment	kind (word), size (word), data	4+data
$00A2	*reserved for Apple use	opcode + 2 bytes data length + data	2+ data length
:	:	:	
:	:	:	
$00AF	*reserved for Apple use	opcode + 2 bytes data length + data	2+ data length
$00B0	*reserved for Apple use	opcode	0
:	:	:	
:	:	:	
$00CF	*reserved for Apple use	opcode	0
$00D0	*reserved for Apple use	opcode + 4 bytes data length + data	4+ data length

Table 3. PICT opcodes (Continued)

Opcode	Name	Description	Data Size (in bytes)
:	:	:	
$00FE	*reserved for Apple use	opcode + 4 bytes data length + data	4+ data length
$00FF	opEndPic	end of picture	2
$0100	*reserved for Apple use	opcode + 2 bytes data	2
:	:	:	
:	:	:	
$01FF	*reserved for Apple use	opcode + 2 bytes data	2
$0200	*reserved for Apple use	opcode + 4 bytes data	4
:	:	:	
$0BFF	*reserved for Apple use	opcode + 4 bytes data	22
$0C00	HeaderOp	opcode	24
$0C01:	*reserved for Apple use	opcode + 4 bytes data	24
:	:	:	
$7F00	*reserved for Apple use	opcode + 254 bytes data	254
:	:	:	
$7FFF	*reserved for Apple use	opcode + 254 bytes data	254
$8000	*reserved for Apple use	opcode	0
:	:	:	
$80FF	*reserved for Apple use	opcode	0
$8100	*reserved for Apple use	opcode + 4 bytes data length + data	4+ data length
:	:	:	
$FFFF	*reserved for Apple use	opcode + 4 bytes data length + data	4+ data length

Notes to Table 3

1. The opcode value has been extended to a word for version 2 pictures. Remember, opcode size = 1 byte for version 1.

2. Because opcodes must be word aligned in version 2 pictures, a byte of 0 (zero) data is added after odd-size data.

3. The size of reserved opcodes has been defined. They can occur only in version 2 pictures.

4. All unused opcodes are reserved for future Apple use and should not be used.

5. For opcodes $0040–$0044: rounded-corner rectangles use the setting of the ovSize point (refer to opcode $000B)

6. For opcodes $0090 and $0091: data is unpacked. These opcodes can only be used for rowbytes less than 8.

7. For opcodes $0100–$7FFF: the amount of data for opcode $nnXX = 2 * nn bytes.

The New Opcodes: Expanded Format

The expanded format of the version 2 PICT opcodes is shown in Table 4 below.

Table 4. Data Format of Version 2 PICT Opcodes

Opcode	Name	Description	Reference to Notes
$0012	BkPixPat	color background pattern	See Note 1
$0013	PnPixPat	color pen pattern	See Note 1
$0014	FillPixPat	color fill pattern	See Note 1
$0015	PnLocHFrac	fractional pen position (word)	If pnLocHFrac <> 1/2, it is always put to the picture before each text drawing operation.
$0016	ChExtra	extra for each character (word)	After chExtra changes, it is put to picture before next text drawing operation.
$001A	RGBFgCol	RGB foreColor (RBGColor)	desired RGB for foreground
$001B	RGBBkCol	RGB backColor (RGBColor)	desired RGB for background
$001D	HiliteColor	RGB hilite color	
$001F	OpColor	RGB OpColor for arithmetic modes	
$001C	HiliteMode	hilite mode flag	No data; this opcode is sent before a drawing operation that uses the hilite mode.
$001E	DefHilite	Use default hilite color	No data; set hilite to default (from low memory).
$0090	BitsRect	copybits, rect clipped	See Note 2,4,5
$0091	BitsRgn	copybits, rgn clipped	See Note 3,4,5
$0098	PackBitsRect	packed copybits, rect clipped	See Note 2,4
$0099	PackBitsRgn	packed copybits, rgn clipped	See Note 3,4

Notes to Table 4

```
    1. if patType = ditherPat
       then
               PatType:  word;        {pattern type = 2}
               Pat1Data: Pattern;     {old pattern data}
               RGB:    RGBColor;      {desired RGB for pattern}
       else
               PatType:  word;        {pattern type = 1}
               Pat1Data: Pattern;     {old pattern data}
               pixMap:                {described in Table 5}
               colorTable:            {described in Table 5}

               pixData:               {described in Table 5}
       end;
```

```
2.    pixMap:                           {described in Table 5}
      colorTable:                       {described in Table 5}
      srcRect:         Rect;            {source rectangle}
      dstRect:         Rect;            {destination rectangle}
      mode:            Word;            {transfer mode (may include new transfer }
                                        { modes)}
      PixData:                          {described in Table 5}

3.    pixMap:                           {described in Table 5 }
      colorTable:                       {described in Table 5 }
      srcRect:         Rect;            {source rectangle}
      dstRect:         Rect;            {destination rectangle}
      mode:            Word;            {transfer mode (may include new transfer }
                                        { modes)}
      maskRgn:         Rgn;             {region for masking}
      PixData:                          {described in Table 5}
```

4. These four opcodes ($0090, $0091, $0098, $0099) are modifications of existing (version 1) opcodes. The first word following the opcode is the rowBytes. If the high bit of the rowBytes is set, then it is a pixMap containing multiple bits per pixel; if it is not set, it is a bitMap containing one bit per pixel. In general, the difference between version 1 and version 2 formats is that the pixMap replaces the bitMap, a color table has been added, and pixData replaces the bitData.

5. Opcodes $0090 and $0091 are used only for rowbytes less than 8.

Table 5. Data Types Found Within New PICT Opcodes Listed in Table 4

Data Type	Field Definitions		Comments
pixMap =	baseAddr:	long;	{unused = 0}
	rowBytes:	word;	{rowBytes w/high byte set}
	Bounds:	rect;	{bounding rectangle}
	version:	word;	{version number = 0}
	packType:	word;	{packing format = 0}
	packSize:	long;	{packed size = 0}
	hRes:	fixed;	{horizontal resolution (default = } { $0048.0000)}
	vRes:	fixed;	{vertical resolution (default= } { $0048.0000)}
	pixelType:	word;	{chunky format = 0}
	pixelSize:	word;	{# bits per pixel (1,2,4,8)}
	cmpCount:	word;	{# components in pixel = 1}
	cmpSize:	word;	{size of each component = pixelSize } { for chunky}
	planeBytes:	long;	{offset to next plane = 0}
	pmTable:	long;	{color table = 0}
	pmReserved:	long;	{reserved = 0}
	end;		

Table 5. Data Types Found Within New PICT Opcodes Listed in Table 4 (Continued)

Data Type	Field Definitions	Comments

```
colorTable = ctSeed:    long;   {id number for color table = 0}
             ctFlags:   word;   {flags word = 0}
             ctSize:    word;   {number of ctTable entries-1 }
                                { ctSize + 1 color table entries }
                                { each entry = pixel value, red, }
                                { green, blue: word}
             end;

pixData: {the following pseudocode describes the pixData data type}
         If rowBytes < 8 then data is unpacked
             data size = rowBytes*(bounds.bottom-bounds.top);
         If rowBytes >= 8 then data is packed.
             Image contains (bounds.bottom-bounds.top) packed
             scanlines.
             Packed scanlines are produced by the PackBits
             routine.
             Each scanline consists of [byteCount] [data].
             If rowBytes > 250 then byteCount is a word,
                 else it is a byte.
             end;
```

SUMMARY OF COLOR QUICKDRAW

Constants

```
CONST

{ Old-style grafPort colors }
   blackColor    = 33;
   whiteColor    = 30;
   redColor      = 205;
   greenColor    = 341;
   blueColor     = 409;
   cyanColor     = 273;
   magentaColor  = 137;
   yellowColor   = 69;

{ Arithmetic transfer modes }
   blend         = 32;
   addPin        = 33;
   addOver       = 34;
   subPin        = 35;
   adMax         = 37;
   subOver       = 38;
   adMin         = 39;

{ Transparent mode constant }

   transparent   = 36;

{ Text mask constant }

   mask          = 64;

{ Highlight constants }

   hilite        = 50;

   pHiliteBit    = 0;   {this is the correct value for use when }
                        { calling the BitClear trap. BClr must use }
                        { the assembly language equate hiliteBit}

{ Constant for resource IDs }

   defQDColors = 127;
```

Data Types

```
TYPE

    RGBColor = RECORD
                   red:      INTEGER;    {red component}
                   green:    INTEGER;    {green component}
                   blue:     INTEGER     {blue component}
               END;

    ColorSpec = RECORD
                    value:   INTEGER;    {index or other value}
                    rgb:     RGBColor    {true color}
                END;

    cSpecArray : ARRAY [0..0] of ColorSpec;

    CTabHandle = ^CTabPtr;
    CTabPtr    = ^ColorTable;
    ColorTable = RECORD
                     ctSeed:   LONGINT; {unique identifier from table}
                     ctFlags:  INTEGER; {high bit is 1 for device, 0 }
                                        { for pixMap}
                     ctSize:   INTEGER; {number of entries -1 in }
                                        { ctTable}
                     ctTable: cSpecArray
                 END;

    CGrafPtr  = ^CGrafPort;
    CGrafPort = RECORD
                    device:       INTEGER;      {device ID for font }
                                               { selection}
                    portPixMap:   PixMapHandle; {port's pixel map}
                    portVersion:  INTEGER;      {highest 2 bits always }
                                               { set}
                    grafVars:     Handle;       {handle to more fields}
                    chExtra:      INTEGER;      {extra characters }
                                               { placed on the end of }
                                               { a string}
                    pnLocHFrac:   INTEGER;      {pen fraction}
                    portRect:     Rect;         {port rectangle}
                    visRgn:       RgnHandle;    {visible region}
                    clipRgn:      RgnHandle;    {clipping region}
                    bkPixPat:     PixPatHandle; {background pattern}
                    rgbFgColor:   RGBColor;     {requested foreground }
                                               { color}
                    rgbBkColor:   RGBColor;     {requested background }
                                               { color}
                    pnLoc:        Point;        {pen location}
                    pnSize:       Point;        {pen size}
```

4 Color QuickDraw

```
                pnMode:       INTEGER;        {pen transfer mode}
                pnPixPat:     PixPatHandle;   {pen pattern}
                fillPixPat:   PixPatHandle;   {fill pattern}
                pnVis:        INTEGER;        {pen visibility}
                txFont:       INTEGER;        {font number for text}
                txFace:       Style;          {text's character style}
                txMode:       INTEGER;        {text's transfer mode}
                txSize:       INTEGER;        {font size for text}
                spExtra:      Fixed;          {extra space}
                fgColor:      LONGINT;        {actual foreground color}
                bkColor:      LONGINT;        {actual background color}
                colrBit:      INTEGER;        {plane being drawn}
                patStretch:   INTEGER;        {used internally}
                picSave:      Handle;         {picture being saved}
                rgnSave:      Handle;         {region being saved}
                polySave:     Handle;         {polygon being saved}
                grafProcs:    CQDProcsPtr     {low-level drawing }
                                              { routines}
          END;

  GrafVars = RECORD
                rgbOpColor:      RGBColor;    {color for addPin, }
                                              { subPin, and blend}
                rgbHiliteColor: RGBColor;     {color for hiliting}
                pmFgColor:       Handle;      {palette handle for }
                                              { foreground color}
                pmFgIndex:       INTEGER;     {index value for }
                                              { foreground}
                pmBkColor:       Handle;      {palette handle for }
                                              { background color}
                pmBkIndex:       INTEGER;     {index value for }
                                              { background}
                pmFlags:         INTEGER;     {flags for Palette }
                                              { Manager}
          END;

PixMapHandle = ^PixMapPtr;
PixMapPtr    = ^PixMap;
PixMap       = RECORD
                baseAddr:   Ptr;       {pointer to pixMap data}
                rowBytes:   INTEGER;   {offset to next row}
                bounds:     Rect;      {boundary rectangle}
                pmVersion:  INTEGER;   {color QuickDraw version }
                                       { number}
                packType:   INTEGER;   {packing format}
                packSize:   LONGINT;   {size of data in packed }
                                       { state}
                hRes:       Fixed;     {horizontal resolution}
                vRes:       Fixed;     {vertical resolution}
                pixelType:  INTEGER;   {format of pixel image}
```

```
                pixelSize:   INTEGER;       {physical bits per }
                                            { pixel}
                cmpCount:    INTEGER;       {logical components per }
                                            { pixel}
                cmpSize:     INTEGER;       {logical bits per }
                                            { component}
                planeBytes:  LONGINT;       {offset to next plane}
                pmTable:     CTabHandle;    {absolute colors for }
                                            { this image}
                pmReserved:  LONGINT        {reserved for future }
                                            { expansion}
            END;

PixPatHandle = ^PixPatPtr;
PixPatPtr    = ^PixPat;
PixPat       = RECORD
                patType:    INTEGER;        {pattern type}
                patMap:     PixMapHandle;   {pattern }
                                            { characteristics}
                patData:    Handle;         {pixel image defining }
                                            { pattern}
                patXData:   Handle;         {expanded pixel image}
                patXValid:  INTEGER;        {flags for expanded }
                                            { pattern data}
                patXMap:    Handle;         {handle to expanded }
                                            { pattern data}
                pat1Data:   Pattern;        {old-style pattern/RGB }
                                            { color}
            END;

CCrsrHandle = ^CCrsrPtr;
CCrsrPtr    = ^CCrsr;
CCrsr       = RECORD
                crsrType:    INTEGER;       {type of cursor}
                crsrMap:     PixMapHandle;  {the cursor's pixMap}
                crsrData:    Handle;        {cursor's data}
                crsrXData:   Handle;        {expanded cursor }
                                            { data}
                crsrXValid:  INTEGER;       {depth of expanded }
                                            { data}
                crsrXHandle: Handle;        {reserved for future }
                                            { use}
                crsr1Data:   Bits16;        {one-bit cursor}
                crsrMask:    Bits16;        {cursor's mask}
                crsrHotSpot: Point;         {cursor's hotspot}
                crsrXTable:  LONGINT;       {private}
                crsrID:      LONGINT;       {ctSeed for expanded }
                                            { cursor}
            END;
```

```
CIconHandle = ^CIconPtr;
CIconPtr    = ^CIcon;
CIcon       = RECORD
                iconPMap:  PixMap;   {the icon's pixMap}
                iconMask:  BitMap;   {the icon's mask bitMap}
                iconBMap:  BitMap;   {the icon's bitMap}
                iconData:  Handle;   {the icon's data}
                iconMaskData: ARRAY[0..0] OF INTEGER; {icon's }
                                     { mask and bitMap data}
              END;

  MatchRec = RECORD
                red:        INTEGER;  {red component}
                green:      INTEGER;  {green component}
                blue:       INTEGER;  {blue component}
                matchData:  LONGINT;
             END;

CQDProcsPtr = ^CQDProcs
CQDProcs    = RECORD
                textProc:    Ptr;
                lineProc:    Ptr;
                rectProc:    Ptr;
                rRectProc:   Ptr;
                ovalProc:    Ptr;
                arcProc:     Ptr;
                polyProc:    Ptr;
                rgnProc:     Ptr;
                bitsProc:    Ptr;
                commentProc: Ptr;
                txMeasProc:  Ptr;
                getPicProc:  Ptr;
                putPicProc:  Ptr;
                opcodeProc:  Ptr;     {fields added to QDProcs}
                newProc1:    Ptr;     {reserved for future use}
                newProc2:    Ptr;     {reserved for future use}
                newProc3:    Ptr;     {reserved for future use}
                newProc4:    Ptr;     {reserved for future use}
                newProc5:    Ptr;     {reserved for future use}
                newProc6:    Ptr;     {reserved for future use}
              END;
```

Routines

Operations on cGrafPorts

```
PROCEDURE OpenCPort  (port: CGrafPtr);
PROCEDURE InitCPort  (port: CGrafPtr);
PROCEDURE CloseCPort (port: CGrafPtr);
```

Setting the Foreground and Background Colors

```
PROCEDURE RGBForeColor (color : RGBColor);
PROCEDURE RGBBackColor (color : RGBColor);
PROCEDURE GetForeColor (VAR color : RGBColor);
PROCEDURE GetBackColor (VAR color : RGBColor);
```

Creating Pixel Maps

```
FUNCTION NewPixMap : PixMapHandle;
PROCEDURE DisposPixMap (pm: PixMapHandle);
PROCEDURE CopyPixMap (srcPM,dstPM: PixMapHandle);
```

Operations on Pixel Maps

```
PROCEDURE CopyBits    (srcBits, dstBits: BitMap; srcRect, dstRect:
                       Rect; mode: INTEGER; maskRgn: RgnHandle);
PROCEDURE CopyMask    (srcBits,maskBits,dstBits: BitMap; srcRect,
                       maskRect, dstRect: Rect);
PROCEDURE SeedCFill   (srcBits, dstBits: BitMap;  srcRect, dstRect:
                       Rect; seedH, seedV: INTEGER; matchProc:
                       ProcPtr; matchData: LONGINT);
PROCEDURE CalcCMask   (srcBits, dstBits: BitMap; srcRect, dstRect:
                       Rect; seedRGB: RGBColor; matchProc: ProcPtr;
                       matchData: LONGINT);
```

Operations on Pixel Patterns

```
FUNCTION  NewPixPat : PixPatHandle;
PROCEDURE DisposPixPat (ppat: PixPatHandle);
FUNCTION  GetPixPat    (patID: INTEGER): PixPatHandle;
PROCEDURE CopyPixPat   (srcPP,dstPP: PixPatHandle);
PROCEDURE MakeRGBPat   (ppat: PixPatHandle; myColor: RGBColor);
PROCEDURE PenPixPat    (ppat: PixPatHandle);
PROCEDURE BackPixPat   (ppat: PixPatHandle);
```

Color Drawing Operations

```
PROCEDURE FillCRect      (r: Rect; ppat: PixPatHandle);
PROCEDURE FillCOval      (r: Rect; ppat: PixPatHandle);
PROCEDURE FillCRoundRect (r: Rect; ovWd,ovHt: INTEGER; ppat:
                          PixPatHandle);
PROCEDURE FillCArc       (r: Rect; startAngle,arcAngle: INTEGER;
                          ppat: PixPatHandle);
PROCEDURE FillCRgn       (rgn: RgnHandle; ppat: PixPatHandle);
PROCEDURE FillCPoly      (poly: PolyHandle; ppat: PixPatHandle);
PROCEDURE GetCPixel      (h,v: INTEGER; VAR cPix: RGBColor);
PROCEDURE SetCPixel      (h,v: INTEGER; cPix: RGBColor);
```

Operations on Color Cursors

```
FUNCTION  GetCCursor     (crsrID: INTEGER): CCrsrHandle;
```

4 Color QuickDraw

```
PROCEDURE SetCCursor    (cCrsr: CCrsrHandle);
PROCEDURE DisposCCursor (cCrsr: \CCrsrHandle);
PROCEDURE AllocCursor;
```

Operations on Icons

```
FUNCTION  GetCIcon      (id: INTEGER): CIconHandle;
PROCEDURE DisposCIcon  (theIcon: CIconHandle);
PROCEDURE PlotCIcon    (theRect: Rect; theIcon: CIconHandle);
```

Operations on cGrafPort Fields

```
PROCEDURE SetPortPix   (pm: PixMapHandle);
PROCEDURE OpColor      (color: RGBColor);
PROCEDURE HiliteColor  (color:RGBColor);
PROCEDURE CharExtra    (extra:Fixed);
PROCEDURE SetStdCProcs (VAR cProcs: CQDProcs);
```

Operations on Color Tables

```
FUNCTION  GetCTable    (ctID: INTEGER): CTabHandle;
PROCEDURE DisposCTable (ctTab: CTabHandle);
```

Color Picture Operations

```
FUNCTION OpenPicture (picFrame: Rect) : PicHandle;
```

Global Variables

```
HiliteMode {if the hilite mode is set, highlighting is on}
HiliteRGB  {default highlight color for the system}
```

Assembly-Language Interface

HiLite Constant

```
hiliteBit EQU 7 ;flag bit in HiliteMode
                ; this is the correct value for use in assembler
                ; programs
```

Equates for Resource IDs

```
defQDColors EQU 127   ;resource ID of clut for default QDColors
```

RGBColor structure

```
red         EQU  $0   ;[word] red channel intensity
```

```
green          EQU    $2      ;[word] green channel intensity
blue           EQU    $4      ;[word] blue channel intensity
rgbColor       EQU    $6      ;size of record
```

ColorSpec structure

```
value          EQU    $0      ;[short] value field
rgb            EQU    $2      ;[rgbColor] rgb values
colorSpecSize  EQU    $8      ;size of record
```

Additional Offsets in a cGrafPort

```
portPixMap   EQU   portBits      ;[long] pixelMap handle
portVersion  EQU   portPixMap+4  ;[word] port version number
grafVars     EQU   portVersion+2 ;[long] handle to new fields
chExtra      EQU   grafVars+4    ;[word] extra characters placed at
                                 ; the end of a string
pnLocHFrac   EQU   chExtra+2     ;[word] pen fraction

bkPixPat     EQU   bkPat         ;[long] handle to bk pattern
rgbFgColor   EQU   bkPixPat+4    ;[6 bytes] RGB components of fg color
rgbBkColor   EQU   RGBFgColor+6  ;[6 bytes] RGB components of bk color

pnPixPat     EQU   $3A           ;[long] handle to pen's pattern
fillPixPat   EQU   pnPixPat+4    ;[long] handle to fill pattern
```

Offsets Within GrafVars

```
rgbOpColor     EQU   0                ;[6 bytes] color for addPin,
                                      ; subPin, and blend
rgbHiliteColor EQU   rgbOpColor+6     ;[6 bytes] color for hiliting
pmFgColor      EQU   rgbHiliteColor+6 ;[4 bytes] Palette handle for
                                      ; foreground color
pmFgIndex      EQU   pmFgColor+4      ;[2 bytes] index value for
                                      ; foreground
pmBkColor      EQU   pmFgIndex+2      ;[4 bytes] Palette handle for
                                      ; background color
pmBkIndex      EQU   pmBkColor+4      ;[2 bytes] index value for
                                      ; background
pmFlags        EQU   pmBkIndex+2      ;[2 bytes] Flags for Palette
                                      ; manager
grafVarRec     EQU   pmFlags+2        ;size of grafVar record
```

PixMap field offsets

```
pmBaseAddr   EQU   $0      ;[long]
pmNewFlag    EQU   $4      ;[1 bit]upper bit of rowbytes is flag
pmRowBytes   EQU   $4      ;[word]
pmBounds     EQU   $6      ;[rect]
pmVersion    EQU   $E      ;[word]  pixMap version number
pmPackType   EQU   $10     ;[word]  defines packing format
pmPackSize   EQU   $12     ;[long]  size of pixel data
pmHRes       EQU   $16     ;[fixed] h. resolution (ppi)
```

```
pmVRes       EQU $1A   ; [fixed]  v. resolution (ppi)
pmPixelType  EQU $1E   ; [word]   defines pixel type
pmPixelSize  EQU $20   ; [word]   # bits in pixel
pmCmpCount   EQU $22   ; [word]   # components in pixel
pmCmpSize    EQU $24   ; [word]   # bits per field
pmPlaneBytes EQU $26   ; [long]   offset to next plane
pmTable      EQU $2A   ; [long]   color map
pmReserved   EQU $2E   ; [long]   must be 0
pmRec        EQU $32   ; size of pixMap record
```

PixPat field offsets

```
patType   EQU $0    ; [word] type of pattern
patMap    EQU $2    ; [long] handle to pixmap
patData   EQU $6    ; [long] handle to data
patXData  EQU $A    ; [long] handle to expanded pattern data
patXValid EQU $E    ; [word] flags whether expanded pattern valid
patXMap   EQU $10   ; [long] handle to expanded pattern data
pat1Data  EQU $14   ; [8 bytes] old-style pattern/RGB color
ppRec     EQU $1C   ; size of pixPat record
```

Pattern Types

```
oldPat     EQU 0       ;foreground/background pattern
newPat     EQU 1       ;self-contained color pattern
ditherPat  EQU 2       ;rgb value to be dithered
oldCrsrPat EQU $8000   ;old-style cursor
CCrsrPat   EQU $8001   ;new-style cursor
```

CCrsr (Color Cursor) field offsets

```
crsrType   EQU 0             ; [word] cursor type
crsrMap    EQU crsrType+2    ; [long] handle to cursor's pixmap
crsrData   EQU crsrMap+4     ; [long] handle to cursor's color
                             ; data
crsrXData  EQU crsrData+4    ; [long] handle to expanded data
crsrXValid EQU crsrXData+4   ; [word] handle to expanded data
                             ; (0 if none)
crsrXHandle EQU crsrXValid+2 ; [long] handle for future use
crsr1Data  EQU crsrXHandle+4 ; [16 words] one-bit data
crsrMask   EQU crsr1Data+32  ; [16 words] one-bit mask
crsrHotSpot EQU crsrMask+32  ; [point] hot-spot for cursor
crsrXTable EQU crsrHotSpot+4 ; [long] private
crsrID     EQU crsrXTable+4  ; [long] color table seed for
                             ; expanded cursor
crsrRec    EQU crsrID+4      ;size of cursor save area
```

CIcon (Color Icon) field offsets

```
iconPMap EQU 0                ; [pixmap] icon's pixMap
iconMask EQU iconPMap+pmRec   ; [bitmap] 1-bit version of icon
                             ; 1-bit mask
iconBMap EQU iconMask+bitmapRec ; [bitmap] 1-bit version of icon
```

```
iconData EQU  iconBMap+bitmapRec ;[long] Handle to pixMap data
                                 ; followed by bMap and mask data
iconRec  EQU  iconData+4         ;size of icon header
```

Extensions to the QDProcs record

```
opcodeProc   EQU  $34   ;[pointer]
newProc1     EQU  $38   ;[pointer]
newProc2     EQU  $3C   ;[pointer]
newProc3     EQU  $40   ;[pointer]
newProc4     EQU  $44   ;[pointer]
newProc5     EQU  $48   ;[pointer]
newProc6     EQU  $4C   ;[pointer]
cqdProcsRec  EQU  $50   ; size of QDProcs record
```

MatchRec structure

```
red           EQU  $0   ; [word] defined in RGBColor
green         EQU  $2   ; [word] defined in RGBColor
blue          EQU  $4   ; [word] defined in RGBColor
matchData     EQU  $6   ; [long]
matchRecSize  EQU  $A   ;size of record
```

Global Variables

```
HiliteMode EQU  $938  ;if the hilite bit is set, highlighting is on
HiliteRGB  EQU  $DA0  ;default highlight color for the system
```

5   GRAPHICS DEVICES

5 Graphics Devices

ABOUT THIS CHAPTER

Because the Macintosh II supports a variable sized screen, different screen depths, and even multiple screens, a new set of data structures and routines has been introduced to support, in a general way, the use of **graphics devices** (called gDevices). These data structures and routines are logically a part of Color QuickDraw, but because they are functionally quite independent of QuickDraw, they appear here in a separate chapter.

A graphics device is used to

- associate a driver with a particular graphics output device

- define the size and color capabilities of the device

- define the position of a video screen with respect to other screens

- change the default matching routine used by the Color Manager

- keep track of the cursor for that device

- allocate a set of colors used by an offscreen bitMap

  Reader's guide: Graphics devices are generally used only by the system. You might need to use the information in this chapter, for example, if your application needs explicit knowledge of the pixel depth of the screen(s) it is drawing to, or if it wants to bring up a window on a particular screen. You might also use the information in this chapter if you want to allocate and maintain an offscreen bitMap.

Before reading this chapter you should be familiar with the material in the chapter on Color QuickDraw. Some of the routine descriptions in this chapter also refer to the Color Manager, the Slot Manager, and the Device Manager chapters; you will only need to refer to those chapters if you are using those routines.

ABOUT GRAPHICS DEVICES

When the system is started up, one handle to a gDevice record (described below) is allocated and initialized for each video card found by the system. These gDevice records are linked together in a linked list, which is called the **DeviceList.**

By default, the gDevice record corresponding to the first video card found is marked as an active device (a device your program can use for drawing); all other devices in the list are marked as inactive. The ways that other devices become active are described below. When drawing is being performed on a device, that device is stored as **theGDevice.**

If you want your application to write into an offscreen pixMap whose pixel depth or set of colors is different from that of the screen, your program must allocate a gDevice to describe the format of the offscreen pixMap. Your application could describe the set of colors that a printer can support, or represent an offscreen version of an image that spans multiple screens. More details of this technique are given below.

GDevices that correspond to video devices have drivers associated with them. These drivers are used, for example, to change the mode of the device from monochrome to color, or to change the pixel depth of the device. GDevices that your application creates won't generally require drivers. The set of calls supported by a video driver is defined and described in *Designing Cards and Drivers for Macintosh II and Macintosh SE*.

DEVICE RECORDS

All information that is needed to communicate with a graphics device is stored in a handle to a gDevice record, called a gdHandle. This information may describe many types of devices, including video displays, printers, or offscreen drawing environments.

The structure of the gDevice record is as follows:

```
TYPE
   GDHandle    = ^GDPtr;
   GDPtr       = ^GDevice;
   GDevice     = RECORD
                 gdRefNum:     INTEGER;       {reference number of driver}
                 gdID:         INTEGER;       {client ID for search }
                                              { procedure}
                 gdType:       INTEGER;       {device type}
                 gdITable:     ITabHandle;    {inverse table}
                 gdResPref:    INTEGER;       {preferred resolution}
                 gdSearchProc: SProcHndl;     {list of search procedures}
                 gdCompProc:   CProcHndl;     {list of complement }
                                              { procedures}
                 gdFlags:      INTEGER;       {grafDevice flags word}
                 gdPMap:       PixMapHandle;  {pixel map for displayed }
                                              { image}
                 gdRefCon:     LONGINT;       {reference value}
                 gdNextGD:     GDHandle;      {handle of next gDevice}
                 gdRect:       Rect;          {device's global bounds}
                 gdMode:       LONGINT;       {device's current mode}
                 gdCCBytes:    INTEGER;       {rowBytes of expanded }
                                              { cursor data}
                 gdCCDepth:    INTEGER;       {rowBytes of expanded }
                                              { cursor data}
                 gdCCXData:    Handle;        {handle to cursor's }
                                              { expanded data}
                 gdCCXMask:    Handle;        {handle to cursor's }
                                              { expanded mask}
                 gdReserved:   LONGINT        {reserved for future }
                                              { expansion}
                 END;
```

Field descriptions

gdRefNum   The gdRefNum is a reference number of the driver for the display device associated with this card. For most display devices, this information is set at system startup time.

gdID   The gdID field contains an application-settable ID number identifying the current client of the port. It is also used for search and complement procedures (see "The Color Manager: Search and Complement Procedures").

gdType   The gdType field specifies the general type of device. Values include:
0 = CLUT device (mapped colors with lookup table)
1 = fixed colors (no lookup table)
2 = direct RGB
These device types are described in the Color Manager chapter.

gdITable   The gdITable contains a handle to the inverse table for color mapping (see "The Color Manager: Inverse Tables").

gdResPref   The gdResPref field contains the preferred resolution for inverse tables (see "The Color Manager: Inverse Tables").

gdSearchProc   The gdSearchProc field is a pointer to the list of search procedures (see "The Color Manager: Search and Complement Procedures"); its value is NIL for a default procedure.

gdCompProc   The gdCompProc field is a pointer to a list of complement procedures (see "The Color Manager: Search and Complement Procedures"; its value is NIL for a default procedure.

gdFlags   The gdFlags field contains the gDevice's attributes. Do not set these flags directly; always use the procedures described in this chapter.

gdPMap   The gdPMap field is a handle to a pixel map giving the dimension of the image buffer, along with the characteristics of the device (resolution, storage format, color depth, color table). For gDevices, the high bit of theGDevice^^.gdPMap^^.pmTable^^.ctFlags is always set.

gdRefCon   The gdRefCon is a field used to pass device-related parameters (see SeedCFill and CalcCMask in the Color QuickDraw chapter). Since a device is shared, you shouldn't store data here.

gdNextGD   The gdNextGD field contains a handle to the next device in the deviceList. If this is the last device in the deviceList, this is set to zero.

gdRect   The gdRect field contains the boundary rectangle of the gDevice. The screen with the menu bar has topLeft = 0,0. All other devices are relative to it.

gdMode   The gdMode field specifies the current setting for the device mode. This is the value passed to the driver to set its pixel depth, etc.

gdCCBytes   The gdCCBytes field contains the rowBytes of the expanded cursor. Applications must not change this field.

gdCCDepth   The gdCCDepth field contains the depth of the expanded cursor. Applications must not change this field.

gdCCXData   The gdCCXData field contains a handle to the cursor's expanded data. Applications must not change this field.

gdCCXMask   The gdCCXMask field contains a handle to the cursor's expanded mask. Applications must not change this field.

gdReserved   The gdReserved field is reserved for future expansion; it must be set to zero for future compatibility.

MULTIPLE SCREEN DEVICES

This section describes how multiple screen devices are supported by the system. It tells how they are initialized, and once initialized, how they're used.

When the system is started up, one of the display devices is selected as the **startup screen,** the screen on which the "happy Macintosh" icon appears. If a startup screen has been indicated in parameter RAM, then that screen is used. Otherwise, the screen whose video card is in the lowest numbered slot is used as the startup screen. By default, the menu bar is placed on the startup screen. The screen with the menu bar is called the **main screen.**

The user can use the Control Panel to set the desired depth of each screen, whether it displays monochrome or color, and the position of that screen relative to the screen with the menu bar. Users can also select which screen should have the menu bar on it. See the Control Panel chapter for more information. All this information is stored in a resource of type 'scrn' (ID=0) in the system file.

When the InitGraf routine is called to initialize QuickDraw, it checks the System file for this resource. If it is found, the screens are organized according to the contents of this resource. If it is not found, then only the startup screen is used. The precise format of a 'scrn' resource is described in the "Graphics Device Resources" section.

When InitWindows is called, it scans through the device list and creates a region that is the union of all the active screen devices (minus the menu bar and the rounded corners on the outermost screens). It saves this region as the global variable **GrayRgn,** which describes and defines the desktop, the area on which windows can be dragged. Programs that paint the desktop should use FillRgn(GrayRgn,myPattern). Programs that move objects around on the desktop should pin to the GrayRgn, not to screenBits.bounds.

Since the Window Manager allows windows to be dragged anywhere within the GrayRgn, windows can span screen boundaries, or be moved to entirely different screens. Despite this fact, QuickDraw can draw to the window's port as if it were all on one screen. In general terms, it works like this: when an application opens a window, the window's port.portBits.baseAddr field is set to be equal to the base address of the main screen. When QuickDraw draws into a grafPort or cGrafPort, it compares the base address of the port to that of the main screen. If they are equal, then QuickDraw might need to draw to multiple screens.

If there are multiple screens, QuickDraw calculates the rectangle, in global coordinates, into which the drawing operation will write. For each active screen device in the device list, QuickDraw intersects the destination rectangle with the device's rectangle (gdRect). If they intersect, the drawing command is issued to that device, with a new pixel value for the foreground and background colors if necessary. In addition, patterns and other structures may be reexpanded for each device.

GRAPHICS DEVICE ROUTINES

The following set of routines allows an application to create and examine gDevice records. Since most device and driver information is automatically set at system startup time, these routines are not needed by most applications that simply draw to the screen.

```
FUNCTION NewGDevice(refNum: INTEGER; mode: LONGINT)  GDHandle;
```

The NewGDevice function allocates a new gDevice data structure and all of its handles, then calls InitGDevice to initialize it for the specified device in the specified mode. If the request is unsuccessful, a NIL handle is returned. The new gDevice and all of its handles are allocated in the system heap. All attributes in the GDFlags word are set to FALSE.

If your application creates a gDevice without a driver, the mode parameter should be set to −1. In this case, InitGDevice is not called to initialize the gDevice. Your application must perform all initialization.

A graphics device's default mode is defined as 128, as described in the Designing Cards and Drivers manual; this is assumed to be a monochrome mode. If the mode parameter is not the default mode, the gdDevType attribute is set TRUE, to indicate that the device is capable of displaying color (see the SetDeviceAttribute call).

This routine doesn't automatically insert the gDevice into the device list. In general, your application shouldn't add devices that it created to the device list.

```
PROCEDURE InitGDevice(gdRefNum: INTEGER; mode: LONGINT; gdh:
        GDHandle);
```

The InitGDevice routine sets the video device whose driver has the specified gdRefNum to the specified mode. It then fills out the gDevice record structure specified by the gdh parameter to contain all information describing that mode. The GDHandle should have been allocated by a call to NewGDevice.

The mode determines the configuration of the device; possible modes for a device can be determined by interrogating the video card's ROM via calls to the Slot Manager (refer to the Slot Manager chapter and the Designing Cards and Drivers manual). Refer to the Device Manager chapter for more details about the interaction of devices and their drivers.

The information describing the new mode is primarily contained in the video card's ROM. If the device has a fixed color table, then that table is read directly from the ROM. If the device has a variable color table, then the default color table for that depth is used (the 'clut' resource with ID=depth).

In general, your application should never need to call this routine. All video devices are initialized at start time and their modes are changed by the control panel. If your program is initializing a device without a driver, this call will do nothing; your application must initialize all fields of the gDevice. It is worth noting that after your program initializes the color table for the device, it needs to call MakeITable to build the inverse table for the device.

```
FUNCTION GetGDevice: GDHandle;
```

The GetGDevice routine returns a handle to the current gDevice. This is useful for determining the characteristics of the current output device (for instance its pixelSize or color table). Note that since a window can span screen boundaries, this call does not return the device that describes a port.

Assembly-language note: A handle to the currently active device is kept in the global variable TheGDevice.

```
PROCEDURE SetGDevice(gdh: GDHandle);
```

The SetGDevice procedure sets the specified gDevice as the current device. Your application won't generally need to use this call except to draw to offscreen gDevices.

```
FUNCTION DisposGDevice: GDHandle;
```

The DisposGDevice function disposes of the current gDevice and releases the space allocated for it, and all data structures allocated by NewGDevice.

5 Graphics Devices

```
FUNCTION GetDeviceList: GDHandle;
```

The GetDeviceList function returns a handle to the first device in the DeviceList.

Assembly-language note: A handle to the first element in the device list is kept in the global variable DeviceList.

```
FUNCTION GetMainDevice: GDHandle;
```

The GetMainDevice function returns the handle of the gDevice that has the menu bar on it. Your application can examine this gDevice to determine the size or depth of the main screen.

Assembly-language note: A handle to the current main device is kept in the global variable MainDevice.

```
FUNCTION GetNextDevice (gdh: GDHandle): GDHandle;
```

The GetNextDevice function returns the handle of the next gDevice in the DeviceList. If there are no more devices in the list, it returns NIL.

```
PROCEDURE SetDeviceAttribute: (gdh: GDHandle; attribute: INTEGER;
          value: BOOLEAN);
```

The SetDeviceAttribute routine can be used to set a device's attribute bits. The following attributes may be set using this call:

```
gdDevType     = 0;  {0 = monochrome, 1 = color}
ramInit       = 10; {set if device has been initialized from RAM}
mainScreen    = 11; {set if device is main screen}
allInit       = 12; {set if devices were initialized from a }
                    { 'scrn' resource}
screenDevice  = 13; {set if device is a screen device}
noDriver      = 14; {set if device has no driver}
screenActive  = 15; {set if device is active}
```

```
FUNCTION TestDeviceAttribute (curDevice: GDHandle; attribute:
          INTEGER) : BOOLEAN;
```

The TestDeviceAttribute function tests a single attribute to see if it is true or not. If your application is scanning through the device list, it would typically use this routine to test if a device is a screen device, and if so, test to see if it's active. Then your application can draw to any active screen devices.

```
FUNCTION GetMaxDevice (globalRect: Rect):GDHandle;
```

The GetMaxDevice routine returns a handle to the deepest device that intersects the specified global rectangle. Your application might use this routine to allocate offscreen pixMaps, as described in the following section.

DRAWING TO OFFSCREEN DEVICES

It's sometimes desirable to perform drawing operations offscreen, and then use CopyBits to transfer the complete image to the screen. One reason to do this is to avoid the flicker that can happen when your program is drawing overlapping objects. Another reason might be to control the set of colors used in the drawing (for instance, if your application performs imaging for a printer that has a different set of colors than the screen). For both these examples, your application needs control of the color environment, and thus needs to make use of gDevices.

First, let's look at the example of drawing a number of objects offscreen, and then transferring the completed image to the screen. In this case, the complicating factor is the possibility that your program may open a window that will span two (or more) screens with different depths. One way to approach the problem is to allocate the offscreen pixMap with a depth that is the same as the deepest screen touched by the window. This allows your program to perform offscreen drawing with the maximum number of colors that is used by any window, giving optimal visual results. Another approach is to allocate the offscreen pixMap with the depth of the screen that contains the largest portion of the window, so that transfers to the screen will be as fast as possible. You might want to alternate between these techniques depending on the position of the window.

Optimizing Visual Results

When allocating a pixMap for the deepest screen, your application should first allocate an offscreen grafPort that has the depth of the deepest screen the window overlaps. To do this, your application must save the current gDevice (GetGDevice), get the deepest screen (GetMaxDevice), set that to be the current gDevice (SetGDevice), create a new cGrafPort (OpenCPort), and then restore the saved gDevice (SetGDevice again). Since OpenCPort initializes its pixMap using TheGDevice, the current grafPort is the same as the deepest screen.

Next, your application must allocate storage for the pixels by setting portPixMap^^.bounds to define the height and width of the desired image, and setting rowBytes to ((width*portPixMap^^.pixelSize)+15)DIV 16*2. (Note that rowBytes must be even, and for optimal performance should be a multiple of four. Your application can adjust portPixMap^^.bounds to achieve this.) Next, define the interior of portPixMap.bounds to which your application can write by setting portRect. Now that the size of the pixMap is defined, the amount of storage is simply the height*portPixMap^^.rowBytes. It is generally better to allocate the storage as a handle. Before writing to it, your application should lock the handle, and place a pointer to the storage in portPixMap^^.baseAddr.

All that remains is to draw to the grafPort. Before drawing, your program should save the current gDevice, and then set TheGDevice to be the maximum device (which was determined earlier). Your application can use SetPort to make this port the current port, and then perform all drawing operations. Remember to have your application restore TheGDevice after drawing is complete.

Keep in mind that all this preparation can be invalidated easily. If the user changes the depth of the screen or moves the window, all your carefully allocated storage may no longer be appropriate. Both changing the depth of the screen and moving the window across device boundaries will cause update events. In your application's update routine, include a test to see if the environment has changed. One good test is to determine whether the color table has changed. Your application can compare the ctSeed field of the new maximum device with that of the old maximum device. (See the Color Manager chapter for more information on this technique.) If ctSeed has changed, your application should check the screen depth, and if it has changed, reallocate the pixMap (possibly repeating the entire process above). If the depth hasn't changed, but the color table has, then your application can just redraw the objects into the offscreen pixMap.

Optimizing Speed

If you decide to optimize for speed instead of appearance, then your application should examine each element in the device list to see how much of the window it intersects. Your application can do this by getting the device list (GetDeviceList), intersecting that device's rectangle with your window's rectangle, and then repeating the examination for each device by calling GetNextDevice. Before examining a device, your application can ensure that it is an active screen device using GetDeviceAttribute. The procedure for allocating the cGrafPort is the same as described above.

Imaging for a Color Printer

Finally, let's look briefly at the example of imaging into an offscreen device that isn't the same as one of the screen devices, which you might do if you were imaging for a color printer. In this case the process is much the same, but instead of relying on an existing gDevice to define the drawing environment, your application must set up a new one. To do this, simply call NewGDevice to allocate a new gDevice data structure. Your application must initialize all fields of the pixMap and color table, as described in the Color QuickDraw chapter. It should call then MakeITable to build the device's inverse table, as described in the Color Manager chapter. As with the example above, your application should set its gDevice as the current device before drawing to the offscreen pixMap. This will guarantee that drawing is done using the set of colors defined by your application's gDevice.

GRAPHICS DEVICE RESOURCES

A new resource type has been added to describe the setup of graphics devices:

'scrn'   Screen resource type

The 'scrn' resource contains all the screen configuration information for a multiple screen system. Only the 'scrn' resource with ID = 0 is used by the system. Normally your application won't have to alter or examine this resource. It's created by the control panel, and is used by InitGraf.

The 'scrn' resource consists of a sequence of records, each describing one screen device. In the following description this sequence of records is represented by a Pascal FOR loop that repeats once for each screen device.

'scrn'   (Screen configuration)

ScrnCount	[word]	number of devices in resource
FOR i := 1 to ScrnCount DO		
spDrvrHw	[word]	Slot Manager hardware ID
slot	[word]	slot number
dCtlDevBase	[long]	dCtlDevBase from DCE
mode	[word]	Slot Manager ID for screen's mode
flagMask	[word]	= $77FE
flags	[word]	indicates device state
		bit 0 = 0 if monochrome; 1 if color
		bit 11=1 if device is main screen
		bit 15=1 if device is active
colorTable	[word]	resource id of desired 'clut'
gammaTable	[word]	resource id of desired 'gama'
global Rect	[rect]	device's global rectangle
ctlCount	[word]	number of control calls
FOR j := 1 to ctlCount DO		
csCode	[word]	control code for this call
length	[word]	number of bytes in param block
param blk	[length]	data to be passed in control call
END;		
END;		

The records in the 'scrn' resource must be in the same order as cards in the slots (starting with the lowest slot). InitGraf scans through the video cards in the slots, and compares them with the descriptors in the 'scrn' resource. If the spDrvrHw, slot, and dCtlDevBase fields all match for every screen device in the system, the 'scrn' resource is used to initialize the video devices. Otherwise the 'scrn' resource is simply ignored. Thus if you move a video card, or add or remove one, the 'scrn' resource will become invalid.

SpDrvrHw is a Slot Manager field that identifies the type of hardware on the card. (The spDrvrSw field on the card must identify it as an Apple-compatible video driver.) Slot is the number of the slot containing the card. DCtlDevBase is the beginning of the device's address space, taken from the device's DCE.

If all video devices match, the rest of the information in the 'scrn' resource is used to configure the video devices. The mode is actually the slot manager ID designating the descriptor for that mode. This same mode number is passed to the video driver to tell it which mode to use.

The flags bits are used to determine whether the device is active (that is, whether it will be used), whether it's color or monochrome, and whether it's the main screen (the one with the menu bar). The flagMask simply tells which bits in the flags word are used.

To use the default color table for a device, set the colorTable field to –1. To use the default gamma table for a device, set the gammaTable field to –1. (Gamma correction is a technique used to select the appropriate intensities of the colors sent to a display device. The default gamma table is designed for the Macintosh II 13-inch color monitor; other manufacturers' color monitors might incorporate their own gamma tables.)

The global rect specifies the coordinates of the device relative to other devices. The main device must have topLeft = 0,0. The coordinates of all other devices are specified relative to this device. Devices may not overlap, and must share at least part of an edge with another device. To support future device capabilities, a series of control calls may be specified. These are issued to the driver in the given order.

SUMMARY OF GRAPHICS DEVICES

Constants

```
{ Values for GDFlags }
clutType     = 0;    {0 if lookup table}
fixedType    = 1;    {1 if fixed table}
directType   = 2;    {2 if direct values}

{ Bit assignments for GDFlags }
gdDevType    = 0;    {0 = monochrome, 1 = color}
ramInit      = 10;   {set if device has been initialized from RAM}
mainScreen   = 11;   {set if device is main screen}
allInit      = 12;   {set if devices were initialized from a 'scrn' }
                     { resource}
screenDevice = 13;   {set if device is a screen device}
noDriver     = 14;   {set if device has no driver}
screenActive = 15;   {set if device is active}
```

Data Types

```
TYPE
    GDHandle   = ^GDPtr;
    GDPtr      = ^GDevice;
    GDevice    = RECORD

                    gdRefNum:     INTEGER;      {reference number of }
                                               { driver}
                    gdID:         INTEGER;      {client ID for search }
                                               { procedure}
                    gdType:       INTEGER;      {device type}
                    gdITable:     ITabHandle;   {inverse table}
                    gdResPref:    INTEGER;      {preferred resolution}
                    gdSearchProc: SProcHndl;    {list of search }
                                               { procedures}
                    gdCompProc:   CProcHndl;    {list of complement }
                                               { procedures}
                    gdFlags:      INTEGER;      {grafDevice flags word}
                    gdPMap:       PixMapHandle; {pixel map for }
                                               { displayed image}
                    gdRefCon:     LONGINT;      {reference value}
                    gdNextGD:     GDHandle;     {handle of next }
                                               { gDevice}
                    gdRect:       Rect;         {device's global }
                                               { bounds}
                    gdMode:       LONGINT;      {device's current mode}
                    gdCCBytes:    INTEGER;      {rowBytes of expanded }
                                               { cursor data}
```

```
            gdCCDepth:     INTEGER;        {depth of expanded }
                                           { cursor data}
            gdCCXData:     Handle;         {handle to cursor's }
                                           { expanded data}
            gdCCXMask:     Handle;         {handle to cursor's }
                                           { expanded mask}
            gdReserved:    LONGINT         {reserved for future }
                                           { expansion}
        END;
```

Routines

```
FUNCTION   NewGDevice           (refNum: INTEGER; mode: LONGINT) :
                                    GDHandle;
PROCEDURE  InitGDevice          (gdRefNum: INTEGER; mode: LONGINT;
                                    gdh: GDHandle);
FUNCTION   GetGDevice:          GDHandle;
PROCEDURE  SetGDevice           (gdh: GDHandle);
PROCEDURE  DisposGDevice        (gdh: GDHandle);
FUNCTION   GetDeviceList:       GDHandle;
FUNCTION   GetMainDevice:       GDHandle;
FUNCTION   GetNextDevice        (curDevice:GDHandle): GDHandle;
PROCEDURE  SetDeviceAttribute   (gdh: GDHandle; attribute: INTEGER;
                                    value: BOOLEAN);
FUNCTION   TestDeviceAttribute  (gdh: GDHandle; attribute: INTEGER):
                                    BOOLEAN;
FUNCTION   GetMaxDevice         (globalRect:Rect): GDHandle;
```

Global Variables

```
DeviceList        {handle to the first element in the device list}
GrayRgn           {contains size and shape of current desktop}
TheGDevice        {handle to current active device}
MainDevice        {handle to the current main device}
```

Assembly Language Information

Values for GDTypes

```
clutType    EQU   0     ;0 if lookup table
fixedType   EQU   1     ;1 if fixed table
directType  EQU   2     ;2 if direct values
```

Bit Assignments for GDFlags

```
gdDevType     EQU   0    ;0 = monochrome, 1 = color
ramInit       EQU   10   ;set if device has been initialized from RAM
mainScreen    EQU   11   ;set if device is main screen
allInit       EQU   12   ;set if devices were initialized from a
                         ; 'scrn' resource
screenDevice  EQU   13   ;set if device is a screen device
noDriver      EQU   14   ;set if device has no driver
screenActive  EQU   15   ;set if device is active
```

GDevice field offsets

```
gdRefNum      EQU   $0   ;[word] unitNum of driver
gdID          EQU   $2   ;[word] client ID for search procs
gdType        EQU   $4   ;[word] fixed/CLUT/direct
gdITable      EQU   $6   ;[long] handle to inverse table
gdResPref     EQU   $A   ;[word] preferred resolution for inverse
                         ; tables
gdSearchProc  EQU   $C   ;[long] search proc (list?) pointer
gdCompProc    EQU   $10  ;[long] complement proc (list?) pointer
gdFlags       EQU   $14  ;[word] grafDevice flags word
gdPMap        EQU   $16  ;[long] handle to pixMap describing
                         ; device
gdRefCon      EQU   $1A  ;[long] reference value
gdNextGD      EQU   $1E  ;handle of next gDevice
gdRect        EQU   $22  ;device's global bounds
gdMode        EQU   $2A  ;device's current mode
gdCCBytes     EQU   $2E  ;rowBytes of expanded cursor data
gdCCDepth     EQU   $30  ;handle to cursor's expanded data
gdCCXData     EQU   $32  ;depth of expanded cursor data
gdCCXMask     EQU   $36  ;handle to cursor's expanded mask
gdReserved    EQU   $3A  ;[long] MUST BE 0
gdRec         EQU   $3E  ;size of GrafDevice record
```

Global Variables

```
DeviceList    EQU   $8A8  ;handle to the first element in the
                          ; device list
GrayRgn       EQU   $9EE  ;contains size and shape of current
                          ; desktop
TheGDevice    EQU   $CC8  ;handle to current active device
MainDevice    EQU   $8A4  ;handle to the current main device
```

5 Graphics Devices

6 THE COLOR MANAGER

ABOUT THIS CHAPTER

The Color Manager supplies color-selection support for Color QuickDraw on the Macintosh II. The software described in this chapter allows specialized applications to fine-tune the color-matching algorithms, and also provides utility functions that are rarely used by applications.

An understanding of Color QuickDraw concepts, terminology, and data structures is essential when using the material in this chapter. You should be familiar with RGB color, pixel maps, pixel patterns, and other material introduced in the Color QuickDraw chapter. You should also be familiar with the material in the Graphics Devices chapter, since the Color Manager routines work on the device level.

Keep in mind that Color Manager routines are the intermediary between high-level software such as Color QuickDraw, the Palette Manager, and the Color Picker, and the lower-level video devices. The majority of applications will never need to use the Color Manager routines directly.

> **Reader's guide:** The material in this chapter is largely for informational purposes only, since Color QuickDraw, the Palette Manager, and the other color Toolbox routines provide a detailed and consistent way to add color to Macintosh programs.

ABOUT THE COLOR MANAGER

The Color Manager is optimized to work with graphics hardware that utilizes a **Color Look-up Table (CLUT),** a data structure that maps color indices, specified using QuickDraw, into actual color values. The exact color capabilities of the Macintosh II depend on the particular video card used. There are three kinds of devices:

- **CLUT devices** contain hardware that converts an arbitrary pixel value stored in the frame buffer to some actual RGB video value, which is changeable. The pixel value could be the index to any of the colors in the current color set for the device, and the color set itself can be changed.

- **Fixed devices** also convert a pixel value to some actual RGB video value, but the hardware colors can't be changed. The pixel value could be the index to any of the colors in the color set, but the color set itself always remains the same.

- **Direct devices** have a direct correlation between the value placed in the frame buffer and the color you see on the screen. The value placed in the frame buffer would produce the same color every time. Direct devices aren't supported in the initial release of Color QuickDraw.

Applications that limit themselves to a small set of colors can use them simply and easily from QuickDraw, with a minimum of overhead. Color QuickDraw accesses the Color Manager to obtain the best available color matches in the lookup table. Applications such as color painting and animation programs, which need greater control over the precise colors they use, can use the Palette Manager to allocate part of the color table for their own exclusive use. The Palette Manager, described in a later chapter, is useful for most applications that use shared color resources, imaging, or color table animation. The Palette Manager is used whenever color is used for objects within windows, while the Color Manager operates on the device level.

> **Note:** Palette Manager routines operate transparently across multiple screens, while Color Manager routines do not. Therefore, always use Palette Manager routines for applications that will run on multiple screens or in a multitasking environment.

The sections that follow describe how the Color Manager converts the RGB values specified using Color QuickDraw into the actual colors available on a device. The pixel value, specifying the number of bits per pixel, is set using the Control Panel.

Graphics Devices

As with Color QuickDraw, the Color Manager accesses a particular graphics device through a data structure known as a gDevice record. Each gDevice record stores information about a particular graphics device; after this record is initialized, the device itself is known to the Color Manager and QuickDraw as a gDevice. See the Graphics Devices chapter for more details on gDevice format and on the routines that allow an application to access a given device. Remember that a gDevice is a logical device, which the software treats the same whether it is a video card, a display device, or an offscreen pixel map.

Color Table Format

The complete set of colors in use at a given time for a particular gDevice is summarized in a color table record. Its format is as follows:

```
TYPE
   CTabHandle = ^CTabPtr;
   CTabPtr    = ^ColorTable;
   ColorTable = RECORD
                   ctSeed:  LONGINT; {unique identifier from table}
                   ctFlags: INTEGER; {high bit is set for a gDevice, }
                                     { clear for a pixMap}
                   ctSize:  INTEGER; {Number of entries in table-1}
                   ctTable: cSpecArray
                END;
```

Field descriptions

ctSeed   The ctSeed field is similar to a version identifier number for a color table. If a color table is created by an application, it should call GetCTSeed to obtain this identifier. The ctSeed should be some unique number higher than minSeed, a predefined constant with a value of 1023. If a color table is created from a resource, its resource number will be used as the initial ctSeed. For 'CLUT' resource, the range of resource numbers should be 0–1023.

ctFlags   The ctFlags field is significant for gDevices only. It contains flags that describe the format of the ctTable. Currently, only the high bit is defined; all others are reserved. Color tables that are part of the gDevice structure always have this bit set. Color tables that are part of pixMaps have this bit clear. Each gDevice has its own pixMap, which has a color table.

ctSize   The ctSize field contains the number of entries in the color table minus one. All counts on color table entries are zero based.

ctTable   The ctTable field contains a cSpecArray, which is an array of ColorSpec entries. Notice that each entry in the color table is a ColorSpec, not simply an RGBColor. The type ColorSpec is composed of an integer value and an RGB color, as shown in the following specification. A color table may include a number of ColorSpec records.

```
TYPE
   cSpecArray = ARRAY [0..0] OF ColorSpec;
   ColorSpec = RECORD
                   value : INTEGER;  {Color representation}
                   rgb   : RGBColor  {Color value}
               END;

   RGBColor  = RECORD
                   red   : INTEGER;  {Red component}
                   green : INTEGER;  {Green component}
                   blue  : INTEGER   {Blue component}
               END;
```

In gDevice color tables, the colorSpec.value field is reserved for use by the Color Manager and Palette Manager. Their interpretation and values are different than the color tables contained in pixMaps.

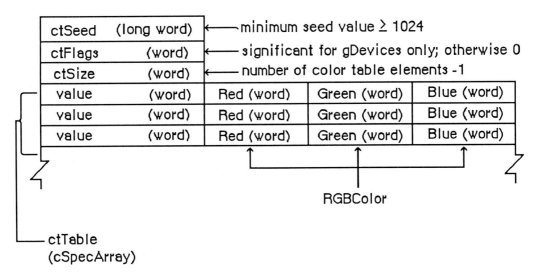

Figure 1. Color Table Format

Note that the colorSpec.value field of the record is only word size (16 bits), even though color index values (as returned by Color2Index) may be long words. The current implementation of Color QuickDraw only supports 16 bits. The components in an RGBColor are left-justified rather than right-justified in a word. Video drivers should respect this convention and extract the appropriate number of bits from the high order side of the component. For example, the Apple Graphics Card uses only the most significant eight bits of each component of the RGBColor record.

Inverse Tables

Reader's guide: The material in this section is provided for informational and debugging purposes, since most programs won't need to use inverse tables.

For normal drawing, Color QuickDraw takes all specifications as absolute RGB triples, by means of the RGBColor record. Internally, these absolute specifications are converted to the appropriate values to be written into the video card. For direct devices, the RGB is separated into its red, green, and blue components, and each of these is written to the video card. On CLUT and fixed devices, however, there isn't always a direct relationship between the specified RGB and the index value written into the frame buffer; in fact, on CLUT devices, the best-match index value may change dynamically as the colors available in the hardware are changed. On these types of devices, Color QuickDraw uses the Color Manager to find the best matches among the colors currently available.

The method used to determine the best available match can be specified by the application or the system on a gDevice by gDevice basis. By default, on CLUT and fixed devices, a special data structure called an **inverse table** is created. An inverse table is a table arranged in such a manner that, given an arbitrary RGB color, the pixel value can be very rapidly looked up.

In the default case, a certain number of the most significant bits of red, green, and blue are extracted, then concatenated together to form an index into the inverse table. At this location is the "best" match to the specified color. The number of bits per color channel that are used to construct this index is known as the resolution of the inverse table, and can be 3, 4, or 5 bits per channel. As the resolution of the inverse table increases, the number of permutations of possible colors increases, as does the size of the inverse table. Three-bit tables occupy 512 bytes, 4-bit tables (the default) occupy 4K bytes, and 5-bit tables occupy 32K bytes.

A disadvantage of this method is that certain colors that are "close" together can become hidden when they differ only in bits that weren't used to construct the inverse table index. For example, even if the color table were loaded with 256 levels of gray, a 4-bit inverse table can only discriminate among 16 of the levels. To solve this problem without having to use special-case sets of colors with hidden colors, inverse tables carry additional information about how to find colors that differ only in the less significant bits. As a result, when the Color2Index routine is called, it can find the best match to the full 48-bit resolution available in a colorSpec. Since examining the extra information takes time, certain parts of Color QuickDraw, notably drawing in the arithmetic transfer modes, don't use this information, and hence won't find the hidden colors.

In most cases, when setting colors using RGBForeColor and RGBBackColor, and when using CopyBits to transfer pixMaps, inverse tables of four bits are sufficient. When using arithmetic transfer modes with certain color tables that have closely-spaced colors, the screen appearance may be improved by specifying inverse tables at 5-bit resolution. Because the format of inverse tables is subject to change in the future, or may not be present on certain devices, applications should not assume the structure of the data.

The data in inverse tables remains valid as long as the color table from which it was built remains unchanged. When a color table is modified, the inverse table must be rebuilt, and the screen should be redrawn to take advantage of this new information. Rather than being reconstructed when the color table is changed, the inverse table is marked invalid, and is automatically rebuilt when next accessed.

Rather than testing each entry of the color table to see if it has changed, the color-matching code compares the ctSeed of the current gDevice's colorTable against the iTabSeed of that gDevice's inverse table. Each routine that modifies the colorTable (with the exception of RestoreEntries) increments the ctSeed field of that colorTable. If the ctSeed and the iTabSeed don't match, the inverse table is reconstructed for that gDevice.

> **Note:** Under normal circumstances, all invalidations are posted and serviced transparently to the application. This method of invalidation is the same as that used to invalidate expanded patterns and cursors elsewhere in Color QuickDraw.

In certain cases, it may be useful to override the inverse table matching code with custom routines that have special matching rules. See the section titled "Custom Search and Complement Procedures" for more details.

The Color Manager performs a color table look-up in the following manner:

1. Builds a table of all possible RGB values;

2. For each position in the table, attempts to get the closest match;

3. Reduces the resolution of the lookup to four bits when constructing the table, but later adds information to get a better resolution.

The Color Manager performs this table-building sequence whenever colors are requested by Color QuickDraw, the Color Picker, or the Palette Manager. This isn't the only color matching method available; a custom search procedure, for example, may not have an inverse table. (See the section titled "Custom Search and Complement Procedures" for more information.) However, inverse tables are the default method for color matching.

When using an inverse table, the table is indexed by concatenating together the high-order bits of the three desired color components; iTabRes tells how many bits of each component are significant. The format of an inverse table is shown below:

```
TYPE
  ITabHandle = ^ITabPtr;
  ITabPtr    = ^ITab;
  ITab       = RECORD
                 iTabSeed: LONGINT;    {copy of color table seed}
                 iTabRes:  INTEGER;    {resolution of table}
                 iTTable:  ARRAY[0..0] OF SignedByte {byte color }
                                       { table index values}
               END;
```

The size of an index table in bytes is $2^{3*iTabRes}$. The table below shows a sample index table:

resolution	RGB color	inverse-table index	size
4-bit	red=$1234, green=$5678, blue=$9ABC	$0159	2^{12} = 4K bytes
5-bit	red=$1234, green=$5678, blue=$9ABC	$0953	2^{15} = 32K bytes

MakeITable only supports 3-bit, 4-bit, and 5-bit resolution. Five bits is the maximum possible resolution, since the indices into a 6-bit table would have to be 18 bits long, more than a full word.

USING THE COLOR MANAGER

In the simplest cases, use of the Color Manager is transparent when invoking the new Color QuickDraw routines. Using RGBForeColor and RGBBackColor, the program requests an RGB color for either the foreground or background. For instance, the following code requests an RGB color of red and sets it in the cGrafPort:

6 Color Manager

```
myColor.red:=$FFFF;
myColor.green:=0;
myColor.blue:=0;
RGBForeColor(myColor); {set pen red}
FrameRect(myRect); {draw in red}
```

Internally the Color Manager finds the best match to a color in TheGdevice's current color table, and sets up the current cGrafPort to draw in this color. At this point, drawing operations can proceed using the selected colors.

The Color Manager routines described in this chapter are designed to operate on a single gDevice. The Palette Manager can perform most of these operations across multiple gDevices. Since the Palette Manager provides more general and portable functionality, applications should use Palette Manager routines whenever possible.

The SetEntries routine is used to change any part of or all of the entries in a device's hardware Color Look-Up Table. The SaveEntries and RestoreEntries routines can make temporary changes to the color table under very specialized circumstances (such as a color selection dialog within an application). These routines aren't needed under normal application circumstances.

SaveEntries allows any combination of colorSpecs to be copied into a special colorTable. RestoreEntries replaces the table created by SaveEntries into the graphics device. Unlike SetEntries, these routines don't perform invalidations of the device's colorTable, so they avoid causing invalidations of cached data structures. When these routines are used, the application must take responsibility for rebuilding and restoring auxiliary structures as necessary.

By convention, when using SetEntries or RestoreEntries, white should be located at color table position 0, and black should be stored in the last color table position available, whether it is 1, 3, 15, or 255. The Palette Manager also enforces this convention.

For precise control over color, or for dedicated color table entries, the Color Manager routines maintain special information in device color tables. Using ProtectEntry and ReserveEntry, an entry may be *protected,* which prevents SetEntries from further changing the entry, or *reserved,* which makes the entry unavailable to be matched by RGBForeColor and RGBBackColor. Routines that change the device table (SetEntries, ProtectEntry, and ReserveEntry, but not RestoreEntries) will perform the appropriate invalidations of QuickDraw data structures. The application must then redraw where necessary.

To inquire if a color exists in a color table, use RealColor. This tells whether an arbitrary color actually exists in the table for that gDevice.

Color2Index returns the index in the current device's colorTable that is the best match to the requested color. Index2Color performs the opposite function—it returns the RGB of a particular index value. These routines can be useful when making copies of the screen frame buffer. InvertColor finds the complement of the provided color. GetSubTable performs a group Color2Index on a colorTable.

The error-handling routine QDError returns the error result from the last QuickDraw or Color Manager call.

COLOR MANAGER ROUTINES

The routines used for color drawing are covered in the chapter "Color QuickDraw". The Color Manager includes routines for color conversion, color table management, and error handling.

Color Conversion

```
FUNCTION Color2Index (rgb: RGBColor): LONGINT;
```

The Color2Index routine finds the best available approximation to a given absolute color, using the list of search procedures in the current device record. It returns a longint, which is a pixel value padded with zeros in the high word. Since the colorSpec.value field is only a word, the result returned from Color2Index must be truncated to fit into a colorSpec. In pixMaps the .value is the low-order word of this index.

Color2Index shouldn't be called from a custom search procedure.

```
PROCEDURE Index2Color (index: LONGINT; VAR rgb: RGBColor);
```

The Index2Color routine finds the RGB color corresponding to a given color table index. The desired pixel value is passed and the corresponding RGB value is returned in RGB. The routine takes a longint, which should be a pixel value padded with zeros in the high word (normally the compiler does this automatically). Normally, the RGB from the current device color table corresponding to the index is returned as the RGBColor. Notice that this is not necessarily the same color that was originally requested via RGBForeColor, RGBBackColor, SetCPixel, or Color2Index. This RGB is read from the current gDevice color table.

```
PROCEDURE InvertColor (VAR theColor: RGBColor);
```

The InvertColor routine finds the complement of an absolute color, using the list of complement procedures in the current device record. The default complement procedure uses the 1's complement of each component of the requested color.

```
FUNCTION RealColor (color: RGBColor) : BOOLEAN;
```

The RealColor routine tells whether a given absolute color actually exists in the current device's color table. This decision is based on the current resolution of the inverse table. For example, if the current iTabRes is four, RealColor returns TRUE if there exists a color that exactly matches the top four bits of red, green, and blue.

```
PROCEDURE GetSubTable (myColors: CTabHandle; iTabRes:INTEGER;
          targetTbl: CTabHandle);
```

The GetSubTable routine takes a ColorTable pointed at by myColors, and maps each RGB value into its nearest available match for each target table. These best matches are returned in the colorSpec.value fields of myColors. The values returned are best matches to the RGBColor in targetTbl and the returned indices are indices into targetTbl. Best matches are calculated using Color2Index and all applicable rules apply. A temporary inverse table is built, and then discarded. ITabRes controls the resolution of the iTable that is built. If targetTbl is NIL, then the current device's color table is used, and the device's inverse table is used rather than building a new one. To provide a different resolution than the current inverse table, provide an explicit targetTbl parameter; don't pass a NIL parameter.

> **Warning:** Depending on the requested resolution, building the inverse table can require large amounts of temporary space in the application heap: twice the size of the table itself, plus a fixed overhead for each inverse table resolution of 3–15K bytes.

```
PROCEDURE MakeITable (colorTab: CTabHandle; inverseTab: ITabHandle;
          res: INTEGER);
```

The MakeITable routine generates an inverse table based on the current contents of the color table pointed to by CTabHandle, with a resolution of res bits per channel. Reserved color table pixel values are not included in the resultant color table. MakeITable tests its input parameters and will return an error in QDError if the resolution is less than three or greater than five. Passing a NIL parameter to CTabHandle or ITabHandle substitutes an appropriate handle from the current gDevice, while passing 0 for res substitutes the current gDevice's preferred table resolution. These defaults can be used in any combination with explicit values, or with NIL parameters.

This routine allows maximum precision in matching colors, even if colors in the color table differ by less than the resolution of the inverse table. Five-bit inverse tables are not needed when drawing in normal QuickDraw modes. However, the new QuickDraw transfer modes (add, subtract, blend, etc.) may require a 5-bit inverse table for best results with certain color tables. MakeITable returns a QDError if the destination inverse table memory cannot be allocated. The 'mitq' resource governs how much memory is allocated for temporary internal structures; this resource type is for internal use only.

> **Warning:** Depending on the requested resolution, building the inverse table can require large amounts of temporary space in the application heap: twice the size of the table itself, plus a fixed overhead for each inverse table resolution of 3–15K bytes.

Color Table Management

```
FUNCTION GetCTSeed : LONGINT;
```

The GetCTSeed function returns a unique seed value that can be used in the ctSeed field of a color table created by an application. This seed value guarantees that the color table will be recognized as distinct from the destination, and that color table translation will be performed properly. The return value will be greater than the value stored in minSeed.

```
PROCEDURE ProtectEntry (index: INTEGER; protect: BOOLEAN);
```

The ProtectEntry procedure protects or removes protection from an entry in the current device's color table, depending on the value of the protect parameter. A protected entry can't be changed by other clients. It returns a protection error if it attempts to protect an already protected entry. However, it can remove protection from any entry.

```
PROCEDURE ReserveEntry (index: INTEGER; reserve: BOOLEAN);
```

The ReserveEntry procedure reserves or dereserves an entry in the current color table, depending on the value of the reserve parameter. A reserved entry cannot be matched by another client's search procedure, and will never be returned to another client by Color2Index or other routines that depend on it (such as RGBForeColor, RGBBackColor, SetCPixel, and so forth). You could use this routine to selectively protect a color for color table animation.

ReserveEntry copies the low byte of gdID into the low byte of ColorSpec.value when reserving an entry, and leaves the high byte alone. It acts like a selective protection, and does not allow any changes if the current gdID is different than the one in the colorSpec.value field of the reserved entry. If a requested match is already reserved, ReserveEntry returns a protection error. Any entry can be dereserved.

```
PROCEDURE  SetEntries(start, count: INTEGER; aTable: CSpecArray);
```

The SetEntries procedure sets a group of color table entries for the current gDevice, starting at a given position for the specified number of entries. The pointer aTable points into a cSpecArray, not into a color table. The colorSpec.value field of the entries must be in the logical range for the target card's assigned pixel depth. Thus, with a 4-bit pixel size, the colorSpec.value fields should be in the range 1 to 15. With an 8-bit pixel size the range is 0 to 255. Note that all values are zero-based; for example, to set three entries, pass two in the count parameter.

> **Note:** Palette Manager routines should be used instead of the SetEntries routine for applications that will run in a multiscreen or multitasking environment.

The SetEntries positional information works in logical space, rather than in the actual memory space used by the hardware. Requesting a change at position four in the color table may not modify color table entry four in the hardware, but it does correctly change the color on the screen for any pixels with a value of four in the video card. The SetEntries mode characterized by a start position and a length is called *sequence mode*. In this case, new colors are sequentially loaded into the hardware in the same order as the aTable, the clientID fields for changed entries are copied from the current device's gdID field, and the colorSpec.value fields are ignored.

The other SetEntries mode is called *index mode*. It allows the cSpecArray to specify where the data will be installed on an entry-by-entry basis. To use this mode, pass –1 for the start position, with a valid count and a pointer to the cSpecArray. Each entry is installed into the color table at the position specified by the colorSpec.value field of each entry in the cSpecArray. In the current device's color table, all changed entries' colorSpec.value fields are assigned the gdID value.

When color table entries are changed, all cached fonts are invalidated, and the seed number is changed so that the next drawing operation will rebuild the inverse table. If any of the requested entries are protected or out of range, a protection error is returned, and nothing happens. If a requested entry is reserved, it can only be changed if the current gdID matches the low byte of the intended ColorSpec.value field.

```
PROCEDURE SaveEntries (srcTable: CTabHandle; ResultTable:
          CTabHandle; VAR  selection: ReqListRec);
```

SaveEntries saves a selection of entries from srcTable into resultTable. The entries to be set are enumerated in the selection parameter, which uses the ReqListRec data structure shown below. (These values are offsets into colorTable, not the contents of the colorSpec.value field.)

```
TYPE
  ReqListRec = RECORD
                    reqLSize: INTEGER;                    {request list }
                                                          { size -1}
                    reqLData: ARRAY [0..0] of INTEGER {request list }
                                                          { data}
                END;
```

If an entry is not present in srcTable, then that position of the requestList is set to colReqErr, and that position of resultTable has random values returned. If one or more entries are not found, then an error code is posted to QDError; however, for every entry in selection which is not colReqErr, the values in resultTable are valid. Note that srcTable and selection are assumed to have the same number of entries.

SaveEntries optionally allows NIL as its source color table parameter. If NIL is used, the current device's color table is used as the source. The output of SaveEntries is the same as the input for RestoreEntries, except for the order.

```
PROCEDURE RestoreEntries (srcTable:CTabHandle;DstTable:CTabHandle;
        VAR selection:RecListRec);
```

RestoreEntries sets a selection of entries from srcTable into dstTable, but doesn't rebuild the inverse table. The dstTable entries to be set are enumerated in the selection parameter, which uses the ReqListRec data structure shown in the SetEntries routine description. (These values are offsets into the srcTable, not the contents of the colorSpec.value field.)

If a request is beyond the end of the dstTable, that position of the requestList is set to colReqErr, and an error is returned. Note that srcTable and selection are assumed to have the same number of entries.

If dstTbl is NIL, or points to the device color table, the current device's color table is updated, and the hardware is updated to these new colors. The seed is not changed, so no invalidation occurs (this may cause RGBForeColor to act strangely). This routine ignores protection and reservation of color table entries.

Generally, the Palette Manager is used to give an application its own set of colors; use of RestoreEntries should be limited to special-purpose applications. RestoreEntries allows you to change the colorTable without changing the ctSeed for the affected colorTable. You can execute the application code and then use RestoreEntries to put the original colors back in. However, in some cases things in the background may appear in the wrong colors, since they were never redrawn. To avoid this, the application must build its own new inverse table and redraw the background. If RestoreEntries were then used, the ctSeed would have to be explicitly changed to clean up correctly.

Error Handling

```
FUNCTION QDError: INTEGER;
```

The QDError routine returns the error result from the last QuickDraw or Color Manager call.

CUSTOM SEARCH AND COMPLEMENT PROCEDURES

Custom search and complement procedures allow an application to override the inverse table matching code. The desired color is specified in the RGBColor field of a ColorSpec record and passed via a pointer on the stack; the procedure returns the corresponding pixel value in the ColorSpec.value field.

A custom search procedure routine can provide its own matching rules. For instance, you might want to map all levels of green to a single green on a monitor. To do this, you could write and install a custom search procedure that is passed the RGB under question by the Color Manager. It can then analyze the color, and if it decides to act on this color, it can return the index of the desired shade of green. Otherwise, it can pass the color back to the Color Manager for matching, using the normal inverse table routine.

Many applications can share the same graphics device, each with its own custom search procedure. The procedures are chain elements in a linked list beginning in the gdSearchProc field of the gDevice port:

```
TYPE
    SProcHndl   = ^SProcPtr;
    SProcPtr    = ^SProcRec;;
    SProcRec    = RECORD
                    nxtSrch:  SProcHndl; {handle to next sProcRec}
                    srchProc: ProcPtr    {pointer to search }
                                         { procedure}
                  END;
```

Any number of search procedures can be installed in a linked list, each element of which will be called sequentially by the Color Manager, and given the chance to act or pass on the color. Since each device is a shared resource, a simple method (the gdID) is provided to identify the caller to the search procedures, as well as routines to add and delete custom procedures from the linked list.

The interface is as follows:

```
    FUNCTION SearchProc (rgb: RGBColor; VAR position: LONGINT):
            BOOLEAN;
```

When attempting to approximate a color, the Color Manager calls each search procedure in the list until the boolean value returns as TRUE. The index value of the closest match is returned by the position parameter. If no search procedure installed in the linked list returns TRUE, the Color Manager calls the default search procedure.

The application can also supply a custom *complement procedure* to find the complement of a specified color. Complement procedures work the same as search procedures, and are kept in a list beginning in the gDevice port's gdCompProc field.

```
TYPE
    CProcHndl   = ^CProcPtr;
    CProcPtr    = ^CProcRec;
    CProcRec    = RECORD
                    nxtComp:  CProcHandle; {pointer to next }
                                           { CProcRec}
                    compProc: ProcPtr      {pointer to complement }
                                           { procedure}
                  END;
```

The default complement procedure simply uses the 1's complement of the RGB color components before looking them up in the inverse table. The interface is as follows:

```
PROCEDURE CompProc (VAR rgb: RGBColor);
```

Operations on Search and Complement Procedures

```
PROCEDURE AddSearch (searchProc: ProcPtr);
PROCEDURE AddComp   (compProc: ProcPtr);
```

The AddSearch and AddComp routines add a procedure to the head of the current device record's list of search or complement procedures. These routines allocate an SProcRec or CProcRec.

```
PROCEDURE DelSearch (searchProc: ProcPtr);
PROCEDURE DelComp   (compProc: ProcPtr);
```

The DelSearch and DelComp procedures remove a custom search or complement procedure from the current device record's list of search or complement procedures. These routines dispose of the chain element, but do nothing to the procPtr.

```
PROCEDURE SetClientID (id: INTEGER);
```

The SetClientID procedure sets the gdID field in the current device record to identify this client program to its search and complement procedures.

SUMMARY OF THE COLOR MANAGER

Constants

```
CONST
  minSeed = 1023; {minimum seed value for ctSeed}
```

Data Types

```
TYPE
    ITabHandle = ^ITabPtr;
    ITabPtr   = ^ITab;
    ITab      = RECORD
                  iTabSeed: LONGINT; {copy of color table seed}
                  iTabRes:  INTEGER; {resolution of table}
                  iTTable:  ARRAY[0..0] OF SignedByte {byte color }
                                                { table index values}
                END;

    SProcHndl = ^SProcPtr;
    SProcPtr  = ^SProcRec;;
    SProcRec  = RECORD
                  nxtSrch:  SProcHndl; {handle to next sProcRec}
                  srchProc: ProcPtr    {pointer to search }
                                       { procedure}
                END;

    CProcHndl = ^CProcPtr;
    CProcPtr  = ^CProcRec;
    CProcRec  = RECORD
                  nxtComp:  CProcHandle; {pointer to next }
                                         { CProcRec}
                  compProc: ProcPtr    {pointer to complement }
                                       { procedure}
                END;

    ReqListRec = RECORD
                  reqLSize: INTEGER;    {request list size -1}
                  reqLData: ARRAY [0..0] of INTEGER {request list }
                                                { data}
                END;
```

Routines

Color Conversion

```
FUNCTION   Color2Index (VAR rgb: RGBColor): LONGINT;
PROCEDURE  Index2Color (index: LONGINT; VAR rgb: RGBColor);
PROCEDURE  InvertColor (VAR theColor: RGBColor);
FUNCTION   RealColor  (color: RGBColor) : BOOLEAN;
PROCEDURE  GetSubTable (myColors: CTabHandle; iTabRes: INTEGER;
                        targetTbl:CTabHandle);
PROCEDURE  MakeITable  (colorTab: CTabHandle; inverseTab: ITabHandle;
                        res: INTEGER);
```

Color Table Management

```
FUNCTION   GetCTSeed: LONGINT;
PROCEDURE  ProtectEntry   (index: INTEGER; protect: BOOLEAN);
PROCEDURE  ReserveEntry   (index: INTEGER; reserve: BOOLEAN);
PROCEDURE  SetEntries     (start, count: INTEGER; aTable:
                           cSpecArray);
PROCEDURE  RestoreEntries (srcTable:CTabHandle;dstTable:CTabHandle;
                           VAR selection:ReqListRec);
PROCEDURE  SaveEntries    (srcTable:CTabHandle;resultTable:CTabHandle;
                           VAR selection:ReqListRec)
```

Operations on Search and Complement Procedures

```
PROCEDURE  AddSearch  (searchProc: ProcPtr);
PROCEDURE  AddComp    (compProc: ProcPtr);
PROCEDURE  DelSearch  (searchProc: ProcPtr);
PROCEDURE  DelComp    (compProc: ProcPtr);
PROCEDURE  SetClientID (id: INTEGER);
```

Error Handling

```
FUNCTION QDError: INTEGER;
```

Assembly Language Information

Constants

```
minSeed     EQU   1023  ;minimum ctSeed value
```

ITab structure

```
iTabSeed    EQU    $0     ;[long] ID of owning color table
iTabRes     EQU    $4     ;[word] client ID
iTTable     EQU    $6     ;table of indices starts here
                         ;in this version, entries are BYTE
```

SProcRec structure

```
nxtSrch     EQU    $0     ;[pointer] link to next proc
srchProc    EQU    $4     ;[pointer] pointer to routine
```

CProcRec structure

```
nxtComp     EQU    $0     ;[pointer] link to next proc
compProc    EQU    $4     ;[pointer] pointer to routine
```

Request list structure

```
reqLSize    EQU    0      ;[word] request list size -1
reqLData    EQU    2      ;[word] request list data
```

7   THE PALETTE MANAGER

ABOUT THIS CHAPTER

This chapter describes the Palette Manager, a new Toolbox addition for the Macintosh II. The Palette Manager, as its name implies, supports the use of a collection of colors when you draw objects with Color QuickDraw. The Palette Manager provides routines your application can call to manage shared color resources, to provide exact colors for imaging, or to initiate color table animation. It also describes the data structures of color palettes and how the Palette Manager communicates with Color QuickDraw.

You should already be familiar with

- the Resource Manager
- the basic concepts and structures behind Color QuickDraw, particularly the calls that set RGB colors and use color patterns
- the Color Manager and the RGB color model used by Color QuickDraw
- the Window Manager

ABOUT THE PALETTE MANAGER

The Palette Manager is responsible for monitoring and establishing the color environment of the Macintosh II. It gives preference to the color needs of the front window, making the assumption that the front window is of greatest interest to the user.

The Palette Manager is initialized during the first InitWindows call after system startup, and continues to run as needed whenever windows are moved. If the front window is an old-style window, or if it has no assigned palette, the Palette Manager establishes the color environment using a default palette.

For many simple applications, the colors in the default palette will suffice. This is especially true of applications that use no color, for the Palette Manager ensures that black and white are always available.

Suppose, as an example, that you wish to draw an object using 32 different shades of gray. The default palette won't provide enough different levels of gray. Color QuickDraw will match your request as well as it can, so the object will look something like you expected, but probably not exactly the way you wanted. What you need is a convenient way to change the color environment for this window automatically, so that plenty of gray colors will be available each time your window comes to the front. The Palette Manager was designed to solve this problem.

You begin by creating a data structure called a color **palette.** This is normally done by creating a resource of type 'pltt', but you can create it within your application using the Palette Manager routines if you prefer. In the palette for the gray drawing, you would include 32 palette entries, each one specifying a different shade of gray. In addition, each entry would contain information telling the Palette Manager that you require the color to be an exact match, a process that is described later in this chapter.

You next use a Palette Manager routine to associate your palette with a particular window. If that window is the front window, or whenever it becomes the front window, the Palette Manager checks the current color environment to determine if the 32 shades of gray are available, exactly as requested. If they aren't available, the Palette Manager changes the color environment, adding as many colors as it can, at the expense of windows in the background. Finally, if the color environment has changed, the Palette Manager updates the background windows.

The Palette Manager routines make each step of this process reasonably simple. The Palette Manager also handles multiple devices and different screen resolutions, so your application need not attempt to provide for all possible machine configurations. In addition, the Palette Manager routines provide for several different uses of color, for example color table animation, by building a color index mode upon the more general Color QuickDraw RGB Model. This color index model is described in the following section.

The Color Index Model

Many video devices implement color using an indexed color model: a pixel value in the video device's memory is used as an index into a color table. The RGB value found in the table at that index position appears on the display device. In general, the resolution of the values in the video card's color look-up table is much higher than the resolution provided by the index itself.

The Palette Manager is primarily designed for use with this indexed color model; it can also be used with direct or fixed video devices. (See the Color Manager chapter for an explanation of the different video device types.) However, the indexed color model has several advantages. It requires less memory than a direct color model. It is also faster because less information must be written to the display device, due to the reduced resolution. In addition, it allows the use of a technique called **color table animation.** Color table animation involves changing the index entries in the video device's color table to achieve a change in color, as opposed to changing the pixel values themselves. All pixel values corresponding to the altered index entries suddenly appear on the display device in the new color. By careful selection of index values and the corresponding colors, you can achieve a number of special animation effects.

The indexed color model also has several disadvantages. Because the range of pixel values is generally low, the number of colors that can be shown at any one time is correspondingly low. Colors on such devices are a shared resource, just as the visible area of a display device is shared by several windows. If desk accessories and application windows wish to use different sets of colors, a problem of color contention arises. If color table animation is also used (assuming the target display device supports it), the problem of contention can become acute.

Although the problems presented by color table animation and color contention can be solved using Color QuickDraw and Color Manager routines, the available solutions are somewhat cumbersome. The Palette Manager handles these problems for your application by providing an indexed color model built upon the more general RGB model. Your application allocates a Palette object and fills it with RGB colors, along with information describing how each color should be managed. When the Palette Manager detects that the target display device allows an indexed color model, it manages the allocation of that device's color resources. As colors are requested and allocated, it updates its information and adjusts the color matching scheme accordingly.

Color Usage

The Palette Manager uses one of four methods for selecting colors:

- **Courteous colors** have no special properties. For such colors, the Palette Manager relies upon Color QuickDraw to select appropriate pixel values. Colors with specified usages that can't be satisfied by the Palette Manager will default to courteous colors. This occurs, for example, when drawing to a device with no color look-up table, such as a direct or fixed device. Courteous colors don't change the color environment in any way.

- **Tolerant colors** cause a change in the color environment unless the fit to the best matching available color falls within a separately specified tolerance value.

- **Animating colors** are reserved by a palette and are unavailable to (and can't be matched by) any other request for color.

- **Explicit colors** always generate the corresponding entry in the device's color table.

These color types are specified when using Palette Manager routines by using the following constants:

```
CONST { Usage constants }

      pmCourteous = $0000;
      pmDithered  = $0001;  {reserved for future use}
      pmTolerant  = $0002;
      pmAnimated  = $0004;
      pmExplicit  = $0008;
```

When you specify colors for a palette within a 'pltt' resource, you will usually assign the same usage value to each color in the palette. However, if for some reason a particular color must be used differently than the other colors in the palette, it can be assigned a different usage value, either within the resource file, or within the application through use of the SetEntryUsage routine.

The sections that follow provide more information on these color types.

Courteous Colors

Courteous colors are provided for two reasons. First, they are a convenient placeholder. If your application uses only a small number of colors you can place each of them in a palette, ordered according to your preference. Suppose you have a palette resource which consists of a set of eight colors, namely white, black, red, orange, yellow, green, blue, and violet, in that order, each with a usage specified as courteous. Assuming further that the palette resource ID number matched that of a color window (myColorWindow) you opened earlier, the following calls will paint a rectangle (myRect) in yellow (palette entry 4, where white is 0):

```
SetPort (myColorWindow);
PmForeColor (4);
PaintRect (myRect);
```

This is exactly analogous to the following sequence of calls made using Color Quickdraw routines, where yellowRGB is of type ColorSpec:

```
with yellowRGB do begin {done once during your initialization}
     red := $FFFF;
     green := $FFFF;
     blue := $0000
     end;

SetPort (myColorWindow);
RGBForeColor (yellowRGB);
PaintRect (myRect);
```

The second reason for providing courteous colors is not immediately apparent. It involves how colors are selected for palettes which use animation. The Palette Manager has access to all palettes used by all windows throughout the system. When deciding which of a device's colors to allocate for animation, it checks each window currently drawn on that device to see which colors the windows are using. It then chooses the color which is least used and reserves that for animation. In the first example shown above, the Palette Manager would try to avoid the eight colors used in your palette, even though they are just courteous colors. In the second example it would have no knowledge of your colors and might steal them unnecessarily, and when your window is redrawn the selected colors might not be as close to the desired colors as they previously were. If you intend to use only a limited number of colors it is therefore best to place them in the window's palette so the Palette Manager will know about them.

Tolerant Colors

Tolerant colors allow you to change the current color environment according to your needs. When your window becomes the frontmost window on a device its palette and the colors contained therein are given preference. Each tolerant color is compared to the best unique match available in the current color environment (for each device on which the window is drawn). When the difference between your color and the best available match is greater than the tolerance you have specified the Palette Manager will modify the color environment to provide an exact match to your color.

The tolerance value associated with each palette entry is compared to a measure of the difference between two RGBColor values. This difference is an approximation of the distance between the two points as measured in a Cartesian coordinate system where the axes are the unsigned red, green, and blue values. The distance formula used is shown below:

$$\Delta\,RGB = \text{maximum of (abs(Red1–Red2), abs(Green1–Green2), abs(Blue1–Blue2))}$$

A value of $5000 is generally sufficient to allow matching without updates in reasonably well-balanced color environments. A tolerance value of $0000 means that only an exact match is acceptable. Any value of $0xxx, other than $0000, is reserved, and should not be used in applications.

If your palette requires more colors than are currently available the Palette Manager will check to see if any other palette has reserved entries for animation. If so it will dereserve them and make them available for your palette. If you ask for more than are available on a device, the Palette Manager cannot honor your request. However, you can still call PmForeColor for such colors; as mentioned earlier, such colors default to courteous colors. Color QuickDraw will still select the best color available, which of course must match one of the colors elsewhere in your palette since the Palette Manager will only run out of colors after it has given your palette all that it has. Two exceptions to this rule are noted below. See the "Black, White, and Palette Customization" section and the "Palette Prioritization" section describing the interaction among colors of different usages in a single palette.

Animating Colors

Animating colors allow you to reserve device indexes for color table animation. Each animating color is checked to see if it already has a reserved index for the target device. If it does not, the Palette Manager attempts to find a suitable index. This is done by checking all windows to see what colors they use, and which device indexes match those colors. The least frequently used indexes are then reserved for your palette. The reservation process is analogous to the Color Manager call ReserveEntry. The device index and its corresponding color value is removed from the matching scheme used by Color Quickdraw; you cannot draw with it by calling RGBForeColor. However, when you call PmForeColor the Palette Manager will locate the reserved index and configure your window's port to draw with it. On multiple devices this will likely be a different index for each device, but this process will be invisible to your application.

After reserving one or more device indexes for each animating entry it detects, the Palette Manager will change the color environment to match the RGB values specified in the palette. To use an animating color you must first draw with it using PmForeColor or PmBackColor. To effect color table animation you can use either AnimateEntry (for a single color) or AnimatePalette (for a contiguous set of colors). These calls are described in the section titled "Palette Manager Routines".

Explicit Colors

Explicit colors are provided as a convenience for users who wish to use colors in very special ways. The RGB value in a palette is completely ignored if a color is an explicit color. Explicit colors cause no change in the color environment and are not counted for purposes of animation. Explicit colors always match the corresponding device index. A PmForeColor call with a parameter of 12 will place a value of (12 modulo (MaxIndex+1)) into the foreground color field of your window's cGrafPort, where MaxIndex is the maximum available index for each device under consideration. When you draw with an explicit color, you get whatever color the device index currently contains.

One interesting use for explicit colors is that it allows you to monitor the color environment on a device. For example, you could draw a grid of 256 explicit colors, 16-by-16, in a small window. The colors shown are exactly those in the device's color table. If color table animation is taking place simultaneously the corresponding colors in the small window will animate as well. If you display such a window on a 4-bit device, the first 16 colors will match the 16 colors available in the device and each row thereafter will be a copy of the first row.

However, the main purpose for explicit colors is to provide a convenient indexed color interface. Using the Color Manager, you can establish a known color environment using the SetEntries routine on each device of interest. You can then easily select any of these colors for drawing by setting your window's palette to contain as many explicit colors as are in the target device with the greatest number of indexes. PmForeColor will configure the cGrafPort to draw with the index of your choice.

> **Warning:** You should not use explicit colors in this fashion if you intend your application to coexist in multi-application environments such as those provided by MultiFinder™ or A/UX™ or when using color desk accessories that depend upon the Palette Manager. However, for certain types of applications, especially those which are written for a known device environment, explicit colors will tend to make indexed color manipulation much more convenient.

Palette Prioritization

To make the best use of the Palette Manager you should understand how it prioritizes the colors you request. Prioritization is important only when the ActivatePalette routine is called. This occurs automatically when your window becomes the front window, or when you call ActivatePalette after changing one or more of the Palette's colors or usage values.

Explicit and courteous colors are ignored and are not considered during prioritization. They are important only during calls to PmForeColor and PmBackColor, or when scanning all palettes to check which colors are in use. Of the remaining two types of colors, animating colors are given preference. Starting with the first entry in your window's palette (entry 0), the Palette Manager checks to see if it is an animating entry. It checks each animating entry to see if the entry has a reserved index for each appropriate device. If the animating entry has no reserved index, the Palette Manager selects an index and reserves it for animation. This process continues until all animating colors have been satisfied or until the available indexes are exhausted.

Tolerant entries are handled next. Each tolerant entry is assigned its own, unique index until all tolerant colors have been satisfied. The Palette Manager then calculates for each entry the difference between the desired color and the color associated with the selected index. If the difference exceeds the tolerance you have specified, the selected device entry is marked to be changed to the desired color.

When as many animating and tolerant entries have been matched as are possible, the Palette Manager checks to see if the color environment needs to be modified. If modifications are needed, it forces the device environment to a known state (overriding any calls made to the Color Manager outside the Palette Manager) and calls the Color Manager to change the device's color environment accordingly (with the SetEntries routine).

Finally, if the color environment on a given device has changed, the Palette Manager checks to see if this change has impacted any other window in the system. If another window was affected, that window is checked to see if it specifies an update in the case of such changes. Applications can use the SetPalette routine to specify if a window should be updated. If so, an InvalRect is performed using the bounding rectangle of the device which has been changed.

As mentioned earlier, when you specify a sequence of tolerant entries, the indexes assigned are guaranteed to be unique provided there are sufficient indexes available. If you specify a pair of tolerant entries that can match each other within tolerance, they will each be matched to a different index, and the color environment changed accordingly (if necessary). If this is not the result you desire, then you should convert one of the two to a courteous entry. In the best case the courteous color will, at drawing time, match the exact color you have requested for it, a service provided automatically by Color Quickdraw. In the worst case, the courteous color will match its tolerant counterpart, because that color is at least guaranteed to be provided when your window is frontmost (again assuming enough entries are available).

Black, White, and Palette Customization

Due to the "first-come, first-served" nature of the Palette Manager, you can prioritize your palettes to customize the color environment automatically for a variety of display depths. Black and white should generally be the first two colors in your palette. Color Quickdraw, in order to support standard Quickdraw features, works best when black and white are located at the end and beginning, respectively, of each device's color table. The Palette Manager enforces this rule, and thus the maximum number of indexes available for animating or tolerant colors is really the maximum number of indexes minus two. However, if black or white are present in your palette, they won't be counted as unique indexes if any of your tolerant entries match them within the specified tolerance.

With black and white as the first two colors in your palette, you have matched the two colors the Palette Manager will allow for a 1-bit device. The next two colors should be assigned to the two you wish to have should the device be a 2-bit device. Likewise the first 16 colors should be the optimal palette entries for a 4-bit device. And, for future expandability, the first 256 colors (if you need that many) should be the optimal palette entries for an 8-bit device. A palette is limited to 4095 entries.

COLOR PALETTE RECORDS

The basic data structure for a color palette is the ColorInfo record. It consists of the following:

```
TYPE
 ColorInfo = RECORD
             ciRGB:       RGBColor;     {absolute RGB values}
             ciUsage:     INTEGER       {color usage information}
             ciTolerance: INTEGER;      {tolerance value}
             ciFlags:     INTEGER;      {private field}
             ciPrivate:   LONGINT;      {private field}
          END;
```

Field descriptions

ciRGB   The ciRGB is the absolute RGB value defined by Color QuickDraw.

ciUsage   The ciUsage field contains color usage information that determines the properties of a color.

ciTolerance The ciTolerance is a value used to determine if a color is close enough to the color chosen; if the tolerance value is exceeded, the preferred color is rendered in the device's color table for the selected index.

ciFlags   The ciFlags field is used internally by the Palette Manager.

ciPrivate   The ciPrivate field is used internally to store information about color allocation: not for use by application.

The data structure for a color palette is made up of an array of ColorInfo records, plus other information relating to the use of the colors within the palette. The 'pltt' resource is an image of the Palette data structure.

Note: The palette is accessed through the Palette Manager routines only: do not attempt to directly access any of the fields in this data structure.

```
TYPE
   PaletteHandle = ^PalettePtr;
   PalettePtr    = ^Palette;
   Palette = RECORD
          pmEntries:   integer;                 {entries in pmInfo}
          pmDataFields: array [0..6] of integer; {private fields}
          pmInfo:      array [0..0] of ColorInfo;
       END;
```

Field descriptions

pmEntries   The pmEntries field contains the number of entries in the pmTable.

pmDataFields   The pmDataFields field contains an array of integers that are used internally by the Palette Manager.

pmInfo   The pmInfo field contains an array of ColorInfo records.

USING THE PALETTE MANAGER

The InitPalettes routine is always called before any other Palette Manager routines. It initializes the Palette Manager, if necessary, and searches the device list to find all active CLUT devices.

Normally, a new color palette is created from a 'pltt' resource, using GetNewPalette. To create a palette from within an application, use NewPalette. Whichever method is used to create the palette, the SetPalette routine can then be used to render the Palette on the display device. The DisposePalette procedure disposes of the entire palette.

The ActivatePalette routine is called by the Window Manager every time your window's status changes. When using the Palette Manager routines, you should use ActivatePalette after you have made changes to a palette. GetPalette is used to return a handle to the palette currently associated with a specified window.

To use color table animation, you can change the colors in a palette and on corresponding devices with the AnimateEntry and AnimatePalette routines. GetEntryColor, SetEntryColor, GetEntryUsage, and SetEntryUsage allow an application to access and modify the fields of a palette.

CTab2Palette copies the specified color table into a palette, while Palette2CTab does the opposite, and copies a palette into a color table. Each routine resizes the target object as necessary.

COLOR PALETTES IN A RESOURCE FILE

The format of a palette resource (type 'pltt') is an image of the palette structure itself. The private fields in both the header and in each ColorInfo record are reserved for future use.

The following table shows a sample palette resource with 16 entries as it would appear within a resource file.

Table 6-1. Sample Palette Resource

Resource Format   **Description**

```
data 'pltt' (1, "My palette resource") {
    $"0010 0000 0000 0000 0000 0000 0000 0000"    /* header - $0010 (16) entries */
    $"FFFF FFFF FFFF 0002 0000 0000 0000 0000"    /* white - used in all screen */
                                                  /*depths */
    $"0000 0000 0000 0002 0000 0000 0000 0000"    /* black */
    $"FC00 F37D 052F 0002 0000 0000 0000 0000"    /* yellow - used in depths >= 2*/
                                                  /* bits/pixel */
    $"FFFF 648A 028C 0002 0000 0000 0000 0000"    /* orange */
    $"0371 C6FF 9EC9 0002 0000 0000 0000 0000"    /* blue green - used in depths */
                                                  /*>= 4 bits/pixel */
    $"0000 A000 0000 0002 0000 0000 0000 0000"    /* green */
    $"0000 0000 D400 0002 0000 0000 0000 0000"    /* blue */
    $"DD6B 08C2 06A2 0002 0000 0000 0000 0000"    /* red */
    $"C000 C000 C000 0002 0000 0000 0000 0000"    /* light gray */
    $"8000 8000 8000 0002 0000 0000 0000 0000"    /* medium gray */
    $"FFFF C3DC 8160 0002 0000 0000 0000 0000"    /* beige */
    $"93FF 281A 12CC 0002 0000 0000 0000 0000"    /* brown */
    $"6524 C2FF 0000 0002 0000 0000 0000 0000"    /* olive green */
    $"0000 FFFF 04F1 0002 0000 0000 0000 0000"    /* bright green */
    $"65DE AD85 FFFF 0002 0000 0000 0000 0000"    /* sky blue */
    $"8000 0000 FFFF 0002 0000 0000 0000 0000"    /* violet */
};
```

PALETTE MANAGER ROUTINES

The Palette Manager routines described in this section are designed for use with the Macintosh II.

Initialization and Allocation

```
PROCEDURE InitPalettes;
```

InitPalettes initializes the Palette Manager. It searches for devices which support a Color Look-Up Table (CLUT) and initializes an internal data structure for each one. This call is made by InitWindows and should not have to be made by your application.

```
FUNCTION NewPalette (entries: INTEGER; srcColors: CTabHandle;
        srcUsage, srcTolerance: INTEGER) : PaletteHandle;
```

NewPalette allocates a new Palette object which contains a table of colors with enough room for "entries" colors. It fills the table with as many RGB values from srcColors as it has or as it can fit. It sets the usage field of each color to srcUsage and the tolerance value of each color to srcTolerance. If no color table is provided (srcColors = NIL) then all colors in the palette are set to black (red = $0000, green = $0000, blue = $0000).

```
FUNCTION GetNewPalette (paletteID: INTEGER) : PaletteHandle;
```

GetNewPalette fetches a Palette object from the Resource Manager and initializes it. If you open a new color window with GetNewCWindow, this routine is called automatically with paletteID equal to the window's resource ID. A palette resource is identified by type 'pltt'. A paletteID of 0 is reserved for the system palette resource which is used as the default palette for noncolor windows and color windows without assigned palettes.

```
PROCEDURE DisposePalette (srcPalette: PaletteHandle);
```

DisposePalette disposes of a Palette object. If the palette has any entries allocated for animation on any display device, these entries are relinquished prior to deallocation of the object.

Interacting With the Window Manager

```
PROCEDURE ActivatePalette (srcWindow: WindowPtr);
```

ActivatePalette is the routine called by the Window Manager when your window's status changes: for example, when it opens, closes, moves, or becomes frontmost. You should call ActivatePalette after making changes to a palette with the utility routines described below. Such changes do not take effect until the next call to ActivatePalette, thereby allowing you to make a series of palette changes without any immediate change in the color environment.

If srcWindow is frontmost, ActivatePalette examines the information stored in the palette associated with srcWindow and attempts to provide the color environment described therein. It determines a list of devices on which to render the palette by intersecting the port rect of the srcWindow with each device. If the intersection is not empty, and if the device has a Color Look-Up Table (CLUT), then ActivatePalette checks to see if the color environment is sufficient. If a change is required, ActivatePalette calls the Color Manager to reserve or modify the device's color entries as required. It then generates update events for all affected windows which desire color updates.

```
PROCEDURE SetPalette (dstWindow: WindowPtr; srcPalette:
        PaletteHandle; cUpdates: BOOLEAN);
```

SetPalette changes the palette associated with dstWindow to srcPalette. It also records whether the window wants to receive updates as a result of a change to its color environment. If you want dstWindow to be updated whenever its color environment changes, set cUpdates to TRUE.

```
FUNCTION GetPalette (srcWindow: WindowPtr) : PaletteHandle;
```

GetPalette returns a handle to the palette associated with srcWindow. If no palette is associated with srcWindow, or if srcWindow is not a color window, GetPalette returns NIL.

Drawing With Color Palettes

These routines enable applications to specify foreground and background drawing colors with the assistance of the Palette Manager. Substitute these for Color Quickdraw's RGBForeColor and RGBBackColor routines when you wish to use a color from a palette. You may still use RGBForeColor and RGBBackColor in the normal way whenever you wish to specify drawing colors, for example when you wish to use a color which is not contained in your palette.

```
PROCEDURE PmForeColor (dstEntry: INTEGER);
```

PmForeColor sets the RGB and index forecolor fields of the current cGrafPort according to the palette entry of the current cGrafPort (window) corresponding to dstEntry. For courteous and tolerant entries, this call performs an RGBForeColor using the RGB color of the palette entry. For animating colors it will select the recorded device index previously reserved for animation (if still present) and install it in the cGrafPort. The RGB forecolor field is set to the value from the palette entry. For explicit colors PmForeColor places (dstEntry modulo (MaxIndex+1)) into the cGrafPort, where MaxIndex is the largest index available in a device's CLUT. When multiple devices are present with different depths, MaxIndex varies appropriately for each device.

```
PROCEDURE PmBackColor (dstEntry: INTEGER);
```

PmBackColor sets the RGB and index backcolor fields of the current cGrafPort according to the palette entry of the current cGrafPort (window) corresponding to dstEntry. For courteous and tolerant entries, this call performs an RGBBackColor using the RGB color of the palette entry. For animating colors it will select the recorded device index previously reserved for animation (if still present) and install it in the cGrafPort. The RGB backcolor field is set to the value from the palette entry. For explicit colors PmBackColor places (dstEntry modulo (MaxIndex+1)) into the cGrafPort, where MaxIndex is the largest index available in a device's color table. When multiple devices are present with different depths, MaxIndex varies appropriately for each device.

Color Table Animation

```
PROCEDURE AnimateEntry (dstWindow: WindowPtr; dstEntry: INTEGER;
        srcRGB: RGBColor);
```

AnimateEntry changes the RGB value of dstEntry in the palette associated with dstWindow to the color specified by srcRGB. Each device for which an index has been reserved is immediately modified to contain the new value. This is not considered to be a change to the device's color environment since no other windows should be using the animated entry. If the palette entry is not an animating color, or if the associated indexes are no longer reserved, no animation is performed.

If you have blocked color updates in a window, by using SetPalette with CUpdates set to FALSE, you may observe undesired animation. This will occur when ActivatePalette reserves device indexes for animation which are already used in the window. Redrawing the window, which normally occurs as the result of a color update event, will remove any animating colors which do not belong to it.

```
PROCEDURE AnimatePalette (dstWindow: WindowPtr; srcCTab:
        CTabHandle; srcIndex,dstEntry,dstLength: INTEGER);
```

AnimatePalette performs a function similar to AnimateEntry, but it acts upon a range of palette entries. Beginning at srcIndex (which has a minimum value of 0), the next dstLength entries are copied from srcCTab to dstWindow's palette, beginning at dstEntry. If srcCTab is not sufficiently large to accommodate the request, as many entries are modified as possible and the remaining entries are left unchanged.

Manipulating Palette Entries

```
PROCEDURE GetEntryColor (srcPalette: PaletteHandle; srcEntry:
        INTEGER; VAR dstRGB: RGBColor);
```

GetEntryColor allows your application to access the color of a palette entry. The color may be modified by using the SetEntryColor routine described below.

```
PROCEDURE SetEntryColor (dstPalette: PaletteHandle; dstEntry:
         INTEGER; srcRGB: RGBColor);
```

SetEntryColor provides a convenient way for your application to modify the color of a single palette entry. When you perform a SetPaletteEntry, the entry is marked as having changed, but no change occurs in the color environment. The change will be effected upon the next call to ActivatePalette. Modified entries are marked such that the palette will be updated even though no update might be required by a change in the color environment.

```
PROCEDURE GetEntryUsage (srcPalette: PaletteHandle; srcEntry:
         INTEGER; VAR dstUsage,dstTolerance: INTEGER);
```

GetEntryUsage allows your application to access the usage fields of a palette entry, namely ciUsage and ciTolerance. These fields may be modified by using the SetEntryUsage routine described below.

```
PROCEDURE SetEntryUsage (dstPalette: PaletteHandle; dstEntry:
         INTEGER; srcUsage,srcTolerance: INTEGER);
```

SetEntryUsage provides a convenient way for your application to modify the color of a single palette entry. When you perform a SetEntryUsage, the entry is marked as having changed, but no change occurs in the color environment. The change will be effected upon the next call to ActivatePalette. Modified entries are marked such that the palette will be updated even though no update might be required by a change in the color environment. If either myUsage or myTolerance are set to $FFFF (–1) they will not be changed.

This call is provided to allow easy modifications to a palette created with NewPalette or modified by CTab2Palette. In such cases the ciUsage and ciTolerance fields are homogeneous since only one value can be designated for each. You will typically call SetEntryUsage after those calls in order to adjust and customize your palette.

```
PROCEDURE CTab2Palette (srcCTab: CTabHandle; dstPalette:
         PaletteHandle; srcUsage,srcTolerance: INTEGER);
```

CTab2Palette is a convenience procedure which copies the fields from an existing ColorTable record into an existing Palette record. If the records are not the same size then the Palette record is resized to match the number of entries in the ColorTable record. If dstPalette has any entries allocated for animation on any display device, these entries are relinquished prior to copying the new colors. If you wish to effect color table animation you can change the colors in a palette, and on corresponding devices, with the AnimateEntry and AnimatePalette routines described above. Changes made to a palette by CTab2Palette don't take effect until the next ActivatePalette is performed. If either the color table handle or the palette handle are NIL, no operation is performed.

```
PROCEDURE Palette2CTab (srcPalette: PaletteHandle; dstCTab:
            CTabHandle);
```

Palette2CTab is a convenience procedure which copies all of the colors from an existing Palette record into an existing ColorTable record. If the records are not the same size then the ColorTable record is resized to match the number of entries in the Palette record. If either the palette handle or the color table handle are NIL, no operation is performed.

SUMMARY OF THE PALETTE MANAGER

Constants

```
CONST { Usage constants }

     pmCourteous = $0000;
     pmDithered = $0001; {not implemented}
     pmTolerant = $0002;
     pmAnimated = $0004;
     pmExplicit = $0008;
```

Data Types

```
TYPE
  ColorInfo = RECORD
          ciRGB:       RGBColor;  {absolute RGB values}
          ciUsage:     INTEGER    {color usage information}
          ciTolerance: INTEGER;   {tolerance value}
          ciFlags:     INTEGER;   {private field}
          ciPrivate:   LONGINT;   {private field}
        END;

  PaletteHandle = ^PalettePtr;
  PalettePtr    = ^Palette;
  Palette = RECORD
          pmEntries:   integer;                      {entries in }
                                                     { pmInfo}
          pmDataFields: array [0..6] of integer; {private }
                                                     { fields}
          pmInfo:      array [0..0] of ColorInfo;
          END;
```

Routines

Initialization and Allocation

```
PROCEDURE InitPalettes;
FUNCTION  NewPalette    (entries: INTEGER; srcColors: CTabHandle;
                         srcUsage,srcTolerance: INTEGER) :
                         PaletteHandle;
FUNCTION  GetNewPalette (paletteID: INTEGER) : PaletteHandle;
PROCEDURE DisposePalette (srcPalette: PaletteHandle);
```

Interacting with the Window Manager

```
PROCEDURE ActivatePalette (srcWindow: WindowPtr);
PROCEDURE SetPalette      (dstWindow: WindowPtr; srcPalette:
                             PaletteHandle; cUpdates: BOOLEAN);
FUNCTION  GetPalette      (srcWindow: WindowPtr) : PaletteHandle;
```

Drawing with Color Palettes

```
PROCEDURE PmForeColor (myEntry: INTEGER);
PROCEDURE PmBackColor (myEntry: INTEGER);
```

Color Table Animation

```
PROCEDURE AnimateEntry  (dstWindow: WindowPtr; dstEntry: INTEGER;
                          srcRGB: RGBColor);
PROCEDURE AnimatePalette (dstWindow: WindowPtr; srcCTab: CTabHandle;
                          srcIndex,dstEntry,dstLength: INTEGER);
```

Manipulating Palettes

```
PROCEDURE GetEntryColor (srcPalette: PaletteHandle; srcEntry: INTEGER;
                          VAR dstRGB: RGBColor);
PROCEDURE SetEntryColor (dstPalette: PaletteHandle; dstEntry: INTEGER;
                          srcRGB: RGBColor);
PROCEDURE GetEntryUsage (srcPalette: PaletteHandle; srcEntry: INTEGER;
                          VAR dstUsage,dstTolerance: INTEGER);
PROCEDURE SetEntryUsage (dstPalette: PaletteHandle; dstEntry: INTEGER;
                          srcUsage,srcTolerance: INTEGER);
PROCEDURE CTab2Palette  (srcCTab: CTabHandle; dstPalette:
                          PaletteHandle; srcUsage,srcTolerance:
                          INTEGER);
PROCEDURE Palette2CTab  (srcPalette: PaletteHandle; dstCTab:
                          CTabHandle);
```

Assembly Language Information

```
; Palette Manager Equates


pmCourteous     EQU     $0000     ;courteous colors
pmDithered      EQU     $0001     ;reserved for future use
pmTolerant      EQU     $0002     ;tolerant colors
pmAnimated      EQU     $0004     ;animating colors
pmExplicit      EQU     $0008     ;explicit colors
```

```
; ColorInfo structure

ciRGB          EQU     $0000       ;absolute RGB values
ciUsage        EQU     $0006       ;color usage information
ciTolerance    EQU     $0008       ;tolerance value
ciFlags        EQU     $000A       ;private field
ciPrivate      EQU     $000C       ;private
ciSize         EQU     $0010       ;size of the ColorInfo data structure

; Palette structure

pmEntries      EQU     $0000       ;entries in pmInfo
pmInfo         EQU     $0010       ;color info
pmHdrSize      EQU     $0010       ;size of Palette header
```

8 THE COLOR PICKER PACKAGE

ABOUT THIS CHAPTER

This chapter describes the Color Picker, a new package that allows applications to present users with a standard interface for color selection. You should be familiar with color on the Macintosh and graphic devices, as discussed in the Color QuickDraw and Graphic Devices chapters of this volume.

THE COLOR PICKER PACKAGE

The Color Picker Package is a tool that applications can use to present a standard user interface for color selection. It also provides routines for converting color values between several different color systems. The Color Picker Package does *not* alter the Color Look-Up Table (CLUT), if any, associated with the current graphics device.

Once the user chooses a color, Color Picker returns it to the application, in the form of an RGBColor value, leaving the graphics device in its original state. The application can do what it likes with the color selection, with as much or as little attention to the available graphics hardware as it deems appropriate. On black and white hardware (or in less than 4-bit mode), the display is in black and white; Color Picker returns the value selected, but does not call any color routines.

On direct device hardware the exact color can be used without extra effort, while on fixed CLUT hardware it can only be approximated. On most hardware, such as Apple's TFB graphics card, which has a variable CLUT, the application decides how faithfully to reproduce the color, because it can replace an entry in the device's CLUT to show it exactly, or treat the table as fixed and approximate the color. Color Picker itself takes advantage of the hardware on such devices, displaying the exact color by borrowing a color table entry. As result, applications that are content to approximate the color will show users colors that differ somewhat from the ones picked.

THE COLOR PICKER DIALOG BOX

Developers can present the Color Picker dialog box, shown in Figure 1 (See frontispiece for a color representation of this dialog box.) to a user by means of the Color Picker routine, described later in this chapter.

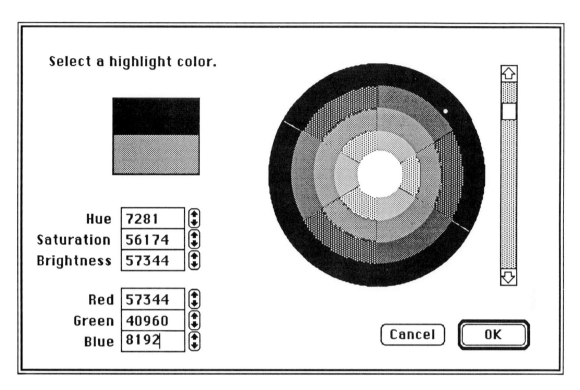

Figure 1. Color Picker Dialog Box

When called by an application, the Color Picker supplies the prompt text, which appears in the upper-left corner, and the initial color, which appears in the bottom of the two rectangles below the prompt. The color being picked, in the upper rectangle, ranges rapidly over the entire color space, in response to the controls in the rest of the dialog. The calling application also supplies the location of the top-left corner of the dialog window.

The user is allowed to select a single color, from the entire range the hardware can produce. The wheel allows users to select a given hue and saturation simultaneously. The center of the wheel displays zero saturation (no hue mixed in); the outer boundary is maximum saturation (no gray mixed in); colors on the edge of the wheel are pure hues. The scroll bar at right controls the brightness (value) of the wheel.

The two groups of text fields (Hue/Saturation/Brightness and Red/Green/Blue) show the parameters of the color being picked in two independent color systems. Brightness represents *value* in the HSV model.

The HSV values are the primary color system, which correspond to the controls in the dialog box. The RGB values are the alternate color system, and the way they vary in response to the dialog controls is not intuitive. Only users who understand both color systems will understand how the RGB values vary in relation to the rest of the dialog. (See the Color Quickdraw chapter for more information.) The alternate color system is intended to make life easier for users accustomed to something other than the HSV model.

The range for all of the component values is 0 to 65,535. Larger values are clipped to the maximum after the user exits the field. When incrementing or decrementing the hue via the arrow controls, 0 wraps around to 65,535, and vice versa, so the user can circumnavigate the wheel unimpeded. The hue value for red is 0; green is 21,845; blue is 43,690.

COLOR PICKER PACKAGE ROUTINES

```
FUNCTION GetColor(where: Point; prompt: Str255; inColor: RGBColor;
        VAR outColor: RGBColor) : BOOLEAN;
```

GetColor displays the Color Picker dialog box on the screen, with its top-left corner located at where. (The where Point should be on the main gDevice.) If where = (0,0), the dialog box is positioned neatly on the screen, centered horizontally, and with one third of the empty space above the box, two thirds below, whatever the screen size.

The prompt string is displayed in the upper-left corner of the dialog box. InColor is the starting color, which the user may want for comparison, and is displayed immediately below the current output color (the one the user is picking). OutColor is set to the last color value the user picked, if and only if the user clicks OK. On entry, it is treated as undefined, so the output color sample originally matches the input. While the color being picked may vary widely, the input color sample remains fixed, and clicking in the input sample resets the output color sample to match it.

GetColor returns TRUE if the user exits via the OK button, or FALSE if the user cancels.

Assembly-language note: the trap macro for the Color Picker Package is _Pack12. The routine selectors are as follows:

```
Fix2SmallFract    .EQU    1
SmallFract2Fix    .EQU    2
CMY2RGB           .EQU    3
RGB2CMY           .EQU    4
HSL2RGB           .EQU    5
RGB2HSL           .EQU    6
HSV2RGB           .EQU    7
RGB2HSV           .EQU    8
GetColor          .EQU    9
```

COLOR PICKER CONVERSION FACILITIES

The Color Picker provides six procedures for converting color values between CMY and RGB, and between HSL or HSV and RGB. Most developers will not need to use these routines.

```
PROCEDURE   CMY2RGB (cColor: CMYColor; VAR rColor: RGBColor);
PROCEDURE   RGB2CMY (rColor: RGBColor; VAR cColor: CMYColor);
PROCEDURE   HSL2RGB (hColor: HSLColor; VAR rColor: RGBColor);
PROCEDURE   RGB2HSL (rColor: RGBColor; VAR hColor: HSLColor);
PROCEDURE   HSV2RGB (hColor: HSVColor; VAR rColor: RGBColor);
PROCEDURE   RGB2HSV (rColor: RGBColor; VAR hColor: HSVColor);
```

For developmental simplicity in switching between the HLS and HSV models, HLS is reordered into HSL. Thus both models start with hue and saturation values; value/lightness/brightness is last.

The CMY, HSL, and HSV structures are defined by ColorPicker with SmallFract values rather than INTEGER values (as in RGBColor). A SmallFract value is the fractional part of a Fixed number, which is the low-order word. The INTEGER values in RGBColor are actually used as unsigned integer-sized values; by using SmallFracts, ColorPicker avoids sign extension problems in the conversion math.

The Color Picker provides two functions for converting between SmallFract and Fixed numbers. Most developers will not need to use these facilities.

```
FUNCTION Fix2SmallFract(f: Fixed): SmallFract;
FUNCTION SmallFract2Fix(s: SmallFract): Fixed;
```

A SmallFract can represent a value between 0 and 65,535. They can be assigned directly to and from INTEGERs.

SUMMARY OF THE COLOR PICKER PACKAGE

Constants

```
CONST
   MaxSmallFract = $0000FFFF;   {maximum SmallFract value, as LONGINT}
```

Data Types

```
TYPE
   SmallFract = INTEGER;   {unsigned fraction between 0 and 1}

   HSVColor   = RECORD
         hue:         SmallFract;   {fraction of circle, red at 0}
         saturation: SmallFract;   {0-1, 0 is gray, 1 is pure color}
         value:       SmallFract;   {0-1, 0 is black, 1 is max }
                                    { intensity}
               END;

   HSLColor = RECORD
      hue:         SmallFract; {fraction of circle, red at 0}
      saturation: SmallFract; {0-1, 0 is gray, 1 is pure color}
      lightness:  SmallFract; {0-1, 0 is black, 1 is white}
      END;

   CMYColor = RECORD  {CMY and RGB are complements}
      cyan:       SmallFract;
      magenta:    SmallFract;
      yellow:     SmallFract;
   END;
```

Routines

```
FUNCTION   GetColor(where: Point; prompt: Str255; inColor: RGBColor;
           VAR outColor: RGBColor): BOOLEAN;
```

Conversion Functions

```
FUNCTION   Fix2SmallFract(f: Fixed): SmallFract;
FUNCTION   SmallFract2Fix(s: SmallFract): Fixed;
```

Color Conversion Procedures

```
PROCEDURE CMY2RGB(cColor: CMYColor; VAR rColor: RGBColor);
PROCEDURE RGB2CMY(rColor: RGBColor; VAR cColor: CMYColor);
PROCEDURE HSL2RGB(hColor: HSLColor; VAR rColor: RGBColor);
PROCEDURE RGB2HSL(rColor: RGBColor; VAR hColor: HSLColor);
PROCEDURE HSV2RGB(hColor: HSVColor; VAR rColor: RGBColor);
PROCEDURE RGB2HSV(rColor: RGBColor; VAR hColor: HSVColor);
```

Assembly-Language Information

Constants

```
Fix2SmallFract   .EQU    1
SmallFract2Fix   .EQU    2
CMY2RGB          .EQU    3
RGB2CMY          .EQU    4
HSL2RGB          .EQU    5
RGB2HSL          .EQU    6
HSV2RGB          .EQU    7
RGB2HSV          .EQU    8
GetColor         .EQU    9
```

Macro

```
_PACK12
```

9 THE FONT MANAGER

9 Font Manager

ABOUT THE FONT MANAGER

The Font Manager has been enhanced. Multibit pixel description for fonts provides color support on the Macintosh II; this includes the ability to create "gray-scale" fonts—character images with shades of gray (instead of merely black and white).

The SetFractEnable routine has been put into ROM, various bugs have been fixed, and a better font search algorithm has been implemented.

FONT MANAGER ROUTINES

One Font Manager routine, SetFractEnable, that was not in the 128K ROM (but was available in the Pascal interfaces) has been added to both the Macintosh SE and Macintosh II ROMs.

Assembly-language note: Assembly-language programmers should call SetFractEnable rather than change the value of the global variable FractEnable.

FRACTIONAL CHARACTER WIDTHS

One correction and two cautionary points should be added to the discussion in Volume IV of how the Font Manager communicates character widths:

- You will get accurate character widths using the QuickDraw routine MeasureText (rather than TextWidth as stated in Volume IV), or by looking in the global width table.

- A font request made with scaling disabled will not necessarily return the same result as an identical request with scaling enabled. The widths are sure to be the same only if fractional widths are enabled, and if the font does not have a font character-width table and is a member of a family record with a family character-width table.

- A font request with either twice the point size or a numerator/denominator scale factor of 2 is not guaranteed to double the widths of the characters exactly. Instead, the widths returned accurately describe how QuickDraw measures and spaces the characters. This is especially noticeable for algorithmically-applied style modifications like boldfacing. Boldfacing makes the character strike one pixel wider, regardless of point size. A font with a family character-width table, however, describes the spacing of the characters correctly.

To cause two different font requests to measure the same, or proportionately, use the QuickDraw routines SpaceExtra and CharExtra to adjust the widths of the spaces and other characters. In most cases, it's sufficient to simply pass the difference of the two measures divided by the number of spaces on the line to SpaceExtra. If the difference is too large or small, or if the line does not contain any spaces, you can adjust the line length with the CharExtra routine.

FONT SEARCH ALGORITHM

When passed a font request, the Font Manager takes a number of steps to provide the desired font; if the font can't be found, it looks for other fonts with which to fill the request. The search order is as follows:

- a 'FOND' resource. It first checks the last used 'FOND', then checks the most recently-used width tables (a handle to them is contained in the global variable WidthListHand), and finally calls GetResource (looking through the chain of open resource files, beginning with the application resource file). The width table it checks is that of the nearest size and font that it found.

- a 'FONT' resource without a corresponding 'FOND' (again calling GetResource)

- the application font

- a "neighborhood" base font. For fonts numbered below 4096, the neighborhood base font is 0. For fonts numbered 4096 and above, it is the next lower font whose number is a multiple of 512.

- the system font

- the Chicago 12 font

FONT MANAGER DATA STRUCTURES

This section describes support for fonts with depth on the Macintosh II; most of the information presented here is useful only to assembly-language programmers.

Just as the Color QuickDraw pixel image lets you use multiple bits to describe each pixel, the Font Manager lets you create fonts whose character images contain multiple bits per pixel. The number of bits per pixel, or the font depth, is specified in the font record (outlined below); font depths of one, two, four, and eight bits are supported.

Drawing to the screen is considerably faster if the font depth matches the screen depth specified by the user in the Control Panel. For speedy access, 4-bit and 8-bit versions of the system font, as well as a 4-bit Geneva font, are stored in the Macintosh II ROM as 'NFNT' resources.

It's not necessary, however, to create separate resources matching each of the possible screen depths for every font family. If a resource (either of type 'FONT' or 'NFNT') with a depth corresponding to the current screen depth can't be found, the Font Manager expands the 1-bit font into a **synthetic font** matching the current screen depth.

A synthetic font list contains information about each synthetic font; the format of an entry in this list is given in Figure 1. The global variable SynListHandle contains a handle to the synthetic font list.

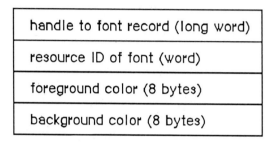

| handle to font record (long word) |
| resource ID of font (word) |
| foreground color (8 bytes) |
| background color (8 bytes) |

Figure 1. Synthetic Font List Entry

Figure 2 shows the relationship between the Font Manager data structures, modifying the figure that was given in Volume IV and adding the synthetic font list.

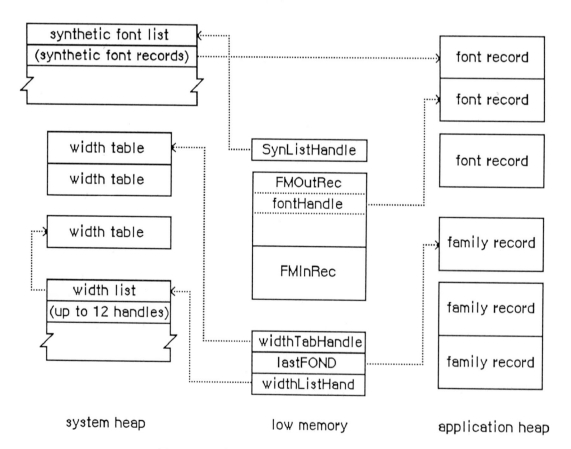

Figure 2. Font Manager Data Structures

Font Color Tables

9 Font Manager

With resources of type 'NFNT', you can specify absolute colors for the font by also supplying a color table. Stored as a resource of type 'fctb' with the same ID as the associated 'NFNT' resource, this table is simply the ColorTable record described in the Color Manager chapter.

A 4-bit font depth provides index values for a color table containing 16 entries. If there are index values for which no corresponding entries are found in the associated color table, the Font Manager assigns colors based on the current port's foreground and background colors. If only one entry is missing, it's assigned the background color. If two entries are missing, the higher index value is assigned the foreground color and the lower value is given the background color. If more than two values are missing, the entries are given shades ranging between the foreground and background colors. Figure 3 shows a hypothetical color table for a 2-bit font in which only five entries have been supplied in the 'fctb' resource.

7	purple
6	fuchsia
5	foreground color
4	gold
3	yellow
2	1/2 foregd, 1/2 backgd
1	background color
0	red

Figure 3. Hypothetical Font Color Table Entries

If no color table is provided, the highest and lowest possible index values for any given screen depth (with a 2-bit screen depth, for example, values 7 and 0) are assigned the foreground and background colors respectively, with the remaining entries given shades in between. This allows gray-scale fonts to be created with as many levels of gray as are needed (since each gray is just a color in between a foreground of black and a background of white) without needing a color table.

Font Records

Several previously unused bits of the fontType field specify the font depth and other related information (the new bits are marked by an asterisk):

	Bit	Meaning
	0	Set if there's an image-height table
	1	Set if there's a character-width table
*	2–3	Font depth (Macintosh II only—must be 0 otherwise)
	4–6	Reserved (should be 0)
*	7	Set if font has an 'fctb' resource (Macintosh II only—must be 0 otherwise)
*	8	Set if a synthetic font (Macintosh II only—must be 0 otherwise)
*	9	Set if font contains colors other than black (Macintosh II only—must be 0 otherwise)
	10–11	Reserved (should be 0)
	12	Reserved (should be 1)
	13	Set for fixed-width font, clear for proportional font
*	14	Set if font is not to be expanded (Macintosh II only—must be 0 otherwise)
	15	Reserved (should be 1)

Bit 2 and 3 specify the font depth and can contain the following values:

Value	Font depth
0	1-bit
1	2-bit
2	4-bit
3	8-bit

The font depth is normally 0, indicating a font intended for a screen one bit deep. If bit 7 is set (and the font is an 'NFNT' resource), a resource of type 'fctb' with the same ID as the font can optionally be provided to assign RGB colors to specific pixel values.

Bit 8 is used only by the Font Manager to indicate a synthetic font, created dynamically from the available font resources in response to a certain color and screen depth combination.

Bit 9 is set if the font contains other than black.

Setting bit 14 indicates that the font should not be expanded by the Font Manager to match the screen depth; some international fonts, such as kanji, are too large for synthetic fonts to be effective or meaningful.

To accommodate multibit font depths, the owTLoc field has been changed to a long word, the nDescent field becoming the high-order word. (For backward compatibility, nDescent is ignored if it's negative.)

Note: The 128K ROM version of the Font Manager limits the strike for a 1-bit font to not quite 128K; this limits the largest practical font to about 127 points. The Macintosh II ROM limits the largest practical font to about 255 points, regardless of the font depth.

Family Records

For Macintosh II only, bits 8 and 9 of the font style word within each font association table specify the font depth; they must contain the same value as bits 2 and 3 of the fontType field of the font record. All other undefined bits remain 0.

The format for resources of type 'FOND' has been extended. The new format is the following (with extension fields indicated by asterisks):

Number of bytes	Contents
2 bytes	FONDFlags field of family record
2 bytes	FONDFamID field of family record
2 bytes	FONDFirst field of family record
2 bytes	FONDLast field of family record
2 bytes	FONDAscent field of family record
2 bytes	FONDDescent field of family record
2 bytes	FONDLeading field of family record
2 bytes	FONDWidMax field of family record
4 bytes	FONDWTabOff of family record
4 bytes	FONDKernOff of family record
4 bytes	FONDStylOff of family record
24 bytes	FONDProperty field of family record
4 bytes	FONDIntl field of family record
2 bytes	*Version number ($02)
m bytes	FONDAssoc field of family record (variable length)
2 bytes	*Number of offsets minus 1
4 bytes	*Offset to bounding box table
n bytes	*Bounding box table
p bytes	FONDWidTable field of family record (variable length)
q bytes	FONDStylTab field of family record (variable length)
r bytes	FONDKerntab field of family record (variable length)

The bounding box table has an entry for each style available in the family. The table as a whole has this form:

Number of bytes   Contents

2 bytes	Number of entries minus 1
10 bytes	First entry
10 bytes	Second entry . . .

Each bounding box entry has this form, giving the bounding box position with respect to the origin of the characters:

Number of bytes   Contents

2 bytes	Style word
2 bytes	Lower left x coordinate
2 bytes	Lower left y coordinate
2 bytes	Upper right x coordinate
2 bytes	Upper right y coordinate

SUMMARY OF THE FONT MANAGER

Variable

SynListHandle   Handle to synthetic font list

10 THE TOOLBOX EVENT MANAGER

10 Toolbox Event

ABOUT THIS CHAPTER

This chapter describes four changes that enhance the ability of the Macintosh II and Macintosh SE to respond to keyboard events:

- Your application can now work with the Macintosh Plus, Macintosh II, and Apple Extended Keyboards, all of which offer several new key functions.

- The event message for keyboard events now distinguishes multiple keyboards.

- A new modifier flag detects the state of the control key on the Macintosh Plus and Apple Extended Keyboards.

- A new Toolbox routine, KeyTrans, helps your application convert key codes into ASCII codes.

NEW STANDARD KEYBOARDS

Three keyboards are now available as standard equipment with Macintosh computers sold in the U.S. They are

- The Macintosh Plus Keyboard, which includes cursor control keys and an integral keypad. Its layout and key coding is shown in Figure 1.

- The Macintosh II Keyboard, also shipped with the Macintosh SE, which adds Esc (Escape) and Control keys and is connected to the Apple Desktop Bus. Its layout and key coding is shown in Figure 2.

- The Apple Extended Keyboard, which the user may connect to the Apple Desktop Bus of any Macintosh II or Macintosh SE computer. Its layout and key coding is shown in Figure 3.

These figures show the **virtual key codes** for each key; they are the key codes that actually appear in keyboard events. In the case of the Macintosh II and Apple Extended Keyboards, however, the hardware produces **raw key codes,** which may be different. Raw key codes are translated to virtual key codes by the 'KMAP' resource in the System Folder. By modifying the 'KMAP' resource you can change the key codes for any keys. Similarly, you can change the ASCII codes corresponding to specific key codes by modifying the 'KCHR' resource in the System Folder. The 'KMAP' and 'KCHR' resources are described in the Resource Manager chapter of this volume.

With both the Macintosh II and the Apple Extended keyboards, the standard 'KMAP' resource supplied in the system folder reassigns the following raw key codes to different virtual key codes:

Key	Raw key code	Virtual key code
Control	36	3B
Left cursor	3B	7B
Right cursor	3C	7C
Down cursor	3D	7D
Up cursor	3E	7E

The standard 'KMAP' resource leaves all other raw key codes and virtual key codes the same.

With the Apple Extended Keyboard, the virtual key codes for three more keys may be easily reassigned, as described below under "Reassigning Right Key Codes".

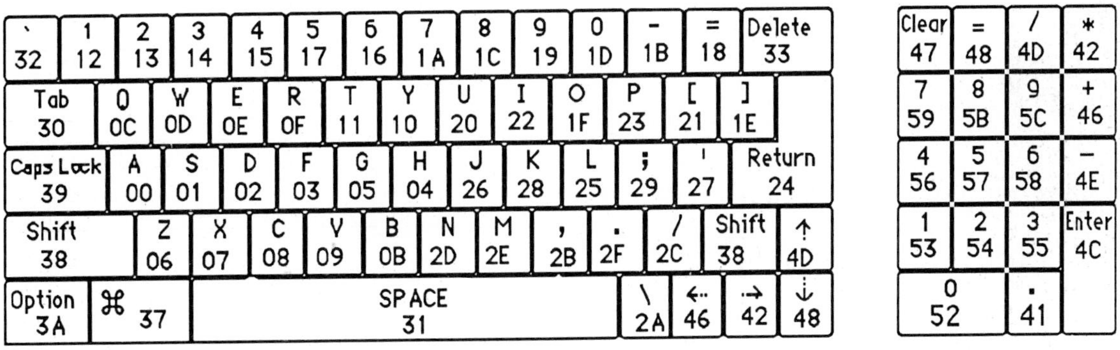

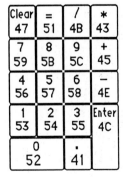

Figure 1. Macintosh Plus Keyboard

Figure 2. Macintosh II Keyboard

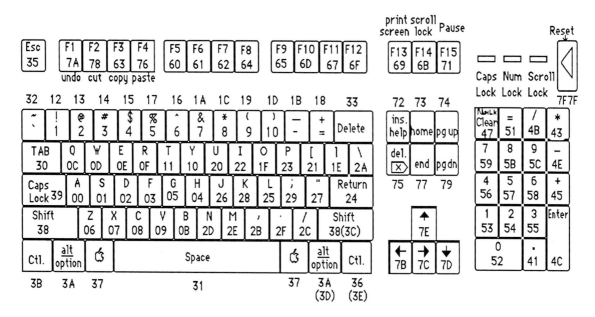

Figure 3. Apple Extended keyboard

The Apple Extended Keyboard

Apple now offers the Extended Keyboard as an option. Besides all the key functions of the present U.S. keyboard and keypad, it contains the following new ones:

- Fifteen general Function keys, labeled F1 through F15. Applications that use Undo, Cut, Copy, and Paste should assign keys F1 through F4 to these operations. Keys F5 through F15 are intended to be defined by the user, not by the application.

- A Control key. This is included for compatibility with applications requiring a Control key, which the Macintosh might access through communication with another operating system. It should not be used by new Macintosh applications. Pressing it sets bit 12 of the modifiers field of the event record for keyboard events, as described below under "New Modifier Flag".

- A Help key. This key is available to the user to request help or instructions from your application.

- A Forward Delete (Fwd Del) key. Pressing this key performs a forward text delete: the character immediately to the right of the insertion point is removed and all subsequent characters are shifted left one place. When the Fwd Del key is held down, the effect is that the insertion point remains stationary while everything ahead of it is "vacuumed" away. If it is pressed while there is a current selection, it removes the selected text.

- A Home key. Pressing the Home key is equivalent to moving the vertical scroll box to the top and the horizontal scroll box to the far left. It has no effect on the current insertion point or on any selected material.

- An End key. Pressing the End key is equivalent to moving the vertical scroll box to the bottom and the horizontal scroll box to the far right. It has no effect on the current insertion point or on any selected material.

- A Page Up key. Pressing the Page Up key is equivalent to clicking in the page-up region of the vertical scroll bar of the active window. It has no effect on the current insertion point or on any selected material.

- A Page Down key. Pressing the Page Down key is equivalent to clicking in the page-down region of the vertical scroll bar of the active window. It has no effect on the current insertion point or on any selected material.

- Duplicated Shift, Option, and Control Keys. On the Apple Extended Keyboard, the Shift, Option, and Control keys occur both to the right and to the left of the space bar. Normally they have the same key codes. However, it is possible to send the keyboard a command that changes the key codes for the keys on the right side. This possibility is discussed under "Reassigning Right Key Codes", below.

Reassigning Right Key Codes

It is possible to reassign the key codes for the Shift, Option, and Control keys on the right side of the Apple Extended keyboard to the following:

Right key	Raw key code	Virtual key code
Shift	$7B	3C
Option	$7C	3D
Control	$7D	3E

Changing these key codes requires changing the value of the Device Handler ID field in the Apple Extended Keyboard's register 3 from 2 to 3. The Device Handler ID is described in the Apple Desktop Bus chapter of this volume.

Warning: This capability is included for compatibility with certain existing operating systems that distinguish the right and left keys. Its use by new applications violates the Apple user interface guidelines and is strongly discouraged.

THE KEYBOARD EVENT MESSAGE

The Apple Desktop Bus chapter of this volume describes how the Macintosh II and Macintosh SE can be connected to multiple keyboards. To identify the origin of keyboard events, the keyboard event message contains a new ADB address field. It now has the structure shown in Figure 4.

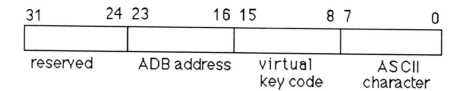

Figure 4. Event Message for Keyboard Events

Warning: The high byte of the event message for keyboard events is reserved for future use, and is not presently guaranteed to be zero.

The event message for non-keyboard events remains the same as described in the Toolbox Event Manager chapter of Volume I.

NEW MODIFIER FLAG

The Modifier Flag structure shown in the Toolbox Event Manager chapter of Volume I has been extended to record the status of the Control key on the Macintosh II and Apple Extended keyboards. The current structure is shown in Figure 5.

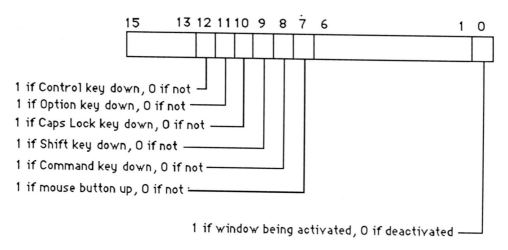

Figure 5. Modifier flags

KEYTRANS

A new routine in the 256K ROM lets your application convert key codes to ASCII values as determined by a 'KCHR' resource. The 'KCHR' resource type is discussed in the Resource Manager chapter of this volume.

```
FUNCTION KeyTrans (transData: Ptr; keycode: Integer; VAR state:
          LONGINT) : LONGINT;
```

TransData points to a 'KCHR' resource, which maps virtual key codes to ASCII values. The keycode parameter is a 16-bit value with the structure shown in Figure 6.

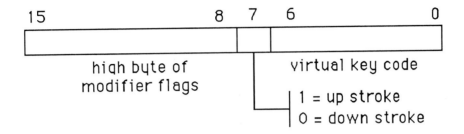

Figure 6. Keycode parameter structure

The state parameter is a value maintained by the Toolbox. Your application should save it between calls to KeyTrans. If your application changes transData to point to a different 'KCHR' resource, it should reset the state value to 0.

KeyTrans returns a 32-bit value with the structure shown in Figure 7. In this structure, ASCII 1 is the ASCII value of the first character generated by the key code parameter; reserved1 is an extension for future "16-bit ASCII" coding. ASCII 2 and reserved2 have the same meanings for a possible second character generated by key code—for example, if key code designates an alphabetic character with a separate accent character.

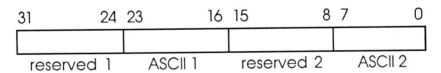

Figure 7. KeyTrans return structure

Assembly-language note: The macro you invoke to call KeyTrans from assembly language is named _KeyTrans. Its parameters are passed on the stack.

SUMMARY OF THE TOOLBOX EVENT MANAGER

Constant

```
ControlKey  =  4096;   {set if Control key down}
```

Routine

```
FUNCTION KeyTrans (transData: Ptr; keycode: Integer;
                  VAR state: LONGINT) : LONGINT;
```

11 THE WINDOW MANAGER

11 Window Manager

ABOUT THIS CHAPTER

This chapter describes the enhancements to the Window Manager provided for the Macintosh Plus, the Macintosh SE, and the Macintosh II. A new set of Window Manager routines for the Macintosh II supports the use of multiple screen desktops and color windows. New data structures and a new resource type, 'wctb', have been introduced to store color window information. All handling of color windows and multiple screens is transparent to applications that aren't using the new features.

To make use of the information in this chapter, you should be familiar with

- the drawing environment described in the Color QuickDraw chapter

- the use of resources in an application program, described in the Resource Manager chapter

For the Macintosh Plus, the Macintosh SE, and the Macintosh II, the following Window Manager routines were changed to support hierarchical menus:

- The InitWindow routine now calls the Menu Manager to calculate menu bar height, and to draw the empty menu bar. The FindWindow routine also makes a call to the Menu Manager when testing to see if a point on the screen has been selected.

For the Macintosh II, the Window Manager has been enhanced to support multiple screen desktops and color windows:

- Color windows can now be created within an application program.

- Because window content regions may be colored on the Macintosh II, each window's area is now erased separately. Formerly, the Window Manager collected the update region of multiple windows into a single region, then erased this single region to white.

- The standard desktop pattern may be a binary deskPattern or a color deskCPattern. If the color desktop pattern is enabled, InitWindows loads the default desktop pixel pattern as well as the standard binary pattern.

- Windows may be dragged from one screen to another on a system configured with multiple screens. Changes to the DragGrayRgn routine allow the object being dragged to be positioned anywhere on the multiscreen desktop. The GetGrayRgn routine provides a handle to the global variable GrayRgn, which contains information about the current desktop.

- The MoveWindow, GrowWindow, and ZoomWindow routines have been modified to ensure that windows will perform properly in a multiscreen environment.

COLOR WINDOW RECORDS

The Window Manager keeps all the information required for drawing color windows in a color window record. The structure and size of a color window record are the same as a regular window record, except that it's now optionally based on a cGrafPort instead of an old-style grafPort. This allows the window structure and content to use the color capability of the Macintosh II.

All standard window definition procedures can now draw window structure information into a color window port, called the WmgrCPort. The WMgrCPort is analogous to the WMgrPort. See the section "Defining Your Own Windows" for more information on how to use the WMgrCPort correctly.

The new data type CWindowRecord is identical to the old WindowRecord except that its port field is a cGrafPort instead of a grafPort. Because both types of port are the same size and follow the same rules, the old-style and new-style window records are also the same size and have all their fields at the same locations within the record. You can access most of the fields of a window record with Window Manager routines, so for most applications you won't need to use the fields listed below.

```
TYPE
  CWindowPtr    = CGrafPtr;
  CWindowPeek   = ^CWindowRecord;
  CWindowRecord = RECORD {all fields remain the same as before}
                    port:           CGrafPort;      {window's CGrafPort}
                    windowKind:     INTEGER;        {window class}
                    visible:        BOOLEAN;        {TRUE if visible}
                    hilited:        BOOLEAN;        {TRUE if highlighted}
                    goAwayFlag:     BOOLEAN;        {TRUE if has go- }
                                                    { away region}
                    spareFlag:      BOOLEAN;        {reserved for future }
                                                    { use}
                    strucRgn:       RgnHandle;      {structure region}
                    contRgn:        RgnHandle;      {content region}
                    updateRgn:      RgnHandle;      {update region}
                    windowDefProc:  Handle;         {window definition}
                                                    { function}
                    dataHandle:     Handle;         {data used by}
                                                    { windowDefProc}
                    titleHandle:    StringHandle;   {window's title}
                    titleWidth:     INTEGER;        {width of title in}
                                                    { pixels}
                    controlList:    ControlHandle;  {window's control }
                                                    { list}
                    nextWindow:     CWindowPeek;    {next window in }
                                                    { window list}
                    windowPic:      PicHandle;      {picture for drawing}
                                                    { window}
```

```
          refCon:        LONGINT        {window's reference}
                                        { value}
     END;
```

All of the old Window Manager routines now accept a CWindowPtr in place of a WindowPtr. If necessary, high-level languages may use **type coercion** to convert one data type to another. (Another method that allows the use of both types is to define a duplicate set of interfaces, substituting a CWindowPtr for a WindowPtr for convenience or code efficiency.) The two types of window may even be mixed on the same screen; the Window Manager will examine each window's port field to see which type it is, and draw it in full RGB colors or the original eight QuickDraw colors.

Auxiliary Window Records

As described in the Window Manager chapter of Volume I, windows consist of two parts: a structure region that includes the frame, titlebar, and other window elements, and a content region enclosed within the frame. Applications draw within the content region, and may draw in color by using the NewCWindow routine. Use of the NewWindow routine limits drawing within the contents region to the eight original QuickDraw colors. On the Macintosh II, the structure region is always drawn in the WMgrCPort and has full color capability, independent of the content region.

A new data structure, the **auxiliary window record,** stores the color information needed for each color window in an independent list. A number of auxiliary window records may exist as a linked list, beginning in the global variable AuxWindowHead. Each auxiliary window record is a relocatable object residing in the application heap. Figure 1 shows an example of a set of auxiliary window records that could be used for an application using a separate window color table for each of the windows. This data structure is known as the AuxWinList, and is simply a linked list where each additional auxiliary window record points to the one after it.

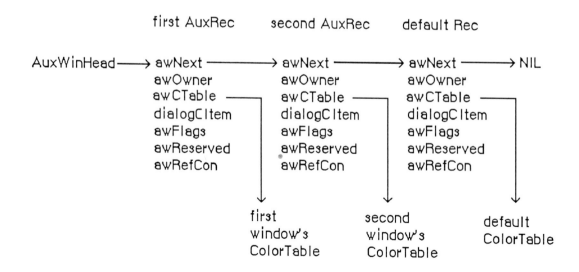

Figure 1. An AuxWinList Structure

The AuxWinRec structure includes a handle to the window's individual color table (see "Window Color Tables" below), as well as the handle to the dialogCItem list. The rest of the record consists of a link to the next record in the list, a pointer to the owning window, and several reserved fields.

```
TYPE
  AuxWinHandle = ^AuxWinPtr;
  AuxWinPtr    = ^AuxWinRec;
  AuxWinRec    = RECORD
              awNext:      AuxWinHandle;  {handle to next record }
                                          { in list}
              awOwner:     WindowPtr;     {pointer to owning }
                                          { window}
              awCTable:    CTabHandle;    {handle to window's }
                                          { color table}
              dialogCItem: CTabHandle;    {private storage for }
                                          { Dialog Manager}
              awFlags:     LONGINT;       {reserved for future use}
              awReserved:  CTabHandle;    {reserved for future use}
              awRefCon:    LONGINT        {reserved for }
                                          { application use}
           END;
```

Field descriptions

awNext   The awNext field is a handle to the next record in the auxiliary window list. If this record is the default auxWinRec, this value will be NIL.

awOwner   The awOwner field is a pointer to the window to which this record belongs. The default auxWinRec awOwner field is always set to NIL.

awCTable   The awCTable is a handle to the window's color table. Normally these are five-element color tables (see "Window Color Tables" below).

dialogCItem The dialogCItem field contains private storage for the Dialog Manager.

awFlags   The awFlags field is reserved for future expansion.

awReserved The awReserved field is reserved for future expansion.

awRefCon   The awRefCon field is a reference constant for use by the application.

The default colors for all windows are loaded from a 'wctb' resource = 0 when InitWindows is called. First the application is checked for a 'wctb' resource, then if none is found, the System file is checked, and finally, ROM Resources is checked for an existing 'wctb'. To change the default colors for any of the windows, use SetWinColor. The standard colors on the system are identical to black-and-white Macintosh windows.

An AuxWinRec specifies the default colorTable for the application's window list. For most types of applications, several windows can use the same auxiliary window record and share the same color table. Separate auxiliary window records are needed only for windows whose color usage differs from the default. Each such nonstandard window must have its own auxiliary record, even if it uses the same colors as another window. Two or more auxiliary records may share the same color table. If a window uses a color table resource, the resource must not be purgeable, and the color table won't be disposed when DisposeWindow is called. However, for an auxiliary record using any color table that is not a resource, the application must avoid deallocating the color table if another window is still using it.

The AuxWinRec is deallocated when DisposeWindow is called. If the resource bit of a color table's handle is set, the color table can only be disposed using the Resource Manager routine ReleaseResource.

A window created with the NewWindow routine will initially have no auxiliary window record. If it is to use nonstandard colors, it must be given an auxiliary record and a color table with SetWinColor (see the "Window Manager Routines" section). Such a window should normally be made invisible at creation and then displayed with ShowWindow or ShowHide after the colors are set. For windows created from a template resource, the color table can be specified as a resource as well.

A/UX systems: For systems using 32-bit mode, each window will have an AuxWinRec. The default AuxWinRec structure is present at the end of the AuxWinList, but is not used. The variant code for the window is no longer stored in the high byte of the windowDefProc field, but is stored in the awFlags field. This allows the defproc to occur anywhere within the 32-bit address space.

WINDOW COLOR TABLES

The contents and meaning of a window's color table are determined by its window definition function (see the "Defining Your Own Windows" section later in this chapter). The CTabHandle parameter used in the Window Manager routines provides a handle to the window color table. The color table containing the window's colorSpecs can have any number of entries, but standard window color tables as stored in the system resource file have five colorSpecs.

The components of a window color table are defined as follows:

```
TYPE
  WTabHandle = ^WCTabPtr;
  WCTabPtr   = ^WinCTab;
  WinCTab    = RECORD
                wCSeed:     LONGINT;   {unique identifier from }
                                       { table}
                wCReserved: INTEGER;   {not used for windows}
                ctSize:     INTEGER;   {number of entries in }
                                       { table -1}
```

```
ctTable:        cSpecArray;  {array of ColorSpec }
                             { records}
    END;
```

Field descriptions

wCSeed
: The wCSeed field is unused in window color tables, and is reserved for Apple's use.

wCReserved
: The wCReserved field is unused in window color tables, and is reserved for Apple's use.

ctSize
: The ctSize field defines the number of elements in the table, minus one. If your application is building a color table for use with the standard definition procedure, this field is always 4. Custom window definition procedures can allocate color tables of any size.

ctTable
: The ctTable field is made of an array of colorSpec records. Each colorSpec contains the partIdentifer and partRGB field, as shown below. The PartIdentifier field holds an integer which associates a colorSpec to a particular part of the window. The definition procedures attempt to find the appropriate partIdentifier when preparing to draw a part. If that partIdentifier is not found, the first color in the table is used to draw the part. The partIdentifiers can appear in any order in the table. The partRGB field specifies a standard RGB color record, indicating what RGB value will be used to draw the window part found in partIdentifier.

The standard window type uses a five-element color table with part identifiers as shown in Figure 2.

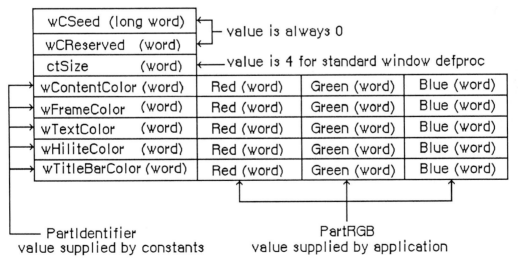

Figure 2. A Window Color Table

The following constants are used for the partIdentifiers in a window color table:

```
wContentColor    =    0;
wFrameColor      =    1;
wTextColor       =    2;
wHiliteColor     =    3;
wTitleBarColor   =    4;
```

The default color table read into the heap at application startup simply contains the right combination of black and white to produce standard black-and-white Macintosh windows. The last record in the auxiliary window list holds a handle to this default color table. Before drawing a window, the standard window definition function searches the list for an auxiliary record whose awOwner points to the window to be drawn. If it finds such a record, it uses the color table designated by that record; if it doesn't find one before reaching the default record at the end of the list, it uses the default color table instead. The default record is recognized by NIL values in both its awNext and awOwner fields; your program must not change these fields.

When creating a color window, the background color is set to the content color. Old-style windows should use a content color of white.

A nonstandard window definition function can explicitly declare a color table of any desired size and define its contents in any way it wishes, except that part identifiers 1 to 127 are reserved for system definition. For compatibility with the defaulting mechanism described above, the customized definition function should either use indices 0 to 4 in the standard way, or else bypass the default by allocating an explicit auxiliary record for every window it creates. To access a nonstandard window color table from Pascal, the handle must be coerced to WCTabHandle.

The 'wctb' resource is an exact image of the window table data structure. This resource is stored in a similar format as 'clut' color table resources. The partIdentifier and partCode fields are stored as the colorSpec.value and colorSpec.RGBColor fields.

USING COLOR WINDOWS

Each color window (excluding those using a colored default) should have its own color table. When an application is initialized, the default colorTable field used is the 'wctb' resource = 0 in the application's resource fork. This allows you to set default window colors on an application basis. If a 'wctb' resource = 0 is not found in the application, or in the System file, a nonchangeable resource is loaded from ROM resources. Normally, the default window colors will be the correct combination of black and white to create standard Macintosh windows.

The GetAuxWin routine is used to return the handle to an individual window color table. CloseWindow will dispose of a window's AuxWinRec, if present.

When a new window is created with the NewCWindow or NewWindow routine, no entry is added to the AuxList, and the window will use the default colors. If SetWinColor is used with a different color table for a window, a new AuxList will be allocated and added to the head of the list. To avoid having a visible window flash to a different color, it is useful to call NewCWindow or NewWindow with the visible field set to FALSE, then to call SetWinColor to change the colors, and finally to call ShowHide to make it visible.

Within an application, a new window is usually created from a resource by using GetNewCWindow or GetNewWindow. GetNewCWindow will attempt to load a 'wctb' resource if it is present. It then executes the SetWinColor call. A new AuxRec is allocated if the resource file contains the 'wctb' resource with the same ResId as the 'WIND' template. Otherwise, the default window colors are used. The Window Manager automatically hides specially-colored visible windows so that they won't flash to a different color.

Any windows created with NewWindow will contain an old-style grafPort in the windowRec, and only the eight original QuickDraw colors can be displayed in the window content. NewCWindow creates a window record based on a cGrafport, thus allowing full use of the Macintosh II color capability.

Advanced Window Manager routines include SetDeskCPat, which allows the Control Panel to set the desktop pattern to a color pattern. This routine should not be used in application programs, but its description here will help you understand how the Window Manager manages desktop patterns. The GetCWMgrPort routine returns the address of the WMgrCPort. In most cases this won't be necessary, since applications should avoid drawing in the Window Manager ports.

Color QuickDraw on the Macintosh II supports drawing to multiple screens that have been configured to act as a single large screen. All window dragging and sizing operations, including the MoveWindow, DragGrayRgn, GrowWindow, SizeWindow, and ZoomWindow routines, have been modified to allow windows to perform properly when dragged across a multiple-screen desktop. If a portion of a window moves across screen boundaries, update events are automatically generated to ensure that the window's contents are drawn in the correct colors.

A special Window Manager variable, the GrayRgn, describes the size and shape of the desktop on all Macintoshes. On a multiple-screen Macintosh II, the GrayRgn variable contains information on all the screens configured into the system. Your application can determine the size of the desktop by checking the GrayRgn's bounding box, and should use this rectangle for dragging and sizing bounds. The GetGrayRgn routine returns a handle to the current desktop GrayRgn. Zooming should be restricted to using the full size of only one screen by using screenbits.bounds for the main screen, or the appropriate GDRect for any other screens. See the section titled "Modifications to Existing Routines" for more details.

DEFINING YOUR OWN WINDOWS

Like standard windows, custom window structures can be drawn in full color. On the Macintosh II, a new data structure known as the WMgrCPort, which opens a cGrafPort, is introduced. This data structure is analogous to the existing WMgrPort, and defines the desktop area of the Window Manager, allowing desktop objects (such as window frames) to be drawn in full color. The standard defprocs included in the Macintosh II ROM and on the system disk, are *universal defprocs* —that is, they support the full color capabilities of the Macintosh II while maintaining full compatibility on noncolor Macintoshes. Since applications can be transported between color and noncolor Macintoshes on disk, custom defprocs associated with applications should be written in this same universal style.

To write a universal defproc, the defproc should, upon entry, identify the capabilities of the machine on which it is running by using the _SysEnvirons call. If the machine doesn't support color, then all previous rules for writing defprocs should be followed as explained in Volume I.

If the machine is equipped with Color QuickDraw, then a number of extra steps should be performed:

- First, the defproc should change the current port from the WMgrPort to the WMgrCPort, to allow the system to draw in the full range of RGBColors.

- Next, the defproc should update certain fields in the WMgrCPort to the values of the corresponding fields in the WMgrPort. The fields that should be updated are the pen attributes, the text attributes, and bkPat. The vis and clip regions are automatically transferred by the Window Manager.

Note: The parallelism of the WMgrPort and the WMgrCPort is maintained only by the defprocs. All defprocs that draw in the WMgrPort should follow these rules even if the changed fields don't affect their operation.

When the two ports are in parallel, the color defproc can proceed with its drawing. Note that the GetAuxWin routine, described below, can be used to get the intended colors for the window parts from the AuxWinList. As with all color objects, highlighting shouldn't be performed by inverting; the forecolor and backcolor should be reversed and the highlighted item redrawn. No special steps need be taken on exit from the defproc. All other features and requirements of defprocs are unchanged and remain as documented in Volume I.

Note: For compatibility with systems using MultiFinder™, no drawing should take place in either the WMgrPort or the WMgrCPort unless the drawing occurs within a definition procedure.

WINDOW MANAGER ROUTINES

This section describes six new routines, modifications to eight existing routines, and two advanced routines.

New Window Manager Routines

The following new routines have been added to the Window Manager:

```
FUNCTION NewCWindow (wStorage: Ptr; boundsRect: Rect; title:
        Str255; visible: BOOLEAN; procID: INTEGER; behind:
        WindowPtr; goAwayFlag: BOOLEAN; refCon: LONGINT) :
        CWindowPtr; [Macintosh II]
```

The NewCWindow routine creates a new color window. This routine is similar to the old routine NewWindow, but creates a window based on a cGrafPort instead of an old-style grafPort.

```
FUNCTION GetNewCWindow (windowID: INTEGER; wStorage: Ptr; behind:
        CWindowPtr) : CWindowPtr; [Macintosh II]
```

The GetNewCWindow routine creates a new color window from a template in a resource file. It's analogous to the old routine GetNewWindow, but it creates a window based on a cGrafPort instead of an old-style grafPort. GetNewCWindow checks the 'wctb' resource, and if it contains the same resource ID, it colors the window. The backColor of the window is set to the new content color. This allows an application to begin its update with an EraseRect without changing the background color.

```
PROCEDURE SetWinColor (theWindow: WindowPtr;
        newColorTable: CTabHandle); [Macintosh II]
```

The SetWinColor routine sets a window's color table. If the window currently has no auxiliary window record, a new one is created with the given color table and added to the head of the auxiliary window list. If there is already an auxiliary record for the window, its color table is replaced by the contents of newColorTable. The window is then automatically redrawn in the new colors. If SetWinColor is performed on a cWindow, it sets the backColor of the window to the new content color. This allows an application to begin its update without changing the background color.

If newColorTable has the same contents as the default color table, the window's existing auxiliary record and color table are removed from the auxiliary window list and deallocated. If theWindow = NIL, the operation modifies the default color table in memory. The system never disposes of color tables that are resources when the resource bit is set; 'wctb' resources can't be purgeable.

```
FUNCTION GetAuxWin (theWindow: WindowPtr;
        VAR colors: CTabHandle) : BOOLEAN; [Macintosh II]
```

The GetAuxWin routine returns a handle to a window's auxiliary window record:

- If the given window has an auxiliary record, its handle is returned in colors and the function returns TRUE.

- If the window has no auxiliary record, a handle to the default record is returned in colors and the function returns FALSE.

- If theWindow = NIL, a handle to the default record is returned in colors and the function returns TRUE.

```
FUNCTION GetWVariant (whichWindow:WindowPtr): INTEGER; [Macintosh Plus,
        Macintosh SE, Macintosh II]
```

GetWVariant returns the variant code for the window described by whichWindow. See the Window Manager chapter in Volume I for more information about variants.

```
FUNCTION GetGrayRgn : regionHandle; [Not in ROM] [Macintosh Plus, Macintosh
        SE, Macintosh II]
```

The GetGrayRgn function returns a handle to the current desktop region stored in the global variable GrayRgn.

Modifications to Existing Routines

The following Window Manager routines are modified to support hierarchical menus within windows, color windows, and multiple-screen desktops:

```
PROCEDURE InitWindows; [Macintosh Plus, Macintosh SE, Macintosh II]
```

The InitWindow procedure now calls the new Menu Bar definition procedure to calculate menu bar height, and to draw the empty menu bar. Since the menu bar definition procedure ('MBDF') actually performs these calculations, InitWindows now calls InitMenus directly. InitMenus has been modified so that it can be called twice in a program without ill effect.

For the Macintosh II, if the color desktop pattern is enabled, InitWindows loads the default desktop pixel pattern as well as the standard binary pattern. It allocates both the WMgrCPort and the WMgrPort, then calculates the union of all active screen devices, and saves this region in the global variable GrayRgn.

```
PROCEDURE FindWindow (thePoint: Point; VAR
        whichWindow:windowPtr):INTEGER; [Macintosh Plus, Macintosh SE,
        Macintosh II]
```

The FindWindow procedure now calls the new menu bar definition procedure to determine whether the point where the mouse button was pressed lies in the menu bar.

```
PROCEDURE PaintOne (window: WindowPeek; clobberedRgn:RgnHandle);
        [Macintosh II]
```

The PaintOne routine is modified to improve the performance of updates when differently colored windows are in use. Formerly, the Window Manager collected the update region of multiple windows into a single region, then erased this single region to white. In a color environment, different windows may need to be erased to different colors, so the previously used monochrome optimization is disabled. Each uncovered window is now erased separately, as if the PaintWhite global variable was always set to TRUE. Software that uses the PaintWhite and SaveUpdate flags may appear slightly different when update events are being processed.

PaintOne tests to see if a window has an old or new grafPort, and sets either the wMgrPort or wMgrCPort as appropriate. This allows color windows the full RGB range when being erased to their content color.

```
PROCEDURE MoveWindow (theWindow:windowPtr; hGlobal, vGlobal:INTEGER;
        front: BOOLEAN); [Macintosh II]
```

The MoveWindow routine formerly copied a window's entire structure region. On multiple-screen systems, MoveWindow now copies only the portion of the window that will remain on the same screen. All other parts of the window are not copied, and are redrawn on the next update event. When a window's content crosses screen boundaries, MoveWindow may post additional updates on multiple screen systems.

For new applications, the specified dragging bounds should be the bounding box of the GrayRgn. To support existing programs, if the dragging bounds passed to MoveWindow are within six pixels of the current screenbits.bounds on the left, right, and bottom, and are within thirty-six pixels of the screenbits.bounds.top, the GrayRgn's bounding box is substituted.

```
FUNCTION DragGrayRgn (theRgn: RgnHandle; startPt: Point; lmitRect,
        slopRect: Rect; axis: INTEGER;
        actionProc:ProcPtr):LONGINT; [Macintosh II]
```

On multiple-screen systems, the Window Manager now checks the screen rectangle (screenBits.bounds) when the DragGrayRgn routine is called. This allows the object being dragged to be positioned anywhere on the multiscreen desktop. If the dragging bounds are based on screenBits.bound, the dragging boundsRect will be changed to the bounding box of the grayRgn. The Window Manager's criteria for modifying the bounds are (1) the left, bottom, and right are within six pixels of screenBits.bound, and (2) the top is within 36 pixels of screenBits.bounds.top. If the dragging bounds are modified, the lmitRect parameter is also similarly modified.

```
FUNCTION GrowWindow (theWindow:windowPtr: startPt:Point; sizeRect:
        Rect):LONGINT; [Macintosh II]
```

On multiple-screen systems, the GrowWindow routine is modified so that windows can be stretched only a small amount onto other screens. This restriction can be removed by holding down the command key while growing the window, allowing windows to cover the full extent of the multiscreen desktop.

```
PROCEDURE ZoomWindow(theWindow:windowPtr; partCode: INTEGER; front:
        BOOLEAN); [Macintosh II]
```

On multiple-screen systems, applications that call ZoomWindow with a new size based on the screen rectangle (screenBits.bounds) will now cause any windows not on the main screen to zoom to full size on the main screen. To perform properly in a multiscreen environment, these applications should test which screen contains the greatest area of the window to be zoomed, and then zoom to the screen rectangle (GDRect) for that screen device. See the Graphics Devices chapter for information on obtaining the GDRect value for a device.

Advanced Routines

```
PROCEDURE GetCWMgrPort (VAR wport: CGrafPtr); [Macintosh II]
```

The WMgrCPort is a parallel structure to the WMgrPort. The GetCWMgrPort returns the address of the WMgrCPort. In Apple-provided 'WDEF' resources, all drawing is done in the WMgrCPort to allow full color drawing, rather than just the eight QuickDraw colors.

```
PROCEDURE SetDeskCPat (deskPixPat: PixPatHandle); [Macintosh II]
```

> **Note:** This routine is not for use by applications, and its description is only included for informational purposes.

The SetDeskCPat procedure sets the desktop pattern to a given pixel pattern, allowing it to be drawn in more than two colors if desired. The desktop is automatically redrawn in the new pattern. If deskPixPat is an old-style binary pattern (patType = 0), it will be drawn in the current foreground and background colors. If the pixPatHandle is NIL, the standard binary deskPat ('ppat' resource = 16) will be used.

The standard desktop painting routines can paint either in the existing binary pattern (kept in global variable DeskPat) or in a new pixel pattern. The desk pattern used at startup is determined by the value of another bit flag called pCDeskPat. If this is pCDeskPat = 0, the new pixel pattern is used; for all other values, the binary pattern is used by default. The color pattern can be changed through use of the Control Panel or through the use of SetDeskCPat, but only the Control Panel changes the value of pCDeskPat in parameter RAM.

SUMMARY OF THE WINDOW MANAGER

Constants

```
{ Window Part Identifiers which correlate color table entries }
{ with window elements }

wContentColor    =    0;
wFrameColor      =    1;
wTextColor       =    2;
wHiliteColor     =    3;
wTitleBarColor   =    4;
```

Data Types

```
TYPE
   CWindowPtr    = CGrafPtr;
   CWindowPeek   = ^CWindowRecord;
   CWindowRecord = RECORD {all fields remains the same as before}
                   port:          CGrafPort;     {window's }
                                                 { CGrafPort}
                   windowKind:    INTEGER;       {window class}
                   visible:       BOOLEAN;       {TRUE if visible}
                   hilited:       BOOLEAN;       {TRUE if }
                                                 { highlighted}
                   goAwayFlag:    BOOLEAN;       {TRUE if has go-}
                                                 { away region}
                   spareFlag:     BOOLEAN;       {reserved for }
                                                 { future use}
                   strucRgn:      RgnHandle;     {structure region}
                   contRgn:       RgnHandle;     {content region}
                   updateRgn:     RgnHandle;     {update region}
                   windowDefProc: Handle;        {window definition }
                                                 { function}
                   dataHandle:    Handle;        {data used by }
                                                 { windowDefProc}
                   titleHandle:   StringHandle;  {window's title}
                   titleWidth:    INTEGER;       {width of title in }
                                                 { pixels}
                   controlList:   ControlHandle; {window's control }
                                                 { list}
                   nextWindow:    CWindowPeek;   {next window in }
                                                 { window list}
                   windowPic:     PicHandle;     {picture for }
                                                 { drawing window}
```

```
                        refCon:        LONGINT              {window's reference }
                                                            { value}
                  END;

  AuxWinHandle = ^AuxWinPtr;
  AuxWinPtr    = ^AuxWinRec;
  AuxWinRec    = RECORD
                  awNext:        AuxWinHandle; {handle to next record }
                                               { in list}
                  awOwner:       WindowPtr;    {pointer to owning }
                                               { window}
                  awCTable:      CTabHandle;   {handle to window's }
                                               { color table}
                  dialogCItem: CTabHandle;     {private storage for }
                                               { Dialog Manager}
                  awFlags:       LONGINT;      {reserved for future }
                                               { use}
                  awReserved:  CTabHandle;     {reserved for future }
                                               { use}
                  awRefCon:      LONGINT       {reserved for }
                                               { application use}
                  END;

  WTabHandle  = ^WCTabPtr;
  WCTabPtr    = ^WinCTab;
  WinCTab     = RECORD
                  wCSeed:        LONGINT;      {unique identifier from }
                                               { table}
                  wCReserved: INTEGER;         {not used for windows}
                  ctSize:        INTEGER;      {number of entries in table -1}
                  ctTable:     cSpecArray;     {array of ColorSpec records}
                  END;
```

Routines

```
FUNCTION NewCWindow      (wStorage: Ptr; boundsRect: Rect; title:
                          Str255; visible: BOOLEAN; procID: INTEGER;
                          behind: WindowPtr; goAwayFlag: BOOLEAN;
                          refCon: LONGINT) : CWindowPtr;

FUNCTION GetNewCWindow (windowID: INTEGER; wStorage: Ptr; behind:
                          CWindowPtr) : CWindowPtr;

PROCEDURE SetWinColor    (theWindow: WindowPtr; newColorTable:
                          CTabHandle);

FUNCTION GetAuxWin       (theWindow: WindowPtr; VAR colors:
                          CTabHandle) : BOOLEAN;

FUNCTION GetWVariant     (whichWindow:WindowPtr): INTEGER;

FUNCTION GetGrayRgn: regionHandle; [Not in ROM]

PROCEDURE GetCWMgrPort (VAR wport: CGrafPtr);
```

```
PROCEDURE SetDeskCPat  (deskPixPat: PixPatHandle);
```

Variables

```
GrayRgn      {Contains information on size and shape of the current }
             { desktop}
AuxWinHead   {Contains handle to the head of the auxiliary window }
             { list}
```

Assembly-Language Information

```
; Window Part Identifiers that correlate color table entries with
; window elements

wContentColor     EQU     0
wFrameColor       EQU     1
wTextColor        EQU     2
wHiliteColor      EQU     3
wTitleBarColor    EQU     4


; auxWinRec structure

nextAuxWin        EQU     $0      ;next in chain [Handle]
auxWinOwner       EQU     $4      ;owner ID [WindowPtr]
awCTable          EQU     $8      ;color table [CTabHandle]
dialogCItem       EQU     $C      ;handle to dialog manager structures
                                  ; [handle]
awFlags           EQU     $10     ;handle for QuickDraw [handle]
awResrv           EQU     $14     ;for expansion [longint]
awRefCon          EQU     $18     ;user constant [longint]

; Global variables

AuxWinHead        EQU     $0CD0   ;[handle] Window Aux List head
GrayRgn           EQU     $9EE    ;contains information on size and shape
                                  ; of the current desktop
```

12 THE CONTROL MANAGER

ABOUT THIS CHAPTER

This chapter describes the enhancements to the Control Manager provided for the Macintosh Plus, Macintosh SE, and Macintosh II. A new set of Control Manager routines now supports the use of color controls. All handling of color controls is transparent to applications that aren't using the new features.

The structure and size of a control record are unchanged. A new data structure, the *auxiliary control record,* has been introduced to carry additional color information for a control, and a new system resource, 'cctb', stores control color table information. Three new routines have been added to support the use of color.

AUXILIARY CONTROL RECORDS

The information needed for drawing controls in color is kept in a linked list of auxiliary control records, beginning in the global variable AuxCtlHead. (Notice that there is just one global list for all controls in all windows, not a separate one for each window.) Each window record has a handle to the list of controls. Figure 1 shows the auxiliary control list structure.

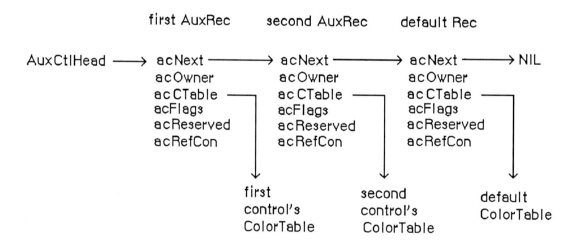

Figure 1. Auxiliary Control List

Each auxiliary control record is a relocatable object residing in the application heap. The most important information it holds is a handle to the control's individual color table (see the "Control Color Tables" section). The rest of the record consists of a link to the next record in the list, a field that identies the control's owner, a 4-byte field reserved for future expansion, and a 4-byte reference constant for use by the application:

```
TYPE
   AuxCtlHandle = ^AuxCtlPtr;
   AuxCtlPtr    = ^AuxCtlRec;
   AuxCtlRec    = RECORD
                     acNext:     AuxCtlHandle;  {handle to next record in }
                                                { list}
                     acOwner:    ControlHandle; {handle to owning control}
                     acCTable:   CCTabHandle;   {handle to control's color }
                                                { table}
                     acFlags:    INTEGER;       {miscellaneous flags; }
                                                { reserved}
                     acReserved: LONGINT;       {reserved for future }
                                                { expansion}
                     acRefCon:   LONGINT        {reserved for application }
                                                { use}
                  END;
```

Field descriptions

acNext   The acNext field contains a handle to the next record in the auxiliary
            control list.

acOwner   The acOwner field contains the handle of the control to which this
            auxiliary record belongs. Used as an ID field.

acCTable   The acCTable contains the handle to the control's color table (see
            "Control Color Tables" below).

acFlags   The acFlags field contains miscellaneous flags for use by the Control
            Manager; this field is reserved.

acReserved The acReserved field is reserved for future expansion; this must be
            set to 0 for future compatibility.

acRefCon   The acRefCon field is a reference constant for use by the application.

Not every control needs an auxiliary control record. When an application is started, a
resource containing a default color table is loaded from the system resource file; this
resource defines a standard set of control colors. Since there is no InitControls routine, this
happens when an application calls InitWindows.

Separate auxiliary control records are needed only for controls whose color usage differs
from the default. Each such nonstandard control must have its own auxiliary record, even
if it uses the same colors as another control. This allows two or more auxiliary records to
share the same control color table. If the control color table is a resource, it won't be
deleted by DisposeControl. When using an auxiliary record that is not stored as a resource,
the application should not deallocate the color table if another control is still using it.

A control created from scratch will initially have no auxiliary control record. If it is to use
nonstandard colors, it must be given an auxiliary record and a color table with SetCtlColor

12 Control Manager

(see the "Control Manager Routines" section). Such a control should normally be made invisible at creation and then displayed with ShowControl after the colors are set. For controls created from a 'CNTL' resource, the color table can be specified as a resource as well. See the section titled "The Control Color Table Resource".

> **A/UX systems:** When using 32-bit mode. every control has its own auxiliary record. If there is no specific set of control colors for this control, the acCTable will point to the default color table.

CONTROL COLOR TABLES

The contents and meaning of a control's color table are determined by its control definition function (see "The Control Color Table Resource" section). The CTabHandle parameter used in the Color Control Manager routines provides a handle to the control color table. The components of a control color table are defined as follows:

```
TYPE
  CCTabHandle = ^CCTabPtr;
  CCTabPtr    = ^CtlCTab;
  CtlCTab     = RECORD
                    ccSeed:      LONGINT;    {not used for controls}
                    ccReserved:  INTEGER;    {not used for controls}
                    ctSize:      INTEGER;    {number of entries in }
                                             { table -1}
                    ctTable:     cSpecArray  {array of ColorSpec records}
                END;
```

Field descriptions

ccSeed   The ccSeed field is unused in control color tables.

ccReserved The ccReserved field is unused in control color tables.

ctSize   The ctSize field defines the number of elements in the table, minus one. For controls drawn with the standard definition procedure, this field is always 3.

ctTable   The ctTable field holds an array of colorSpec records. Each colorSpec is made up of a partIdentifier field and a partRGB field. The partIdentifier field holds an integer which associates an RGBColor to a particular part of the control. The definition procedures attempt to find the appropriate part identifier when preparing to draw a part. If that part identifier is not found, the first color in the table is used to draw the part. The part identifiers can appear in any order in the table. The partRGB field specifies a standard RGB color record, indicating what absolute color will be used to draw the control part found in the partIdentifier field.

A standard control color table is shown in Figure 2.

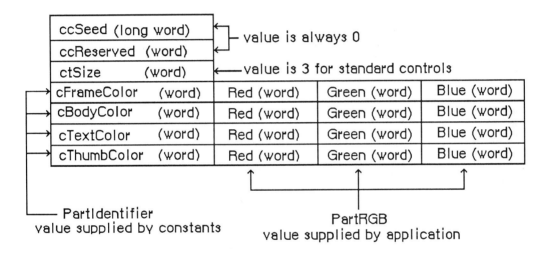

Figure 2. Control Color Table

The 'cctb' resource is an exact image of this control table data structure, and is stored in the same format as 'clut' color table resources.

Standard buttons, check boxes, and radio buttons use a four-element color table with part identifiers as shown below:

    cFrameColor (0)   Frame color

    cBodyColor (1)   Fill color for body of control

    cTextColor (2)   Text color

    cThumbColor (3)   Unused

When highlighted, plain buttons exchange their body and text colors (colors 1 and 2); check boxes and radio buttons change their appearance without changing colors. All three types indicate deactivation by dimming their text with no change in colors.

Standard scroll bars use a four-element color table with part identifiers as shown below:

cFrameColor (0)	Frame color, foreground color for shaft and arrows
cBodyColor (1	Background color for shaft and arrows
cTextColor (2)	Unused
cThumbColor (3)	Fill color for thumb

When highlighted, the arrows are filled with the foreground color (color 0) within the arrow outline. A deactivated scroll bar shows no indicator, and displays its shaft in solid background color (color 1), with no pattern.

The 'cctb' resource = 0 is read into the application heap when the application starts, and serves as the default control color table. The last record in the auxiliary control list points to the default 'cctb' resource. When drawing a control, the standard control definition function searches the list for an auxiliary control record whose acOwner points to the control being drawn. If it finds such a record, it uses the color table designated by that record; if it doesn't find one before reaching the default record at the end of the list, it uses the default color table instead. All types of controls share the same default record. The default auxiliary control record is recognized by NIL values in both its acNext and acOwner fields; the application must not change these fields.

A nonstandard control definition function can use color tables of any desired size and define their contents in any way it wishes, except that part indices 1 to 127 are reserved for system definition. Any such nonstandard function should take care to bypass the defaulting mechanism just described, by allocating an explicit auxiliary record for every control it creates.

USING COLOR CONTROLS

The following caveats apply to the use of color with controls:

- Each colored control (excluding those using the default colors) should have its own color table.
- Controls are drawn in the window port, which by default is an old-style grafPort. This limits color matching to the eight old QuickDraw colors. To achieve full RGB display with controls, the window must be opened with a cGrafPort, using the NewCWindow routine.

Since there is no "InitControls" call, a default AuxCtlRec is created and intialized on the application heap when InitWindows is executed. When a new control is created with the NewControl routine, no entry is added to the AuxList, and the control will use the default colors. If SetCtlColor is used with a different color set of a control, a new AuxList will be allocated and added to the head of the list. The CloseControl routine disposes of the AuxCtlRec.

Often a new control is created from a 'CNTL' resource, using GetNewControl. A new AuxRec is allocated if the resource file contains a 'cctb' resource type with the same resource ID as the 'CNTL' resource. Otherwise, the default colors are used.

The Control Manager supports controls that have color tables with more than four elements. To create a control with more than four colors, you must create a custom 'CDEF' that can access a larger color table. The interpretation of the partIdentifiers is determined by the 'CDEF'. If your application includes a 'CDEF' that recognizes more than four partIdentifiers, it should use partIdentifiers 0–3 in the same way as the standard control defprocs. An application with a custom 'CDEF" should use the _SysEnvirons routine upon entry to the defproc to determine the configuration of the system.

THE CONTROL COLOR TABLE RESOURCE

The system default control colors are stored in the System file and ROMResources as 'cctb' resource = 0. By including a 'cctb' resource = 0 in your application, it is possible to change the default colors that will be used for all controls, unless a specific 'cctb' exists for a control defined within the application.

When you use GetNewControl for the control resource 'CNTL', GetNewControl will attempt to load a 'cctb' resource with the same ID as the 'CNTL' resource ID, if one is present. It then executes the SetCtlColor call.

The following part identifiers for control elements should be present in the ColorSpec.value field:

cFrameColor (0)	Frame color
cBodyColor (1)	Fill color for body of control
cTextColor (2)	Text color
cThumbColor (3)	Thumb color

These identifiers may be present in any order; for instance, the text or indicator color values may be stored before the fill and frame colors in the ColorSpec record structure. If a part identifier is not found, then the first color in the color table will be used.

CONTROL MANAGER ROUTINES

The following new Control Manager routines can be used as noted below for the Macintosh Plus, the Macintosh SE, and the Macintosh II.

```
FUNCTION GetCVariant (theControl: ControlHandle) : INTEGER;
      [Macintosh Plus, Macintosh SE, and Macintosh II]
```

The GetVariant function returns the variant control value for the control described by theControl. This value was formerly stored in the high four bits of the control defproc handle; for future compatibility, use the GetCVariant routine to access this value.

```
PROCEDURE SetCtlColor (theControl: ControlHandle; newColorTable:
      CCTabHandle); [Macintosh II]
```

The SetCtlColor procedure sets or modifies a control's color table. If the control currently has no auxiliary control record, a new one is created with the given color table and added to the head of the auxiliary control list. If there is already an auxiliary record for the control, its color table is replaced by the contents of newColorTable.

If newColorTable has the same contents as the default color table, the control's existing auxiliary record and color table are removed from the auxiliary control list and deallocated. If theControl = NIL, the operation modifies the default color table itself. If the control is visible, it will be redrawn by SetCtlColor using the new color table.

```
FUNCTION GetAuxCtl (theControl: ControlHandle; VAR acHndl:
      AuxCtlHndl) : BOOLEAN; [Macintosh II]
```

The GetAuxCtl function returns a handle to a control's color table:

- If the given control has its own color table, the function returns TRUE.
- If the control used the default color set, the function returns FALSE.
- If the control asked to receive the default color set (theControl = NIL), then the function returns TRUE.

SUMMARY OF THE CONTROL MANAGER

Constants

```
CONST
      cFrameColor =        0;
      cBodyColor  =        1;
      cTextColor  =        2;
      cThumbColor =        3;
```

Data Types

```
TYPE
  AuxCtlHandle = ^AuxCtlPtr;
  AuxCtlPtr    = ^AuxCtlRec;
  AuxCtlRec    = RECORD
                    acNext:      AuxCtlHandle;   {handle to next record }
                                                 { in list}
                    acOwner:     ControlHandle;  {handle to owning }
                                                 { control}
                    acCTable:    CCTabHandle;    {handle to control's }
                                                 { color table}
                    acFlags:     INTEGER;        {miscellaneous flags; }
                                                 { reserved}
                    acReserved:  LONGINT;        {reserved for future }
                                                 { expansion}
                    acRefCon:    LONGINT         {reserved for }
                                                 { application use}
                 END;

  CCTabHandle = ^CCTabPtr;
  CCTabPtr    = ^CtlCTab;
  CtlCTab     = RECORD
                   ccSeed:      LONGINT;   {not used for controls}
                   ccReserved:  INTEGER;   {not used for controls}
                   ctSize:      INTEGER;   {number of entries in table -1}
                   ctTable:     cSpecArray {array of ColorSpec records}
                END;
```

Routines

```
PROCEDURE SetCtlColor (theControl:  ControlHandle; newColorTable:
       CCTabHandle);
FUNCTION  GetAuxCtl (theControl:  ControlHandle; VAR acHndl:
       AuxWinHndl): BOOLEAN;
FUNCTION  GetCVariant (theControl: ControlHandle) : INTEGER;
```

Global Variables

AuxWinHead Contains a pointer to the linked list of auxiliary control records.

Assembly Language Information

```
;auxCtlRec structure

acnext        EQU    $0     ;[handle] next in chain
acOwner       EQU    $4     ;[ControlHandle] owner ID
acCTable      EQU    $8     ;[CTabHandle] color table
acFlags       EQU    $C     ;[word] miscellaneous flags
acReserved    EQU    $E     ;[LONGINT] for expansion
acRefCon      EQU    $18    ;[LONGINT] user constant
auxWinSize    EQU    $1C    ;size of record

; Equates for the colors of control parts

cFrameColor EQU       0
cBodyColor  EQU       1
cTextColor  EQU       2
cThumbColor EQU       3

; Global variable

AuxCtlHead  EQU    $0CD4   ;Control Aux List head
```

13 THE MENU MANAGER

ABOUT THIS CHAPTER

This chapter describes the enhancements to the Menu Manager for the Macintosh II. All changes are backward-compatible with the Macintosh Plus and the Macintosh SE, so your existing programs using Menu Manager routines will continue to work and produce the same screen display as before. All new features, except for color menus, will work on the Macintosh Plus and Macintosh SE using System 4.1 and later.

To best use the material presented in this chapter, you should be familiar with QuickDraw, and should also know how to use resources in your application programs.

For the Macintosh Plus, Macintosh SE, and Macintosh II, the new Menu Manager provides these features:

- Menus can include submenus. This feature is known as **hierarchical menus**. Hierarchical menu items have a small filled black triangle pointing to the right, indicating that a submenu exists.

- Pop-up menus are supported.

- Scrolling menus are marked with a filled black triangle indicator at the top or bottom of the menu, to indicate which direction the menu may scroll.

- Within menus, font names for international scripts are printed in the actual script rather than in the system font when the Script Manager is installed.

- A new definition procedure (defproc), called the Menu Bar Defproc, handles such functions as drawing the menu bar and saving and restoring bits behind a menu.

- It is now possible to determine if a user has chosen a disabled menu item.

For the Macintosh II, the new Menu Manager provides these features:

- Color can be added to menus. When the menu title is the appleMark, a color apple is displayed instead of the system font appleMark. Applications may provide additional colors in menus if desired.

A bug in the DrawMenuBar procedure has been fixed; formerly, DrawMenuBar would redraw incorrectly when a menu was highlighted. If your application called HiliteMenu or FlashMenuBar to correct this, the result will now be overcompensation, and the menu title will be unhighlighted. Another change overcomes a limitation in the original menu data structure; the EnableItem and DisableItem routines now refer to the menu title and the first 31 items only, and all items beyond 31 are always enabled.

The following sections define and describe the new hierarchical, pop-up, and color menus. The remainder of the chapter describes the data structures and routines used to implement the new Menu Manager features.

Hierarchical Menus

A **hierarchical menu** is a menu that includes, among its various menu choices, the ability to display a submenu. In most cases the submenu appears to the right of the menu item used to select it, and is marked with a filled triangle indicator. Throughout this chapter, there is a distinction made between a menu and a hierarchical menu. If the word *hierarchical* is not used, then the reference is to a nonhierarchical menu. At times, though, the term *normal* or *regular* menu may appear when referring to a nonhierarchical menu. The term *submenu* is used to describe any menu that is the "offspring" of a previous menu.

Several illustrations of hierarchical menus appear in the Macintosh User Interface Guidelines chapter, with recommendations for their use.

Pop-Up Menus

The PopUpMenuSelect routine allows an application to create a pop-up menu. A pop-up menu is one that isn't in the menu bar, but appears somewhere else on the screen (usually in a dialog box) when the user presses in a particular place. A pop-up menu may be colored like any other menu, and it may have submenus. Pop-up menus are typically used for lists of items, for example, a list of fonts. See the Macintosh User Interface Guidelines chapter for a more complete description of how to use pop-up menus in your application.

Color Menus

For the Macintosh II, color can be added to menus in video modes with a resolution of two bits or greater. Your application can specify the menu bar color, menu title colors, the background color of a pulled down menu, and a separate color for each menu item's mark, name, and command character. As the Macintosh II is shipped, the only user observable menu color is the color Apple symbol, which appears in the 4-bit and 8-bit modes. If the menu title is the appleMark (a one-character string containing the appleMark character $14) the color Apple symbol appears instead of the system font appleMark.

Multicolor menus should be used with discretion: user testing has shown that the use of many arbitrary colors can cause user confusion and slow down menu item recognition. See the Macintosh User Interface Guidelines chapter for more information on using color in applications.

The user can specify system-wide menu colors along with a colored desktop pattern with the Control Panel, and applications should avoid overriding the user choices. The system-wide menu colors are specified in the 'mctb' resource = 0 in the System file, and include

- the menu bar color
- a default color for menu titles
- a default color for the background of a pulled-down menu
- a default color for menu items.

The user-specified default colors may be overridden by a separate 'mctb' resource = 0 in the application's resource file.

Of course, a user can also use a resource editor to completely color an application's menus by adding or changing its 'mctb' resource(s). If your application doesn't need color menus, it should not try to override the user's default color choices. However, if the application needs specific colors that might clash with a user's default choices, the user should be prompted for an alternate choice of colors. An application should only override a user's choices as a last resort; let the user's color preferences prevail.

MENU MANAGER DATA STRUCTURES

There are two existing Menu Manager data structures. The MenuList contains data describing which menus are in the menu bar. Each menu has a MenuInfo structure describing the items in that menu. For backward compatibility, the MenuInfo structure has not been changed, although several of its fields have new meanings for hierarchical menus. The MenuList has also kept its general structure to provide backward compatibility, and still contains six bytes of header information and six bytes of information for each menu; however, each menu entry is now allocated dynamically. There is also additional storage at the end of the MenuList for hierarchical and pop-up menus.

Except where explicitly noted, the data structures in this section are listed for information only; applications should never interrogate or change them directly. The Menu Manager routines provide all needed functions.

Data Structures for Hierarchical Menus

A new MenuList data structure accommodates hierarchical menus. It dynamically allocates storage space as menus and hierarchical menus are added and deleted.

> **Warning:** The MenuList data structure is listed for information only; applications should never access it directly.

The following TYPE definition is for conceptual purposes only; there is no such data structure in the Menu Manager:

```
TYPE InitialMenuList = RECORD
                    lastMenu:   INTEGER;  {offset}
                    lastRight:  INTEGER;  {pixels}
                    mbResID:    INTEGER;  {upper 13 bits used as }
                                          { mbarproc resource ID }
                                          { low 3 bits used as }
                                          { mbVariant }
                    lastHMenu:  INTEGER;  {offset}
```

```
menuTitleSave: pixMapHandle {handle to }
                            { bits behind inverted }
                            { menu title}
            END;
```

Field descriptions

lastMenu   The lastMenu field contains the offset to the last regular menu in the
                  MenuList.

lastRight   The lastRight field contains the pixel location of the right edge of the
                  rightmost menu in the menu bar.

mbResID   The mbResID field stores the resource ID of the menu bar defproc
                  used by the application. Its default value is zero. The upper 13 bits
                  are used as the resource ID. The low three bits are passed to the
                  menu bar defproc ('MBDF') as the mbVariant.

lastHMenu   The lastHMenu field contains the offset to the last hierarchical menu
                  in the MenuList.

menuTitleSave   The menuTitleSave field stores a PixMapHandle to the saved "bits
                  behind" the selected menu title.

When the MenuList data structure is initialized, there is no space allocated for menu handles
or hierarchical menu handles. When a menu is allocated, six bytes are inserted between the
mbResID and lastHMenu fields. As each menu is allocated or deleted, the space between
mbResID and lastHMenu grows or shrinks accordingly. Space is allocated for hierarchical
menus after the MenuTitleSave field, and its space is also dynamic.

A sample MenuList Data Structure with X menus and Y hierarchical menus appears below.

Warning: The sample MenuList structure is not a valid Pascal type because of its
dynamic size; it's shown for conceptual purposes only.

```
TYPE MenuRec = RECORD
                 menuOH:        Menuhandle; {menu's data}
                 menuLeft:      INTEGER;    {pixels}
               END;

     HMenuRec = RECORD
                 menuHOH:       Menuhandle; {hierarchical menu's }
                                            { data}
                 reserved:      INTEGER;    {reserved for future }
                                            { use}
               END;

     DynamicMenuList = RECORD
                 lastMenu:      INTEGER;    {offset}
```

```
                lastRight:      INTEGER;     {pixels}
                mbResID:        INTEGER;
                menu:           ARRAY [1..X] OF MenuRec;
                                             {X is the number of }
                                             { menus}
                lastHMenu:      INTEGER;     {offset}
                menuTitleSave: PixMapHandle {handle to bits behind }
                                             { inverted menu title}
                hMenu:          ARRAY [1..Y] OF HMenuRec;
                                             {Y is the number of }
                                             { submenus used}

                END;
```

The initial MenuList data structure is allocated by InitMenus each time an application is started. Any subsequent calls to InitMenus, while the application is running, don't cause the MenuList data structure to be reallocated.

The MenuInfo data structure is shown below; this version is similar to what is shown in Volume 1, but includes additional information about menu items.

Warning: The MenuInfo data structure is listed for information only; applications should never access it directly. This structure is not a valid Pascal type because of its dynamic size; it's shown for conceptual purposes only.

```
TYPE MenuInfo = RECORD
                menuID:         INTEGER;     {menu ID}
                menuWidth:      INTEGER;     {pixels}
                menuHeight:     INTEGER;     {pixels}
                menuProc:       Handle;      {handle}
                enableFlags:    LONGINT;     {bit string}
                menuTitle:      String;      {menu title name}
                itemData:       ARRAY [1..X] OF
                                itemString: string; {item name}
                                itemIcon:   BYTE;   {iconnum-256}
                                itemCmd:    char;   {item cmd key}
                                itemMark:   char;   {item mark is a }
                                                    { byte value }
                                                    { for hierachical }
                                                    { menus}
                                itemStyle:  Style;  {bit string}
                endMarker:      Byte;               {zero-length }
                                                    { string }
                                                    { indicates no }
                                                    { more menu items}

                END;
```

Field descriptions

menuID   The menuID field contains the menu ID of the menu.

menuWidth   The menuWidth field contains the width in pixels of the menu.

menuHeight The menuHeight field contains the height in pixels of the menu.

menuProc   The menuProc field contains a handle to the menu's definition procedure.

enableFlags The enableFlags field is a bit string which allows the menu and the first 31 items to be enabled or disabled. All items beyond 31 are always enabled.

menuTitle   The menuTitle field is a string containing the menu title.

itemData   The itemData field is an array containing the following information for each menu item: item name, item icon number, item command key equivalent, item mark, and item style. For hierarchical menus, the itemMark field is a byte value.

endMarker   The endMarker field is a byte value, which contains zero if there are no more menu items.

The contents of the itemData array are the same for hierarchical and nonhierarchical menus, but for hierarchical menus the itemMark field is a byte value, which limits hierarchical menu menuID values to between 0 and 255. Hierarchical menus numbered 236 to 255 are reserved for use by desk accessories. Desk accessories must remove their hierarchical menus from the MenuList each time their window is not the frontmost, to prevent hierarchical menu collisions with other desk accessories.

Color Menu Data Structures

For the Macintosh II, menus can be colored in 2-bit mode or higher, in both color and gray-scale. The menu color information is contained in a table format, but because this format is different from the standard color table format, it is referred to as the menu color information table, rather than the menu color table. A menu color information table is composed of several entries, each of which is an MCEntry record. These data structures are shown below:

```
TYPE MCEntryPtr = ^MCEntry;
    MCEntry    = RECORD
                    mctID:      INTEGER;    {menu ID. ID = 0 is }
                                            { the menu bar}
                    mctItem:    INTEGER;    {menu entry. Item = 0 }
                                            { is a title}
                    mctRGB1:    RGBColor;   {usage depends on ID }
                                            { and Item}
```

13 Menu Manager

```
                     mctRGB2:      RGBColor;   {usage depends on ID }
                                               { and Item}
                     mctRGB3:      RGBColor;   {usage depends on ID }
                                               { and Item}
                     mctRGB4:      RGBColor;   {usage depends on ID }
                                               { and Item}
                     mctReserved: INTEGER;     {reserved for internal }
                                               { use}
                END;

     MCTable      = ARRAY [0..0] of MCEntry; {The menu entries are }
                                             { represented in this }
                                             { array}
     MCTablePtr   = ^MCTable;
     MCTableHandle = ^MCTablePtr;
```

Field descriptions

mctID   The mctID field contains the menu ID of the menu. A value of
                 mctID = 0 means that this is the menu bar.

mctItem   The mctItem field contains the menu item. A value of item = 0
                 means that the item is a menu title.

mctRGB1   The mctRGB1 field contains a color value which depends on the
                 mctID and mctItem. See the description in the following section.

mctRGB2   The mctRGB2 field contains a color value which depends on the
                 mctID and mctItem. See the description in the following section.

mctRGB3   The mctRGB3 field contains a color value which depends on the
                 mctID and mctItem. See the description in the following section.

mctRGB4   The mctRGB4 field contains a color value which depends on the
                 mctID and mctItem. See the description in the following section.

mctReserved   The mctReserved field is used internally; applications must not use
                 this field.

The color information table is created at InitMenus time, and its handle is stored in the
global variable MenuCInfo ($D50). Like the MenuList data structure, it is only created the
first time InitMenus or InitProcMenu is called for an application.

A menu color information table is shown in Figure 1.

Menu Elements	Menu Color Table Entries						
	ID	Item	RGB1	RGB2	RGB3	RGB4	Reserved
menu bar	0	0	default title	default background	default items	bar color	reserved
title	N <> 0	0	title color	bar color	default items	background color	reserved
item	N <> 0	M <> 0	mark color	name color	command color	background color	reserved
last entry	-99	reserved	reserved	reserved	reserved	reserved	reserved

Figure 1. Menu Color Information Table

There is always at least one entry in the color table, the last entry, which has the arbitrary value –99 in the ID field as an "end-of-table" marker. (This means that the value –99 cannot be used as an ID by an application.) Note that the other fields in the "end-of-table" entry are reserved by use for Apple. Each entry in the color information table has seven fields.

The first two fields define the entry's menu and item. The last field is used internally and has no information for use by programmers. The other fields define colors depending on what type of menu element the entry describes. All colors are specified as RGB colors. There are three types of entries in the menu color information table: one type for the menu bar, one type for menu titles, and one type for menu items.

The **menu bar entry** has ID = 0, Item = 0. There will be at most one menu bar entry in the color information table. If there is no menu bar entry, the default menu bar colors are black text on a white background. The fields in a menu bar entry are as follows:

- mctRGB1 is the default color for menu titles. If a menu title doesn't have an entry in the table, then this is the color used to draw the title.

- mctRGB2 is the default color for the background of a pulled down menu. If a menu title doesn't have an entry in the table, this color is used as the menu's background color.

- mctRGB3 is the default color for the items in a pulled down menu. If a menu item doesn't have an entry in a table, and if the title for that menu item doesn't also have an entry, this color will be used to color the mark, name, and Command-key equivalent of the item.

- mctRGB4 is the menu bar color.

The **menu title entry** has ID <> 0, Item = 0. There will be at most one title entry for each menu in the color information table. If there is no title entry, the title, menu background, and menu items are drawn using the defaults found in the menu bar entry. If there is no menu bar entry, the default colors are black on white. The fields in a title entry areas follows:

■ mctRGBG1 is the title color.

■ mctRGB2 is the menu bar color. This is duplicated here from the menu bar entry to speed menu drawing.

■ mctRGB3 is the default color for the menu items. If a menu item doesn't have an entry in the table, this color will be used to color the mark, name, and Command-key equivalent of the item.

■ mctRGB4 is the menu's background color.

The **menu item entry** has ID <> 0, Item <> 0. There will be at most one item entry for each menu item in the color information table. If there is no entry for a particular item, the item mark, name, and Command-key equivalent are drawn using the defaults found in the title entry. If there is no title entry, the information in the menu bar entry is used. If there is no menu bar entry, the mark, name, and Command-key equivalent are drawn in black. The fields in an item entry are as follows:

■ mctRGB1 is the mark color.

■ mctRGB2 is the name color.

■ mctRGB3 is the Command-key equivalent.

■ mctRGB4 is the menu's background color. It's duplicated here to speed menu drawing.

It's not possible to specify an icon's color. Black and white icons are drawn in the item's name color. Icons may be colored using a 'cicn' resource instead of an 'ICON' resource. When an icon is drawn in a menu, the menu defproc attempts to load the 'cicn' resource first, and if it isn't found, searches for the 'ICON' resource. The menu defproc checks a color icon's size, and won't display it if it's larger than 32-by-32. See the QuickDraw chapter for more information on color icons.

Menu Color Information Table Resource Format

The resource type for a menu color information table is 'mctb'. Once read into memory, this data is transferred into the application's menu color information table. The resource data format is identical to an MCTable, with the addition of a leading word that contains the number of entries in the resource:

```
TYPE MenuCRsrc = RECORD
    numEntries: integer;
    data:        array [1..numEntries] of MCEntry;
    END;
```

The 'mctb' resource is loaded automatically by two routines. InitMenus attempts to load an 'mctb' resource = 0, and if it is successful, adds the colors to the application's menu color information table. GetMenu attempts to load an 'mctb' resource with the same resource ID as the menu it has loaded, and if it succeeds, it adds the colors to the application's menu color information table.

USING THE MENU MANAGER

This section describes how to use the new Menu Manager routines implemented for the Macintosh Plus, Macintosh SE, and Macintosh II. It also explains how changes to previously existing routines affect Menu Manager functions. Several of the new features and calls have interesting side effects that aren't immediately obvious. If your application is running on a machine that can only produce a black-and-white display, any color information is ignored, and color icons won't be displayed.

Enable and Disable

The EnableItem and DisableItem routines have been changed so that they affect only the menu and the first 31 items. All items beyond 31 are always enabled. The DrawMenuBar routine properly highlights the selected menu title, if one exists.

When a user chooses a disabled menu item—that is, when the mouse-up event occurs over a disabled item—MenuSelect returns a zero result. In the past, there was no way for an application to determine which disabled item was chosen. A new routine, MenuChoice, can now be called after MenuSelect returns a zero result, to determine if the mouse was over a disabled item, and if so, what were the menu ID and item number.

Fonts

The AddResMenu and InsertResMenu routines can recognize when an added 'FONT' or 'FOND' resource is the name of an International font. If the Script Manager is installed, the font name will be displayed in the actual script. GetItemIcon may be used to determine the script number of a font item that names an International script. SetItemIcon should never be called for font items that are International scripts.

Custom Menu Bars

You should only use the InitProcMenu routine if your application has a custom menu bar defproc. The effect of this routine lasts for the duration of the application program only, and the default menu bar defproc is used afterwards.

Highlighting

Menu highlighting has been modified, and this affects the MenuSelect, MenuKey, HiliteMenu, and FlashMenuBar routines. Previously, a menu title was selected by inverting the rectangle that contained the menu title; when the menu became deselected, the same rectangle was merely inverted again, returning the title to its original state. This menu title inversion was changed for color menus. In the color world, it is no longer proper to merely invert the title's rectangle. Color inversion often produces unpleasing and/or unreadable results. Your application should set the foreground and background colors before drawing a selected menu, and then reset the foreground and background colors before drawing the deselected (i.e., normal) menu. One important result of this new highlighting scheme is that only one menu may be highlighted at a time.

Hierarchical and Pop-up Menus

Using hierarchical menus in an application is straightforward. Hierarchical menus may be stored as 'MENU' resources, just as regular menus are. To specify that a particular menu is hierarchical, pass a "beforeID" of –1 to the InsertMenu routine. When InsertMenu gets a –1, it places the menu in the hierarchical portion of the MenuList. Pop-up menus are also stored in the hierarchical portion of the MenuList, and like hierarchical menus, are specified by passing a "beforeID" of –1 to InsertMenu. DeleteMenu may be used to remove a hierarchical or pop-up menu from the MenuList.

A submenu is associated with a menu item by reusing two of the fields in the MenuInfo data structure. When the itemCmd field has the hex value $1B, the itemMark field contains the menuID of the associated hierarchical menu. (These two fields are used because an item with a submenu never has a check mark, and doesn't have a Command-key equivalent.)

The itemMark field is a byte value, which limits hierarchical menu menuIDs to values between 0 and 255. The menuIDs 0–235 (inclusive) may be used by applications; numbers 236–255 are reserved for desk accessories.

Because there is no way to arbitrate among desk accessories, each desk accessory is responsible for inserting its hierarchical menus when it becomes active, and deleting them when it is deactivated. The problem with this scheme is that some desk accessories, such as a spelling checker, need to be activated all the time; this kind of desk accessory can't use hierarchical menus, since it has no way to determine when it should add or delete its menus.

Attaching a submenu to a menu item is done in one of two ways. One way is to place a $1B in the Command-key equivalent byte in the 'MENU' resource. To specify which hierarchical menu is the submenu, the hierarchical menu's resource ID is placed in the character mark byte in the 'MENU' resource.

The other way to attach a submenu to a menu item is to call AppendMenu or InsMenuItem.The value $1B may be placed after the Command key metacharacter (/) to signify that an item has a submenu. The value of the character following the mark metacharacter (!) is taken as the menu ID of the submenu.

The MenuKey routine has been modified to search for Command-key equivalents in hierarchical menus. To accomodate future extensions to the Menu Manager, the Command key values $1B (Control-[ ) through $1F (Control-_) are reserved for use by Apple Computer. The MenuKey procedure ignores these five values as Command-key equivalents. Until the Apple Standard Keyboard was implemented, it was impossible for the user to type a Control-key sequence, so reserving these five values will not impose limitations on existing applications.

Two new procedures, GetItemCmd and SetItemCmd, have been included to facilitate hierarchical menu manipulation. GetItemCmd can be used to determine if a menu item has a submenu attached. SetItemCmd can be used to attach a submenu to a menu item. GetItemMark can be used to determine the ID of the hierarchical menu associated with an item. SetItemMark can be used to change the ID of the hierarchical menu associated with an item. The GetMHandle routine can be used to get a menu handle for a menu, pop-up menu, or hierarchical menu.

Color

A number of existing routines have been modified for color menus; these changes affect only the Macintosh II. The InitMenus routine attempts to load a menu color resource, 'mctb' resource = 0, and if it succeeds, stores those colors in the application's menu color information table. This allows the user to specify a set of menu colors that will exist across all applications.

Calling the GetMenu, GetMenuBar, SetMenuBar, and GetNewMBar routines affects the menu color information table. Clear MenuBar disposes both the current MenuList and the current menu color information table.

GetMenu has been modified: it looks for a 'MENU' resource with the resource ID equal to the parameter "menuID" and returns a handle to the menu. It also looks for a 'mctb' resource with the resource ID equal to the parameter "menuID", and if one is found, adds the colors to the current menu color information table. DeleteMenu removes all entries from the menu color information table for the menuID specified.

A set of new routines provides access to the menu color information table. SetMCEntries allows an application to add new menu colors and GetMCEntry allows the application to query a particular menu color. DelMCEntries deletes specified menu color information table entries.

GetMCInfo makes a copy of the current menu color information table, and returns a handle to the copy. While GetMenuBar returns the handle to the current MenuList, you must also call GetMCInfo if you want the handle to the current menu color information table.

SetMCInfo copies a table of menu color entries into the current table, after first disposing of the current table; this routine can be used to set a new menu color information table, or restore a table previously saved by GetMCInfo. SetMenuBar first disposes of the current MenuList, then makes a copy of the MenuList passed as a parameter and makes it the current MenuList. If you also want to set the menu color information table, your application must call SetMCInfo.

GetNewMBar first calls GetMenuBar to store the current MenuList. Next, it calls ClearMenuBar, thus disposing of the current MenuList as well as the current menu color information table. Then it calls GetMenu and InsertMenu for every menu in the menu bar. This builds not only a new MenuList, but a new menu color information table. Finally, GetNewMBar restores the old MenuList by calling SetMenuBar. Notice that it doesn't store

13 Menu Manager

the current menu color information table before it begins, nor does it restore it upon leaving. Applications should bracket a call to GetNewMBar with calls to GetMCInfo and SetMCInfo, as shown in the following example:

```
CurMCTable := GetMCInfo;            {save current menu color info }
                                    { table}
NewMenuBar := GetNewMenuBar(4);     {get new menu bar #4}
NewMCTable := GetMCInfo;            {get new menu color info table}
SetMCInfo (CurMCTable);             {restore previous menu color info }
                                    { table}
```

MENU MANAGER ROUTINES

The Menu Manager routines listed in the following sections are implemented for the Macintosh Plus, Macintosh SE, and Macintosh II where noted.

New Menu Manager Routines

PROCEDURE InitProcMenu (mbResID: INTEGER); [Macintosh Plus, Macintosh SE, Macintosh II]

> **Note:** The mbVariant field is contained in the low three bits of the mbResID. The high order 13 bits are used to load the proper 'MBDF'.

The InitProcMenu routine is called when an application has a custom menu bar defproc, 'MBDF'. InitProcMenu allocates a new MenuList if it hasn't already been allocated by a previous call to InitMenus, and the mbResID is stored in the mbResID field in the MenuList (note that InitWindows calls InitMenus, so that it can obtain the menu bar height).

The effect of InitProcMenu lasts for the duration of the application only; the next InitMenus call will replace the mbResID field in the MenuList with the default value of zero. This affects applications such as development systems, which use multiple heaps and whose "applications" call InitMenus.

> **Note:** Apple reserves mbResID values $000–$100 for its own use.

PROCEDURE DelMCEntries (MenuID, menuItem: INTEGER); [Macintosh II]

The DelMCEntries routine deletes entries from the menu color information table based on the given menuID and menuItem. If the entry is not found, no entry is removed. If the menuItem is mctAllItems (–98), then all Items for the specified ID are removed.

Applications must, of course, never delete the last entry in the menu color information table.

FUNCTION GetMCInfo: MCTableHandle; [Macintosh II]

The GetMCInfo routine creates a copy of the current menu color information table and returns a handle to the copy. It doesn't affect the current menu color information table. If the copy fails, a NIL handle is returned.

PROCEDURE SetMCInfo (menuCTbl : MCTableHandle); [Macintosh II]

The SetMCInfo routine copies the given menu color information table to the current menu color information table. It first disposes of the current menu color information table, so your application shouldn't explicitly dispose the current table. If the copy fails, the global variable MemErr contains the error code, and the procedure doesn't dispose the current menu color information table. Applications should call the MemError function to determine if this call failed.

You can use this procedure to restore a menu color information table previously saved by GetMCInfo. Be sure to call DrawMenuBar to update the menu bar if a new menu bar color or menu title colors have been specified.

PROCEDURE DispMCInfo (menuCTbl : MCTableHandle); [Macintosh II]

Given a handle to a menu color information table, the DispMCInfo routine disposes of the table. No checking is done to determine whether the handle is valid. While this procedure currently only calls DisposHandle, to ensure compatibility with any updates to the color portion of the menu manager, it's a good idea to use this call.

FUNCTION GetMCEntry (menuID, menuItem : INTEGER): MCEntryPtr;
        [Macintosh II]

The GetMCEntry routine finds the entry of the specified menuID and menuItem in the menu color information table, and returns a pointer into the table. If the entry is not found, a NIL pointer is returned.

Note: Entries are not removed from the table. Applications must not remove entries from the table directly; they should always use the procedure DelMCEntries to remove entries.

Warning: The menu color information table is relocatable, so the GetMCEntry return value may not be valid across traps that move or purge memory. Applications should make a copy of the record in this case.

PROCEDURE SetMCEntries (numEntries: INTEGER; menuCEntries:
        MCTablePtr); [Macintosh II]

The SetMCEntries procedure takes a pointer to an array of color information records. The array may be of any size, so it's necessary to also pass the number of entries in the array.

The ID and Item of each entry in the color information record array are checked to see if the entry already exists in the menu color information table. If it exists, the information in the entry is used to update the entry in the color table. If the entry doesn't exist in the color information table, the entry is added to the table.

> **Warning:** SetMCEntries makes memory management calls that may move or purge memory; therefore the array menuCEntries should be nonrelocatable for the duration of this call.

```
FUNCTION MenuChoice : LONGINT;  [Macintosh II]
```

The MenuChoice routine is called only after the result from MenuSelect is zero. It determines if the mouse-up event that terminated MenuSelect was in a disabled menu item. When the mouse button is released over a disabled item in an application menu, MenuChoice returns a long integer whose high-order word is the menuID of the menu, and whose low-order word is the menu item number for the disabled item "chosen". If the item number is zero, then the mouse-up event occurred when the mouse was either in the menu title or completely outside the menu; there is no way to distinguish between the two.

> **Note:** This information is available on the Macintosh Plus and Macintosh SE by directly querying the long word stored in the global variable MenuDisable ($B54).

This feature has been added to MenuChoice to make it possible for applications to provide better help facilities. For example, when the Finder calls MenuChoice, and determines that a user has chosen the disabled menu item "Empty Trash" with the Finder, the application could display a message telling the user that it can't empty the trash because there is nothing currently in the trash.

The new MenuChoice capability is implemented by continual updates of the global variable MenuDisable ($B54) whenever a menu is down. As the mouse moves over each item, MenuDisable is updated to reflect the current menu and item ID. The code that changes the value in MenuDisable resides in the standard menu defproc. The return value is undefined when the menu uses a custom menu defproc, unless the custom defproc also supports this feature.

```
PROCEDURE GetItemCmd (theMenu: menuHandle; item:INTEGER; VAR
        cmdChar:Char);  [Macintosh Plus, Macintosh SE, Macintosh II]
```

The GetItemCmd routine may be used to determine whether a menu item has a submenu attached. For a menu item with a submenu, the returned cmdChar will have the value $1B.

```
PROCEDURE SetItemCmd (theMenu: menuHandle; item:INTEGER;
        cmdChar:Char);   [Macintosh Plus, Macintosh SE, Macintosh II]
```

The SetItemCmd routine allows the application to attach a submenu to a menu by passing the character $1B. You should be careful about arbitrarily adding or removing a submenu from a menu item; see the Macintosh User Interface Guidelines chapter for recommendations. Notice that SetItemMark can be used to change the ID of the submenu that is associated with the menu item.

> **Note**: SetItemCmd must never be used to change the Command-key value of a menu item that doesn't have a submenu; users must always be free to change their Command-key preferences.

```
FUNCTION PopUpMenuSelect (theMenu:menuHandle;
        Top,Left,PopUpItem:INTEGER): LONGINT;    [Macintosh Plus,
        Macintosh SE, Macintosh II]
```

The PopUpMenuSelect routine allows an application to create a pop-up menu anywhere on the screen. This menu may be colored like any other menu, and it may have submenus. The return value is the same as that for MenuSelect, where the low word is the menu item selected, and the high word is the menu ID. Unlike MenuSelect, PopUpMenuSelect doesn't highlight any of the menus in the menu bar, so HiliteMenu(0) doesn't have to be called after completing the chosen task.

Pop-up menus are typically used for lists of items, for example, fonts. See the Macintosh User Interface Guidelines chapter for a description of how to use pop-up menus in your application. See MenuSelect for information about the return value when the menu chosen is a hierarchical menu.

TheMenu is a handle to the menu that you want "popped up". The PopUpItem is typically the currently selected item, that is, the last item selected, or the first item if nothing was selected. Doing this allows the user to click on a pop-up menu and release again quickly, without changing the item selection by mistake. The parameters Top and Left define where the top left corner of the PopUpItem is to appear, in global coordinates. Typically, these will be the top left coordinates of the pop-up box, so that the menu item appears on top of the pop-up box. See Figure 2 for an example.

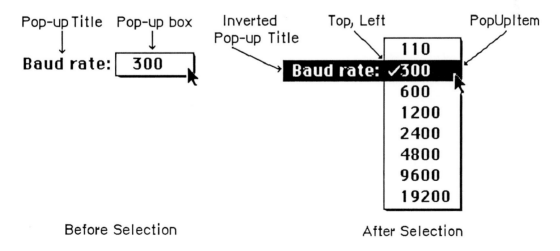

Figure 2. Pop-up Box Parameters

Drawing the Pop-Up Box

Your application is responsible for drawing the pop-up box. A pop-up box is a rectangle that is the same height as the menu item, is wide enough to show the currently selected item, and has a one-pixel-wide drop shadow.

The pop-up box must be the same height as a menu item so that when the menu appears, the cursor will be in the previously chosen item. If the pop-up box is too tall, the user could click once quickly in a pop-up box and unintentionally choose a different menu item. The height of a menu item in the system font is the ascent + descent + leading.

The pop-up box has a title to its left. The application is responsible for recognizing a mouse-down event in the pop-up box, and highlighting the title to the left of the pop-up menu box before calling MenuSelect. Similarly, the application is responsible for highlighting the title if the pop-up menu has Command-key equivalents.

Before calling PopUpMenuSelect, the pop-up menu must be installed in the hierarchical portion of the MenuList by passing a value of –1 as the "beforeID" to InsertMenu.

The following is a sample psuedocode stub that might be used to track a pop-up menu:

```
if mouse is in popUpMenuRect then
   myInvertPopUpTitle();                {invert title of pop-up menu}
   InsertMenu(popupMenuHandle, -1);     {-1 means hierarchical menu}
   Result = PopUpMenuSelect(popUpMenuHandle, popUpRect.Top,
                            popUpRect.Left, lastItemSelected);
   DeleteMenu(popUpMenuID);
   myInvertPopUpTitle();                {return pop-up title to normal}
endif
```

Notice that PopUpMenuSelect's sole function is to display the pop-up menu and track the mouse during a mouse-down event. It is the application's responsibility to handle all other pop-up menu functions, such as drawing the pop-up box, drawing and highlighting the title, and changing the entry in the pop-up box after an item has been chosen from the pop-up menu. This could all be handled by creating a pop-up menu control within the application.

When calling PopUpMenuSelect, the pop-up menu must be in the MenuList for the duration of the call. The code above shows a call the InsertMenu before, and a call to DeleteMenu after, the call to PopUpMenuSelect. The InsertMenu must be used at some time before the call to PopUpMenuSelect, but it's not necessary to call DeleteMenu immediately afterwards; the pop-up menu may be left in the MenuList if desired.

Pop-up menu items can have Command-key equivalents. The application must provide sufficient visual feedback, normally provided by using MenuKey, by inverting the pop-up title.

Changes to Existing Routines

PROCEDURE InitMenus;

The InitMenus routine now allocates a dynamic MenuList structure with no menus or hierarchical menus. After allocating the initial MenuList, it attempts to load an 'mctb' resource = 0. If the user has chosen default menu color values, this 'mctb' resource = 0 will exist in the System file. If the 'mctb' is loaded, the information contained in the resource is added to the menu color information table by making a call to SetMCEntries. If there is an 'mctb' resource = 0 among the application's resources, this will be loaded instead of the default 'mctb' in the System file.

FUNCTION GetMenu (resourceID: INTEGER) : MenuHandle;

After loading a 'MENU' resource, GetMenu attempts to load an 'mctb' resource with the same resource ID. If an 'mctb' is loaded, all of the entries are added to the application's menu color information table by making a call to SetMCEntries.

PROCEDURE AppendMenu (theMenu: MenuHandle; data: Str255);

PROCEDURE InsNewItem (theMenu: MenuHandle; itemString: Str255;
        afterItem);

When adding an item to a menu using the AppendMenu or InsMenuItem routines, a submenu may be attached to the item by using $1B as the command character, and the menu ID of the attached submenu as the mark character.

PROCEDURE AddResMenu (theMenu: MenuHandle; theType: ResType);

PROCEDURE InsertResMenu (theMenu: MenuHandle; theType: ResType;
        afterItem: INTEGER);

When AddResMenu or InsertResMenu is called for 'FONT' or 'FOND' resources, special processing occurs for fontNumbers greater than or equal to $4000, as is the case for international fonts. If the script associated with the font is currently active, then the ItemCmd and ItemIcon fields are used to store information allowing the font names to be displayed in the correct script.

There is a known problem with the AddResMenu and InsertResMenu routines, and with the menu enable flags, when the number of items is greater than 31. Applications should explicitly reenable or redisable all items after calling AddResMenu or InsertResMenu. This is because only the first 31 items are affected by the enable flags: all items 32 and greater are always enabled.

```
PROCEDURE InsertMenu (theMenu:  MenuHandle; beforeID:  INTEGER);
```

The InsertMenu routine can be used to add a hierarchical menu to the Menulist. If beforeID is equal to –1, the menu is a hierarchical menu. If beforeID is greater than or equal to zero, the menu is a nonhierarchical menu.

It isn't necessary for every menu in the hierarchical menu portion of the MenuList to be currently in use; that is, attached to a menu item. Hierarchical menus that are currently unused, but may be used some time later by the application, may be stored there, and attached to menu items only as needed. You should realize that this can cause problems if the unattached submenus have items with Command-key equivalents, because MenuKey will find these equivalents even though the menu is unattached.

```
PROCEDURE DrawMenuBar;
```

The warning about DrawMenuBar in Volume I is no longer true; DrawMenuBar now properly highlights the selected menu title, if there is one. If your application program assumed that DrawMenuBar would redraw the menu incorrectly, and called HiliteMenu or FlashMenuBar to compensate, what happens now is that the menu bar is redrawn properly, and the next call to HiliteMenu or FlashMenuBar causes the highlighted title to become unhighlighted.

```
PROCEDURE DeleteMenu (menuID:  INTEGER);
```

The DeleteMenu routine removes all color entries from the menu color information table for the specified menuID. It first checks the hierarchical portion of the MenuList for the menuID and, if it finds it, deletes the menu; it then returns. If the menu is not found in the hierarchical portion of the MenuList, the regular portion is checked.

The hierarchical portion of the MenuList is always checked first, so that any desk accessories whose hierarchical menu IDs conflict with an application's regular menu IDs can call DeleteMenu without deleting the application's menus.

```
PROCEDURE DelMenuItem (menuItemID:  INTEGER);
```

DelMenuItem removes the item's color entry from the menu color information table, and then deletes the item.

```
FUNCTION MenuSelect (startPt:  Point) :  LONGINT;
```

If the user chooses an item with a submenu, MenuSelect returns zero, meaning that no item was selected. If the user selects an item from a hierarchical menu, the menuID of the hierarchical menu and the menuItem of the item chosen are returned, just as though the item had been in a regular menu.

If MenuSelect returns zero, an application may call MenuChoice to determine whether the mouse was released over either a disabled menu item or an item with a submenu.

Note: The global variable TheMenu contains the ID of the highlighted menu in the menu bar. If an item from a hierarchical menu is chosen, TheMenu contains the ID of the "owner" menu, not the ID of the hierarchical menu.

```
FUNCTION MenuKey (ch:  CHAR) :  LONGINT;
```

The MenuKey routine first searches for the given key in the regular portion of the MenuList, and if it doesn't find it there, searches for the key in the hierarchical portion of the MenuList. If the key is in a hierarchical menu, MenuKey highlights the menu title of the menu that "owns" the hierarchical menu. Ownership in this case means the menu in the menu bar that the user would first encounter on the way to the item with the given Command-key equivalent. Because several levels of hierarchy are possible, this traversal may not always be obvious to the user. As before, after performing the chosen task, your application should call HiliteMenu(0) to remove the highlighting from the menu title.

Note: The Command-key codes $1B (Control-[ ) through $1F (Control- _) are reserved by Apple Computer to indicate meanings other than Command-key equivalents. These key codes are ignored by MenuKey, and a result of zero is always returned. Applications must never use these codes for their own use.

The global variable TheMenu contains the ID of the highlighted menu in the menu bar. If an item from a hierarchical menu is chosen, TheMenu contains the ID of the "owner" menu, not the ID of the hierarchical menu.

It's possible, although undesirable, to define so-called "circular" hierarchical menus. A circular hierarchical menu is one in which a submenu has an "ancestor" that is also one of its "offspring". If MenuKey detects circular hierarchical menus, a SysError = 86 = #DSHMenuFndErr is generated.

```
PROCEDURE HiliteMenu (menuID:  INTEGER);
```

Previously, highlighting a menu title meant inverting the title rectangle, and dehighlighting it meant reinverting it, so that it returned to normal. With color titles, color inversion is usually aesthetically unacceptable, so there is a need to draw the highlighted menu title.

HiliteMenu begins by restoring the bits behind the currently highlighted title (if there is one). It then saves the bits behind the title rectangle, and draws the highlighted title. HiliteMenu(0) dehighlights the currently highlighted menu by restoring the bits behind the title.

Note: Because an application can only save the bits behind the menu title, only one menu title can be highlighted at a time.

```
PROCEDURE DisableItem (theMenu:  MenuHandle; item:  INTEGER);
PROCEDURE EnableItem (theMenu:  MenuHandle; item:  INTEGER);
```

The EnableItem and DisableItem routines provide enable flags that can handle the title and 31 menu items. All items greater than 31 will be ignored by these calls and will always be enabled.

```
PROCEDURE SetItemMark (theMenu:  MenuHandle; item:  INTEGER;
        markChar:  CHAR);
```

The SetItemMark procedure allows the application to change the submenu associated with a menu item.

```
PROCEDURE GetItemMark (theMenu:  MenuHandle; item:  INTEGER; VAR
        markChar:  CHAR);
```

The GetItemMark procedure may be used to determine the ID of the hierarchical menu associated with a menu item.

```
PROCEDURE SetItemIcon (theMenu:  MenuHandle; item:  INTEGER; icon:
        Byte);
```

The SetItemIcon procedure should never be called for font items that are international scripts, unless the intention is to change the script number (there should never be any need to do this).

```
PROCEDURE GetItemIcon (theMenu:  MenuHandle; item:  INTEGER; VAR
        icon:  Byte);
```

The GetItemIcon procedure may be used to determine the script number of a font item that is the name of an international script.

```
FUNCTION GetMHandle (menuID:  INTEGER) :  MenuHandle;
```

The GetMHandle routine looks for the menu in the hierarchical portion of the MenuList first, and if it isn't found, looks in the regular portion of the MenuList. The routine has no way to determine whether the returned menu is associated with a menu, pop-up, or hierarchical menu. Presumably the application will contain that information.

```
PROCEDURE FlashMenuBar (menuID:  INTEGER);
```

FlashMenuBar(0) still inverts the complete menu bar. Strange colors may result if HiliteMenu, or FlashMenuBar with a nonzero parameter, are called while the menu bar is inverted.

FlashMenuBar has been modified so that only one menu may be highlighted at a time (see HiliteMenu). If no menu is currently highlighted, calling FlashMenuBar with a nonzero parameter highlights that menu. If the highlighted menu is different than the one being "flashed", the previously highlighted menu is first restored to normal, and the new menu is highlighted.

```
PROCEDURE ClearMenuBar (menuID:  INTEGER);
```

ClearMenuBar clears both the MenuList and the application's menu color information table.

```
FUNCTION GetNewMBar (menuID:  INTEGER): Handle;
```

GetNewMBar begins by calling ClearMenuBar, which clears both the MenuList and the application's menu color information table. Before returning the Handle to the new MenuList, it restores the previous MenuList. It doesn't restore the previous menu color information table. If that is desired, the application must use GetMCInfo before calling GetNewMBar, and call SetMCInfo afterwards.

```
PROCEDURE GetItemStyle (theMenu: MenuHandle; item: INTEGER; VAR
        chStyle: Style);
```

There is a possible bug in this routine, depending on the interpretation of the address of the VAR parameter chStyle. GetItemStyle assumes that the address on the stack points to a word with chStyle in the low byte. MPW Pascal passes the byte address of chStyle regardless of whether it's in the high or low byte of a word. Since there has never been a bug report for this "problem", it is listed here for information only.

THE STANDARD MENU DEFINITION PROCEDURE

This section describes changes made to the default menu definition procedure 'MDEF' resource = 0, for all Macintoshes except the 64K and 512K versions. The 'MDEF' resource has been modified to ignore all undefined messages. Any custom 'MDEF' should do the same. This allows Apple to define new messages (as described below for pop-up menus) without impacting custom 'MDEF' resources. Apple recognizes that applications may want to call their custom defprocs for information, and has reserved all messages above and including 128 for application use. Apple's defprocs will ignore all messages above and including 128.

For the latest standard 'MDEF', the version number = 10. Version 10 and all later versions include the features listed below.

For hierarchical menus:

- The triangular marker indicating that an item has a submenu appears in the location where the Command-key equivalent is normally shown.

- The Command-key values $1B (Control-[ ) through $1F (Control-_) are reserved by Apple to have meanings other than command keys.

For scrolling menus:

- When a menu is scrollable, scrolling indicators appear. If the menu scrolls up, a triangular indicator appears in place of the last item in the list, and if the menu scrolls down, an indicator appears in place of the first item in the list. The menu scrolls when the cursor is moved into the area of the indicator, or is directly above or below the menu.

For pop-up menus:

- A new message has been added to the standard 'MDEF' resource. Message #3, pop-up menu placement, asks the defproc to calculate the menu rectangle of the pop-up menu.

Parameter	On Entry	Return Value
message	3	
theMenu	menuHandle	
menuRect		Pop-up menu's rectangle
hitPt	Top left of PopupItem	
whichItem	PopupItem	Top of menu if menu scrolls

When a pop-up menu appears, the menu is adjusted on the screen so that the previously selected item appears on top of the pop-up menu box. The previously selected item is passed in the parameter whichItem, and the top left corner of the pop-up menu box is passed in hitPt. On exit, the rectangle in which the pop-up menu is to appear is returned in menuRect. If the menu is so large that it scrolls, then the actual top of the menu is returned in whichItem.

■ When a defproc draws a pop-up menu, its scrolling information must be placed in the global variables TopMenuItem and AtMenuBottom.

For color menus (Macintosh II only):

■ When menu items are drawn, the background of the menu has already been erased to the color specified for that menu in the menu color information table, or to white if none is specified. When the mark, item, and Command-key equivalent fields are drawn, the menu defproc checks the menu color information table for the colors to use. If there is an item entry, those colors are used. If there is no item entry, then the default from the title entry is used. If there is no title entry, then the default from the menu bar entry is used. If there is no menu bar entry, then black on white is used.

■ When an item is chosen, the background color and the item color are reversed, and the item is redrawn in those colors. When an item is chosen, the background color and item color are reset, and the item is redrawn in those colors.

■ If your application uses the standard menu bar defproc to draw menu items into menus after saving the bits behind and drawing the drop shadow, it must erase the menu's background to the correct color. If this isn't done when the user has set default menu colors, incorrect colors and unreadable items can result.

■ Custom menu defprocs that use color items must provide the menu background color. When the standard 'MBDF' clears the menu background and draws the drop shadow, it clears the menu background to whatever color is specified in the menu color information table. Custom menu defprocs should either (1) support color items by accessing the menu color information table or (2) erase the background of the menu to white before drawing color items.

All menus:

■ The menu defproc sets the global variable MenuDisable ($B54) each time a new item is highlighted. After MenuSelect returns a zero, your application can query MenuDisable directly, or use MenuChoice, to determine which menu ID and menu item were chosen.

■ The value returned by MenuChoice will be undefined if the last menu displayed has a custom 'MDEF'. When including a custom 'MDEF' in your application, you should consider supporting MenuChoice so that desk accessories providing on-line help for the application will be able to support all its menus.

■ Any application that uses the standard 'MDEF' to draw menu items must set the global variable TopMenuItem ($A0A). This variable is used by the standard 'MDEF' to determine if scrolling is necessary. If TopMenuItem isn't set properly, scrolling might occur when it shouldn't. TopMenuItem should contain global coordinates indicating where the first item in the menu is to be drawn; typically this is the same as the top of the menu rectangle. However, your application can use other coordinates if you don't want the first menu item to appear at the top of the menu rectangle.

THE STANDARD MENU BAR DEFINITION PROCEDURE

To give application writers more control over custom menus, a default menu bar definition procedure has been added. This section describes the default menu bar definition procedure ('MBDF' resource = 0). On the Macintosh II, the menu bar defproc provides support for color, pop-up, and hierarchical menus, as well as standard menus. This new defproc supplements the existing standard 'MDEF' resource.

All menu drawing-related activities, previously included in the routines DrawMenuBar, MenuSelect, MenuKey, HiliteMenu, and FlashMenuBar, have been removed from the menu manager code, and placed in the menu bar defproc. Using the menu bar defproc with the menu defproc gives the application writer complete control over the appearance and use of menus.

An application that specifies its own menu bar defproc should call InitProcMenu instead of InitMenus, which then loads the appropriate 'MBDF' resource.

There are currently 13 messages defined for the menu bar defproc:

Msg #	Msg	Description
0	Draw	Draws the menu bar or clears the menu bar.
1	Hit	Tests to see if the mouse is in the menu bar or any currently displayed menus.
2	Calc	Calculates the left edges of each menu title in the MenuList data structure.
3	Init	Initializes any menu bar defproc data structures.
4	Dispos	Disposes of any menu bar defproc data structures.
5	Hilite	Highlights the specified menu title, or inverts the whole menu bar.
6	Height	Returns the menu bar height.
7	Save	Saves the bits behind a menu and draws the menu structure.
8	Restor	Restores the bits behind a menu.
9	Rect	Calculates the rectangle of a menu.
10	SaveAlt	Saves more information about a menu after it has been drawn.
11	ResetAlt	Resets information about a menu.
12	MenuRgn	Returns a region for the menu bar.

Custom 'MBDF' defprocs should ignore messages that are not currently defined in this documentation. Messages numbered 128 and above are reserved for custom defprocs.

You may choose any name you wish for the menu bar defproc. The following example declares a menu bar defproc named MyMenuBar:

```
FUNCTION MyMenuBar ( selector: INTEGER;
        message: INTEGER;
        parameter1: INTEGER:
        parameter2: LONGINT): LONGINT;
```

Parameters for Menu Bar Defproc Messages

This section lists the parameters for each message. Note that the menu bar defproc draws directly into the window manager port, or color window manager port if there is one. Any time the menu bar defproc draws in the Window Manager port (or color port) it clips the port to full open before it returns. *Full open* is defined to be the portRect of the Window Manager, or the color Window Manager port. The exception to this rule is that the Draw message leaves the Window Manager port (or color port) clipped to the menu bar when parameter2 = –1. See the individual message descriptions for more information.

Message #0: Draw:

Called By	Selector	Parameter1	Parameter2	Result
Window Manager DrawMenuBar	mbVariant	none	–1 = clear bar 0 = draw bar	none

When parameter2 = 0 (zero), the menu bar is cleared to the proper color, the titles are drawn, and the window manager port clip region is set to full open. After all of the titles are drawn, if one of the titles is currently selected (its menuID is contained in the global variable TheMenu ($A26)), then the title is highlighted. DrawMenuBar passes parameter2 = 0.

When parameter2 = –1 the menu bar is cleared to the proper color, no titles are drawn, and the Window Manger port clip region is set to the menu bar. The Window Manager passes parameter2 = –1.

Message #1: Hit

Called By	Selector	Parameter1	Parameter2	Result
FindWindow	mbVariant	none	mouse pt	0 = in bar, no title hit
MenuSelect				–1 = not in bar <pos> = six-byte offset

The mouse point to be tested for its location is passed in parameter2. First this message checks to see whether the mouse point is in the menu bar. If it is in the menu bar, then the message further checks whether the mouse is in any menu title. If the mouse is in the menu bar but not in a title, the result is 0. If the mouse is in a title, the result is the offset of the title in the menuList. The notation <pos> refers to a result which is a positive value (greater than zero). A six-byte offset refers to the offset of a menu in the menuList data structure.

If the mouse is not in the menu bar, this message tests whether mouse point is in any currently visible menu. If more than one menu is visible—that is, one or more hierarchical menus are visible—the message searches through those menus backwards, checking the topmost hierarchical menu first. If the mouse pcint is found to be in a currently visible menu, the result is the six-byte offset of that menu in the menuList.

Message #2: Calc

Called By	Selector	Parameter1	Parameter2	Result
InsertMenu DeleteMenu	mbVariant	none	0 = all <pos> = six-byte offset	none

This message calculates the lastRight and menuLeft fields in the menuList. If parameter2 = 0 then the calculation is done for all of the menus. If parameter2 = the offset of a title in the menuList, then the calculation begins with that menu and continues for all following menus. A six-byte offset refers to the offset of a menu in the menuList data structure. The notation <pos> refers to a result which is a positive value (greater than zero).

Message #3: Init

Called By	Selector	Parameter1	Parameter2	Result
InitMenus InitProcMenu	mbVariant	none	none	none

This message creates a data structure in the system heap the first time it is called after system startup. It clears the field lastMBSave in that data structure at every call thereafter.

This message is called by InitProcMenu if the MenuList data structure hasn't been allocated. Applications that switch menu defprocs on the fly, and call InitProcMenu to do so, will need to call the 'MBDF' with the "Init" message to execute this message.

Message #4: Dispose

Called By	Selector	Parameter1	Parameter2	Result
—	mbVariant	none	none	none

Currently, this message does nothing.

Message #5: Hilite

Called By	Selector	Parameter1	Parameter2	Result
MenuSelect HiliteMenu FlashMenuBar	mbVariant	none	<packed>	none

Parameter2 contains a packed value: the high word contains the highlight state desired, and the low word contains the menu to be highlighted, which is its six-byte offset in the menuList. The <packed> notation refers to the following: high word 0 = normal, high word 1 = selected, low word 0 = flipbar. A highlight state of 1 (one) means the title is to be selected, and a highlight state of 0 (zero) means that the title is to be returned to normal.

When a menu is selected, the bits behind the title are saved. Next, the color of the title and the color of the menu bar are reversed, and the title is redrawn in these reversed colors. Reversing the colors simply means setting the background color to the title color and the foreground color to the menu bar color. This is necessary because merely inverting the title rectangle with a call to InvertRect, as was done on previous machines, often produces unpleasing and/or unreadable results.

When a menu is deselected—that is, the highlight state is 0 (zero)—the bits behind the title are restored. If there was not enough memory to save the bits behind the title, DrawMenuBar is called to redraw the whole menu bar.

If the low word of parameter2 is zero, the whole menu bar is inverted. FlashMenuBar uses this feature.

Message #6: Height

Called By	Selector	Parameter1	Parameter2	Result
Window Manager	mbVariant	none	none	none

This calculates the menu bar height by looking at the size of the system font, and stores that value in the global variable MBarHeight ($BAA). Note that the Window Manager assumes that the menu bar is at the top of the screen.

Message #7: Save

Called By	Selector	Parameter1	Parameter2	Result
MenuSelect PopUpMenuSelect	mbVariant	six-byte offset	menuRect	none

Parameter2 is the rectangle into which the menu is to be drawn. Parameter1 is the offset into the menuList of the menu to be drawn. A six-byte offset refers to the offset of the menu into the menuList data structure. First the bits behind the menu are saved. Next the menu rectangle is erased to the proper background color, and the menu structure (i.e., shadow) is drawn. Finally, various information about the menu is stored in the menu bar defproc's data structure.

Message #8: Restore

Called By	Selector	Parameter1	Parameter2	Result
MenuSelect PopUpMenuSelect	mbVariant	none	none	none

No parameters are passed; the assumption is that the last displayed menu will always be the first one restored. If there was not enough memory to save the bits behind the menu, an update event is generated for the menu rectangle.

Message #9: GetRect

Called By	Selector	Parameter1	Parameter2	Result
MenuSelect PopUpMenuSelect	mbVariant	none	<packed2>	menuRect

Parameter2 contains the offset into the menuList data structure for the menu whose rectangle is to be calculated, as well as information about whether this is for a regular menu or a hierarchical menu. The <packed2> notation refers to the following: high word 0 = regular menu, high word nonzero = mouse pt/hierarchical menu, low-word = six-byte offset of a menu in the MenuList. If the menu is currently showing on the screen, then its rectangle need not be recalculated, since it is stored in the menu bar defproc's data structure.

If the menu is not currently showing on the screen, the rectangle is calculated. If it is the first menu up, the menu drops from the menu bar. If it is a hierarchical menu, an attempt is made to line up the top of the hierarchical menu with the item that is the "parent" of this submenu.

Message #10: SaveAlt

Called By	Selector	Parameter1	Parameter2	Result
MenuSelect PopUpMenuSelect	mbVariant	none	six-byte offset	none

This message is called after message #7 (Save) has been executed and the menu defproc has been called to draw the menu items. It currently saves data about the menu's scrolling position. A six-byte offset refers to the offset of the menu into the menuList data structure.

Message #11: ResetAlt

Called By	Selector	Parameter1	Parameter2	Result
MenuSelect PopUpMenuSelect	mbVariant	none	six-byte offset	none

This message is currently used to restore the global variables TopMenuItem ($A0A) and AtMenuBottom ($A0C) for the menu where the mouse is currently located. When a hierarchical menu is drawn, its scrolling information will be in the global variables TopMenu Item and AtMenuBottom. For menu scrolling to work properly, the scrolling information *for the menu where the mouse is currently located* must be in those global variables. A six-byte offset refers to the offset of menu into the menuList data structure.

Message #12: MenuRgn

Called By	Selector	Parameter1	Parameter2	Result
—	mbVariant	none	region handle	region handle

A handle to an empty region is passed in parameter2. The same handle is returned as the result, and the region is the menu bar's region.

13 Menu Manager

SUMMARY OF THE MENU MANAGER

Constants

```
CONST

hMenuCmd       = $1B;  {itemCmd == $1B ==> hierarchical menu }
                       { attached to this item}
hierMenu       = -1;   {for use as "beforeID" with InsertMenu}
hPopUpMsg      =  3;   {pop-up menu placement, asks the defproc to }
                       { calculate the menu rectangle of the }
                       { pop-up menu}
mctAllItems    = -98;  {for use as a "menuItem" with DelMCEntries}
mctLastIDIndic = -99;  {last color table entry has this in ID field}
dsMBarNFnd     = 85;   {SysErr code indicating MBDF not found. Used }
                       { by InitProcMenu and InitMenu}
dsHMenuFindErr = 86;   {SysErr code indicating recursive }
                       { hierarchical menus defined. Used by }
                       { MenuKey.}
```

Data Types

```
TYPE MCEntryPtr = ^MCEntry;
     MCEntry    = RECORD
                    mctID:       INTEGER;  {menu ID. ID = 0 is the }
                                           { menu bar}
                    mctItem:     INTEGER;  {menu entry. Item = 0 is }
                                           { a title}
                    mctRGB1:     RGBColor; {usage depends on ID and }
                                           { Item}
                    mctRGB2:     RGBColor; {usage depends on ID and }
                                           { Item}
                    mctRGB3:     RGBColor; {usage depends on ID and }
                                           { Item}
                    mctRGB4:     RGBColor; {usage depends on ID and }
                                           { Item}
                    mctReserved: INTEGER;  {reserved for internal }
                                           { use}
                  END;

     MCTable        = ARRAY [0..0] of MCEntry; {the menu entries are }
                                               { represented in this }
                                               { array}
     MCTablePtr     = ^MCTable;
     MCTableHandle  = ^MCTablePtr;
```

Routines

```
PROCEDURE  InitProcMenu     (mbResID: INTEGER);
PROCEDURE  DelMCEntries     (menuID, menuItem: INTEGER);
FUNCTION   GetMCInfo:       MCTableHandle;
PROCEDURE  SetMCInfo        (menuCTbl: MCTableHandle);
PROCEDURE  DispMCInfo       (menuCTbl: MCTableHandle);
FUNCTION   GetMCEntry       (menuID, menuItem: INTEGER): MCEntryPtr;
FUNCTION   MenuChoice:      LONGINT;
PROCEDURE  SetMCEntries     (numEntries: INTEGER; menuCEntries:
                             MCTablePtr);
PROCEDURE  GetItemCmd       (theMenu:MenuHandle; item:INTEGER; VAR
                             cmdChar: CHAR);
PROCEDURE  SetItemCmd       (theMenu:MenuHandle; item:INTEGER;
                             cmdChar: CHAR);
FUNCTION   PopUpMenuSelect  (theMenu: MenuHandle; Top, Left,
                             PopupItem: INTEGER;) LONGINT;
```

Global Variables

MBarHeight	Contains menu bar height derived from the size of the system font.
MenuCInfo	Contains handle to the menu color information table.
MenuDisable	Contains the menu ID for last menu item chosen, whether or not it's disabled.
TheMenu	Contains the ID of the highlighted menu in the menu bar.
TopMenuItem	Contains information on top menu item for menu scrolling.
AtMenuBottom	Contains information on bottom menu item for menu scrolling.

Assembly-Language Information

Menu Color Information Table Structure

```
mctID          EQU    $0
mctItem        EQU    $2
mctRGB1        EQU    $4
mctRGB2        EQU    $A
mctRGB3        EQU    $10
mctRGB4        EQU    $16
mctReserved    EQU    $1C
mctEntrySize   EQU    $1E
```

Miscellaneous equates for hierarchical menus

```
HMenuCmd       EQU  $1B  ;itemCmd == $1B ==> hierarchical menu for
                         ; this item
ScriptMenuCmd EQU  $1C  ;itemCmd == $1C ==> item to be displayed in
                         ; script font
AltMenuCmd1    EQU  $1D  ;itemCmd == $1D ==> unused indicator
                         ; reserved for future Apple use
AltMenuCmd2    EQU  $1E  ;itemCmd == $1E ==> unused indicator
                         ; reserved for future Apple use
AltMenuCmd3    EQU  $1F  ;itemCmd == $1F ==> unused indicator
                         ; reserved for future Apple use
hierMenu       EQU  -1   ;InsertMenu(handle, hierMenu), when
                         ; beforeID ==hierMenu, the handle is
                         ; inserted in the hierarchical menuList
hPopUpMsg      EQU  3    ;pop-up menu placement, asks the defproc to
                         ; calculate the menu rectangle of the pop-up
                         ; menu
```

Color table search messages

```
mctAllItems    EQU   -98  ;search for all items for the given ID
mctLastIDIndic EQU   -99  ;last entry in color table has this in ID
                          ; field
```

Global Variables

```
MBarHeight     EQU  $BAA  ;contains menu bar height derived from the
                          ; size of the system font
MenuCInfo      EQU  $0D50 ;handle to menu color information table
MenuDisable    EQU  $0B54 ;contains the menu ID for last menu item
                          ; chosen, whether or not it's disabled
TheMenu        EQU  $A26  ;contains the ID of the highlighted menu
                          ; in the menu bar
TopMenuItem    EQU  $A0A  ;pixel value of top of scrollable menu
AtMenuBottom   EQU  $A0C  ;pixel value of bottom of scrollable menu
```

14 TEXTEDIT

ABOUT THIS CHAPTER

This chapter describes the enhanced version of TextEdit for the Macintosh Plus, the Macintosh SE and Macintosh II. The new TextEdit routines allow text attributes such as font, size, style, and color to vary from one character to another. The changes are backward compatible with earlier Macintosh versions: all existing programs using TextEdit routines should still work. TextEdit is also fully compatible with the Script Manager.

DATA STRUCTURES

The structure and size of the edit record are unchanged, but a few of its fields are interpreted in different ways. All records have a 32K maximum size. A new data structure, the *style record,* has been introduced to carry the style information for the edit record's text, along with various subsidiary data structures: the *style run,* the *style table* and its *style elements,* the *line-height table* and its *line-height elements,* and the *null-style record.* In addition, there is the *text style* record for passing style information to and from TextEdit routines, and the *style scrap record* for writing style information to the desk scrap.

The Edit Record

Most fields of the edit record have the same meanings as in the old TextEdit, with the following exceptions:

txSize	Used as a flag telling whether the edit record has style information associated with it:
≥0	Old-style edit record; all text set in a single font, size, and face; all fields (including txSize itself) have their old, natural meanings.
−1	Edit record has associated style information; the txFont and txFace fields have new meanings as described below.
txFont, txFace	Combine to hold a handle to the associated style record (see "The Style Record" below). Use new routines GetStylHandle and SetStylHandle to access or change this handle in Pascal.
lineHeight fontAscent	Controls whether vertical spacing is fixed or may vary from line to line, depending on specific text styles:
>0	Fixed line height or font ascent, as before.

−1   Line height or font ascent calculated independently for
            each line, based on maximum value for any individual
            style on that line.

The new routine TEStylNew, which creates a new edit record with style information, sets
txSize, lineHeight, and fontAscent to −1, allocates a style record, and stores a handle to the
style record in the txFont and txFace fields. The old routine TENew still creates a new edit
record without style information, initializing these fields from the current graphics port as
before.

The Style Record

The **style record,** located via a handle kept in the txFont and txFace fields of the edit
record, specifies the styles for the edit record's text. The text is divided into *runs* of
consecutive characters in the same style, summarized in a table in the runs field of the style
record. Each entry in this table gives the starting character position of a run and an index
into the style table (described in the next section). The length of the run is found by
subtracting its start position from that of the next entry in the table. A dummy entry at the
end of the table delimits the length of the last run; its start position is equal to the overall
number of characters in the text, plus 1.

```
TYPE
  TEStyleHandle = ^TEStylePtr;
  TEStylePtr    = ^TEStyleRec;
  TEStyleRec    = RECORD
                    nRuns:    INTEGER;      {number of style runs}
                    nStyles:  INTEGER;      {number of distinct }
                                            { styles stored in }
                                            { style table}
                    styleTab: STHandle;     {handle to style table}
                    lhTab:    LHHandle;     {handle to line-height }
                                            { table}
                    teRefCon: LONGINT;      {reserved for }
                                            { application use}
                    nullStyle: nullSTHandle; {handle to style set }
                                            { at null selection}
                    runs:     ARRAY [0..0] OF StyleRun
                  END;


  StyleRun = RECORD
               startChar: INTEGER; {starting character position}
               styleIndex: INTEGER {index in style table}
             END;
```

Field descriptions

nRuns   The nRuns field specifies the number of style runs in the text.

nStyles   The nStyles field contains the number of distinct styles used in the text; this forms the size of the style table.

styleTab   The StyleTab field contains a handle to the style table (see "The Style Table" below).

lhTab   The lhTab field contains a handle to the line-height table (see "The Line-Height Table" below).

teRefCon   The teRefCon field is a reference constant for use by applications.

nullStyle   The nullStyle field contains a handle to a data structure used to store the style information for a null selection.

runs   The runs field contains an indefinite-length array of style runs.

The Style Table

The style table contains one entry for each distinct style used in an edit record's text. The size of the table is given by the nStyles field of the style record. There is no duplication; each style appears exactly once in the table. A reference count tells how many times each style is used within the text.

```
TYPE
  STHandle    = ^STPtr;
  STPtr       = ^TEStyleTable;
  TEStyleTable= ARRAY [0..0] OF STElement;


  STElement = RECORD
              stCount:   INTEGER;     {number of runs in }
                                      { this style}
              stHeight:  INTEGER;     {line height}
              stAscent:  INTEGER;     {font ascent}
              stFont:    INTEGER;     {font (family) number}
              stFace:    Style;       {character style}
              stSize:    INTEGER;     {size in points}
              stColor:   RGBColor     {absolute (RGB) color}
            END;
```

Field descriptions

stCount   The stCount field contains a reference count of character runs using this style.

stHeight   The stHeight field contains the line height for this style, in points.

stAscent   The stAscent field contains the font ascent for this style, in points.

stFont   The stFont field is the font (family) number.

stFace   The stFace field is the character style (bold, italic, and so forth).

stSize   The stSize field is the text size in points.

stColor   The stColor field is the RGB color; see Chapter 6, "The Color Manager", for further information.

The Line-Height Table

The line-height table holds vertical spacing information for an edit record's text. This table parallels the lineStarts table in the edit record itself. Its length is given by the edit record's nLines field plus 1 for a dummy entry at the end, just as the line starts array ends with a dummy entry that has the same value as the length of the text. The table's contents are recalculated whenever the line starts themselves are recalculated with TECalText, or whenever an editing action causes recalibration.

The line-height table is used only if the lineHeight and fontAscent fields in the edit record are negative; positive values in those fields specify fixed vertical spacing, overriding the information in the table.

```
TYPE
  LHHandle = ^LHPtr;
  LHPtr    = ^LHTable;
  LHTable  = ARRAY [0..0] OF LHElement;

  LHElement = RECORD
              lhHeight:    INTEGER;    {maximum height in line}
              lhAscent:    INTEGER     {maximum ascent in line}
            END;
```

Field descriptions

lhHeight   The lhHeight field contains the line height in points; this is the
                maximum value for any individual style in a line.

lhAscent   The lhAscent field contains the font ascent in points; this is the
                maximum value for any individual style in a line.

If you want, you can override TextEdit's line-height calculation and store your own height
and ascent values into the line-height table. Any table entry with the high bit set in the
lhHeight field will be used as-is (both height and ascent), overriding whatever values
TextEdit would have used. The high bit of lhHeight is masked out to arrive at the true line
height, but the high bit of lhAscent is *not* masked, so you should never set it; the one in
lhHeight serves as a flag for both fields. Notice that you can selectively set some lines for
yourself and let TextEdit do the rest for you. This technique is intended to be used for
static, unchanging text, such as in text boxes; if you use it on text that can change
dynamically, be sure to readjust your line-height values whenever the line breaks in the text
are recalculated. Otherwise, if new lines are created as a result of a text insertion, their line
heights and ascents will be computed by TextEdit.

The Null-Style Record

The **null-style record** is used to store the style information for a null selection. If
TESetStyle is called when setStart equals setEnd, the input style information is stored in the
nullStyle handle. The nStyles field of nullScrap is set to 1, and the style information is
stored as the ScrpSTElement. If text is then entered (pasted, inserted, or typed), the style is
entered into the runs array, and nStyles is reset to 0. The nStyles field is also reset if the
selection offsets are changed (by TEClick, for example).

```
TYPE
  NullSTHandle = ^NullSTPtr;
  NullSTPtr    = ^NullSTRec;
  NullSTRec = RECORD
             TEReserved: LONGINT;       {reserved for future }
                                        { expansion}
             nullScrap:  STScrpHandle   {handle to scrap style }
                                        { table}
           END;
```

Field descriptions

teReserved   The teReserved field is reserved for future expansion.

nullScrap   The nullScrap field contains a handle to the scrap style table.

Text Styles

Text style records are used for communicating style information between the application program and the TextEdit routines. They carry the same information as the STElement records in the style table, but without the reference count, line height, and font ascent:

```
TYPE
  TextStyle= RECORD
              tsFont:  INTEGER;   {Font (family) number}
              tsFace:  Style;     {Character style}
              tsSize:  INTEGER;   {Size in points}
              tsColor: RGBColor   {Absolute (RGB) color}
            END;
```

Field descriptions

tsFont   The tsFont field is the font (family) number.

tsFace   The tsFace field is the character style (bold, italic, and so forth).

tsSize   The tsSize field is the text size in points.

tsColor   The tsColor field contains the RGB color; see Chapter 6, "The Color Manager", for further information.

The Style Scrap

A new scrap type, 'styl', is used for storing style information in the desk scrap along with the old 'TEXT' scrap. The format of the **style scrap** is defined by a style scrap record:

```
TYPE
  StScrpHandle = ^StScrpPtr;
  StScrpPtr    = ^StScrpRec;
  StScrpRec    = RECORD
              scrpNStyles: INTEGER;       {number of distinct }
                                          { styles in scrap}
              scrpStyleTab: ScrpSTTable   {table of styles for }
                                          { scrap}
            END;
```

Field descriptions

scrpNStyles   The scrpNStyles field is the number of distinct styles used in text; this forms the size of the style table.

scrpSTTable   The scrpSTTable is the table of text styles: see the data structure shown below.

Unlike the main style table for an edit record, the table in the style scrap may contain duplicate elements; the entries in the table correspond one-to-one with the character runs in the text. The scrpStartChar field of each entry gives the starting character position for the run.

The ScrpSTTable is a separate data structure defined for style records in the scrap. Its format is:

```
TYPE
  ScrpSTTable  = array [0..0] of ScrpSTElement;
  ScrpSTElement = RECORD
                scrpStartChar: LONGINT;   {offset to start of }
                                          { style}
                scrpHeight:    INTEGER;   {line height}
                scrpAscent:    INTEGER;   {font ascent}
                scrpFont:      INTEGER;   {font (family) number}
                scrpFace:      Style;     {character style}
                scrpSize:      INTEGER;   {size in points}
                scrpColor:     RGBColor;  {absolute (RGB) color}
              END;
```

Field descriptions

scrpStartChar   The scrpStartChar field is the offset to the beginning of a style record in the scrap.

scrpHeight   The scrpHeight field contains the line height.

scrpAscent   The scrpAscent field contains the font ascent.

scrpFont   The scrpFont is the font's family number.

scrpFace   The scrpFace is the character style for the style scrap.

scrpSize   The scrpSize field contains the size in points.

scrpColor   The scrpColor field contains the RGB color for the style scrap.

CUTTING AND PASTING

For new TextEdit records created using TEStylNew, the routines TECut and TECopy will write both the text and its associated style information directly to the desk scrap, under scrap types 'TEXT' and 'styl', respectively. (For compatibility with existing applications, they also write a handle to the text to the old global TEScrapHandle.) For old TextEdit records, TECopy and TEPaste will work as they did before, copying and pasting via the private TextEdit scrap only.

A new routine, TEStylPaste, reads both text and style back from the desk scrap and pastes them into the document at the current selection range or insertion point. The old TEPaste reads the text only, ignoring any style information found in the scrap; instead it uses the style of the first character in the selection range being replaced, or that of the preceding character if the selection is an insertion point. (TEStylPaste defaults to the same behavior if it doesn't find a 'styl' entry in the desk scrap.) The old routines TEFromScrap and TEToScrap, for transferring text between the desk and internal scraps, are no longer needed, but are still supported for backward compatibility. The GetStylScrap and TEStylInsert routines can now be used to access the text and style information associated with a given selection without destroying the current contents of the desk scrap.

TEXTEDIT ROUTINES

The Macintosh Plus, Macintosh SE, and Macintosh II versions of TextEdit support all previous TextEdit routines, as well as the new routines described below.

Assembly-language note: All but two of the new routines share a single trap, _TEDispatch ($A83D). The routines are distinguished by an integer *routine selector* passed on the stack, after the last argument:

TEStylPaste	0
TESetStyle	1
TEReplaceStyle	2
TEGetStyle	3
GetStylHandle	4
SetStylHandle	5
GetStylScrap	6
TEStylInsert	7
TEGetPoint	8
TEGetHeight	9

The Pascal interface supplies the routine selectors automatically, as do the macros for calling these routines from assembly language. The remaining two new TextEdit routines have traps of their own: _TEStylNew ($A83E) and _TEGetOffset ($A83C).

```
FUNCTION  TEStylNew  (destRect,viewRect: Rect) : TEHandle;
```

The TEStylNew routine creates a new-style edit record with associated style information. It initializes the new record's txSize, lineHeight, and fontAscent fields to –1; allocates a style record and stores a handle to it in the txFont and txFace fields.

```
PROCEDURE SetStylHandle (theHandle: TEStyleHandle; hTE: TEHandle);
```

The SetStylHandle procedure sets an edit record's style handle, stored in the txFont and txFace fields. SetStylHandle has no effect on an old-style edit record. Applications should always use SetStylHandle rather than manipulating the fields of the edit record directly.

```
FUNCTION  GetStylHandle (hTE: TEHandle) : TEStyleHandle;
```

The GetStylHandle function gets an edit record's style handle, stored in the txFont and txFace fields. GetStylHandle returns NIL when used with an old-style edit record. Applications should always use this function rather than manipulating the fields of the edit record directly.

```
FUNCTION  GetStylScrap (hTE: TEHandle) : StScrpHandle;
```

The GetStylScrap routine allocates a block of type StScrpRec and copies the style information associated with the current selection into it. This is the same as TECopy, except that no action is performed on the text, and the handle to the 'styl' scrap is output in this case. Unlike TECopy, the StScrpRec is not copied to the desk scrap.

GetStylScrap will return a NIL value if called with an old style TEHandle, or if the selection is NIL (stylStart equals stylEnd).

```
PROCEDURE TEStylInsert (text: Ptr; length: LONGINT; hST:
          stScrpHandle; hTE: TEHandle);
```

The TEStylInsert procedure takes the specified text and inserts it just before the selection range into the text indicated by hTE, redrawing the text as necessary. If hST is not NIL and hTE is a TextEdit record created using TEStylNew, the style information indicated by hST will also be inserted to correspond with the inserted text. When hST is NIL and/or hTE has not been created using TEStylNew, there is no difference between this procedure and TEInsert. TEStylInsert does not affect either the current selection range or the scrap.

```
FUNCTION  TEGetOffset (pt: Point; hTE: TEHandle) : INTEGER;
```

The TEGetOffset routine finds the character offset in an edit record's text corresponding to the given point. TEGetOffset works for both old-style and new-style edit records.

```
FUNCTION TEGetPoint  (offset: INTEGER; hTE: TEHandle) : POINT;
```

The TEGetPoint routine returns the point corresponding to the given offset into the text. The point returned is to the bottom (baseline) left of the character at the specified offset. TEGetPoint works for both old- and new-style edit records.

```
FUNCTION TEGetHeight (endLine, startLine: LONGINT; hTE: TEHandle) :
       INTEGER;
```

The TEGetHeight routine returns the total height of all the lines in the text between and including startLine and endLine. TEGetHeight works for both old- and new-style edit records.

```
PROCEDURE TEGetStyle (offset: INTEGER; VAR theStyle: TextStyle;
       VAR lineHeight,fontAscent: INTEGER; hTE: TEHandle);
```

The TEGetStyle procedure returns the style information, including line height and font ascent, associated with a given character in an edit record's text. For an old-style edit record, it returns the record's global text characteristics.

```
PROCEDURE TEStylPaste (hTE: TEHandle);
```

The TEStylPaste procedure pastes text from the desk scrap into the edit record's text at the current insertion point or replaces the current selection. The text is styled according to the style information found in the desk scrap; if there is none, it is given the same style as the first character of the replaced selection (or that of the preceding character if the selection is an insertion point). In an old-style edit record, just the text is pasted without its accompanying style.

```
PROCEDURE TESetStyle (mode: INTEGER; newStyle: TextStyle; redraw:
       BOOLEAN;  hTE: TEHandle);
```

The TESetStyle procedure sets the style of the current selection to that specified by newStyle. (It has no effect on an old-style edit record.) The mode parameter controls which style attributes to set; it may be any additive combination of the following constants:

```
CONST
    doFont  =  1;    {set font (family) number}
    doFace  =  2;    {set character style}
    doSize  =  4;    {set type size}
    doColor =  8;    {set color}
    doAll   = 15;    {set all attributes}
    addSize = 16;    {adjust type size}
```

In the last case (addSize), the value of newStyle.tsSize is added to all type sizes within the current selection instead of replacing them; this value may be either positive or negative. (If present, addSize overrides doSize.) If redraw = TRUE, the affected text will be redrawn in the new style.

```
PROCEDURE TEReplaceStyle (mode: INTEGER; oldStyle,newStyle:
        TextStyle; redraw: BOOLEAN; hTE: TEHandle);
```

The TEReplaceStyle procedure replaces the style specified by oldStyle with that given by newStyle within the current selection. (It has no effect on an old-style edit record.) The mode parameter takes the same values as TESetStyle (above), except that addSize has no meaning here. All styles for which the combination of attributes designated by mode have the values given by oldStyle are changed to have the corresponding values from newStyle instead. Style changes are made directly to the style-table elements within the table itself. If mode = doAll, newStyle simply replaces oldStyle outright.

SUMMARY OF TEXTEDIT

Constants

```
CONST
  doFont   =    1; {set font (family) number}
  doFace   =    2; {set character style}
  doSize   =    4; {set type size}
  doColor  =    8; {set color}
  doAll    =   15; {set all attributes}
  addSize  =   16; {adjust type size}
```

Data Types

```
TYPE
  TEStyleHandle = ^TEStylePtr;
  TEStylePtr    = ^TEStyleRec;
  TEStyleRec    = RECORD
                    nRuns:     INTEGER;        {number of style runs}
                    nStyles:   INTEGER;        {size of style table}
                    styleTab:  STHandle;       {handle to style table}
                    lhTab:     LHHandle;       {handle to line-height }
                                               { table}
                    teRefCon:  LONGINT;        {reserved for }
                                               { application use}
                    nullStyle: nullSTHandle;   {handle to style set at }
                                               { null selection}
                    runs:      ARRAY [0..0] OF StyleRun
                  END;

  StyleRun = RECORD
                startChar:  INTEGER;   {starting character position}
                styleIndex: INTEGER    {index in style table}
             END;

  STHandle     = ^STPtr;
  STPtr        = ^TEStyleTable;
  TEStyleTable = ARRAY [0..0] OF STElement;

  STElement    = RECORD
                   stCount:  INTEGER;   {number of runs in this style}
                   stHeight: INTEGER;   {line height}
                   stAscent: INTEGER;   {font ascent}
                   stFont:   INTEGER;   {font (family) number}
                   stFace:   Style;     {character style}
                   stSize:   INTEGER;   {size in points}
                   stColor:  RGBColor   {absolute (RGB) color}
                 END;
```

```
LHHandle      = ^LHPtr;
LHPtr         = ^LHTable;
LHTable       = ARRAY [0..0] OF LHElement;

LHElement     = RECORD
                    lhHeight: INTEGER;        {maximum height in line}
                    lhAscent: INTEGER         {maximum ascent in line}
                END;

NullSTHandle = ^NullSTPtr;
NullSTPtr     = ^NullSTRec;
NullSTRec     = RECORD
                    TEReserved: LONGINT;        {reserved for future }
                                                { expansion}
                    nullScrap:  STScrpHandle {handle to scrap style }
                                                { table}
                END;

TextStyle     = RECORD
                    tsFont:   INTEGER;      {font (family) number}
                    tsFace:   Style;        {character style}
                    tsSize:   INTEGER;      {size in points}
                    tsColor:  RGBColor      {absolute (RGB) color}
                END;

StScrpHandle = ^StScrpPtr;
StScrpPtr     = ^StScrpRec;
StScrpRec     = RECORD
                    scrpNStyles: INTEGER;   {number of distinct styles }
                                            { in scrap}
                    scrpStyleTab: ScrpSTTable {table of styles for }
                                            { scrap}
                END;

ScrpSTTable   = ARRAY [0..0] OF scrpSTElement;
ScrpSTElement = RECORD
                    scrpStartChar: LONGINT; {offset to start of style}
                    scrpHeight:  INTEGER;   {line height}
                    scrpAscent:  INTEGER;   {font ascent}
                    scrpFont:    INTEGER;   {font (family) number}
                    scrpFace:    Style;     {character style}
                    scrpSize:    INTEGER;   {size in points}
                    scrpColor:   RGBColor;  {absolute (RGB) color}
                END;
```

Routines

```
FUNCTION    TEStylNew       (destRect,viewRect: Rect) : TEHandle;
PROCEDURE   SetStylHandle   (theHandle: TEStyleHandle; hTE: TEHandle);
FUNCTION    GetStylHandle   (hTE: TEHandle) : TEStyleHandle;
FUNCTION    GetStylScrap    (hTE: TEHandle) : StScrpHandle;
PROCEDURE   TEStylInsert    (text: Ptr; length: LONGINT; hST:
                             stScrpHandle; hTE: TEHandle);
FUNCTION    TEGetOffset     (pt: Point; hTE: TEHandle) : INTEGER;
FUNCTION    TEGetPoint      (offset: INTEGER; hTE: TEHandle) : POINT;
FUNCTION    TEGetHeight     (endLine, startLine: LONGINT; hTE:
                             TEHandle) : INTEGER;
PROCEDURE   TEGetStyle      (offset: INTEGER; VAR theStyle:
                             TextStyle;VAR lineHeight,fontAscent:
                             INTEGER; hTE: TEHandle);
PROCEDURE   TEStylPaste     (hTE: TEHandle);
PROCEDURE   TESetStyle      (mode: INTEGER; newStyle: TextStyle;
                             redraw: BOOLEAN;hTE: TEHandle);
PROCEDURE   TEReplaceStyle  (mode: INTEGER; oldStyle,newStyle:
                             TextStyle;redraw: BOOLEAN; hTE: TEHandle);
```

Assembly-Language Information

Set/Replace style modes

```
fontBit     EQU   0           ;set font
faceBit     EQU   1           ;set face
sizeBit     EQU   2           ;set size
clrBit      EQU   3           ;set color
addSizeBit  EQU   4           ;add size mode
teStylesH   EQU   teFont      ;replaces teFont/teFace
```

Offsets into TEStyleRec

```
nRuns       EQU     0   ;[integer] # of entries in styleStarts array
nStyles     EQU     2   ;[integer] # of distinct styles
styleTab    EQU     4   ;[STHandle] handle to distinct styles
lhTab       EQU     8   ;[LHHandle] handle to line heights
teRefCon    EQU    12   ;[longint] reserved
nullStyle   EQU    16   ;[nullSTHandle] Handle to style set at null
                        ; selection
runs        EQU    20   ;array of styles
```

Offsets into StyleRun array

```
startChar   EQU     0   ;[INTEGER] offset into text to start of
                        ; style
styleIndex  EQU     2   ;[INTEGER] style index
stStartSize EQU     4   ;size of a styleStarts entry
```

Offsets into STElement

```
stCount     EQU     0   ;[integer] # of times this style is used
stHeight    EQU     2   ;[integer] line height
stAscent    EQU     4   ;[integer] ascent
stFont      EQU     6   ;[integer] font
stFace      EQU     8   ;[style] face
stSize      EQU    10   ;[integer] size
stColor     EQU    12   ;[RGBColor] color
stRecSize   EQU    18   ;size of a teStylesRec
```

Offsets into TextStyle

```
tsFont      EQU     0   ;[integer] font
tsFace      EQU     2   ;[style] face
tsSize      EQU     4   ;[integer] size
tsColor     EQU     6   ;[RGBColor] color

styleSize   EQU    12   ;size of a StylRec
```

Offsets into StScrpRec

```
scrpNStyles  EQU     0   ;[integer] # of styles in scrap
scrpStyleTab EQU     2   ;[ScrpSTTable] start of scrap styles array
```

Offsets into scrpSTElement

```
scrpStartChar EQU   0   ;[longint] char where this style starts
scrpHeight    EQU   4   ;[integer] line height
scrpAscent    EQU   6   ;[integer]ascent
scrpFont      EQU   8   ;[integer]font
scrpFace      EQU  10   ;[style] face
scrpSize      EQU  12   ;[integer]size
scrpColor     EQU  14   ;[RGBColor] color

scrpRecSize   EQU  20   ;size of a scrap record
```

15 THE DIALOG MANAGER

ABOUT THIS CHAPTER

This chapter describes the enhancements to the Dialog Manager for the Macintosh II. A new Dialog Manager routine now provides color dialog and item support. The new resource types 'dctb', 'actb', and 'ictb', which are auxiliary data structures to 'DITL', 'ALRT', and 'DLOG', allow color dialog boxes and alert boxes to be stored as resources. If the 'ALRT', 'DLOG', or 'DITL' resources are missing, the Dialog Manager will gracefully return from the Alert, NoteAlert, CautionAlert, StopAlert, and GetNewDialog calls.

COLOR ALERT AND DIALOG RESOURCES

You don't have to call any new routines to create color alert or dialog boxes. Additional resources of types 'actb', 'dctb', and 'ictb' complement the existing 'ALRT', 'DLOG', and 'DITL' resources, and provide all the information needed to color dialog windows, controls, and text.

To create a dialog or alert box, the Dialog Manager needs the same information about the box as the Window Manager needs when it creates a new window. The structure of dialog color tables and alert color tables is similar to the window color table described in the Window Manager chapter, as shown in Figure 1.

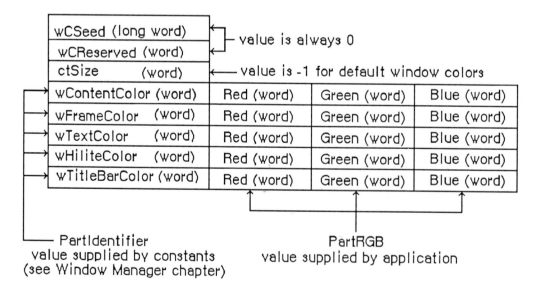

Figure 1. Color Table for Dialogs and Alerts

The calls Alert, CautionAlert, StopAlert, and NoteAlert look for a resource of type 'actb' with the same resource ID as the alert. GetNewDialog looks for a resource of type 'dctb' with the same resource ID as the dialog. These resources contain color tables identical to the 'wctb' color tables described in the Window Manager GetNewCWindow call. If an 'actb' or 'dctb' resource is present, then the window created will be a cGrafPort, created with a NewCWindow call. If the ctSize field of a 'dctb' or 'actb' resource is –1, the default window colors will be used.

To include a color icon in a dialog box, add a resource of type 'cicn' with the same resource ID as an old-style icon. The Dialog Manager will then access the icon with the QuickDraw routine GetCIcon.

To include a version 2 picture in a dialog, create a color table for the dialog to cause the dialog to use a cGrafPort. See the Color QuickDraw chapter for more information on the use of color pictures.

To color controls in a dialog, or to change the color, style, font, or size of text within a dialog, include an 'ictb' resource as described in the following section.

Color table resources 'actb' and 'dctb' are treated the same as 'ALRT' resources and 'DLOG' resources. The 'ictb' resource is handled just like the 'DITL' resource. These resources are preloaded and made nonpurgeable by CouldAlert and CouldDialog, and their original purge state is restored by FreeAlert and FreeDialog.

COLOR DIALOG ITEM LISTS

This section discusses the contents of an item list after it's been read into memory from a resource file. If a resource of type 'ictb' is present with the same resource ID as the 'DITL' resource (in addition to the presence of the 'dctb' or 'actb' resources), then the statText, editText, and control items in the dialog or alert boxes are drawn using the colors and text styles indicated by the item color table record contained in the resource.

> **Note**: Neither the display device nor the dialog box needs to be in color, but a dialog or alert color table must exist to include an item color table (even if the item color table only describes statText and editText style changes and has no actual color information).

Figure 2 shows how a dialog color table stores item color table records.

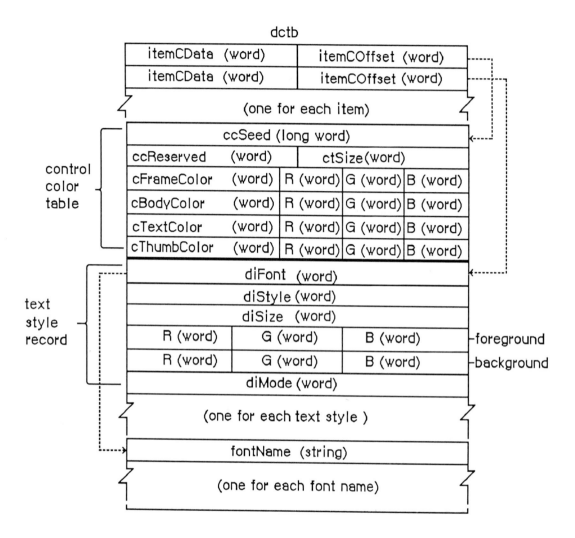

Figure 2. Color Table for Dialogs and Alerts

The record starts with an array of two-word entries for each item in the matching dialog item list. The first word (itemCData) is the length of the entry if the item is a control, or it is a word of flags if the item is an editText or statText item. The second word (itemCOffset) is an offset from the beginning of the record to the color item entry. This color record is used only for controls and text; icons and pictures have a different method of describing associated colors. Set the itemCData and itemCOffset fields to zero for controls or text without colors or font changes.

If the item is an editText or statText item, the bits in the itemCData field determine which fields of the text style record to use; these bit equates are listed in the following table.

Bit   Meaning

0   Change the font family
1   Change the font face
2   Change the font size
3   Change the font forecolor
4   Add the font size
13   Change the font backcolor
14   Change the font mode
15   The font field is an offset to the name.

Note: Multiple text items can share the same font name.

The itemCData field for text items contains a superset of the flags passed as the mode word to the TextEdit routine TESetStyle. The constants defined for that routine include:

```
CONST
{ Constants for TextEdit and dialog boxes }
  TEdoFont    = 1;        {set font (family) number}
  TEdoFace    = 2;        {set character style}
  TEdoSize    = 4;        {set type size}
  TEdoColor   = 8;        {set foreground color}
  TEdoAll     = 15;       {set all attributes}
  TEaddSize   = 16;       {adjust type size}

{ Constants for dialog boxes only }
  doBColor    = 8192;     {set backgound color}
  doMode      = 16384;    {set txMode}
  doFontName  = 32768;    {set txFont from name}
```

The text style record indicated by itemCOffset must be 20 bytes long, as shown in Figure 2. Multiple statText and editText items can use the same text style record. To display text in the standard font, color, size, and style, set the itemCData and itemCOffset to zero. Allocate space for all fields in the style table, even if they are not used. Even if only the first few items of the dialog box have color style information, there must be room for all of the items actually in the box (with the data and offset words of the unused entries set to zero).

For controls, the colors are described by a color table identical to the contents of a 'cctb' resource used by a GetNewCControl call. Multiple controls can use the same color table. To display a control in the default colors, set the itemCData and itemCOffset fields to zero. The length of the control color table should be the header size of eight bytes plus the eight-byte ColorSpec record for each entry in the color table.

The doFontName array is optional. However, it's important to point to the name of the font instead of just including the font number. Fonts may be renumbered by font installers like the Font/DA Mover as the fonts are moved, so it is safest to rely on getting the right font by referring to the name.

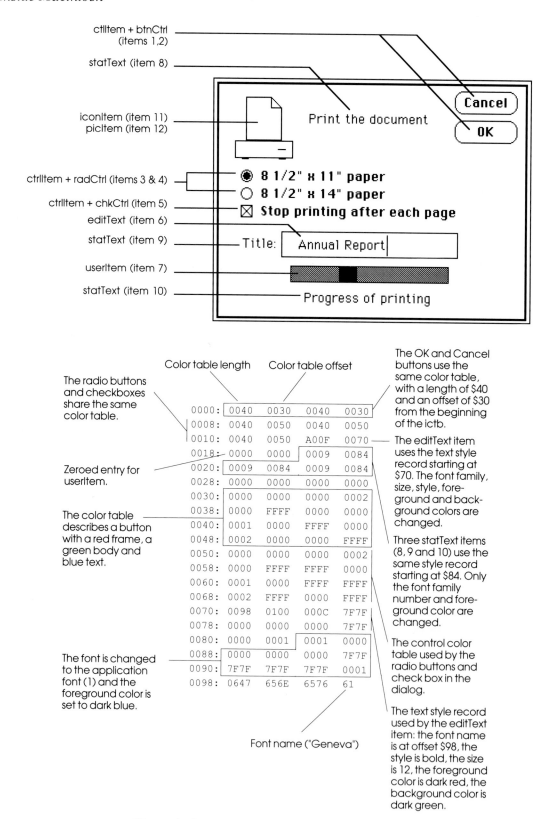

Figure 3. Sample Dialog with Color Dialog Items

USING COLOR DIALOGS AND ALERTS

The dialog box shown in Figure 3 contains 12 different dialog items. Some of these items—the OK and Cancel buttons, the radio buttons and the check box, and the editText and statText items—contain color information. The table shown in the figure contains the hexadecimal description of the dialog items. PicItems, iconItems, resCtrls and userItems should have zeroed entries for both fields. All items in the dialog should have a field, whether or not the item uses the new features.

> **Note**: The dialog box shown in Figure 3 is just a colored version of the original sample dialog box given in Chapter 13 of Volume I (Figure 5). It does not illustrate a standard printer dialog and does not conform to the current Macintosh user interface guidelines set forth in Chapter 2.

Your application can create a dialog or alert, with color dialog items, within a resource file, and then use the GetNewDialog routine with the dialog's resource ID. You can also use the NewCDialog routine to create a dialog or alert within an application, passing a handle to the dialog's item list.

DIALOG MANAGER ROUTINES

A new routine, NewCDialog, has been created, and several existing routines have been modified for use with color.

New Dialog Manager Routine

```
FUNCTION NewCDialog (dStorage:  Ptr; boundsRect:  Rect;
        title:  Str255; visible:  BOOLEAN; procID:  INTEGER;
        behind:  WindowPtr; goAwayFlag:  BOOLEAN; refCon:  LONGINT;
        items:  Handle) : CDialogPtr;
```

A new Dialog Manager routine has been added to support color dialogs: NewCDialog. Its parameters are identical to NewDialog, except that a cGrafPort is allocated through a NewCWindow call instead of a call to NewWindow.

NewCDialog creates a dialog box as specified by its parameters and returns a cDialogPtr to the new dialog. The first eight parameters (dStorage through refCon) are passed to the Window Manager function NewCWindow, which creates the dialog window. The items parameter is a handle to the dialog's item list. You can get the items handle by calling the Resource Manager to read the item list from the resource file into memory.

After calling NewCDialog, you can use SetWinColor to add a color table to the dialog. This creates an auxiliary window record (auxWinRec) for the dialog window. You can access this record with the GetAuxWin routine. The dialogCItem handle within the auxWinRec points to the dialog item color table.

If the dialog's content color isn't white, it's a good idea to call NewCDialog with the visible flag set to FALSE. After the color table and color item list are installed, use ShowWindow to display the dialog if the dialog is the frontmost window. If the dialog is not in front, use ShowHide to display the dialog.

Modifications to Existing Routines

```
FUNCTION GetNewDialog (dialogID: INTEGER; dStorage: Ptr; behind:
        WindowPtr) : DialogPtr;
```

The GetNewDialog routine will attempt to load a 'dctb' resource and returns a pointer to a color grafPort if the resource exists. If no 'dctb' resource is present, GetNewDialog returns a pointer to an old grafPort.

The dialog color table is copied before it is passed to SetWinSize unless its ctSize field is equal to –1, indicating that the default window colors are to be used instead. The copy is made so that the color table resource can be purged without affecting the dialog.

The color dialog item list resource is duplicated as well, so it can be purgeable.

```
FUNCTION Alert (alertID: INTEGER; filterProc: ProcPtr) : INTEGER;
```

The Alert function looks for a resource of type 'actb' with the same ID as the alert. The alert color table is copied before it is passed to SetWinSize unless its ctSize field is equal to –1, indicating that the default window colors are to be used instead. The copy is made so that the color table resource can be purged without affecting the alert.

The color dialog item list resource is duplicated as well, so it can be purgeable.

```
FUNCTION CautionAlert (alertID: INTEGER; filterProc: ProcPtr) :
                       INTEGER;
FUNCTION StopAlert (alertID: INTEGER; filterProc: ProcPtr) :
                    INTEGER;
FUNCTION NoteAlert (alertID: INTEGER; filterProc: ProcPtr) :
                    INTEGER;
```

The calls CautionAlert, StopAlert, and NoteAlert look for a resource of type 'actb' with the same ID as the alert.

```
PROCEDURE CouldDialog (dialogID: INTEGER);
```

The CouldDialog procedure makes the dialog color table template unpurgeable (reading it into memory if it isn't already there), if it exists. It does the same for the dialog's color item list, if it has one.

Warning: CouldDialog doesn't load or make 'FONT' or 'FOND' resources indicated in the color item list unpurgeable.

```
PROCEDURE FreeDialog (dialogID: INTEGER);
```

Given the resource ID of a dialog template previously specified in a call to CouldDialog, the FreeDialog routine undoes the effect of CouldDialog, by restoring the original purge state of the color table and color item list resources.

```
PROCEDURE CouldAlert (alertID: INTEGER);
```

The CouldAlert routine makes the alert color table template unpurgeable (reading it into memory if it isn't already there), if it exists. It does the same for the alert's color item list, if it has one.

> **Warning:** Like CouldDialog, CouldAlert doesn't load or make 'FONT' or 'FOND' resources indicated in the color item list unpurgeable.

```
PROCEDURE FreeAlert (alertID: INTEGER);
```

Given the resource ID of an alert template previously specified in a call to CouldAlert, the FreeAlert routine undoes the effect of CouldAlert, by restoring the original purge state of the color table and color item list resources.

SUMMARY OF THE DIALOG MANAGER

Constants

```
CONST
{ Constants for TextEdit and dialog boxes }
    TEdoFont    = 1;      {set font (family) number}
    TEdoFace    = 2;      {set character style}
    TEdoSize    = 4;      {set type size}
    TEdoColor   = 8;      {set foreground color}
    TEdoAll     = 15;     {set all attributes}
    TEaddSize   = 16;     {adjust type size}

{ Constants for dialog boxes only }
    doBColor    = 8192;   {set background color}
    doMode      = 16384;  {set txMode}
    doFontName  = 32768;  {set txFont from name}
```

Routines

```
FUNCTION NewCDialog (dStorage:  Ptr; boundsRect:  Rect; title:
                    Str255; visible:  BOOLEAN; procID:  INTEGER;
                    behind:  WindowPtr; goAwayFlag:  BOOLEAN;
                    refCon:  LONGINT; items:  Handle) :
                    CDialogPtr;
```

16 THE INTERNATIONAL UTILITIES PACKAGE

16 International Utilities

ABOUT THE INTERNATIONAL UTILITIES PACKAGE

The International Utilities Package has been extended to work in conjunction with the Script Manager, described in this volume. In addition, several new formatting options provide added flexibility in specifying exactly how dates and times are to be displayed. The string comparison capabilities have also been extended to handle non-Roman writing systems, such as Arabic and Japanese.

Reader's guide: You need the information in this chapter if you are using one or more of the following in your application:

■ a non-Roman writing system

■ non-English date or time formats

■ routines that compare strings containing accented characters

INTERNATIONAL RESOURCES

The 'INTL' resources with ID numbers 0 and 1 have been used in the past for international formats. The Script Manager now allows multiple formats to be used with the same system by adding multiple international script resources, as described in the Script Manager chapter of this volume. The new international resources are of types 'itl0', 'itl1', 'itl2', 'itlb', and 'itlc'. Each installed script has an associated list of international resource numbers, generally in the range used for its fonts. For example, the Arabic script has the resources 'itl0', 'itl1', and 'itl2' with numbers in the range $4600 to $47FF; the Roman script has the resources 'itl0', 'itl1', and 'itl2' with numbers in the range $2 to $3FFF.

In the default case, the resources used by the International Utilities package are determined by the script designated for the system font. However, you can force them to be determined by the font script (the script of the font in thePort), by clearing the IntlForce flag to 0. You can set and clear the IntlForce flag by using the SetEnvirons routine described in the Script Manager chapter of this volume. The selected resources will then be used internally by the International Utilities package.

The 'itl0' and 'itl1' resources basically correspond to the former 'INTL' 0 and 1; the 'itl2' resource contains new procedures for sorting, which are discussed below. The IUSetIntl call described in the International Utilities chapter of Volume I still uses the 'INTL' 0 and 1 resources. IUGetIntl, however, uses the 'itl0', 'itl1' and 'itl2' resources.

For compatibility, the 'INTL' 0 and 1 resources are still present in the System file and remain the same; an 'INTL' 2 has been added to correspond to the 'itl2'. Applications can access these resources by means of GetResource.

Note: The one exception to the correspondence between an 'itl0' or 'itl1' and 'INTL' 0 or 'INTL' 1 is that the lengths of the former may be increased at some future date: they are not guaranteed to remain the same length, although the positions of the existing fields will not change.

The 'itlb' resource is a script bundle resource that determines which keyboard and which international formats are to be used. The 'itlc' resource determines the system script.

Using the International Resources

Note: Before using any of the international resources, or using the Binary to Decimal routines, verify that the thePort and thePort^.txFont are set correctly, or that the intlForce flag is on.

To make it easy to localize your application to different scripts and languages, use the international utilities for Date/Time/Number formatting.When formatting numbers, use the fields in the international resources to find out the decimal, thousands or list separators for the given script.

```
{Make sure the font is set properly in thePort, then}
myHandle := intl0Hndl(IUGetIntl(0)); {don't use GetResource!}
myDecimal := myHandle^^.decimalPt;   {as in 1.234 in English}
myThousands := myHandle^^.thousSep;  {as in 1,234,567 in English}
myList := myHandle^^.listSep;        {as in (3;4;5) in English}
```

These three separators should always be distinct; they can be used for parsing. Programs that do not support input of numbers with thousands separators may want to override the list separator and use commas. The program should keep any overriding characters in a resource, so they can be changed if necessary. Before using the resource, it should first check to see that the decimal separator is not the same.

When sorting a list of text items having different scripts, first sort the items by script, producing sublists. Then within each sublist sort the text items, using the International Utilities comparison routine described later in this chapter, with the intlForce off and the font in thePort set to one of the fonts in the sublist.

Where performance is critical, such as when you are sorting very large amounts of data in memory, it may be advantageous to use a straight ASCII comparison instead of the International Utilities comparison routines. In this case, give the user a choice of sorting style (quick versus accurate) in a preferences dialog. The stored default setting can be determined when localizing the application.

FORMATTING OPTIONS

New options are available for time cycle and dates.

Time Cycle

A new constant value, zeroCycle, is provided for the timeCycle field in the Intl0Rec data structure to allow specification of 0:00 AM/PM rather than 12:00 or 24:00.

Short Date Format

Three new constant values, MYD, DYM, YDM, for the dateOrder field in the Intl0Rec data structure now allow the exact specification of the short date format, as follows:

Constant	Format
MYD	Month Year Day
DYM	Day Year Month
YDM	Year Day Month

Long Date Format

New values allow specification of the exact order of the elements in the long date format. If the byte value of the lngDateFmt field in the Intl1Rec data structure is neither 0 nor $FF, then its value is divided into four fields of two bits each. The least significant bit field (bits 0 and 1) corresponds to the first element in the long date format, while the most significant bit field (bits 6 and 7) specifies the last (fourth) element in the format. Four new constants (longDay, longWeek, longMonth, longYear) may be used to set each bit field to the appropriate value.

For example, to specify the order day-of-week/day-of-month/month/year, you would set the value of lngDateFmt to:

```
longWeek*1          {sets bits 0 and 1 to longWeek}
+ longDay*4         {sets bits 2 and 3 to longDay}
+ longMonth*16      {sets bits 4 and 5 to longMonth}
+ longYear*64       {sets bits 6 and 7 to longYear}
```

Suppress Day

New values are available for the suppressDay field in the Intl1Rec data structure to enable suppression of any part of the date. If its value does not equal 0 or $FF, the field is treated as a bitmap. The values supDay, supWeek, supMonth and supYear may be used to set the appropriate bits in the suppressDay byte. For example, to suppress both the month and the year, the value of suppressDay would be: supMonth + supYear.

SORTING ROUTINES

The international sorting routines handle cases where letters are equal in **primary ordering** but different in **secondary ordering** (e.g., 'ä' and 'a'). They also handle cases where one character sorts as if it were two (e.g., 'æ' as 'ae'). The 'itl2' resource has been added to generalize the sorting process for non-Roman scripts.

This is the process that the International Utilities Package now uses to compare two strings:

- Starting with the first character, it fetches corresponding characters from the two strings and compares them.
- If the characters are identical, the comparison continues.
- If the characters are not identical, and if one or both is part of a secondary ordering (e.g., 'ä' and 'a'), their primary characters are compared.
- If the characters are not identical but their primary characters are equal, the comparison continues.
- If neither the original characters nor their primary characters are equal, the comparison ends and the ordering of the original characters is returned.
- If the foregoing comparison continues and one string ends before the other, then the shorter string is less.
- If the comparison continues to the end of strings that are the same length and if the strings contain no characters that are equal in primary ordering but different in secondary ordering, then the strings are identical.
- If the comparison continues to the end of strings that are the same length and contain one or more characters that are equal in primary ordering but different in secondary ordering, then the first such pair of characters is compared by secondary ordering to determine the final ordering.

Note: It is possible to create your own ordering routine, using hook routines contained in the 'itl2' resource. For guidance on doing this, contact Apple Technical Support.

SUMMARY OF THE INTERNATIONAL UTILITIES

Constants

```
zeroCycle    = 1;    {0:00 AM/PM format}

MYD          = 3;    {month, day, year}
DYM          = 4;    {day, year, month}
YDM          = 5;    {year, day, month}

longDay      = 0;    {day of the month}
longWeek     = 1;    {day of the week}
longMonth    = 2;    {month of the year}
longYear     = 3;    {year}

supDay       = 1;    {suppress day of month}
supWeek      = 2;    {suppress day of week}
supMonth     = 4;    {suppress month}
supYear      = 8;    {suppress year}
```

Assembly-Language Information

```
zeroCycle    EQU    1       ;use 0:00 AM/PM format

MYD          EQU    3       ;use month, year, day
DYM          EQU    4       ;use day, year, month
YDM          EQU    5       ;use year, day, month

longDay      EQU    0       ;day of month
longWeek     EQU    1       ;day of week
longMonth    EQU    2       ;month of year
longYear     EQU    3       ;year

supDay       EQU    0       ;suppress day of month
supWeek      EQU    2       ;suppress day of week
supMonth     EQU    4       ;suppress month
supYear      EQU    8       ;suppress year
```

17 THE SCRIPT MANAGER

ABOUT THIS CHAPTER

This chapter describes the Script Manager, a set of general text manipulation routines that let applications function correctly with non-Roman writing systems such as Japanese and Arabic, as well as Roman (or Latin-based) alphabets such as English, French, and German. The Script Manager works with one or more Script Interface Systems, each of which contains the rules for a specific method of writing.

> **Reader's guide:** Most applications do not need to call the Script Manager routines directly, since they can handle text by means of TextEdit, which functions correctly with the Script Manager. Applications that need to call the new routines are those that directly manipulate text, such as word processors or programs that parse ordinary language.

You should already be familiar with

- QuickDraw's text manipulation functions
- the International Utilities package
- the Binary-Decimal Conversion package

It may also be helpful to have a general understanding of how the Font Manager provides font support for QuickDraw and how TextEdit handles word selection and justification.

The process of adapting an application to different languages, called **localization,** is made easier if certain principles are kept in mind when you create the application. For example, you should place quoted strings in resources separate from program code, and you should avoid implicit assumptions about the language that the application uses, such as the number of characters in its alphabet. General guidelines for writing applications that are easy to localize are presented in *Human Interface Guidelines,* available through the Apple Programmers and Developers Association (APDA). They are summarized in the "Compatibility Guidelines" chapter of this volume.

ABOUT THE SCRIPT MANAGER

The Script Manager is a set of extensions to the standard Macintosh Toolbox and operating system that does two things:

- It provides standard, easy-to-use tools for the sophisticated manipulation of ordinary text.
- It makes it easy to translate an application into another writing system.

A **script** is a writing system. Roman scripts are writing systems whose alphabets have evolved from Latin. Non-Roman scripts, (such as Japanese, Chinese, and Arabic) have quite different characteristics. For example, Roman scripts generally have less than 256 characters, whereas the Japanese script contains more than 40,000. Characters of Roman scripts are relatively independent of each other, but Arabic characters change form depending on surrounding characters.

For example, Figure 1 shows how Key Caps looks in Arabic script.

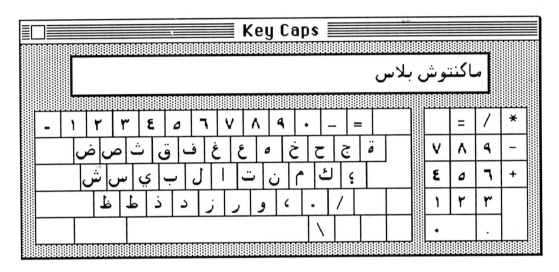

Figure 1. Key Caps in Arabic Script

The Script Manager is the low-level software that enables Macintosh applications to work with such different scripts. It includes utilities and initialization code to create an environment in which scripts of all kinds can be handled. In order for an application to use a particular script, a **Script Interface System** to support that script must also be present. All the currently available Script Interface Systems are written by Apple. Macintosh computers normally use the Roman script, so the Roman Interface System (RIS) is in the System file and always present. On some models it may be in ROM. Other Script Interface Systems are the Kanji Interface System (KIS, also called KanjiTalk), which allows applications to write in Japanese; the Arabic Interface System (AIS); and the Hanze Interface System (HIS) for Chinese.

A Script Interface System typically provides the following:

- fonts for the target language
- keyboard mapping tables
- special routines to perform character input, conversion, sorting, and text manipulation
- a desk accessory utility for system maintenance and control

The Script Manager calls a Script Interface System to perform specific procedure calls for a given script. How a typical call (in this case, Pixel2Char) is passed from an application through the Script Manager to a Script Interface System and back is shown in Figure 2.

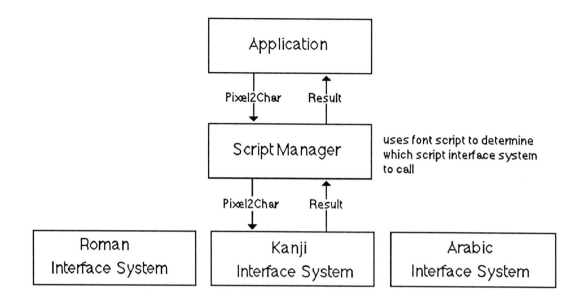

Figure 2. Example of a Procedure Call

In many cases the versatility provided by Script Interface Systems allows applications to be localized for non-Roman languages with no change to their program code (assuming they were written to permit localization to Roman script). Up to 64 different Script Interface Systems can be installed at one time on the Macintosh, allowing an application to switch back and forth between different scripts. When more than one Script Interface System is installed, an icon symbolizing the script in use appears at the right side of the menu bar.

The Script Manager provides the functions needed to extend Macintosh's text manipulation capabilities beyond any implicit assumptions that would limit it to Roman scripts. The areas in which these limitations appear are:

- **Character set size.** Large character sets, such as Japanese, require two-byte codes for computer storage in place of the one-byte codes that are sufficient for Roman scripts. Script Manager routines permit applications to run without knowing whether one-byte or two-byte codes are being used.

- **Writing direction.** The Script Manager provides the capability to write from right to left, as required by Arabic, Hebrew, and other languages, and to mix right-to-left and left-to-right directions within lines and blocks of text.

- **Context dependence.** Context dependence means that characters may be modified by the values of preceding and following characters in the input stream. In Arabic, for example, many characters change form depending on other characters nearby. Context analysis is usually handled by the appropriate Script Interface System under the control of the Script Manager.

- **Word demarcation.** Words in Roman scripts are generally delimited by spaces and punctuation marks. In contrast, Japanese scripts may have no word delimiters, so the Script Manager provides a more sophisticated method of finding word boundaries. TextEdit calls may be intercepted by the Script Manager, which calls the appropriate

Script Interface System routines to perform selection, highlighting, dragging, and word wrapping correctly for the current script.

■ **Text justification.** Justification (spreading text out to fill a given line width) is usually performed in Roman text by increasing the size of the interword spaces. Arabic, however, inserts extension bar characters between joined characters and widens blank characters to fill any remaining gap. The Script Manager provides routines that take these alternate justification methods into account when drawing, measuring, or selecting text.

TEXT MANIPULATION

Applications that do extensive text handling and analysis, such as word processors, may need to use Script Manager routines directly and work in close interaction with Script Interface Systems. This section describes some potential problems with such applications and provides general guidelines for handling them.

Determining the Script in Use

The characteristics of different scripts require that text manipulation functions be handled according to the script in use. Every script has a unique identification number, as shown in the following list:

Constant	Value	Script
smRoman	0	Normal ASCII alphabet
smKanji	1	Japanese
smChinese	2	Chinese
smKorean	3	Korean
smArabic	4	Arabic
smHebrew	5	Hebrew
smGreek	6	Greek
smRussian	7	Cyrillic
smReserved1	8	Reserved
smDevanagari	9	Devanagari
smGurmukhi	10	Gurmukhi
smGujarati	11	Gujarati
smOriya	12	Oriya
smBengali	13	Bengali
smTamil	14	Tamil
smTelugu	15	Telugu
smKannada	16	Kannada
smMalayalam	17	Malayalam
smSinhalese	18	Sinhalese

Constant	Value	Script
smBurmese	19	Burmese
smKhmer	20	Cambodian
smThai	21	Thai
smLaotian	22	Laotian
smGeorgian	23	Georgian
smArmenian	24	Armenian
smMaldivian	25	Maldivian
smTibetan	26	Tibetan
smMongolian	27	Mongolian
smAmharic	28	Ethiopian
smSlavic	29	Non-Cyrillic Slavic
smVietnamese	30	Vietnamese
smSindhi	31	Sindhi
smUninterp	32	Uninterpreted symbols (such as MacPaint palette symbols)

The Script Manager looks for one of these values in the font field of the current grafPort (thePort) to determine which script the application is using. The script specified by the font of thePort is referred to as the **font script.** For example, if thePort's font is Geneva, the font script will be Roman. If thePort's font is Kyoto, the font script will be Japanese. If the mapping from font to script results in a request for a Script Interface System that is not available, the font script defaults to Roman.

> **Note:** Be sure to set the font in the current grafPort correctly so the Script Manager will know what script it is working with. Otherwise the results it returns will be meaningless (for example, if a block of Arabic text is treated as if it were kanji).

The font script is not to be confused with the **key script,** which is maintained by the system. The key script value determines which keyboard layout and input method to use, but has no effect on characters drawn on the screen or on the operations performed by the Script Manager routines. The key and font scripts are not always the same. For example, while an international word processing application is using the Arabic Interface System for keyboard input, it may also be drawing kanji and Roman text on the screen. For further information about keyboard characters translation, see the System Resource File chapter in this volume.

Drawing and Measuring

The drawing and measuring of Roman and non-Roman text is handled correctly by standard Toolbox routines working in conjunction with the current Script Interface System and the Script Manager. For example, the QuickDraw routine TextWidth can always be used to find the width of a given line of text, since the Script Interface System that is currently in use modifies the routine if necessary to give proper results.

For an application to be able to handle non-Roman as well as Roman scripts, however, it is important for text to be drawn and measured in blocks, rather than as individual characters.

> **Warning:** Since non-Roman scripts can have multibyte characters, breaking apart a string into individual bytes will have unpredictable results. This is not a good idea even on standard Roman systems: scaled or fractional-width characters cause incorrect results if measured and/or drawn one at a time. Also, it takes longer to measure the widths of several characters one at a time (using CharWidth) than it does to measure them together (using TextWidth or MeasureText).

In addition to supporting the standard trap routines for drawing and measuring text, the Script Manager provides routines for handling text that is fully justified. These routines behave the same as the standard drawing and measuring routines, but they have the extra ability to spread the text out evenly on the line.

Parsing

One problem in evaluating or searching non-Roman text is that the low byte of a double-byte character may be treated as though it were a valid character. For example, 93 (the ASCII code for a right bracket) is the value of the low byte for up to 60 double-byte kanji characters. If an application uses this character as a delimiter and searches through double-byte text, it can produce invalid results. To prevent invalid character evaluation results, applications should use the Script Manager routine CharByte to determine whether the character in question is one byte of a double-byte character.

A related problem occurs when text is broken up into arbitrary chunks. This is a problem for scripts whose characters are more than one byte long, or that change their appearance based on surrounding context. The best solution is to avoid breaking text into physical chunks. If it is necessary to draw the text in sections, it should be done using the clipping facility of QuickDraw.

For example, suppose a graphics program needs to draw a string that has been rotated to 45°, and it must use a temporary buffer to draw the original text before drawing the rotated text on the screen. The solution is to create a grafPort whose bit image is the buffer and set the clipping region or bitmap bounding rectangle to the dimensions of the buffer. The text can then be drawn into the grafPort, with the starting pen position set up so that the desired segment of the text appears in the buffer. The text can be drawn in the buffer as many times as is necessary, with a different starting pen position for each segment, until the entire text has been drawn on the screen.

This method lets the Script Interface System correctly draw the characters each time, regardless of any double-byte character or context problems. It also ensures that fractional width characters will be drawn correctly.

Character Codes

An application may, for some reason, need to use a character code or range of codes to represent non-character data (such as field delimiters). Character codes below $20 are never affected by the Script Interface System, and therefore can be used safely for these special purposes. Note, however, that certain characters in this range are already assigned special meanings by parts of the Macintosh Toolbox (TextEdit) or certain languages (C). The following low-ASCII characters should be avoided:

Character	ASCII Code
Null	0
Enter	3
Backspace	8
Tab	9
Line feed	10
Carriage return	13
System characters	17, 18, 19, 20
Clear	27
Cursor keys	28, 29, 30, 31

Key-Down Event Handling

Double-byte characters are passed to an application by two key-down events. With double-byte scripts, the Script Interface System extends TextEdit as necessary to handle character buffering.

Text-processing routines should check to see whether a key-down event is the first byte of a double-byte character by using CharByte. If so, they should buffer the first byte and wait for the second byte. When the second byte arrives, the character can be inserted in the text and drawn correctly.

TextEdit performance can be improved significantly, even with Roman scripts, if the application program buffers characters. Each time through the event loop, if the current event is a keyDown or autoKey, place the byte in a buffer. Whenever the event is anything else (including the null event), insert the buffer (call TEDelete to remove the current selection range, call TEInsert to add the buffered characters, then clear the buffer).

Writing Direction

The standard writing direction at a given time is determined by the low-memory global teSysJust. Setting teSysJust is handled by the Script Interface System, which provides user control through a desk accessory. For Roman text teSysJust is set to 0; if it is –1, the user (or the Script Interface System) has specified right-to-left as the standard system direction. The value of this global has two results:

- TextEdit, the Menu Manager, and the Control Manager's radio buttons and check boxes will all justify on the right instead of the left. For compatibility, the meaning of teJustLeft (0) changes. In that case, 0 causes the text to be right-justified, so teJustLeft actually represents default justification. The parameter teForceLeft should be used if the application really needs to force the justification to be left. This is also the case for the TextEdit routine TextBox.

- Bidirectional fonts, such as Arabic and Hebrew, will draw blocks from right to left. Within blocks of Arabic or Hebrew, QuickDraw is patched to order text from right to left. That is, text is drawn from the given penLoc towards the right as normal, but the order of the characters within that text may be reversed.

When constructing dialog boxes, if the user sets teSysJust through the Script Interface System desk accessory, everything in dialog boxes will be lined up on the right edges of the individual item rectangles. If a column of buttons, for example, is supposed to line up in either writing direction, both the left and the right boundaries should be aligned.

When a word processor displays different text fonts and styles within a line, the pieces should be drawn (and measured) in different order, depending on the teSysJust value.

Partitioning Text

You should be careful when text needs to be partitioned or analyzed. With the Script Manager, bytes may be mapped to different fonts in order to display non-Roman characters. This mapping is also not fixed, because it can depend on the context around the byte. Moreover, with Japanese and Chinese double-byte characters, a single byte may be only part of a character. Here is a list of situations requiring extra care:

- Applications should not assume that a given character code will always have the same width. With certain scripts, for example, using the new Font Manager cached width tables may give inaccurate results. The new QuickDraw routine MeasureText will return correct results with all current scripts.

- Applications should not assume that a monospaced font always produces monospaced text. For example, the user might insert a wide Japanese character within a line of Monaco text.

- Applications should be capable of processing zero-width characters. Zero-width characters should never be divided from the previous character in the text when partitioning text. When truncating a string to fit into a horizontal space, the correct algorithm is to truncate from the end of the string toward the beginning, one byte at a time, until the total width is small enough. This avoids cutting text before a zero-width character.

- Script Manager utility routines should be used any time a line of text is to be partitioned, as in selection, searching, or word wrapping. If a line is to be truncated within a cell, for example, Pixel2Char should be used to find the point where the line should be broken. If a line of text is broken into pieces, as when a word processor displays different text fonts and styles within a line, Pixel2Char and Char2Pixel can be applied to each piece in succession to find the character offset or pixel width.

- Applications should use the FindWord routine for word selection and word wrapping, since some languages do not use spaces between words. TextEdit breaks words properly because it is extended by the Script Interface System to handle the current script.

Numeric Strings

The characters that can appear in a numeric string depend on the script in which the string is written. Applications that want to check ASCII strings to see if they are valid numeric fields, or convert ASCII strings into their equivalent numeric values, should use the SANE routines to do so. These routines will always return the correct result, regardess of the script in which the number is written. SANE routines are described in the *Apple Numerics Manual*.

Note: As with the international sorting and date/time routines, the interpretation of numbers depends on the font for the current port. See "Script Information", later in this chapter.

USING THE SCRIPT MANAGER

This section outlines the routines provided by the Script Manager and explains some of the basic concepts you need to use them. The actual routines are presented later in this chapter.

Script Information

FontScript tells your application to which script the font of the current grafPort belongs. IntlScript is similar to FontScript but is used by the International Utilities package to determine the number, date, time, currency, and sorting formats.

> **Note:** Application programs can examine the international parameter blocks that determine the number, date, time, currency, and sorting formats by calling the IUGetIntl routine in the International Utilities package. Applications should not try to access the international parameter blocks directly (via the Resource Manager routine GetResource).

KeyScript is used to change the keyboard script, which determines the layout of the keyboard. Word processors and other text-intensive programs should use this routine to change the keyboard script when the user changes the current font. For example, if the user selects Al Qahira (Cairo) as the current font or selects a run of text that uses the Al Qahira font, the application should set the keyboard script to Arabic. This can be done by using FontScript to find the script for the font, then using KeyScript to set the keyboard.

> **Note:** With many scripts, the user can also change the keyboard script by using the script desk accessory. Alternatively, your application can check the keyscript (using GetEnvirons) in its main event loop; if it has changed, the application can set the current font to the system font of the new keyscript (determined by a call to GetScript). This saves the user from having to do it manually.

Character Information

With scripts that use two-byte characters, such as kanji, it is necessary to be able to determine what part of a character a single byte represents. CharByte tells you whether a particular byte is the first or second byte of a two-byte character, or a single-byte character code.

Here is an example of adding an extra step to a search procedure, similar to a check for whole words, to handle double-byte characters:

17 Script Manager

```
{Search for text at keyPtr with size keySize}

done := false;
newLocation := -1;
repeat
   newLocation := Munger(mainHandle, newLocation+1,
      keyPtr, keySize, nil, 0); {find the raw text}
   if newLocation < 0 then done := true
   {only use CharByte when ScriptManager is installed}
   else if (scriptsInstalled <= 1) |
      (CharByte(mainHandle^,newLocation) <= 0) then done := true
         {note that CharByte doesn't touch the heap}
until done;
if newLocation >= 0 then {we really got it, so do something}
```

To make an extra test for whole words, the following code can be inserted instead of the done := true statement after CharByte:

```
if not testWord then done := true     {if no word testing}
else begin                            {test whole word}
   HLock(mainHandle);                 {FindWord may touch heap}
   FindWord(mainHandle^, GetHandleSize(mainHandle),
      newLocation, false, nil, myOffsets);
   if myOffsets[0] = newLocation then
       if myOffsets[1] = newLocation+keySize then done:= true;
   HUnlock(mainHandle);               {restore}
   end;                               {whole word test}
```

The CharType routine is similar to CharByte; it tells you what kind of character is indicated given a text buffer pointer and an offset. CharType returns additional information about the character, such as to which script it belongs and whether it's uppercase or lowercase.

Text Editing

Pixel2Char converts a screen position (given in pixels) to a character offset. This is useful for determining the character position of a mouse-down event.

The Char2Pixel routine finds the screen position (in pixels) of insertion points, selections, and so on, given a text buffer pointer and a length.

The FindWord routine can be used to find word boundaries within text. It takes an optional breakTable parameter which can be used to change its function for a particular script. For word wrapping or selection, application programs can call Pixel2Char to find a character offset and FindWord to find the boundaries of a word.

The HiliteText routine is used to find the appropriate sections of text to be highlighted. It allows applications to be independent of the direction of text. The right-to-left languages are actually bidirectional, with mixed blocks of left-to-right and right-to-left text. Using this routine allows applications to highlight properly with left-to-right or with bidirectional scripts.

The DrawJust and MeasureJust routines can be used to draw and measure text that is fully justified. These routines take a **justification gap** argument, which determines how much justification is to be done. The justification gap is the difference between the normal width of the text, as measured by TextWidth, and the desired margins after justification has taken place. A justification gap of zero causes these routines to behave like the QuickDraw DrawText and MeasureText routines.

Pixel2Char and Char2Pixel also take the justification gap argument, so they can be used on fully justified text.

Advanced Routines

The Transliterate routine converts text to the closest approximation in a different script or type of character. The primary use of this routine for developers is to convert uppercase text to lowercase and vice versa.

The Font2Script routine can be used to map an arbitrary font number to the appropriate script. By using Font2Script and KeyScript, for example, your program can set the keyboard to correspond to the user's font selection.

System Routines

The GetEnvirons and SetEnvirons routines can be used to retrieve or to modify the global variables maintained for all scripts. Each script also has its own set of local variables and routine vectors. The GetScript and SetScript routines perform the same functions as GetEnvirons and SetEnvirons, but they work with the local area of the specified script.

> **Warning:** Changing the local variables of a script while it is running can be dangerous. Be sure you know what you are doing before attempting it, following the guidelines in the documentation for the particular Script Interface System. Save the original values of the variables you change, and restore them as soon as possible.

The GetEnvirons and SetEnvirons routines either pass or return a long integer. The actual values that are loaded or stored can be long integers, integers, or signedBytes. If the value is not a long integer, then it is stored in the low-order word or byte of the long integer. The remaining bytes in the value should be zero with SetScript and SetEnvirons, and are set to zero with GetScript and GetEnvirons.

The GetDefFontSize, GetSysFont, GetAppFont, GetMBarHeight, and GetSysJust functions return the current values of specific Script Manager variables. SetSysJust is a procedure that lets you adjust the system script justification.

SCRIPT MANAGER ROUTINES

The Script Manager provides routines that support text manipulation with scripts of all kinds.

Assembly-language note: You can invoke each of the Script Manager routines with a macro of the same name preceded by an underscore. These macros, however, aren't trap macros themselves; instead they expand to invoke the trap macro _ScriptUtil. The Script Manager then determines the routine to execute from the **routine selector,** a long integer that's pushed on the stack. The routine selectors are listed in the Script Manager equates included with the Macintosh Programmer's Workshop, Version 2.0 and higher.

CharByte

```
FUNCTION CharByte  (textBuf: Ptr; textOffset: Integer) : Integer;
```

CharByte is used to check the character type of the byte at the given offset (using an offset of zero for the first character in the buffer). It can return the following values:

Value	Meaning
−1	First byte of a multibyte character
0	Single-byte character
1	Last byte of multibyte character
2	Middle byte of multibyte character

CharType

```
FUNCTION CharType (textBuf: Ptr; textOffset: Integer) : Integer;
```

CharType is an extension of CharByte which returns more information about the given byte.

Note: If the byte indicated by the offset is not the last or the only byte of a character, the offset should be incremented until the CharType call is made for the lowest-order byte.

The format of the return value is an integer with the following structure:

Bits	Contents
0–3	Character type
4–7	Reserved
8–11	Character class (subset of type)
12	Reserved
13	Direction
14	Character case
15	Character size

Each Script Interface System defines constants for the different types of characters. The following predefined constants are available to help you access the CharType return value for the Roman script:

```
CONST
        { CharType character types }
        smCharPunct    = 0;
        smCharAscii    = 1;
        smCharEuro     = 7;
        { CharType character classes }
        smPunctNormal = $0000;
        smPunctNumber = $0100;
        smPunctSymbol = $0200;
        smPunctBlank  = $0300;
        { CharType directions }
        smCharLeft     = $0000;
        smCharRight    = $2000;
        { CharType character case }
        smCharLower    = $0000;
        smCharUpper    = $4000;
        { CharType character size (1 or 2 byte) }
        smChar1byte    = $0000;
        smChar2byte    = $8000;
```

For example, if the character indicated were an uppercase "A" (single-byte), then the value of the result would be smCharAscii + smCharUpper. Blank characters are indicated by a type smCharPunct and a class smCharBlank.

Pixel2Char

```
FUNCTION Pixel2Char    (textBuf: Ptr; textLen, slop, pixelWidth:
        Integer; VAR leftSide: Boolean) : Integer;
```

Pixel2Char should be used to find the nearest character offset within a text buffer corresponding to a given pixel width. It returns the offset of the character that pixelWidth is closest to. It is the inverse of the Char2Pixel routine.

The leftSide flag is set if the pixel width falls within the left side of a character. This flag can be used for word selection, and for positioning the cursor correctly at the end of lines. For example, during word selection if the character offset is at the end of a word and the leftSide flag is on, then the double click was actually on the following character, and the ⸴ preceding word should not be selected.

The slop argument is used for justified text. It specifies how many extra pixels must be added to the length of the string. If the text is not justified, pass a slop value of zero.

Char2Pixel

```
FUNCTION Char2Pixel (textBuf: Ptr; textLen, slop, offset: Integer;
        direction: SignedByte): Integer;
```

Char2Pixel is the inverse of Pixel2Char ; it should be used to find the screen position of carets and selection points, given the text and length. For left-to-right scripts (including kanji), this routine works the same way as TextWidth. For other scripts, it works differently. The parameters are the same as in Pixel2Char, except for the direction.

The direction argument indicates whether Char2Pixel is being called to determine where the caret should appear or to find the endpoints for highlighting. For unidirectional scripts such as Roman, it should have the value 1. The following predefined constants are available for specifying the direction:

```
CONST
        smLeftCaret    =  0;      {place caret for left block}
        smRightCaret   = -1;      {place caret for right block}
        smHilite       =  1;      {direction is TESysJust}
```

Like Pixel2Char, this routine can handle fully justified text. If the text is not justified, pass a slop value of zero.

Although Char2Pixel uses TextWidth (with Roman script), the arguments passed are not the same. TextWidth, for ease of calling from Pascal, takes a byteCount argument which is redundant. The length and offset for Char2Pixel are not equivalent; the routine needs the context of the complete text in order to determine the correct value. For example, if myPtr is a pointer to the text 'abcdefghi', with the cursor between the 'd' and the 'e' (and no justification), the call would be

```
pixelWidth := Char2Pixel(myPtr, 9, 0, 4, 1);
```

When Char2Pixel is used to blink the insertion, the direction parameter to Char2Pixel should depend on the keyboard script. The call can look like this:

```
keyDirection := GetScript(GetEnvirons(smKeyScript),smScriptRight);
pixelWidth := Char2Pixel(myPtr, 9, 0, 4, keyDirection);
```

However, the keyboard script may change between drawing and erasing the insertion point. An application should remember the position where it drew the cursor, then erase (invert) at that position again. This can be done by remembering the keyDirection, the pixel width, or even the whole rectangle. For example, if the application remembers the keyDirection by declaring it as a global variable, code like this could be used:

```
drawingInsertion := true; {when window is activated}
.
.
.
{to blink the insertion point}
IF drawingInsertion THEN
  BEGIN{drawing}
   keyDirection := GetScript(GetEnvirons(smKeyScript),smScriptRight);
   pixelWidth := Char2Pixel(myPtr, myLength, mySlop, keyDirection);
   {Get the vertical position for the insertion point, then invert }
   { the appropriate rectangle}
  END
ELSE
  BEGIN {erasing}
   pixelWidth := Char2Pixel(myPtr, myLength, mySlop, keyDirection);
   {Get the vertical position for the insertion point, then invert }
   { the appropriate rectangle}
  END; {blinking}
drawingInsertion := not drawingInsertion;
```

FindWord

```
PROCEDURE FindWord(textPtr: Ptr; textLength, offset: Integer
          leftSide: Boolean; breaks: BreakTable; var offsets:
          OffsetTable);
```

FindWord takes a text string, passed in the textPtr and textLength parameters, and a position in the string, passed as an offset. The leftSide flag has the same meaning here as in the Pixel2Char routine. FindWord returns two offsets in the offset table which specify the boundaries of the word selected by the offset and leftSide. For example, if the text "This is it" were passed with an offset and leftSide that selected the first word, the offset pair returned would be (0,4).

FindWord uses a **break table**—a list of word-division templates—to determine the boundaries of a word. If the breaks parameter is NIL, the default word-selection break table for the current script is used. If it is POINTER(–1), then the default word-wrapping break table is used. If the breaks parameter has another value, it should point to a valid break table, which will be used in place of the default table. For information about constructing alternate break tables, contact Apple Technical Support.

Word-selection break tables are used to find boundaries of words for word selection, dragging, spelling checking, and so on. **Word-wrapping break tables** are used to distinguish words for finding the widths of lines for wrapping. Word selection generally makes finer distinctions than word wrapping. For example, the default word-selection break table for Roman script yields three words in the string (here): (, here, and). For word wrapping, on the other hand, this string is considered to be one word.

HiLiteText

```
PROCEDURE HiliteText (textPtr: Ptr; textLength, firstOffset,
        secondOffset: Integer; VAR offsets: OffsetTable);
```

HiliteText is used to find the characters between two offsets that should be highlighted. The offsets are passed in firstOffset and secondOffset, and returned in offsetTable.

The offsetTable can be thought of as a set of three offset pairs. If the two offsets in any pair are equal, the pair is empty and can be skipped. Otherwise the pair identifies a run of characters. Char2Pixel can be used to convert the offsets into pixel widths, if necessary.

The offsetTable requires three offset pairs because in bidirectional scripts a single selection may comprise up to three physically discontinuous segments. In the Arabic script, for example, Arabic words are written right-to-left while English words in the same line are written left-to-right. Thus the selection of a section of Arabic containing an English word can appear as shown in Figure 3.

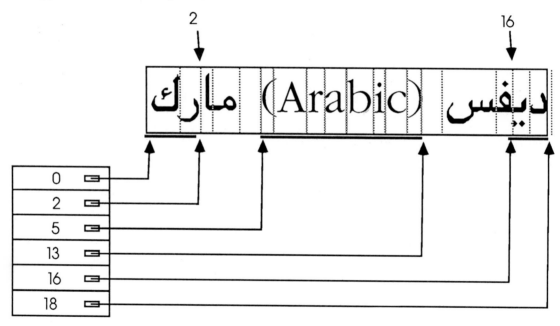

Figure 3. Example of Bidirectional Selection

HiLiteText returns the specific regions to be highlighted in this case as an offset table.

DrawJust

```
PROCEDURE DrawJust (textPtr: Ptr; textLength, slop: Integer);
```

DrawJust is similar to the QuickDraw DrawText routine. It draws the given text at the current pen location in the current font, style, and size. The slop parameter indicates how many extra pixels are to be added to the width of the string when it is drawn. This is useful for justifying text.

MeasureJust

```
PROCEDURE MeasureJust (textPtr: Ptr; textLength, slop: Integer;
        charLocs: Ptr);
```

MeasureJust is similar to the QuickDraw MeasureText routine. The charLocs parameter should point to an array of textLength+1 integers; MeasureJust will fill it with the TextWidths of the first textLength characters of the text pointed to by textPtr. The first entry in the array will return the width of zero characters, the second the width of the first character, the third the width of the first and second characters, and so forth.

Transliterate

```
FUNCTION Transliterate (srcHandle, dstHandle: Handle; target:
        Integer; srcMask: Longint): Integer;
```

Transliterate converts the given text to the closest possible approximation in a different script or type of character. It is the caller's responsibility to provide storage and dispose of it. The srcMask indicates which character types (scripts) in the source are to be converted. For example, Japanese text may contain Roman, hiragana, katakana, and kanji characters. The source mask could be used to limit transliteration to hiragana characters only.

The target value specifies what the text is to be transliterated into. The low byte of the target is the format to convert to. A value of –1 means the system script. The high byte contains modifiers, which depend on the specific script number. The following predefined constants are available to help you specify target values:

Constant	Value	Meaning
smTransAscii	0	Target is Roman script
smTransNative	1	Target is non-Roman script
smTransCase	2	Switch case for any target
smTransLower	16384	Target becomes lowercase
smTransUpper	32768	Target becomes uppercase
smMaskAscii	1	Convert only Roman script
smMaskNative	2	Convert only non-Roman script
smMaskAll	–1	Convert all text

The result is 0 for noErr or –1 for transliteration not available.

Transliteration is performed on a "best effort" basis: typically it will be designed to give a unique transliteration into the non-Roman script. This may not be the most phonetic or natural transcription, since those transcriptions are usually ambiguous (for example, in certain transcriptions "th" may refer to the sound in *the,* the sound in *thick,* or the sounds in *boathouse*).

On Roman systems, this routine is typically used to change case. For example, to convert all the characters in a block of text to single-byte Roman (uppercase), the value of srcMask would be smMaskAll, and target would be smTransUpper+smTransAscii. Each of the Script Interface Systems defines additional target constants to be used during transliteration.

Here are some examples of the effects of transliteration:

to uppercase	------►	TO UPPERCASE
TO LOWERCASE	------►	to lowercase
Mixed 漢字	------►	MIXED 漢字
romaji	------►	r o m a j i
ニホン	------►	にほん
にほん	------►	nihonn

GetScript

```
FUNCTION GetScript (script, verb: Integer) : LongInt;
```

GetScript is used to retrieve the values of the local script variables and routine vectors. The following predefined constants are available for the verb parameter:

Constant	Value	Meaning
smScriptVersion	0	Software version
smScriptMunged	2	Script entry changed count
smScriptEnabled	4	Script enabled flag
smScriptRight	6	Right-to-left flag
smScriptJust	8	Justification flag
smScriptRedraw	10	Word redraw flag
smScriptSysFond	12	Preferred system font
smScriptAppFond	14	Preferred application font
smScriptNumber	16	Script 'itl0' ID, from dictionary
smScriptDate	18	Script 'itl1' ID, from dictionary
smScriptSort	20	Script 'itl2' ID, from dictionary
smScriptRsvd1	22	Reserved
smScriptRsvd2	24	Reserved
smScriptRsvd3	26	Reserved
smScriptRsvd4	28	Reserved
smScriptRsvd5	30	Reserved
smScriptKeys	32	Script 'KEYC' ID, from dictionary
smScriptIcon	34	Script 'SICN' ID, from dictionary
smScriptPrint	36	Script printer action routine
smScriptTrap	38	Trap entry pointer
smScriptCreator	40	Script file creator

smScriptFile	42	Script file name
smScriptName	44	Script name

Verb values unique to a script are defined by the applicable Script Interface System. GetScript returns 0 if the verb value is not recognized or if the specified script is not installed.

SetScript

```
FUNCTION SetScript (script, verb: Integer; param: LongInt) : OSErr;
```

SetScript is the opposite of GetScript. It is used to change the local script variables and routine vectors and uses the same verb values as GetScript. The value smVerbNotFound is returned if the verb value is not recognized or the script specified is not installed. Otherwise, the function result will be noErr. It is a good idea to first retrieve the original value of the global variable that you want to change, using GetScript. The original value can then be restored with a second call to SetScript as soon as possible.

GetEnvirons

```
FUNCTION GetEnvirons (verb: Integer) : LongInt;
```

GetEnvirons is used to retrieve the values of the global Script Manager variables and routine vectors. The following predefined constants are available for the verb argument:

Constant	Value	Meaning
smVersion	0	Environment version
smMunged	2	Globals changed count
smEnabled	4	Environment enabled flag
smBiDirect	6	Set if scripts of different directions are installed together
smFontForce	8	Force font flag
smIntlForce	10	Force international utilities flag
smForced	12	Current script forced to system script
smForced	14	Current script defaulted to Roman script
smPrint	16	Printer action routine
smSysScript	18	System script
smAppScript	20	Application script
smKeyScript	22	Keyboard script
smSysRef	24	System folder reference number
smKeyCache	26	Keyboard table cache pointer
smKeySwap	28	Swapping table pointer

This routine returns 0 if the verb is not recognized.

SetEnvirons

```
FUNCTION SetEnvirons (verb: Integer; param: LongInt) : OSErr;
```

SetEnvirons is the opposite of GetEnvirons. It is used to change the global Script Interface System variables and routine vectors; it uses the same verbs as GetEnvirons. The value smVerbNotFound is returned if the verb is not recognized. Otherwise, the function result will be noErr.

It is a good idea to first retrieve the original value of the global variable that you want to change, using GetEnvirons. The original value can then be restored with a second call to SetEnvirons as soon as possible.

FontScript

```
FUNCTION FontScript: Integer;
```

FontScript returns the script code for the font script. The font script is determined by the font of the current grafPort.

IntlScript

```
FUNCTION IntlScript: Integer;
```

IntlScript returns the script code for the International Utilities script. Like the font script, the International Utilities script is determined by the font of the current grafPort. If the Script Manager global IntlForce is off, then IntlScript is the same as the font script; if IntlForce is on, IntlScript is the system script. For further information, see the International Utilities Package chapter in this volume.

KeyScript

```
PROCEDURE KeyScript(scriptCode: Integer);
```

KeyScript is used to set the keyboard script. This routine also changes the keyboard layout to that of the new keyboard script and draws the script icon for the new keyboard script in the upper-right corner of the menu bar.

> **Warning:** Applications can also change the keyboard script without changing the keyboard layout or the script icon in the menu bar, by calling the SetEnvirons routine with the smKeyScript verb. However, this method should only be used to momentarily change the keyboard script to perform a special operation. Changing the keyboard script without changing the keyboard layout violates the user interface paradigm and will cause problems for other Script Manager routines.

Font2Script

```
FUNCTION Font2Script(fontNumber: Integer): Integer;
```

Font2Script translates a font identification number into a script code. This routine is useful for determining to which script a particular font belongs and which fonts are usable under a particular script.

GetDefFontSize

```
FUNCTION GetDefFontSize: Integer;
```

GetDefFontSize fetches the size of the current default font. This routine is in the Pascal interface, not in ROM; it cannot be used with the 64K ROM.

GetSysFont

```
FUNCTION GetSysFont: Integer;
```

GetSysFont fetches the identification number of the current system font. This routine is in the Pascal interface, not in ROM; it cannot be used with the 64K ROM.

GetAppFont

```
FUNCTION GetAppFont: Integer;
```

GetAppFont fetches the identification number of the current application font. This routine is in the Pascal interface, not in ROM.

GetMBarHeight

```
FUNCTION GetMBarHeight: Integer;
```

GetMBarHeight fetches the height of the menu bar as required to hold menu titles in its current font. This routine is in the Pascal interface, not in ROM; it cannot be used with the 64K ROM.

GetSysJust

```
FUNCTION GetSysJust: Integer;
```

GetSysJust returns the value of a global variable that represents the direction in which lines written in the system script are justified: 0 for left justification (the default case) or –1 for right justification. This routine is in the Pascal interface, not in ROM; it cannot be used with the 64K ROM.

SetSysJust

```
PROCEDURE SetSysJust (newJust: Integer);
```

GetSysJust sets a global variable that represents the direction in which lines written in the system script are justified: 0 for left justification (the default case) or –1 for right justification. This routine is in the Pascal interface, not in ROM; it cannot be used with the 64K ROM.

HINTS FOR USING THE SCRIPT MANAGER

This section contains two programming suggestions you may find useful when using the Script Manager.

Note: In a work of this scope it is impossible to cover all aspects of script manipulation. It is strongly advised that you obtain the latest version of the Script Manager Developer's Package before trying to write an application that uses the Script Manager. This documentation is available through the Apple Programmer's and Developer's Association (APDA).

Testing for the Script Manager

Verify that the Script Manager is installed by checking to see if the Script Manager trap is implemented. To identify the number of scripts currently enabled, use the verb smEnabled. There is always at least one enabled script—Roman. Programs can use this information to optimize performance for the Roman version:

```
{ Globals }

Const
   UnimplCoreRoutine = $9F;     {unimplemented core routine}
   ScriptUtil = $B5;            {the Script Manager trap}
Var
   scriptsInstalled : Integer;  {global for testing throughout }
                                { application}
   .
   .
   .
{ Initialization: find out whether we can use the Script Manager }

scriptsInstalled := 0;
if GetTrapAddress(UnimplCoreRoutine) <>
   GetTrapAddress(ScriptUtil)
then scriptsInstalled := GetEnvirons(smEnabled);
```

```
    .
    .
    .
{ Code: we can then bracket sections of the code that use the }
{ Script Manager }

if scriptsInstalled > 1
then begin
    {use CharByte}
end else begin
    {don't use CharByte}
end;
```

Most script systems other than Roman will not install themselves on 64K ROMs, but the Roman interface system and utility routines will always be present if the Script Manager is installed.

Setting the Keyboard Script

When the user selects a font from a menu, or clicks in text of a different script, the application should set the keyboard script. Key Caps Version 2.0 does this, for example. Use the following code:

```
{ Set the font for the item or port to myFont }
{ Set the keyboard to agree with the current script, if different}

if scriptsInstalled > 1 then begin              {only if 2+ }
                                                { scripts}
    if myFont <> oldFont then begin             {quick check for }
                                                { speed}
        newScript := Font2Script(myFont);       {find the }
                                                { script}
        if newScript <> oldScript then begin    {if different}
            if multiFont or                     { always switch }
                                                { mixed fonts}
                (GetEnvirons(smKeyScript) <> smRoman) {don't }
                                                { switch if not}
            then KeyScript(newScript);          {switch the }
                                                { keyboard}
            oldScript := newScript;             {save global}
        end;
        oldFont := myFont;                      {save global}
    end;
end;
```

Roman script is a special case with single-script text. Non-Roman scripts typically include the 128 ASCII characters, and users will alternate between the Roman keyboard and the native keyboard. Hence the Roman keyboard should be left alone when switching. With mixed-script text this is not true, since users will be using a Roman font when they want Roman text. For this case, you do not need to test for Roman.

To get the current keyboard script, and the system or application font for that script, use the code:

```
{ For the system font }
if scriptsInstalled <= 1 then scriptFont := systemFont
{default to system font}
else scriptFont := GetScript(GetEnvirons(smKeyScript),
                    smScriptSysFond);

{ For the application font }
if scriptsInstalled <= 1 then scriptFont := applFont
{default to application font}
else scriptFont := GetScript(GetEnvirons(smKeyScript),
                    smScriptAppFond);
```

This code can be used if your application does not have an interface that lets users change fonts but still needs to provide for different scripts.

SUMMARY OF THE SCRIPT MANAGER

Constants

```
CONST { Values of thePort.font }

     smRoman        =  0;    {normal ASCII alphabet}
     smKanji        =  1;    {Japanese}
     smChinese      =  2;    {Chinese}
     smKorean       =  3;    {Korean}
     smArabic       =  4;    {Arabic}
     smHebrew       =  5;    {Hebrew}
     smGreek        =  6;    {Greek}
     smRussian      =  7;    {Cyrillic}
     smReserved1    =  8;    {reserved}
     smDevanagari   =  9;    {Devanagari}
     smGurmukhi     = 10;    {Gurmukhi}
     smGujarati     = 11;    {Gujarati}
     smOriya        = 12;    {Oriya}
     smBengali      = 13;    {Bengali}
     smTamil        = 14;    {Tamil}
     smTelugu       = 15;    {Telugu}
     smKannada      = 16;    {Kannada}
     smMalayalam    = 17;    {Malayalam}
     smSinhalese    = 18;    {Sinhalese}
     smBurmese      = 19;    {Burmese}
     smKhmer        = 20;    {Khmer}
     smThai         = 21;    {Thai}
     smLaotian      = 22;    {Laotian}
     smGeorgian     = 23;    {Georgian}
     smArmenian     = 24;    {Armenian}
     smMaldivian    = 25;    {Maldivian}
     smTibetan      = 26;    {Tibetan}
     smMongolian    = 27;    {Mongolian}
     smAmharic      = 28;    {Ethiopian}
     smSlavic       = 29;    {non-Cyrillic Slavic}
     smVietnamese   = 30;    {Vietnamese}
     smSindhi       = 31;    {Sindhi}
     smUninterp     = 32;    {uninterpreted symbols}

     { CharType character types }

     smCharPunct    = 0;
     smCharAscii    = 1;
     smCharEuro     = 7;

     { CharType character classes }

     smPunctNormal  = $0000;
     smPunctNumber  = $0100;
```

```
smPunctSymbol  = $0200;
smPunctBlank   = $0300;

{ CharType directions }

smCharLeft     = $0000;
smCharRight    = $2000;

{ CharType character case }

smCharLower    = $0000;
smCharUpper    = $4000;

{ CharType character size (1 or 2 byte) }

smChar1byte    = $0000;
smChar2byte    = $8000;

{ Transliterate targets }

smTransAscii   = 0          {target is Roman script}
smTransNative  = 1          {target is non-Roman script}
smTransLower   = 16384      {target becomes lowercase}
smTransUpper   = 32768      {target becomes uppercase}
smMaskAscii    = 1          {convert only Roman script}
smMaskNative   = 2          {convert only non-Roman script}
smMaskAll      = -1         {convert all text}

{ GetScript verbs }

smScriptVersion  = 0        {software version}
smScriptMunged   = 2        {script entry changed count}
smScriptEnabled  = 4        {script enabled flag}
smScriptRight    = 6        {right-to-left flag}
smScriptJust     = 8        {justification flag}
smScriptRedraw   = 10       {word redraw flag}
smScriptSysFond  = 12       {preferred system font}
smScriptAppFond  = 14       {preferred application font}
smScriptNumber   = 16       {script 'itl0' ID, from dictionary}
smScriptDate     = 18       {script 'itl1' ID, from dictionary}
smScriptSort     = 20       {script 'itl2' ID, from dictionary}
smScriptRsvd1    = 22       {reserved}
smScriptRsvd2    = 24       {reserved}
smScriptRsvd3    = 26       {reserved}
smScriptRsvd4    = 28       {reserved}
smScriptRsvd5    = 30       {reserved}
smScriptKeys     = 32       {script 'KEYC' ID, from dictionary}
smScriptIcon     = 34       {script 'SICN' ID, from dictionary}
smScriptPrint    = 36       {script printer action routine}
smScriptTrap     = 38       {trap entry pointer}
smScriptCreator  = 40       {script file creator}
smScriptFile     = 42       {script file name}
smScriptName     = 44       {script name}

{ GetEnvirons verbs }

smVersion      = 0          {environment version}
smMunged       = 2          {globals changed count}
```

```
smEnabled          = 4       {environment enabled flag}
smBiDirect         = 6       {set if scripts of both directions are }
                             { installed}
smFontForce        = 8       {force font flag}
smIntlForce        = 10      {force intl flag}
smForced           = 12      {current script forced to system }
                             { script}
smForced           = 14      {current script defaulted to Roman }
                             { script}
smPrint            = 16      {printer action routine}
smSysScript        = 18      {system script}
smAppScript        = 20      {application script}
smKeyScript        = 22      {keyboard script}
smSysRef           = 24      {system folder reference number}
smKeyCache         = 26      {keyboard table cache pointer}
smKeySwap          = 28      {swapping table pointer}
```

Routines

Script Information Routines

```
FUNCTION   FontScript : Integer;
FUNCTION   IntlScript : Integer;
PROCEDURE  KeyScript(scriptCode: Integer);
```

Character Information Routines

```
FUNCTION CharByte (textBuf: Ptr; textOffset: Integer) : Integer;
FUNCTION CharType (textBuf: Ptr; textOffset: Integer) : Integer;
```

Text Editing Routines

```
FUNCTION Pixel2Char      (textBuf: Ptr; textLen, slop,pixelWidth:
                         Integer ; VAR leftSide: Boolean): Integer;
FUNCTION Char2Pixel      (textBuf: Ptr; textLen, slop,offset: Integer;
                         direction: SignedByte) : Integer;
PROCEDURE FindWord       (textPtr: Ptr; textLength, offset: Integer;
                         leftSide: Boolean; breaks: BreakTable; var
                         offsets: OffsetTable);
PROCEDURE HiliteText     (textPtr: Ptr; textLength, firstOffset,
                         secondOffset: Integer; VAR offsets:
                         OffsetTable);
PROCEDURE DrawJust       (textPtr: Ptr; textLength, slop: Integer);
PROCEDURE MeasureJust    (textPtr: Ptr; textLength, slop: Integer;
                         charLocs: Ptr);
```

Advanced Routines

```
FUNCTION Transliterate (srcHandle, dstHandle: Handle; target:
                        Integer; srcMask: Longint) : Integer;
FUNCTION Font2Script    (fontNumber: Integer) : Integer;
```

System Routines

```
FUNCTION   GetScript (script, verb: Integer) : LongInt;
FUNCTION   SetScript (script, verb: Integer; param: LongInt) : OSErr;
FUNCTION   GetEnvirons (verb: Integer) : LongInt;
FUNCTION   SetEnvirons (verb: Integer; param: LongInt) : OSErr;
FUNCTION   GetDefFontSize: Integer;
FUNCTION   GetSysFont: Integer;
FUNCTION   GetAppFont: Integer;
FUNCTION   GetMBarHeight: Integer;
FUNCTION   GetSysJust: Integer;
PROCEDURE  SetSysJust (newJust: Integer);
```

Assembly-Language Information

Constants

```
; Routine selectors for _ScriptUtil trap

    smFontScript    EQU    0
    smIntlScript    EQU    2
    smKybdScript    EQU    4
    smFont2Script   EQU    6
    smGetEnvirons   EQU    8
    smSetEnvirons   EQU    10
    smGetScript     EQU    12
    smSetScript     EQU    14
    smCharByte      EQU    16
    smCharType      EQU    18
    smPixel2Char    EQU    20
    smChar2Pixel    EQU    22
    smTranslit      EQU    24
    smFindWord      EQU    26
    smHiliteText    EQU    28
    smDrawJust      EQU    30
    smMeasureJust   EQU    32
```

Trap Macro Name

_ScriptUtil

Note: You can invoke each of the Script Manager routines with a macro that has the same name as the routine preceded by an underscore.

18 THE CONTROL PANEL

ABOUT THIS CHAPTER

The Control Panel has been made extendible: developers can now supply new user controls for the Control Panel to display.

The new Control Panel presents a scrollable list of control devices, or **cdevs,** rather than a single panel. Each cdev is self-contained. When the user selects a control device, controls for the previous cdev disappear and most of the Control Panel's window is turned over to the newly selected one.

This chapter describes how to write a cdev that the new Control Panel will recognize and allow users to access. It concludes with the code for a very simple example cdev. (Several cdevs are standard on the System Disk; they contain all of the functions that were in the old Control Panel, and more.)

THE CONTROL PANEL

Rather than presenting a fixed set of controllable items displayed in a single, sectioned window, the new Control Panel presents a scrollable list of cdevs in the left quarter of the window. Selecting an icon in the list brings up the controls for that cdev on the right side of the panel. When the Control Panel is opened, it searches the System Folder for cdevs. Since each cdev appears with its own icon in the System Folder, users can easily add or throw away items as they need.

Before going into the details of their construction, you should consider the most basic fact about cdevs: they are parts of the Control Panel, and should perform functions that belong there—primarily the occasional setting and resetting of machine or system preferences. Before designing something as a cdev, you should think carefully about whether it belongs in the Control Panel.

You should also think carefully about the user interface. If the default settings are well chosen, most users will rarely need to use the Control Panel. Because cdevs are not used routinely, designers should make the user interface to their cdevs as straightforward as possible.

Figure 1 shows the new, extendible Control Panel.

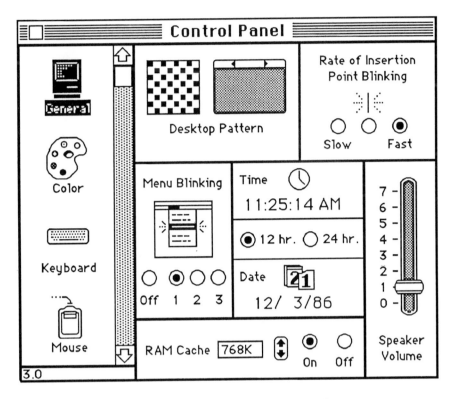

Figure 1. Extendible Control Panel

OPERATION

When the Control Panel is opened it scans the System Folder for resource files of type cdev. Upon finding a cdev file it takes the file's icon and name and adds it to the list at the left quarter of the Control Panel window. When the Control Panel has found all the cdev files, it puts General at the top of the list and opens the General cdev.

The factory-issue Control Panel has six cdevs in the scrollable list. The initial cdevs are, in order of appearance:

- General   (all Macintoshes)
- Keyboard   (all Macintoshes)
- Monitors   (Macintosh II only)
- Mouse   (all Macintoshes)
- Sound   (Macintosh II only)
- Startup device (Macintosh SE and II)

The General cdev is always first, and comes up selected the first time the user opens the Control Panel.

Each cdev is self-contained, with a standard structure and interface that is supported by the Control Panel. The Control Panel handles actions that are common to all cdevs, such as putting up a dialog window and responding to window-related events, displaying dialog items and tracking controls. The cdev itself simply describes what's in the dialog (except the cdev icon), and contains code for controlling whatever that cdev was designed to do. The division of labor between Control Panel and the individual cdevs follows.

The Control Panel will

- manage the modeless dialog window for the Control Panel as a whole, and respond to events for the window, such as dragging or closing it
- query cdevs initially, to see if they should be displayed on the current hardware
- manage the list of cdev icons, and respond to user actions on the list, such as picking which cdev to run
- track user actions on cdev controls
- if requested by a cdev, draw rectangles within the cdev portion of the window, and blank out (with light gray) any area of the window not needed by the current cdev
- if requested by a cdev, display selected error conditions
- draw dialog items belonging to the cdev that's displayed
- signal the current cdev to do its part in responding to specific events

The cdev should

- supply the standard resources that the Control Panel needs to run any cdev (described below)
- draw and respond to user items
- be prepared to handle errors, as described later in this chapter
- initialize and shut down when signalled by Control Panel to do so
- do any updating, activating, deactivating that can't be done automatically for dialog items
- respond to user keystrokes and hits on dialog items or controls, when signalled by the Control Panel
- perform whatever actions that cdev was designed to do

When the user clicks a new control device to select it, the Control Panel signals the current cdev to shut down and removes any items in the dialog that belong it. For the new cdev, the Control Panel then loads its code, splices its dialog items into the dialog's item list and draws them, signals the cdev to initialize, and begins signalling the new cdev, as needed, in response to user actions.

Contents of Cdev Files

The cdev interface to the Control Panel has two parts: a standard set of resources that describe the cdev, and are contained in the cdev resource file; second, one of those resources is code, which contains a function that must respond to a well-defined set of messages that may be passed to the cdev by the Control Panel.

To be adopted by the Control Panel, a cdev file must contain at least these seven resources:

1. 'DITL' (ID = −4064)
2. 'mach' (ID = −4064)
3. 'nrct' (ID = −4064)
4. 'ICN#' (ID = −4064)
5. 'BNDL' (ID = −4064)
6. 'FREF' (ID = −4064)
7. 'cdev' (ID = −4064)   the code resource

These standard resources, and others that are unique to the cdev, fall in two halves of the same resource ID range, −4033 through −4064. IDs that fall in the range −4064 through −4049 are reserved for the resources in the Control Panel's cdev interface. IDs in the range −4048 through −4033 can be used by individual cdevs. Cdevs that encroach on the Control Panel's range risk conflicting with future releases of the Control Panel.

The rest of this subsection describes the standard cdev resources and the messages that the cdev can expect from the Control Panel. The sample cdev file at the end of this chapter has examples of the seven resources.

'BNDL', ICN#', and 'FREF' Resources

The 'BNDL', 'ICN#' and 'FREF' resources enable the cdev to appear both in the Finder™ and Control Panel displays. (An owner resource is also needed for the cdev to display its correct icon in the Finder.)

'DITL' Resource

The 'DITL' is a standard dialog item list, including all of the items in your cdev. When a cdev is opened, the Control Panel concatenates the 'DITL' to its own. The coordinates of a cdev's dialog items are relative to the entire Control Panel window, not just the cdev portion of the window to the right of the list. To fall in the cdev section of the window, items must be entirely within the rectangle (1, 89, 253, 320).

18 Control Panel

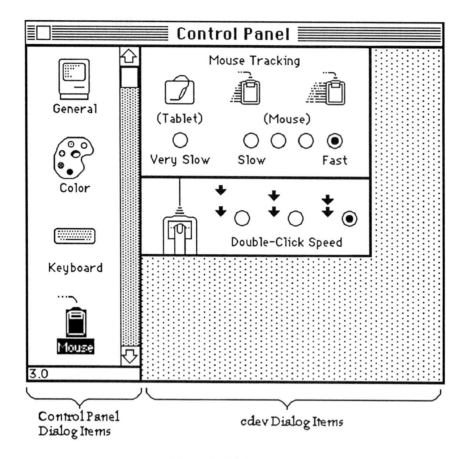

Figure 2. Dialog Items

'mach' Resource

The 'mach' resource is used by the Control Panel to determine the machines on which this cdev can run. It contains two word-sized masks: the Softmask is compared to the global variable ROM85 to test for toolbox features (such as Color Quickdraw); the Hardmask is compared to the low memory global HwCfgFlgs to determine which hardware features are available. The cdev will show up if every bit that is 0 in the Softmask is 0 in ROM85 and every bit that is 1 in the Hardmask is 1 in HwCfgFlgs. If the Softmask is 0 and the Hardmask is $FFFF then the Control Panel sends the cdev a macDev call (described below), otherwise it does not. Mask examples:

Softmask	Hardmask	Action
0	$FFFF	always call cdev with macDev message
$FFFF	$0000	appear on all machines
$7FFF	$0400	appear on machines with ADB
$3FFF	$0000	appear on Macintosh II only

The 'mach' resource enables the Control Panel to cache information about each cdev. (The user can force a rebuild of the cache by holding down Command-Option while opening the Control Panel.)

'nrct' Resource

The 'nrct' resource is a list of rectangles. The first word of the resource is the number of rectangles in the list; the rest of the resource contains the rectangle definitions, using eight bytes per rectangle in (top, left, bottom, right) order.

The Control Panel starts out with a light gray background pattern and then uses the rectangles to clear white space for the controls and to draw frames around them. The 'nrct' resource, along with the 'DITL' resource, defines the look of the cdev panel.

Rectangle coordinates are relative to the entire Control Panel window. To use all of the available space in the cdev area, use one rectangle with coordinates (–1, 87, 255, 322). (The coordinates differ from those given in 'DITL' by exactly two pixels, which is the width of the frame Control Panel draws around each rectangle.) To join two panels neatly, overlap their rectangles by one pixel on the side where they meet, so that the rectangle frames overlap too. For example, the two cdev rectangles in Figure 2 have the coordinates (–1, 87, 100, 266) and (98, 87, 159, 266).

If the number or sizes of rectangles you want varies (as in the Macintosh II Monitors cdev), the easiest way to manage it is to define rectangles covering the maximum area, and paint out those you don't want at run time with the same gray pattern Control Panel uses, or frame them yourself.

'cdev' Code Resource

The 'cdev' code resource contains all of your code to handle the other part of the cdev interface, the events that are passed to you by Control Panel. The very first piece of code in this resource must be the cdev function, as described below.

CDEV CALL

The cdev function should be the first piece of code in your 'cdev' resource. Its calling sequence is as follows:

```
FUNCTION cdev(message, Item, numItems, CPanelID: INTEGER;
        VAR theEvent: EventRecord; cdevValue: LONGINT; CPDialog:
                    DialogPtr) : LONGINT;
```

Field descriptions

message
: A message number, from the list defined below, that allows the Control Panel to tell the cdev what event has just taken place.

Item
: For hitDev messages only: the dialog item number of the item that was hit. Since the cdev's DITL is appended to the Control Panel's DITL, the number of items preceding the cdev's must be subtracted to get a value that is meaningful to the cdev. (See the hitDev message, described below.)

numItems
: The number of items in the DITL, belonging to the Control Panel, that precede the cdev's dialog items in the item list.

CPanelID
: The base resource ID of the Control Panel driver. This value is private to the Control Panel.

theEvent
: For hit, null, activate, deactivate, and key events: the event record for the event that caused the message. See the Toolbox Event Manager in Volume I for details of the EventRecord structure.

cdevValue
: The value the cdev returned the last time it was called by the Control Panel, or a return message from the Control Panel. When a cdev is initialized it typically allocates some storage for state information or other data it needs to run. Since desk accessories in general and the Control Panel in particular—and therefore cdevs—cannot have global variables, the cdevValue, which is passed to the cdev for every message, is often used for storing data. The cdevValue is also used by the Control Panel to communicate error handling action to the cdev. See "Storage in a Cdev" and "Cdev Error Checking" later in this chapter.

CPDialog
: The Control Panel DialogPtr. This may be a color dialog on Macintoshes that support color windows.

The function value returned will be one of three kinds. The Control Panel's initial call to a cdev will be a macDev call, described below. The cdev responds with a function value that tells the Control Panel whether the cdev should be displayed or not. In subsequent calls the cdev function result may be an error code, or data that needs to be kept until the Control Panel's next call. The function result is generally passed back to the cdev in the cdevValue parameter at the next cdev function call.

The cdev will be called with the current resource file set to the cdev file, the current grafPort set to the Control Panel's dialog, and the default volume set to the System Folder of the current startup disk. The cdev must preserve all of these. Also note that the Control Panel sets the cursor to the cross cursor whenever it is above the cdev area of the Control Panel window. Your cdev thus has control of the cursor only during the call; if you change it, the Control Panel will immediately reset it.

Your cdev may be reentered, especially if you put up dialog or alert boxes. The Dialog Manager calls SystemEvent and SystemTask, which may cause a deactivate message to be sent while your cdev is still processing the previous message.

Messages

The following cdev message values have been defined:

```
CONST
      initDev    = 0;   {initialization}
      hitDev     = 1;   {user clicked dialog item}
      closeDev   = 2;   {user selected another cdev or CP closed}
      nulDev     = 3;   {desk accessory run}
      updateDev  = 4;   {update event}
      activDev   = 5;   {activate event}
      deActivDev = 6;   {deactivate event}
      keyEvtDev  = 7;   {key-down or auto-key event}
      macDev     = 8;   {check machine characteristics}
      undoDev    = 9;   {standard Edit menu undo}
      cutDev     =10;   {standard Edit menu cut}
      copyDev    =11;   {standard Edit menu copy}
      pasteDev   =12;   {standard Edit menu paste}
      clearDev   =13;   {standard Edit menu clear}
```

The messages are described below.

Before dispatching to handle a specific message, all cdevs should have some common defensive behavior, for example ensuring that they have enough memory to run. Public-minded cdevs keep a minimum of memory allocated between calls, and memory that was free may be consumed by other applications while Control Panel is inactive, so it is important to check that there is enough memory available on every message.

As part of their memory check, cdevs that depend on various Toolbox packages should ensure that there's still room to load them. Cdevs should also ignore any messages (except macDev) received before initialization, or after shutdown or an error.

Your cdev, as part of a desk accessory that may move from one invocation to another, cannot use global variables. This in turn means that you cannot set user item procedures for drawing user items in the 'DITL', because the procedure pointers will dangle if the code moves. Instead, you must draw your user items in response to update messages. Also, you must find Quickdraw globals by means of thePort if you need to reference them.

See the sample cdev for examples.

The macDev Message

If the 'mach' resource has a 0 in Softmask and a −1 ($FFFF) in Hardmask, the first message a cdev will get is a macDev message. This is an opportunity for the cdev to determine whether it can run, and whether it should appear in the Control Panel's cdev list. The cdev can do its own check to see which machine it is being run on, what hardware is connected, and what is in the slots (if it has slots). The cdev must then return a function result of 1 or 0. If a 0 is returned, the Control Panel will not display the cdev in the icon list. (Note that the Control Panel does not interpret this 0 or 1 as an error message as described under "Cdev Error Checking".)

The macDev call happens only once, and only when Softmask and Hardmask are 0 and FFFF. It is always the first call made to the cdev.

The initDev Message

InitDev is an initialization message sent to allow the cdev to allocate its private storage (if any) and do any initial settings to buttons or controls. This message is sent when the user clicks on the cdev's icon.

Note that the dialog, cdev list, and all of the items in the cdev's 'DITL' except user items will already have been drawn when the initDev message is sent.

If your cdev doesn't need any storage it should return the value that was passed to it in cdevValue.

The activDev Message

An activDev message is sent to the cdev on every activate event. It allows the cdev to reset any items that may have changed while the Control Panel was inactive. It also allows the cdev to send things such as "lists activate" messages.

The updateDev Message

An updateDev message is sent to the cdev on every update event. It allows the cdev to perform any updating necessary aside from the standard dialog item updating provided by the Dialog Manager. For example, if the cdev resource contains a picture of the sound control bar, it will probably be a user item, and the picture of the control bar and the volume knob should be redrawn in response to update events.

Note that there is no mechanism for determining what to update, as the update region has already been reset. You must redraw all of your user items completely.

The nulDev Message

A nulDev message is sent to the cdev on every Control Panel run event. This allows the cdev to perform tasks that need to be executed continuously (insertion point blinking, for example).

A cdev cannot assume any particular timing of calls from applications. Don't use nulDev to refresh settings; see activDev, above.

The hitDev Message

A hitDev message is sent when the user has clicked an enabled dialog item that belongs to the cdev. The dialog item number of the item hit is passed in the Item parameter. Remember that the Control Panel's items precede yours, so you'll want (Item − numItems) to determine which of your items was hit. If the Control Panel itself has *n* items, the first of the cdev's items will be *n*+1 in the combined dialog item list. A cdev should not depend on any hardcoded value for numItems, since the number of items in Control Panel's 'DITL' is likely to change in the future.

Factoring in numItems need not mean an increase in your code size, or passing and adding numItems everywhere, or foregoing the constants that most developers use to identify specific items. You can do it easily, and neatly, as follows:

1. Subtract numItems from Item right away, and refer to your dialog items with constants as usual throughout the cdev.

2. Write simple envelope routines to enclose Dialog Manager procedures that require item number arguments. Add numItems only locally, within those routines and for the Dialog Manager calls only.

This is demonstrated in the sample cdev.

The keyEvtDev Message

A keyEvtDev message is sent to the cdev on every keyDown event and autoKey event. It allows the cdev to process key events. On return to the Control Panel, the key event will be processed by a call to dialogSelect in the Dialog Manager. A cdev that does not want the Toolbox Event Manager to do any further processing should change the what field of the EventRecord to nullEvent before returning to the Control Panel.

The deActivDev Message

A deActivDev message is sent to the cdev on every deactivate event. It allows the cdev to send deactivate messages to items such as lists.

The closeDev Message

A closeDev message is sent to the cdev when either the Control Panel is closed or the user selects another cdev. When a cdev receives a closeDev message it should dispose of any storage it has allocated, including the handle stored in cdevValue, if any.

The Standard Edit Menu Messages

Values 9 through 13 have been defined in order to provide the standard Edit menu functions of Undo, Cut, Copy, Paste, and Clear for applications that need to implement them.

STORAGE IN A CDEV

Since normal global storage is not available, the Control Panel, like all desk accessories, uses a special mechanism to store values between calls. The cdevValue parameter in the cdev call extends this storage mechanism to cdevs.

If a cdev needs to store information between calls it should create a handle during the initDev call, and return it as the cdev function result. The Control Panel always returns such handles in the cdevValue parameter at the next call.

If the cdev is called with a closeDev message, or if it needs to shut down because of an error, then this handle and any pointers or handles within the storage area should be disposed of before returning to the Control Panel.

CDEV ERROR CHECKING

Because a desk accessory may be called into many strange and wonderful situations, careful attention must be paid to error checking. The two most common error conditions are missing resources and lack of memory. Some error reporting and recovery facilities have been provided in the Control Panel to help with errors encountered in a cdev.

Because the Control Panel has no direct information about the cdev, the cdev's code must be able to detect and recover from error conditions on its own. If the recovery cannot be effected the cdev must dispose of any memory it has allocated, and exit back to the Control Panel with an error code.

Following a shutdown, the Control Panel can help report the error condition to the user and prevent accidental reentry into the cdev that might result from such things as an update event. A cdev can request three different error reporting mechanisms from the Control Panel:

- If a memory error has occured, then, after the cdev has safely shut itself down, it may request the Control Panel to issue an out-of-memory error message and gray out (paint over with the background pattern) the cdev area of the Control Panel window. It will remain grayed until another cdev is selected. The Control Panel window itself is not closed since other cdevs may still be able to function in the environment.

- If a resource error is detected, the cdev may request that a can't-find-needed-resource error message be issued.

■ The cdev may display its own error message and then call on the Control Panel to gray its area.

The Control Panel uses the cdevValue parameter to send status information to the cdev, and a proper cdev uses its function value to send information back to the Control Panel. In the absence of errors, the same value passes back and forth: the Control Panel puts the last function value it received into cdevValue when it calls the cdev; the çdev returns the value it finds there as the function value. The cdev may want to keep a handle to its own storage, in which case passing it as the function value ensures its availability, since the Control Panel will pass it back in cdevValue at the next call.

Four constants have been defined for this cdev/Control Panel communication:

```
CONST
     cdevUnset  =   3; {initial value passed in cdevValue}
     cdevGenErr = -1; {generic cdev error}
     cdevMemErr =   0; {insufficient memory for cdev execution}
     cdevResErr =   1; {missing resource needed by cdev}
```

After the macDev call, the Control Panel sends cdevUnset in cdevValue, so that until an error occurs or the cdev uses its function value as a handle, cdevUnset is passed back and forth. If the cdev encounters an error, it should dispose of all handles and pointers it has set up, strip the stack back to the same position as a normal exit, and return one of the three error codes as the function result. The Control Panel will respond as follows:

Function Result	Message to Control Panel	Control Panel Action
cdevGenErr	The cdev has encountered an error from which it cannot recover, but do not put up an error dialog.	Gray out the cdev's area, send a 0 in cdevValue in succeding cdev calls.
cdevMemErr	The cdev has determined that there is not enough memory to execute; please put up a memory error dialog.	Gray out cdev's area, put up error dialog, send a 0 in cdevValue in succeeding cdev calls.
cdevResErr	The cdev can't find a needed resource; please put up a resource error dialog.	Gray out cdev's area, put up error dialog, send a 0 in cdevValue in succeeding cdev calls.
all other values, either handles or cdevUnset	No error conditions.	Send the value back in cdevValue.

The cdev code should check cdevValue at entry. A 0 means that the Control Panel has responded to a cdev error message by shutting down the cdev and displaying an error dialog if one was requested. The cdev should immediately exit.

Once the Control Panel has responded to an error message from a cdev it will no longer respond to any return values until another cdev is launched.

The sample cdev code presented next includes error checking.

SAMPLE CDEV

Following is a REZ resource file containing resource definitions for a sample cdev. The cdev code resource is provided by the Pascal code that follows. When executed, the cdev puts up a control window that has two buttons, and displays how many messages it has received, as shown in Figure 3.

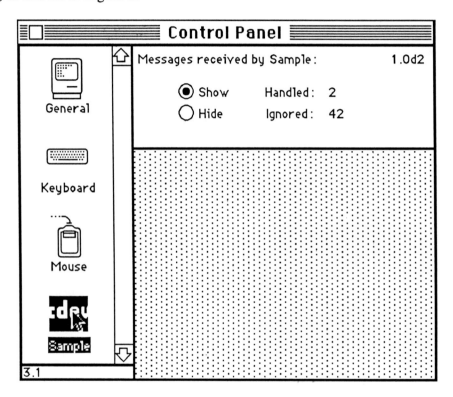

Figure 3. Sample cdev

```
/*
 * File Sample.r
 * Copyright © 1986, 1987 Apple Computer, Inc.  All rights reserved.
 *
 * Sample cdev rez file
 */

#include "Types.r"

type 'samp' as 'STR ';

type 'nrct' {
  integer = $$CountOf(RectArray);
  array RectArray { rect; };
```

```
};

type 'mach' {
  unsigned hex integer;        /* Softmask */
  unsigned hex integer;        /* Hardmask */
};

/* The owner resource (related to the BNDL below).  See Inside
      Macintosh Volume IV for more information. */
resource 'samp' (0, purgeable) {
  "Sample cdev 1.0d2, June 23, 1987"
};

resource 'BNDL' (-4064, purgeable) {
  'samp', 0,
  {  'ICN#', {0, -4064},
     'FREF', {0, -4064}
  }
};

resource 'ICN#' (-4064, purgeable) {
  {  /* array: 2 elements */
      /* [1] */
      $"FFFF FFFF 8000 0001 8000 0001 8000 0001"
      $"800E 0001 800E 0001 800E 0001 800E 0001"
      $"800E 0000 78FE 3E33 F9FE 7F33 F9FE 6333"
      $"E1CE 7F33 E1CE 7F33 E1CE 603F F9FE 7F1E"
      $"F9FE 7F1E 78FE 3F0C 8000 0001 8000 0001"
      $"8000 0001 8000 0001 8000 0001 8000 0001"
      $"8000 0001 8000 0001 8000 0001 8000 0001"
      $"FFFF FFFF 0000 0000 0000 0000 0000 0000",
      /* [2] */
      $"FFFF FFFF FFFF FFFF FFFF FFFF FFFF FFFF"
      $"FFFF FFFF FFFF FFFF FFFF FFFF FFFF FFFF"
      $"FFFF FFFE 7FFF FFFF FFFF FFFF FFFF FFFF"
      $"FFFF FFFF FFFF FFFF FFFF FFFF FFFF FFFE"
      $"FFFF FFFE 7FFF FFFE FFFF FFFF FFFF FFFF"
      $"FFFF FFFF FFFF FFFF FFFF FFFF FFFF FFFF"
      $"FFFF FFFF FFFF FFFF FFFF FFFF FFFF FFFF"
      $"FFFF FFFF 0000 0000 0000 0000 0000 0000"
  }
};

resource 'FREF' (-4064, purgeable) {
  'cdev', 0, ""
};

resource 'mach' (-4064, purgeable) {
  0xFFFF,
  0
};

resource 'nrct' (-4064, purgeable) {
  {  /* array RectArray: 1 elements */
      {-1, 87, 79, 322}
  }
```

```
};

resource 'DITL' (-4064, purgeable) {
   {  /* array DITLarray: 8 elements */
        {4,   287, 16, 320}, StaticText    {disabled, "1.0d2"};
        {4,    92, 16, 280}, StaticText    {disabled, "Messages }
                                           { received by Sample:"};
        {26, 122, 43, 170}, Control        {enabled,  -4048};
        {42, 122, 59, 170}, Control        {enabled,  -4047};
        {29, 190, 41, 230}, StaticText     {disabled, "Handled:"};
        {45, 190, 57, 230}, StaticText     {disabled, "Ignored:"};
        {29, 240, 39, 300}, UserItem       {disabled};
        {45, 240, 55, 300}, UserItem       {disabled}
   }
};


/*==================================================================
 * Resources that are private to the Sample cdev (IDs for these
 * must fall in the range -4048 to -4033).  All those above (-4064
 * to -4049) are standard for every cdev, and specified by Control
 * Panel. */

resource 'CNTL' (-4048, purgeable) {
   {26, 122, 43, 170}, 0, visible, 1, 0, radioButProcUseWFont, 0, }
   { "Show"
};

resource 'CNTL' (-4047, purgeable) {
   {42, 122, 59, 170}, 0, visible, 1, 0, radioButProcUseWFont, 0, }
   { "Hide"
};
```

The Pascal source code for the 'cdev' code resource:

```
{Copyright © 1986, 1987 Apple Computer, Inc.  All rights reserved.}

{Sample: A small cdev code resource for use by Control Panel 3.0. The }
{ cdev has two radio buttons, labeled "Hide" and "Show", which cause }
{ four other items to be visible or invisible.  The four }
{ visible/hidden items are the number of messages handled by the cdev, }
{ the number ignored, and titles for those two counts.  Note that }
{ Sample violates the prime directive for cdevs, i.e. that it do }
{ something that's really useful in Control Panel…}


{$D+} {turn debugging symbols on}

UNIT cdev;

INTERFACE

USES
        MemTypes, QuickDraw, OSIntf, ToolIntf, PackIntf;

FUNCTION Sample    (message, item, numItems, CPanelID: INTEGER;
                         theEvent: EventRecord; cdevValue: LONGINT;
                         CPDialog: DialogPtr) : LONGINT;


IMPLEMENTATION

CONST
        { Constants for all of Sample's dialog items }
        iVersion =        1;          {cdev's version number is just }
                                      { staticText}
        iTitle =          2;          {title for Sample is just }
                                      { staticText}
        iShowCounts =     3;          {show the events handled/ignored}
        iHideCounts =     4;          {hide the events handled/ignored}
        iTitleHandled =   5;          {title for events handled count}
        iTitleIgnored =   6;          {title for events ignored count}
        iHandled =        7;          {user item for number of events }
                                      { handled}
        iIgnored =        8;          {user item for number of events }
                                      { ignored}

TYPE
        SampleStorage = RECORD
            dlgPtr:         DialogPtr;
            dlgItems:       INTEGER;
            countShown:     BOOLEAN;
            msgHandled:     INTEGER;
            msgIgnored:     INTEGER;
            END;
        SamplePtr = ^SampleStorage;
        SampleHdl = ^SamplePtr;
```

```
FUNCTION  InitSample (CPDialog: DialogPtr;
                         numItems: INTEGER): LONGINT; FORWARD;
FUNCTION  EnoughRoomToRun (VAR cdevValue: LONGINT) : BOOLEAN; FORWARD;
PROCEDURE CountMessage (ourHandle: SampleHdl; handledIt: BOOLEAN);
                         FORWARD;
PROCEDURE HitSample (ourHandle: SampleHdl; item: INTEGER); FORWARD;
PROCEDURE DrawSampleItem (ourHandle: SampleHdl; item: INTEGER); FORWARD;
FUNCTION  IGetCtlHand (ourHandle: SampleHdl;
                         item: INTEGER): ControlHandle; FORWARD;
PROCEDURE IGetRect (ourHandle: SampleHdl; item: INTEGER;
                     VAR itemRect: Rect); FORWARD;
PROCEDURE IHide (ourHandle: SampleHdl; item: INTEGER); FORWARD;
PROCEDURE IShow (ourHandle: SampleHdl; item: INTEGER); FORWARD;
PROCEDURE IInvalidate (ourHandle: SampleHdl; item: INTEGER); FORWARD;


{--------------------------------------------------------------------}
{Sample: the cdev dispatch function, as documented above.  The cdev }
{ function MUST be the first code in the code resource; Control Panel }
{ jumps to the first location in the 'cdev' code resource to dispatch }
{ messages to the cdev. }


FUNCTION Sample (message, item, numItems, CPanelID: INTEGER; theEvent:
                 EventRecord; cdevValue: LONGINT; CPDialog: DialogPtr)
                   : LONGINT;
VAR
      i:               INTEGER;
      handledIt:       BOOLEAN;
      ourHandle:       SampleHdl;
      storageExpected: BOOLEAN;
BEGIN
      {Do a validity check before trying to handle the message. }
      { cdevValue is initialized to cdevUnset by Control Panel; zero }
      { is the new cdevValue after any error return.}

      storageExpected := NOT ((message = initDev)
            OR (message = macDev));
      IF storageExpected AND ((cdevValue = 0)
            OR (cdevValue = cdevUnset))
            THEN  cdevValue := 0
      {Equally important, we must check that there's still enough }
      { memory available for Sample to run, on every message. Memory }
      { can easily be consumed by other apps, etc, between messages, }
      { and (to be neighborly) we don't keep anything around between }
      { messages  except the handle in cdevValue.}

      ELSE IF storageExpected & NOT EnoughRoomToRun (cdevValue) THEN
            BEGIN
            {We're past initialization, and have been hit with a memory }
            { squeeze. Escape now, averting mayhem.}
            END

      ELSE
            BEGIN
            handledIt := TRUE;
            ourHandle := SampleHdl (cdevValue);
```

```
            CASE message OF
                initDev:      IF EnoughRoomToRun (cdevValue) THEN
                                          BEGIN
                                          cdevValue := InitSample
                                              (CPDialog, numItems);
                                          ourHandle := SampleHdl
                                              (cdevValue);
                                          END;
                closeDev:     IF ourHandle <> NIL THEN
                                          BEGIN
                                          DisposHandle (Handle
                                              (ourHandle));
                                          cdevValue := 0;
                                          ourHandle := NIL;
                                          END;
                hitDev:       HitSample (ourHandle, item - numItems);
                updateDev:    FOR i := iHandled TO iIgnored DO
                                          DrawSampleItem (ourHandle, i);
                OTHERWISE     handledIt := FALSE;
                END;
                IF ourHandle <> NIL THEN
                CountMessage(ourHandle, handledIt);
                END;

      Sample := cdevValue;
END;

{------------------------------------------------------------------}
{InitSample: Initialize the cdev}


FUNCTION InitSample (CPDialog: DialogPtr; numItems: INTEGER): LONGINT;
VAR
      i:            INTEGER;
      ourHandle:    SampleHdl;
BEGIN
      ourHandle := SampleHdl (NewHandle (SIZEOF (SampleStorage)));
      IF ourHandle <> NIL THEN
          BEGIN
          WITH ourHandle^^ DO
              BEGIN
              dlgPtr := CPDialog;
              dlgItems := numItems;
              msgHandled := 0;
              msgIgnored := 0;
              countShown := TRUE;
              END;
          FOR i := iShowCounts TO iHideCounts DO
              SetCtlValue (IGetCtlHand (ourHandle, i), ORD (i =
                              iShowCounts));
          END;
      InitSample := ORD4 (ourHandle);
END;

{------------------------------------------------------------------}
{EnoughRoomToRun: check that we still have room to run; close up if not }
```

```
FUNCTION EnoughRoomToRun (VAR cdevValue: LONGINT) : BOOLEAN;
VAR
      error:       INTEGER;
      packHand:    Handle;
BEGIN
      {Make sure there is still room for the maximum amount of memory }
      { needed to process any event, AND for any packages or other }
      { resources you need at the same time.  If you allocate lots  of }
      { storage, you should account for that also if it hasn't  been }
      { allocated yet.  Sample needs the Binary/Decimal  conversion }
      { package to display the event counts. }
      { In the interest of simplicity, this does NOT take into account }
      { the fact that PACK 7 may be in ROM; it really should.}
      packHand := GetResource ('PACK', 7);
      IF packHand <> NIL THEN
            BEGIN
            EnoughRoomToRun := TRUE;
            EXIT (EnoughRoomToRun);
            END
      ELSE IF ResError = resNotFound
            THEN error := cdevResErr      {a needed resource is missing}
            ELSE error := cdevMemErr;      {assume memFull otherwise}

      {There's too little memory to load the package.  Try to fail }
      { gracefully, disposing of our storage if it's already been }
      { allocated, because the error code we return to Control Panel }
      { will replace cdevValue.}
      IF (cdevValue <> cdevUnset) AND (Handle (cdevValue) <> NIL) THEN
            DisposHandle (Handle (cdevValue));
      cdevValue := error;
      EnoughRoomToRun := FALSE;
END;


{---------------------------------------------------------------------}
{CountMessage: count message from Control Panel as handled/ignored}


PROCEDURE CountMessage (ourHandle: SampleHdl; handledIt: BOOLEAN);
BEGIN
      IF ourHandle <> NIL THEN
            WITH ourHandle^^ DO
                  IF handledIt THEN
                        BEGIN
                        msgHandled := msgHandled + 1;
                        DrawSampleItem (ourHandle, iHandled);
                        END
                  ELSE
                        BEGIN
                        msgIgnored := msgIgnored + 1;
                        DrawSampleItem (ourHandle, iIgnored);
                        END
END;
{---------------------------------------------------------------------}
{HitSample: Handle a hit in one of our DITL items}
```

```
PROCEDURE HitSample (ourHandle: SampleHdl; item: INTEGER);
VAR
        i:              INTEGER;
BEGIN
        WITH ourHandle^^ DO
                IF countShown <> (item = iShowCounts)
                        THEN countShown := (item = iShowCounts)
                        ELSE EXIT (HitSample);

        FOR i := iShowCounts TO iHideCounts DO
                SetCtlValue (IGetCtlHand (ourHandle, i), ORD (i = item));
        FOR i := iTitleHandled TO iIgnored DO
                BEGIN
                IF item = iShowCounts
                        THEN IShow (ourHandle, i)
                        ELSE IHide (ourHandle, i);
                IInvalidate (ourHandle, i);
                END;
END;


{------------------------------------------------------------------------}
{DrawSampleItem: Draw one of our DITL user items}


PROCEDURE DrawSampleItem (ourHandle: SampleHdl; item: INTEGER);
VAR
        itemRect:    Rect;
        s:           Str255;
BEGIN
        {Note that Sample draws its user items explicitly, rather than }
        { installing a pointer to the draw procedure in the dialog item. }
        { Since the cdev's code may move between messages, the pointer }
        { would become invalid (Control Panel often calls the dialog }
        { manager before the cdev, so there's no chance to refresh the }
        { pointer either).}
        IGetRect (ourHandle, item, itemRect);
        WITH ourHandle^^ DO
                BEGIN
                SetPort (dlgPtr);
                IF item = iHandled
                        THEN NumToString (msgHandled, s)
                        ELSE NumToString (msgIgnored, s);
                END;
        WITH itemRect DO
                MoveTo (left, bottom);
        TextMode (srcCopy);
        DrawString (s);
        TextMode (srcOr);
END;
```

```
{--------------------------------------------------------------------}
{Simple routines enclosing the dialog manager functions we need, to}
{ tack on numItems (so we can refer to our items with constants }
{ everywhere else). }

{IGetCtlHand: get control handle for given dialog item}
{IGetRect: get rectangle for given dialog item}
{IHide: hide dialog item}
{IShow: show dialog item}
{IInvalidate: erase & invalidate dialog item}


FUNCTION IGetCtlHand (ourHandle: SampleHdl; item: INTEGER):
ControlHandle;
VAR
       itemHand:   Handle;
       itemRect:   Rect;
       itemType:   INTEGER;
BEGIN
       WITH ourHandle^^ DO
             GetDItem (dlgPtr, item + dlgItems, itemType, itemHand,
                                 itemRect);
       IGetCtlHand := ControlHandle (itemHand);
END;

PROCEDURE IGetRect (ourHandle: SampleHdl; item: INTEGER; VAR itemRect:
                                 Rect);
VAR
       itemType:   INTEGER;
       itemHand:   Handle;
BEGIN
       WITH ourHandle^^ DO
             GetDItem (dlgPtr, item + dlgItems, itemType, itemHand,
                                 itemRect);
END;

PROCEDURE IHide (ourHandle: SampleHdl; item: INTEGER);
BEGIN
       WITH ourHandle^^ DO
             HideDItem (dlgPtr, item + dlgItems);
END;

PROCEDURE IShow (ourHandle: SampleHdl; item: INTEGER);
BEGIN
       WITH ourHandle^^ DO
             ShowDItem (dlgPtr, item + dlgItems);
END;

PROCEDURE IInvalidate (ourHandle: SampleHdl; item: INTEGER);
VAR
       itemRect:   Rect;
```

```
BEGIN
      IGetRect (ourHandle, item, itemRect);
      EraseRect (itemRect);
      InvalRect (itemRect);
END;

END.
```

SUMMARY OF THE CONTROL PANEL

Constants

```
CONST

{ messages }

        initDev     = 0;   {initialization}
        hitDev      = 1;   {user clicked on dialog item}
        closeDev    = 2;   {user selected another cdev or CP closed}
        nulDev      = 3;   {desk accessory run}
        updateDev   = 4;   {update event}
        activDev    = 5;   {activate event}
        deActivDev  = 6;   {deactivate event}
        keyEvtDev   = 7;   {key down or autokey event}
        macDev      = 8;   {check machine characteristics}
        undoDev     = 9;   {standard Edit menu undo}
        cutDev      =10;   {standard Edit menu cut}
        copyDev     =11;   {standard Edit menu copy}
        pasteDev    =12;   {standard Edit menu paste}
        clearDev    =13;   {standard Edit menu clear}

{ Special cdevValue values }

        cdevGenErr  = -1;  {general error; gray cdev w/o alert}
        cdevMemErr  =  0;  {memory shortfall; alert user please}
        cdevResErr  =  1;  {couldn't get a needed resource; alert}
        cdevUnset   =  3;  {cdevValue is initialized to this}
```

Routines

```
FUNCTION cdev(message, Item, numItems, CPanelID :
              INTEGER; VAR theEvent : EventRecord;
              cdevValue : LONGINT; CPDialog : DialogPtr)
              : LONGINT;
```

19 THE START MANAGER

ABOUT THIS CHAPTER

This chapter describes the Start Manager, which coordinates the initialization and system startup procedures of the Macintosh SE and Macintosh II.

> **Reader's guide:** The Start Manager is operated entirely by the standard Macintosh operating system. The only time you might need to understand the Start Manager is if you were implementing a different operating system on the Macintosh.

INITIALIZATION

When the Macintosh SE or Macintosh II are turned on or restarted, the Start Manager goes through the following initialization procedures (steps specific to the Macintosh II are noted as such):

- A set of diagnostic routines test the critical hardware components (VIA1, VIA2, SCC, IWM, SCSI, and ASC); if the diagnostics succeed, the familiar startup tone is issued and the hardware components are initialized.

- Memory is tested in two stages, depending on whether the machine is being turned on or the system is being restarted. A complete test of RAM is done only when the system is first turned on; on a system restart, only a quick 1K RAM test is performed.

- The Start Manager determines which microprocessor is installed and the rate at which it's running. The global variable CPUFlag will contain the value 0, 1, or 2, indicating that the processor is an MC68000, 68010, or 68020 respectively. If the MC68020 is present, the instruction cache is enabled. Several global variables are initialized with timing information (see below for details).

- Global variables needed by the system and interrupt dispatch tables are initialized.

- On the Macintosh II, the system is put in 24-bit mode for compatibility with existing Macintosh software. (For information on how to convert to 32-bit address mode, see the Operating System Utilities chapter in this volume.)

- A small system heap is created; this heap will grow in order to accommodate additional drivers.

- The ROM resources, Package Manager, and Time Manager are initialized.

- On the Macintosh II, the Slot Manager is initialized and the initialization code on the declaration ROM of each inserted card is executed.

- The Apple Desktop Bus Manager is initialized.

- On the Macintosh II, the Start Manager looks for a video card to use as the main video display. It first tries the device specified by the user via the Control Panel. If no device has been specified, or if the specified card isn't found, it looks for the first available video sResource. (SResources are described in the Slot Manager chapter.) QuickDraw is initialized and the desktop is drawn.

- The SCSI Manager, Disk Manager, and Sound Manager are initialized.

- The cursor is made available. (If no video card was found, the global variable ScrnBase is set to 0.)

SYSTEM STARTUP

After initialization has been completed, the Start Manager performs the following system startup procedures:

- The drive number of the internal SCSI drive is obtained from parameter RAM. The Start Manager then pauses from 15 to 31 seconds to allow the device to power up. (The amount of time that the system waits can be obtained and changed with the GetTimeout and SetTimeout procedures, described below.)

- The Start Manager looks for an appropriate start device. It first checks the 3.5-inch drives, starting with the internal drive; if no disk is found, the device specified as the default start device by the user (via the Control Panel) is used. If no default is specified, or if the specified device is no longer connected, it checks for devices on the SCSI bus, beginning with the internal drive (the drive number of the internal drive is contained in parameter RAM). The remaining drives are then checked, beginning with drive 6 and ending with drive 0. For each device, the appropriate driver is read in and entered in the drive queue.

- Once a start device has been selected, system startup information is read from the device. On the Macintosh II, a slot device may take over the system startup process instead of providing system startup information; for details, see the Device Manager chapter in this volume.

- If the system startup information is dispatchable (version $44), the code is executed; otherwise, the information is read in. (The format of the system startup information is given below.)

- Using this information, the System file is used to initialize the Resource Manager, and the System Error Handler and Font Manager are then initialized.

- The system startup screen, if present, is displayed (the name of the startup screen, typically "StartUpScreen", is contained in the system startup information).

- The debugger, if present, is loaded (the name of the debugger, typically "MacsBug", is contained in the system startup information).

- ROM patches are loaded from resources of type 'PTCH'.

- If the machine uses the Apple Desktop Bus, all resources of type 'ADBS' are loaded and executed.

- Tracking of mouse movement begins.

- Drivers read in from slot devices are opened if the flag fOpenAtStart in the sRsrc_Flags field of the device's sResource is set. This flag is discussed under

"Installing a Driver at Startup" in the Driver Design chapter of *Designing Cards and Drivers for Macintosh II and Macintosh SE*.

■ The RAM cache specified in the Control Panel is installed, and the application heap is initialized.

■ All 'INIT' resources are loaded and executed (see below for details).

■ The system heap size (determined by the system startup information) and default folder are set.

■ The startup application is launched; if this fails, the Finder is launched.

SPECIAL TOPICS

This section gives additional information about various aspects of initialization and system startup.

System Startup Information

Each Macintosh-initialized volume must contain system startup information in logical blocks 0 and 1 (sometimes referred to as the "boot blocks"). This information consists of certain configurable system parameters, such as the capacity of the event queue, the initial size of the system heap, and the number of open files allowed. Figure 1 gives the format of the first 16 fields of this system startup information.

byte 0	system startup information ID (word)
2	entry point of boot code (long word)
6	system startup version number (word)
8	used internally - should be 0 (word)
A	name of system resource code file (bytes)
1A	name of system shell (bytes)
2A	name of debugger (bytes)
3A	name of debugger (bytes)
4A	name of system startup screen (bytes)
5A	name of first program to run (bytes)
6A	name of scrap file on disk (bytes)
7A	number of file control blocks (word)
7C	number of events in event queue (word)
7E	system heap size for 128K system (long word)
82	reserved (long word)
86	system heap size for 512K system (long word)

Figure 1. System Startup Information

The System file contains standard values for these fields that are used in formatting a volume. (The values for certain fields, such as the number of file control blocks and the system heap size, depend on the machine that's running and are computed at system startup time.) You should have no reason to access the information in these fields; they're shown only for your information.

The system startup information ID is used to verify that the blocks contain system startup information.

The version number distinguishes between different versions of system startup information. A version number of $44 means that the blocks contain executable code. The code typically directly follows the startup information, and the entry code for such code is stored just before the version number (at byte 2).

Following the version number are a number of names that identify standard files used or executed during system startup. These names can be up to 15 characters long, and must be preceded by a length byte.

'INIT' Resource 31

The 'INIT' 31 resource (introduced in chapter 29 of Volume IV) has been modified to provide a way for 'INIT' resources to request space in the system heap zone. Whenever 'INIT' 31 opens your file of type 'INIT' or 'RDEV', it now looks for a resource of type 'sysz' with an ID = 0. The 'sysz' resource can be any size you like, as long as the first long word contains the number of bytes of system heap space needed by the 'INIT' resources in your 'RDEV' or 'INIT' file. 'INIT' 31 calls the SetApplBase procedure as needed to meet the space request. For each 'INIT' resource loaded from the 'RDEV' or 'INIT' file, 'INIT' 31 guarantees at least 16K of contiguous space in the system heap.

Although chapter 29 of Volume IV discussed allocation of space from the address contained in the global variable BufPtr, programmers are encouraged to take advantage of the 'sysz' resource for the memory needs of their 'INIT' resources.

Timing Information

At system startup, a number of global variables are initialized with timing information useful to assembly-language programmers:

Variable	Contents
TimeDBRA	The number of times the DBRA instruction can be executed per millisecond.
TimeSCCDB	The number of times the SCC can be accessed per millisecond.
TimeSCSIDB	The number of times the SCSI can be accessed per millisecond.

Access of the SCC and SCSI chips consists of the following two instructions (where register A0 points at the base address of the respective chips):

```
@1    BTST    #0,(A0)
      DBRA    D0,@1
```

START MANAGER ROUTINES

The routines described below are used by the Start Manager for configuring the system startup process. Only a very few advanced programmers who wish to implement a different operating system on the Macintosh will ever need to use these routines.

GetDefaultStartup, SetDefaultStartup, GetTimeout, and Set Timeout are implemented for both the Macintosh SE and the Macintosh II. GetVideoDefault, SetVideoDefault, GetOSDefault, and SetOSDefault are implemented only on the Macintosh II.

Routine parameters for GetDefaultStartup, SetDefaultStartup, GetVideoDefault, SetVideoDefault, GetOSDefault, and SetOSDefault are passed and returned using parameter blocks.

Assembly-language note: When you call GetDefaultStartup, SetDefaultStartup, GetVideoDefault, SetVideoDefault, GetOSDefault, and SetOSDefault, A0 must point to a parameter block that will contain the parameters passed to, or returned by, the routine.

The DefStartRec parameter block used by GetDefaultStartup and SetDefaultStartup has the following structure:

```
TYPE DefStartType  = (slotDev,scsiDev);

     DefStartRec   = RECORD
                        CASE DefStartType OF
                          slotDev:
                           sdExtDevID:  SignedByte; {external device ID}
                           sdPartition: SignedByte; {reserved}
                           sdSlotNum:   SignedByte; {slot number}
                           sdSRsrcID:   SignedByte; {SResourceID}
                          scsiDev:
                           sdReserved1: SignedByte; {reserved}
                           sdReserved2: SignedByte; {reserved}
                           sdRefNum:    INTEGER     {driver reference }
                                                    { number}
                      END;

     DefStartPtr  = ^DefStartRec
```

The two variants of the StartDevPBRec correspond to two types of devices that can currently be connected. The slotDev variant contains information about slot devices, while the scsiDev variant describes a device connected through the SCSI port.

```
PROCEDURE GetDefaultStartup (paramBlock: DefStartPtr);
```

←	0	sdExtDevID	byte	or	←	0	sdReserved1	byte
←	1	sdPartition	byte		←	1	sdReserved2	byte
←	2	sdSlotNum	byte		←	2	sdRefNum	word
←	3	sdSRsrcID	byte					

GetDefaultStartup returns information about the default startup device from parameter RAM. To determine which variant to use, you need to look at the sdRefNum field. If this field contains a negative number, it's the driver reference number for an SCSI device, which is all you need to know. (SDReserved1 and sdReserved2 are reserved for future use.)

If sdRefNum contains a positive number, you'll need to access the information in the slotDev variant. SDExtDevID is specified by a slot's driver; it identifies one of perhaps several devices that are connected through a single slot. SDSlotNum is the slot number ($9 thru E) and sdSRsrcID is the sResource ID; see the Slot Manager chapter for details.

```
PROCEDURE SetDefaultStartup (paramBlock: DefStartPtr);
```

				or					
→	0	sdExtDevID	byte		→	0	sdReserved1	byte
→	1	sdPartition	byte		→	1	sdReserved2	byte
→	2	sdSlotNum	byte		→	2	sdRefNum	word
→	3	sdSRsrcID	byte					

SetDefaultStartup specifies a device as the default startup device. For a slot device, sdExtDevID (specified by the slot's driver) identifies one of perhaps several devices that are connected through a single slot. SDSlotNum is the slot number ($9 thru E) and sdSRsrcID is the sResource ID; see the Slot Manager chapter for details.

In the case of an SCSI device, sdRefNum contains the reference number; to specify no device as default (meaning that the first available device will be chosen at startup), pass 0 in sdRefNum. SDReserved1 and sdReserved2 are reserved for future use and should be 0.

The GetVideoDefault and SetVideoDefault calls use the following parameter block to pass information about the default video device:

```
TYPE DefVideoRec = RECORD
                     sdSlot:      SignedByte;  {slot number}
                     sdSResource: SignedByte;  {sResource ID}
                   END;

     DefVideoPtr = ^DefVideoRec
```

```
PROCEDURE GetVideoDefault (paramBlock: DefVideoPtr);
```

Trap macro   _GetVideoDefault

Parameter block
←	0	sdSlot	byte
←	1	sdSResource	byte

GetVideoDefault returns the slot number and sResourceID of the default video device. If sdSlot returns 0, there is no default video device and the first available video device will be chosen.

```
PROCEDURE SetVideoDefault (paramBlock: DefVideoPtr);
```

Trap macro   _SetVideoDefault

Parameter block
  →   0   sdSlot   byte
  →   1   sdSResource   byte

SetVideoDefault makes the device with the given slot number and sResourceID the default video device.

The GetOSDefault and SetOSDefault calls use the following parameter block to pas information about the default operating system:

```
TYPE DefOSRec = RECORD
                  sdReserved: SignedByte;  {reserved--should be 0}
                  sdOSType:   SignedByte;  {operating system type}
                END;

     DefOSPtr = ^DefOSRec
```

```
PROCEDURE GetOSDefault (paramBlock: DefOSPtr);
```

Trap macro   _GetOSDefault

Parameter block
  ←   0   sdReserved   byte
  ←   1   sdOSType   byte

GetOSDefault returns a value in sdOSType identifying the operating system to be used at startup. The sdReserved parameter currently returns 0; it's reserved for future use. This call is generally used only with partitioned devices containing multiple operating systems; for more details, see the SCSI Manager chapter in this volume.

```
PROCEDURE SetOSDefault (paramBlock: DefOSPtr);
```

Trap macro   _SetOSDefault

Parameter block
  →   0   sdReserved   byte
  →   1   sdOSType   byte

SetOSDefault specifies in sdOSType the operating system to be used at startup. The sdReserved parameter is reserved for future use and should be 0. This call is generally used only with partitioned devices containing multiple operating systems; for details, see the SCSI Manager chapter in this volume.

```
PROCEDURE GetTimeout (VAR count: INTEGER);
```

Trap macro   _GetTimeout

On exit   D0: count (word)

Note: The _GetTimeout macro is actually not a trap, but expands to invoke the trap macro _InternalWait with a routine selector of 0 pushed on the stack.

GetTimeout returns in count the number of seconds the system will wait for the internal hard disk to respond. A value of 0 indicates the default timeout of 15 seconds.

```
PROCEDURE SetTimeout (count: INTEGER);
```

Trap macro   _SetTimeout

On entry   D0: count (word)

Note: The _SetTimeout macro is actually not a trap, but expands to invoke the trap macro _InternalWait with a routine selector of 1 pushed on the stack.

SetTimeout lets you specify in count the number of seconds the system should wait for the internal hard disk to respond. The maximum value is 31 seconds; a value of 0 indicates the default timeout of 15 seconds.

Routines

Trap macro	On entry	On Exit
_GetVideoDefault	A0: ptr to param block	A0: ptr to param block
_SetVideoDefault	A0: ptr to param block	A0: ptr to param block
_GetOSDefault	A0: ptr to param block	A0: ptr to param block
_SetOSDefault	A0: ptr to param block	A0: ptr to param block
_GetTimeout		D0: count (word)
_SetTimeout	D0: count (word)	

Note: The GetTimeout and SetTimeout macros expand to invoke the trap macro _InternalWait with routine selectors of 0 and 1 respectively pushed on the stack.)

Variables

CPUFlag	Microprocessor in use (word)
TimeDBRA	Number of times the DBRA instruction can be executed per millisecond (word)
TimeSCCDB	Number of times the SCC can be accessed per millisecond (word)
TimeSCSIDB	Number of times the SCSI can be accessed per millisecond (word)

19 Start Manager

20 THE APPLE DESKTOP BUS

ABOUT THIS CHAPTER

This chapter tells you how to accomplish low-level communication with peripheral devices that are connected to the Apple Desktop Bus (ADB).

> **Reader's guide:** The standard mouse and keyboard drivers automatically take care of all required ADB access functions. When the user manipulates the mouse or keyboard, the system calls the appropriate driver and the application never uses the ADB Manager. Hence you need the information in this chapter only if you are writing a special driver, such as a driver for a new user-input device.

The ADB is a simple local-area network that connects low-speed input-only devices to the operating system. In the Macintosh II and Macintosh SE computers, the ADB is used to communicate with one or more keyboards, the mouse, and other user input devices.

Keys located on multiple keyboards are distinguished by the keyboard event message, as described in the Toolbox Event Manager chapter of this volume.

> **Note:** An ADB, using the same operating protocols, is also part of the Apple IIGS computer.

This chapter contains three principal sections:

- a description of the Apple Desktop Bus and how it works
- a description of the ADB Manager. This section of system ROM contains the routines that a driver must use to access devices connected to the ADB.
- a discussion of the special requirements for drivers that support devices connected to the ADB

You should already be familiar with

- the hardware interface to the Apple Desktop Bus, described in the *Macintosh Family Hardware Reference*
- events generated by ADB keyboard devices (described in the Toolbox Event Manager chapter in this volume) if your driver communicates with one or more keyboards

ABOUT THE APPLE DESKTOP BUS

The Apple Desktop Bus connects up to 16 low-speed input-only devices to the Macintosh II or Macintosh SE computer. Each device can maintain up to four variable-size registers, whose contents can be read from or written to by the ADB network. Each register may contain from two to eight bytes. Two of the device registers have an assigned meaning and a standardized format: register 0, used for interrupt information, and register 3, containing the device's identification number. The other two device registers have no assigned meaning, and may have different meanings for read and write operations.

The system communicates with the Apple Desktop Bus through the system's Versatile Interface Adapter chip (VIA). The VIA is described in the Macintosh Hardware chapter of Volume III.

> **Warning:** The ADB does not support connecting a device while the computer is running. The result may be to reinitialize all devices on the bus without informing the system.

The system always controls the bus. It issues commands to specific devices on the bus and they respond by accepting data, sending data, or changing their configuration. These commands are discussed below.

> **Note:** Devices connected to the ADB contain their own single-chip microprocessors, which handle both device routines and the ADB interface. If the system sends commands to a device with a duty cycle of more than 50%, the device's microprocessor may become overloaded.

Bus Commands

Each bus command consists of a byte that the system sends to a device connected to the ADB. Applications may place bus commands on the network by calling the routine ADBOp, discussed under "ADB Manager Routines" later in this chapter. There are four bus commands; their bit layouts are shown in Figure 1. All other bit layouts are reserved.

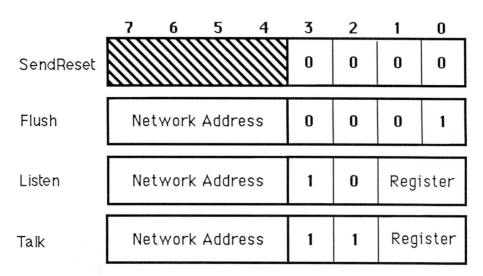

Figure 1. ADB Command Formats

The individual commands are discussed below.

Warning: Values of the low bytes of the ADB command formats other than those shown in Figure 1 are reserved, and should not be used.

SendReset

The SendReset command forces a hardware reset of all devices connected to the ADB. Such a reset clears all pending device actions and places the devices in their startup state. All devices are able to accept new ADB commands and user inputs immediately thereafter. All devices ignore the high-order four bits of the SendReset command.

Flush

The Flush command flushes data from the single device specified by the network address in its high-order four bits. Network addresses are discussed below, under "Device Addressing". It purges any pending user inputs and make the device ready to accept new commands and input data.

Listen

The Listen command is used to send instructions to devices connected to the ADB. It transfers data from a buffer in system RAM to a register in the device specified by the network address in its high-order four bits. The device register is specified by the low-order two bits of the Listen command.

Talk

The Talk command is used to fetch user inputs from devices connected to the ADB. It is the complement of the Listen command. It transfers data from a register in the device specified by the network address in its high-order four bits to a buffer in system RAM. The device register is specified by the low-order two bits of the Talk command.

Device Registers

Each device connected to the ADB contains four registers, each of which may store from two to eight bytes of data. Each register is identified by the value of the low-order two bits in a Listen or Talk command. Registers 0 and 3 have dedicated functions; registers 1 and 2 are used for purposes specific to each device, and need not be present in a device.

Note: ADB device registers are virtual registers; they need not be implemented physically. The device firmware must only respond to register commands as if a register were present.

Register 0

Device register 0 is reserved for input data. If the device has user-input data to be fetched, it places the data in register 0 and initiates an interrupt. It continues to generate interrupts until the system retrieves its data. The system responds to data-input interrupts with the following polling sequence:

- It generates a Talk command for register 0 in each device connected to the ADB.

- If the device has data to send, it responds. The system does not poll the next device until the data is exhausted.

- If the device has no data to send, or if its data is exhausted, the VIA generates an interrupt. The system then polls the next device.

Register 3

Device register 3 is reserved for device identification data and operating flags. Application programs may set this data with Listen commands and read it with Talk commands. Register 3 stores 16 bits, divided into the fields shown in Figure 2.

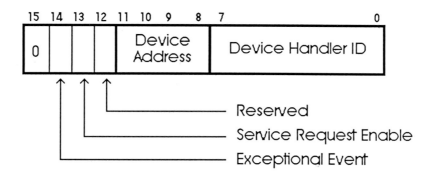

Figure 2. Format of Device Register 3

Except for commands that contain certain reserved device handler ID values (listed below), every command to register 3 changes the entire register contents. Hence to change part of the register, you should first fetch its current contents with a Talk command and then send it an updated value with Listen. You can change part of the contents of register 3 by using special device handler ID values, as described below.

The **device handler ID** field indicates the device's type. With certain devices, an application can change the device's mode of operation by sending it a new ID value. If the device supports the new mode, it stores the new value in this field.

> **Warning:** You must register new device handler ID values with Apple, so they do not conflict with the values of other devices that may be connected to the ADB at the same time.

When certain reserved values are sent to the device handler ID field by a Listen command, they are not stored in the field; instead, they cause specific device actions. Hence these values cannot be used as device ID values. They are the following:

Value	Action
$00	Change bits 8–13 of register 3 to match the rest of the command; leave Device Handler ID value unchanged.
$FD	Change Device Address to match bits 8–11 if the device activator has been depressed; leave Device Handler ID value and flags unchanged.
$FE	Change Device Address to match bits 8–11 if the result produces no address duplication on the bus; leave Device Handler ID value and flags unchanged.
$FF	Initiate device self-test. If self-test succeeds, leave register 3 unchanged; if self-test fails, clear Device Handler ID field to $00.

Other Device Handler ID values may be stored in the field.

Note: Device Handler ID values below $20 are reserved by Apple.

The **Device Address** field indicates the device's location within the 16 possible device locations of the ADB. An application may change its value with a Listen command. When this field is interrogated with a Talk command, it returns a random value. This helps you separate multiple devices that have the same ADB address; for further information, see "Device Addressing", below.

The **Service Request Enable** bit is set by the device to request an interrupt poll.

Device Addressing

There are 16 possible direct addresses, $00–$0F, for devices connected to the ADB. However, it is possible to connect more than one device to an address; this might happen, for example, in a system with two alternate keyboards.

When several devices share a single ADB address, but there are free addresses available in the net, the system will automatically reassign addresses until they are all different. It will do this every time the ADB Manager is initiated or reinitiated. To find out a device's new address, use the calls GetIndADB or GetADBInfo, described later in this chapter.

Standard ADB Device Drivers

The Macintosh II and Macintosh SE systems contain two standard ADB drivers:

- the mouse driver, which supports the ADB mouse. The Apple mouse normally has an ADB address of 3.

- the universal keyboard driver, which supports all Apple ADB keyboards. The Apple keyboard normally has an ADB address of 2, with a Device Handler ID of 1 for the

Macintosh II keyboard and 2 for the Apple Extended Keyboard. These keyboards are described in the Toolbox Event Manager chapter of this volume.

These drivers reside in the system ROM. In addition, ADB address 0 is reserved for the ADB chip itself. You can change the ADB addresses of the mouse or keyboard, as described above under "Device Registers".

Assembly-language note: The ADB address of the keyboard on which the last-typed character was entered is now stored in the global variable KbdLast. The type of the keyboard on which the last-typed character was entered is stored in the global variable KbdType. The value of KbdType is the Device Handler ID value in Register 3 of the device; values below $20 are reserved by Apple.

The requirements for writing new ADB device drivers are discussed later in this chapter.

ADB MANAGER ROUTINES

The ADB Manager consists of six routines located in the 256K ROM. You would use them only if you needed to access bus devices directly or communicate with a special device.

Some of these routines access and update information in the **ADB device table,** a structure placed in the system heap by ROM code during system startup. It lists for each device the device's type, its original ADB address, its current ADB address, the address of the routine that services the device, and the address of the area in RAM used for temporary data storage by its driver. The ADB device table is accessible only through ADB Manager routines.

```
PROCEDURE ADBReInit;
```

Trap macro	_ADBReInit

ADBReInit reinitializes the entire Apple Desktop Bus. It clears the ADB device table to zeros and places a SendReset command on the bus to reset all devices to their original addresses. ADBReInit has no parameters.

ADBReInit is intended to be used only by installer programs that permit a new device to be connected to the ADB while the system is running. Because it does not deallocate ADB resources on the system heap, ADBReInit should not be used for routine bus initialization.

ADBReInit also calls a routine pointed to by the low memory global JADBProc at the beginning and end of its execution. You can insert your own preprocessing/ postprocessing routine by changing the value of JADBProc; ADBReInit conditions it by setting D0 to 0 for preprocessing and to 1 for postprocessing. Your procedure must restore the value of D0 and branch to the original value of JADBProc on exit. The complete ADBReInit sequence is therefore the following:

- JSR to JADBProc with D0 set to 0
- reinitialize the Apple Desktop Bus
- clear the ADB device table
- JSR to JADBProc with D0 set to 1

```
FUNCTION ADBOp (data: Ptr; compRout: ProcPtr; buffer: Ptr;
        commandNum: INTEGER) : OSErr;
```

Trap macro	_ADBOp

On entry: A0: pointer to parameter block
              D0: commandNum (byte)

Parameter block
  →   0   buffer   pointer
  →   4   compRout   pointer
  →   8   data   pointer

On exit: D0: result code (byte)

The completion routine pointed to by compRout will be passed the following parameters on entry:

              D0: commandNum (byte)
              A0: pointer to data stored as a Pascal string (maximum
                    8 bytes data preceded by one length byte)
              A1: pointer to completion routine
              A2: pointer to optional data area

ADBOp transmits over the bus the command byte whose value is given by commandNum. The structure of the command byte is given earlier in Figure 1. ADBOp executes only when the ADB is otherwise idle; otherwise it is held in a command queue. It returns an error if the command queue is full. The length of the data buffer pointed to by buffer is contained in its first byte, like a Pascal string. The optional data area pointed to by data is for local storage by the completion routine pointed to by compRout.

Result codes	noErr	No error
	−1	Unsuccessful completion

```
FUNCTION CountADBs: INTEGER;
```

Trap macro	_CountADBs
On exit:	D0: number of devices (byte)

CountADBs returns a value representing the number of devices connected to the ADB by counting the number of entries in the device table. It has no arguments and returns no error codes.

```
FUNCTION GetIndADB (VAR info: ADBDataBlock; devTableIndex: INTEGER) :
       ADBAddress;
```

Trap macro	_GetIndADB		
On entry:	A0: pointer to parameter block		
	D0: entry index number; range = 1..CountADBs (byte)		
Parameter block			
←	0	device type	byte
←	1	original ADB address	byte
←	2	service routine address	pointer
←	6	data area address	pointer
On exit:	D0: positive value: current ADB address (byte)		
	negative value: error code (byte)		

GetIndADB returns information from the ADB device table entry whose index number is given by devTableIndex. ADBDataBlock has this form:

```
TYPE ADBDataBlock =
          PACKED RECORD
            devType:      SignedByte; {device type}
            origADBAddr:  SignedByte; {original ADB address}
            dbServiceRtPtr: Ptr;     {service routine address}
            dbDataAreaAddr: Ptr      {data area address}
          END;
```

GetIndADB returns the current ADB address of the device. If it is unable to complete execution successfully, GetIndADB returns a negative value.

```
FUNCTION GetADBInfo (VAR info: ADBDataBlock; ADBAddr: ADBAddress) :
        OsErr;
```

Trap macro	_GetADBInfo

On entry: A0: pointer to parameter block
                     D0: ADB address of the device (byte)

Parameter block

←	0	device handler ID	byte
←	1	original ADB address	byte
←	2	service routine address	pointer
←	6	data area address	pointer

On exit: D0: result code (byte)

GetADBInfo returns information from the ADB device table entry of the device whose ADB address is given by ABDAddr. The structure of ADBDataBlock is given above under "GetIndADB".

Result codes   noErr   No error

```
FUNCTION SetADBInfo (VAR info: ADBSetInfoBlock; ADBAddr:
        ADBAddress) : OsErr;
```

Trap macro	_SetADBInfo

On entry: A0: pointer to parameter block
                     D0: ADB address of the device (byte)

Parameter block

→	0	service routine address	pointer
→	4	data area address	pointer

On exit: D0: result code (byte)

SetADBInfo sets the service routine address and the data area address in the ADB device table entry for the device whose ADB address is given by ABDAddr. ADBSetInfoBlock has this form:

```
TYPE ADBSetInfoBlock =
                RECORD
                  siServiceRtPtr: Ptr;   {service routine address}
                  siDataAreaAddr: Ptr    {data area address}
                END;
```

Result codes   noErr   No error

Warning: You should send a Flush command to the device after calling it with SetADBInfo, to prevent it sending old data to the new data area address.

WRITING ADB DEVICE DRIVERS

Drivers for devices connected to the ADB have the following special requirements:

- Each ADB device driver must reside in a resource of type 'ADBS'. This type has two sections: initialization and driver code.
- The initialization section of each ADB device driver must support the installation procedure described below.

When the system calls an ADB device driver, it passes it the following values:

- Register A0 points to the data buffer, which is formatted as a Pascal string.
- Register A1 points to the driver's completion routine.
- Register A2 points to the optional data area.
- Register D0 contains the ADB command that resulted in the driver being called.

The ADB driver should handle the ADB command passed to it and store any resulting input data by an appropriate action, such as by posting an event or moving the cursor.

Note: Events posted from keyboards connected to the ADB now have an expanded structure. For more information, see the Toolbox Event Manager chapter in this volume.

Installing an ADB Driver

The Start Manager (described in this volume) finds all the ADB devices connected to the system and places their device types and ADB addresses in the ADB device table. It then calls the initialization section of each ADB device driver by executing the initialization code in its 'ADBS' resource.

As a minimum, the initialization section of each ADB device driver must do the following:

- The driver must allocate all the memory required by the driver code in one or more nonrelocatable blocks in the system heap area.
- The driver must install its own preprocessing/postprocessing routine (if any) as described above under "ADBReInit".
- Finally, the driver must initialize the service routine address and data area address of its entry in the ADB device table, using SetADBInfo.

SUMMARY OF THE ADB MANAGER

Data Types

```
TYPE ADBDataBlock =
        PACKED RECORD
                    devType:         SignedByte; {device type}
                    origADBAddr:     SignedByte; {original ADB }
                                                 { address}
                    dbServiceRtPtr:  Ptr;        {service routine }
                                                 { address}
                    dbDataAreaAddr:  Ptr         {data area address}
        END;

    ADBSetInfoBlock =
        RECORD
            siServiceRtPtr:  Ptr;  {service routine address}
            siDataAreaAddr:  Ptr   {data area address}
        END;
```

Routines

Initializing the ADB Manager

```
PROCEDURE ADBReInit; INLINE $A07B;
```

Communicating Through the ADB

```
FUNCTION ADBOp (data: Ptr; compRout: ProcPtr; buffer: Ptr;
            commandNum: INTEGER) : OSErr;
```

Getting ADB Device Information

```
FUNCTION CountADBs: INTEGER;
FUNCTION GetIndADB  (VAR info: ADBDataBlock; devTableIndex:
                INTEGER) : ADBAddress;
FUNCTION GetADBInfo (VAR info: ADBDataBlock; ADBAddr: ADBAddress) :
                OsErr;
```

Setting ADB Device Information

```
FUNCTION SetADBInfo (VAR info: ADBSetInfoBlock; ADBAddr:
                ADBAddress) : OsErr;
```

Assembly-Language Information

Variables

JADBProc	Pointer to ADBReInit preprocessing/postprocessing routine
KbdLast	ADB address of the keyboard last used (byte)
KbdType	Keyboard type of the keyboard last used (byte)

Routines

Trap macro	On entry	On Exit
_ADBReInit		
_ADBOp	A0: pointer to parameter block buffer (pointer) compRout (pointer) data (pointer) D0: commandNum (byte)	D0: result code (byte)
_CountADBs		D0: result code (byte)
_GetIndADB	A0: pointer to parameter block device type (byte) original ADB address (byte) service routine address (pointer) data area address (pointer) D0: entry index number; range = 1..CountADBs (byte)	D0: positive value: current ADB address (byte) negative value: error code (byte)
_GetADBInfo	A0: pointer to parameter block device handler ID (byte) original ADB address (byte) service routine address (pointer) data area address (pointer) D0: ADB address of the device (byte)	D0: result code (byte)
_SetADBInfo	A0: pointer to parameter block service routine address (pointer) data area address (pointer) D0: ADB address of the device (byte)	D0: result code (byte)

21 FILE MANAGER EXTENSIONS IN A SHARED ENVIRONMENT

ABOUT THIS CHAPTER

This chapter presents a set of new file access routines that support application execution in a shared environment. A shared environment can mean a number of workstations connected to a file server; it can also mean a multitasking operating system or a system program that allows sharing applications or data. The discussion in this chapter focuses on AppleShare™. This chapter describes how the old access modes are translated into the new ones, discusses some aspects of file access implementation in a shared environment, and presents the format of the routines.

> **Reader's guide:** Since virtually any application may someday find itself executing in a shared environment, all developers should have some understanding of the information in this chapter. Readers should be familiar with the following chapters from *Inside Macintosh:*
>
> ■ Volume II and V: The AppleTalk Manager
>
> ■ Volume II and V: The Device Manager
>
> ■ Volume IV: The File Manager and The Standard File Package

Further information on Apple networking and file servers may be obtained from

■ *Inside AppleTalk,* Section XI: AppleTalk Session Protocol (ASP)

■ AppleTalk Filing Protocol, Version 1.1

■ *AppleShare User's Guide*

■ *AppleShare Administrator's Guide*

ABOUT THE FILE MANAGER EXTENSIONS

> **Warning:** Currently, only a startup volume with the AppleShare file located in its System Folder supports the File Manager extensions. Future versions of the File Manager may or may not support these calls.

When the File Manager was originally designed, only three file-access modes were thought to be necessary: read/write, read only, and whatever's available (of the first two). These modes operated under a basic rule of file access known as "single writer and/or multiple readers". In a world with file servers and multitasking systems, where more than one application might have access to a document simultaneously, this rule and these access modes are not sufficiently flexible.

In addition to specifying the access required by the caller, the new access modes give the caller the ability to *deny* access to other users. The new modes are therefore known as *deny modes.* They operate by setting bits in the permissions byte instead of using a constant value as a message. The new access modes are implemented by ten new calls and one modified call (PBGetCatInfo) described later in this chapter.

So that existing applications will work, the external file system used by AppleShare translates the old modes into the new. For the majority of applications, this translation will be sufficient.

OVERVIEW OF THE NEW FILE ACCESS METHODS

This overview first describes the new access modes and how they might be used, and then how the old permissions are translated into the new.

Opening Files

The combination of access and deny requests in the new open calls creates four opening possibilities: browsing, exclusive access, single writer with multiple readers, and multiple writers. The best way to open a file depends on how the application is going to use it. Figure 1 charts the opening possibilities, including whether range locking is needed. (Range locking is described later in this chapter.)

Application	Write	Read	LockRng
browsing only	none allowed	read/ deny write	no
exclusive access (one at a time)	read/write/ deny read/deny write	none allowed	no
single writer, multiple readers	read/write/ deny write	read	yes
shared (many writers)	read/write	read	yes

Figure 1. Opening Files

Browsing

Browsing is traditional read-only access. Browsing access permits multiple readers but no writers. Browsing access is useful for common files, such as help files, configuration files that don't often change, and dictionaries. Developers may wish to add a "Browse Only" checkbox to the SFGetFile dialog, so that the user may explicitly open a file in this manner.

Note that the new deny flags take into account both existing access paths to a file and future attempts to open new paths. For example, if you attempt to open a file for browsing (read/deny-write permission), your call will succeed only if no write access paths currently exist to the file. Also, all future attempts to open the file with write access will fail (with a message that you already have a read/deny-write path) until you close the first read/deny-write path.

Exclusive Access

This is the access mode that most unshared-data applications will use. (Most existing applications use fsCurPerm permissions, which are translated to exclusive access if it's available, as described below.) An exclusive-access open call will succeed only if there are no existing paths to the file. All future attempts to establish access paths to the file will be denied until the exclusive-access path is closed.

> **AppleShare note:** an exclusive-access open call will fail if you try to open a path to a file in a folder to which you do not have both "see files" and "make changes" privileges. In such a case, you could offer the user the choice of opening a browse-only copy of the file, and try again using browsing access. Or you could attempt browsing access as soon as exclusive access fails, to avoid offering a choice that won't work. If the browsing access fails, report that the file cannot be opened; if it succeeds, offer the user the browse-only file.

Single Writer, Multiple Readers

This access method allows additional users to gain read-only access to browse a document being modified by the initial writer. The writer's application is responsible for range-locking the file before writing to it, to protect the readers from reading when the file is inconsistent. Likewise, the reader's application must explicitly check for errors in reading the file, to warn the user that the file was in the process of being updated and to try again later.

Single writer, multiple readers is a step toward shared data, one that may be easy to accomplish for existing applications, especially those that are memory based. (A memory-based application is one that, when it opens a document, reads the entire document into memory. Note that it should not close the document's file, as this could lead to checkout problems, as described below under "Network Programming Guidelines".)

Shared Access

Shared access should be used by an application that supports full multi-user access to its documents. Range locking is needed by each user's application to prevent other users from accessing information undergoing change. Each user must check for and handle errors resulting from other users' access. Some applications may prefer to use a semaphore to flag records in a document as checked out, rather than using range locking exclusively.

Shared access is usually designed into an application. It is not easy to modify an existing application to support full multi-user access to documents, except for memory-based applications, as discussed above.

Translation of Permissions

AppleShare uses the deny-mode permissions exclusively. So that old applications will work, the external file system used by AppleShare (on each workstation) translates the classic permissions into the new permissions.

To keep applications from damaging each other's files, the basic rule of file access (in translating permissions for AppleShare volumes) was changed to "single writer OR multiple readers, but not both." Because of this change, two applications cannot both have access to the same file unless both are read only; this eliminates the danger of reading from a file when it is inconsistent.

> **Note**: This change in the basic rule currently applies only to AppleShare volumes. Should a future version of the File Manager incorporate this change for local volumes, then an application expecting to get more than one path to a file (with at least one read/write) will fail.

Figure 2 shows how the classic permissions described in the File Manager chapter of Volume IV are translated into the new deny-mode permissions.

Standard HFS Permissions	Deny-Mode Permissions
fsRdPerm (read only)	browsing (read/deny write)
fsRdWrPerm (read/write) fsWrPerm (write only) fsCurPerm (whatever's available)	exclusive (read/write/deny read/deny write) or browsing (read/deny write)
fsRdWrShPerm (shared read/write)	shared (read/write/deny none)

Figure 2. Access Mode Translations

FsRdPerm acts as you would expect: browsing access is achieved if there is no existing write access path to the file.

The *or* in the middle translations means that if the call cannot be completed successfully with exclusive access, it is automatically retried using browsing access.

For fsCurPerm, this is also what you'd expect: "whatever's available" has always meant "read/write if you can, otherwise, read only". The deny portions of the translation are important for enforcing the updated basic rule of file access: if there's an existing read or write access path to a file being opened with fsCurPerm, the first set of permissions will fail; the second set, browsing access, will then succeed only if there is no existing write access path to the file.

Both fsRdWrPerm and fsWrPerm (which has always been translated into fsRdWrPerm, since write-only access has little utility) are also retried as read-only, to simulate the case where a file is being opened from a locked disk. Volume IV points out that fsRdWrPerm is granted even if the volume is locked, and that an error won't be returned until a PBWrite (or SetEOF or PBAllocate) call is made. The same is now true for a read-only folder on an AppleShare volume. (An exception is that if you eject a disk, you can then write to an open file on it; changing access privileges of a folder does not change the access established for an open path to a file in that folder.)

THE SHARED ENVIRONMENT

A file server such as AppleShare allows users to share data, applications, and disk storage over a network. A file server is a combination of a computer, special software, and one or more large-capacity disks attached to other computers via a network. In the file server context, the other computers are known as workstations. The computer network allows communication between the file server and the workstations. Users have easy access to programs, data, and disk storage provided by the file server.

AppleShare

The server application available from Apple Computer is AppleShare. Explanation of the AppleShare file server environment should provide parallels for other shared environments.

Each hard disk attached to the server's computer is called a file server volume. A selected server volume will appear on the workstation's desktop as an icon and can be used just like any Macintosh disk.

Access to the information contained in folders on the disk can be controlled by use of access privileges. In the AppleShare file server environment, access privileges control who has what kind of access to the contents of the folders contained on a volume. The access privileges are assigned on a folder-by-folder basis. A folder may be kept private, shared by a group of registered users, or shared with all users on the network.

New users are registered, given passwords, and organized into groups. Users can belong to more than one group. Information about users and groups is stored in a data base on the server and is used to determine the access privileges the user or group has when they access an object on the server. The owner of a folder specifies that folder's access privileges for the following user categories:

- Owner—the user who owns the folder (or who currently holds ownership)

- Group—any group established by the AppleShare administrator (folders have only one group designation per folder)

- Everyone—every user who has access to the file server (registered users and guests)

- See Folders—see other folders in the folder

■ See Files—see the icons and open documents or applications in that folder as well

■ Make Changes—create, modify, rename, or delete any file or folder contained in the particular folder (Note: folder deletion requires other privileges as well.)

An extensive discussion of access privileges can be found in the *AppleShare User's Guide.*

Resource Availability

The availability of resources in a network or shared environment cannot be assumed. Certain file system operations taken for granted in a single-user environment must be monitored to ensure their successful completion, and appropriate error messages should be returned to the user if they fail. Some examples of failure are

■ a file read or write fails because the file has been removed, the file server has been shut down, or a break in the network has occurred

■ creation of a file on the server fails due to an existing duplicate name that is invisible to the user (it's in a folder to which the user does not have search access)

■ a file cannot be opened for use because another user has already opened the file or the user does not have the proper access privileges

Preflighting system operations becomes important in the shared environment. Preflighting, a term derived from the careful world of aviation, means checking the availability of a resource before you attempt to use it. For example, if an application creates temporary files, the application should check to see if the names it gives to the temporary files already exist. If the name already exists, the application can then give the temporary files other names or warn the user of the impending problem. This example is especially relevant for computers attached to a network because file storage may not be local to the computer.

Sharing

Sharing may mean sharing both data and the application itself:

■ An example of data file sharing would be a project schedule that would be read by many users simultaneously but could be updated by only one user at a time. Simultaneous updates to such a file must be prevented in order to protect the data.

■ An example of application file sharing would be a word processor shared as a read only file among many users. A correctly written application, with a proper site license, would allow many users to use the same copy of the application at the same time.

Data files may be shared at the file or subfile level. The latter would be appropriate for applications such as data bases and spreadsheets in which several parts of the file could be updated by users simultaneously, but each part of the file can be updated by only one user at a time.

Range Locking

Range locking is available through the PBLockRange function (_LockRng macro) described in Volume IV. By using byte-range locking

- you can lock and unlock ranges within a file at any time while you have it open
- you can keep other users from reading from or writing to a range
- all range locks set by you are removed automatically when you close the file

The LockRng call locks a range of bytes in an open file opened with shared read/write permission. Calling LockRng before writing to the file prevents another user from reading from or writing to the locked range while you are making your changes.

On a file opened with a shared read/write permission, LockRng uses the same parameter block (HParamBlockRec) as both the Read and Write calls; by calling it immediately before Read or Write, you can use the information present in the parameter block for the Read or Write call. When calling LockRng, the ioPosMode field of HParamBlockRec specifies the position mode; bits 0 and 1 indicate how to position the start of the range.

When your application finishes using the range, be sure it calls UnlockRng to free up that portion of the file for other users. Since the ioPosOffset field is modified by the Read and Write calls it must be set up again before making an UnlockRng call.

When updating a particular record and that update affects other records within the file, first determine the range of bytes affected by the updated information. Then call LockRng to lock out any other user from accessing this range of data. If the lock request succeeds, the required changes to the data can be made. Then release the lock and make the data available to other users again. If the lock fails, several retries should be done. After several unsuccessful retries, an error message could be issued to indicate that the file is busy and the user should try again later.

To append data to a file, lock a range including the logical end-of-file and the last possible addressable byte of the file ($7FFFFFFF-Hex), and then write to that range. This actually locks a range where data does not exist. Practically speaking, locking the entire unused addressable range of a file prevents another user from appending data until you unlock it.

To truncate a file, lock the entire file, truncate the data, and then unlock the file. This will prevent another user from using a portion of the file while you are in the process of truncating it.

Sharing Applications

The shared environment may involve not only applications that allow multiple access to a file, but applications that themselves have multiple users. Some definitions may help sort this out:

- **Single-user** (private data) applications allow only one user at a time to make changes to a file.

- **Multi-user** (shared data) applications allow two or more users to concurrently make changes to the same file.

- **Single-launch** applications allow only one user at a time to launch and use a single copy of the application.

- **Multi-launch** applications allow two or more users at a time to launch and use a single copy of the application.

When *single-user* and *multi-user* are seen as describing data file sharing modes and *single-launch* and *multi-launch* describe the launching characteristic of the applications, four categories of network applications emerge, as shown in Figure 3.

		File Sharing Mode	
		Single User (private)	Multi-User (shared)
Application Sharing Mode	**Single Launch**	The single launch / single user application follows ■ Only one user at a time to launch and use a single copy of the application ■ Only one user at a time to make changes to a file.	The single launch / single user application follows ■ Only one user at a time to launch and use a single copy of the application ■ Two or more users to concurrently make changes to the same file.
	Multi-Launch	The multi-launch / single user application follows ■ Two or more users to concurrently launch and use a single copy of the application ■ Only one user at a time to make changes to the file.	The multi-launch / single user application follows ■ Two or more users to concurrently launch and use a single copy of the application ■ Two or more users to concurrently make changes to the same file.

Figure 3. Sharing Applications

The multi-user application needs to

- Lock records correctly while they are being modified. Allowing and coordinating multiple writers to a single document can be accomplished by keeping the document open while it is in use and by using an open mode in the file system that specifically allows subsequent users of the document write access.

- Include an update mechanism so that all users of a document receive updates when a record is changed.

- Use byte-range locking to permit only one writer in a byte range at a time.

The multi-launch application needs to

- Use ResEdit or FEdit to set the multi-launch or shared bit in the application's finder information.

- Consider limiting the total number of concurrent users of a given copy of the application.

Limiting the number of concurrent users requires that the application implement some method to count the users as they launch and quit the application. Counting can become complex; for example, counting temporary files is a workable approach, but the temporary files may not all be in the same place and may in fact be in the user's boot volumes. Counting temporary files would also require checking whether or not the temporary files in existence were really in use or merely the remnants of a user crash.

One method to make things easier for the programmer is to require that a multi-launch application be able to create temporary files in the folder containing the application. You would, of course, have to document this so users would know that the application could not be launched from a read-only folder.

Shared Environment Guidelines

This section contains some do's and don't's for developers working in a network environment. Keep in mind that for most applications, the translated standard permissions will work fine.

Things to Do

1. If using the new calls, try them first.

   Structure your code such that you try the new open calls first, then check to see if paramErr is returned. A paramErr indicates that the file does not reside on a server volume. If that is the case, make the equivalent old style open call. Attempts to make the new calls specifying a local (non-AppleShare) volume will return a paramErr indicating that the local file system does not know how to handle the call.

2. Inform the user what access was granted during the open process.

   Shared environment applications should respond appropriately to errors returned by the file system. A more precise error reporting mechanism is used to communicate between the file server and an application program running in a workstation.

Applications should be prepared to respond to this error reporting mechanism correctly.

3. Use the Scrap Manager to access the Scrapbook.

Don't implement your own scrap mechanism. Use the ROM Scrap Manager so that resources in the scrap can be shared among applications.

4. Keep program segmentation swapping to a minimum.

The effect of program segmentation swapping is exaggerated when the application is launched from the file server, because segments are dynamically swapped in over the network. This can reduce the performance of the file server.

Things to Avoid

1. An application should not write to itself (either to data or to resource forks).

Applications should not save information by writing into their own file. When information specific to one user is saved in the the application's own file and that application is shared by two or more users, information owned by the first user may be overwritten by the second user, and so on.

2. Multi-user applications should not use the Resource Manager to structure their data in a resource fork.

The Resource Manager assumes that when it reads the resource map into memory (during OpenResFile), it will be the only one modifying that file. If two write-access paths existed to a resource fork, neither would have any way of notifying the other that the file had changed (and in fact, no way to reread the map). If your application uses resource files for document storage, you cannot share data (for multi-user access); if you want to create a multi-user or multi-launch version of your application you must find another way to store your data.

3. Don't close a file while in the process of making changes to its contents.

An application that opens a file, reads the file's contents into memory, and then closes the file, has checked out a copy of the file. After the file is closed, another user can open the file, read the contents of the file into memory, and then close it. Two copies of the file are now *checked out* to two different users. Each user, after changing the checked-out copy of the file, may decide to save the changes to the original file: user one opens the file and writes the changes back into the original and closes the file, then user two does the same thing. The second user's write operation wipes out the first. Neither user is aware of what has happened and neither has a way of finding out.

Applications should keep the file open while in use. This will prevent other users from obtaining an access path and modifying the file while it's currently open.

4. Don't give temporary files fixed names.

Many programs that create and open temporary files give them fixed names. If such an application is shared by many users, the program may attempt to create temporary files with duplicate names. One solution is not to create any temporary files on disk, holding all information in memory. Another is to save them in the System Folder of the user's boot volume (startup disk) which is usually available for the System file writing. This solution is not perfect, however, since a person's boot volume may be a disk with extremely limited space.

5. Do not directly examine or manipulate system data structures, such as file control blocks (FCB) or volume control blocks (VCB), in memory.

Use File Manager calls to access FCB and VCB information.

When the application directly examines the list of data structures related to volumes that are currently mounted without using the appropriate calls to the File Manager, it is possible that these structures will not accurately reflect the structure of the data on file server volumes.

To give the file system the opportunity to update information, use GetVolInfo to determine volume information and GetFCBInfo to determine open file information.

6. The Allocate function is not supported by AppleShare.

Instead, use SetEOF to extend a file by setting the logical end-of-file.

THE SHARED ENVIRONMENT CALLS

This section describes the interface to the new calls used in supporting shared environments. Though the calls are not necessarily specific to AppleShare, the example descriptions keep the implementation of AppleShare in mind.

For AppleShare startup volumes, these calls get installed by an 'INIT' resource patch contained within the AppleShare file. This means that only startup volumes with the AppleShare file located in its System Folder will support the shared environment calls. Since the patch currently handles only external file system volumes, making the new calls to local volumes will return with an error; however, the AppleShare external file system code will get all calls made to AppleShare volumes.

Assembly-language note: You can invoke each of these routines with a macro, whose name is presented with the call description. The macros expand to HFSDispatch ($A260) calls with an index value passed in register D0. (The File Manager chapter of Volume IV describes how to make HFSDispatch calls.) The routine selectors are as follows:

Macro Name	Call number
_GetCatInfo	$09
_GetVolParms	$30
_GetLogInInfo	$31
_GetDirAccess	$32
_SetDirAccess	$33
_MapID	$34
_MapName	$35
_CopyFile	$36
_MoveRename	$37
_OpenDeny	$38
_OpenRFDeny	$39

HFS Support

The simplest way to determine if your HFS supports these new calls is to make the PBHGetVolParms call to a mounted volume. If a paramErr error is returned and you have set the correct parameters, then the volume does not support these new calls.

Making successive PBHGetVolParms calls to each mounted volume is a good way to tell if any of the volumes support these calls. Once you find a volume that returns noErr to the call, examine the information to see if that volume supports various functions (such as access privileges and PBHCopyFile) that you may need.

Error Reporting

Most error codes returned by these calls map directly into existing Macintosh error equates, but some cannot, and new error equates have been defined for them:

VolGoneErr	−124	Connection to the server volume has been disconnected, but the VCB is still around and marked offline.
AccessDenied	−5000	The operation has failed because the user does not have the correct access to the file/folder.
DenyConflict	−5006	The operation has failed because the permission or deny mode conflicts with the mode in which the fork has already been opened.
NoMoreLocks	−5015	Byte range locking has failed because the server cannot lock any additional ranges.
RangeNotLocked	−5020	User attempted to unlock a range that was not locked by this user.
RangeOverlap	−5021	User attempted to lock some or all of a range that is already locked.

The AppleTalk AFP protocol returns errors in the range of –5000 to –5030. Since it is possible, though unlikely, to receive error codes in this range, it would be wise to handle these undocumented error codes in a generic fashion. If you require it, the complete list of these error codes can be found in the AppleTalk AFP Protocol specification document.

Data Structures

Some of the new data structures used by these calls are described below. Specific information about the placement and setting of parameters is described with the call.

For PBHGetLogInInfo, ioObjType contains the log in method, where the following values are recognized:

1	guest user
2	registered user—clear text password
3	registered user—scrambled password
4–127	reserved by Apple for future use
128–255	user-defined values

For PBHMapName and PBHMapID, ioObjType contains a mapping code. The PBHMapID call recognizes these codes:

1	map owner ID to owner name
2	map group ID to group name

and MapName recognizes these codes:

3	map owner name to owner ID
4	map group name to group ID

For PBHGetDirAccess and PBHSetDirAccess, ioACAccess is a long integer that contains access rights information in the format uueeggoo, where uu = user's rights, ee = everyone's rights, gg = group's rights, and oo = owner's rights.

> **Note:** In AppleShare 1.0 and 1.1, the Write bit represents Make Changes privileges, the Read bit represents See Files privileges, and the Search bit represents See Folders privileges.

Unused bits should always be cleared. A pictorial representation is shown in Figure 4 (high-order bit on the left).

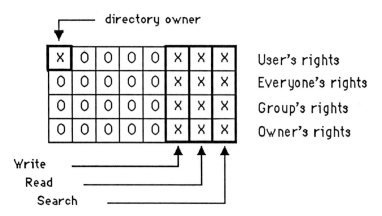

Figure 4. Access Rights in IoACAccess

Bit 7   If set, user is not the owner of the directory.
            If clear, user is the owner of the directory.
    6–3   Reserved; this is returned set to zero.
    2   If set, user does not have Write privileges to the directory.
            If clear, user has Write privileges to the directory.
    1   If set, user does not have Read privileges to the directory.
            If clear, user has Read privileges to the directory.
    0   If set, user does not have Search privileges to the directory.
            If clear, user has Search privileges to the directory.

The User's rights information is the logical OR of Everyone's rights, Group's rights, and Owner's rights. It is only returned from the GetDirAccess call; it is never passed by the SetDirAccess call. Likewise, the Owner bit is only returned in the GetDirAccess call. To change a folder's owner, you must change the Owner ID field of the SetDirAccess call.

For PBHOpenDeny and PBHOpenRFDeny, ioDenyModes contain a word of permissions information, as pictured in Figure 5 (high order bit on the left).

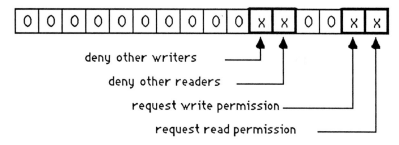

Figure 5. Permission Bits

Bit 15–6   Reserved; this should be set to zero.
    5   If set, deny other writers to this file.
    4   If set, deny other readers to this file.
    3–2   Reserved; this should be set to zero.
    1   If set, requesting write permission.
    0   If set, requesting read permission.

For PBGetCatInfo, ioACUser (a new byte field) returns the user's access rights information for a directory whose volume supports access controls in the format shown in Figure 6.

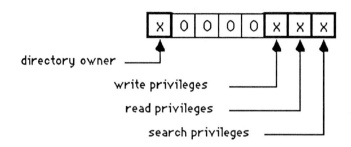

Figure 6. Access Rights in ioACUser

Bit 7   If set, user is not the owner of the directory.
                 If clear, user is the owner of the directory.
       6–3   Reserved; this is returned set to zero.
       2   If set, user does not have Write privileges to the directory.
                 If clear, user has Write privileges to the directory.
       1   If set, user does not have Read privileges to the directory.
                 If clear, user has Read privileges to the directory.
       0   If set, user does not have Search privileges to the directory.
                 If clear, user has Search privileges to the directory.

HParamBlockRec, described in the File Manager chapter of Volume IV, has been extended by the addition of AccessParam, ObjParam, CopyParam, and WDParam, as shown below. (The complete HParamBlockRec data type is shown in the summary.)

```
AccessParam:
     (filler3:       INTEGER;
     ioDenyModes:    INTEGER;         {access rights data}
     filler4:        INTEGER;
     filler5:        Signed Byte;
     ioACUser:       Signed Byte;     {access rights for directory only}
     filler6:        LONGINT;
     ioACOwnerID:    LONGINT;         {owner ID}
     ioACGroupID:    LONGINT;         {group ID}
     ioACAccess:     LONGINT);        {access rights}
ObjParam:
     (filler7:       INTEGER;
     ioObjType:      INTEGER;         {function code}
     ioObjNamePtr:   Ptr;            {ptr to returned creator/group name}
     ioObjID:        LONGINT;         {creator/group ID}
     ioReqCount:     LONGINT;         {size of buffer area}
     ioActCount:     LONGINT);        {length of vol parms data}
CopyParam:
     (ioDstVRefNum: INTEGER;         {destination vol identifier}
     filler8:        INTEGER;
     ioNewName:      Ptr;            {ptr to destination pathname}
     ioCopyName:     Ptr;            {ptr to optional name}
```

```
    ioNewDirID:    LONGINT);        {destination directory ID}
WDParam:
    (filler9:      INTEGER;
    ioWDIndex:     INTEGER;
    ioWDProcID:    LONGINT;
    ioWDVRefNum:   INTEGER;
    filler10:      INTEGER;
    filler11:      LONGINT;
    filler12:      LONGINT;
    filler13:      LONGINT;
    ioWDDirID:     LONGINT);
```

Modified Existing HFS Call

```
FUNCTION PBGetCatInfo(paramBlock: CInfoPBPtr; aSync: BOOLEAN):
        OSErr;
```

Trap macro   _GetCatInfo

Parameter block

←   31   ioACUser   byte   access rights for directory only

PBGetCatInfo returns information about the file and directories in a file catalog. See the File Manager chapter of Volume IV for the exact format of the parameter block.

For server volume directories, in addition to the normal return parameters the ioACUser field returns the user's access rights in the following format:

Bit		
	7	if set, user is not the owner of the directory.
		if clear, user is the owner of the directory.
	6–3	Reserved; this is returned set to zero.
	2	If set, user does not have Make Changes privileges to the directory.
		If clear, user has Make Changes privileges to the directory.
	1	If set, user does not have See Files privileges to the directory.
		If clear, user has See Files privileges to the directory.
	0	If set, user does not have See Folders privileges to the directory.
		If clear, user has See Folders privileges to the directory.

For example, if ioACUser returns zero for a given server volume directory, you know that the user is the owner of the directory and has complete privileges to it.

New Shared Volume HFS Calls

```
FUNCTION PBHGetVolParms (paramBlock:   HParmBlkPtr; async: BOOLEAN):
        OSErr;
```

Trap macro   _GetVolParms

Parameter block

→	12	ioCompletion	long	optional completion routine ptr
←	16	ioResult	word	error result code
→	18	ioFileName	long	volume name specifier
→	22	ioVRefNum	word	volume refNum
←	32	ioBuffer	long	ptr to vol parms data
→	36	ioReqCount	long	size of buffer area
←	40	ioActCount	long	length of vol parms data

The PBHGetVolParms call is used to return volume level information. ioVRefNum or ioFileName contain the volume identifier information. ioReqCount and ioBuffer contain the size and location of the buffer in which to place the volume parameters. The actual size of the information is returned in ioActCount.

The format of the buffer is described below. Version 01 of the buffer is shown below along with offsets into the buffer and their equates:

offset	0	vMVersion	word	version number (currently 01)
	2	vMAttrib	long	attributes (detailed below)
	6	vMLocalHand	long	handle used to keep information necessary for shared volumes
	10	vMServerAdr	long	AppleTalk server address (zero if not supported)

On creation of the VCB (right after mounting), vMLocalHand will be a handle to a 2 byte block of memory. The Finder uses this for its local window list storage, allocating and deallocating memory as needed. It is disposed of when the volume is unmounted.

For AppleTalk server volumes, vMServerAdr contains the AppleTalk internet address of the server. This can be used to tell which volumes are for which server.

vMAttrib contains attributes information (32 flag bits) about the volume. These bits and their equates are defined as follows:

bit	31	bLimitFCBs	If set, Finder limits the number of FCBs used during copies to 8 (instead of 16).
	30	bLocalWList	If set, Finder uses the returned shared volume handle for its local window list.
	29	bNoMiniFndr	If set, Mini Finder menu item is disabled.
	28	bNoVNEdit	If set, volume name cannot be edited.
	27	bNoLclSync	If set, volume's modification date is not set by any Finder action.

26	bTrshOffLine	If set, anytime volume goes offline, it is zoomed to the Trash and unmounted.
25	bNoSwitchTo	If set, Finder will not switch launch to any application on the volume.
24–21		Reserved—server volumes should return these bits set, all other disks should return these bits cleared.
20	bNoDeskItems	If set, no items may be placed on the Finder desktop.
19	bNoBootBlks	If set, no boot blocks on this volume—not a startup volume. SetStartup menu item will be disabled; bootblocks will not be copied during copy operations.
18	bAccessCntl	If set, volume supports AppleTalk AFP access control interfaces. The calls GetLoginInfo, GetDirAccess, SetDirAccess, MapID, and MapName are supported. Special folder icons are used. Access Privileges menu item is enabled for disk and folder items. The privileges field of GetCatInfo calls are assumed to be valid.
17	bNoSysDir	If set, volume doesn't support a system directory; no switch launch to this volume.
16	bExtFSVol	If set, this volume is an external file system volume. Disk init package will not be called. Erase Disk menu item is disabled.
15	bHasOpenDeny	If set, supports _OpenDeny and _OpenRFDeny calls. For copy operations, source files are opened with enable read/deny write and destination files are opened enable write/deny read and write.
14	bHasCopyFile	If set, _CopyFile call supported. _CopyFile is used in copy and duplicate operations if both source and destination volumes have same server address.
13	bHasMoveRename	If set, _MoveRename call supported.
12	bHasNewDesk	If set, all of the new desktop calls are supported (for example, OpenDB, AddIcon, AddComment).
11–0		Reserved—these bits should be returned cleared.

```
FUNCTION PBHGetLogInInfo (paramBlock: HParmBlkPtr; async: BOOLEAN)
        : OSErr;
```

Trap macro   _GetLogInInfo

Parameter block

→	12	ioCompletion	long	optional completion routine ptr
←	16	ioResult	word	error result code
→	22	ioVRefNum	word	volume refNum
←	26	ioObjType	word	log in method
←	28	ioObjNamePtr	long	ptr to log in name buffer

PBHGetLogInInfo returns the method used for log-in and the user name specified at log-in time for the volume. The log-in user name is returned as a Pascal string in ioObjNamePtr. The maximum size of the user name is 31 characters. The log-in method type is returned in ioObjType.

```
FUNCTION PBHGetDirAccess (paramBlock: HParmBlkPtr; async: BOOLEAN):
        OSErr;
```

Trap macro   _GetDirAccess

Parameter block

→	12	ioCompletion	long	optional completion routine ptr
←	16	ioResult	word	error result code
→	18	ioFileName	long	directory name
→	22	ioVRefNum	word	volume refNum
←	36	ioACOwnerID	long	owner ID
←	40	ioACGroupID	long	group ID
←	44	ioACAccess	long	access rights
→	48	ioDirID	long	directory ID

PBHGetDirAccess returns access control information for the folder pointed to by the ioDirID/ioFIleName pair. ioACOwnerID will return the ID for the folder's owner. ioACGroupID will return the ID for the folder's primary group. The access rights are returned in ioACAccess.

A fnfErr is returned if the pathname does not point to a valid directory. An AccessDenied error is returned if the user does not have the correct access rights to examine this directory.

```
FUNCTION PBHSetDirAccess (paramBlock: HParmBlkPtr; async: BOOLEAN)
        : OSErr;
```

Trap macro   _SetDirAccess

Parameter block

→	12	ioCompletion	long	optional completion routine ptr
←	16	ioResult	word	error result code
→	18	ioFileName	long	pathname identifier
→	22	ioVRefNum	word	volume refNum
→	36	ioACOwnerID	long	owner ID
→	40	ioACGroupID	long	group ID
→	44	ioACAccess	long	access rights
→	48	ioDirID	long	directory ID

PBHSetDirAccess allows you to change the access rights to a folder pointed to by the ioFileName/ioDirID pair. IOACOwnerID contains the new owner ID. IOACGroupID contains the group ID. IOACAccess contains the folder's access rights. You cannot set the owner bit or the user's rights of the directory. To change the owner or group, you should set the ioACOwnerID or ioACGroupID field with the appropriate ID of the new owner/group. You must be the owner of the directory to change the owner or group ID.

A fnfErr is returned if the pathname does not point to a valid directory. An AccessDenied error is returned if you do not have the correct access rights to modify the parameters for this directory. A paramErr is returned if you try to set the owner bit or user's rights bits.

```
FUNCTION PBHMapID (paramBlock: HParmBlkPtr; async: BOOLEAN): OSErr;
```

Trap macro   _MapID

Parameter block

→	12	ioCompletion	long	optional completion routine ptr
←	16	ioResult	word	error result code
→	18	ioFileName	long	pathname identifier
→	22	ioVRefNum	word	volume refNum
→	26	ioObjType	word	function code
←	28	ioObjNamePtr	long	ptr to retrnd creator/group name
→	32	ioObjID	long	creator/group ID

PBHMapID returns the name of a user or group given its unique ID. IOObjID contains the ID to be mapped. The value zero for ioObjID is special cased and will always return a NIL name. AppleShare uses this to signify <Any User>. IOObjType is the mapping function code; it's 1 if you're mapping an owner ID to owner name or 2 if you're mapping a group ID to a group name. The name is returned as a Pascal string in ioObjNamePtr. The maximum size of the name is 31 characters.

A fnfErr is returned if an unrecognizable owner or group ID is passed.

```
FUNCTION PBHMapName (paramBlock: HParmBlkPtr; async: BOOLEAN) :
        OSErr;
```

Trap macro   _MapName

Parameter block

→	12	ioCompletion	long	optional completion routine ptr
←	16	ioResult	word	error result code
→	18	ioFileName	long	volume identifier (may be NIL)
→	22	ioVRefNum	word	volume refNum

→	28	ioObjNamePtr	long	owner or group name
→	26	ioObjType	word	function code
←	32	ioObjID	long	creator/group ID

PBHMapName returns the unique user ID or group ID given its name. The name is passed as a string in ioObjNamePtr. If a NIL name is passed, the ID returned will always be zero. The maximum size of the name is 31 characters. IOObjType is the mapping function code; it's 3 if you're mapping an owner name to owner ID or 4 if you're mapping a group name to a group ID. IOObjID will contain the mapped ID.

A fnfErr is returned if an unrecognizable owner or group name is passed.

```
FUNCTION PBHCopyFile (paramBlock: HParmBlkPtr; async: BOOLEAN) :
        OSErr;
```

Trap macro   _CopyFile

Parameter block

→	12	ioCompletion	long	optional completion routine ptr
←	16	ioResult	word	error result code
→	18	ioFileName	long	ptr to source pathname
→	22	ioVRefNum	word	source vol identifier
→	24	ioDstVRefNum	word	destination vol identifier
→	28	ioNewName	long	ptr to destination pathname
→	32	ioCopyName	long	ptr to optional name (may be NIL)
→	36	ioNewDirID	long	destination directory ID
→	48	ioDirID	long	source directory ID

PBHCopyFile duplicates a file on the volume and optionally renames it. It is an optional call for AppleShare file servers. You should examine the returned flag information in the PBHGetVolParms call to see if this volume supports CopyFile.

For AppleShare file servers, the source and destination pathnames must indicate the same file server; however, it may point to a different volume for that file server. A useful way to tell if two file server volumes are on the same file server is to make the GetVolParms call and compare the server addresses returned. The server will open source files with read/deny write enabled and destination files with write/deny read and write enabled.

IOVRefNum contains a source volume identifier. The source pathname is determined by the ioFileName/ioDirID pair. IODstVRefNum contains a destination volume identifier. AppleShare 1.0 required that it be an actual volume reference number; however, on future versions it can be a WDRefNum. The destination pathname is determined by the ioNewName/ioNewDirID pair. IOCopyName may contain an optional string used in renaming the file. If it is non-NIL then the file copy will be renamed to the specified name in ioCopyName.

A fnfErr is returned if the source pathname does not point to an existing file or the destination pathname does not point to an existing directory. An AccessDenied error is returned if the user does not have the right to read the source or write to the destination. A dupFnErr is returned if the destination already exists. A DenyConflict error is returned if either the source or destination file could not be opened under the access modes described above.

```
FUNCTION PBHMoveRename (paramBlock: HParmBlkPtr; async: BOOLEAN) :
        OSErr;
```

Trap macro   _MoveRename

Parameter block

→	12	ioCompletion	long	optional completion routine ptr
←	16	ioResult	word	error result code
→	18	ioFileName	long	ptr to source pathname
→	22	ioVRefNum	word	source vol identifier
→	28	ioNewName	long	ptr to destination pathname
→	32	ioBuffer	long	ptr to optional name (may be NIL)
→	36	ioNewDirID	long	destination directory ID
→	48	ioDirID	long	source directory ID

PBHMoveRename allows you to move (not copy) an item and optionally to rename it. The source and destination pathnames must point to the same file server volume.

IOVRefNum contains a source volume identifier. The source pathname is specified by the ioFileName/ioDirID pair. The destination pathname is specified by the ioNewName/ioNewDirID pair. IOBuffer may contain an optional string used in renaming the item. If it is non-NIL then the moved object will be renamed to the specified name in ioBuffer.

A fnfErr is returned if the source pathname does not point to an existing object. An AccessDenied error is returned if the user does not have the right to move the object. A dupFnErr is returned if the destination already exists. A badMovErr is returned if an attempt is made to move a directory into one of its descendent directories.

```
FUNCTION PBHOpenDeny (paramBlock: HParmBlkPtr; async: BOOLEAN):
        OSErr;
```

Trap macro   _OpenDeny

Parameter block

→	12	ioCompletion	long	optional completion routine ptr
←	16	ioResult	word	error result code
→	18	ioFileName	long	ptr to pathname
→	22	ioVRefNum	word	vol identifier
←	24	ioRefNum	word	file refNum
→	26	ioDenyModes	word	access rights data
→	48	ioDirID	long	directory ID

PBHOpenDeny opens a file's data fork under specific access rights. It creates an access path to the file having the name pointed to by ioFileName/ioDirID. The path reference number is returned in ioRefNum.

IODenyModes contains a word of access rights information. The format for these access rights is:

bits	15–6	Reserved—should be cleared.
	5	If set, other writers are denied access.
	4	If set, other readers are denied access.
	3–2	Reserved—should be cleared.
	1	If set, write permission requested.
	0	If set, read permission requested.

A fnfErr is returned if the input specification does not point to an existing file. A permErr is returned if the file is already open and you cannot open it under the deny modes that you have specified. An opWrErr is returned if you have asked for write permission and the file is already opened by you for write. The already opened path reference number is returned in ioRefNum. An AccessDenied error is returned if you do not have the right to access the file.

```
FUNCTION PBHOpenRFDeny (paramBlock: HParmBlkPtr; async: BOOLEAN) :
        OSErr;
```

Trap macro   _OpenRFDeny

Parameter block

→	12	ioCompletion	long	optional completion routine ptr
←	16	ioResult	word	error result code
→	18	ioFileName	long	ptr to pathname
→	22	ioVRefNum	word	vol identifier
←	24	ioRefNum	word	file refNum
→	26	ioDenyModes	word	access rights data
→	48	ioDirID	long	directory ID

PBHOpenRFDeny opens a file's resource fork under specific access rights. It creates an access path to the file having the name pointed to by ioFileName/ioDirID. The path reference number is returned in ioRefNum. The format of the access rights data contained in ioDenyModes is described under the OpenDeny call.

A fnfErr is returned if the input specification does not point to an existing file. A permErr is returned if the file is already open and you cannot open it under the deny modes that you have specified. An opWrErr is returned if you have asked for write permission and the file is already opened by you for write. The already-opened path reference number is returned in ioRefNum. An AccessDenied error is returned if you do not have the right to access the file.

SUMMARY OF THE FILE MANAGER EXTENSIONS

Result Codes

Name	Value	Meaning
VolGoneErr	–124	Connection to the server volume has been disconnected, but the VCB is still around and marked offline.
AccessDenied	–5000	The operation has failed because the user does not have the correct access to the file/folder.
DenyConflict	–5006	The operation has failed because the permission or deny mode conflicts with the mode in which the fork has already been opened.
NoMoreLocks	–5015	Byte range locking has failed because the server cannot lock any additional ranges.
RangeNotLocked	–5020	User has attempted to unlock a range that was not locked by this user.
RangeOverlap	–5021	User attempted to lock some or all of a range that is already locked.

Constants

```
; Bits in vMAttrib about the volume

bHasNewDesk     .EQU  12    ;If set, all of the new desktop calls are
                            ; supported (for example, OpenDB, AddIco,
                            ; AddComment).
bHasMoveRename  .EQU  13    ;If set, _MoveRename call supported.
bHasCopyFile    .EQU  14    ;If set, _CopyFile call supported.
                            ; _CopyFile is used in copy and duplicate
                            ; operations if both source and
                            ; destination volumes have same server
                            ; address.
bHasOpenDeny    .EQU  15    ;If set, supports _OpenDeny and
                            ; _OpenRFDeny calls. For copy operations,
                            ; source files are opened with enable
                            ; read/deny write and destination files
                            ; are opened enable write/deny read and
                            ; write.
bExtFSVol       .EQU  16    ;If set, this volume is an external file
                            ; system volume. Disk init package will
                            ; not be called. Erase Disk menu item is
                            ; disabled.
bNoSysDir       .EQU  17    ;If set, volume doesn't support a system
                            ; directory; no switch launch to this
                            ; volume.
```

```
                      ; GetLoginInfo, GetDirAccess,
                      ; SetDirAccess, MapID, and MapName are
                      ; supported. Special folder icons are
                      ; used. Access Privileges menu item is
                      ; enabled for disk and folder items. The
                      ; privileges field of GetCatInfo calls are
                      ; assumed to be valid.
bNoBootBlks    .EQU 19   ;If set, no boot blocks on this volume--
                      ; not a startup volume. SetStartup menu
                      ; item will be disabled; boot blocks will
                      ; not be copied during copy operations.
bNoDeskItems   .EQU 20   ;If set, no items may be places on the
                      ; Finder desktop
bNoSwitchTo    .EQU 25   ;If set, Finder will not switch launch to
                      ; any application on the volume.
bTrshOffLine   .EQU 26   ;If set, anytime volume goes offline, it
                      ; is zoomed to the Trash and unmounted
bNoLclSync     .EQU 27   ;If set, volume's modification date is not
                      ; set by any Finder action.
bNoVNEdit      .EQU 28   ;If set, volume name cannot be edited.
bNoMiniFndr    .EQU 29   ;If set, MiniFinder menu item is
                      ; disabled.
bLocalWList    .EQU 30   ;If set, Finder uses the returned shared
                      ; volume handle for its local window list.
bLimitFCBs     .EQU 31   ;If set, Finder limits the number of FCBs
                      ; used during copies to 8 (instead of 16).
```

Data Types

```
HParamBlockRec = RECORD
{12 byte header used by the file system}
    qLink:          QElemPtr;
    qType:          INTEGER;
    ioTrap:         INTEGER;
    ioCmdAddr:      Ptr;
{common header to all variants}
    ioCompletion:   ProcPtr;        {completion routine, or NIL if none}
    ioResult:       OSErr;          {result code}
    ioNamePtr:      StringPtr;      {ptr to pathname}
    ioVRefNum:      INTEGER;        {volume refnum}

{different components for the different type of parameter blocks}
CASE ParamBlkType OF
IOParam:
    (ioRefNum:      INTEGER;        {refNum for I/O operation}
    ioVersNum:      SignedByte;     {version number}
    ioPermssn:      SignedByte;     {Open: permissions (byte)}
    ioMisc:         Ptr;            {HRename: new name}
                                    { HOpen: optional ptr to buffer}
    ioBuffer:       Ptr;            {data buffer Ptr}
    ioReqCount:     LONGINT;        {requested byte count}
    ioActCount:     LONGINT;        {actual byte count completed}
    ioPosMode:      INTEGER;        {initial file positioning}
    ioPosOffset:    LONGINT);       {file position offset}
```

```
FileParam:
    (ioFRefNum:      INTEGER;            {reference number}
    ioFVersNum:      SignedByte;         {version number, normally 0}
    filler1:         SignedByte;
    ioFDirIndex:     INTEGER;            {HGetFInfo directory index}
    ioFlAttrib:      SignedByte;         {HGetFInfo: in-use bit=7, lock bit=0}
    ioFlVersNum:     SignedByte;         {file version number returned by }
                                         { GetFInfoz}
    ioFlFndrInfo:    FInfo;              {information used by the Finder}
    ioDirID:         LONGINT;            {directory ID}
    ioFlStBlk:       INTEGER;            {start file block (0 if none)}
    ioFlLgLen:       LONGINT;            {logical length (EOF)}
    ioFlPyLen:       LONGINT;            {physical length}
    ioFlRStBlk:      INTEGER;            {start block rsrc fork}
    ioFlRLgLen:      LONGINT;            {file logical length rsrc fork}
    ioFlRPyLen:      LONGINT;            {file physical length rsrc fork}
    ioFlCrDat:       LONGINT;            {file creation date & time (32 bits }
                                         { in secs)}
    ioFlMdDat:       LONGINT);           {last modified date and time}
VolumeParam:
    (filler2:        LONGINT;
    ioVolIndex:      INTEGER;            {volume index number}
    ioVCrDate:       LONGINT;            {creation date and time}
    ioVLsMod:        LONGINT;            {last date and time volume was flushed}
    ioVAtrb:         INTEGER;            {volume attrib}
    ioVNmFls:        INTEGER;            {number of files in directory}
    ioVBitMap:       INTEGER;            {start block of volume bitmap}
    ioAllocPtr:      INTEGER;            {HGetVInfo: length of dir in blocks}
    ioVNmAlBlks:     INTEGER;            {HGetVInfo: num blks (of alloc size)}
    ioVAlBlkSiz:     LONGINT;            {HGetVInfo: alloc blk byte size}
    ioVClpSiz:       LONGINT;            {HGetVInfo: bytes to allocate at a }
                                         { time}
    ioAlBlSt:        INTEGER;            {starting disk(512-byte) block in }
                                         { block map}
    ioVNxtCNID:      LONGINT;            {HGetVInfo: next free file number}
    ioVFrBlk:        INTEGER;            {HGetVInfo: # free alloc blks for this }
                                         { vol}
    ioVSigWord:      INTEGER;            {volume signature}
    ioVDrvInfo:      INTEGER;            {drive number}
    ioVDRefNum:      INTEGER;            {driver refNum}
    ioVFSID:         INTEGER;            {ID of file system handling this }
                                         { volume}
    ioVBkUp:         LONGINT;            {last backup date (0 if never backed }
                                         { up)}
    ioVSeqNum:       INTEGER;            {sequence number of this volume in }
                                         { volume set}
    ioVWrCnt:        LONGINT;            {volume write count}
    ioVFilCnt:       LONGINT;            {volume file count}
    ioVDirCnt:       LONGINT;            {volume directory count}
    ioVFndrInfo:     ARRAY [1..8] OF LONGINT); {Finder info. for volume}
AccessParam:
    (filler3:        INTEGER;
    ioDenyModes:     INTEGER;            {access rights data}
    filler4:         INTEGER;
    filler5:         Signed Byte;
    ioACUser:        Signed Byte;        {access rights for directory only}
```

```
      filler6:         LONGINT;
      ioACOwnerID:     LONGINT;          {owner ID}
      ioACGroupID:     LONGINT;          {group ID}
      ioACAccess:      LONGINT);         {access rights}
ObjParam:
      (filler7:        INTEGER;
      ioObjType:       INTEGER;          {function code}
      ioObjNamePtr:    Ptr;             {ptr to returned creator/group name}
      ioObjID:         LONGINT;          {creator/group ID}
      ioReqCount:      LONGINT;          {size of buffer area}
      ioActCount:      LONGINT);         {length of vol parms data}
CopyParam:
      (ioDstVRefNum:   INTEGER;          {destination vol identifier}
      filler8:         INTEGER;
      ioNewName:       Ptr;             {ptr to destination pathname}
      ioCopyName:      Ptr;             {ptr to optional name}
      ioNewDirID:      LONGINT);         {destination directory ID}
WDParam:
      (filler9:        INTEGER;
      ioWDIndex:       INTEGER;
      ioWDProcID:      LONGINT;
      ioWDVRefNum:     INTEGER;
      filler10:        INTEGER;
      filler11:        LONGINT;
      filler12:        LONGINT;
      filler13:        LONGINT;
      ioWDDirID:       LONGINT);
END; {HParamBlockRec}
```

Routines

```
FUNCTION PBGetCatInfo(paramBlock: CInfoPBPtr; aSync: BOOLEAN) :
      OSErr;
```

Parameter Block's new field:

←	31	ioACUser	byte

```
FUNCTION PBHGetVolParms (paramBlock:  HParmBlkPtr; async: BOOLEAN)
      : OSErr;
```

→	12	ioCompletion	long
←	16	ioResult	word
→	18	ioFileName	long
→	22	ioVRefNum	word
←	32	ioBuffer	long
→	36	ioReqCount	long
←	40	ioActCount	long

```
FUNCTION PBHGetLogInInfo (paramBlock: HParmBlkPtr; async: BOOLEAN) :
        OSErr;
```

→	12	ioCompletion	long
←	16	ioResult	word
→	22	ioVRefNum	word
←	26	ioObjType	word
←	28	ioObjNamePtr	long

```
FUNCTION PBHGetDirAccess (paramBlock: HParmBlkPtr; async: BOOLEAN)
        : OSErr;
```

→	12	ioCompletion	long
←	16	ioResult	word
→	18	ioFileName	long
→	22	ioVRefNum	word
←	36	ioACOwnerID	long
←	40	ioACGroupID	long
←	44	ioACAccess	long
→	48	ioDirID	long

```
FUNCTION PBHSetDirAccess (paramBlock: HParmBlkPtr; async: BOOLEAN)
        : OSErr;
```

→	12	ioCompletion	long
←	16	ioResult	word
→	18	ioFileName	long
→	22	ioVRefNum	word
→	36	ioACOwnerID	long
→	40	ioACGroupID	long
→	44	ioACAccess	long
→	48	ioDirID	long

```
FUNCTION PBHMapID (paramBlock: HParmBlkPtr; async: BOOLEAN) :
        OSErr;
```

→	12	ioCompletion	long
←	16	ioResult	word
→	18	ioFileName	long
→	22	ioVRefNum	word
→	26	ioObjType	word
←	28	ioObjNamePtr	long
→	32	ioObjID	long

```
FUNCTION PBHMapName (paramBlock: HParmBlkPtr; async: BOOLEAN) :
        OSErr;
```

→	12	ioCompletion	long
←	16	ioResult	word
→	18	ioFileName	long
→	22	ioVRefNum	word
→	28	ioObjNamePtr	long
→	26	ioObjType	word
←	32	ioObjID	long

```
FUNCTION PBHCopyFile (paramBlock: HParmBlkPtr; async: BOOLEAN) :
        OSErr;
```

→	12	ioCompletion	long
←	16	ioResult	word
→	18	ioFileName	long
→	22	ioVRefNum	word
→	24	ioDstVRefNum	word
→	28	ioNewName	long
→	32	ioCopyName	long
→	36	ioNewDirID	long
→	48	ioDirID	long

```
FUNCTION PBHMoveRename (paramBlock: HParmBlkPtr; async: BOOLEAN) :
        OSErr;
```

→	12	ioCompletion	long
←	16	ioResult	word
→	18	ioFileName	long
→	22	ioVRefNum	word
→	28	ioNewName	long
→	32	ioBuffer	long
→	36	ioNewDirID	long
→	48	ioDirID	long

```
FUNCTION PBHOpenDeny (paramBlock: HParmBlkPtr; async: BOOLEAN) :
        OSErr;
```

→	12	ioCompletion	long
←	16	ioResult	word
→	18	ioFileName	long
→	22	ioVRefNum	word
←	24	ioRefNum	word
→	26	ioDenyModes	word
→	48	ioDirID	long

```
FUNCTION PBHOpenRFDeny (paramBlock: HParmBlkPtr; async: BOOLEAN) :
        OSErr;
```

→	12	ioCompletion	long
←	16	ioResult	word
→	18	ioFileName	long
→	22	ioVRefNum	word
←	24	ioRefNum	word
→	26	ioDenyModes	word
→	48	ioDirID	long

Assembly-Language Information

Shared Environment Macros

Pascal Name	Macro Name	Call Number
PBGetCatInfo	_GetCatInfo	$09
PBHGetVolParms	_GetVolParms	$30
PBHGetLogInInfo	_GetLogInInfo	$31
PBHGetDirAccess	_GetDirAccess	$32
PBHSetDirAccess	_SetDirAccess	$33
PBHMapID	_MapID	$34
PBHMapName	_MapName	$35
PBHCopyFile	_CopyFile	$36
PBHMoveRename	_MoveRename	$37
PBHOpenDeny	_OpenDeny	$38
PBHOpenRFDeny	_OpenRFDeny	$39

2 2 THE PRINTING MANAGER

ABOUT THE PRINTING MANAGER

The Printing Manager has been enhanced and made easier to use through these changes: ·

- Its code has been moved from a linked file into the 256K ROM.
- New low-level printer control calls have been added, in the form of new predefined parameter constants for PrCtlCall.
- A generic procedure called PrGeneral now lets your application perform several advanced printer configuration tasks.

CALLING THE PRINTING MANAGER IN ROM

All the Printing Manager routines are now accessible through the single trap _PrGlue, available in System file version 4.1 and later. To use trap calls with *all* System file versions, link your application to PRGlue, available in the MPW 2.0 file Interface.o.

Here are the Printing Manager trap calls as they appear in the Pascal interface:

```
PROCEDURE PrOpen;
PROCEDURE PrClose;
PROCEDURE PrintDefault (hPrint: THPrint);
FUNCTION  PrValidate  (hPrint: THPrint) : Boolean;
FUNCTION  PrStlDialog (hPrint: THPrint) : Boolean;
FUNCTION  PrJobDialog (hPrint: THPrint) : Boolean;
PROCEDURE PrJobMerge  (hPrintSrc, hPrintDst: THPrint);
FUNCTION  PrOpenDoc   (hPrint: THPrint; pPrPort: TPPrPort;
                       pIOBuf: Ptr): TPPrPort;
PROCEDURE PrCloseDoc  (pPrPort: TPPrPort);
PROCEDURE PrOpenPage  (pPrPort: TPPrPort; pPageFrame: TPRect);
PROCEDURE PrClosePage (pPrPort: TPPrPort);
PROCEDURE PrPicFile   (hPrint: THPrint; pPrPort: TPPrPort; pIOBuf:
                       Ptr; pDevBuf: Ptr; VAR PrStatus: TPrStatus);
FUNCTION  PrError: Integer;
PROCEDURE PrSetError  (iErr: Integer);
PROCEDURE PrDrvrOpen;
PROCEDURE PrDrvrClose;
PROCEDURE PrCtlCall   (iWhichCtl: Integer; lParam1, lParam2,
                       lParam3: LongInt);
FUNCTION  PrDrvrDCE:  Handle;
FUNCTION  PrDrvrVers: Integer;
```

You can still call Printing Manager routines with the formats given in the Printing Manager chapter of Volume II by using one of the following interface files:

- PrintTraps.p for Pascal
- PrintTraps.h for C
- PrintTraps.a for assembly language

Assembly-language note: You can invoke each of the Printing Manager routines by pushing a longint called a **routine selector** on the stack and then executing the _PrGlue trap ($A8FD). The routine selectors are the following:

```
PrOpen          EQU        $C8000000
PrClose         EQU        $D0000000
PrintDefault    EQU        $20040480
PrValidate      EQU        $52040498
PrStlDialog     EQU        $2A040484
PrJobDialog     EQU        $32040488
PrJobMerge      EQU        $5804089C
PrOpenDoc       EQU        $04000C00
PrCloseDoc      EQU        $08000484
PrOpenPage      EQU        $10000808
PrClosePage     EQU        $1800040C
PrPicFile       EQU        $60051480
PrError         EQU        $BA000000
PrSetError      EQU        $C0000200
PrDrvrOpen      EQU        $80000000
PrDrvrClose     EQU        $88000000
PrCtlCall       EQU        $A0000E00
PrDrvrDCE       EQU        $94000000
PrDrvrVers      EQU        $9A000000
```

NEW LOW-LEVEL PRINTER CONTROLS

New values have been added for PrCtlCall parameters. The complete list is now the following:

```
CONST
    iPrBitsCtl = 4;              {the Bitmap Print Proc's ctl number}
    lScreenBits = $00000000;     {the Bitmap Print Proc's Screen Bitmap }
                                 { param}
    lPaintBits = $00000001;      {the Bitmap Print Proc's Paint }
                                 { (sq pix) param}
    lHiScreenBits = $00000002;   {the Bitmap Print Proc's Screen Bitmap }
                                 { param}
    lHiPaintBits = $00000003;    {the Bitmap Print Proc's Paint }
                                 { (sq pix) param}
    iPrIOCtl = 5;                {the Raw Byte IO Proc's ctl number}
```

```
        iPrEvtCtl = 6;                  {the PrEvent Proc's ctl number; use }
                                        { with Sony printers and one of these }
                                        { CParams:}
        lPrEvtAll = $0002FFFD;          {PrEvent Proc's CParam for the whole }
                                        { screen}
        lPrEvtTop = $0001FFFD           {PrEvent Proc's CParam for the top }
                                        { window}
        iPrDevCtl = 7;                  {the PrDevCtl Proc's ctl number}
        lPrReset = $00010000;           {the PrDevCtl Proc's CParam for reset}
        lPrDocOpen = $00010000;         {alias for reset}
        lPrPageEnd = $00020000;         {the PrDevCtl Proc's CParam for end }
                                        { page}
        lPrPageClose = $00020000;       {alias for end page}
        lPrLineFeed = $00030000;        {the PrDevCtl Proc's CParam for paper }
                                        { advance}
        lPrLFStd = $0003FFFF;           {the PrDevCtl Proc's CParam for std }
                                        { paper adv}
        lPrPageOpen = $00040000;        {the PrDevCtl Proc's CParam for }
                                        { PageOpen}
        lPrDocClose = $00050000;        {the PrDevCtl Proc's CParam for }
                                        { DocClose}
```

Other values that may be shown in the interface file are used only by the Macintosh system.

PRGENERAL

The Printing Manager has been expanded to include a new procedure called PrGeneral. It provides advanced, special-purpose features, intended to solve specific problems for those applications that need them. You can use PrGeneral with version 2.5 and later of the ImageWriter driver and version 4.0 and later of the LaserWriter driver. The Pascal declaration of PrGeneral is

```
PROCEDURE PrGeneral (pData: Ptr);
```

The pData parameter is a pointer to a data block. The structure of the data block is declared as follows:

```
TGnlData = RECORD
            {1st 8 bytes are common for all PrGeneral calls);
            iOpCode:    Integer;     {input}
            iError:     Integer;     {output}
            lReserved: LongInt;     {reserved for future use}
            {more fields here, depending on particular call}
           END;
```

The first field in the TGnlData record is a 2-byte opcode, iOpCode, which acts somewhat like a routine selector. The currently available opcodes are these:

- GetRslData (get resolution data): iOpCode = 4

- SetRsl (set resolution): iOpCode = 5
- DraftBits (bitmaps in draft mode): iOpCode = 6
- NoDraftBits (no bitmaps in draft mode): iOpCode = 7
- GetRotn (get rotation): iOpCode = 8

GetRslData and SetRsl allow the application to find out what physical resolutions the printer supports, and then specify a supported resolution. DraftBits and noDraftBits invoke a new feature of the ImageWriter, allowing bitmaps (imaged via CopyBits) to be printed in draft mode. GetRotn lets an application know whether landscape orientation has been selected. These routines are described in the next sections.

The second field in the TGnlData record is the error result, iError, returned by the print code. This error only reflects error conditions that occur during the PrGeneral call. For example, if you use an opcode that isn't implemented in a particular printer driver then you will get an OpNotImpl error. Here are the error codes:

```
CONST
    NoErr      = 0;  {no error}
    NoSuchRsl  = 1;  {the resolution you chose isn't available}
    OpNotImpl  = 2;  {the driver doesn't support this opcode}
```

After calling PrGeneral you should always check PrError. If NoErr is returned, then you can proceed. If ResNotFound is returned, then the current printer driver doesn't support PrGeneral and you should proceed appropriately.

IError is followed by a four byte reserved field. The contents of the rest of the data block depends on the opcode that the application uses.

GetRslData

GetRslData (iOpCode = 4) returns a record that lets the application know what resolutions are supported by the current printer. The application can then use SetRsl to tell the printer driver which one it will use. These calls introduce a good deal of complexity into your application's code, and should be used only when necessary.

This is the format of the input data block for the GetRslData call:

```
TRslRg = RECORD {used in TGetRslBlk}
            iMin:  Integer;   {0 if printer supports only discrete }
                              { resolutions}
            iMax:  Integer;   {0 if printer supports only discrete }
                              { resolutions}
         END;

TRslRec = RECORD {used in TGetRslBlk}
            iXRsl: Integer;   {a discrete, physical X resolution}
            iYRsl: Integer;   {a discrete, physical Y resolution}
          END;
```

```
TGetRslBlk = RECORD {data block for GetRslData call}
    iOpCode:  Integer; {input; = getRslDataOp}
    iError:   Integer; {output}
    lReserved: LongInt; {reserved for future use}
    iRgType:  Integer; {output; version number}
    XRslRg:   TRslRg; {output; range of X resolutions}
    YRslRg:   TRslRg; {output; range of Y resolutions}
    iRslRecCnt: Integer; {output; how many RslRecs follow}
    rgRslRec: ARRAY[1..27] OF TRslRec; {output; number filled }
                                        { depends on printer type}
          END;
```

The iRgType field is much like a version number; it determines the interpretation of the data that follows. An iRgType value of 1 applies both to the LaserWriter and to the ImageWriter.

For variable-resolution printers like the LaserWriter, the resolution range fields XRslRg and YRslRg express the ranges of values to which the X and Y resolutions can be set. For discrete-resolution printers like the ImageWriter, the values in the resolution range fields are zero.

Note: In general, X and Y in these records are the horizontal and vertical directions of the printer, not the document. In "landscape" orientation, X is horizontal on the printer but vertical on the document.

After the resolution range information there is a word which gives the number of resolution records that contain information. These records indicate the physical resolutions at which the printer can actually print dots. Each resolution record gives an X value and a Y value.

When you call PrGeneral, use the following data block:

OpCode = 4	1 word
Error Code	1 word
Reserved	2 words
RangeType = 1	1 word
X Resolution Range: min = 0, max = 0	2 words
Y Resolution Range: min =0, max = 0	2 words
Resolution Record Count =0	1 word
Resolution Record #1: X = 0, Y = 0	2 words
Resolution Record #2..27	

Here is the data block returned by the LaserWriter:

OpCode = 4	1 word
Error Code (0 = okay)	1 word
Reserved	2 words
RangeType = 1	1 word
X Resolution Range: min = 72, max = 1500	2 words
Y Resolution Range: min = 72, max = 1500	2 words
Resolution Record Count = 1	1 word
Resolution Record #1: X = 300, Y = 300	2 words

Notice that all the resolution range numbers are the same for this printer. There is only one resolution record, which gives the physical X and Y resolutions of the printer (300 x 300).

Below is the data block returned by the ImageWriter.

OpCode = 4	1 word
Error Code (0 = okay)	1 word
Reserved	2 words
RangeType = 1	1 word
X Resolution Range: min =0, max = 0	2 words
Y Resolution Range: min = 0, max = 0	2 words
Resolution Record Count = 4	1 word
Resolution Record #1: X = 72, Y = 72	2 words
Resolution Record #2: X =144, Y = 144	2 words
Resolution Record #3: X = 80, Y = 72	2 words
Resolution Record #4: X = 160, Y = 144	2 words

All the resolution range values are zero, because only discrete resolutions can be specified for the ImageWriter. There are four resolution records giving these discrete physical resolutions.

GetRslData always returns the same information for a particular printer type—it is not dependent on what the user does or on printer configuration information.

SetRsl

SetRsl (iOpCode = 5) is used to specify the desired imaging resolution, after using GetRslData to determine a workable pair of values. Below is the format of the data block:

```
TSetRslBlk = RECORD {data block for SetRsl call}
   iOpCode:   Integer;  {input; = setRslOp}
   iError:    Integer;  {output}
   lReserved: LongInt;  {reserved for future use}
   hPrint:    THPrint;  {input; handle to a valid print record}
   iXRsl:     Integer;  {input; desired X resolution}
   iYRsl:     Integer;  {input; desired Y resolution}
END;
```

The hPrint parameter contains the handle of a print record that has previously been passed to PrValidate. If the call executes successfully, the print record is updated with the new resolution; the data block comes back with 0 for the error and is otherwise unchanged. If the desired resolution is not supported, the error is set to noSuchRsl and the resolution fields are set to the printer's default resolution

You can undo the effect of a previous call to SetRsl by making another call that specifies an unsupported resolution (such as 0 x 0), forcing the default resolution.

DraftBits

DraftBits (iOpCode = 6) is implemented on both the ImageWriter and the LaserWriter. On the LaserWriter it does nothing, because the LaserWriter is always in draft mode and can always print bitmaps. Here is the format of the data block:

```
TDftBitsBlk = RECORD {data block for DraftBits and NoDraftBits }
                     { calls}
   iOpCode:   Integer;  {input; = draftBitsOp or noDraftBitsOp}
   iError:    Integer;  {output}
   lReserved: LongInt;  {reserved for future use}
   hPrint:    THPrint;  {input; handle to a valid print record}
END;
```

The hPrint parameter contains the handle of a print record that has previously been passed to PrValidate.

This call forces draft-mode (immediate) printing, and will allow bitmaps to be printed via CopyBits calls. The virtue of this is that you avoid spooling large masses of bitmap data onto the disk, and you also get better performance.

The following restrictions apply:

- This call should be made before bringing up the print dialog boxes because it affects their appearance. On the ImageWriter, calling DraftBits disables the landscape icon in the Style dialog, and the Best, Faster, and Draft buttons in the Job dialog box.

- If the printer does not support draft mode, already prints bitmaps in draft mode, or does not print bitmaps at all, this call does nothing.

- Only text and bitmaps can be printed.

- As in the normal draft mode, landscape format is not allowed.

- Everything on the page must be strictly Y-sorted; that is, no reverse paper motion between one string or bitmap and the next. This means you can't have two or more objects (text or bitmaps) side by side; the top boundary of each object must be no higher than the bottom of the preceding object.

The last restriction is important. If you violate it, you will not like the results. However, if you want two or more bitmaps side by side, you can combine them into one before calling CopyBits to print the result. Similarly, if you are just printing bitmaps you can rotate them yourself to achieve landscape printing.

NoDraftBits

NoDraftBits (iOpCode = 7) is implemented on both the ImageWriter and the LaserWriter. On the LaserWriter it does nothing, since the LaserWriter is always in draft mode and can always print bitmaps. The format of the data block is the same as that for the DraftBits call. This call cancels the effect of any preceding DraftBits call. If there was no preceding DraftBits call, or the printer does not support draft-mode printing anyway, this call does nothing.

GetRotn

GetRotn (iOpCode = 8) is implemented on the ImageWriter and LaserWriter. Here is the format of the data block:

```
TGetRotnBlk = RECORD {data block for GetRotn call}
    iOpCode:  Integer;      {input; = getRotnOp}
    iError:   Integer;      {output}
    lReserved: LongInt;     {reserved for future use}
    hPrint:   THPrint;      {input; handle to a valid print record}
    fLandscape: Boolean;    {output; Boolean flag}
    bXtra:    SignedByte;   {reserved}
END;
```

The hPrint parameter contains a handle to a print record that has previously been passed to PrValidate.

If landscape orientation is selected in the print record, then fLandscape is true.

Using PrGeneral

SetRsl and DraftBits calls may require the print code to suppress certain options in the Style and/or Job dialog boxes, therefore they should always be called before any call to the Style or Job dialogs. An application might use PrGeneral as follows:

- Get a new print record by calling PrintDefault, or take an existing one from a document and call PrValidate on it.

- Call GetRslData to find out what the printer is capable of, and decide what resolution to use. Check PrError to be sure the PrGeneral call is supported on this version of the print code; if the error is ResNotFound, you have older print code and must print accordingly. But if the PrError return is 0, proceed as follows:

- Call SetRsl with the print record and the desired resolution if you wish.

- Call DraftBits to invoke the printing of bitmaps in draft mode if you wish.

If you call either SetRsl or DraftBits, you should do so before the user sees either of the printing dialog boxes.

SUMMARY OF THE PRINTING MANAGER

Constants

```
CONST
{PrtCtlCall parameters}
    iPrBitsCtl = 4;              {the Bitmap Print Proc's ctl number}
    lScreenBits = $00000000;     {the Bitmap Print Proc's Screen Bitmap }
                                 { param}
    lPaintBits = $00000001;      {the Bitmap Print Proc's Paint }
                                 { (sq pix) param}
    lHiScreenBits = $00000002;   {the Bitmap Print Proc's Screen Bitmap }
                                 { param}
    lHiPaintBits = $00000003;    {the Bitmap Print Proc's Paint }
                                 { (sq pix) param}
    iPrIOCtl = 5;                {the Raw Byte IO Proc's ctl number}
    iPrEvtCtl = 6;               {the PrEvent Proc's ctl number}
    lPrEvtAll = $0002FFFD;       {PrEvent Proc's CParam for the whole }
                                 { screen}
    lPrEvtTop = $0001FFFD        {PrEvent Proc's CParam for the top }
                                 { folder}
    iPrDevCtl = 7;               {the PrDevCtl Proc's ctl number}
    lPrReset = $00010000;        {the PrDevCtl Proc's CParam for reset}
    lPrDocOpen = $00010000;      {alias for reset}
    lPrPageEnd = $00020000;      {the PrDevCtl Proc's CParam for end }
                                 { page}
    lPrPageClose = $00020000;    {alias for end page}
    lPrLineFeed = $00030000;     {the PrDevCtl Proc's CParam for paper }
                                 { advance}
    lPrLFStd = $0003FFFF;        {the PrDevCtl Proc's CParam for std }
                                 { paper adv}
    lPrPageOpen = $00040000;     {the PrDevCtl Proc's CParam for }
                                 { PageOpen}
    lPrDocClose = $00050000;     {the PrDevCtl Proc's CParam for }
                                 { DocClose}
{PrGeneral iOpCode values}
    GetRslData = 4;              {get resolution data}
    SetRsl = 5;                  {set resolution}
    DraftBits = 6;               {bitmaps in draft mode}
    NoDraftBits = 7;             {no bitmaps in draft mode}
    GetRotn = 8;                 {get rotation}
{PrGeneral error codes}
    NoErr = 0;       {no error}
    NoSuchRsl = 1; {the resolution you chose isn't available}
    OpNotImpl = 2; {the driver doesn't support this opcode}
```

Data Structures

```
TGnlData = RECORD    {1st 8 bytes are common for all PrGeneral calls}
            iOpCode:    Integer;     {input}
            iError:     Integer;     {output}
            lReserved:  LongInt;     {reserved for future use}
            {more fields here, depending on particular call}
         END;


TRslRg = RECORD {used in TGetRslBlk}
          iMin:  Integer;  {0 if printer only supports discrete }
                           { resolutions}
          iMax:  Integer;  {0 if printer only supports discrete }
                           { resolutions}
       END;

TRslRec = RECORD   {used in TGetRslBlk}
            iXRsl: Integer;  {a discrete, physical X resolution}
            iYRsl: Integer;  {a discrete, physical Y resolution}
         END;

TGetRslBlk = RECORD  {data block for GetRslData call}
            iOpCode:    Integer;     {input; = getRslDataOp}
            iError:     Integer;     {output}
            lReserved:  LongInt;     {reserved for future use}
            iRgType:    Integer;     {output; version number}
            XRslRg:     TRslRg;      {output; range of X resolutions}
            YRslRg:     TRslRg;      {output; range of Y resolutions}
            iRslRecCnt: Integer;     {output; how many RslRecs follow}
            rgRslRec:   ARRAY[1..27] OF TRslRec;  {output; number }
                                     { filled depends on printer type}
         END;


TSetRslBlk = RECORD   {data block for SetRsl call}
            iOpCode:    Integer; {input; = setRslOp}
            iError:     Integer; {output}
            lReserved:  LongInt; {reserved for future use}
            hPrint:     THPrint; {input; handle to a valid print }
                                 { record}
            iXRsl:      Integer; {input; desired X resolution}
            iYRsl:      Integer; {input; desired Y resolution}
         END;


TDftBitsBlk = RECORD   {data block for DraftBits and NoDraftBits calls}
            iOpCode:    Integer;   {input; = draftBitsOp or }
                                   { noDraftBitsOp}
            iError:     Integer;   {output}
            lReserved:  LongInt;   {reserved for future use}
            hPrint:     THPrint;   {input; handle to a valid print }
                                   { record}
         END;
```

```
TGetRotnBlk = RECORD {data block for GetRotn call}
                iOpCode:    Integer;      {input; = getRotnOp}
                iError:     Integer;      {output}
                lReserved:  LongInt;      {reserved for future use}
                hPrint:     THPrint;      {input; handle to a valid }
                                          { print record}
                fLandscape: Boolean;      {output; Boolean flag}
                bXtra:      SignedByte;    {reserved}
             END;
```

Routines

```
PROCEDURE PrOpen;
PROCEDURE PrClose;
PROCEDURE PrintDefault  (hPrint: THPrint);
FUNCTION  PrValidate    (hPrint: THPrint) : Boolean;
FUNCTION  PrStlDialog   (hPrint: THPrint) : Boolean;
FUNCTION  PrJobDialog   (hPrint: THPrint) : Boolean;
PROCEDURE PrJobMerge    (hPrintSrc, hPrintDst: THPrint);
FUNCTION  PrOpenDoc     (hPrint: THPrint; pPrPort: TPPrPort; pIOBuf:
                          Ptr): TPPrPort;
PROCEDURE PrCloseDoc    (pPrPort: TPPrPort);
PROCEDURE PrOpenPage    (pPrPort: TPPrPort; pPageFrame: TPRect);
PROCEDURE PrClosePage   (pPrPort: TPPrPort);
PROCEDURE PrPicFile     (hPrint: THPrint; pPrPort: TPPrPort; pIOBuf:
                          Ptr; pDevBuf: Ptr; VAR PrStatus: TPrStatus);
FUNCTION  PrError: Integer;
PROCEDURE PrSetError    (iErr: Integer);
PROCEDURE PrDrvrOpen;
PROCEDURE PrDrvrClose;
PROCEDURE PrCtlCall     (iWhichCtl: Integer; lParam1, lParam2, lParam3:
                          LongInt);
FUNCTION  PrDrvrDCE: Handle;
FUNCTION  PrDrvrVers: Integer;
PROCEDURE PrGeneral     (pData: Ptr);
```

23 THE DEVICE MANAGER

23 Device Manager

ABOUT THE DEVICE MANAGER

New modifications have been made to the Device Manager to support slot devices.

Reader's guide: You need the information in this chapter only if your application uses a specific card (other than a standard video card) that plugs into a NuBus™ slot on the Macintosh II.

This chapter covers the following subjects:

- the parts of the system startup procedure that affect slot devices
- how the Open call now handles slot devices
- how interrupts originating in slot devices are processed
- how the new Chooser works with slot devices

You'll also need to be familiar with

- the Device Manager information in Volumes II and IV
- the Start Manager
- the Slot Manager
- the parts of the book *Designing Cards and Drivers for Macintosh II and Macintosh SE* that pertain to the device your application uses.

THE STARTUP PROCESS

The Macintosh II ROM searches for the startup device using an algorithm described in the Start Manager chapter of this volume. It will attempt to start from a NuBus card only when certain values are set in its parameter RAM. These values can be accessed by using Start Manager routines.

When the Macintosh starts up from a card in a NuBus slot, it uses startup code found in an sResource in the configuration ROM on the card. Otherwise, the normal Macintosh startup process occurs. Configuration ROMs and sResources are described in the Slot Manager chapter of this volume and in the book *Designing Cards and Drivers for Macintosh II and Macintosh SE*.

If parameter RAM specifies a valid sResource ID and slot, and if that sResource has an sBootRecord, it is used for startup. The ROM loads the slot startup code into memory and calls its entry point to execute it. For non-Macintosh operating systems that take over the machine, this code is either the operating system itself or a startup program. For instance, a traditional UNIX® startup process would bring in the secondary startup program, which prompts for a device name or filename to execute. The ROM would never receive control again.

The sBootRecord code is first called early in the ROM-based startup sequence, before any access to the internal drive. It is passed an seBlock pointed to by register A0. If a non-Macintosh operating system is being installed, the sBootRecord can pass control to it. In this case, control never returns to the normal start sequence in the Macintosh ROM. When the Macintosh operating system is started up, the sBootRecord is called twice. The first time, when the value of seBootState is 0, the startup code tries to load and open at least one driver for the card-based device and install it in the disk drive queue. It returns the refnum of the driver. That driver becomes the initial one used to install the Macintosh operating system. During the second call to the sBootRecord (when the value of seBootState is 1), which happens after system patches have been installed but before 'INIT' resources have been executed, the sBootRec must open any remaining drivers for devices on the card.

The sBootRecord can use the HOpen call to open the driver and install it into the unit table. The HOpen call will either fetch the driver from the sDriver directory, or call the sLoadDriver record if one exists. In any case, the driver's open code must install the driver into the drive queue. This process is discussed in more detail in the Card Firmware chapter of the book *Designing Cards and Drivers for Macintosh II and Macintosh SE*.

Automatic Driver Installation

During the startup process the system installs the default video and startup drivers, as described in the Start Manager chapter of this volume. Immediately prior to installing the 'INIT' resources, the system searches the NuBus slots looking for other device drivers to install. The sRsrcDir data structure in each card's configuration ROM describes all devices on that card. For each device there is a sRsrcList structure which contains the resource name (sRsrcName) and the offset to a table of drivers. These structures are described in the Slot Manager chapter of this volume.

For each sResource, the search for drivers during startup takes place in the following steps:

1. The operating system looks for an sRsrc_Flags field in the sResource list.

2. If no sRsrc_Flags field exists, or if an sRsrc_Flags field exists and the field's fOpenAtStart bit is set to 1, the operating system searches for a driver, as described below in steps 3 and 4. If the value of fOpenAtStart is 0, the operating system does not search for a driver; it goes on to the next sResource.

3. The system searches the sResource list for a driver load record (sRsrc_LoadRec)— a routine designed to copy a driver into the Macintosh system heap. If such a routine exists, the system copies it from the card's ROM to the heap and executes it. The system passes this routine a pointer in A0 to an seBlock; on exit, the routine must return a handle in the seResult field of the same seBlock to the driver it has loaded. If the value of the seStatus field is 0, the system then installs the new driver.

4. If there is no driver load record, the system searches the sResource list for a driver directory entry (sRsrc_DrvrDir). If there is such an entry and the directory contains a

driver of the type sMacOS68000 or sMacOS68020, the system reads the driver from the card's ROM and installs it in the Macintosh system heap.

To install a driver, the Macintosh II ROM first loads it into the system heap and locks it if the dNeedsLock bit in the driver flags (drvrFlags) word is set. It then installs the driver with a DrvrInstall system call and initializes it with an Open call. If the driver returns an error from the Open call, it is marked closed, the refNum field is cleared in the ioParameter block, and the driver is unlocked. Note that this procedure guarantees that driver initialization code will be executed before the system starts executing applications.

The video driver used at the beginning of system startup (the one that makes the "happy Macintosh" appear) must be taken from a video card's configuration ROM because the System file is not yet accessible. If a system contains multiple video cards, the one used first is determined by parameter RAM or, by default, by selecting the lowest slot number. To override this initial driver, the user must install an 'INIT' 31 resource that explicitly closes the driver from the configuration ROM and loads a new driver from a file.

The unit table data structure has been extended from 48 devices to 64 to accommodate installing slot devices. If more than 64 entries are needed, the table automatically expands up to a maximum of 128 entries.

When a driver serves a device that is plugged into a NuBus slot, it needs to know the slot number, the sResource ID number and the ExtDevID number. These numbers are discussed in the Slot Manager chapter of this volume. The Slot Manager provides values for five new entries on the end of the Device Control Entry (DCE) data structure for each sResource. These new entries are

■ a byte containing the slot number (dCtlSlot)

■ a byte containing the RsrcDir ID number for the sResource (dCtlSlotID)

■ a pointer for the driver to use for the device base address (dCtlDevBase)

■ a reserved field for future use

■ a byte containing the external device ID (dCtlExtDev)

The Device Control Entry now looks like this:

```
AuxDCE = PACKED RECORD
            dCtlDriver: Ptr;         {ptr to ROM or handle to RAM driver}
            dCtlFlags: INTEGER;      {flags}
            dCtlQHdr: QHdr;          {driver's i/o queue}
            dCtlPosition: LONGINT;   {byte pos used by read and write }
                                     { calls}
            dCtlStorage: Handle;     {hndl to RAM drivers private }
                                     { storage}
            dCtlRefNum: INTEGER;     {driver's reference number}
            dCtlCurTicks: LONGINT;   {counter for timing system task }
                                     { calls}
            dCtlWindow: Ptr;         {ptr to driver's window if any}
            dCtlDelay: INTEGER;      {number of ticks btwn sysTask calls}
            dCtlEMask: INTEGER;      {desk acessory event mask}
```

```
        dCtlMenu: INTEGER;          {menu ID of menu associated with }
                                    { driver}
        dCtlSlot: Byte;             {slot}
        dCtlSlotId: Byte;           {slot ID}
        dCtlDevBase: LONGINT;       {base address of card for driver}
        reserved: LONGINT;          {reserved; should be 0}
        dCtlExtDev: Byte;           {external device ID}
        fillByte: Byte;             {reserved}
    END; {SlotDCE}
  AuxDCEPtr = ^AuxDCE;
  AuxDCEHandle = ^AuxDCEPtr;
```

All Device Control Entries are set before the driver's Open routine is called.

Use of the base address pointer dCtlDevBase in the DCE is optional. On a card with multiple instances of the same device, the driver can use this pointer to distinguish between devices. Because the DCE address is passed to the driver on every call from the Device Manager, the presence of this pointer in the DCE simplifies location of the correct device. This pointer is the address of the base of the card's slot space plus an optional offset obtained from the MinorBaseOS field of the sResource. This field frees the driver writer from the necessity of locating the hardware for simple slot devices. The system makes no other references to it.

OPENING SLOT DEVICES

The low-level PBOpen routine has been extended to let you open devices in NuBus slots. A new call has been defined: OpenSlot is the equivalent of PBOpen except that it sets the IMMED bit, which signals an extended parameter block.

```
FUNCTION OpenSlot(paramBlock: paramBlkPtr; aSync: BOOLEAN) : OsErr;
```

If the slot sResource serves a single device (for example, a video device), clear all the bits of the ioFlags field and use the following parameter block:

Parameter block

→	12	ioCompletion	pointer
←	16	ioResult	word
→	18	ioNamePtr	pointer
←	22	ioRefNum	word
→	27	ioPermssn	byte
→	28	ioMix	pointer
→	32	ioFlags	word
→	34	ioSlot	byte
→	35	ioId	byte

In the extension fields, ioMix is a pointer reserved for use by the driver open routine. The ioSlot parameter contains the slot number of the device being opened, in the range 9..$E; if a built-in device is being opened, ioSlot must be 0. The ioId parameter contains the sResource ID. Slot numbers and sResources are discussed in the Slot Manager chapter of this volume.

If the slot sResource serves more than one device (for example, a chain of disk drives), set the fMulti bit in the ioFlags field (clearing all other flags bits to 0) and use the following parameter block:

Parameter block

→	12	ioCompletion	pointer
←	16	ioResult	word
→	18	ioNamePtr	pointer
←	22	ioRefNum	word
→	27	ioPermssn	byte
→	28	ioMix	pointer
→	32	ioFlags	word
→	34	ioSEBlkPtr	pointer

Here the new parameter ioSEBlkPtr is a pointer to an external parameter block (described in the Slot Manager chapter of this volume) that is customized for the devices installed in the slot. The pointer value is passed to the driver.

SLOT DEVICE INTERRUPTS

Slot interrupts enter the system by way of the Macintosh II VIA2 chip, which contains an 8-bit register that has a bit for each slot. This means that there is effectively one interrupt line per card. You can tell almost instantly which card requested the interrupt, but not which device on the card. To locate the interrupt to a device, the Slot Manager provides the polling procedure described below.

The Device Manager maintains an interrupt queue for each slot. The queue elements are ordered by priority and contain pointers to polling routines. Upon receipt of a slot interrupt the Device Manager goes through the slot's interrupt queue, calling each polling routine, until it gets an indication that the interrupt has been satisfied. If no such indication occurs, a system error dialog is displayed.

The format for a slot interrupt queue element is the following:

```
SQLink    EQU   0      ;link to next element (pointer)
SQType    EQU   4      ;queue type ID for validity (word)
SQPrio    EQU   6      ;priority (low byte of word)
SQAddr    EQU   8      ;interrupt service routine (pointer)
SQParm    EQU   12     ;optional A1 parameter (long)
```

The SQLink field points to the next queue entry; it is maintained by the system. The SQType field identifies the structure as an element of a slot interrupt queue. It should be set to SIQType. The SQPrio field is an unsigned byte that determines the order in which slots are polled and routines are called. Higher value routines are called sooner. Priority values 200–255 are reserved for Apple devices. The SQAddr field points to the interrupt polling routine.

The SQParm field is a value which is loaded into A1 before calling an interrupt service routine. This could be a handle to the driver's DCE, for example.

NEW ROUTINES

The Device Manager provides two new routines to implement the interrupt queue process just described: SIntInstall and SIntRemove. They are described below.

```
FUNCTION SIntInstall(sIntQElemPtr: SQElemPtr; theSlot: INTEGER) : OsErr;
```

Trap macro	_SIntInstall
On entry	D0: slot number (word)
	A0: address of slot queue element
On exit	D0: error code

SIntInstall adds a new element (pointed to by sIntQElemPtr) to the interrupt queue for the slot whose number is given in theSlot. As explained in the Slot Manager chapter of this volume, slots are numbered from 9 to $E.

Assembly-language note: From assembly language, this routine has the following calling sequence (assuming A0 points to a slot queue element):

```
        LEA         PollRoutine,A1      ;get routine address
        MOVE.L      A1,SQAddr(A0)       ;set address
        MOVE.W      Prio,SQPrio(A0)     ;set priority
        MOVE.L      A1Parm, SQParm(A0)  ;save A1 parameter
        MOVE.W      Slot,D0             ;set slot number
        _SIntInstall                    ;do installation
```

This code causes the routine at label PollRoutine to be called as a result of an interrupt from the specified slot (9..$E). The Device Manager will poll the slot which has the highest priority first if two or more slots request an interrupt simultaneously.

```
FUNCTION SIntRemove(sIntQElemPtr: SQElemPtr; theSlot: INTEGER) : OsErr;
```

Trap macro	_SIntRemove
On entry	D0: slot number (word)
	A0: address of slot queue element
On exit	D0: error code

SIntRemove removes an element (pointed to by sIntQElemPtr) from the interrupt queue for the slot whose number is given in theSlot. As explained in the Slot Manager chapter of this volume, slots are numbered from 9 to $E.

Assembly-language note: From assembly language, this routine has the following calling sequence (assuming A0 points to a slot queue element):

```
    LEA         MySQE1,A0           ;pointer to queue element
    _SIntRemove                     ;remove it
```

This routine lets you remove an interrupt handler from the system without causing a crash.

Your driver polling routine will be called with the following assembly-language code:

```
    MOVE.L      A1Parm,A1           ;load A1 Parameter
    JSR         PollRoutine         ;call polling routine
```

Your polling routine should preserve the contents of all registers except A1 and D0. It should return to the Device Manager with an RTS instruction. D0 should be set to zero to indicate that the polling routine did not service the interrupt, or nonzero to indicate the interrupt has been serviced. The polling routine should not set the processor priority below 2, and should return with the processor priority equal to 2. The Device Manager resets the VIA2 int flag and executes an RTE to the interrrupted task when a polling routine indicates that the interrupt is satisfied; otherwise, it calls the next lower-priority polling routine for that slot. If none exists, a system error results.

CHOOSER CHANGES

Three new facilities for user-written device packages have been added to the Chooser:

- In addition to specifying and setting their names, a device package can now position one or both buttons.
- A device package can now supply a custom list definition for the device list. The custom list can include icons, pictures, or small icons next to the name.

■ Applications that do their own housekeeping can now bypass the warning message brought up whenever a different device is chosen.

Figure 1 shows the new window displayed by the Chooser.

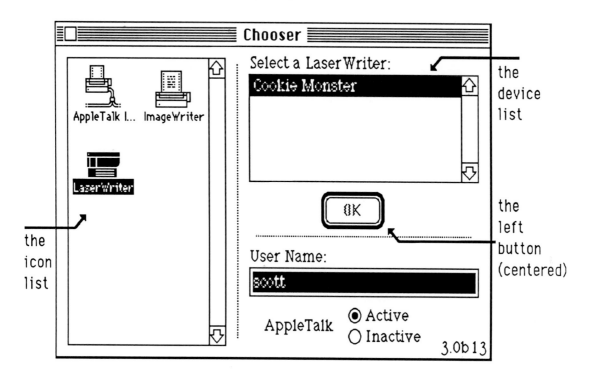

Figure 1. The Chooser Window

As described in the Device Manager chapter of Volume IV, the Chooser can also prompt the user for which AppleTalk network zone to communicate with. See Figure 2.

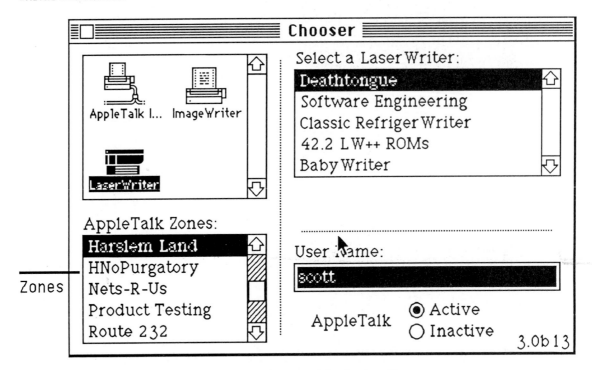

Figure 2. The Chooser Displaying Zones

Buttons

A device package can choose to have 0, 1, or 2 buttons, as determined by bits 27 and 26 in the flag field of the device ID. The two buttons are not the same. The button set by bit 27 is called the Left Button, and the button set by bit 26 the Right Button, because these are their default positions.

The Left Button has a double border, and if it is highlighted (the title string is dark, not gray), then a Return, Enter, or double click are equivalent to clicking the button. The Left Button is highlighted only when one or more devices are selected in the device list. The Right Button has a single border, never dims its title, and can be activated only by clicking it.

Buttons can be positioned by having a resource type 'nrct' with an ID of –4096 in the device file. The first word of the resource is the number of rectangles in the list, in this case two; the rest of the resource contains the rectangle definitions. The first rectangle is the Left Button, the second is the Right Button.

Each rectangle definition is eight bytes long and contains the rectangle coordinates in the order [top, left, bottom, right] order. The default values are [112, 206, 132, 266] for the Left Button, and [112, 296, 132, 356] for the Right Button. Substituting 'nrct' values of [112, 251, 132, 311], for example, would center a single button.

There's an additional button-related change: in the ButtonMsg parameter, the low order byte of the P2 parameter has a value of 1 or 2 depending on whether the Left Button or

Right Button was clicked. The high order word of P2 now contains modifier bits from the event.

List Definition Procedure

The Chooser uses the List Manager to produce and display the standard device list. The programmer can now supply a list definition procedure, which could, for example, include pictures or icons. The application should provide an 'LDEF' resource with an ID of –4096.

Also, with Chooser 3.0 and above the device may use the refCon field of the device list for its own purposes. Remember that the list will be disposed of whenever the user changes device types or changes the current zone.

Before the list is disposed of, the device package will be called with the terminate message.

See the List Manager section in Volume IV for the mechanics of list construction and the list record data structure.

Page Setup

The Chooser normally issues a warning message whenever a different printer type is selected:

```
Be sure to choose Page Setup and confirm the settings so that
the application can format documents correctly for the  <printer>.
```

Since some applications handle the page resetup correctly on their own, the Chooser now offers a way for applications to bypass the message.

```
FUNCTION SetChooserAlert (f:BOOLEAN) : BOOLEAN;
```

If f is true, the Chooser will put up the page setup alert; if f is false it won't. SetChooserAlert returns the original alert state. The application should restore the original alert state when it exits.

Assembly-language note: If the psAlert bit of the low-memory global HiliteMode is 0 then no page setup alert will be generated. Applications that set or clear this bit must be sure not to affect any other bits in the byte and to restore the bit as they leave.

```
HiliteMode   equ    $938
psAlert      equ    6
bclr         #psAlert,HiliteMode
bset         #psAlert,HiliteMode
```

Device Package Function

When the device package is called, the device file will be the current resource file, the Chooser's window will be the current grafPort, and the System Folder of the current startup disk will be the default volume. The device package must preserve all of these.

SUMMARY OF THE DEVICE MANAGER

Routines

```
FUNCTION OpenSlot(paramBlock: paramBlkPtr; aSync: BOOLEAN) : OsErr;
FUNCTION SIntInstall(sIntQElemPtr: SQElemPtr; theSlot: INTEGER ) : OsErr;
FUNCTION SIntRemove(sIntQElemPtr: SQElemPtr; theSlot: INTEGER) : OsErr;
```

Assembly-Language Information

Device Control Entry Data Structure

dCtlFlags	Flags (word)
dCtlQueue	Queue flags: low-order byte is driver's version number (word)
dCtlQHead	Pointer to first entry in driver's I/O queue
dCtlQTail	Pointer to last entry in driver's I/O queue
dCtlPosition	Byte position used by Read and Write calls (long)
dCtlStorage	Handle to RAM driver's private storage
dCtlRefNum	Driver's reference number (word)
dCtlWindow	Pointer to driver's window
dCtlDelay	Number of ticks between periodic actions (word)
dCtlEMask	Desk accessory event mask (word)
dCtlMenu	Menu ID of menu associated with driver (word)
dCtlSlot	Slot number (byte)
dCtlSlotID	Resource directory ID number for sResource (byte)
dCtlDevBase	Device base address (pointer)
reserved	Longint reserved for future use (should be 0)
dCtlExtDev	External device ID (byte)

Slot Queue Element

```
SQLink      EQU    0     ;link to next element (pointer)
SQType      EQU    4     ;queue type ID for validity (word)
SQPrio      EQU    6     ;priority (low byte of word)
SQAddr      EQU    8     ;interrupt service routine (pointer)
SQParm      EQU    12    ;optional A1 parameter (long)

SIQType     EQU    6     ;slot interrupt queue element type
```

OpenSlot Parameter Blocks

If fMulti bit in ioFlags = 0:

→	12	ioCompletion	pointer
←	16	ioResult	word
→	18	ioNamePtr	pointer
←	22	ioRefNum	word
→	26	ioPermssn	byte
→	28	ioMix	pointer
→	32	ioFlags	word
→	34	ioSlot	byte
→	35	ioId	byte

If fMulti bit in ioFlags = 1:

→	12	ioCompletion	pointer
←	16	ioResult	word
→	18	ioNamePtr	pointer
←	22	ioRefNum	word
→	26	ioPermssn	byte
→	28	ioMix	pointer
→	32	ioFlags	word
→	34	ioSEBlkPtr	pointer

Macro Names

Pascal Name	Macro Name
sIntInstall	_sIntInstall
sIntRemove	_sIntRemove

24 THE SLOT MANAGER

ABOUT THIS CHAPTER

This chapter describes the Slot Manager section of the Macintosh II ROM. The Slot Manager contains routines that let your program identify cards plugged into NuBus slots in the Macintosh II and communicate with the firmware on each card.

Note: The Macintosh SE computer also has slots, but they work differently. For an explanation of Macintosh SE slots, see the book *Designing Cards and Drivers for Macintosh II and Macintosh SE*.

Reader's guide: You need the information in this chapter only if you are writing an application, driver, or operating system that must access a slot card directly. Otherwise, the standard Macintosh Toolbox and Operating System routines normally take care of all slot card management, making the Slot Manager transparent to most applications.

The Slot Manager routines described in this chapter are divided into three sections:

■ The section "Principal Slot Manager Routines" describes routines that you might need if you are writing an application or a driver.

■ The section "Specialized Slot Manager Routines" describes routines that you might need if you are writing a driver.

■ The section "Advanced Slot Manager Routines" describes routines that are normally used only by the operating system. This section is included for completeness of documentation.

Note: When accessing NuBus cards directly, it is important that you use the standard Slot Manager routines. If you try to bypass them, your application may conflict with other applications and probably will not work in future Apple computers.

Before trying to use the information in this chapter, you should already be familiar with the Device Manager. If you are writing a driver, you should also be familiar with

■ the information in the book *Designing Cards and Drivers for Macintosh II and Macintosh SE*

■ the architecture and mode of operation of the specific card or cards your driver will access

SLOT CARD FIRMWARE

Most of the routines described in this chapter let you access data or code structures residing in the firmware of all NuBus plug-in cards. These structures are described in detail in the book *Designing Cards and Drivers for Macintosh II and Macintosh SE*. They have certain uniform features that create a standard interface to the Slot Manager. The principal card firmware structures are the following:

- A **format block,** containing format and identification information for the card's firmware and an offset to its sResource directory

- An **sResource directory,** containing an identification number and offset for each sResource list in the firmware

- A **Board sResource list,** containing information about the slot card itself

- One or more other **sResource lists,** each of which contains information about a single **sResource** in the card's firmware

Don't confuse sResources on plug-in cards with standard Macintosh resources; they are different, although related conceptually. Every sResource has a type and a name. It may also have an icon and driver code in firmware, and may define a region of system memory allocated to the card it is in. Such sResources are treated like devices. Some sResources, however, may contain only data—for example, special fonts. You must understand the specific nature of an sResource before trying to access it with the Slot Manager.

The physical location of a slot card's firmware is called its **declaration ROM.** The Slot Manager maintains a table, called the **Slot Resource Table,** of all sResources currently available in the system.

For full details about slot card firmware, see the book *Designing Cards and Drivers for Macintosh II and Macintosh SE.*

SLOT MANAGER ROUTINES

The Slot Manager is a section of the Macintosh II ROM containing routines that communicate with NuBus card firmware. This section discusses them under three headings:

- the four principal routines—those used by virtually any driver or application that needs to manage a NuBus card directly

- the specialized routines—those that might be used by a driver

- the advanced routines—those normally used only by the Macintosh II operating system

Assembly-language note: You can invoke each of the Slot Manager routines with a macro of the same name preceded by an underscore. These macros, however, aren't trap macros themselves; instead they expand to invoke the trap macro _SlotManager. The Slot Manager then determines the routine to execute from the **routine selector,** a long integer that's passed in register D0. The routine selectors are the following:

```
SReadByte          EQU    0
SReadWord          EQU    1
SReadLong          EQU    2
SGetCString        EQU    3
SGetBlock          EQU    5
SFindStruct        EQU    6
SReadStruct        EQU    7
SReadInfo          EQU    16
SReadPRAMRec       EQU    17
SPutPRAMRec        EQU    18
SReadFHeader       EQU    19
SNextRsrc          EQU    20
SNextTypesRsrc     EQU    21
SRsrcInfo          EQU    22
SCkCardStatus      EQU    24
SReadDrvrName      EQU    25
SFindDevBase       EQU    27
InitSDeclMgr       EQU    32
SPrimaryInit       EQU    33
SCardChanged       EQU    34
SExec              EQU    35
SOffsetData        EQU    36
InitPRAMRecs       EQU    37
SReadPBSize        EQU    38
SCalcStep          EQU    40
InitsRsrcTable     EQU    41
SSearchSRT         EQU    42
SUpdateSRT         EQU    43
SCalcsPointer      EQU    44
SGetDriver         EQU    45
SPtrToSlot         EQU    46
SFindsInfoRecPtr   EQU    47
SFindsRsrcPtr      EQU    48
SdeleteSRTRec      EQU    49
```

At the time the trap macro is called, register A0 must contain a pointer to the Slot Parameter Block, described in the next section. On exit, the routine leaves a result code in register D0.

Data Types

The following data types are used for communication with the Slot Manager routines:

Data type **Description**

Byte   8 bits, signed or unsigned
Word   16 bits, signed or unsigned

Long	32 bits, signed or unsigned
cString	One-dimensional array of bytes, the last of which has the value $00
sBlock	Data structure starting with a 4-byte header that gives the total sBlock size

The bit formats of the word, long, and sBlock data types are shown in Figure 1.

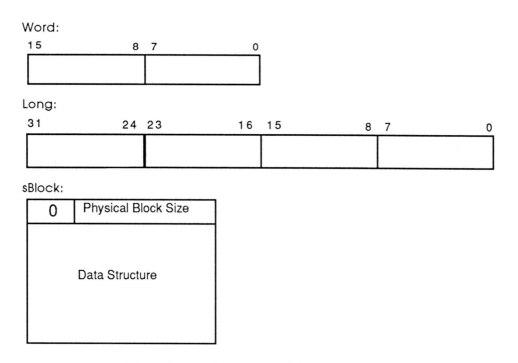

Figure 1. Word, Long, and sBlock Data Types

Note: Pointers are always of type long. The value of a null pointer is $00000000.

Slot Parameter Block

Data transfer between the Slot Manager and card firmware takes place through the **Slot Parameter Block,** which has this structure:

```
TYPE
  SpBlockPtr = ^SpBlock;
  SpBlock    = PACKED RECORD
                spResult: LONGINT;        {FUNCTION result used by }
                                          { every function}
                spsPointer: Ptr;          {structure pointer}
                spSize: LONGINT;          {size of structure}
                spOffsetData: LONGINT;    {offset/data field used by }
                                          { sOffsetData}
                spIOFileName: Ptr;        {pointer to IOFile name used }
                                          { by sDisDrvrName}
```

```
                spsExecPBlk: Ptr;            {pointer to sExec parameter }
                                             { block}
                spStackPtr: Ptr;             {old Stack pointer}
                spMisc: LONGINT;             {misc field for SDM}
                spReserved: LONGINT;         {reserved for future }
                                             { expansion}
                spIOReserved: INTEGER;       {reserved field of Slot }
                                             { Resource Table}
                spRefNum: INTEGER;           {RefNum}
                spCategory: INTEGER;         {sType:Category}
                spCType: INTEGER;            {sType:Type}
                spDrvrSW: INTEGER;           {sType:DrvrSW}
                spDrvrHW: INTEGER;           {sType:DrvrHW}
                spTBMask: SignedByte;        {type bit mask (Bits 0..3 }
                                             { mask words 0..3}
                spSlot: SignedByte;          {slot number}
                spID: SignedByte;            {structure ID}
                spExtDev: SignedByte;        {ID of the external device}
                spHWDev: SignedByte;         {ID of the hardware device}
                spByteLanes: SignedByte;     {ByteLanes from format block }
                                             { in card ROM}
                spFlags: SignedByte;         {standard flags}
                spKey: SignedByte;           {internal use only}
            END;
```

Assembly-language note: The Slot Parameter Block has the following structure in assembly language:

spResult	Function result (long)
spsPointer	Structure pointer (long)
spOffsetData	Offset/Data field (long)
spIOFileName	Pointer to IOFileName (long)
spsExecBlk	Pointer to sExec parameter block (long)
spStackPtr	Old stack pointer (long)
spMisc	Reserved for Slot Manager (long)
spReserved	Reserved (long)
spIOReserved	Reserved field of Slot Resource Table (word)
spRefNum	Slot Resource Table reference number (word)
spCategory	sResource type: Category (word)
spType	sResource type: Type (word)
spDrvrSW	sResource type: Driver software identifier (word)
spDrvrHW	sResource type: Driver hardware identifier (word)
spTBMask	Type bit mask (byte)
spSlot	Slot number (byte)
spId	sResource list ID (byte)
spExtDev	External device identifier (byte)
spHWDev	Hardware device identifier (byte)
spByteLanes	ByteLanes value from format block in card firmware (byte)
spFlags	Standard flags (byte)
spKey	Reserved (byte)
spBlockSize	Size of Slot Parameter Block

SExec Block

For the routine sExec, data transfer between the Slot Manager and card firmware also takes place through the **SExec Block,** which has this structure:

```
SEBlockPtr  = ^SEBlock;
SEBlock     = PACKED RECORD
                  seSlot:        SignedByte;   {slot number}
                  sesRsrcId:     SignedByte;   {sResource Id}
                  seStatus:      INTEGER;      {status of code executed by }
                                              { sExec}
                  seFlags:       SignedByte;   {flags}
                  seFiller0:     SignedByte;   {filler--SignedByte to align }
                                              { on word boundary}
                  seFiller1:     SignedByte;   {filler}
                  seFiller2:     SignedByte;   {filler}
                  seResult:      LONGINT;      {result of sLoad}
                  seIOFileName:  LONGINT;      {pointer to IOFile name}
                  seDevice:      SignedByte;   {which device to read from}
                  sePartition:   SignedByte;   {the partition}
                  seOSType:      SignedByte;   {type of OS}
                  seReserved:    SignedByte;   {reserved field}
                  seRefNum:      SignedByte;   {RefNum of the driver}
                  seNumDevices:  SignedByte;   {number of devices to load}
                  seBootState:   SignedByte;   {state of StartBoot code}
              END;
```

Assembly-language note: The SExec Block has the following structure in assembly language:

seSlot	Slot number (byte)
sesRsrcId	sResource list ID (byte)
seStatus	Status of code executed by sExec (word)
seFlags	Flags (byte)
seFiller0	Filler (byte)
seFiller1	Filler (byte)
seFiller2	Filler (byte)
seResult	Result of sLoad (long)
seIOFileName	Pointer to IOFile name (long)
seDevice	Which device to read from (byte)
sePartition	Device partition (byte)
seOSType	Operating system type (byte)
seReserved	Reserved (byte)
seRefNum	RefNum of the driver (byte)
seNumDevices	Number of devices to load (byte)
seBootState	Status of the StartBoot code (byte)

The seOSType parameter has these values:

Name	Value	Description
sMacOS68000	1	Load routine will run on a Macintosh computer with MC68000 processor
sMacOS68020	2	Load routine will run on a Macintosh computer with MC68020 processor

Other values may be used for future Macintosh family operating systems.

Principal Slot Manager Routines

The routines described in this section are available to drivers and applications that need to perform slot management tasks beyond those automatically provided by the system. Their principal purpose is to find slot devices and open their drivers.

The description of each Slot Manager routine specifies which parameters are required for communication with the routine. A right-pointing arrow indicates that the parameter is an input to the routine; a left-pointing arrow indicates that it is an output. Other parameters whose values may be affected by the routine are also listed. Parameters not mentioned remain unchanged.

Assembly-language note: All Slot Manager routines return a status result in the low-order word of register D0 after execution. A D0 value of zero indicates successful execution. Other D0 values are listed under "Status Results" later in this section. All routines report fatal errors (those that halt program execution); some may also report nonfatal errors. The description of each routine specifies if it can return status values indicating nonfatal errors.

```
FUNCTION SRsrcInfo(spBlkPtr: SpBlockPtr) : OSErr;
```

Trap macro: _SRsrcInfo

Required Parameters	←	spsPointer
	←	spIOReserved
	←	spRefNum
	←	spCategory
	←	spCType
	←	spDrvrSW
	←	spDrvrHW
	→	spSlot
	→	spId
	→	spExtDev
	←	spHWDev

The trap macro SRsrcInfo returns an sResource list pointer (spsPointer), plus the sResource type (category, cType, software, and hardware), driver reference number (spRefNum), and Slot Resource Table ioReserved field (spIOReserved) for the sResource specified by the slot number spSlot, sResource list identification number spId, and external device identifier spExtDev. This call is most often used to return the driver reference number.

```
FUNCTION SNextsRsrc(spBlkPtr: SpBlockPtr) : OSErr;
```

Trap macro: _SNextsRsrc

Required Parameters	↔	spSlot
	↔	spId
	↔	spExtDev
	←	spsPointer
	←	spRefNum
	←	spIOReserved
	←	spCategory
	←	spCType
	←	spDrvrSW
	←	spDrvrHW
	←	spHWDev

Starting from a given slot number spSlot, sResource list identification number spId, and external device identifier spExtDev, the trap macro SNextsRsrc returns the slot number, sResource list identification number, sResource type (category, cType, software, and hardware), driver reference number (spRefNum), and Slot Resource Table ioReserved field (spIOReserved) for the next sResource. If there are no more sResources, SNextsRsrc returns a nonfatal error status. This routine can be used to determine the set of all sResources in a given slot card or NuBus configuration.

```
FUNCTION SNextTypesRsrc(spBlkPtr: SpBlockPtr) : OSErr;
```

Trap macro: _SNextTypesRsrc

Required Parameters	↔	spSlot
	↔	spId
	↔	spExtDev
	→	spTBMask
	←	spsPointer
	←	spRefNum
	←	spIOReserved
	↔	spCategory
	↔	spCType
	↔	spDrvrSW
	↔	spDrvrHW
	↔	spHWDev

Given an sResource type (category, cType, software, and hardware) and spTBMask, and starting from a given slot number spSlot and sResource list identification number spId, the trap macro SNextTypesRsrc returns the slot number spSlot, sResource list identification

24 Slot Manager

number spId, sResource type, driver reference number (spRefNum), and Slot Resource
Table ioReserved field (spIOReserved) for the next sResource of that type, as masked. If
there are no more sResources of that type, SNextTypesRsrc returns a nonfatal error report.

The spTBMask field lets you mask off specific fields of the sResource type that you don't
care about, by setting any of bits 0–3. Bit 3 masks off the spCategory field; bit 2 the
spCType field; bit 1 the spDrvrSW field; and bit 0 the spDrvrHW field.

This procedure behaves the same as sNextsRsrc except that it returns information only
about sResources of the specified type.

```
FUNCTION SReadDrvrName(spBlkPtr: SpBlockPtr) : OSErr;
```

Trap macro: _SReadDrvrName

Required Parameters	→	spSlot
	→	spId
	→	spResult

Other Parameters Affected	spSize
	spsPointer

The trap macro SReadDrvrName reads the name of the sResource corresponding to the slot
number spSlot and sResource list identification number spId, prefixes a period to the value
of the cString and converts its type to Str255. It then reads the result into a Pascal string
variable declared by the calling program and pointed to by spResult. The final driver name
is compatible with the Open routine.

Specialized Slot Manager Routines

The routines described in this section are used only by drivers. They find data structures in
slot card firmware.

```
FUNCTION SReadByte(spBlkPtr: SpBlockPtr) : OSErr;
```

Trap macro: _SReadByte

Required Parameters	→	spsPointer
	→	spId
	←	spResult

Other Parameters Affected	spOffsetData
	spByteLanes

The trap macro SReadByte returns in spResult an 8-bit value identified by spId from the
sResource list pointed to by spsPointer. This routine's low-order byte can return nonfatal
error reports.

```
FUNCTION SReadWord(spBlkPtr: SpBlockPtr) : OSErr;
```

Trap macro: _SReadWord

Required Parameters   →   spsPointer
                      →   spId
                      ←   spResult

Other Parameters Affected   spOffsetData
                                spByteLanes

The trap macro SReadWord returns in the low-order word of spResult a 16-bit value identified by spId from the sResource list pointed to by spsPointer. This routine can return nonfatal error reports.

```
FUNCTION sReadLong(spBlkPtr: SpBlockPtr) : OSErr;
```

Trap macro: _SReadLong

Required Parameters   →   spsPointer
                      →   spId
                      ←   spResult

Other Parameters Affected   spOffsetData
                                spByteLanes
                                spSize

The trap macro SReadLong returns in spResult a 32-bit value identified by spId from the sResource list pointed to by spsPointer. This routine can return nonfatal error reports.

```
FUNCTION SGetCString(spBlkPtr: SpBlockPtr) : OSErr;
```

Trap macro: _SGetCString

Required Parameters   →   spsPointer
                      →   spId
                      ←   spResult

Other Parameters Affected   spOffsetData
                                spByteLanes
                                spSize
                                spFlags

The trap macro SGetCString copies a cString identified by spId from the sResource list pointed to by spsPointer to a buffer pointed to by spResult. Memory for this buffer is automatically allocated by SGetCString.

```
FUNCTION SGetBlock(spBlkPtr: SpBlockPtr) : OSErr;
```

Trap macro: _SGetBlock

Required Parameters	→	spsPointer
	→	spId
	←	spResult

Other Parameters Affected		spOffsetData
		spByteLanes
		spSize
		spFlags

The trap macro SGetBlock copies the sBlock from the sResource list pointed to by spsPointer and identified by spId into a new block and returns a pointer to it in spResult. The pointer in spResult should be disposed of by using the Memory Manager routine DisposPtr.

```
FUNCTION SFindStruct(spBlkPtr: SpBlockPtr) : OSErr;
```

Trap macro: _ sFindStruct

| Required Parameters | → | spId |
| | ↔ | spsPointer |

| Other Parameters Affected | | spByteLanes |

The trap macro SFindStruct returns a pointer to the data structure defined by spId in the sResource list pointed to by spsPointer.

```
FUNCTION SReadStruct(spBlkPtr: SpBlockPtr) : OSErr;
```

Trap macro: _SReadStruct

Required Parameters	→	spsPointer
	→	spSize
	→	spResult

| Other Parameter Affected | | spByteLanes |

The trap macro sReadStruct copies a structure of size spSize from the sResource list pointed to by spsPointer into a new block allocated by the calling program and pointed to by spResult.

```
FUNCTION SReadInfo(spBlkPtr: SpBlockPtr) : OSErr;
```

Trap macro: _SReadInfo

| Required Parameters | → | spSlot |
| | → | spResult |

Other Parameter Affected   spSize

The trap macro SReadInfo reads the sInfo record identified by spSlot into a new record allocated by the calling program and pointed to by spResult. Here is the structure of the sInfo record:

```
TYPE
  SInfoRecPtr  = ^SInfoRecord;
  SInfoRecord  = PACKED RECORD
                 siDirPtr:        Ptr;         {pointer to directory}
                 siInitStatusA:   INTEGER;     {initialization error}
                 siInitStatusV:   INTEGER;     {status returned by }
                                               { vendor init code}
                 siState:         SignedByte;  {initialization state}
                 siCPUByteLanes:  SignedByte;  {0=[d0..d7], }
                                               { 1=[d8..d15],  ...}
                 siTopOfROM:      SignedByte;  {top of ROM = $FsFFFFFx, }
                                               { where x is TopOfROM}
                 siStatusFlags:   SignedByte;  {bit 0--card is changed}
                 siTOConstant:    INTEGER;     {timeout constant for }
                                               { bus error}
                 siReserved:      SignedByte;  {reserved}
               END;
```

Assembly-language note: The sInfo record has the following structure in assembly language:

siDirPtr	Pointer to sResource directory (long)
siInitStatusA	Fundamental error (word)
siInitStatusV	Status returned by vendor init code (word)
siState	Initialization state—primary, secondary (byte)
siCPUByteLanes	Each bit set signifies a byte lane used (byte)
siTopOfROM	x such that Top of ROM = $FsFFFFFx (byte)
siStatusFlags	Bit 0 indicates if card has been changed (byte)
siTOConst	Timeout constant for bus error (word)
siReserved	Reserved—must be 0 (byte)
sInfoRecSize	Size of sInfo record

The siDirPtr field of the sInfo record contains a pointer to the sResource directory in the configuration ROM. The siInitStatusA field indicates the result of efforts to initialize the card. A zero value indicates that the card is installed and operational. A non-zero value is the Slot Manager error code indicating why the card could not be used.

The siInitStatusV field contains the value returned by the card's primary initialization code (in the seStatus field of the seBlock). Negative values cause the card to fail initialization. Zero or positive values indicate that the card is operational.

The siState field is used internally to indicate what initialization steps have occurred so far.

The siCPUByteLanes field indicate which byte lanes are used by the card.

The siTopOfROM field gives the last nibble of the address of the actual ByteLanes value in the fHeader record.

The siStatusFlags field gives status information about the slot. Currently only the fCardIsChanged bit has meaning. A value of 1 indicates that the board ID of the installed card did not match the ID saved in parameter RAM—in other words, the card has been changed.

The siTOConstant field contains the number of retries that will be performed when a bus error occurs while accessing the declaration ROM. It defaults to 100, but may be set to another value with the TimeOut field in the board sResource of the card.

The siReserved field is reserved and should have a value of 0.

```
FUNCTION SReadPRAMRec(spBlkPtr: SpBlockPtr) : OSErr;
```

Trap macro: _SReadPRAMRec

Required Parameters	→	spSlot
	→	spResult

Other Parameter Affected   spSize

The trap macro SReadPRAMRec copies the sPRAM record data for the slot identified by spSlot to a new record allocated by the calling program and pointed to by spResult.

One sPRAM record for each slot resides in the Macintosh II parameter RAM. The sPRAM record is initialized during startup by InitsPRAMRecs, described below under "Advanced Routines". Here is its structure:

```
TYPE
  SPRAMRecPtr  =  ^SPRAMRecord;
  SPRAMRecord  =  PACKED RECORD
              boardID:    INTEGER;     {Apple-defined card }
                                       { identification}
           vendorUse1: SignedByte;  {reserved for vendor use}
           vendorUse2: SignedByte;  {reserved for vendor use}
           vendorUse3: SignedByte;  {reserved for vendor use}
           vendorUse4: SignedByte;  {reserved for vendor use}
           vendorUse5: SignedByte;  {reserved for vendor use}
           vendorUse6:  SignedByte; {reserved for vendor use}
          END;
```

Assembly-language note: The sPRAM record has the following structure in assembly language:

boardID	Apple-defined card indentification (word)
vendorUse1	Reserved for vendor use (byte)
vendorUse2	Reserved for vendor use (byte)
vendorUse3	Reserved for vendor use (byte)

vendorUse4	Reserved for vendor use (byte)
vendorUse5	Reserved for vendor use (byte)
vendorUse6	Reserved for vendor use (byte)

If a card is removed from its slot, the corresponding sPRAM record is cleared at the next system startup. If a different card is plugged back into the slot, the corresponding sPRAM record is reinitialized. A flag is set each time an sPRAM record is initialized, to alert the Start Manager.

```
FUNCTION SPutPRAMRec(spBlkPtr: SpBlockPtr) : OSErr;
```

Trap macro: _SPutPRAMRec

Required Parameters → spSlot
→ spsPointer

The trap macro SPutPRAMRec copies the logical data from the block referenced by spsPointer into the sPRAM record for the slot identified by spSlot. This updates the Macintosh PRAM for that slot. The sPRAM record is defined above under SReadPRAMRec. In this record, the field boardId is an Apple-defined field and is protected during execution of SPutPRAMRec.

```
FUNCTION SReadFHeader(spBlkPtr: SpBlockPtr) : OSErr;
```

Trap macro: _SReadFHeader

Required Parameters → spSlot
→ spResult

Other Parameters Affected   spsPointer
spByteLanes
spSize
spOffsetData

The trap macro SReadFHeader copies the format block data for the slot designated by spSlot to an FHeader record allocated by the calling program and pointed to by spResult. Here is the structure of FHeader:

```
TYPE
  FHeaderRecPtr = ^FHeaderRec;
  FHeaderRec    = PACKED RECORD
              fhDIROffset: LONGINT;    {offset to directory}
              fhLength:    LONGINT;    {length of ROM}
              fhCRC:       LONGINT;    {CRC}
              fhROMRev:    SignedByte; {revision of ROM}
              fhFormat:    SignedByte; {format - 2}
              fhTstPat:    LONGINT;    {test pattern}
              fhReserved:  INTEGER;    {reserved}
              fhByteLanes: SignedByte; {ByteLanes}
            END;
```

Assembly-language note: The FHeader record has the following structure in assembly language:

fhDIROffset	Offset to sResource directory (long)
fhLength	Length of card's declaration ROM (long)
fhCRC	Declaration ROM checksum (long)
fhROMRev	ROM revision number (byte)
fhFormat	ROM format number (byte)
fhTstPat	Test Pattern (long)
fhReserved	Reserved (byte)
fhByteLanes	Byte lanes used (byte)
fhSize	Size of the FHeader record

The fHeader record exists at the highest address of a card's declaration ROM, and should therefore be visible at the highest address in the card's slot space. The Slot Manager uses the fHeader record to verify that a card is installed in the slot, to determine its physical connection to NuBus (which byte lanes are used), and to locate the sResource directory.

The fhDIROffset field of the fHeader record is a self-relative signed 24-bit offset to the sResource directory. The high order byte must be 0, or a card initialization error occurs.

The fhLength field gives the size of the configuration ROM.

The fhCRC field gives the cyclic redundancy check (CRC) value of the declaration ROM. The CRC value itself is taken as zero in the CRC calculation.

The fhRomRev field gives the revision level of this declaration ROM. Values greater than 9 cause a card initialization error.

The fhFormat field identifies the format of the configuration ROM. Only the value 1 (appleFormat) is currently recognized as valid.

The fhTstPat field is used to verify that the fhByteLanes field is correct.

The fhReserved field must be zero.

The fhByteLanes field indicates what NuBus byte lanes are used by the card. Byte lanes are described in the "Access to Address Space" chapter of *Designing Cards and Drivers for Macintosh II and Macintosh SE*.

```
FUNCTION SCkCardStatus(spBlkPtr: SpBlockPtr) : OSErr;
```

Trap macro: _SCkCardStatus

Required Parameter   →   spSlot

Other Parameter Affected   spResult

The trap macro SCkCardStatus checks the InitStatusA field of the sInfo record of the slot designated by spSlot, which also reflects the value of InitStatusV. If this field contains a nonzero value, SCkCardStatus returns a zero value. The sInfo record is described above under SReadInfo. The sCkCardStatus routine can return nonfatal error reports.

Trap macro: _SFindDevBase

Required Parameters   →   spSlot
                       →   spId
                       ←   spResult

The trap macro SFindDevBase returns a pointer in spResult to the base of a device whose slot number is in spSlot and whose sResource id is in spId. The base address of a device may be in either slot or superslot space but not in both. Slot or superslot slot spaces are discussed in the book *Designing Cards and Drivers for Macintosh II and Macintosh SE.*

```
FUNCTION SDeleteSRTRec(spBlkPtr: SpBlockPtr) : OSErr;
```

Trap macro: _SDeleteSRTRec

Required Parameters   →   spSlot
                       →   spId
                       →   spExtDev

The trap macro SDeleteSRTRec deletes from the system's Slot Resource Table the sResource defined by spId,spSlot, and spExtDev.

```
FUNCTION SPtrToSlot(spBlkPtr: SpBlockPtr) : OSErr;
```

Trap macro: _SPtrToSlot

Required Parameters   →   spsPointer
                       ←   spSlot

The trap macro SPtrToSlot returns in spSlot the slot number of the card whose declaration ROM is pointed to by spsPointer. The value of spsPointer must have the form Fsxx xxxx, where s is a slot number.

Advanced Slot Manager Routines

The routines described in this section are used only by the Macintosh II operating system. They are described here just for completeness of documentation.

```
FUNCTION InitSDeclMgr(spBlkPtr: SpBlockPtr) : OSErr;
```

Trap macro: _InitSDeclMgr

The trap macro InitSDeclMgr initializes the Slot Manager. The contents of the parameter block are undefined. This procedure allocates the sInfo array and checks each slot for a card. If a card is not present, an error is logged in the initStatusA field of the sInfoRecord for that slot; otherwise the card's firmware is validated, and the resulting data is placed in the slot's sInfoRecord. The sInfoRecord is described above under SReadInfo.

```
FUNCTION SPrimaryInit(spBlkPtr: SpBlockPtr) : OSErr;
```

Trap macro: _SPrimaryInit

Required Parameter   →   spFlags

The trap macro SPrimaryInit initializes each slot having an sPrimaryInit record. It passes the spFlags byte to the initialization code via seFlags. Within that byte the fWarmStart bit should be set to 1 if a warm start is being performed.

```
FUNCTION SCardChanged(spBlkPtr: SpBlockPtr) : OSErr;
```

Trap macro: _SCardChanged

Required Parameters   →   spSlot
                       ←   spResult

The trap macro SCardChanged returns a value of true in spResult if the card in slot spSlot has been changed (that is, if its sPRAMRecord has been initialized); otherwise it returns false.

```
FUNCTION SExec(spBlkPtr: SpBlockPtr) : OSErr;
```

Trap macro: _SExec

Required Parameters   →   spsPointer
                       →   spId
                       →   spsExecPBlk

Other parameters affected: spResult

The trap macro SExec loads an sExec code block from the sResource list pointed to by spsPointer and identified by spId to the current heap zone, checks its revision level, checks its CRC field, and executes the code. The status is returned in seStatus. The spsExecPBlk field is presumed to hold a pointer to an sExecBlock (described in the Card Firmware chapter of *Designing Cards and Drivers for Macintosh II and Macintosh SE*), and is passed to the sExec block code in register A0.

```
FUNCTION SOffsetData(spBlkPtr: SpBlockPtr) : OSErr;
```

Trap macro: _SOffsetData

Required Parameters	→	spsPointer
	→	spId
	←	spOffsetData
	←	spByteLanes

Other Parameters Affected	spResult
	spFlags

The trap macro SOffsetData returns (in spOffsetData) the contents of the offset/data field from the sResource list identified by spId and pointed to by spsPointer. The parameter spsPointer returns a pointer to the fields's identification number in the sResource list.

```
FUNCTION SReadPBSize(spBlkPtr: SpBlockPtr) : OSErr;
```

Trap macro: _SReadPBSize

Required Parameters	→	spsPointer
	→	spId
	→	spFlags
	←	spSize
	←	spByteLanes

Other Parameter Affected	spResult

The trap macro SReadPBSize reads the physical block size of the sBlock pointed to by spsPointer and identified by spId. It also checks to see that the upper byte is 0 if the fckReserved flag is set. The parameter spsPointer points to the resulting logical block when SReadPBSize is done.

```
FUNCTION SCalcStep(spBlkPtr: SpBlockPtr) : OSErr;
```

Trap macro: _SCalcStep

Parameters Required	→	spsPointer
	→	spByteLanes
	→	spFlags
	←	spResult

The trap macro SCalcStep calculates the field sizes in the block pointed to by spBlkPtr. It is used for stepping through the card firmware one field at a time. If the fConsecBytes flag is set it calculates the step value for consecutive bytes; otherwise it calculates it for consecutive IDs.

```
FUNCTION InitsRsrcTable(spBlkPtr: SpBlockPtr) : OSErr;
```

Trap macro: _InitsRsrcTable

The trap macro InitsRsrcTable initializes the Slot Resource Table. It scans each slot and inserts the slot, type, sRsrcId, sRsrcPtr, and HWDevID values into the table for every sResource. It sets all other fields to zero. The contents of the parameter block are undefined.

```
FUNCTION InitPRAMRecs(spBlkPtr: SpBlockPtr) : OSErr;
```

Trap macro: _InitPRAMRecs

The trap macro InitPRAMRecs scans every slot and checks its BoardId value against the value stored for it in its sPRAM record. If the values do not match, then the CardIsChanged flag is set and the Board sResource list is searched for an sPRAMInitRecord. If one is found, the sPRAMRecord for the slot is initialized with this data; otherwise it is initialized with all zeros.

```
FUNCTION SSearchSRT(spBlkPtr: SpBlockPtr) : OSErr;
```

Trap macro: _SSearchSRT

Parameters Required	→	spSlot
	→	spId
	→	spExtDev
	→	spFlags
	→	spsPointer

The trap macro SSearchSRT searches the Slot Resource Table for the record corresponding to the sResource in slot spSlot with list spId and external device identifier spExtDev, and returns a pointer to it in spsPointer. If the fckForNext bit of spFlags has a value of 0, it searches for that record; if it has a value of 1, it searches for the next record.

```
FUNCTION SUpdateSRT(spBlkPtr: SpBlockPtr) : OSErr;
```

Trap macro: _SUpdateSRT

Parameters Required	→	spSlot
	→	spId
	→	spExtDev
	→	spRefNum
	→	spIOReserved

Other Parameters Affected	spsPointer
	spFlags
	spSize
	spResult

The trap macro SUpdateSRT updates the Slot Resource Table records spRefNum and spIOReserved with information about the sResource in slot spSlot with list spId and external device identifier spExtDev. This routine is called by IOCore whenever the driver for a slot device is opened or closed.

```
FUNCTION SCalcSPtr(spBlkPtr: SpBlockPtr) : OSErr;
```

Trap macro: _SCalcSPtr

Parameters Required   →   spsPointer
                               →   spOffsetData
                               →   spByteLanes

The trap macro SCalcSPtr returns a pointer to a given byte in a card's declaration ROM, given the pointer to a current byte and an offset (spOffsetData) in bytes.

```
FUNCTION SGetDriver(spBlkPtr: SpBlockPtr) : OSErr;
```

Trap macro: _SGetDriver

Parameters Required   →   spSlot
                               →   spId
                               →   spExtDev
                               →   spsExecPBlk
                               ←   spResult

Other Parameters Affected   spFlags
                                          spSize

The trap macro SGetDriver loads the driver corresponding to the sResource designated by the slot number spSlot and the sResource list identification number spId into a relocatable block on the system heap and returns a handle to it in spResult (referenced by A0 in assembly language). The driver can come from either of two sources:

- First, the sResource sLoad directory is checked for a Macintosh sLoadRecord. If one is found, then the sLoad record is loaded into RAM and executed.

- If no sLoad record exists, the sResource sDriver directory is checked for an sDriverRecord. If one is found, then the sDriver record is loaded into RAM.

```
FUNCTION SFindsInfoRecPtr(spBlkPtr: SpBlockPtr) : OSErr;
```

Trap macro: _SFindsInfoRecPtr

Parameters Required   →   spSlot
                               ←   spResult

The trap macro SFindsInfoRecPtr returns a pointer to the sInfoRecord identified by spSlot. The sInfoRecord is described under SReadInfo.

```
FUNCTION SFindsRsrcPtr(spBlkPtr: SpBlockPtr): OSErr;
```

Trap macro: _SFindsRsrcPtr

Parameters Required	←	spsPointer
	→	spSlot
	→	spId

Other Parameter Affected   spResult

The trap macro SFindsRsrcPtr returns a pointer to the sRsrc list for the sRsrc identified by spSlot, spID, and spExtDev.

Status Results

All Slot Manager routines return a status result in register D0 upon completion. Its value is zero if execution was successful; otherwise it is one of the values listed below.

Fatal Errors

In the event of a serious execution error (one that halts program execution), the Slot Manager returns one of the following status values:

Value	Name	Description
–300	smEmptySlot	No card in this slot.
–301	smCRCFail	CRC check failed.
–302	smFormatErr	The format of the card's declaration ROM is wrong.
–303	smRevisionErr	The revision of the card's declaration ROM is wrong.
–304	smNoDir	There is no sResource directory.
–306	smNosInfoArray	The SDM was unable to allocate memory for the sInfo array.
–307	smResrvErr	A reserved field of the declaration ROM was used.
–308	smUnExBusErr	An unexpected bus error occurred.
–309	smBLFieldBad	A valid ByteLanes field was not found.
–312	smDisposePErr	An error occurred during execution of DisposPointer.
–313	smNoBoardsRsrc	There is no board sResource.
–314	smGetPRErr	An error occurred during execution of sGetPRAMRec.
–315	smNoBoardId	There is no board Id.
–316	smInitStatVErr	The InitStatus_V field was negative after Primary Init.
–317	smInitTblErr	An error occurred while trying to initialize the sResource Table.
–318	smNoJmpTbl	Slot Manager jump table could not be created.
–319	smBadBoardId	BoardId was wrong; reinit the PRAM record.

Nonfatal Errors

Some (but not all) of the Slot Manager routines may also indicate nonfatal execution problems by returning one of the status values listed below. The discussion of each routine earlier in this chapter indicates whether or not it can return a nonfatal error.

Value	Name	Description
–330	smBadRefId	Reference ID was not found in the given sResource list.
–331	smBadsList	The IDs in the given sResource list are not in ascending order.
–332	smReservedErr	A reserved field was not zero.
–333	smCodeRevErr	The revision of the code to be executed by sExec was wrong.
–334	smCPUErr	The CPU field of the code to be executed by sExec was wrong.
–335	smsPointerNil	The sPointer is NIL. No sResource list is specified.
–336	smNilsBlockErr	The physical block size (of an sBlock) was zero.
–337	smSlotOOBErr	The given slot was out of bounds (or does not exist).
–338	smSelOOBErr	Selector is out of bounds.
–339	smNewPErr	An error occurred during execution of NewPointer.
–341	smCkStatusErr	Status of slot is bad (InitStatus_A,V).
–342	smGetDrvrNamErr	An error occurred during execution of sGetDrvrName.
–344	smNoMoresRsrcs	No more sResources.
–345	smGetDrvrErr	An error occurred during execution of sGetDrvr.
–346	smBadsPtrErr	A bad sPointer was presented to a SDM call.
–347	smByteLanesErr	Bad ByteLanes value was passed to an SDM call.
–350	smSRTOvrFlErr	Slot Resource Table overflow.
–351	smRecNotFnd	Record not found in the Slot Resource Table.

24 Slot Manager

SUMMARY OF THE SLOT MANAGER

Constants

```
CONST { seOSType parameter values }
     sMacOS68000  = 1      {driver will run with 68000 processor}
     sMacOS68020  = 2      {driver will run with 68020 processor}
```

Data Types

```
TYPE
  SpBlockPtr = ^SpBlock;
  SpBlock    = PACKED RECORD
                  spResult:      LONGINT;    {FUNCTION result used by }
                                             { every function}
                  spsPointer:    Ptr;        {structure pointer}
                  spSize:        LONGINT;    {size of structure}
                  spOffsetData:  LONGINT;    {offset/data field used by }
                                             { sOffsetData}
                  spIOFileName:  Ptr;        {pointer to IOFile name used }
                                             { by sDisDrvrName}
                  spsExecPBlk:   Ptr;        {pointer to sExec parameter }
                                             { block}
                  spStackPtr:    Ptr;        {old Stack pointer}
                  spMisc:        LONGINT;    {misc field for SDM}
                  spReserved:    LONGINT;    {reserved for future }
                                             { expansion}
                  spIOReserved:  INTEGER;    {reserved field of Slot }
                                             { Resource Table}
                  spRefNum:      INTEGER;    {RefNum}
                  spCategory:    INTEGER;    {sType:  Category}
                  spCType:       INTEGER;    {sType:  Type}
                  spDrvrSW:      INTEGER;    {sType:  DrvrSW}
                  spDrvrHW:      INTEGER;    {sType:  DrvrHW}
                  spTBMask:      SignedByte; {type bit mask (Bits 0..3 }
                                             { mask words 0..3}
                  spSlot:        SignedByte; {slot number}
                  spID:          SignedByte; {structure ID}
                  spExtDev:      SignedByte; {ID of the external device}
                  spHWDev:       SignedByte; {ID of the hardware device}
                  spByteLanes:   SignedByte; {ByteLanes from format block }
                                             { in card ROM}
                  spFlags:       SignedByte; {standard flags}
                  spKey:         SignedByte; {internal use only}
                END;
```

```
SInfoRecPtr = ^SInfoRecord;
SInfoRecord = PACKED RECORD
                siDirPtr:           Ptr;          {pointer to }
                                                  { directory}
                siInitStatusA:      INTEGER;      {initialization }
                                                  { error}
                siInitStatusV:      INTEGER;      {status returned by }
                                                  { vendor init code}
                siState:            SignedByte;   {initialization }
                                                  { state}
                siCPUByteLanes:     SignedByte;   {0=[d0..d7], }
                                                  { 1=[d8..d15], ...}
                siTopOfROM:         SignedByte;   {Top of ROM = }
                                                  { $FssFFFFx, where x }
                                                  { is TopOfROM.}
                siStatusFlags:      SignedByte;   {bit 0 - card is }
                                                  { changed}
                siTOConstant:       INTEGER;      {timeout constant }
                                                  { for bus error}
                siReserved:         SignedByte;   {reserved}
              END;


SeBlockPtr  = ^SeBlock;
SeBlock     = PACKED RECORD
                seSlot:         SignedByte;   {slot number}
                sesRsrcId:      SignedByte;   {sResource Id}
                seStatus:       INTEGER;      {Status of code executed }
                                              { by sExec.}
                seFlags:        SignedByte;   {flags}
                seFiller0:      SignedByte;   {filler--SignedByte to }
                                              { align on word boundary}
                seFiller1:      SignedByte;   {filler}
                seFiller2:      SignedByte;   {filler}
                seResult:       LONGINT;      {result of sLoad}
                seIOFileName:   LONGINT;      {pointer to IOFile name}
                seDevice:       SignedByte;   {which device to read }
                                              { from}
                sePartition:    SignedByte;   {the partition}
                seOSType:       SignedByte;   {type of OS}
                seReserved:     SignedByte;   {reserved field}
                seRefNum:       SignedByte;   {RefNum of the driver}
                seNumDevices:   SignedByte;   {number of devices to }
                                              { load}
                seBootState:    SignedByte;   {state of StartBoot }
                                              { code.}
              END;
```

```
SPRAMRecPtr = ^SPRAMRecord;
SPRAMRecord = PACKED RECORD
                boardID:    INTEGER;    {Apple-defined card }
                                        { identification}
              vendorUse1:  SignedByte;  {reserved for vendor use}
              vendorUse2:  SignedByte;  {reserved for vendor use}
              vendorUse3:  SignedByte;  {reserved for vendor use}
              vendorUse4:  SignedByte;  {reserved for vendor use}
              vendorUse5:  SignedByte;  {reserved for vendor use}
              vendorUse6:  SignedByte;  {reserved for vendor use}
            END;


FHeaderRecPtr = ^FHeaderRec;
FHeaderRec    = PACKED RECORD
              fhDIROffset:  LONGINT;    {offset to directory}
              fhLength:     LONGINT;    {length of ROM}
              fhCRC:        LONGINT;    {CRC}
              fhROMRev:     SignedByte; {revision of ROM}
              fhFormat:     SignedByte; {format - 2}
              fhTstPat:     LONGINT;    {test pattern}
              fhReserved:   INTEGER;    {reserved}
              fhByteLanes:  SignedByte; {ByteLanes}
            END;
```

Routines

Principal Routines

```
FUNCTION SRsrcInfo         (spBlkPtr: SpBlockPtr) : OSErr;
FUNCTION SNextsRsrc        (spBlkPtr: SpBlockPtr) : OSErr;
FUNCTION SNextTypesRsrc    (spBlkPtr: SpBlockPtr) : OSErr;
FUNCTION SReadDrvrName     (spBlkPtr: SpBlockPtr) : OSErr;
```

Specialized Routines

```
FUNCTION SReadByte         (spBlkPtr: SpBlockPtr) : OSErr;
FUNCTION SReadWord         (spBlkPtr: SpBlockPtr) : OSErr;
FUNCTION SReadLong         (spBlkPtr: SpBlockPtr) : OSErr;
FUNCTION SGetcString       (spBlkPtr: SpBlockPtr) : OSErr;
FUNCTION SGetBlock         (spBlkPtr: SpBlockPtr) : OSErr;
FUNCTION SFindStruct       (spBlkPtr: SpBlockPtr) : OSErr;
FUNCTION SReadStruct       (spBlkPtr: SpBlockPtr) : OSErr;
FUNCTION SReadInfo         (spBlkPtr: SpBlockPtr) : OSErr;
FUNCTION SReadPRAMRec      (spBlkPtr: SpBlockPtr) : OSErr;
FUNCTION SPutPRAMRec       (spBlkPtr: SpBlockPtr) : OSErr;
FUNCTION SReadFHeader      (spBlkPtr: SpBlockPtr) : OSErr;
FUNCTION SCkCardStatus     (spBlkPtr: SpBlockPtr) : OSErr;
FUNCTION SFindDevBase      (spBlkPtr: SpBlockPtr) : OSErr;
FUNCTION SDeleteSRTRec
FUNCTION SPtrToSlot        (spBlkPtr: SpBlockPtr) : OSErr;
```

Advanced Routines

```
FUNCTION InitSDeclMgr     (spBlkPtr: SpBlockPtr) : OSErr;
FUNCTION SPrimaryInit     (spBlkPtr: SpBlockPtr) : OSErr;
FUNCTION SCardChanged     (spBlkPtr: SpBlockPtr) : OSErr;
FUNCTION SExec            (spBlkPtr: SpBlockPtr) : OSErr;
FUNCTION SOffsetData      (spBlkPtr: SpBlockPtr) : OSErr;
FUNCTION SReadPBSize      (spBlkPtr: SpBlockPtr) : OSErr;
FUNCTION SCalcStep        (spBlkPtr: SpBlockPtr) : OSErr;
FUNCTION InitsRsrcTable   (spBlkPtr: SpBlockPtr) : OSErr;
FUNCTION InitPRAMRecs     (spBlkPtr: SpBlockPtr) : OSErr;
FUNCTION SSearchSRT       (spBlkPtr: SpBlockPtr) : OSErr;
FUNCTION SUpdateSRT       (spBlkPtr: SpBlockPtr) : OSErr;
FUNCTION SCalcSPointer
FUNCTION SGetDriver       (spBlkPtr: SpBlockPtr) : OSErr;
FUNCTION SFindSInfoRecPtr
FUNCTION SFindSRsrcPtr
```

Assembly-Language Information

Constants

```
; Routine selectors for _SlotManager trap
    sReadByte        EQU     0
    sReadWord        EQU     1
    sReadLong        EQU     2
    sGetcString      EQU     3
    sGetBlock        EQU     5
    sFindStruct      EQU     6
    sReadStruct      EQU     7
    sReadInfo        EQU     16
    sReadPRAMRec     EQU     17
    sPutPRAMRec      EQU     18
    sReadFHeader     EQU     19
    sNextRsrc        EQU     20
    sNextTypesRsrc   EQU     21
    sRsrcInfo        EQU     22
    sDisposePtr      EQU     23
    sCkCardStatus    EQU     24
    sReadDrvrName    EQU     25
    sFindDevBase     EQU     27
    InitSDeclMgr     EQU     32
    sPrimaryInit     EQU     33
    sCardChanged     EQU     34
    sExec            EQU     35
    sOffsetData      EQU     36
    InitPRAMRecs     EQU     37
    sReadPBSize      EQU     38
    sCalcStep        EQU     40
    InitsRsrcTable   EQU     41
    sSearchSRT       EQU     42
    sUpdateSRT       EQU     43
    sCalcsPointer    EQU     44
```

```
sGetDriver          EQU     45
sPtrToSlot          EQU     46
sFindsInfoRecPtr    EQU     47
sFindsRsrcPtr       EQU     48
sdeleteSRTRec       EQU     49
```

Slot Parameter Block Structure

spResult	Function result (long)
spsPointer	Structure pointer (long)
spOffsetData	Offset/Data field (long)
spIOFileName	Pointer to IOFileName (long)
spsExecBlk	Pointer to sExec parameter block (long)
spStackPtr	Old stack pointer (long)
spMisc	Reserved for Slot Manager (long)
spReserved	Reserved (long)
spIOReserved	Reserved field of Slot Resource Table (word)
spRefNum	Slot Resource Table reference number (word)
spCategory	sResource type: Category (word)
spType	sResource type: Type (word)
spDrvrSW	sResource type: Driver software identifier (word)
spDrvrHW	sResource type: Driver hardware identifier (word)
spTBMask	Type bit mask (byte)
spSlot	Slot number (byte)
spId	sResource list ID (byte)
spExtDev	External device identifier (byte)
spHWDev	Hardware device identifier (byte)
spByteLanes	ByteLanes value from format block in card firmware (byte)
spFlags	Standard flags (byte)
spKey	Reserved (byte)
spBlockSize	Size of Slot Parameter Block

Slot Executive Block Structure

seSlot	Slot number (byte)
sesRsrcId	sResource list ID (byte)
seStatus	Status of code executed by sExec (word)
seFlags	Flags (byte)
seFiller0	Filler (byte)
seFiller1	Filler (byte)
seFiller2	Filler (byte)
seResult	Result of sLoad (long)
seIOFileName	Pointer to IOFile name (long)
seDevice	Which device to read from (byte)
sePartition	Device partition (byte)
seOSType	Operating system type (byte)
seReserved	Reserved (byte)
seRefNum	RefNum of the driver (byte)
seNumDevices	Number of devices to load (byte)
seBootState	Status of the StartBoot code (byte)

SInfo Record Structure

siDirPtr	Pointer to sResource directory (long)
siInitStatusA	Fundamental error (word)
siInitStatusV	Status returned by vendor init code (word)
siState	Initialization state—primary, secondary (byte)
siCPUByteLanes	Each bit set signifies a byte lane used (byte)
siTopOfROM	Top of ROM = $FssFFFFx, where x is siTopOfROM (byte)
siStatusFlags	Bit 0 indicates if card has been changed (byte)
siTOConst	Timeout constant for bus error (word)
siReserved	Reserved—must be 0 (byte)
sInfoRecSize	Size of sInfo record

FHeader Record Structure

fhDIROffset	Offset to sResource directory (long)
fhLength	Length of card's declaration ROM (long)
fhCRC	Declaration ROM checksum (long)
fhROMRev	ROM revision number (byte)
fhFormat	ROM format number (byte)
fhTstPat	Test Pattern (long)
fhReserved	Reserved (byte)
fhByteLanes	Byte lanes used (byte)
fhSize	Size of the FHeader record

SPRAM Record Structure

boardID	Apple-defined card indentification (word)
vendorUse1	Reserved for vendor use (byte)
vendorUse2	Reserved for vendor use (byte)
vendorUse3	Reserved for vendor use (byte)
vendorUse4	Reserved for vendor use (byte)
vendorUse5	Reserved for vendor use (byte)
vendorUse6	Reserved for vendor use (byte)

Trap Macro Name

_SlotManager

25 THE DEFERRED TASK MANAGER

ABOUT THIS CHAPTER

This chapter describes the Deferred Task Manager, which provides improved interrupt handling by allowing lengthy tasks to be deferred.

> **Reader's guide:** Lengthy tasks are usually initiated by slot cards. Hence you normally need the information in this chapter only if your program deals with slot card interrupts.

ABOUT THE DEFERRED TASK MANAGER

The Deferred Task Manager provides a way to defer the execution of interrupt tasks until interrupts have been reenabled (processor priority level 0). It maintains a deferred task queue; instead of performing a task immediately, you can place the information describing the task into the queue by calling the DTInstall procedure. All system interrupt handlers check this queue just before returning. If there are tasks in the queue and interrupts are about to be reenabled, the tasks are removed and then executed with all interrupts enabled.

While useful for all types of interrupt tasks, the Deferred Task Manager is especially handy for slot interrupts. Interrupts from NuBus slot devices are received and decoded by the VIA2, a second Versatile Interface Adapter (Rockwell 6522) chip on the Macintosh Iı. The VIA2 generates level-2 interrupts and, due to the way the VIA chip works, interrupts must be serviced before the processor priority level can be lowered (otherwise, a system error will occur). During this period (which could be quite long depending on the slot device) other level-2 interrupts such as those for sound, as well as all level-1 interrupts, are blocked. By using the Deferred Task Manager, the processing of slot interrupts can be deferred until all the slots are scanned; just before returning, the slot interrupt handler dispatches to any tasks in the deferred task queue.

The deferred task queue is a standard Macintosh Operating System queue, as described in chapter 13 of Volume II. Each entry in the deferred task queue has the following structure:

```
TYPE DeferredTask = RECORD
                qLink:      QElemPtr;  {next queue entry}
                qType:      INTEGER;   {queue type}
                dtFlags:    INTEGER;   {reserved}
                dtAddr:     ProcPtr;   {pointer to task}
                dtParm:     LONGINT;   {optional parameter}
                dtReserved: LONGINT    {reserved--should be 0}
            END;
```

QLink points to the next entry in the queue, and qType indicates the queue type, which must always be ORD(dtQType).

DTAddr contains a pointer to the task. DTParm is useful only from assembly language.

Assembly-language note: DTParm lets you pass an optional parameter to be loaded into register A1 just before the task is executed.

DEFERRED TASK MANAGER ROUTINES

```
FUNCTION DTInstall (dtTaskPtr: QElemPtr) : OSErr;
```

Trap macro	_DTInstall
On entry	A0: dtTaskPtr (pointer)
On exit	D0: result code (word)

Note: To reduce overhead at interrupt time, instead of executing the _DTInstall trap you can load the jump vector jDTInstall into an address register other than A0 and execute a JSR instruction using that register.

DTInstall adds the specified task to the deferred task queue. Your application must fill in all fields of the task except qLink. DTInstall returns one of the result codes listed below.

Result codes	noErr	No error
	vTypErr	Invalid queue element

SUMMARY OF THE DEFERRED TASK MANAGER

Data Types

```
TYPE DeferredTask = RECORD
                    qLink:      QElemPtr;  {next queue entry}
                    qType:      INTEGER;   {queue type}
                    dtFlags:    INTEGER;   {reserved}
                    dtAddr:     ProcPtr;   {pointer to task}
                    dtParm:     LONGINT;   {optional parameter}
                    dtReserved: LONGINT    {reserved--should be 0}
                END;
```

Routines

```
FUNCTION DTInstall (dtTaskPtr: QElemPtr) : OSErr;
```

Assembly-Language Information

Routines

Trap macro	On entry	On exit
_DTInstall	A0: dtTaskPtr (ptr)	D0: result code (word)

Structure of Deferred Task Manager Queue Entry

qLink	Pointer to next queue entry
qType	Queue type (word)
dtFlags	Reserved (word)
dtAddr	Address of task
dtParm	Optional parameter (long)
dtResrvd	Reserved—should be 0 (long)
dtQElSize	Size in bytes of queue element

Variables

DTQueue	Deferred task queue header (10 bytes)
JDTInstall	Jump vector for DTInstall routine

26 THE DISK DRIVER

26 Disk Driver

CHANGES TO THE DISK DRIVER

In earlier versions of the Disk Driver, each drive, whether electrically connected or not, is assigned its own, hard-coded drive number—the internal and external 3.5-inch drives have drive numbers 1 and 2, while Hard Disk 20 drives have drive numbers 3 and 4.

The new Disk Driver determines which drives are electrically connected and then dynamically assigns drive numbers, leaving no gaps for missing drives. This translation from drive to logical drive number means that a drive number might not correspond to the drive's physical, or electrical, address. For instance, on a Macintosh SE with one internal drive and one external drive, without translation the internal drive would be given drive number 1 and the external drive number 3 (drive number 2 belonging to the missing internal drive). With translation, the two connected drives are assigned logical drive numbers 1 and 2.

> **Warning**: Programs (such as copy-protection programs) that expect a given physical drive to have a permanently-assigned drive number will need to be modified in order to run under the new Disk Driver.

USING THE DISK DRIVER

Two advanced control calls have been added to the Disk Driver and one existing call has been extended.

csCode = 21   csParam = ptr (long)

This call previously worked only with the Hard Disk 20; with drive number translation, it's been extended to support all drives. For the drive whose drive number (remember, this will be a *logical* drive number) is specified in ioDrvNum, this call returns a pointer to a data structure consisting of an icon, a mask icon, and a Pascal string. This icon typically describes the disk media. The string is used in the Get Info dialog (after the word "Where:") to specify the physical drive associated with the icon. The Disk Driver leaves this string null, letting the Finder fill in this information. (Your own driver would need to supply this string.)

csCode = 22   csParam = ptr (long)

For the drive whose drive number is specified in ioDrvNum, this call returns a pointer to an icon and a mask icon. This icon typically describes the physical drive.

csCode = 23   csParam = long

This call returns information about the drive's physical location, size, and other characteristics. The low-order byte of csParam specifies the drive type and can contain one of the following values:

Value Meaning

0	No such drive
1	Unspecified drive
2	400K drive
3	800K drive
4	Reserved
5	Reserved
6	Reserved
7	Hard Disk 20

Bits 8 through 11 of csParam specify the drive attributes, as follows:

Bit Meaning

8	Set for external drives, clear for internal drive
9	Set if SCSI drive, clear if IWM
10	Set if drive is fixed, clear if drive can be removed
11	Set for secondary drives, clear for primary drive

The remaining bits of csParam are reserved for future use.

SUMMARY OF THE DISK DRIVER

Advanced Control Calls

csCode	csParam	Effect
21	ptr (long)	Fetches icon for media
22	ptr (long)	Fetches icon for physical drive
23	long	Fetches drive information

27 THE SOUND MANAGER

ABOUT THIS CHAPTER

This chapter describes the Sound Manager, which replaces the 64K and 128K ROM Sound Driver. While supporting the old Sound Driver data structures, routines, and synthesizers, the Sound Manager offers a more flexible way of doing the same things, often with new features and options and with less programming effort.

> **Reader's guide:** Most applications (other than music synthesizers) do not use complex sound effects, and hence have no need of the Sound Manager. For cautions about using complex sounds in ordinary applications, see the Macintosh User Interface Guidelines chapter in this volume.

ABOUT THE SOUND MANAGER

A major innovation of Sound Manager is the introduction of sound resources. Sound resources can specify just about anything—from a simple beep to a digital recording with the quality of a compact disk. Playing a sound resource is as simple as loading the resource and passing its handle to the SndPlay routine.

In addition, the synthesizers of the Sound Manager, utilizing the power of the new Apple Sound Chip, use only a fraction of the processing time of the MC68020.

Overview

With the Sound Manager, sounds are created by sending commands to a synthesizer. A synthesizer is like a device driver. The commands specify the sounds you want, and the synthesizer takes care of playing them on a particular piece of hardware (a speaker, for instance).

Commands are passed to a synthesizer through a special kind of queue, known as a channel. Every channel belongs to a particular synthesizer. To produce complex sounds like music and speech, several sounds may need to be produced at the same time; for this reason, the wave table, MIDI, and sampled sound synthesizers can have multiple channels.

Before being passed to the synthesizer, commands may also be processed by one or more routines, known as modifiers. Modifiers are typically used to synchronize the flow of commands between multiple channels, or to modify a sound before it reaches the synthesizer. To accomplish this, the Sound Manager provides modifiers with an additional set of commands.

The path of a typical Sound Manager command is shown in Figure 1.

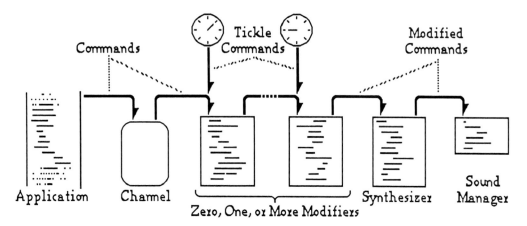

Figure 1. Sound Manager Command Path

Synthesizers

Which synthesizer you use depends on how complex a sound you want. If you just want
to play a simple melody, you can use the **note synthesizer.** Each note of the melody is
described by its frequency, or pitch (middle C, for instance), its amplitude (how loud), and
its duration.

With the note synthesizer, however, you can only play one note at a time; it's not possible
to play a chord. In addition, the range of available timbres is limited.

> **Note:** The note synthesizer is functionally equivalent to the old square-wave
> synthesizer.

To produce more complex sounds, you can use the **wave table synthesizer.** As the
name indicates, the wave table synthesizer lets you supply a wave table that describes the
harmonic content, or timbre, of a note at any point in time. It also lets you play multiple
notes at the same time by opening several channels.

> **Note:** Using the old four-tone synthesizer results in four channels of wave table
> synthesis.

The **sampled sound synthesizer** lets you play digitally recorded (or computed) music
and speech. (The sampled sound synthesizer is functionally equivalent to the old free-form
synthesizer.) Rather than specifying actual notes and corresponding wave tables, you pass
a pointer to a buffer that contains samples of the sound to be played. By changing the rate
at which the samples are played, notes of different pitches and durations are produced.

> **Note:** It's beyond the scope of this chapter to describe how to create a wave table or
> a sampled sound buffer. A good book to get started with is *Computer Music,
> Synthesis, Composition, and Performance* by Charles Dodge and Thomas A. Jerse.

An external **MIDI synthesizer** can be connected to the Apple serial ports, using an
adaptor. It lets you play music created by external synthesis. The Musical Instrument

Digital Interface (**MIDI**) is a world-wide standard for controlling external music synthesizers. It allows them to be controlled remotely, from a computer or another synthesizer. In addition, many of the parameters of the typical MIDI synthesizer can be altered and controlled in real time, giving it some of the features of a played instrument.

USING THE SOUND MANAGER

The Sound Manager has seven routines. Many applications will need to use only a few of these routines, since sound resources take care of much of the work. Two types of sound resources are available: 'snth' and 'snd '. (A detailed description of the format of the 'snd ' resource is given later in the chapter.)

A 'snth' resource contains executable code; the code is a function whose entry point is at the beginning of the resource. Synthesizers and modifiers are typically stored as 'snth' resources. A synthesizer is specified to the Sound Manager by its number, which must be the same as the resource ID of the 'snth' resource that contains it.

> **Note:** Numbers for 'snth' resources in the range 0 through 255 are reserved for Apple; others may be used freely. The 'snd ' resources 1 through 4 are defined to be the standard system beep and three variants of it. Numbers for 'snd ' resources in the range of 0 through 8191 are reserved for Apple.

The 'snd ' resource is both powerful and flexible. It can contain one or all of the following:

- a list of modifiers and synthesizers ('snth' resources) to load

- some or all of the commands needed to produce a sound

- data tables (consisting of either wave tables or sampled sound buffers) to be used with certain commands

By having only commands, a 'snd ' resource can describe a simple melody that can be played on almost any channel. In this case, the channel must first be set up with a synthesizer using the routine SndNewChannel. (It's never necessary to open a channel for the note synthesizer.) To dispose of the channel when you're done with it, call SndDisposeChannel.

Another possibility is to have the 'snd ' resource contain a single digitized sound, such as recorded music or speech. In this case, the resource also contains a few commands that start the sound (which is contained in a data table) playing at its natural sampling rate.

Another method is to provide the synthesizer and modifiers to be used, as well as the sounds to play. To "play" such a resource, you need only load it into memory and pass its handle to the SndPlay routine. SndPlay will open a channel, load the specified 'snth' resources, and pass the commands to the channel.

To add a modifier to a channel from your application (instead of from a 'snd ' resource), you can call SndAddModifier. The modifier can be a 'snth' resource, or simply a routine in memory to which you pass a pointer.

As mentioned above, commands can be placed in a 'snd ' resource and played using SndPlay. An application can also send commands with the routine SndDoCommand. If there's a command you want to pass immediately to the synthesizer (and any modifiers), bypassing the commands currently in the channel, call SndDoImmediate.

SndControl is intended for passing special commands directly to a modifier or synthesizer; currently, the only command that can be sent with SndControl is availableCmd (described below).

SOUND MANAGER ROUTINES

```
FUNCTION SndPlay (chan: SndChannelPtr; sndHdl: Handle; async:
        BOOLEAN): OSErr;
```

SndPlay plays the 'snd ' resource specified by sndHdl. If the resource specifies a synthesizer and any modifiers to be used, the appropriate 'snth' resources are loaded and linked to the channel. The commands in the 'snd ' resource are then passed to the channel.

If chan is NIL and no modifiers are specified in the 'snd ' resource, SndPlay allocates a channel defaulting to the note synthesizer. This channel is released after the commands in the resource have been processed (in other words, after the sounds have been played).

If you specify a channel in chan, you can call SndPlay asynchronously by passing TRUE in async. If chan is NIL, you must pass FALSE in async.

Result codes	noErr	No error
	resProblem	Problem loading resource
	badFormat	Handle to 'snd ' resource was invalid
	badChannel	Invalid channel queue length

```
FUNCTION SndNewChannel (VAR chan: SndChannelPtr; synth: INTEGER;
        init: LONGINT; userRoutine: ProcPtr) : OSErr;
```

SndNewChannel opens a new channel. If you pass NIL for the chan parameter, the Sound Manager opens a channel for you and returns a pointer to it.

Advanced programmers: If you're particularly concerned with memory management, you may want to allocate a SndChannel record yourself and pass a pointer to it in chan; for details on doing this, see "Sound Manager Data Structures" below.

Synth indicates the synthesizer to be used; the following standard values have been defined:

```
CONST noteSynth        = 1;   {note synthesizer}
      waveTableSynth   = 3;   {wave table synthesizer}
      sampledSynth     = 5;   {sampled sound synthesizer}
      MIDISynthIn      = 7;   {MIDI synthesizer in}
      MIDISynthOut     = 9;   {MIDI synthesizer out}
```

If you pass 0 for synth, no synthesizer is linked to the channel; you'd do this only if you intended to process commands using modifiers alone.

The init parameter is sent to the synthesizer as the second parameter of the initCmd command; its possible values are given in the description of initCmd below. The init parameter lets you request a channel with certain characteristics; this is only a request. To determine whether the requested characteristics were available, you can send the availableCmd command (described below) using the SndControl function.

If you want to supply a "call-back" routine, pass a pointer to it in userRoutine; if you pass NIL, callBackCmd commands are ignored (see "User Routines" below for a discussion of the call back routine).

Result codes	noErr	No error
	resProblem	Problem loading resource
	badChannel	Invalid channel queue length

```
FUNCTION SndAddModifier (chan: SndChannelPtr; modifier: ProcPtr;
       id: INTEGER; init: LONGINT) : OSErr;
```

SndAddModifier lets you add a modifier to an open channel. Chan contains a pointer to the channel. SndAddModifier always adds the modifier in front of the synthesizer, and in front of any modifiers previously installed.

If you want to load a 'snth' resource and add it as a modifier, pass NIL in the modifier parameter and pass the resource ID in id. The Sound Manager will load the resource, lock it, and link it to the channel.

> **Note:** The Sound Manager saves the state of the pointer (with HGetState) and restores it when SndDisposeChannel is called (using HSetState).

If you want to add your own procedure as a modifier (instead of using an 'snth' resource), simply pass a pointer to it in the modifier parameter. The format of a modifier procedure is given in "User Routines" below.

> **Warning:** Having too many modifiers per channel may degrade performance.

Result codes	noErr	No error
	resProblem	Problem loading resource
	badChannel	Invalid channel queue length

```
FUNCTION SndDoCommand (chan: SndChannelPtr; cmd: SndCommand;
        noWait: BOOLEAN) : OSErr;
```

SndDoCommand inserts the given command at the end of the channel. If you specify
FALSE for the noWait parameter and the queue is full, SndDoCommand waits for room in
the queue. If you pass TRUE and the queue is full, SndDoCommand will not insert the
command, and the result code queueFull will be returned.

Result codes   noErr   No error
                   queueFull   No room in the queue
                   badChannel   Invalid channel queue length

```
FUNCTION SndDoImmediate (chan: SndChannelPtr; cmd: SndCommand) :
        OSErr;
```

SndDoImmediate bypasses the queue and passes the given command directly to the
modifiers and synthesizer.

Note: SndDoImmediate passes the command on even if the channel is waiting in
response to a waitCmd or syncCmd command (described below).

Result codes   noErr   No error
                   badChannel   Invalid channel queue length

```
FUNCTION SndControl (id: INTEGER; VAR cmd: SndCommand) : OSErr;
```

SndControl sends the given command directly to the modifier or synthesizer whose
resource ID is in id. The result, if any, is returned in cmd. (Currently, only the
availableCmd command is sent with SndControl; it's described below.)

Result codes   noErr   No error
                   badChannel   Invalid channel queue length

```
FUNCTION SndDisposeChannel (chan: SndChannelPtr; quitNow: BOOLEAN)
        : OSErr;
```

SndDisposeChannel closes a channel, releasing all data structures associated with it, as
well as any 'snth' resources held by it. (Remember that if you allocated the SndChannel
record yourself, the Sound Manager will simply restore the pointer to its original state with
a call to HSetState.)

If you specify FALSE for quitNow, SndDispose channel simply places a quietCmd in the
queue; commands already in the queue are processed. If you specify TRUE for quitNow,
a flushCmd is passed, flushing all commands from the queue, and then a quietCmd is
placed in the queue.

Result codes   noErr   No error
                   badChannel   Invalid channel queue length

User Routines

Warning: These user routines may be called at interrupt level and must preserve all registers other than A0, A1, and D0–D2. They must not make any calls to the Memory Manager, directly or indirectly, and can't depend on handles to unlocked blocks being valid. If they use application globals, they must also ensure that register A5 contains the address of the boundary between the application globals and the application parameters; for details, see the SetUpA5 and RestoreA5 routines.

The SndNewChannel function lets you provide a "call-back" routine. A special command, callBackCmd, works like a flag; whenever this command is received by the Sound Manager, your call-back routine is called. Your call-back routine should be of the form

```
PROCEDURE MyCallBack (chan: SndChannelPtr; cmd: SndCommand);
```

The chan parameter contains a pointer to the channel; this lets you use the same call-back procedure with multiple channels. The callBackCmd command (described below) itself is passed in the cmd parameter; allowing you to pass information to your call-back routine.

The SndAddModifier function lets you add your own function as a modifier (without having to create an actual 'snth' resource). Your modifier function should be of the form

```
FUNCTION MyModifier (chan: SndChannelPtr; VAR cmd: SndCommand; mod:
        ModifierStubPtr) : BOOLEAN;
```

Each time a command reaches your modifier, your function is called. Chan contains a pointer to the channel; this lets you use the modifier with multiple channels. Mod contains a pointer to the modifier stub; you can use the modifier stub to store global variables used by the modifier.

The cmd parameter contains the command. To pass the command along, simply return FALSE (without altering the command). If you want to replace the command with another one, place the new command in cmd and return FALSE. To prevent a command from going on, replace it with the nullCmd command and return FALSE.

If you want to pass along an additional command, return TRUE. The Sound Manager will call your function again, this time passing the requestNextCmd command. You can then replace this command with a different command. You can return TRUE as many times as you like. The requestNextCmd command indicates how many times in a row it has been sent to your function.

SOUND MANAGER DATA STRUCTURES

This section describes two data structures: the channel and the modifier stub.

Reader's guide: Application programmers rarely need to access these structures.

The SndChannel Record

When you pass NIL for the chan parameter in the SndNewChannel function, the Sound Manager allocates a SndChannel record for you. This record is a locked, nonrelocatable block that's released when SndDisposeChannel is called.

If you're particularly concerned with memory allocation, you may want to allocate the SndChannel record yourself and pass a pointer to it in the SndNewChannel call. The structure of the SndChannel record is as follows:

```
TYPE SndChannel = RECORD
                nextChan:   Ptr;          {pointer to next channel}
                firstMod:   Ptr;          {pointer to first }
                                          { modifier}
                callBack:   ProcPtr;      {pointer to channel's }
                                          { call back procedure}
                userInfo:   LONGINT;      {free for use}
                wait:       Time;         {used internally}
                cmdInProg:  SndCommand;   {used internally}
                flags:      INTEGER;      {used internally}
                qLength:    INTEGER;      {queue length}
                qHead:      INTEGER;      {used internally}
                qTail:      INTEGER;      {used internally}
                queue:      ARRAY[0..stdQLength-1] OF SndCommand
            END;
```

CallBack contains a pointer to your call back routine (specified in the userRoutine parameter of SndNewChannel). UserInfo is free for your use.

The wait field, used internally by the Sound Manager, is of type Time; this data type is declared as follows:

```
TYPE Time = LONGINT;
```

QLength specifies the number of commands that the channel can hold; it must always be ORD(stdQLength).

The remaining fields of the SndChannel record are used by the Sound Manager and should not be manipulated.

When you've allocated the SndChannel record yourself, the Sound Manager saves the state information from the pointer you pass, (calling HGetState). It locks the block while it's in use (with HLock), and then restores the state when SndDisposeChannel is called (using HSetState).

The Modifier Stub

Each modifier linked to a channel must have a modifier stub that describes it; the structure of a modifier stub is as follows:

```
TYPE ModifierStub = RECORD
                    nextStub: Ptr;         {pointer to next modifier}
                    code:     ProcPtr;     {pointer to modifier code}
                    userInfo: LONGINT;     {free for modifier to use}
                    count:    Time;        {used internally}
                    every:    Time;        {used internally}
                    flags:    SignedByte;  {used internally}
                    hState:   SignedByte   {used internally}
                  END;
```

NextStub points to the modifier stub of the next modifier in the list; this field is maintained by the Sound Manager and should not be modified. Code must contain a pointer to the modifier code itself.

UserInfo is free for your modifier to use. If the modifier is used with more than one channel, this field could be used to maintain state information about each channel. It can be a longint or a pointer.

A modifier could, for instance, transpose music by altering the pitch of every note that gets passed to it. It could also create a "trill" effect by periodically altering the pitch of a note; to do this a modifier might generate a frequencyCmd in response to a tickleCmd (these commands are described below).

SOUND MANAGER COMMANDS

The Sound Manager commands are as follows:

```
CONST nullCmd         = 0;
      initCmd         = 1;
      freeCmd         = 2;
      quietCmd        = 3;
      flushCmd        = 4;
      waitCmd         = 10;
      pauseCmd        = 11;
      resumeCmd       = 12;
      callBackCmd     = 13;
      syncCmd         = 14;
      emptyCmd        = 15;
      tickleCmd       = 20;
      requestNextCmd  = 21;
      howOftenCmd     = 22;
      wakeUpCmd       = 23;
      availableCmd    = 24;
      noteCmd         = 40;
      restCmd         = 41;
```

```
freqCmd            = 42;
ampCmd             = 43;
timbreCmd          = 44;
waveTableCmd       = 60;
phaseCmd           = 61;
soundCmd           = 80;
bufferCmd          = 81;
rateCmd            = 82;
midiDataCmd        = 100;
```

Commands are always eight bytes in length, and are specified using the following record:

```
TYPE SndCommand = PACKED RECORD
               cmd:      INTEGER;    {command number}
               param1:   INTEGER;    {first parameter}
               param2:   LONGINT;    {second parameter}
            END;
```

If the high-order of the cmd field is set, param2 contains a pointer to some other memory block.

Most applications only need to know about a few of the above commands. The complete set of commands, along with the parameters they take, is described below under "Command Descriptions". The next three sections introduce the commands that actually produce sound.

Basic Note Commands

The basic note commands are noteCmd, restCmd, freqCmd, ampCmd, and timbreCmd; these commands are understood by all four synthesizers. They are also the only commands used by the note synthesizer.

With noteCmd, you specify a note by its pitch, amplitude, and duration. Pitch can be specified in two ways. One way is to supply a value between 0 and 127; this value is then converted into a frequency as follows. The value 60 is considered to be middle C on a piano keyboard. Adding 1 raises the pitch by one semitone; in other words, a value of 61 represents a C sharp above middle C. Subtracting 1 lowers the pitch by one semitone; in other words, a value of 59 represents a B below middle C. Adding or subtracting 12 raises or lowers the pitch by one octave respectively.

> **Note:** This method limits one to an equal-tempered scale (just like a piano keyboard) but is perfectly acceptable for many needs.

A second way of specifying pitch is with the actual frequency of the note; this method does not limit one to the equal-tempered scale. The frequency of middle C, as an example, is 261.6256 Hz, and concert A (A440) is 440 Hz.

When specifying pitch as a value between 0..127, the value is stored in the low-order byte of param2; the other two bytes must be 0. When supplying an actual frequency, all three bytes are used. The two high-order bytes represent the integer portion of the frequency and the low-order byte contains the fraction (in other words, $01 = 1/256 and $FF = 255/256). For example, middle C would be represented as $0105A0 and A440 would be $01B800.

Duration is specified in half-milliseconds. To translate this into real terms, suppose you want to play a piece at 120 beats per minute and each quarter note is one beat. This means a quarter note occurs every 500 milliseconds, so the duration would be 1000 (half-milliseconds). If you wanted 60 beats per minute, the duration would be doubled.

Amplitude is specified as a value between 0 and 255 with 255 meaning maximum amplitude and 0 meaning silence.

NoteCmd, unlike all the other commands, needs two different values specified in param2: the amplitude in the high-order byte and the pitch or frequency in the three low-order bytes. To do this, you can assign the two values to temporary LONGINT fields, with the value for the high-order byte preshifted, and then assign the sum of the fields to param2. An example of doing this, assuming a desired amplitude of 255 (maximum amplitude) and a pitch of 60 (middle C on a piano), is as follows:

```
myAmplitude, myPitch:  LONGINT;
myAmplitude := $FF000000;
myPitch := $000105A0;
mySndCmd.param2 := myAmplitude + myPitch;
```

RestCmd produces silence for a given duration.

FreqCmd, ampCmd, and timbreCmd change the pitch, amplitude, and timbre of the sound that's currently playing.

Wave Table Synthesizer

In addition to the basic sound commands, the wave table synthesizer uses waveTableCmd and phaseCmd. WaveTableCmd specifies the wave table to be used, while phaseCmd lets you tell where in the table to begin producing the sound.

The wave table describes the timbre, or harmonic content, of a sound at any point in time. The table consists of a sequence of bytes spanning a single oscillation of sound. A length of 512 bytes is recommended for optimum performance, but the synthesizer will convert other sizes into an equivalent table of the correct frequency that's 512 bytes long. The samples are to be represented in offset binary format; that is, $80 is considered zero, $00 the largest negative value, and $FF the largest positive value. (This is just like the old Sound Driver.) For example, a wave table consisting of a sine timbre would look like that in Figure 2.

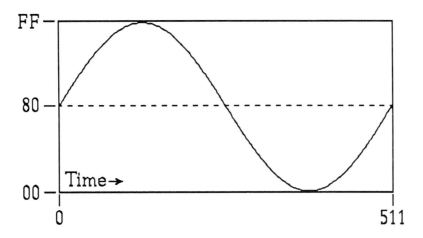

Figure 2. Wave Form for a Sine Timbre

In addition to the standard method of playing out a wave table continuously, the wave table synthesizer can be used in a "one-shot" mode. When this mode is enabled, the waveform is output once per trigger command. Voice and other natural-sounding pulsed sounds can be achieved by placing one period of the sound in the wave table and triggering it to play in a nonregular fashion. One-shot mode may also be used to play a short sound (practically speaking, a tenth of a second or less), such as a game bleep, with very little overhead.

> **Note:** Using the old four-tone synthesizer results in four channels of wave table synthesis. The techniques for suppressing clicks with the old four-tone synthesizer are still supported when the old interface is used; these techniques are discouraged, however, as they are costly in time and space. The wave table synthesizer provides equivalent functionality with more power.

Sampled Sound Synthesizer

The sampled sound synthesizer plays out digitally recorded (or computed) sounds. The sounds are passed to the synthesizer in buffers containing samples of the sound (also in offset binary format).

The buffers may be played out at the original sampling rate (producing the same pitch), or they can be played at higher or lower rates (producing higher or lower pitches). The rate may be changed over time. The amplitude, as well as whether the sound is left, middle, or right, may also be specified and changed over time. The format for these buffers is shown in Figure 5.

Playing two or more buffers end-to-end is guaranteed to sound just as though the buffers had been concatenated into a longer buffer as long as the buffers are longer than 256 bytes each and are presented to the Sound Manager quickly enough. For this reason, the techniques and restrictions for playing continuous sound with the old free-form synthesizer no longer apply and are discouraged.

Alternatively, a single buffer of sound may be passed to the synthesizer. NoteCmd commands can then be sent to play the buffer out at different pitches and durations. The pitch is changed by altering the rate used to play out the buffer. The duration is changed by looping (playing over and over) some segment of the buffer. This segment is specified by loop points given when the buffer is passed to the synthesizer in the 'snd ' resource. For notes of a given duration, the loop is repeated such that the end portion will fit within the duration. For notes of unknown duration, the loop is simply repeated until a new note or rest is played; in the case of a rest, the end portion plays then.

Command Descriptions

cmd = nullCmd   **param1 = NIL**   **param2 = NIL**

The Sound Manager simply absorbs the nullCmd. To prevent a command from going on, replace it with nullCmd.

cmd = initCmd   **param1 = NIL**   **param2 = init**

Sent by the Sound Manager to a modifier or synthesizer when it's linked to a channel. If the application passed the init parameter when calling SndNewChannel or SndAddModifier, this information is passed in param2.

The note synthesizer does not accept initialization parameters. The other three standard synthesizers can be sent a request for certain characteristics in the low-order byte of init; the following masks are provided:

```
CONST initChanLeft      = $02; {left stereo channel}
      initChanRight     = $03; {right stereo channel}
      initChan0         = $04; {channel 0--Wave Table only}
      initChan1         = $05; {channel 1--Wave Table only}
      initChan2         = $06; {channel 2--Wave Table only}
      initChan3         = $07; {channel 3--Wave Table only}
      initSRate22k      = $20; {sampling rate of 22kHz}
      initSRate44k      = $30; {sampling rate of 44kHz}
      initMono          = $80; {monophonic channel}
      initStereo        = $C0; {stereo channel}
```

Warning: InitCmd is only a request; to determine whether the requested characteristics were available, you can send availableCmd (described below) using the SndControl function.

cmd = freeCmd   **param1 = NIL**   **param2 = NIL**

Sent by the Sound Manager in response to a SndDisposeChannel call, freeCmd causes the synthesizer and modifiers to stop processing commands after the current sound has completed playing.

Note: Neither initCmd nor freeCmd will be called at interrupt level, so you're free to call the Memory Manager.

cmd = quietCmd   **param1 = NIL**   **param2 = NIL**

Sent by the application, quietCmd causes the synthesizer and modifiers to stop processing commands immediately, stopping any sound in progress.

cmd = flushCmd   **param1 = NIL**   **param2 = NIL**

Sent by the application, flushCmd causes all commands to be flushed immediately from the channel.

cmd = waitCmd   **param1 = duration** **param2 = NIL**

Sent by either the application or a modifier, waitCmd suspends the processing of commands for the specified duration.

cmd = pauseCmd   **param1 = NIL**   **param2 = NIL**

Sent by a modifier, pauseCmd suspends the processing of commands indefinitely; typically the channel will "wake up" only in response to a tickleCmd or resumeCmd. PauseCmd is intended for synthesizers that want to halt processing until the current command is processed when the duration is not known in advance.

cmd = resumeCmd   **param1 = NIL**   **param2 = NIL**

Sent by a modifier, resumeCmd causes command processing to resume on a channel that was paused due to a pauseCmd.

cmd = callBackCmd **param1 = user-defined param2 = user-defined**

Sent by an application, callBackCmd causes the call-back routine specified in the SndNewChannel function to be executed. Param1 and param2 can be used to pass information to the call-back routine.

The callBackCmd is like a marker; when the call back routine gets called, it knows a particular point in the command stream has been reached. A game might want, for instance, to display something on the screen immediately after a certain sound has been made. A callBackCmd could be placed after the particular noteCmd; the call-back routine is alerted after the note has sounded, and is given control to perform the screen activity.

cmd = syncCmd   **param1 = count**   **param2 = identifier**

Sent by an application, syncCmd suspends processing of commands in this channel until syncCmd commands with the same identifier have been received for count other channels. Figure 3 illustrates the use of syncCmd.

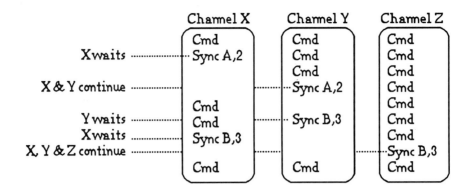

Figure 3. Use of the SyncCmd

cmd = emptyCmd   **param1 = NIL**   **param2 = NIL**

EmptyCmd is sent only by the Sound Manager. The synthesizers expect resumeCmd to be
followed by another command; if there are no commands to follow, the Sound Manager
sends an emptyCmd.

cmd = tickleCmd   **param1 = NIL**   **param2 = NIL**

Sent by the Sound Manager to modifiers and synthesizers that request periodic action; the
period at which the tickleCmd is sent is specified by the howOftenCmd.

cmd = requestNextCmd   param1 = count   **param2 = NIL**

Sent by the Sound Manager in response to a modifier returning a TRUE result (indicating
that it wants to send another command). Count is the number of times in a row that this
modifier has asked to send another command.

cmd = howOftenCmd   **param1 = period**   **param2 = pointer**

Sent by a modifier, howOftenCmd instructs the Sound Manager to periodically send a
tickleCmd to a modifier. Param1 contains the period, specified in half milliseconds.
Param2 contains a pointer to the modifier stub.

cmd = wakeUpCmd   **param1 = period**   **param2 = pointer**

Sent by a modifier, wakeUpCmd requests a single tickleCmd after the number of
milliseconds specified in param1 have elapsed. Param2 contains a pointer to the modifier
stub.

> **Note:** HowOftenCmd and wakeUpCmd are mutually exclusive; sending one will
> cancel the other.

cmd = availableCmd   **param1 = status**   **param2 = init**

Sent by an application, availableCmd can be used to determine whether the initialization parameters requested by initCmd were available. Init specifies the same characteristics as in the initCmd. Status returns a boolean result of TRUE if the characteristics were available and FALSE if they weren't.

> **Note:** AvailableCmd can be sent only with the SndControl routine (it can't be sent with SndDoCommand).

cmd = noteCmd   **param1 = duration**   **param2 = amplitude + frequency**

Play a note with the specified frequency and amplitude for the given duration. On a monophonic channel, this suspends the processing of commands until the note is finished. On a polyphonic channels, subsequent commands will continue to processed.

cmd = restCmd   **param1 = duration**   **param2 = NIL**

Causes the channel to rest for the given duration. (This may not result in silence since the decay of the previous note may continue to sound.) RestCmd differs from waitCmd in that it allows a playing sound to finish (go into release and decay stages) whereas waitCmd causes the Sound Manager to physically cut off the sound.

cmd = frequencyCmd   **param1 = NIL**   **param2 = frequency**

Changes the frequency of the currently playing sound. If no sound is playing, a sound of indefinite duration is started at the given frequency and the last-requested amplitude. Specifying a frequency of 0 results in silence; it's equivalent to sending a waitCmd. The frequency is specified in the low-order three bytes of the long argument (the high-order byte must be zero).

cmd = ampCmd   **param1 = amplitude**   **param2 = NIL**

Changes the amplitude of the currently playing sound. If no sound is playing, the amplitude of the next sound, unless otherwise specified, will be set. The amplitude is specified in param1 (unlike noteCmd, where it's given in the high-order byte of param2)

cmd = timbreCmd   **param1 = timbre**   **param2 = NIL**

TimbreCmd is supported only by the note synthesizer. It lets you request a change in the waveform, where 0 represents a sine wave and 255 represents a square wave. This is only a request.

cmd = waveTableCmd   **param1 = length**   **param2 = ptr**

Sent by an application, waveTableCmd specifies the wave table to be used with succeeding note commands. Param2 contains a pointer to the table and param1 specifies the length of the table.

cmd = phaseCmd

PhaseCmd lets you specify which byte in the wave table to begin playing on.

cmd = soundCmd   **param1 = NIL**   **param2 = pointer**

Sent by an application, soundCmd specifies the sound to be played by succeeding note commands. Param2 contains a pointer to the bytes describing the sound.

cmd = bufferCmd   **param1 = NIL**   **param2 = pointer**

Sent by an application, bufferCmd plays the buffer pointed to by param2 at the last set frequency and amplitude. The buffer format is shown in Figure 5. The channel pauses until the sound has played.

> **Note:** The channel will actually be started again just before the sound has finished, so that multiple buffers will be continuous.

cmd = rateCmd   **param1 = NIL**   **param2 = rate**

Sets the rate at which succeeding buffer commands will be played. RateCmd is similar to frequencyCmd except that it lets you specify the rate as a multiplier of the original sampling rate; in other words, a rate of 2 is an octave higher, 0.667 a fifth lower. The rate is specified as a fixed-point number (of type Fixed).

SOUND RESOURCES

This section describes two standard formats of the 'snd ' resources type: format 1 and format 2.

> **Note:** Numbers for 'snd ' resources in the range of 0 through 8191 are reserved for Apple.

Format 1 'snd' Resources

Figure 4 shows the structure of a format 1 'snd ' resource.

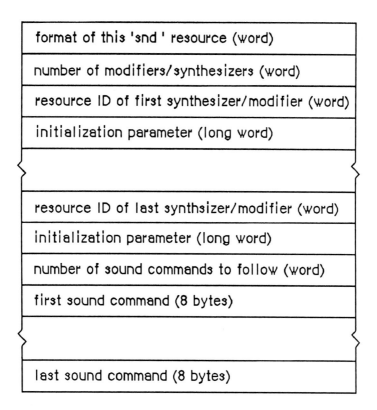

| format of this 'snd' resource (word) |
| number of modifiers/synthesizers (word) |
| resource ID of first synthesizer/modifier (word) |
| initialization parameter (long word) |
| |
| resource ID of last synthsizer/modifier (word) |
| initialization parameter (long word) |
| number of sound commands to follow (word) |
| first sound command (8 bytes) |
| |
| last sound command (8 bytes) |

Figure 4. A Format 1 'snd' Resource

The first word is the format number; in this case, it's $0001. The next field tells how many synthesizers and modifiers are used by this 'snd' resource. For each synthesizer or modifier, there follows the resource ID (of the corresponding 'snth' resource) and an optional initialization parameter.

The synthesizers and modifiers are listed in the reverse of the order in which they are to sit in the channel: the synthesizer first, followed by modifiers, ending with the first modifier. (The Sound Manager runs down this list calling SndAddModifier, which places the new modifier in front of those previously installed.)

The number of commands in the resource comes next, immediately followed by the commands themselves. As described above in "Sound Manager Commands", commands consist of three fields totaling eight bytes.

The commands are followed by data tables (if any). A command with additional data is marked by setting the high-order bit of the command number field, with the third (long word) argument containing the offset of the data from the start of the 'snd' resource.

Note: The offset is calculated as 6 bytes plus the number of synthesizers/modifiers times 6 plus the number of commands times 8. When passed to a channel by the SndPlay routine, this offset will be converted into an actual address.

Example

By providing a synthesizer and list of modifiers, and a few commands to initialize them, a 'snd ' resource becomes an instrument. After calling SndPlay to install the instrument, the calling program can issue a series of noteCmd commands to play a tune using this timbre. Since there are no noteCmd commands in the resource itself, the installation does not make any noise.

For the sampled sound synthesizer, an instrument has only a soundCmd and the corresponding data table. The data table usually contains a single digitized note, to be played over and over at different pitches and durations. Note: It can only play one note at a time (one voice) per channel. In this example, a 'snd ' resource specifies the sampled sound synthesizer and a hypothetical modifier. It plays one instrument for two notes and two rests, and a second instrument for one note and rest. The soundCmd sets the instrument for subsequent notes and points to the actual samples stored in the data table portion of the resource. The calling program brings the resource into memory and calls the Sound Manager, as follows:

```
ResHndl := GetNamedResource ('snd ','Harpsichord');
SndPlay (NIL,ResHndl,TRUE);
```

Since the call does not specify a channel, the Sound Manager allocates one and destroys it afterwards. The third argument tells the Sound Manager to play the sound asynchronously, returning control immediately to the calling program. Because it specifies both a synthesizer and notes, the 'snd ' resource in this example is a self-contained sound and could be used for a sysbeep or bootbeep. The contents of this 'snd ' resource are as follows:

Value	Size	Meaning
1	word	A format 1 'snd ' resource
2	word	Install two synthesizers/modifiers in the channel
5	word	Resource ID of the sampled sound synthesizer
0	long	NIL initialization parameter
12	word	Resource ID of hypothetical modifier
0	long	NIL initialization parameter
8	word	Eight sound commands (eight bytes each) to follow

(sound commands)

$8050, 0, 82	SoundCmd (offset is 6 bytes plus 2 synthesizers/modifiers times 6 bytes plus 8 bytes times 8 commands)
40, 400, 60	NoteCmd, play for 400 half-milliseconds, a middle C note
41, 400, 0	RestCmd, rest for 0.2 seconds (while the note decays)
40, 400, 64	NoteCmd, play for 400 half-milliseconds, an E note
41, 400, 0	RestCmd, rest for 0.2 seconds (while the note decays)
$8050, 0, 82+3022	SoundCmd, with offset to the second data table (the first sound is 3022 bytes long)

41, 400, 0   RestCmd, rest for 0.2 seconds (while the note decays)

(first sampled sound data table)

0	long	Pointer to the data (though it follows immediately)
3000	long	Number of samples in the sound (1 byte per sample)
$56EE8BA4	long	Sampling rate (22K samples per second)
2000	long	Start of loop, for when duration is longer than samples
2200	long	End of the loop (jump back to start). The remaining 800 samples are the decay portion.
60	word	BaseNote (the pitch of the sound in half steps when the samples are played at the sampling rate)
3000 bytes		Sound samples (with $80 the resting value, $FF the maximum positive amplitude, and $00 the maximum negative amplitude)

(second sampled sound data table)

0	long	Pointer to the data (though it follows immediately)
1500	long	Number of samples in the sound (1 byte per sample)
$56EE8BA4	long	Sampling rate (22K samples per second)
500	long	Start of loop when duration is longer than samples
600	long	End of the loop (jump back to start). The remaining 900 samples are the decay portion.
55	word	BaseNote (the pitch of the sound in half steps when the samples are played at the sampling rate)
1500 bytes		Sound samples for 1500 more bytes

Format 2 'snd ' Resources

A format 2 'snd ' represents either an instrument or a digitally recorded sound. After installing it on a sound channel that uses the sampled synthesizer, an application can send note and rest commands to the channel to play a tune. If the resource contains speech or a sound effect, the application can play it once at its natural pitch for its natural length.

Developers of music applications are strongly encouraged to adopt the format 2 'snd ' resource as a standard. As "non-music" developers incorporate 'snd ' resources into their applications, they will come to depend on tools for creating and editing those sounds. Adding to your music application the ability to write sounds out as format 2 'snd ' resources is thus highly desirable.

Format 2 'snd ' resources work only with the sampled sound synthesizer. They assume that the sampled sound synthesizer and any relevant modifiers are already installed on a preexisting channel (unlike format 1 resources which can let the Sound Manager take care of allocating and releasing a channel). After setting up the channel and synthesizer, the calling program will most likely set up an instrument, play some notes, and then install a different instrument and play more notes. Format 2 resources hold either the instrument, a list of notes without an instrument, or both. Format 2 resources do not disturb the setup of the channel and synthesizer; this allows additional format 2 resources to be played. (This saves time, prevents clicks, and keeps memory from getting fragmented.) The structure of a format 2 resource is given in Figure 5.

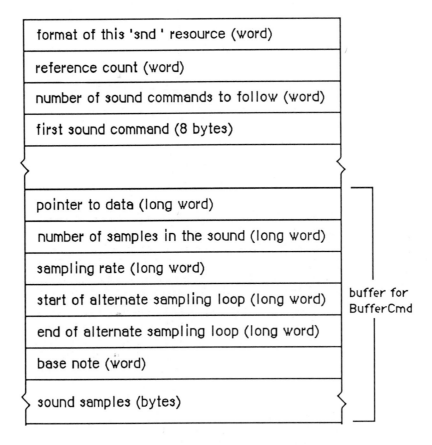

Figure 5. A Format 2 'snd ' Resource

The 'snd ' resource for each instrument must be locked and unpurgeable so the synthesizer can find the samples. It must be released, however, when the sound is over so that memory does not become fragmented. Since the notes are played asynchronously of the calling program, the caller does not know when the sound has finished. In addition, the same resource may be queued for playing many times. For these reasons, format 2 resources have a special field in which the calling program can keep a reference count for each 'snd ' resource that contains an instrument; when the count falls to zero, the resource can be unlocked and made purgeable.

When a format 2 resource is used solely as an instrument description (itself not specifying any notes), it expects the calling program to send a series of noteCmds to the channel just after it's installed.

Example

Value	Size	Meaning
2	word	A format 2 'snd ' resource.
0	word	Space for the reference count. Must start out 0 for the resource to be freed. Put 256+1 here to force the calling program to keep it in memory permanently.
1	word	One sound command to follow.

(sound command)

$8050, 0, 14   SoundCmd (offset is 6 bytes plus 8 bytes times 1 command)

(NoteCmd commands could be placed here but would be played every time the timbre is installed. NoteCmd commands without a soundCmd make up a tune that could be played after another instrument has been installed.)

(sampled sound data table)

0	long	Pointer to the data (it follows immediately, not indirect)
3000	long	Number of samples in the sound (1 byte per sample)
$56EE8BA4	long	The sample rate (22K samples per second)
2000	long	Start of loop when duration is longer than samples
2200	long	End of the loop (jump back to start). The remaining 800 samples are the decay portion.
60	word	BaseNote (the pitch of the sound in half steps when the samples are played at the sampling rate)
3000 bytes		Sound samples (with $80 the resting value, $FF the maximum positive amplitude, and $00 the maximum negative amplitude)

'snth' Resources

Sound Manager synthesizers and modifiers are both stored as resources of type 'snth'. Low-number 'snth' resource IDs are reserved for use by Apple. High-number 'snth' resource IDs are available for use by developers.

A modifier has the same format as a synthesizer. The main difference is a functional one. While a synthesizer controls hardware to produce some sort of effect, a modifier resides in the Sound Manager channel and modifies commands.

There are several cases where being able to modify a command is desirable. In the case of MIDI a modifier is used to convert MIDI messages into Sound Manager commands. A modifier may be written to play a chord based on a note sent down a channel.

The synthesizers currently included on the Macintosh II System Disk have the following resource IDs:

    1 = Note Synthesizer
    3 = WaveTable Synthesizer
    5 = Sampling Synthesizer
    7 = MIDI Input Synthesizer
    9 = MIDI Output Synthesizer

All 'snth' resources conform to the following Pascal call:

```
FUNCTION MySynth (chan : SndChannelPtr; VAR comm : SndCommand; mod:
        ModifierStubPtr) : Boolean;
```

The synthesizer passes information along the channel by altering the value of the VAR parameter comm.

The boolean result of a synthesizer or modifier tells the Sound Manager if it should send a RequestNextCmd. If the result is TRUE, then a RequestNextCmd is sent. In general, most synthesizers and modifiers return FALSE.

There are three commands that every synth or modifier must handle. These are InitCmd, FreeCmd, and NullCmd.

InitCmd is sent to a synthesizer or modifier at the time it is linked to the channel. It is never sent at interrupt time so it is safe for the synthesizer or modifier to allocate memory. During an interrupt your synthesizer or modifier should initialize any global data, try to take control of the hardware and allocate any necessary memory. The modifier stub contains a 4-byte user field. If more than four bytes of storage are needed, a pointer to memory can be stored here. It is important to note that any storage being allocated by the synthesizer or modifier should be locked, since the memory manager cannot be called during an interrupt. When InitCmd is passed to the synthesizer, as described above under "Command Descriptions", Param2 may contain a synthesizer-specific init parameter.

FreeCmd tells the synthesizer or modifier to free any data structures it may have allocated and release control of the hardware after making sure that the hardware is quiet. FreeCmd will never be called at interrupt time so it is safe to call the memory manager to dispose of allocated memory. Neither the InitCmd or the FreeCmd are passed on.

The correct response to a NullCmd is simply to pass it on. You can use the NullCmd to insure that a command is passed on by subsequent synthesizers or modifiers. The general rule for all synthesizers and modifiers is to pass on all commands that they cannot process.

MIDI IMPLEMENTATION

This section describes in detail how the MIDI Input and Output Modifiers currently work under the Sound Manager. It is likely that the handling of some MIDI messages will change in future versions of the Macintosh system.

MIDI input is accomplished through a 'snth' resource with ID=7 that converts Sound Manager commands to MIDI commands. MIDI output is accomplished through a 'snth' resource with ID = 9 that converts MIDI commands to Sound Manager commands.

Note: For details of the MIDI interface, refer to the MIDI 1.0 Specification, available directly from the International MIDI Association.

MIDI Input Modifier

The MIDI Input Modifier is designed to allow an application using the Sound Manager to receive information via MIDI.

When it receives an InitCmd, the Input Modifier allocates storage for internal state information, sets up a periodic wakeup, and allows the following constants to be passed in param2:

```
CONST MidiInitChannel   = n;      {MIDI Channel to init $0..$F}
      MidiInitChanFilter = $10;   {set to initialize a MIDI Channel}
      MidiInitRawMode    = $100;  {set to send raw MIDI data}
```

If MidiInitChanFilter is set, only information coming in on the MIDI channel specified in MidiInitChannel will be passed along. Otherwise all MIDI input is passed along, equivalent to MIDI omni mode.

MidiInitRawMode is set if the channel should be sent raw MIDI data. Normally the MIDI Synthesizer interprets Sound Manager commands and sends the equivalent MIDI commands. By setting MidiInitRawMode, raw MIDI data can be passed back to the application.

FreeCmd disposes of all data structures allocated by the modifier during InitCmd, and shuts down transmission of MIDI data.

TickleCmd and RequestNextCmd cause the modifier to receive MIDI input and pass it down the channel, converting it to Sound Manager commands if MidiInitRawMode was not set in InitCmd. This can be useful in two ways:

- when using the MIDI Input Modifier to play a Sound Manager synthesizer
- when using the MIDI Input Modifier to accept raw MIDI data

These two possibilities are discussed below.

Playing a Sound Manager Synthesizer

When playing a Sound Manager synthesizer, the MIDI Input Modifier retrieves a command from the MIDI input buffer each time the modifier receives a TickleCmd or a RequestNextCmd, as diagrammed in Figure 6.

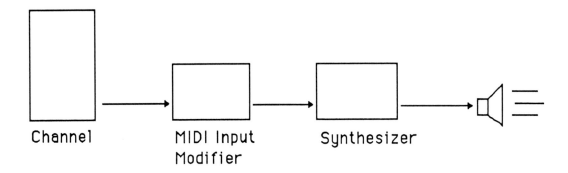

Figure 6. Playing a Sound Manager Synthesizer

Each MIDI command is converted to a Sound Manager command according to the rules listed below.

Channel Voice Messages:

- NoteOn events are converted to FreqCmd. Note that this is done since we cannot determine the correct duration for a NoteCmd.

- NoteOff events are converted to FreqCmd with Param2 = 0. This will turn off any notes playing on the channel.

- The following events are not currently processed:
    Polyphonic Key Pressure/Aftertouch
    Control Change
    Program Change
    Channel Presssure (Aftertouch)
    Pitch Wheel Change

System Common Messages:

- The following messages are not currently processed:
    System Exclusive
    Song Position Pointer
    Song Select
    Tune Request
    EOX "End of System Exclusive" flag

System Real Time Messages:

- Start and Continue messages are converted to ResumeCmd.

- Stop messages are converted to PauseCmd.

- System Reset will reset the MIDI input queue. It is not passed along through the channel.

- The following messages are not currently processed:
    Timing Clock
    Active Sensing

Accepting Raw MIDI Data

An application can use the MIDI Input Modifier to receive raw MIDI data, as diagrammed in Figure 7. This is useful for applications that want to handle MIDI messages in a special way or want to take control of the translation from MIDI message to Sound Manager commands.

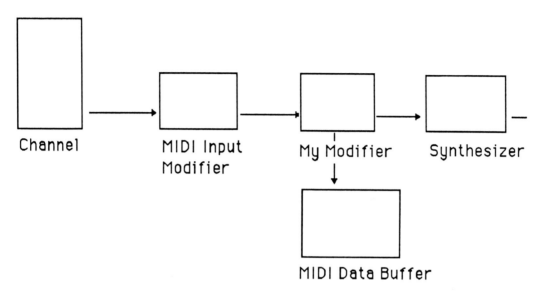

Figure 7. Accepting Raw MIDI Data

If the application has set MidiInitRawMode in InitCmd, then the MIDI Input Modifier will pass raw MIDI data down the channel in Param2.

MIDI Output Modifier

The MIDI Output Modifier is very similar to the MIDI Input Modifier. It provides a way for an application to make Sound Manager calls and have them be converted to MIDI messages, as diagrammed in Figure 8. It is also possible to send MIDI messages as raw data.

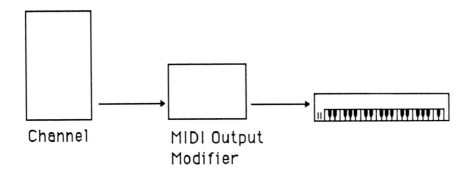

Figure 8. MIDI Output Modifier

The Sound Manager commands that can be used with the MIDI Output Modifier are listed below.

InitCmd

■ Allocates storage for internal state information.

■ Allows an InitParam to be passed in Param2, using these constants:

```
CONST  MidiInitChannel    = n;        {MIDI Channel to init $0 .. $F}
       MidiInitChanFilter = $10;      {set to initialize a MIDI Channel}
```

MidiInitChannel will contain the number of the MIDI channel to be initialized.

MidiInitChanFilter must be set. Monovoice information will be sent on the MIDI channel specified in MidiInitChannel. This is equivalent to MIDI transmit mode 4.

The MIDI velocity used is initialized to 64 by InitCmd.

FreeCmd

Disposes of all data structures allocated by the modifier during InitCmd. Shuts down transmission of MIDI data.

NoteCmd
FreqCmd

A MIDI NoteOff message is sent for the last note played. The note is played using a fixed velocity. The amplitude supplied in the high byte of Param2 for NoteCmd is ignored. The low three bytes of Param2 must contain a MIDI semitone value (0 .. 127); frequency values are not permitted. The duration supplied with NoteCmd is processed correctly.

EmptyCmd

A MIDI NoteOff message is sent for the last note played.

QuietCmd

A MIDI AllNotesOff message is sent.

AmpCmd

The fixed velocity used in the translation of FreqCmd and NoteCmd is changed to the supplied value. This value will be used for all subsequent MIDI messages requiring a velocity.

MidiDataCmd

Param2 is treated as raw MIDI data and sent to the MIDI output stream.

SUMMARY OF THE SOUND MANAGER

Constants

```
CONST { Command numbers for SndDoCommand }

        nullCmd           = 0;
        initCmd           = 1;
        freeCmd           = 2;
        quietCmd          = 3;
        flushCmd          = 4;
        waitCmd           = 10;
        pauseCmd          = 11;
        resumeCmd         = 12;
        callBackCmd       = 13;
        syncCmd           = 14;
        emptyCmd          = 15;
        tickleCmd         = 20;
        requestNextCmd    = 21;
        howOftenCmd       = 22;
        wakeUpCmd         = 23;
        availableCmd      = 24;
        noteCmd           = 40;
        restCmd           = 41;
        freqCmd           = 42;
        ampCmd            = 43;
        timbreCmd         = 44;
        waveTableCmd      = 60;
        phaseCmd          = 61;
        soundCmd          = 80;
        bufferCmd         = 81;
        rateCmd           = 82;
        midiDataCmd       = 100;

        { Synthesizer numbers for SndNewChannel }

        noteSynth         = 1; {note synthesizer}
        waveTableSynth    = 3; {wave table synthesizer}
        sampledSynth      = 5; {sampled sound synthesizer}
        MIDISynthIn       = 7; {MIDI synthesizer in}
        MIDISynthOut      = 9; {MIDI synthesizer out}

        { Param2 values }

        MidiInitChannel    = n;      {MIDI Channel to init $0 .. $F}
        MidiInitChanFilter = $10;    {set to initialize a MIDI Channel}
        MidiInitRawMode    = $100;   {set to send raw MIDI data}

        { Queue length }

        StdQLength         = 128     {standard queue length}
```

Data Types

```
TYPE SndCommand = PACKED RECORD
                cmd:         INTEGER;    {command number}
                param1:      INTEGER;    {first parameter}
                param2:      LONGINT;    {second parameter}
              END;

     Time =     LONGINT;

     SndChannel = RECORD
                nextChan:   SndChannelPtr;    {pointer to next }
                                              { channel}
                firstMod:   ModifierStubPtr;  {pointer to first }
                                              { modifier}
                callBack:   ProcPtr;          {pointer to channel's }
                                              { call back procedure}
                userInfo:   LONGINT;          {free for use}
                wait:       Time;             {used internally}
                cmdInProg:  SndCommand;       {used internally}
                flags:      INTEGER;          {used internally}
                qLength:    INTEGER;          {queue length}
                qHead:      INTEGER;          {used internally}
                qTail:      INTEGER;          {used internally}
                queue:      ARRAY[0..stdQLength-1] OF SndCommand
              END;

     ModifierStub = RECORD
                nextStub:   ModifierStubPtr; {pointer to next }
                                             { modifier}
                code:       ProcPtr;         {pointer to modifier }
                                             { code}
                userInfo:   LONGINT;         {free for modifier to }
                                             { use}
                count:      Time;            {used internally}
                every:      Time;            {used internally}
                flags:      SignedByte;      {used internally}
                hState:     SignedByte       {used internally}
              END;
```

Routines

```
FUNCTION  SndPlay        (chan: SndChannelPtr; sndHdl: Handle;
                          async: BOOLEAN) : OSErr;
FUNCTION  SndNewChannel  (VAR chan: SndChannelPtr; synth:
                          INTEGER; init: LONGINT; userRoutine:
                          ProcPtr) : OSErr;
FUNCTION  SndAddModifier (chan: SndChannelPtr; modifier: ProcPtr;
                          id: INTEGER; init: LONGINT) : OSErr;
FUNCTION  SndDoCommand   (chan: SndChannelPtr; cmd: SndCommand;
                          noWait: BOOLEAN) : OSErr;
```

```
FUNCTION   SndDoImmediate   (chan: SndChannelPtr; cmd: SndCommand) :
                            OSErr;
FUNCTION   SndControl       (id: INTEGER; VAR cmd: SndCommand) :
                            OSErr;
FUNCTION   SndDisposeChannel (chan: SndChannelPtr; quietNow: BOOLEAN)
                            : OSErr;
PROCEDURE  MyCallBack       (chan: SndChannelPtr; cmd: SndCommand);
FUNCTION   MyModifier       (chan: SndChannelPtr; VAR cmd:
                            SndCommand; mod: ModifierStub) :
                            BOOLEAN;
```

Result Codes

Name	Value	Meaning
badChannel	–205	Invalid channel queue length
badFormat	–206	Handle to 'snd ' resource was invalid
noHardware	–200	No hardware support for the specified synthesizer
notEnoughHardware	–201	No more channels for the specified synthesizer
queueFull	–203	No room in the queue
resProblem	–204	Problem loading the resource

Assembly-Language Information

Constants

```
; Command numbers for SndDoCommand

nullCmd          .EQU   0
initCmd          .EQU   1
freeCmd          .EQU   2
quietCmd         .EQU   3
flushCmd         .EQU   4
waitCmd          .EQU   10
pauseCmd         .EQU   11
resumeCmd        .EQU   12
callBackCmd      .EQU   13
syncCmd          .EQU   14
emptyCmd         .EQU   15
tickleCmd        .EQU   20
requestNextCmd   .EQU   21
howOftenCmd      .EQU   22
wakeUpCmd        .EQU   23
availableCmd     .EQU   24
noteCmd          .EQU   40
restCmd          .EQU   41
freqCmd          .EQU   42
ampCmd           .EQU   43
timbreCmd        .EQU   44
waveTableCmd     .EQU   60
phaseCmd         .EQU   61
```

```
soundCmd          .EQU  80
bufferCmd         .EQU  81
rateCmd           .EQU  82
midiDataCmd       .EQU  100

; Synthesizer numbers for SndNewChannel

noteSynth         .EQU  1   ;note synthesizer
waveTableSynth    .EQU  3   ;wave table synthesizer
sampledSynth      .EQU  5   ;sample sound synthesizer
MIDISynthIn       .EQU  7   ;MIDI synthesizer in
MIDISynthOut      .EQU  9   ;MIDI synthesizer out
```

Structure of Sound Command

cmdNum	Command number (word)
param1	First argument (word)
param2	Second argument (long)
sndCSize	Size of sound command

Structure of Sound Channel

commandNum	Command number (word)
nextChan	Pointer to next channel
firstMod	Pointer to first modifier
callBack	Pointer to channel's call back procedure
userInfo	Free for use (long)
wait	Used internally (long)
cmdInProg	Used internally (8 bytes)
flags	Used internally (word)
qLength	Queue length (word)
qHead	Used internally (word)
qTail	Used internally (word)
queue	Array of sound commands

Structure of Modifier Stub

nextStub	Pointer to next modifier
code	Pointer to modifier code
userInfo	Free for modifier to use (long)
count	Used internally (long)
every	Used internally (long)
flags	Used internally (byte)
hState	Used internally (byte)

28 THE APPLETALK MANAGER

ABOUT THIS CHAPTER

The AppleTalk Manager has been enhanced through the implementation of new protocols and an increase in the functionality of the existing interface. This chapter describes these enhancements beginning with a brief summary of the changes that have been made. The remainder of the chapter provides detailed information about these changes.

> **Reader's guide:** The AppleTalk Manager provides services that allow Macintosh programs to interact with clients in devices connected to an AppleTalk network. Hence you need the information in this chapter only if your application uses AppleTalk.

The following is a brief summary of the changes that have been made to the AppleTalk Manager interface.

- New parameter block–style Pascal calls have been added for the entire AppleTalk Manager. These new calls give the application programmer better control of AppleTalk operation within an application.

- At open time, the .MPP driver can be told to pick a node number in the server range. This is a more time consuming but more thorough operation than is selecting a node number in the workstation range, and it is required for devices acting as servers.

- Multiple concurrent NBP requests are now supported (just as multiple concurrent ATP requests have been supported). The KillNBP command has been implemented to abort an outstanding NBP request.

- ATP requests can now be sent *through* client-specified sockets, instead of having ATP pick the socket itself.

- The ability to send packets to one's own node is supported (although this functionality is, in the default case, disabled).

- Two new ATP abort calls have been added: KillSendReq and KillGetReq. KillSendReq is functionally equivalent to RelTCB, although its arguments are different. KillGetReq is a new call for aborting outstanding GetRequests.

- Additional machine-dependent resources have been added to support, for example, more dynamic sockets and more concurrent ATP requests.

- A new protocol called the Echo Protocol (EP) is supported.

- A new driver, .XPP, has been added. The .XPP driver implements the workstation side of the AppleTalk Session Protocol (ASP) and a small portion of the AppleTalk Filing Protocol.

To determine if your application is running on a machine that supports these enhanced features, check the version number of the .MPP driver (at offset DCtlQueue+1 in the Device Control Entry). A version number of 48 (NCVersion) or greater indicates the presence of the new drivers.

CHANGES TO THE APPLETALK MANAGER

The changes to the AppleTalk manager increase functionality and resources. Two interfaces for the AppleTalk Manager calls are discussed: the new or preferred interface and the alternate interface. Picking a node address in the server range, sending packets to one's own node, multiple concurrent NBP requests, sending ATP requests through a specified socket and two new ATP calls are also discussed in this section.

New AppleTalk Manager Pascal Interface

In addition to the interface documented in Volume II, a new parameter block–style interface to the AppleTalk Manager is now available for Pascal programmers. This new interface, referred to as the **preferred interface,** is available in addition to the interface described in Volume II which is referred to as the **alternate interface.** All AppleTalk Manager calls, old and new, are supported by the preferred interface.

The alternate interface has not been extended to support the new AppleTalk Manager calls. However, the alternate interface provides the only implementation of LAPRead and DDPRead. These are higher-level calls not directly supported through the assembly-language interface. Developers will wish to use the alternate interface for these calls, and also for compatibility with previous applications. In all other cases, it is recommended that the new preferred interface be used.

Using Pascal

All AppleTalk Manager calls in the preferred interface are essentially equivalent to the corresponding assembly-language calls. Their form is

```
FUNCTION MPPCall (pbPtr: Ptr; asyncFlag: BOOLEAN) : OSErr;
```

where pbPtr points to a device manager parameter block, and asyncFlag is TRUE if the call is to be executed asynchronously. Three parameter block types are provided by the preferred interface (MPP, ATP, and XPP). The MPP parameter block is shown below. The ATP parameter block is shown in the following section, and the XPP parameter block is shown in Figure 4 in the "Calling the .XPP Driver" section of this document. The field names in these parameter blocks are the same as the parameter block offset names defined in the assembly-language section (except as documented below). The caller fills in the parameter block with the fields as specified in that section and issues the appropriate call. The interface issues the actual device manager control call.

On asynchronous calls, the caller may pass a completion routine pointer in the parameter block, at offset ioCompletion. This routine will be executed upon completion of the call. It is executed at interrupt level and must not make any memory manager calls. If it uses application globals, it must ensure that register A5 is set up correctly; for details see

SetupA5 and RestoreA5 in the Operating System Utilities chapter of Volume II. If no completion routine is desired, ioCompletion should be set to NIL.

Asynchronous calls return control to the caller with result code of noErr as soon as they are queued to the driver. This isn't an indication of successful completion. To determine when the call is actually completed, if you don't want to use a completion routine, you can poll the ioResult field; this field is set to 1 when the call is made, and receives the actual result code upon completion.

Refer to the AppleTalk Manager chapter in Volume II for the parameter blocks used by each MPP and ATP call. As different MPP and ATP calls take different arguments in their parameter block, two Pascal variant records have been defined to account for all the different cases. These parameter blocks are shown in the sections that follow. The first four fields (which are the same for all calls) are automatically filled in by the device manager. The csCode and ioRefnum fields are automatically filled in by the interface, depending on which call is being made, except in XPP where the caller must fill in the ioRefnum. The ioVRefnum field is unused.

There are two fields that at the assembly-language level have more than one name. These two fields have been given only one name in the preferred interface. These are entityPtr and ntqelPtr, which are both referred to as entityPtr, and atpSocket and currBitmap, which are both referred to as atpSocket. These are the only exceptions to the naming convention.

MPP Parameter Block

```
MPPParamBlock = PACKED RECORD
        qLink:          QElemPtr;       {next queue entry}
        qType:          INTEGER;        {queue type}
        ioTrap:         INTEGER;        {routine trap}
        ioCmdAddr:      Ptr;            {routine address}
        ioCompletion:   ProcPtr;        {completion routine}
        ioResult:       OSErr;          {result code}
        ioNamePtr:      StringPtr;      {command result (ATP user bytes) }
                                        { [long]}
        ioVRefNum:      INTEGER;        {volume reference or drive number}
        ioRefNum:       INTEGER;        {driver reference number}
        csCode:         INTEGER;        {call command code AUTOMATICALLY }
                                        { SET}
        CASE MPPParmType OF
        LAPWriteParm:
                    (filler0:INTEGER;
                    wdsPointer:Ptr);    {->Write Data Structure}
        AttachPHParm,DetachPHParm:
                    (protType:Byte;     {ALAP Protocol Type}
                    filler1:Byte;
                    handler:Ptr);       {->protocol handler routine}
        OpenSktParm,CloseSktParm,WriteDDPParm:
                    (socket:Byte;       {socket number}
                    checksumFlag:Byte;  {checksum flag}
                    listener:Ptr);      {->socket listener routine}
        RegisterNameParm,LookupNameParm,ConfirmNameParm,RemoveNameParm:
                    (interval:Byte;     {retry interval}
```

```
                        count:Byte;          {retry count}
                        entityPtr:Ptr;       {->names table element or }
                                             { ->entity name}
                     CASE MPPParmType OF
                     RegisterNameParm:
                             (verifyFlag:Byte; {set if verify needed}
                              filler3:Byte);
                     LookupNameParm:
                                 (retBuffPtr:Ptr;    {->return buffer}
                                  retBuffSize:INTEGER; {return }
                                                     { buffer size}
                             maxToGet:INTEGER; {matches to get}
                             numGotten:INTEGER); {matched }
                                                  { gotten}
                     ConfirmNameParm:
                                 (confirmAddr:AddrBlock; {->entity}
                             newSocket:Byte; {socket number}
                             filler4:Byte));

        SetSelfSendParm:
                    (newSelfFlag:Byte; {self-send toggle flag}
                    oldSelfFlag:Byte); {previous self-send state}
        KillNBPParm:
                    (nKillQEl:Ptr);      {ptr to Q element to cancel}
        END;
```

ATP Parameter Block

```
ATPParamBlock = PACKED RECORD
        qLink:              QElemPtr;   {next queue entry}
        qType:              INTEGER;    {queue type}
        ioTrap:             INTEGER;    {routine trap}
        ioCmdAddr:          Ptr;        {routine address}
        ioCompletion:       ProcPtr;    {completion routine}
        ioResult:           OSErr;      {result code}
        userData:           LONGINT;    {ATP user bytes [long]}
        reqTID:             INTEGER;    {request transaction ID}
        ioRefNum:           INTEGER;    {driver reference number
        csCode:             INTEGER;    {Call command code }
                                        { AUTOMATICALLY SET}
        atpSocket:          Byte;       {currBitMap or socket number}
        atpFlags:           Byte;       {control information}
        addrBlock:          AddrBlock;  {source/dest. socket address}
        reqLength:          INTEGER;    {request/response length}
        reqPointer:         Ptr;        {-> request/response data}
        bdsPointer:         Ptr;        {-> response BDS}
        CASE MPPParmType OF
            SendRequestParm,NSendRequestParm:
                (numOfBuffs:Byte;    {numOfBuffs}
                timeOutVal:Byte;     {timeout interval}
                numOfResps:Byte;     {number responses actually }
                                     { received}
                retryCount:Byte;     {number of retries}
```

```
              intBuff:INTEGER);      {used internally for }
                                     { NSendRequest}
          SendResponseParm:
              (filler0:Byte;         {number of responses being }
                                     { sent}
              bdsSize:Byte;          {number of BDS elements}
              transID:INTEGER);      {transaction ID}
          GetRequestParm:
              (bitMap:Byte;          {bit map}
              filler1:Byte);
          AddResponseParm:
              (rspNum:Byte;          {sequence number}
              filler2:Byte);
          KillSendReqParm,KillGetReqParm:
              (aKillQEl:Ptr);        {ptr to Q element to cancel}
      END;
```

The following table is a complete list of all the parameter block calls provided by the preferred interface.

AppleTalk Manager Routine	Preferred Interface Call
AttachPH	Function PAttachPH (thePBptr: MPPPBPtr; async: BOOLEAN) : OSErr;
DetachPH	Function PDetachPH (thePBptr: MPPPBPtr; async: BOOLEAN) : OSErr;
WriteLAP	Function PWriteLAP (thePBptr: MPPPBPtr; async: BOOLEAN) : OSErr;
OpenSkt	Function POpenSkt (thePBptr: MPPPBPtr; async: BOOLEAN) : OSErr;
CloseSkt	Function PCloseSkt (thePBptr: MPPPBPtr; async: BOOLEAN) : OSErr;
WriteDDP	Function PWriteDDP (thePBptr: MPPPBPtr; async: BOOLEAN) : OSErr;
RegisterName	Function PRegisterName (thePBptr: MPPPBPtr; async: BOOLEAN) : OSErr;
LookupName	Function PLookupName (thePBptr: MPPPBPtr; async: BOOLEAN) : OSErr;
ConfirmName	Function PConfirmName (thePBptr: MPPPBPtr; async: BOOLEAN) : OSErr;
RemoveName	Function PRemoveName (thePBptr: MPPPBPtr; async: BOOLEAN) : OSErr;
OpenATPSkt	Function POpenATPSkt (thePBptr: ATPPBPtr; async: BOOLEAN) : OSErr;
CloseATPSkt	Function PCloseATPSkt (thePBptr: ATPPBPtr; async: BOOLEAN) : OSErr;
SendRequest	Function PSendRequest (thePBptr: ATPPBPtr; async: BOOLEAN) : OSErr;
GetRequest	Function PGetRequest (thePBptr: ATPPBPtr; async: BOOLEAN) : OSErr;
SendResponse	Function PSendResponse (thePBptr: ATPPBPtr; async: BOOLEAN) : OSErr;

```
AddResponse       Function PAddResponse(thePBptr: ATPPBPtr; async:
                           BOOLEAN) : OSErr;
ReltCB            Function PRelTCB (thePBptr: ATPPBPtr; async: BOOLEAN) :
                           OSErr;
RelRspCB          Function PRelRspCB (thePBptr: ATPPBPtr; async:
                           BOOLEAN) : OSErr;
SetSelfSend       Function PSetSelfSend (thePBptr: MPPPBPtr; async:
                           BOOLEAN) : OSErr;
NSendRequest      Function PNSendRequest (thePBptr: ATPPBPtr; async:
                           BOOLEAN) : OSErr;
KillSendReq       Function PKillSendReq (thePBptr: ATPPBPtr; async:
                           BOOLEAN) : OSErr;
KillGetReq        Function PKillGetReq (thePBptr: ATPPBPtr; async:
                           BOOLEAN) : OSErr;
KillNBP           Function PKillNBP (thePBptr: MPPPBPtr; async: BOOLEAN) :
                           OSErr;
```

Building Data Structures

Because it is difficult for Pascal to deal with certain assembly-language structures, the
preferred interface provides a number of routines for building these structures. These
routines are summarized below. See Volume II for details of these data structures.

```
PROCEDURE BuildLAPwds (wdsPtr,dataPtr: Ptr;
        destHost,protoType,frameLen: INTEGER);
```

This routine builds a single-frame write data structure LAP WDS for use with the
PWriteLAP call. Given a buffer of length frameLen pointed to by dataPtr, it fills in the
WDS pointed to by wdsPtr and sets the destination node and protocol type as indicated by
destHost and protoType, respectively. The WDS indicated must contain at least two
elements.

```
PROCEDURE BuildDDPwds  (wdsPtr,headerPtr,dataPtr: Ptr; destAddress:
        AddrBlock; DDPType : INTEGER; dataLen: INTEGER);
```

This routine builds a single-frame write data structure DDP WDS, for use with the
PWriteDDP call. Given a header buffer of at least 17 bytes pointed to by headerPtr and a
data buffer of length dataLen pointed to by dataPtr, it fills in the WDS pointed to by
wdsPtr, and sets the destination address and protocol type as indicated by destaddress and
DDPtype, respectively. The WDS indicated must contain at least 3 elements.

```
PROCEDURE NBPSetEntity (buffer: Ptr; nbpObject,nbpType,nbpZone:
        Str32);
```

This routine builds an NBP entity structure, for use with the PLookupNBP and
PConfirmName calls. Given a buffer of at least the size of the EntityName data structure
(99 bytes) pointed to by buffer, this routine sets the indicated object, type, and zone in that
buffer.

```
PROCEDURE NBPSetNTE (ntePtr: Ptr; nbpObject,nbpType,nbpZone: Str32;
        Socket: INTEGER);
```

This routine builds an NBP names table entry, for use with the PRegisterName call. Given
a names table entry of at least the size of the EntityName data structure plus nine bytes (108
bytes) pointed to by ntePtr, this routine sets the indicated object, type, zone, and socket in
that names table entry.

```
FUNCTION NBPExtract (theBuffer: Ptr; numInBuf: INTEGER; whichOne:
        INTEGER; VAR abEntity: EntityName; VAR address: AddrBlock) :
        OSErr;
```

This routine is provided in the alternate interface, but can be used as provided for extracting
NBP entity names from a look-up response buffer.

```
FUNCTION GetBridgeAddress: INTEGER;
```

This routine returns the current address of a bridge in the low byte, or zero if there is none.

```
FUNCTION BuildBDS (buffPtr,bdsPtr: Ptr; buffSize: INTEGER) : INTEGER;
```

This routine builds a BDS, for use with the ATP calls. Given a data buffer of length
buffSize pointed to by buffPtr, it fills in the BDS pointed to by bdsPtr. The buffer will be
broken up into pieces of maximum size (578 bytes). The user bytes in the BDS are not
modified by this routine. This routine is provided only as a convenience; generally the
caller will be able to build the BDS completely from Pascal without it.

Picking a Node Address in the Server Range

Normally upon opening, the node number picked by the AppleTalk manager will be in the
node number range ($01–$7F). It is possible to indicate that a node number in the server
range ($80–$FE) is desired. Picking a number in the server range is a more time-
consuming but more thorough process, and it's required for server nodes because it greatly
decreases the possibility of a node number conflict.

To open AppleTalk with a server node number, an extended open call is used. An
extended open call is indicated by having the immediate bit set in the Open trap itself. In
the extended open call, the high bit (bit 31) of the extension longword field (ioMix)
indicates whether a server or workstation node number should be picked. Set this bit to 1
to request a server node number. The rest of this field should be zero, as should all other
unused fields in the queue element. A server node number can only be requested on the
first Open call to the .MPP driver.

Sending Packets to One's Own Node

Upon opening, the ability to send a packet to one's own node (intranode delivery) is disabled. This feature of the AppleTalk Manager can be manipulated through the SetSelfSend function. Once enabled, it is possible, at all levels, to send packets to entities within one's own node. An example of where this might be desirable is an application sending data to a print spooler that is actually running in the background on the same node.

Enabling (or disabling) this feature affects the entire node and should be performed with care. For instance, a desk accessory may not expect to receive names from within its own node as a response to an NBP look-up; enabling this feature from an application could break the desk accessory. All future programs should be written with this feature in mind.

```
FUNCTION PSetSelfSend (thePBptr: MPPPBPtr; async: BOOLEAN) : OSErr;
```

Parameter Block

→	26	csCode	word	Always PSetSelfSend
→	28	newSelfFlag	byte	New SelfSend flag
←	29	oldSelfFlag	byte	Old SelfSend flag

PSetSelfSend enables or disables the intranode delivery feature of the AppleTalk Manager. If newSelfFlag is nonzero, the feature will be enabled; otherwise it will be disabled. The previous value of the flag will be returned in oldSelfFlag.

Result Codes	noErr	No error

ATP Driver Changes

Changes to the ATP driver include the ability to send an ATP request through a specific socket rather than having ATP open a new socket, a new call to abort outstanding SendRequest calls, and a new call to abort specific outstanding GetRequest calls.

Sending an ATP Request Through a Specified Socket

ATP requests can now be sent through client-specified sockets. ATP previously would open a dynamic socket, send the request through it, and close the socket when the request was completed. The client can now choose to send a request through an already-opened socket; this also allows more than one request to be sent per socket. A new call, PNSendRequest, has been added for this purpose. The function of the old SendRequest call itself remains unchanged.

```
FUNCTION PNSendRequest (thePBptr: ATPBPtr; async: BOOLEAN) : OSErr;
```

Parameter block

→	18	userData	longword	User bytes
←	22	reqTID	word	Transaction ID used in request
→	26	csCode	word	Always sendRequest
↔	28	atpSocket	byte	Socket to send request on or current bitmap
↔	29	atpFlags	byte	Control information
→	30	addrBlock	longword	Destination socket address
→	34	reqLength	word	Request size in bytes
→	36	reqPointer	pointer	Pointer to request data
→	40	bdsPointer	pointer	Pointer to response BDS
→	44	numOfBuffs	byte	Number of responses expected
→	45	timeOutVal	byte	Timeout interval
←	46	numOf Resps	byte	Number of responses received
↔	47	retryCount	byte	Number of retries
←	48	intBuff	word	Used internally

The PNSendRequest call is functionally equivalent to the SendRequest call, however PNSendRequest allows you to specify, in the atpSocket field, the socket *through* which the request is to be sent. This socket must have been previously opened through an OpenATPSkt request (otherwise a badATPSkt error will be returned). Note that PNSendRequest requires two additional bytes of memory at the end of the parameter block, immediately following the retryCount. These bytes are for the internal use of the AppleTalk Manager and should not be modified while the PNSendRequest call is active.

There is a machine-dependent limit as to the number of concurrent PNSendRequests that can be active on a given socket. If this limit is exceeded, the error tooManyReqs is returned.

One additional difference between SendRequest and PNSendRequest is that a PNSendRequest can only be aborted by a PKillSendReq call (see below), whereas a SendRequest can be aborted by either a RelTCB or KillSendReq call.

Result Codes	noErr	No error
	reqFailed	Retry count exceeded
	tooManyReqs	Too many concurrent requests
	noDataArea	Too many outstanding ATP calls
	reqAborted	Request cancelled by user

Aborting ATP SendRequests

The RelTCB call is still supported, but only for aborting SendRequests. To abort PNSendRequests, a new call, PKillSendReq, has been added. This call will abort both SendRequests and PNSendRequests. PKillSendReq's only argument is the queue element pointer of the request to be aborted. The queue element pointer is passed at the offset of the PKillSendReq queue element specified by aKillQEl.

```
FUNCTION PKillSendReq (thePBptr: ATPPBPtr; async: BOOLEAN) : OSErr;
```

Parameter block

→	26	csCode	word	Always PKillSendReq
→	44	aKillQEl	pointer	Pointer to queue element

PKillSendReq is functionally equivalent to RelTCB, except that it takes different arguments and will abort both SendRequests and PNSendRequests. To abort one of these calls, place a pointer to the queue element of the call to abort in aKillQEl and issue the PKillSendReq call.

Result Codes	noErr	No error
	cbNotFound	aKillQEl does not point to a SendReq or NSendReq queue element

Aborting ATP GetRequests

ATP GetRequests can now be aborted through the PKillGetReq call. This call looks and works just like the PKillSendReq call, and is used to abort a specific GetRequest call. Previously it was necessary to close the socket to abort all GetRequest calls on the socket.

```
FUNCTION PKillGetReq (thePBptr: ATPPBPtr; async: BOOLEAN) : OSErr;
```

Parameter block

→	26	csCode	word	Always PKillGetReq
→	44	aKillQEl	pointer	Pointer to queue element

PKillGetReq will abort a specific outstanding GetRequest call (as opposed to closing the socket, which aborts all outstanding GetRequests on that socket). The call will be completed with a reqAborted error. To abort a GetRequest, place a pointer to the queue element of the call to abort in aKillQEl and issue the PKillGetReq call.

Result Codes	noErr	No error
	cbNotFound	aKillQEl does not point to a GetReq queue element

Name Binding Protocol Changes

Changes to the Name Binding Protocol include supporting multiple concurrent requests and a means for aborting an active request.

Multiple Concurrent NBP Requests

NBP now supports multiple concurrent active requests. Specifically, a number of LookupNames, RegisterNames and ConfirmNames can all be active concurrently. The maximum number of concurrent requests is machine dependent; if it is exceeded the error tooManyReqs will be returned. Active requests can be aborted by the PKillNBP call.

KillNBP function

```
FUNCTION PKillNBP (thePBptr: ATPPBPtr; async: BOOLEAN) : OSErr;
```

Parameter block

→	26	csCode	word	Always PKillNBP
→	28	aKillQEl	pointer	Pointer to queue element

PKillNBP is used to abort an outstanding LookupName, RegisterName or ConfirmName request. To abort one of these calls, place a pointer to the queue element of the call to abort in a KillQEl and issue the PKillNBP call. The call will be completed with a ReqAborted error.

Result Codes	noErr	No error
	cbNotFound	aKillQEl does not point to a valid NBP queue element

Variable Resources

The table below lists machine-dependent resources for the different Macintosh system configurations. The RAM-based resources are available through the AppleShare Server.

Resource	Macintosh Plus	RAM-Based	Macintosh SE	Macintosh II
Protocol Handlers	4	8	8	8
Statically Assigned Sockets	14*	12	12	14
Concurrent ATP SendRequests	6	12	12	12
ATP Sockets	6	32	32	126

Resource	Macintosh Plus	RAM-Based	Macintosh SE	Macintosh II
Concurrent ATP Responses	8	16	16	32
Concurrent NBP Requests	1	6	6	10
Concurrent ASP Sessions	N/A	5	10	20
Concurrent ATP NSendRequests Per Socket **	N/A	9	14	62

* Includes dynamic sockets
** Determined dynamically at runtime based on CPU speed.
N/A : Not Applicable

NEW APPLETALK PROTOCOLS

The following protocols have been added to the AppleTalk Manager:

- Echo Protocol
- AppleTalk Session Protocol (workstation side)
- AppleTalk Filing Protocol (small portion of the workstation side)

The AppleTalk system architecture consists of a number of protocols arranged in layers. Each protocol in a specific layer provides services to higher-level layers (known as the protocol's clients) by building on the services provided by the lower-level layers. Figure 1 shows the AppleTalk Protocols and their corresponding network layers.

In Figure 1, the lines indicate the interaction between the protocols. Notice that like the Routing Table Maintenance Protocol, the Echo Protocol is not directly accessible to Macintosh programs.

The details of these protocols are provided in *Inside AppleTalk*.

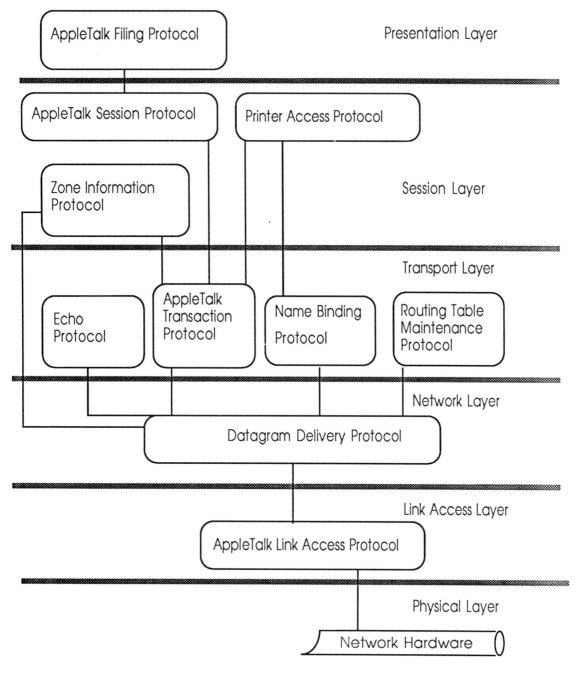

Figure 1. AppleTalk Protocols and OSI Network Layers

Echo Protocol

The **Echo Protocol** (EP) provides an echoing service through static socket number 4 known as the **echoer socket.** The **echoer** listens for packets received through this socket. Any correctly formed packet sent to the echoer socket on a node will be echoed back to its sender.

This simple protocol can be used for two important purposes:

■ EP can be used by any Datagram Delivery Protocol (DDP) client to determine if a particular node (known to have an echoer) is accessible over an internet.

■ EP is useful in determining the average time it takes for a packet to travel to a remote node and back. This is very helpful in developing client-dependent heuristics for estimating the timeouts to be specified by clients of ATP, ASP, and other protocols.

Programs cannot access EP directly via the AppleTalk Manager. The EP implementation exists solely to respond to EP requests sent by other nodes. EP is a DDP client residing on statically-assigned socket 4, the echoing socket. Clients wishing to send EP requests (and receive EP responses) should use the Datagram Delivery Protocol (DDP) to send the appropriate packet. For more information about the EP packet format, see *Inside AppleTalk.*

AppleTalk Session Protocol

The **AppleTalk Session Protocol** (ASP) provides for the setting up, maintaining and closing down of a **session.** A session is a logical relationship between two network entities, a **workstation** and a **server.** The workstation tells the server what to do, and the server responds with the appropriate actions. ASP makes sure that the session dialog is maintained in the correct sequence and that both ends of the conversation are properly participating.

ASP will generally be used between two communicating network entities where one is providing a service to the other (for example, a server is providing a service to a workstation) and the service provided is *state-dependent*. That is, the response to a particular request from an entity is dependent upon other previous requests from that entity. For example, a request to read bytes from a file is dependent upon a previous request to open that file in the first place. However, a request to return the time of day is independent of all such previous requests.

When the service provided is state-dependent, requests must be delivered to the server in the same order as generated by the workstation. ASP guarantees requests are delivered to the server in the order in which they are issued, and that duplicate requests are never delivered (another requirement of state-dependent service).

What ASP Does

ASP is an asymmetric protocol, providing one set of services to the workstation and a different set of services to the server.

ASP workstation clients initiate (open) sessions, send requests (commands) on that session, and close sessions down. ASP server clients receive and respond (through command replies) to these requests. ASP guarantees that these requests are delivered in the same order as they are made, and without duplication. ASP is also responsible for closing down the session if one end fails or becomes unreachable, and will inform its client (either server or workstation) of the action.

ASP also provides various additional services, such as allowing a workstation to obtain server status information without opening a session to a server, writing blocks of data from the workstation to the server end of the session, and providing the ability for a server to send an attention message to the workstation.

ASP assumes that the workstation client has a mechanism for looking up the network address of the server with which it wants to set up a session. (Generally this is done using the AppleTalk Name Binding Protocol.)

Both ends of the session periodically check to see that the other end of the session is still responsive. If one end fails or becomes unreachable the other end closes the session.

ASP is a client of ATP and calls ATP for transport services.

What ASP Does Not Do

ASP does not

- ensure that consecutive commands *complete* in the order in which they were sent (and delivered) to the server

- understand or interpret the syntax or the semantics of the commands sent to the server by the workstation

- allow the server to send commands to the workstation (The server is allowed to alert the workstation through the server's *attention* mechanism only.)

   Note: The .XPP driver does implement the workstation side of the AppleTalk Filing Protocol login command.

AppleTalk Filing Protocol

The AppleTalk Filing Protocol (AFP) allows a workstation on an AppleTalk network to access files on an AFP file server. AFP specifies a remote filing system that provides user authentication and an access control mechanism that supports volume and folder-level access rights. For details of AFP, refer to the *AFP Technical Notes*.

EXTENDED PROTOCOL PACKAGE DRIVER

The Extended Protocol Package (XPP) driver is intended to implement several AppleTalk communication protocols in the same package for ease of use. The .XPP driver currently consists of two modules that operate on two levels: the low-level module implements the workstation side of AppleTalk Session Protocol, and the high-level module implements a small portion of the workstation side of the AppleTalk Filing Protocol.

This driver adds functionality to the AppleTalk manager by providing services additional to those provided in the .MPP and .ATP drivers. Figure 2 shows the Macintosh AppleTalk drivers and the protocols accessible through each driver.

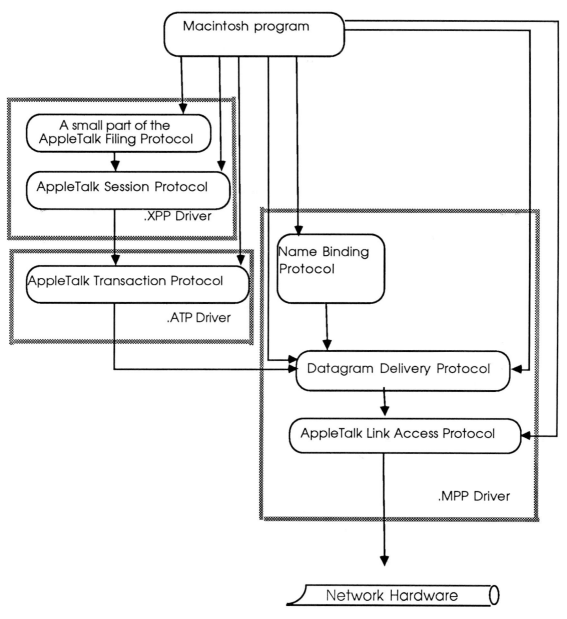

Figure 2. Macintosh AppleTalk Drivers

The .XPP driver maps an AFP call from the client workstation into one or more ASP calls. .XPP provides one client-level call for AFP.

The implementation of AFP in the .XPP driver is very limited. Most calls are a very simple one-to-one mapping from an AFP call to an ASP command without any interpretation of the syntax of the AFP command by the .XPP driver. Refer to the "Mapping AFP Commands" section of this chapter for further information.

Version

The .XPP driver supports ASP Version (hex) $100, as described in *Inside AppleTalk*.

Error Reporting

Errors are returned by the .XPP driver in the ioResult field of the Device Manager Control calls.

The error conditions reported by the .XPP driver may represent the unsuccessful completion of a routine in more than just one process involved in the interaction of the session. System-level, .XPP driver, AppleTalk, and server errors can all turn up in the ioResult field.

AFP calls return codes indicating the unsuccessful completion of AFP commands in the Command Result field of the parameter block (described below).

An application using the .XPP driver should respond appropriately to error conditions reported from the different parts of the interaction. As shown in Figure 3, the following errors can be returned in the ioResult field:

1. System-level errors

   System errors returned by the .XPP driver indicate such conditions as the driver not being open or a specific system call not being supported. For a complete list of result codes returned by the Macintosh system software, refer to Volume II, Appendix A.

2. XPP errors (for example, "Session not opened")

   The .XPP driver can also return errors resulting from its own activity (for example, the referenced session isn't open). The possible .XPP driver errors returned are listed in the .XPP driver results codes section with each function that can return the code.

3. AppleTalk Errors (returned from lower-level protocols)

   .XPP may also return errors from lower-level protocols (for example, "Socket not open").

Possible error conditions and codes are described in Volume II, chapter 10, "The
AppleTalk Manager."

4. An ASP-specific error could be returned from an ASP server in response to a failed
OpenSession call. Errors of this type, returned by the server to the workstation, are
documented both in *Inside AppleTalk,* section 11, "AppleTalk Session Protocol",
and in the .XPP driver results code section of this chapter.

5. The AppleTalk Filing Protocol defines errors that are returned from the server to the
workstation client. These errors are returned in the cmdResult field of the parameter
block (error type 5 in Figure 3). This field is valid if no system-level error is returned
by the call. Note that at the ASP level, the cmdResult field is client-defined data and
may not be an error code.

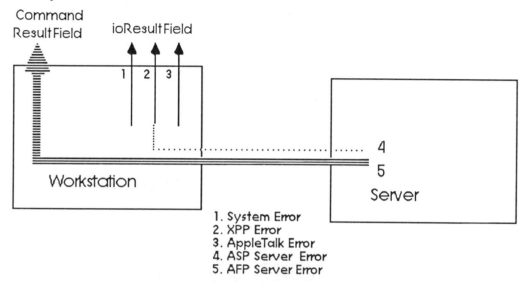

Figure 3. Error Reporting

.XPP Driver Functions Overview

The paragraphs below describe the implementation of ASP in the .XPP driver. For more
detailed information about ASP, refer to *Inside AppleTalk,* Section 11, "AppleTalk Session
Protocol (ASP)".

Using AppleTalk Name Binding Protocol

A server wishing to advertise its service on the AppleTalk network calls ATP to open an
ATP responding socket known as the *session listening socket* (SLS). The server then calls
the Name Binding Protocol (NBP) to register a name on this socket. At this point, the
server calls the server side of ASP to pass it the address of the SLS. Then, the server
starts listening on the SLS for session opening requests coming over the network.

Opening and Closing Sessions

When a workstation wishes to access a server, the workstation must call NBP to discover the SLS for that server. Then the workstation calls ASP to open a session with that server.

After determining the SLS (address) of the server, the workstation client issues an OpenSession (or AFPLogin) call to open a session with that server. As a result of this call, ASP sends a special OpenSession packet (an ATP request) to the SLS; this packet carries the address of a workstation socket for use in the session. This socket is referred to as the workstation session socket (WSS). If the server is unable to set up the session, it returns an error. If the request is successful, the server returns no error, and the session is opened. The open session packet also contains a version number so that both ends can verify that they are speaking the same version of ASP.

The AbortOS function can be used to abort an outstanding OpenSession request before it has completed.

The workstation client closes the session by issuing a CloseSession (or AFPLogout). The CloseSession call aborts any calls that are active on the session and closes the session. The session can also be closed by the server or by ASP itself, such as when one end of the session fails. The CloseAll call (which should be used with care) aborts every session that the driver has active.

Session Maintenance

A session will remain open until it is explicitly terminated by the ASP client at either end or until one of the sessions ends, fails, or becomes unreachable.

Commands on an Open Session

Once a session has been opened, the workstation client can send a sequence of commands over the session to the server end. The commands are delivered in the same order as they are issued at the workstation end, and replies to the commands are returned to the workstation end.

Three types of commands can be made on an open session. These commands are UserCommand, UserWrite, and AFPCall functions described in the following paragraphs.

UserCommand calls are similar to ATP requests. The workstation client sends a command (included in a variable size command block) to the server client requesting it to perform a particular function and send back a variable size command reply. Examples of such commands vary from a request to open a particular file on a file server, to reading a certain range of bytes from a device. In the first case, a small amount of reply data is returned; in the second case a multiple-packet reply might be generated.

The .XPP driver does not interpret the command block or in any way participate in executing the command's function. It simply conveys the command block, included in a higher-level format, to the server end of the session, and returns the command reply to the workstation-end client. The command reply consists of a four-byte command result and a variable size command reply block.

UserWrite allows the workstation to convey blocks of data to the server. UserWrite is used to transfer a variable size block of data to the server end of the session and to receive a reply.

The AFPCall function provides a mechanism for passing an AFP command to the server end of an open session and receiving a reply. The first byte of the AFPCall command buffer contains the code for the AFP command that is to be passed to the server for execution. Most AFP calls are implemented through a very simple one-to-one mapping that takes the call and makes an ASP command out of it.

The AFPCall function can have one of four different, but very similar, formats.

Getting Server Status Information

ASP provides a service to allow its workstation clients to obtain a block of service status information from a server without the need for opening a session. The GetStatus function returns a status block from the server identified by the indicated address. ASP does not impose any structure on the status block. This structure is defined by the protocol above ASP.

Attention Mechanism

Attentions are defined in ASP as a way for the server to alert the workstation of some event or critical piece of information. The ASP OpenSession and AFPLogin calls include a pointer to an attention routine in their parameter blocks. This attention routine is called by the .XPP driver when it receives an attention from the server and also when the session is closing as described below.

In addition, upon receiving an OpenSession call or AFPLogin call, the .XPP driver sets the first two bytes of the session control block (SCB) to zero. When the .XPP driver receives an attention, the first two bytes of the SCB are set to the attention bytes from the packet (which are always nonzero).

> **Note:** A higher-level language such as Pascal may not wish to have a low-level attention routine called. A Pascal program can poll the attention bytes, and if they are ever nonzero, the program will know that an attention has come in. (It would then set the attention bytes back to zero.) Of course, two or more attentions could be received between successive polls, and only the last one would be recorded.

The .XPP driver also calls the attention routine when the session is closed by either the server, workstation, or ASP itself (if the ASP session times out). In these cases, the attention bytes in the SCB are unchanged.

The Attention Routine

The attention routine is called at interrupt level and must observe interrupt conventions. Specifically, the interrupt routine can change registers A0 through A3 and D0 through D3 and it must not make any Memory Manager calls.

It will be called with

- D0 (word) equal to the SessRefnum for that session (see OpenSession Function)
- D1 (word) equal to the attention bytes passed by the server (or zero if the session is closing)

Return with an RTS (return from subroutine) to resume normal execution.

The next section describes the calls that can be made to the .XPP driver.

CALLING THE .XPP DRIVER

This section describes how to use the .XPP driver and how to call the .XPP driver routines from assembly language and Pascal.

Using XPP

The .XPP driver implements the workstation side of ASP and provides a mechanism for the workstation to send AppleTalk Filing Protocol (AFP) commands to the server.

Allocating Memory

Every call to the .XPP driver requires the caller to pass in whatever memory is needed by the driver for the call, generally at the end of the queue element. When a session is opened, the memory required for maintenance of that session (that is, the Session Control Block) is also passed in.

For standard Device Manager calls, a queue element of a specific size equal to IOQElSize is allocated. When issuing many calls to XPP, it is the caller's responsibility to allocate a queue element that is large enough to accommodate the .XPP driver's requirements for executing that call, as defined below. Once allocated, that memory can't be modified until the call completes.

Opening the .XPP Driver

To open the .XPP driver, issue a Device Manager Open call. (Refer to Volume II, chapter 6, "The Device Manager".) The name of the .XPP driver is '.XPP'. The original Macintosh ROMs require that .XPP be opened only once. With new ROMs, the .XPP unit number can always be obtained through an Open call. With old ROMs only, the .XPP unit number must be hard coded to XPPUnitNum (40) since only one Open call can be issued to the driver.

The .XPP driver cannot be opened unless AppleTalk is open. The application must ensure that the .MPP and .ATP drivers are opened, as described in Volume II, pages 304–305.

The xppLoaded bit (bit 5) in the PortBUse byte in low memory indicates whether or not the .XPP driver is open.

Example

The following is an example of the procedure an application might use to open the .XPP driver.

```
; Routine: OpenXPP
;
;    Open the .XPP driver and return the driver refNum for it.
;
;    Exit:   D0 = error code (ccr's set)
;            D1 = XPP driver refNum (if no errors)
;
;    All other registers preserved
;
xppUnitNum   EQU   40                    ;default XPP driver number
xppTfRNum    EQU   -(xppUnitNum+1)       ;default XPP driver refNum

OpenXPP
     MOVE.L  A0-A1/D2,-(SP)     ;save registers
     MOVE    ROM85,D0           ;check ROM type byte
     BPL.S   @10                ;branch if >=128K ROMs
     BTST    #xppLoadedBit,PortBUse ;is the XPP driver open already?
     BEQ.S   @10                ;if not open, then branch to Open code
     MOVE    #xppTfRNum,D1       ;else use this as driver refnum
     MOVEQ   #0,D0              ;set noErr
     BRA.S   @90                ;and exit
;
; XPP driver not open. Make an _Open call to it. If using a 128K
; ROM machine and the driver is already open, we will make another
; Open call to it just so we get the correct driver refNum.
;
```

```
@10   SUB       #ioQElSize,SP          ;allocate temporary param block
      MOVE.L    SP,A0                  ;A0 -> param block
      LEA       XPPName, A1            ;A1 -> XPP (ASP/AFP) driver name
      MOVE.L    A1,ioFileName(A0)      ;driver name into param block
      CLR.B     ioPermssn(A0)          ;clear permissions byte
      _Open
      MOVE      ioRefNum(A0),D1        ;D1=driver refNum (invalid if error)
      ADD       #ioQElSize,SP          ;deallocate temp param block
@90   MOVE.L    (SP)+,A0-A1/D2         ;restore registers
      TST       D0                     ;error? (set ccr's)
      RTS

XPPName   DC.B 4                       ;length of string
          DC.B '.XPP'                  ;driver name
```

From Pascal, XPP can be opened through the OpenXPP call, which returns the driver's reference number:

```
FUNCTION OpenXPP (VAR xppRefnum: INTEGER) : OSErr;
```

Open Errors

Errors returned when calling the Device Manager Open routine if the function does not execute properly include the following:

- errors returned by System
- portInUse is returned if the AppleTalk port is in use by a driver other than AppleTalk or if AppleTalk is not open.

Closing the .XPP Driver

To close the .XPP driver, call the Device Manager Close routine.

> **Warning:** There is generally no reason to close the driver. Use this call sparingly, if at all. This call should generally be used only by system-level applications.

Close Errors

Errors returned when calling the Device Manager Close routine if the function does not execute properly include the following:

- errors returned by System

- closeErr (new ROMs only) is returned if you try to close the driver and there are sessions active through that driver. When sessions are active, closeErr is returned and the driver remains open.

- on old ROMs the driver is closed whether or not sessions are active and no error is returned. Results are unpredictable if sessions are still active.

Session Control Block

The session control block (SCB) is a nonrelocatable block of data passed by the caller to XPP upon session opening. XPP reserves this block for use in maintaining an open session. The SCB size is defined by the constant scbMemSize. The SCB is a locked block, and as long as the session is open, the SCB cannot be modified in any way by the application. There is one SCB for each open session. This block can be reused once a CloseSess call is issued and completed for that session or when the session is indicated as closed.

How to Access the .XPP Driver

This section contains information for programmers using Pascal and assembly-language routines.

All .XPP driver routines can be executed either synchronously (meaning that the application can't continue until the routine is completed) or asynchronously (meaning that the application is free to perform other tasks while the routine is executing).

XPP calls are made from Pascal in the same manner as MPP and ATP calls, with the exception that when making XPP calls the caller must set the XPP driver's refnum. This refnum is returned in the XPPOpen call's parameter block.

A Pascal variant record has been defined for all XPP calls. This parameter block is detailed in Figure 4. The first four fields (which are the same for all calls) are automatically filled in by the device manager. The csCode field is automatically filled in by Pascal, depending on which call is being made. The caller must, however, set the ioRefnum field to XPP's reference number, as returned in the OpenXPP call. The ioVRefnum field is unused.

Note that the parameter block is defined so as to be the maximum size used by any call. Different calls take different size parameter blocks, each call requiring a certain minimum size. Callers are free to abbreviate the parameter block where appropriate.

General

With each routine, a list of the parameter block fields used by the call is also given. All routines are invoked by Device Manager Control calls with the csCode field equal to the code corresponding to the function being called. The number next to each field name indicates the byte offset of the field from the start of the parameter block pointed to by A0; only assembly-language programmers need to be concerned with it. An arrow next to each parameter name indicates whether it's an input, output, or input/output parameter:

Arrow   Meaning

←	Parameter is passed
←	Parameter is returned
↔	Parameter is passed and returned

All Device Manager Control calls return an integer result code in the ioResult field. Each routine description lists all the applicable result codes, along with a short description of what the result code means. Refer to the section "XPP Driver Result Codes" for an alphabetical list of result codes returned by the .XPP driver.

Each routine description includes a Pascal form of the call. Pascal calls to the .XPP Driver are of the form:

```
FUNCTION XPPCall (paramBlock: XPPParmBlkPtr,async: BOOLEAN) :
        OSErr;
```

XPPCall is the name of the routine.

The parameter paramBlock points to the actual I/O queue element used in the _Control call, filled in by the caller with the parameters of the routine.

The parameter async indicates whether or not the call should be made asynchronously. If async is TRUE, the call is executed asynchronously; otherwise the call is executed synchronously.

The routine returns a result code of type OSErr.

```
XPPParamBlock = PACKED RECORD
   qLink:          QElemPtr;   {next queue entry}
   qType:          INTEGER;    {queue type}
   ioTrap:         INTEGER;    {routine trap}
   ioCmdAddr:      Ptr;        {routine address}
   ioCompletion:   ProcPtr;    {completion routine}
   ioResult:       OSErr;      {result code}
   cmdResult:      LONGINT;    {command result (ATP user bytes) [long]}
   ioVRefNum:      INTEGER;    {volume reference or drive number)
   ioRefNum:       INTEGER;    {driver reference number)
   csCode:         INTEGER;    {Call command code}
   CASE XPPPrmBlkType OF
     ASPAbortPrm:
       (abortSCBPtr:   Ptr);      {SCB pointer for AbortOS [long]}
     ASPSizeBlk:
       (aspMaxCmdSize: INTEGER;   {for SPGetParms [word]
        aspQuantumSize: INTEGER;  {for SPGetParms [word]}
        numSesss:      INTEGER);  {for SPGetParms [word]}
     XPPPrmBlk:
       (sessRefnum:    INTEGER;   {offset to session refnum [word]}
        aspTimeout:    Byte;      {timeout for ATP [byte]}
        aspRetry:      Byte;      {retry count for ATP [byte]}
        CASE XPPSubPrmType OF
          ASPOpenPrm:
             (serverAddr: AddrBlock;  {server address block [longword]}
              scbPointer: Ptr;        {SCB pointer [longword]}
              attnRoutine: Ptr);      {attention routine pointer [long]}
          ASPSubPrm:
             (cbSize:    INTEGER;   {command block size [word]}
              cbPtr:     Ptr;       {command block pointer [long]}
              rbSize:    INTEGER;   {reply buffer size [word]}
              rbPtr:     Ptr;       {reply buffer pointer [long]}
              CASE XPPEndPrmType OF
                AFPLoginPrm:
                   (afpAddrBlock:  AddrBlock;  {address block in }
                                               { AFPlogin [long]}
                    afpSCBPtr:      Ptr;       {SCB pointer in }
                                               { AFPlogin [long]}
                    afpAttnRoutine: Ptr);      {attn routine pointer }
                                               { in AFPlogin}
                ASPEndPrm:
                   (wdSize:         INTEGER;   {write data size }
                                               { [word]}
                    wdPtr:          Ptr;       {write data pointer }
                                               { [long]}
                    ccbStart:  ARRAY[0..295] OF Byte))); {CCB memory }
                                                         { for driver}
   {Write max size(CCB) = 296; all other calls = 150}
END;
```

Figure 4. .XPP Driver Parameter Block Record

AppleTalk Session Protocol Functions

This section contains descriptions of the .XPP driver functions that you can call. Each function description shows the required parameter block fields, their offsets within the parameter block and a brief definition of the field. Possible result codes are also described.

Note on Result Codes

An important distinction exists between the aspParamErr and aspSessClose result codes that may be returned by the .XPP driver.

When the driver returns aspParamEr to a call that takes as an input a session reference number, the session reference number does not relate to a valid open session. There could be several reasons for this, such as the workstation or server end closed the session or the server end of the session died.

The aspSessClosed result code indicates that even though the session reference number relates to a valid session, that particular session is in the process of closing down (although the session is not yet closed).

```
FUNCTION ASPOpenSession (xParamBlock: XPPParmBlkPtr; async:
        BOOLEAN) : OSErr;
```

Parameter block

←	26	csCode	word	Always ASPOpenSess
←	28	sessRefnum	word	Session reference number
←	30	aspTimeout	byte	Retry interval in seconds
←	31	aspRetry	byte	Number of retries
←	32	serverAddr	long word	Server socket address
←	36	scbPointer	pointer	Pointer to session control block
←	40	attnRoutine	pointer	Pointer to attention routine

ASPOpenSession initiates (opens) a session between the workstation and a server. The required parameter block is shown above. A brief definition of the fields follows.

SessRefnum is a unique number identifying the open session between the workstation and the server. The SessRefnum is returned when the function completes successfully and is used in all calls to identify the session.

ASPTimeOut is the interval in seconds between retries of the open session request.

ASPRetry is the number of retries that will be attempted.

ServerAddr is the network identifier or address of the socket on which the server is listening.

SCBPointer points to a nonrelocatable block of data for the session control block (SCB) that the .XPP driver reserves for use in maintaining an open session. The SCB size is defined by the constant scbMemSize. The SCB is a locked block and as long as the session is open, the SCB cannot be modified in any way by the application. There is one

SCB for each open session. This block can be reused when a CloseSess call is issued and completed for that session, or when the session is indicated as closed through return of aspParamErr as the result of a call for that session.

AttnRoutine is a pointer to a routine that is invoked if an attention from the server is received, or upon session closing. If this pointer is equal to zero, no attention routine will be invoked.

Result codes	aspNoMoreSess	Driver cannot support another session
	aspParamErr	Server returned bad (positive) error code
	aspNoServers	No servers at that address, or the server did not respond to the request
	reqAborted	OpenSess was aborted by an AbortOS
	aspBadVersNum	Server cannot support the offered version number
	aspServerBusy	Server cannot open another session

Note: The number of sessions that the driver is capable of supporting depends on the machine that the driver is running on.

```
FUNCTION ASPCloseSession (xParamBlock: XPPParmBlkPtr; async:
        BOOLEAN) : OSErr;
```

Parameter block

←	26	csCode	word	Always ASPCloseSession
←	28	sessRefnum	word	Session reference number

ASPCloseSession closes the session identified by the sessRefnum returned in the ASPOpenSession call. ASPCloseSession aborts any calls that are active on the session, closes the session, and calls the attention routine, if any, with an attention code of zero (zero is invalid as a real attention code).

Result codes	aspParamErr	Parameter error, indicates an invalid session reference number
	aspSessClosed	Session already in process of closing

```
FUNCTION ASPAbortOS (xParamBlock: XPPParmBlkPtr; async: BOOLEAN) :
        OSErr;
```

Parameter block

←	26	csCode	word	Always ASPAbortOS
←	28	abortSCBPointer	pointer	Pointer to session control block

ASPAbortOS aborts a pending (not yet completed) ASPOpenSession call. The aborted ASPOpenSession call will return a reqAborted error.

AbortSCBPointer points to the original SCB used in the the pending ASPOpenSession call.

Result codes   cbNotFound   SCB not found, no outstanding open session to be aborted. Pointer did not point to an open session SCB.

```
FUNCTION ASPGetParms (xParamBlock: XPPParmBlkPtr; async: BOOLEAN):
       OSErr;
```

Parameter block

←	26	csCode	word	Always ASPGetParms
←	28	aspMaxCmdSize	word	Maximum size of command block
←	30	aspQuantumSize	word	Maximum data size
←	32	numSesss	word	Number of sessions

ASPGetParms returns three ASP parameters. This call does not require an open session.

ASPMaxCmdSize is the maximum size of a command that can be sent to the server.

ASPQuantumSize is the maximum size of data that can be transferred to the server in a Write request or from the server in a command reply.

NumSess is the number of concurrent sessions supported by the driver.

```
FUNCTION ASPCloseAll (xParamBlock: XPPParmBlkPtr; async: BOOLEAN) :
       OSErr;
```

Parameter block

←	26	csCode	word	Always ASPCloseAll

ASPCloseAll closes every session that the driver has active, aborting all active requests and invoking the attention routines where provided. This call should be used carefully. ASPCloseAll can be used as a system level resource for making sure all sessions are closed prior to closing the driver.

```
FUNCTION ASPUserWrite (xParamBlock: XPPParmBlkPtr; async: BOOLEAN):
       OSErr;
```

Parameter block

←	18	cmdResult	long word	ASP command result
←	26	csCode	word	Always UserWrite
←	28	sessRefnum	word	Session reference number
←	30	aspTimeout	byte	Retry interval in seconds
←	32	cbSize	word	Command block size
←	34	cbPtr	pointer	Command block pointer
↔	38	rbSize	word	Reply buffer size and reply size
←	40	rbPtr	pointer	Reply buffer pointer
↔	44	wdSize	word	Write data size
←	46	wdPtr	pointer	Write data pointer
←	50	ccbStart	record	Start of memory for CCB

ASPUserWrite transfers data on a session. ASPUserWrite is one of the two main calls that can be used to transfer data on an ASP session. The other call that performs a similar data transfer is ASPUserCommand described below. The ASPUserWrite command returns data in two different places. Four bytes of data are returned in the cmdResult field and a variable size reply buffer is also returned.

CmdResult is four bytes of data returned by the server.

SessRefnum is the session reference number returned in the ASPOpenSession call.

ASPTimeOut is the interval in seconds between retries of the call. Notice that there is no aspRetry field (retries are infinite). The command will be retried at the prescribed interval until completion or the session is closed.

CBSize is the size in bytes of the command data that is to be written on the session. The size of the command block must not exceed the value of aspMaxCmdSize returned by the ASPGetParms call. Note that this buffer is not the data to be written by the command but only the data of the command itself.

CBPtr points to the command data.

RBSize is passed and indicates the size of the reply buffer in bytes expected by the command. RBSize is also returned and indicates the size of the reply that was actually returned.

RBPtr points to the reply buffer.

WDSize is passed and indicates the size of the write data in bytes to be sent by the command. WDSize is also returned and indicates the size of the write data that was actually written.

WDPointer points to the write data buffer.

CCBStart is the start of the memory to be used by the .XPP driver for the command control block. The size of this block is equal to a maximum of 296 bytes. To determine the exact requirement, refer to the CCB Sizes section of this document.

Result codes	aspParamErr	Invalid session number, session has been closed
	aspSizeErr	Command block size is bigger than MaxCmdSize
	aspSessClosed	Session is closing
	aspBufTooSmall	Reply is bigger than response buffer; the buffer will be filled, data will be truncated

```
FUNCTION ASPUserCommand (xParamBlock: XPPParmBlkPtr; async:
        BOOLEAN) : OSErr;
```

Parameter block

←	18	cmdResult	long word	ASP command result
←	26	csCode	word	Always ASPUserCommand
←	28	sessRefnum	word	Session number
←	30	aspTimeout	byte	Retry interval in seconds
←	32	cbSize	word	Command block size

←	34	cbPtr	pointer	Command block pointer
↔	38	rbSize	word	Reply buffer and reply size
←	40	rbPtr	pointer	Reply buffer pointer
←	50	ccbStart	record	Start of memory for CCB

ASPUserCommand is used to send a command to the server on a session.

SessRefnum is the session reference number returned in the ASPOpenSession call.

ASPTimeOut is the interval in seconds between retries of the call. Notice that there is no aspRetry field (retries are infinite). The command will be retried at the prescribed interval until completion or the session is closed.

CBSize is the size in bytes of the block of data that contains the command to be sent to the server on the session. The size of the command block must not exceed the value of aspMaxCmdSize returned by the ASPGetParms call.

CBPointer points to the block of data containing the command that is to be sent to the server on the session.

RBSize is passed and indicates the size of the reply buffer in bytes expected by the command. RBSize is also returned and indicates the size of the reply that was actually returned.

RBPtr points to the reply buffer.

CCBStart is the start of the memory to be used by the .XPP driver for the command control block. The size of this block is equal to a maximum of 150 bytes. To determine the exact requirement refer to the CCB Sizes section of this document.

Result codes	aspParamErr	Invalid session number, session has been closed
	aspSizeErr	Command block size is bigger than MaxCmdSize
	aspSessClosed	Session is closing
	aspBufTooSmall	Reply is bigger than response buffer; the buffer will be filled, data will be truncated.

```
FUNCTION ASPGetStatus (xParamBlock: XPPParmBlkPtr; async: BOOLEAN) :
        OSErr;
```

Parameter block

←	26	csCode	word	Always ASPGetStatus
←	30	aspTimeout	byte	Retry interval in seconds
←	31	aspRetry	byte	Number of retries
←	32	serverAddr	long word	Server socket address
↔	38	rbSize	word	Reply buffer and reply size
←	40	rbPtr	pointer	Reply buffer pointer
←	50	ccbStart	record	Start of memory for CCB

ASPGetStatus returns server status. This call is also used as GetServerInfo at the AFP level. This call is unique in that it transfers data over the network without having a session open. This call does not pass any data but requests that server status be returned.

ASPTimeOut is the interval in seconds between retries of the call.

ASPRetry is the number of retries that will be attempted.

ServerAddr is the network identifier or address of the socket on which the server is listening.

RBSize is passed and indicates the size of the reply buffer in bytes expected by the command. RBSize is also returned and indicates the size of the reply that was actually returned.

RBPtr points to the reply buffer.

CCBStart is the start of the memory to be used by the .XPP driver for the command control block. The size of this block is equal to a maximum of 150 bytes. To determine the exact requirement refer to the CCB Sizes section of this document.

Result codes	aspBufTooSmall	Reply is bigger than response buffer, or Replysize is bigger than ReplyBuffsize
	aspNoServer	No response from server at address used in call

AFP Implementation

The AFPCall function (called AFPCommand in Pascal) passes a command to an AFP server. The first byte of the AFPCall command buffer (the AFP command byte) must contain a valid AFP command code.

Note: Server information should be gotten through an ASPGetStatus call (described above). ASPGetStatus is equivalent to the AFPGetSrvrInfo. Making an AFP GetSrvrInfo call using AFPCommand results in an error.

Mapping AFP Commands

Most AFP calls are implemented by XPP through a very simple one-to-one mapping of an AFP call to an ASP call without interpretation or verification of the data.

The .XPP driver maps AFP command codes to ASP commands according to the following conventions:

AFP Command Code	Comment
$00	Invalid AFP command
$01–$BE (1–190)	Mapped to UserCommand (with the exceptions listed below)
$BF (191)	Mapped to UserCommand (Reserved for developers; will never be used by Apple)
$C0–$FD (192–253)	Mapped to UserWrite
$FE (254)	Mapped to UserWrite (will never be used by Apple)
$FF (255)	Invalid AFP command

The following AFP calls are exceptions to the above conventions:

AFP Command (Code/Decimal)	Comment
getSrvrInfo (15)	Mapped to ASPGetStatus (Use ASPGetStatus to make this call)
login (18)	Mapped to appropriate log-in dialog including ASPOpenSession call
loginCont (19)	Mapped to appropriate log-in dialog
logout (20)	Mapped to ASPCloseSession
write (33)	Mapped to ASPUserWrite

The following AFP calls can pass or return more data than can fit in quantumSize bytes (eight ATP response packets) and may be broken up by XPP into multiple ASP calls.

AFP Command (Code/Decimal)	Comment
read (27)	Can return up to the number of bytes indicated in reqCount
write (33)	Can pass up to the number of bytes indicated in reqCount

AFPCall Function

The AFPCall function can have one of the following command formats.

- General
- Login
- AFPWrite
- AFPRead

General Command Format

```
FUNCTION AFPCommand (xParamBlock: XPPParmBlkPtr; async: BOOLEAN) :
        OSErr;
```

Parameter block

←	18	cmdResult	long word	AFP command result
←	26	csCode	word	Always AFPCall
←	28	sessRefnum	word	Session reference number
←	30	aspTimeout	byte	Retry interval in seconds
←	32	cbSize	word	Command buffer size
←	34	cbPtr	pointer	Command buffer
↔	38	rbSize	word	Reply buffer size and reply size
←	40	rbPtr	pointer	Reply buffer pointer
↔	44	wdSize	word	Write data size
←	46	wdPtr	pointer	Write data pointer
←	50	ccbStart	record	Start of memory for CCB

The general command format for the AFPCall function passes an AFP command to the server. This format is used for all AFP calls except AFPLogin, AFPRead, and AFPWrite. Note that from Pascal this call is referred to as AFPCommand.

CmdResult is four bytes of data returned from the server containing an indication of the result of the AFP command.

SessRefnum is the session reference number returned in the AFPLogin call.

ASPTimeOut is the interval in seconds between retries of the call by the driver.

CBSize is the size in bytes of the block of data that contains the command to be sent to the server on the session. The size of the command block must not exceed the value of aspMaxCmdSize returned by the ASPGetParms call.

CBPtr points to start of the block of data (command block) containing the command that is to be sent to the server on the session. The first byte of the command block must contain the AFP command byte. Subsequent bytes in the command buffer contain the parameters associated with the command as defined in the AFP document.

RBSize is passed and indicates the size of the reply buffer in bytes expected by the command. RBSize is also returned and indicates the size of the reply that was actually returned.

RBPtr points to the reply buffer.

WDSize is the size of data to be written to the server (only used if the command is one that is mapped to an ASPUserWrite).

WDPtr points to the write data buffer (only used if the command is one that is mapped to an ASPUserWrite).

CCBStart is the start of the memory to be used by the .XPP driver for the command control block. The size of this block is equal to a maximum of 296 bytes. To determine the exact requirement refer to the CCB Sizes section of this document.

Result codes	aspParamErr	Invalid session number; session has been closed
	aspSizeErr	Command block size is bigger than MaxCmdSize
	aspSessClosed	Session is closing
	aspBufTooSmall	Reply is bigger than response buffer or buffer will be filled, data will be truncated
	afpParmError	AFP command block size is equal to zero. This error will also be returned if the command byte in the command block is equal to 0 or $FF (255) or GetSrvrStatus (15).

Login Command Format

The AFP login command executes a series of AFP operations as defined in the AFP Draft Proposal. For further information, refer to the AFP document.

```
FUNCTION AFPCommand (xParamBlock: XPPParmBlkPtr; async: BOOLEAN):
          OSErr;
```

Parameter block

←	18	cmdResult	long word	AFP command result
←	26	csCode	word	Always AFPCall
←	28	sessRefnum	word	Session reference number
←	30	aspTimeout	byte	Retry interval in seconds
←	31	aspRetry	byte	Number of retries
←	32	cbSize	word	Command buffer size
←	34	cbPtr	pointer	Command buffer
↔	38	rbSize	word	Reply buffer size and reply size
←	40	rbPtr	pointer	Reply buffer pointer
←	44	afpAddrBlock	long word	Server address block
↔	48	afpSCBPtr	pointer	SCB pointer
↔	52	afpAttnRoutine	pointer	Attention routine pointer
←	50	ccbStart	record	Start of command control block

CmdResult is four bytes of data returned from the server containing an indication of the result of the AFP command.

SessRefnum is the session reference number (returned by the AFPLogin call).

ASPTimeOut is the interval in seconds between retries of the call.

ASPRetry is the number of retries that will be attempted.

CBSize is the size in bytes of the block data that contains the command to be sent to the server on the session. The size of the command block must not exceed the value of aspMaxCmdSize returned by the ASPGetParms call.

CBPtr points to the block of data (command block) containing the AFP login command that is to be sent to the server on the session. The first byte of the command block must be the AFP login command byte. Subsequent bytes in the command buffer contain the parameters associated with the command.

RBSize is passed and indicates the size of the reply buffer in bytes expected by the command. RBSize is also returned and indicates the size of the reply that was actually returned.

RBPtr points to the reply buffer.

AFPServerAddr is the network identifier or address of the socket on which the server is listening.

AFPSCBPointer points to a locked block of data for the session control block (SCB). The SCB size is defined by scbMemSize. The SCB is a locked block, and as long as the session is open, the SCB cannot be modified in any way by the application. There is one SCB for each open session.

AFPAttnRoutine is a pointer to a routine that is invoked if an attention from the server is received. When afpAttnRoutine is equal to zero, no attention routine will be invoked.

CCBStart is the start of the memory to be used by the .XPP driver for the command control block. The size of this block is equal to a maximum of 150 bytes. To determine the exact requirement refer to the CCB Sizes section later in this chapter.

Note: In the parameter block, the afpSCBPointer and the afpAttnRoutine fields overlap with the start of the CCB and are modified by the call.

Result codes

aspSizeErr	Command block size is bigger than MaxCmdSize
aspBufTooSmall	Reply is bigger than response buffer; or buffer will be filled, data will be truncated
aspNoServer	Server not responding
aspServerBusy	Server cannot open another session
aspBadVersNum	Server cannot support the offered ASP version number
aspNoMoreSess	Driver cannot support another session.

AFPWrite Command Format

The AFPWrite and AFPRead command formats allow the calling application to make AFP-level calls that read or write a data block that is larger than a single ASP-level call is capable of reading or writing. The maximum number of bytes of data that can be read or written at the ASP level is equal to quantumSize.

```
FUNCTION AFPCommand (xParamBlock: XPPParmBlkPtr; async: BOOLEAN) :
        OSErr;
```

Parameter block

←	18	cmdResult	long word	AFP command result
←	26	csCode	word	Always AFPCall
←	28	sessRefnum	word	Session number
←	30	aspTimeout	byte	Retry interval in seconds
←	32	cbSize	word	Command buffer size
←	34	cbPtr	pointer	Command buffer
↔	38	rbSize	word	Reply buffer size and reply size
←	40	rbPtr	pointer	Reply buffer pointer
←	44	wdSize	word	(used internally)
↔	46	wdPtr	pointer	Write data pointer (updated)
←	50	ccbStart	record	Start of memory for CCB

CmdResult is four bytes of data returned from the server containing an indication of the result of the AFP command.

SessRefnum is the session reference number returned in the AFPLogin call.

ASPTimeOut is the interval in seconds between retries of the call.

CBSize is the size in bytes of the block data that contains the command to be sent to the server on the session. The size of the command block must not exceed the value of aspMaxCmdSize returned by the aspGetParms call.

CBPtr points to the block of data (see command block structure below) containing the AFP write command that is to be sent to the server on the session. The first byte of the Command Block must contain the AFP write command byte.

RBSize is passed and indicates the size of the reply buffer in bytes expected by the command. RBSize is also returned and indicates the size of the reply that was actually returned.

RBPtr points to the reply buffer.

WDSize is used internally.

> **Note:** This command does not pass the write data size in the queue element but in the command buffer. XPP will look for the size in that buffer.

WDPtr is a pointer to the block of data to be written. Note that this field will be updated by XPP as it proceeds and will always point to that section of the data which XPP is currently writing.

CCBStart is the start of the memory to be used by the XPP driver for the command control block. The size of this block is equal to a maximum of 296 bytes. To determine the exact requirement refer to the CCB Sizes section later in this chapter.

Command Block Structure: The AFP write command passes several arguments to XPP in the command buffer itself. The byte offsets are relative to the location pointed to by cbPtr.

←	0	cmdByte	byte	AFP call command byte
←	1	startEndFlag	byte	Start/end Flag
↔	4	rwOffset	long word	Offset within fork to write
↔	8	reqCount	long word	Requested count

CmdByte is the AFP call command byte and must contain the AFP write command code.

StartEndFlag is a one-bit flag (the high bit of the byte) indicating whether the rwOffset field is relative to the beginning or the end of the fork (all other bits are zero).

　　0 = relative to the beginning of the fork

　　1 = relative to the end of the fork

RWOffset is the byte offset within the fork at which the write is to begin.

ReqCount indicates the size of the data to be written and is returned as the actual size written.

The rwOffset and reqCount fields are modified by XPP as the write proceeds and will always indicate the current value of these fields.

The Pascal structure of the AFP command buffer follows:

```
AFPCommandBlock = PACKED RECORD
                cmdByte:        Byte;
                startEndFlag:   Byte;
                forkRefNum:     INTEGER;      {used by server}
                rwOffset:       LONGINT;
                reqCount:       LONGINT;
                newLineFlag:    Byte;         {unused by write}
                newLineChar:    CHAR;         {unused by write}
            END;
```

Result codes   aspParamErr   Invalid session number
               aspSizeErr   Command block size is bigger than MaxCmdSize
               aspSessClosed   Session is closing
               aspBufTooSmall   Reply is bigger than response buffer

AFPRead Command Format

The AFPWrite and AFPRead command formats allow the calling application to make AFP-level calls that read or write a data block that is larger than a single ASP-level call is capable of reading or writing. The maximum number of bytes of data that can be read or written at the ASP level is equal to quantumSize.

```
FUNCTION AFPCommand (xParamBlock: XPPParmBlkPtr; async: BOOLEAN) :
        OSErr;
```

Parameter block

←	18	cmdResult	long word	ASP command result
←	26	csCode	word	Always AFPCall
←	28	sessRefnum	word	Session number
←	30	aspTimeout	byte	Retry interval in seconds
←	32	cbSize	word	Command buffer size
←	34	cbPtr	pointer	Command buffer
←	38	rbSize	word	Used internally
↔	40	rbPtr	pointer	Reply buffer pointer (updated)
←	50	ccbStart	record	Start of memory for CCB

CmdResult is four bytes of data returned from the server containing an indication of the result of the AFP command.

SessRefnum is the session reference number returned in the AFPLogin call.

ASPTimeOut is the interval in seconds between retries of the call.

CBSize is the size in bytes of the block data that contains the command to be sent to the server on the session. The size of the command block must not exceed the value of aspMaxCmdSize returned by the GetParms call.

CBPtr points to the block of data (command block) containing the AFP read command that is to be sent to the server on the session. The first byte of the command block must contain the AFP read command byte. The command block structure is shown below.

RBSize is used internally.

> **Note:** This command does not pass the read size in the queue element but in the command buffer. XPP will look for the size in that buffer.

RBPtr points to the reply buffer. Note that this field will be updated by XPP as it proceeds and will always point to that section of the buffer that XPP is currently reading into.

CCBStart is the start of the memory to be used by the .XPP driver for the command control block. The size of this block is equal to a maximum of 150 bytes. To determine the exact requirement refer to The CCB Sizes section later in this chapter.

Command Block Structure: The AFP read command passes several arguments to XPP in the command buffer itself. The byte offsets are relative to the location pointed to by cbPointer.

←	0	cmdByte	byte	AFP call command byte
↔	4	rwOffset	long word	Offset within fork to read
↔	8	reqCount	long word	Requested count
←	12	newLineFlag	byte	Newline Flag
←	13	newLineChar	byte	Newline Character

CmdByte is the AFP call command byte and must contain the AFP read command code.

RWOffset is the byte offset within the fork at which the read is to begin.

ReqCount indicates the size of the read data buffer and is returned as the actual size read.

The rwOffset and reqCount fields are modified by XPP as the read proceeds and will always indicate the current value of these fields.

NewLineFlag is a one-bit flag (the high bit of the byte) indicating whether or not the read is to terminate at a specified character (all other bits are zero).

0 = no Newline Character is specified

1 = a Newline Character is specified

NewLineChar is any character from $00 to $FF (inclusive) that, when encountered in reading the fork, causes the read operation to terminate.

The Pascal structure of the AFPCommand follows:

```
AFPCommandBlock = PACKED RECORD
                cmdByte:        Byte;
                startEndFlag:   Byte;      {unused for read}
                forkRefNum:     INTEGER;   {used by server}
                rwOffset:       LONGINT;
                reqCount:       LONGINT;
                newLineFlag:    Byte;
                newLineChar:    CHAR;

            END;
```

Result codes	aspParamErr	Invalid session number
	aspSizeErr	Command block size is bigger than MaxCmdSize
	aspSessClosed	Session is closing
	aspBufTooSmall	Reply is bigger than response buffer

CCB Sizes

The .XPP driver uses the memory provided at the end of the UserWrite, UserCommand, and GetStatus functions parameter blocks as an internal command control block (CCB). Using the maximum block sizes specified in the call descriptions will provide adequate space for the call to execute successfully. However, this section is provided for developers who wish to minimize the amount of memory taken up by the CCB in the queue element.

Specifically, this memory is used for building data structures to be used in making calls to the ATP driver. This includes parameter blocks and buffer data structures (BDS). The structure of the BDS is detailed in the AppleTalk Manager chapter of Volume II. The exact size of this memory depends on the size of the response expected, and, in the case of UserWrite, on the size of data to be written.

In the UserCommand and GetStatus cases (along with all AFP calls which map to UserCommand), a BDS must be set up to hold the response information. The number of entries in this BDS is equal to the size of the response buffer divided by the maximum number of data bytes per ATP response packet (578), rounded up. As described in the ASP chapter in *Inside AppleTalk,* ASP must ask for an extra response in the case where the response buffer is an exact multiple of 578. Of course, no BDS can be larger than eight elements. XPP also needs bytes for the queue element to call ATP with, so the minimum size of a CCB, as a function of the response buffer size (rbSize) is

> bdsSize = MIN (((rbSize DIV 578) + 1),8) * bdsEntrySz
> ccbSize = ioQElSize + 4 + bdsSize

With UserWrite (and AFP calls mapping to UserWrite), XPP must create an additional BDS and queue element to use in sending the write data to the server. Therefore the minimum size of a UserWrite CCB, as a function of the response buffer and write data sizes (rbSize and wdSize) is:

> wrBDSSize = MIN (((wdSize DIV 578) + 1),8) * bdsEntrySz
> wrCCBSize = (2 * ioQElSize) + 4 + bdsSize + wrBDSSize

Note: BDSEntrySz is equal to 12; ioQelSize is equal to 50.

.XPP Driver Result Codes

Result Code	Comment	Returned by
aspBadVersNum	Server cannot support the offered version number.	ASPOpenSession AFPCall (Login)
aspBufTooSmall	Reply is bigger than response buffer. Buffer will be filled, data may be truncated.	ASPUserWrite ASPUserCommand ASPGetStatus AFPCall
aspNoMoreSess	Driver cannot support another session.	ASPOpenSessION AFPCall (Login)
aspNoServers	No servers at that address. The server did not respond to the request.	ASPGetStatus ASPOpenSession AFPCall (Login)
aspParamErr	Parameter error, server returned bad (positive) error code. Invalid Session Reference Number.	ASPOpenSession ASPCloseSess ASPUserWrite ASPUserCommand AFPCall
aspServerBusy	Server cannot open another session.	ASPOpenSession AFPCall (Login)
aspSessClosed	Session already in process of closing.	ASPCloseSession ASPUserWrite ASPUserCommand AFPCall
aspSizeErr	Command block size is bigger than maxParamSize.	ASPUserWrite ASPUserCommand AFPCall
cbNotFound	SCB not found, no outstanding open session to be aborted. Pointer did not point to an open session SCB.	ASPAbortOS
afpParmError	AFP Command Block size is less than or equal to zero. Command byte in the Command block is equal to 0 or $FF (255) or GetSrvrStatus (15).	AFPCall
reqAborted	Open session was aborted by an Abort Open Session.	ASPOpenSession AFPCall (Login)

SUMMARY OF THE APPLETALK MANAGER

Data Types

```
MPPParamBlock = PACKED RECORD
        qLink:          QElemPtr;   {next queue entry}
        qType:          INTEGER;    {queue type}
        ioTrap:         INTEGER;    {routine trap}
        ioCmdAddr:      Ptr;        {routine address}
        ioCompletion:   ProcPtr;    {completion routine}
        ioResult:       OSErr;      {result code}
        ioNamePtr:      StringPtr;  {command result (ATP user bytes) }
                                    { [long]}
        ioVRefNum:      INTEGER;    {volume reference or drive number}
        ioRefNum:       INTEGER;    {driver reference number}
        csCode:         INTEGER;    {call command code AUTOMATICALLY SET}
        CASE MPPParmType OF
        LAPWriteParm:
                        (filler0:INTEGER;
                        wdsPointer:Ptr);        {->Write Data Structure}
        AttachPHParm,DetachPHParm:
                        (protType:Byte;         {ALAP Protocol Type}
                        filler1:Byte;
                        handler:Ptr);           {->protocol handler routine}
        OpenSktParm,CloseSktParm,WriteDDPParm:
                        (socket:Byte;           {socket number}
                        checksumFlag:Byte;      {checksum flag}
                        listener:Ptr);          {->socket listener routine}
        RegisterNameParm,LookupNameParm,ConfirmNameParm,RemoveNameParm:
                        (interval:Byte;         {retry interval}
                        count:Byte;             {retry count}
                        entityPtr:Ptr;          {->names table element or }
                                                { ->entity name}
                        CASE MPPParmType OF
                        RegisterNameParm:
                                (verifyFlag:Byte;       {set if verify }
                                                        { needed}
                                filler3:Byte);
                        LookupNameParm:
                                (retBuffPtr:Ptr;        {->return buffer}
                                retBuffSize:INTEGER;    {return buffer }
                                                        { size}
                                maxToGet:INTEGER;       {matches to get}
                                numGotten:INTEGER);     {matched gotten}
                        ConfirmNameParm:
                                (confirmAddr:AddrBlock; {->entity}
                                newSocket:Byte;         {socket number}
                                filler4:Byte));
        SetSelfSendParm:
```

```
                    (newSelfFlag:Byte;    {self-send toggle flag}
                    oldSelfFlag:Byte);    {previous self-send state}
        KillNBPParm:
                    (nKillQEl:Ptr);       {ptr to Q element to cancel}
        END;


ATPParamBlock = PACKED RECORD
        qLink:        QElemPtr;   {next queue entry}
        qType:        INTEGER;    {queue type}
        ioTrap:       INTEGER;    {routine trap}
        ioCmdAddr:    Ptr;        {routine address}
        ioCompletion: ProcPtr;    {completion routine}
        ioResult:     OSErr;      {result code}
        userData:     LONGINT;    {ATP user bytes [long]}
        reqTID:       INTEGER;    {request transaction ID}
        ioRefNum:     INTEGER;    {driver reference number }
        csCode:       INTEGER;    {call command code AUTOMATICALLY }
                                  { SET}
        atpSocket:    Byte;       {currBitMap or socket number}
        atpFlags:     Byte;       {control information}
        addrBlock:    AddrBlock;  {source/dest. socket address}
        reqLength:    INTEGER;    {request/response length}
        reqPointer:   Ptr;        {-> request/response data}
        bdsPointer:   Ptr;        {-> response BDS}
        CASE MPPParmType OF
                SendRequestParm,NSendRequestParm:
                        (numOfBuffs:Byte;  {numOfBuffs}
                        timeOutVal:Byte;   {timeout interval}
                        numOfResps:Byte;   {number responses actually }
                                           { received}
                        retryCount:Byte;   {number of retries}
                        intBuff:INTEGER);  {used internally for }
                                           { NSendRequest}
                SendResponseParm:
                        (filler0:Byte;     {number of responses being }
                                           { sent}
                        bdsSize:Byte;      {number of BDS elements}
                        transID:INTEGER);  {transaction ID}
                GetRequestParm:
                        (bitMap:Byte;      {bit map}
                        filler1:Byte);
                AddResponseParm:
                        (rspNum:Byte;      {sequence number}
                        filler2:Byte);
                KillSendReqParm,KillGetReqParm:
                        (aKillQEl:Ptr);    {ptr to Q element to }
                                           { cancel}
        END;


XPPParamBlock = PACKED RECORD
        qLink:        QElemPtr; {next queue entry}
        qType:        INTEGER;  {queue type}
        ioTrap:       INTEGER;  {routine trap}
        ioCmdAddr:    Ptr;      {routine address}
        ioCompletion: ProcPtr;  {completion routine}
        ioResult:     OSErr;    {result code}
```

```
cmdResult:        LONGINT;     {command result (ATP user bytes) }
                               { [long]}
ioVRefNum:        INTEGER;     {volume reference or drive number)
ioRefNum:         INTEGER;     {driver reference number)
csCode:           INTEGER;     {call command code}
CASE XPPPrmBlkType OF
  ASPAbortPrm:
               (abortSCBPtr:   Ptr);      {SCB pointer for }
                                          { AbortOS [long] }
  ASPSizeBlk:
               (aspMaxCmdSize: INTEGER;   {for SPGetParms }
                                          { [word]}
               aspQuantumSize: INTEGER;   {for SPGetParms }
                                          { [word]}
               numSesss:       INTEGER);  {for SPGetParms }
                                          { [word]}
  XPPPrmBlk:
               (sessRefnum:    INTEGER;   {offset to session }
                                          { refnum [word]}
               aspTimeout:     Byte;      {timeout for ATP }
                                          { [byte]}
               aspRetry:       Byte;      {retry count for ATP }
                                          { [byte]}
               CASE XPPSubPrmType OF
                 ASPOpenPrm:
                      (serverAddr: AddrBlock; {server address }
                                              { block }
                                              { [longword]}
                      scbPointer:  Ptr;       {SCB pointer }
                                              { [longword]}
                      attnRoutine: Ptr);      {attention routine }
                                              { pointer [long]}
                 ASPSubPrm:
                      (cbSize:     INTEGER;   {command block }
                                              { size [word]}
                      cbPtr:       Ptr;       {command block }
                                              { pointer [long]}
                      rbSize:      INTEGER;   {reply buffer size }
                                              { [word]}
                      rbPtr:       Ptr;       {reply buffer }
                                              { pointer [long]}
                           CASE XPPEndPrmType OF
                             AFPLoginPrm:
                                  (afpAddrBlock: AddrBlock;
                                       {address block in }
                                       { AFPlogin [long]}
                                  afpSCBPtr:     Ptr;
                                       {SCB pointer in }
                                       { AFPlogin [long]}
                                  afpAttnRoutine: Ptr);
                                       {attn routine }
                                       { pointer}
                                       { in AFPlogin}
                             ASPEndPrm:
                                  (wdSize:  INTEGER;
                                     {write data size [word] }
```

```
                                                 wdPtr:    Ptr;
                                                   {write data pointer
                                                   { [long] }
                                                 ccbStart: ARRAY[0..295] OF
                                                            Byte)));
                                                   {CCB memory for driver}
                                                   {Write max size(CCB) =
                                                   { 296; all other calls =
                                                   { 150}

              END;

AFPCommandBlock = PACKED RECORD
        cmdByte:         Byte;
        startEndFlag:    Byte;
        forkRefNum:      INTEGER;   {used by server}
        rwOffset:        LONGINT;
        reqCount:        LONGINT;
        newLineFlag:     Byte;      {unused by write}
        newLineChar:     CHAR;      {unused by write}

        END;

AFPCommandBlock = PACKED RECORD
        cmdByte:         Byte;
        startEndFlag:    Byte;      {unused for read}
        forkRefNum:      INTEGER;   {used by server}
        rwOffset:        LONGINT;
        reqCount:        LONGINT;
        newLineFlag:     Byte;
        newLineChar:     CHAR;

        END;
```

AppleTalk Manager Routines

```
FUNCTION PSetSelfSend (thePBptr: MPPPBPtr; async: BOOLEAN) : OSErr;
```

→	26	csCode	word	Always PSetSelfSend
→	28	newSelfFlag	byte	New SelfSend flag
←	29	oldSelfFlag	byte	Old SelfSend flag

AppleTalk Transaction Protocol Functions

```
FUNCTION PNSendRequest (thePBptr: ATPBPtr; async: BOOLEAN) : OSErr;
```

→	18	userData	longword	User bytes
←	22	reqTID	word	Transaction ID used in request
→	26	csCode	word	Always sendRequest
↔	28	atpSocket	byte	Socket to send request on or Current bitmap
↔	29	atpFlags	byte	Control information
→	30	addrBlock	longword	Destination socket address

→	34	reqLength	word	Dequest size in bytes
→	36	reqPointer	pointer	Pointer to request data
→	40	bdsPointer	pointer	Pointer to response BDS
→	44	numOfBuffs	byte	Number of responses expected
→	45	timeOutVal	byte	Timeout interval
←	46	numOf Resps	byte	Number of responses received
↔	47	retryCount	byte	Number of retries
←	48	intBuff	word	Used internally

```
FUNCTION PKillSendReq (thePBptr: ATPPBPtr; async: BOOLEAN) : OSErr;
```

→	26	csCode	word	Always PKillSendReq
→	44	aKillQEl	pointer	Pointer to queue element

```
FUNCTION PKillGetReq (thePBptr: ATPPBPtr; async: BOOLEAN) : OSErr;
```

→	26	csCode	word	Always PKillGetReq
→	44	aKillQEl	pointer	Pointer to queue element

Name Binding Protocol Functions

```
FUNCTION PKillNBP (thePBptr: ATPPBPtr; async: BOOLEAN) : OSErr;
```

→	26	csCode	word	Always PKillNBP
→	28	nKillQEl	pointer	Pointer to queue element

AppleTalk Session Protocol Functions

```
FUNCTION ASPOpenSession (xParamBlock: XPPParmBlkPtr; async: BOOLEAN) :
        OSErr;
```

→	26	csCode	word	Always ASPOpenSession
←	28	sessRefnum	word	Session reference number
→	30	aspTimeout	byte	Retry interval in seconds
→	31	aspRetry	byte	Number of retries
→	32	serverAddr	long word	Server socket address
→	36	scbPointer	pointer	Pointer to session control block
→	40	attnRoutine	pointer	Pointer to attention routine

```
FUNCTION ASPCloseSession (xParamBlock: XPPParmBlkPtr; async: BOOLEAN) :
        OSErr;
```

→	26	csCode	word	Always ASPCloseSess
→	28	sessRefnum	word	Session reference number

```
FUNCTION ASPAbortOS (xParamBlock: XPPParmBlkPtr; async: BOOLEAN) :
        OSErr;
```

→	26	csCode	word	Always ASPAbortOS
→	28	abortSCBPointer	pointer	Pointer to session control block

```
FUNCTION ASPGetParms (xParamBlock: XPPParmBlkPtr; async: BOOLEAN) :
        OSErr;
```

→	26	csCode	word	Always ASPGetParms
←	28	aspMaxCmdSize	word	Maximum size of command block
←	30	aspQuantumSize	word	Maximum data size
←	32	numSesss	word	Number of sessions

```
FUNCTION ASPCloseAll (xParamBlock: XPPParmBlkPtr; async: BOOLEAN) :
        OSErr;
```

→	26	csCode	word	Always ASPCloseAll

```
FUNCTION ASPUserWrite (xParamBlock: XPPParmBlkPtr; async: BOOLEAN) :
        OSErr;
```

←	18	cmdResult	long word	ASP command result
→	26	csCode	word	Always ASPUserWrite
→	28	sessRefnum	word	Session reference number
→	30	aspTimeout	byte	Retry interval in seconds
→	32	cbSize	word	Command block size
→	34	cbPtr	pointer	Command block pointer
↔	38	rbSize	word	Reply buffer size and reply size
→	40	rbPointer	pointer	Reply buffer pointer
↔	44	wdSize	word	Write data size
→	46	wdPtr	pointer	Write data pointer
←	50	ccbStart	record	Start of memory for CCB

```
FUNCTION ASPUserCommand (xParamBlock: XPPParmBlkPtr; async: BOOLEAN) :
        OSErr;
```

←	18	cmdResult	long word	ASP command result
→	26	csCode	word	Always ASPUserCommand
→	28	sessRefnum	word	Session number
→	30	aspTimeout	byte	Retry interval in seconds
→	32	cbSize	word	Command block size
→	34	cbPtr	pointer	Command block pointer
↔	38	rbSize	word	Reply buffer and reply size
→	40	rbPointer	pointer	Reply buffer pointer
←	50	ccbStart	record	Start of memory for CCB

```
FUNCTION ASPGetStatus (xParamBlock: XPPParmBlkPtr; async: BOOLEAN) :
        OSErr;
```

→	26	csCode	word	Always ASPGetStatus
→	30	aspTimeout	byte	Retry interval in seconds
→	31	aspRetry	byte	Number of retries
→	32	serverAddr	long word	Server socket address
↔	38	rbSize	word	Reply buffer and reply size
→	40	rbPointer	pointer	Reply buffer pointer
←	50	ccbStart	record	Start of memory for CCB

General Command Format

```
FUNCTION AFPCommand (xParamBlock: XPPParmBlkPtr; async: BOOLEAN) :
        OSErr;
```

Parameter block

←	18	cmdResult	long word	AFP command result
→	26	csCode	word	Always AFPCall
→	28	sessRefnum	word	Session reference number
→	30	aspTimeout	byte	Retry interval in seconds
→	32	cbSize	word	Command buffer size
→	34	cbPtr	pointer	Command buffer
↔	38	rbSize	word	Reply buffer size and reply size
→	40	rbPtr	pointer	Reply buffer pointer
↔	44	wdSize	word	Write data size
→	46	wdPtr	pointer	Write data pointer
←	50	ccbStart	record	Start of memory for CCB

Login Command Format

```
FUNCTION AFPCommand (xParamBlock: XPPParmBlkPtr; async: BOOLEAN) :
        OSErr;
```

←	18	cmdResult	long word	AFP command result
→	26	csCode	word	Always AFPCall
←	28	sessRefnum	word	Session reference number
→	30	aspTimeout	byte	Retry interval in seconds
→	31	aspRetry	byte	Number of retries
→	32	cbSize	word	Command buffer size
→	34	cbPtr	pointer	Command buffer
↔	38	rbSize	word	Reply buffer size and reply size
→	40	rbPtr	pointer	Reply buffer pointer
→	44	afpAddrBlock	long word	Server address block
↔	48	afpSCBPtr	pointer	SCB pointer
↔	52	afpAttnRoutine	pointer	Attention routine pointer
←	50	ccbStart	record	Start of command control block

AFPWrite Command Format

```
FUNCTION AFPCommand (xParamBlock: XPPParmBlkPtr; async: BOOLEAN) :
        OSErr;
```

←	18	cmdResult	long word	AFP command result
→	26	csCode	word	Always AFPCall
→	28	sessRefnum	word	Session number
→	30	aspTimeout	byte	Retry interval in seconds
→	32	cbSize	word	Command buffer size
→	34	cbPtr	pointer	Command buffer
↔	38	rbSize	word	Reply buffer size and reply size
→	40	rbPtr	pointer	Reply buffer pointer
←	44	wdSize	word	(used internally)
↔	46	wdPtr	pointer	Write data pointer (updated)
←	50	ccbStart	record	Start of memory for CCB

Command Block Structure

→	0	cmdByte	byte	AFP call command byte
→	1	startEndFlag	byte	Start/end Flag
↔	4	rwOffset	long word	Offset within fork to write
↔	8	reqCount	long word	Requested count

AFPRead Command Format

```
FUNCTION AFPCommand (xParamBlock: XPPParmBlkPtr; async: BOOLEAN): OSErr;
```

←	18	cmdResult	long word	ASP command result
→	26	csCode	word	Always AFPCall
→	28	sessRefnum	word	Session number
→	30	aspTimeout	byte	Retry interval in seconds
→	32	cbSize	word	Command buffer size
→	34	cbPtr	pointer	Command buffer
→	38	rbSize	word	Used internally
↔	40	rbPtr	pointer	Reply buffer pointer (updated)
←	50	ccbStart	record	Start of memory for CCB

Command Block Structure

→	0	cmdByte	byte	AFP call command byte
↔	4	rwOffset	long word	Offset within fork to read
↔	8	reqCount	long word	Requested count
→	12	newLineFlag	byte	Newline Flag
→	13	newLineChar	byte	Newline Character

Constants

Offsets in User Bytes

```
aspCmdCode     EQU     0       ;offset to command field
aspWSSNum      EQU     1       ;WSS number in OpenSessions
aspVersNum     EQU     2       ;ASP version number in OpenSessions
aspSSSNum      EQU     0       ;SSS number in OpenSessReplies
aspSessID      EQU     1       ;session ID (requests &OpenSessReply)
aspOpenErr     EQU     2       ;OpenSessReply error code

aspSeqNum      EQU     2       ;sequence number in requests
aspAttnCode    EQU     2       ;attention bytes in attentions
```

Offsets in ATP data part

```
aspWrBSize     EQU     0       ;offset to write buffer size
                               ; (WriteData)
aspWrHdrSz     EQU     ASPWrBSize+2 ;size of data part
```

ASP command codes

```
aspCloseSess     EQU   1                     ;close session
aspCommand       EQU   2                     ;user-command
aspGetStat       EQU   3                     ;get status
aspOpenSess      EQU   4                     ;open session
aspTickle        EQU   5                     ;tickle
aspWrite         EQU   6                     ;write
aspDataWrite     EQU   7                     ;writedata (from server)
aspAttention     EQU   8                     ;attention (from server)
```

ASP miscellaneous

```
aspVersion       EQU   $0100       ;ASP version number
MaxCmdSize       EQU   ATPMaxData  ;maximum command block size
QuantumSize      EQU   ATPMaxData*ATPMaxNum ;maximum reply size
XPPLoadedBit     EQU   ATPLoadedBit+1 ;XPP bit in PortBUse
XPPUnitNum       EQU   40          ;unit number for XPP (old ROMs)
```

ASP errors codes

```
aspBadVersNum    EQU   -1066  ;server cannot support this ASP version
aspBufTooSmall   EQU   -1067  ;buffer too small
aspNoMoreSess    EQU   -1068  ;no more sessions on server
aspNoServers     EQU   -1069  ;no servers at that address
aspParamErr      EQU   -1070  ;parameter error
aspServerBusy    EQU   -1071  ;server cannot open another session
aspSessClosed    EQU   -1072  ;session closed
aspSizeErr       EQU   -1073  ;command block too big
aspTooMany       EQU   -1074  ;too many clients
aspNoAck         EQU   -1075  ;no ack on attention Request
```

Control codes

```
openSess         EQU   255    ;open session
closeSess        EQU   254    ;close session
userCommand      EQU   253    ;user command
userWrite        EQU   252    ;user write
getStatus        EQU   251    ;get status
afpCall          EQU   250    ;AFP command (buffer has command code)
getParms         EQU   249    ;get parameters
abortOS          EQU   248    ;abort open session request
closeAll         EQU   247    ;close all open sessions
```

ASP queue element standard structure: arguments passed in the CSParam area

```
sessRefnum      EQU     $1C    ;offset to session refnum [word]
aspTimeout      EQU     $1E    ;timeout for ATP [byte]
aspRetry        EQU     $1F    ;retry count for ATP [byte]
serverAddr      EQU     $20    ;server address block [longword]
scbPointer      EQU     $24    ;SCB pointer [longword]
attnRoutine     EQU     $28    ;attention routine pointer [long]

cbSize          EQU     $20    ;command block size [word]
cbPtr           EQU     $22    ;command block pointer [long]
rbSize          EQU     $26    ;reply buffer size [word]
rbPtr           EQU     $28    ;reply buffer pointer [long]
wdSize          EQU     $2C    ;write data size [word]
wdPtr           EQU     $2E    ;write data pointer [long]
ccbStart        EQU     $32    ;start of memory for CCB

aspMaxCmdSize   EQU     $1C    ;for SPGetParms [word]
aspQuantumSize  EQU     $1E    ;for SPGetParms [word]
abortSCBPtr     EQU     $1F    ;SCB pointer for AbortOS [long]

cmdResult       EQU     $12    ;command result (ATP user
                               ; bytes)[long]

afpAddrBlock    EQU     $2C    ;address block in AFP login[long]
afpSCBPtr       EQU     $30    ;SCB pointer in AFP login [long]
afpAttnRoutine  EQU     $34    ;attn routine pointer in AFP login

scbMemSize      EQU     $C0    ;size of memory for SCB
```

AFPCall command codes

```
afpLogin        EQU     18;
afpContLogin    EQU     19;
afpLogout       EQU     20;
afpRead         EQU     27;
afpWrite        EQU     33;
```

Offsets for certain parameters in Read/Write calls

```
startEndFlag   EQU   $1 ;write only; offset relative to start or end
rwOffset       EQU   $4 ;offset at which to start read or write
reqCount       EQU   $8 ;count of bytes to read or write
newLineFlag    EQU   $C ;read only; newline character flag
newLineChar    EQU   $D ;read only; newline character
lastWritten    EQU   $0 ;write only; last written  (returned)
```

Miscellaneous

```
afpUseWrite  EQU  $C0   ;first call in range that maps to an
                        ; ASPWrite
```

Preferred Interface Routines

```
AttachPH      Function PAttachPH      (thePBptr: MPPPBPtr; async:
                                       BOOLEAN) : OSErr;
DetachPH      Function PDetachPH      (thePBptr: MPPPBPtr; async:
                                       BOOLEAN) : OSErr;
WriteLAP      Function PWriteLAP      (thePBptr: MPPPBPtr; async:
                                       BOOLEAN) : OSErr;
OpenSkt       Function POpenSkt       (thePBptr: MPPPBPtr; async:
                                       BOOLEAN) : OSErr;
CloseSkt      Function PCloseSkt      (thePBptr: MPPPBPtr; async:
                                       BOOLEAN) : OSErr;
WriteDDP      Function PWriteDDP      (thePBptr: MPPPBPtr; async:
                                       BOOLEAN) : OSErr;
RegisterName  Function PRegisterName  (thePBptr: MPPPBPtr; async:
                                       BOOLEAN) : OSErr;
LookupName    Function PLookupName    (thePBptr: MPPPBPtr; async:
                                       BOOLEAN) : OSErr;
ConfirmName   Function PConfirmName   (thePBptr: MPPPBPtr; async:
                                       BOOLEAN) : OSErr;
RemoveName    Function PRemoveName    (thePBptr: MPPPBPtr; async:
                                       BOOLEAN) : OSErr;
OpenATPSkt    Function POpenATPSkt    (thePBptr: ATPPBPtr; async:
                                       BOOLEAN) : OSErr;
CloseATPSkt   Function PCloseATPSkt   (thePBptr: ATPPBPtr; async:
                                       BOOLEAN) : OSErr;
SendRequest   Function PSendRequest   (thePBptr: ATPPBPtr; async:
                                       BOOLEAN) : OSErr;
GetRequest    Function PGetRequest    (thePBptr: ATPPBPtr; async:
                                       BOOLEAN) : OSErr;
SendResponse  Function PSendResponse  (thePBptr: ATPPBPtr; async:
                                       BOOLEAN) : OSErr;
AddResponse   Function PAddResponse   (thePBptr: ATPPBPtr; async:
                                       BOOLEAN) : OSErr;
ReLTCB        Function PRelTCB        (thePBptr: ATPPBPtr; async:
                                       BOOLEAN) : OSErr;
RelRspCB      Function PRelRspCB      (thePBptr: ATPPBPtr; async:
                                       BOOLEAN) : OSErr;
SetSelfSend   Function PSetSelfSend   (thePBptr: MPPPBPtr; async:
                                       BOOLEAN) : OSErr;
NSendRequest  Function PNSendRequest  (thePBptr: ATPPBPtr; async:
                                       BOOLEAN) : OSErr;
KillSendReq   Function PKillSendReq   (thePBptr: ATPPBPtr; async:
                                       BOOLEAN) : OSErr;
KillGetReq    Function PKillGetReq    (thePBptr: ATPPBPtr; async:
                                       BOOLEAN) : OSErr;
KillNBP       Function PKillNBP       (thePBptr: MPPPBPtr; async:
                                       BOOLEAN) : OSErr;
```

```
PROCEDURE BuildLAPwds (wdsPtr,dataPtr: Ptr;
          destHost,protoType,frameLen: INTEGER);

PROCEDURE BuildDDPwds  (wdsPtr,headerPtr,dataPtr: Ptr; destAddress:
          AddrBlock; DDPType : INTEGER; dataLen: INTEGER);

PROCEDURE NBPSetEntity (buffer: Ptr; nbpObject,nbpType,nbpZone:
          Str32);

PROCEDURE NBPSetNTE (ntePtr: Ptr; nbpObject,nbpType,nbpZone: Str32;
          Socket: INTEGER);

FUNCTION   NBPExtract (theBuffer: Ptr; numInBuf: INTEGER; whichOne:
          INTEGER; VAR abEntity: EntityName; VAR address:
          AddrBlock) : OSErr;

FUNCTION   GetBridgeAddress: INTEGER;

FUNCTION   BuildBDS (buffPtr,bdsPtr: Ptr; buffSize: INTEGER) :
          INTEGER;
```

29 THE VERTICAL RETRACE MANAGER

CHANGES TO THE VERTICAL RETRACE MANAGER

With the advent of slots, a variety of screens are available, each with potentially different vertical retrace periods. The Vertical Retrace Manager has been extended to provide flexible, slot-specific video-interrupt handling on the Macintosh II. These changes are mostly transparent to existing applications.

Several video cards can be installed on a single system. The user can, at any time, designate a particular slot as the primary video slot for the system. If at system startup, no device is designated, the Start Manager selects one (see the Start Manager chapter in this volume for details).

Instead of maintaining a single vertical retrace queue, the Vertical Retrace Manager now maintains a separate queue for each connected video device; associated with each queue is the rate at which the device's vertical retrace interrupt occurs. When interrupts occur for a particular video slot, the Vertical Retrace Manager executes any tasks in the queue for that slot.

For compatibility with existing software, a special system-generated interrupt handles the execution of tasks previously performed during the vertical retrace interrupt. This special interrupt, generated 60.15 times a second (identical to the retrace rate on the Macintosh Plus), mimics the vertical retrace interrupt and ensures that application tasks installed with the VInstall function, as well as periodic system tasks such as updating the tick count and checking whether the stack has expanded into the heap, are performed as usual.

You can still use the VInstall function as a way of performing recurrent tasks based on ticks. Be aware, however, that these tasks will no longer be tied to the actual retrace rate of the video screen.

To install a task whose execution is tied to the vertical retrace period of a particular video device, call SlotVInstall using the VBLTask queue element; as before qType must be ORD(vType). The Vertical Retrace Manager interprets the vblCount field in terms of the rate that the specified slot generates vertical retrace interrupts. On the current Macintosh II monitors, for instance, the interrupt occurs every 1/67th of a second; specifying a vblCount of 10 means that the task will be executed every 10/67ths of a second. The value of vblCount is decremented every 1/67th of a second until it reaches 0, at which point the task is called. To remove a slot-specific task, call SlotVRemove.

The AttachVBL function is used primarily by the Start Manager and Control Panel for designating the primary video device; only applications that shift between multiple video cards will need to call this routine.

Slot interrupt handlers for video cards need to call the DoVBLTask function; this causes the Vertical Retrace Manager to execute any tasks in the queue for that slot.

VERTICAL RETRACE MANAGER ROUTINES

```
Function AttachVBL (theSlot: INTEGER) : OSErr;
```

Trap macro	_AttachVBL
On entry	D0: theSlot (word)
On exit	D0: result code (word)

AttachVBL makes theSlot the primary video slot, allowing correct cursor updating.

Result codes	noErr	No error
	slotNumErr	Invalid slot number

```
Function SlotVInstall (vblTaskPtr: QElemPtr; theSlot:INTEGER) :
        OSErr;
```

Trap macro	_SlotVInstall
On entry	A0: vblTaskPtr (pointer)
	D0: theSlot (word)
On exit	D0: result code (word)

SlotVInstall is identical in function to the VInstall function except that it installs the task in the queue for the device specified by theSlot.

Result codes	noErr	No error
	vTypErr	Invalid queue element
	slotNumErr	Invalid slot number

```
Function SlotVRemove (vblTaskPtr: QElemPtr; theSlot: INTEGER) :
        OSErr;
```

Trap macro	_SlotVRemove
On entry	A0: vblTaskPtr (pointer)
	D0: theSlot (word)
On exit	D0: result code (word)

SlotVRemove is identical in function to the VRemove function except that it removes the task from the queue for the slot specified by theSlot.

Result codes	noErr	No error
	vTypErr	Invalid queue element
	slotNumErr	Invalid slot number

```
Function DoVBLTask (theSlot: INTEGER) : OSErr;
```

Trap macro	_DoVBLTask
On entry	D0: theSlot (word)
On exit	D0: result code (word)

Note: To reduce overhead at interrupt time, instead of executing the _DoVBLTask trap you can load the jump vector jDoVBLTask into an address register and execute a JSR instruction using that register.

DoVBLTask causes any VBL tasks in the queue for the specified slot to be executed. If the specified slot is the primary video slot, the position of the cursor will also be updated.

Result codes	noErr	No error
	slotNumErr	Invalid slot number

SUMMARY OF THE VERTICAL RETRACE MANAGER

Routines

```
FUNCTION AttachVBL    (theSlot: INTEGER) : OSErr;
FUNCTION SlotVInstall (vblTaskPtr: QElemPtr; theSlot:INTEGER) :
                       OSErr;
FUNCTION SlotVRemove  (vblTaskPtr: QElemPtr; theSlot: INTEGER) :
                       OSErr;
FUNCTION DoVBLTask    (theSlot: INTEGER) : OSErr;
```

Assembly-Language Information

Routines

Trap macro	On entry	On exit
_AttachVBL	D0: theSlot (word)	D0: result code (word)
_SlotVInstall	A0: vblTaskPtr (pointer) D0: theSlot (word)	D0: result code (word)
_SlotVRemove	A0: vblTaskPtr (pointer) D0: theSlot (word)	D0: result code (word)
_DoVBLTask	D0: theSlot (word)	D0: result code (word)

Variables

jDoVBLTask   Jump vector for DoVBLTask routine

30 THE SYSTEM ERROR HANDLER

30 System Error

NEW ERROR CODES

The following new error codes may be reported by the procedure SysError:

ID   **Explanation**

31   Not the requested disk
33   Negative ZcbFree value
84   A menu has been purged

Assembly-Language Information

Constants

```
dsNotThe1        EQU    31      ;not the requested disk
negZcbFreeErr    EQU    33      ;ZcbFree is negative
menuPrgErr       EQU    84      ;happens when a menu is purged
```

31 THE SCSI MANAGER

31 SCSI Manager

CHANGES TO THE SCSI MANAGER

On the Macintosh SE and Macintosh II, the SCSIRBlind and SCSIWBlind functions have hardware support; this ensures that they will work reliably with most third-party SCSI drives.

> **Warning**: SCSI drivers that jump directly to the ROM will crash on any machine other than a Macintosh Plus.

Three new routines support the message phases of the SCSI standard.

Several new result codes have been defined:

- If arbitration fails because the bus is busy during the SCSIGet function, the result code scArbNBErr is returned. If the SCSI Manager is busy with another operation when SCSIGet is called, the result code scMgrBusyErr is returned.

- If the data doesn't come ready within the bus timeout period during the SCSIRBlind and SCSIWBlind functions, the result code scBusTOErr is returned.

- If the bus is not in the Status phase during the SCSIComplete function, the result code scComplPhaseErr is returned (indicating either that filler bytes were written or bytes were read and lost).

- If an attempted operation is out of sequence (calling SCSISelect without first calling SCSIGet, for instance), the result code scSequenceErr is returned.

USING THE SCSI MANAGER

Three new routines support the message phase of the SCSI standard. SCSISelAtn lets you select a device, alerting the device that you want to send a message. SCSIMsgOut sends a message byte to the device, and SCSIMsgIn receives a message byte from the device.

SCSI MANAGER ROUTINES

> **Assembly-language note:** Unlike most other Operating System routines, the SCSI Manager routines are stack-based. You can invoke each of the SCSI routines with a macro that has the same name as the routine preceded by an underscore. These macros, however, aren't trap macros themselves; instead they expand to invoke the trap macro _SCSIDispatch. The SCSI Manager determines which routine to execute from the **routine selector,** an integer that's passed to it in a word on the stack. The routine selectors for the new routines are as follows:

```
scsiSelAtn      .EQU    11
scsiMsgIn       .EQU    12
scsiMsgOut      .EQU    13
```

If you specify a routine selector that's not defined, the System Error Handler is called with the system error ID dsCoreErr.

```
FUNCTION SCSISelAtn (targetID: INTEGER) : OSErr;
```

SCSISelAtn is identical in function to SCSISelect except that it asserts the Attention line during selection, signaling that you want to send a message to the device.

```
FUNCTION SCSIMsgIn (VAR message: INTEGER) : OSErr;
```

SCSIMsgIn gets a message from the device. The message is contained in the low-order byte of the message parameter; message values are listed in the ANSI documentation for SCSI.

SCSIMsgIn leaves the Attention line undisturbed if it's already asserted upon entry.

```
FUNCTION SCSIMsgOut (message: INTEGER) : OSErr;
```

SCSIMsgOut sends a message byte to the target device; message values are listed in the ANSI documentation for SCSI.

TRANSFER MODES

The Macintosh Plus SCSI Manager implements two transfer modes: polled and blind. The polled mode checks the DRQ signal on the 5380 SCSI chip before each byte is transferred (on both read and write operations). While slower than blind mode, the polled mode is completely safe since the SCSI Manager will wait indefinitely for each byte sent to or from the peripheral.

The blind mode does not poll the DRQ line and is therefore about 50% faster. Use of this mode imposes certain timing constraints, however, making it unreliable for some peripherals. Once a transfer is underway, if the peripheral's controller cannot send (or receive) a byte every 2 microseconds, the SCSI Manager may either read invalid data or write data faster than the peripheral can accept it, resulting in the loss of data.

Programmers writing SCSI device drivers must be familiar with the limits of their peripherals. If the peripheral has internal interrupts, for instance, or if it has processing overhead at unpredictable points within a block transfer, the blind mode should not be used.

Note: If the peripheral has a regular pause at a specific byte number within a block, it's possible to use a transfer information block containing two or more data transfer pseudoinstructions. Since the SCSI Manager will handshake the first byte at the beginning of each data transfer operation, this can be used to synchronize with the peripheral's internal processing.

The Macintosh SE and Macintosh II have additional hardware support for SCSI data transfers. For compatibility, the faster transfer routines are still called SCSIRBlind and SCSIWBlind; these routines do, however, take advantage of the hardware handshaking available on the new machines. Use of the hardware handshake, however, imposes other timing constraints. If the time between any two bytes in a data transfer exceeds a certain period—between 265 and 284 milliseconds on the Macintosh SE and approximately 16 microseconds on the Macintosh II—a CPU bus error is generated. If your peripheral cannot meet this constraint, you should use the polled mode calls, SCSIRead and SCSIWrite.

DISK PARTITIONING

The SCSI Manager chapter of Volume IV introduces the subject of booting from SCSI devices. It presents two data structures needed in the first two physical blocks of the device. The first data structure, the driver descriptor map, identifies the various device drivers available for loading. The second structure, the device partition map, presents a scheme for describing the allocation, or partitioning, of the blocks of a device between multiple operating systems.

The driver descriptor map is unchanged. In order to support multiple operating systems on a single disk, however, the device partition map has been redesigned. The old partition map format is still supported, but developers are encouraged to adopt the new format (see below).

Driver Descriptor Map

A driver descriptor map must always be located at the start of physical block 0; its format is given in Figure 1.

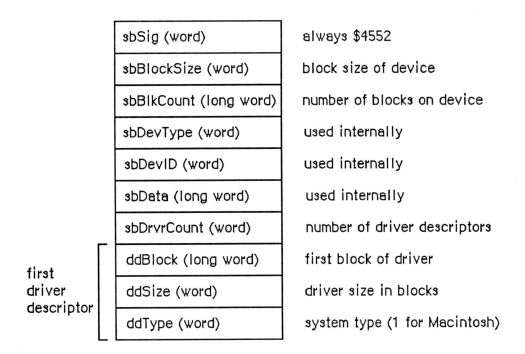

Figure 1. Driver Descriptor Map

SBSig contains the signature; it's used to verify that the block is valid (that is, the disk has been formatted) and should always be $4552.

SBDrvrCount specifies the number of drivers that may be used for this disk; more than one driver may be needed when multiple operating systems or processors are supported.

There must be a driver descriptor for each driver on the device (as well as a partition map entry, as explained below). DDBlock is the address of the first physical block of the driver code. DDSize contains the size of the driver in blocks. DDType identifies the operating system or processor supported by the driver. The Macintosh Operating System has the value 1; values 0 through 15 are reserved for use by Apple.

To specify a particular operating system for use at system startup, you'll need to call the Start Manager routine SetOSDefault using the same value in ddType (see the Start Manager chapter in this volume).

Partition Map

For the purposes of this discussion, a partition is simply a series of blocks that have been allocated to a particular operating system, file system, or device driver. (Another way to look at it is that a single physical disk is divided into a number of logical disks.) The partition map organizes, or maps, this allocation of the physical blocks of a disk. It is *strongly recommended* that all operating systems that run on the Macintosh II use and support the partition map presented here. This will ensure the peaceful coexistence and operation of different operating systems on a single disk, and will enable the transfer of files between partitions.

To support the variety of disk types and sizes that can be attached to the Macintosh II, you should either allow for a variable number of partitions (to be determined at disk initialization), or allocate a large number (greater than 100) of fixed partition slots.

With the exception of physical block zero, every block on a disk must be accounted for as belonging to a partition.

The partition map contains a number of physical blocks (as mentioned above, the old device partition map, located at physical block 1, has become logical block 0 of the partition map). For each partition on a disk, the partition map has one block that describes the partition. The partition map is itself a partition and contains a partition map entry describing itself. Figure 2 gives an example of a partitioned disk.

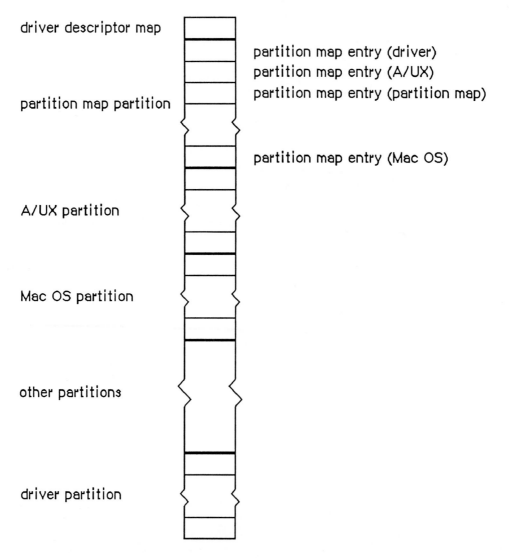

Figure 2. An Example of Disk Partitioning

The information about a partition is contained in a **partition map entry**; it's shown in Figure 3.

byte 0	*	pmSig (word)	always $504D
2		pmSigPad (word)	reserved for future use
4	*	pmMapBlkCnt (long word)	number of blocks in map
8	*	pmPyPartStart (long word)	first physical block of partition
C	*	pmPartBlkCnt (long word)	number of blocks in partition
10	*	pmPartName (32 bytes)	partition name
30	*	pmPartType (32 bytes)	partition type
50		pmLgDataStart (long word)	first logical block of data area
54		pmDataCnt (long word)	number of blocks in data area
58		pmPartStatus (long word)	partiton status information
5C		pmLgBootStart (long word)	first logical block of boot code
60		pmBootSize (long word)	size in bytes of boot code
64		pmBootLoad (long word)	boot code load address
68		pmBootLoad2 (long word)	additional boot load information
6C		pmBootEntry (long word)	boot code entry point
70		pmBootEntry2 (long word)	additional boot entry information
74		pmBootCksum (long word)	boot code checksum
78		pmProcessor (16 bytes)	processor type
88		(128 bytes)	boot-specific arguments

Figure 3. Partition Map Entry

The information in the fields marked with asterisks is used and expected by the Start Manager. The other fields may or may not be currently used; they've been defined to provide a convenient and standard way of storing information specific to your driver or operating system. To permit communication between partitions, it's recommended that you use these fields as described below.

PMSig should always contain $504D to identify the block as containing a partition map entry. (The old partition map format, with a signature of $5453, is still supported but is discouraged.)

PMMapBlkCnt should contain the size in blocks of the partition map. The partition map entry for the partition map is not necessarily the first entry in the map. The number of blocks in the partition map is maintained in each entry, so that you can determine the size of the partition map from any entry in the map.

PMPyPartStart should give the physical block number of the first block of the partition and pmPartBlkCnt should contain the number of blocks in the partition.

PMPartName and pmPartType are both ASCII strings of 1 to 32 bytes in length; case is not significant. If either name is less than 32 characters long, it must be terminated by the NUL character (ASCII code 0). You can specify an empty name or type by setting the first byte to the NUL character.

PMPartName is similar to the handwritten label on a floppy disk; you can use this field to store a user-defined name (which may or may not be the same name used by the operating system).

PMPartType should indicate the operating system or driver using the partition. Types beginning with the string Apple_name are reserved by Apple; the following standard types have been defined:

Type	Meaning
Apple_MFS	Flat file system (64K ROM)
Apple_HFS	Hierarchical file system (128K ROM and later)
Apple_Unix_SVR2	Partition for UNIX
Apple_partition_map	Partition containing partition map
Apple_Driver	Partition contains a device driver
Apple_PRODOS	Partition designated for an Apple IIGS
Apple_Free	Partition unused and available for assignment
Apple_Scratch	Partition empty and free for use

Programmers who wish to take advantage of a checksum verification performed by the Start Manager should give a partition type of Apple_Driver and a partition name beginning with the letters "MACI" (for Macintosh). PMBootSize must contain the size in bytes of the boot code, while pmBootChecksum the checksum for that code, using the following algorithm:

```
DoCksum
        moveq.l    #0,D0       ;initialize sum register
        moveq.l    #0,D7       ;zero-extended byte
        bra.s      CkDecr      ;handle 0 bytes
CkLoop
        move.b     (A0)+,D7    ;get a byte
        add.w      D7,D0       ;add to checksum
        rol.w      #1,D0       ;and rotate
```

```
CkDecr
        dbra       D1,CkLoop  ;next byte
        tst.w      D0         ;convert a checksum of 0
        bne.s      @1         ; into $FFFF
        subq.w     #1,D0      ;
@1
```

With some operating systems—for instance Apple's A/UX™ operating system—the file system may not begin at logical block 0 of the partition. You should use pmLgDataStart to store the logical block number of the first block containing the file system data and pmDataCnt to specify the size in blocks of that data area.

The low-order byte of pmPartStatus (currently used only by A/UX) contains status information about the partition, as follows:

Bit	Meaning
0	Set if a valid partition map entry
1	Set if partition is already allocated; clear if available
2	Set if partition is in use; might be cleared after a system reset
3	Set if partition contains valid boot information
4	Set if partition allows reading
5	Set if partition allows writing
6	Set if boot code is position independent
7	Free for your use

The high-order byte of pmPartStatus is reserved for future use.

PMLgBootStart specifies the logical block number of the first block containing boot code.

PMBootLoad specifies the memory address where the boot code is to be loaded; pmBootLoad2 contains additional load information.

PMBootEntry specifies the memory address to which the boot code will jump after being loaded into memory; pmBootEntry2 contains additional information about this address.

PMProcessor identifies the type of processor that will execute the boot code. It's an ASCII string of 1 to 16 bytes in length; case is not significant. If the type is less than 16 characters long, it must be terminated by the NUL character (ASCII code 0). You can specify an empty processor type by setting the first byte to the NUL character. The following processor types have been defined:

```
68000
68008
68010
68012
68020
```

Partitioning Guidelines

Developers writing disk partitioning (or repartitioning) programs should remember the following basic guidelines:

- Every block on a disk, with the exception of physical block 0, *must* belong to a partition. Unused blocks are given the partition type Apple_Free.

- Every partition must have a partition map entry describing it. Remember that the partition map is itself a partition, with a partition map entry describing it. Partition map entries can be in any particular order, and need not correspond to the order in which the partitions they describe are located on the disk.

- Each device driver must be placed in its own partition (as opposed to being in the partition of the operating system associated with it). This simplifies the updating of the driver descriptor map when the driver is moved.

- Repartitioning of a disk is a two-step process where existing partitions must be combined to form new partitions. The existing partitions to be combined must first be marked as type Apple_Free. As part of freeing a partition, you must set to zero the first eight blocks (copying the contents of the partition somewhere else) to ensure that the partition is not mistaken for an occupied partition. Once freed, the existing partitions can be combined with adjacent free partitions to make a single, larger partition.

- If, as a result of repartitioning, the partition map needs additional room, the other existing partitions can be shifted towards the "end" of the disk. The partition map is the only partition that can be extended without first destroying its contents.

SUMMARY OF THE SCSI MANAGER

Routines

```
FUNCTION SCSISelAtn     (targetID: INTEGER) : OSErr;
FUNCTION SCSIMsgIn      (VAR message: INTEGER) : OSErr;
FUNCTION SCSIMsgOut     (message: INTEGER) : OSErr;
```

Result Codes

Name	Value	Meaning
scArbNBErr	3	Arbitration failed during SCSIGet; bus busy
scBusTOErr	9	Bus timeout before data ready on SCSIRBlind and SCSIWBlind
scComplPhaseErr	10	SCSIComplete failed; bus not in Status phase
scMgrBusyErr	7	SCSI Manager busy with another operation when SCSIGet was called
scSequenceErr	8	Attempted operation is out of sequence; e.g., calling SCSISelect before doing SCSIGet

Assembly-Language Information

Constants

```
; Routine selectors
; (Note:  You can invoke each of the SCSI Manager routines with a
; macro that has the same name as the routine preceded by an
; underscore.)

scsiSelAtn      .EQU  11
scsiMsgIn       .EQU  12
scsiMsgOut      .EQU  13
```

Structure of Driver Descriptor Map

sbSig	Always $4552 (word)
sbBlockSize	Block size of device (word)
sbBlkCount	Number of blocks on device (long)
sbDevType	Used internally (word)
sbDevID	Used internally (word)
sbData	Used internally (long)
sbDrvrCount	Number of driver descriptors (word)

Driver Descriptor Structure

ddBlock   First block of driver (long)
ddSize   Driver size in blocks (word)
ddType   System type; 1 for Macintosh

Structure of Partition Map Entry

pmSig   Always $504D (or $5453 for old format) (word)
pmSigPad   Reserved for future use (word)
pmMapBlkCnt   Number of blocks in partition map (long)
pmPyPartStart   First physical block of partition (long)
pmPartBlkCnt   Number of blocks in partition (long)
pmPartName   Partition name (1–32 bytes)
pmPartType   Partition type (1–32 bytes)
pmLgDataStart   First logical block of data area (long)
pmDataCnt   Number of blocks in data area (long)
pmPartStatus   Partition status information (long)
pmLgBootStart   First logical block of boot code (long)
pmBootSize   Size in bytes of boot code (long)
pmBootLoad   Boot code load address (long)
pmBootLoad2   Additional boot load information (long)
pmBootEntry   Boot code entry point (long)
pmBootEntry2   Additional boot code entry information (long)
pmBootCksum   Optional checksum (long)
pmProcessor   Processor type (1–16 bytes)
Additional boot-specific arguments (128 bytes)

3 2 THE SHUTDOWN MANAGER

32 Shutdown Manager

ABOUT THIS CHAPTER

This chapter describes the Shutdown Manager, which gives applications a chance to perform any necessary housekeeping before the machine is rebooted or turned off. The Shutdown Manager also provides the user with a consistent interface for restarting and turning off the different versions of the Macintosh.

ABOUT THE SHUTDOWN MANAGER

With earlier versions of the System file, the Shut Down (a misnomer) menu item in the Special menu resulted in the restarting of the machine. There was no way to turn the machine off from software; the user needed to choose Shut Down and manually toggle the power switch before the machine had begun to reboot.

On the Macintosh II, two options are available: the Restart menu item results in a reboot, while the Shut Down menu item actually turns off power to the machine.

The Macintosh SE does not have power-off capability from software. When the user chooses Restart, the machine is rebooted. When the user chooses Shut Down, the Shutdown Manager blackens the screen and calls the System Error Handler with an error code of 42. This causes an alert to be presented, telling the user it's safe to turn off the machine.

The Shutdown Manager is contained in the System Resource File (System file version 3.3 or later) and is compatible with all earlier versions of the Macintosh. If the Shutdown Manager is present and the user chooses Restart, the machine is rebooted. On all earlier machines (with the exception of the Macintosh XL), if the user chooses Shut Down, the Shutdown alert is presented. On the Macintosh XL, Shut Down fades the screen and turns off the power.

USING THE SHUTDOWN MANAGER

The ShutDwnPower procedure turns the machine off; if the Macintosh must be turned off manually, the Shutdown alert is presented to the user. The ShutDwnStart procedure causes the machine to reboot.

> **Warning**: ShutDwnPower and ShutDwnStart are used by the Finder and other system software; your application should have no need to call these two routines.

Both ShutDwnPower and ShutDwnStart check to see if Switcher is running; if it is, the ExitToShell procedure is called, exiting Switcher and returning control to the Finder. Otherwise, they perform standard system housekeeping prior to reboot or power off; this housekeeping can be divided into two phases. In the first phase, the unit table is searched for open drivers (including desk accessories). For each driver, if the dNeedGoodbye bit in the drvrFlags field is set (see chapter 6 of Volume II for details), a Control call with csCode equal to –1 is sent to the driver's control routine. Then, the UnloadScrap function is called, writing the desk scrap to the disk.

> **Note**: While the Finder does not currently read the scrap at boot time, it may do so in the future.

In the second phase of housekeeping, the volume-control-block queue is searched; for each mounted volume, the UnmountVol and Eject routines are called.

The ShutDwnInstall procedure lets you install your own shutdown procedure(s) prior to either of these two system housekeeping phases, as well as just prior to rebooting and/or power off. The ShutDwnRemove procedure lets you remove your shutdown procedures.

SHUTDOWN MANAGER ROUTINES

Assembly-language note: You can invoke each of the Shutdown Manager routines with a macro that has the same name as the routine preceded by an underscore. These macros expand to invoke the _Shutdown trap macro. The _Shutdown trap determines which routine to execute from a routine selector, an integer that's passed to it in a word on the stack. The routine selectors are as follows:

```
sdPowerOff .EQU   1
sdRestart  .EQU   2
sdInstall  .EQU   3
sdRemove   .EQU   4
```

```
PROCEDURE ShutDwnPower;
```

ShutDwnPower performs system housekeeping, executes any shutdown procedures you may have installed with ShutDwnInstall, and turns the machine off. (If the machine must be turned off manually, the shutdown alert is presented.)

```
PROCEDURE ShutDwnStart;
```

ShutDwnPower performs system housekeeping, executes any shutdown procedures you may have installed with ShutDwnInstall, and reboots the machine.

Assembly-language note: ShutDwnStart results in the execution of the Reset instruction, followed by a jump to the ROM boot code (the address is the value of the global variable ROMBase + 10).

```
PROCEDURE ShutDwnInstall (shutDwnProc: ProcPtr; flags: INTEGER);
```

ShutDwnInstall installs the shutdown procedure pointed to by shutDwnProc. The flags parameter indicates where in the shutdown process to execute your shutdown procedure. The following masks are provided for setting the bits of the flags parameter:

```
CONST sdOnPowerOff    = 1;  {call procedure before power off}
      sdOnRestart     = 2;  {call procedure before restart}
      sdOnUnmount     = 4;  {call procedure before unmounting}
      sdOnDrivers     = 8;  {call procedure before closing }
                            { drivers}
      sdRestartOrPower = sdOnPowerOff + sdOnRestart {call }
                            { procedure before either power off or }
                            { restart}
```

```
PROCEDURE ShutDwnRemove (shutDwnProc: ProcPtr);
```

ShutDwnRemove removes the shutdown procedure pointed to by shutDwnProc.

Note: If the procedure was marked for execution at a number of points in the shutdown process (say, for instance, at unmounting, restart, and power off), it will be removed at all points.

SUMMARY OF THE SHUTDOWN MANAGER

Constants

```
CONST { Masks for ShutDwnInstall procedure }

        sdOnPowerOff       = 1;   {call procedure before power off}
        sdOnRestart        = 2;   {call procedure before restart}
        sdOnUnmount        = 4;   {call procedure before unmounting}
        sdOnDrivers        = 8;   {call procedure before closing }
                                  { drivers}
        sdRestartOrPower  = sdOnPowerOff + sdOnRestart; {call }
                                  { procedure before either power off or }
                                  { restart}
```

Routines

```
PROCEDURE  ShutDwnPower;
PROCEDURE  ShutDwnStart;
PROCEDURE  ShutDwnInstall    (shutDwnProc: ProcPtr; flags: INTEGER);
PROCEDURE  ShutDwnRemove     (shutDwnProc: ProcPtr);
```

Assembly-Language Information

Constants

```
; Masks for ShutDwnInstall procedure

sdOnPowerOff        .EQU  1    ;call procedure before power off
sdOnRestart         .EQU  2    ;call procedure before restart
sdOnUnmount         .EQU  4    ;call procedure before unmounting
sdOnDrivers         .EQU  8    ;call procedure before closing drivers
sdRestartOrPower    .EQU   sdOnPowerOff + sdOnRestart   ;call procedure
                                ; before either power off or restart

; Routine selectors
; (Note:  You can invoke each of the Shutdown Manager routines with
; a macro that has the same name as the routine preceded by an
; underscore.)

sdPowerOff  .EQU  1
sdRestart   .EQU  2
sdInstall   .EQU  3
sdRemove    .EQU  4
```

32 Shutdown Manager

Trap Macro Name

_Shutdown

(Note: You can invoke each of the Shutdown Manager routines with a macro that has the same name as the routine preceded by an underscore. Also, be aware that the _Shutdown macro is not in ROM.)

33 THE OPERATING SYSTEM UTILITIES

33 OS Utilities

CHANGES TO THE OPERATING SYSTEM UTILITIES

When the Sound Manager is installed, the SysBeep procedure causes the alert sound setting specified in the Control Panel to be played. The duration parameter is ignored.

Existing Macintosh applications operate in a 24-bit addressing mode. For access to slot card devices, the Macintosh II also supports the full 32-bit addressing capability of the MC68020. Two new routines, GetMMUMode and SwapMMUMode, let you determine, change, and restore the addressing mode, using the following constants:

```
CONST false32b = 0;   {24-bit addressing mode}
      true32b  = 1;   {32-bit addressing mode}
```

The Start Manager puts the system in 24-bit addressing mode by default.

The 32-bit addressing mode is provided primarily so that drivers can gain full slot-card access. Be aware, however, that you cannot use the Memory Manager when in this mode, and that some Toolbox routines may not function properly. (Interrupt handlers will function properly in either mode.)

Warning: To be compatible with future versions of the Macintosh, you should not depend on 24-bit addressing mode.

A new routine, StripAddress, will mask the high-order byte of an address when in 24-bit addressing mode, but will do nothing if 32-bit mode is in effect.

OPERATING SYSTEM UTILITY ROUTINES

```
FUNCTION GetMMUMode (VAR mode: INTEGER);   [Not in ROM]
```

GetMMUMode returns the address translation mode currently in use.

Assembly-language note: Assembly-language programmers can determine the current address mode by testing the contents of the global variable MMU32Bit; it's TRUE if 32-bit mode is in effect.

```
PROCEDURE SwapMMUMode (VAR mode: Byte);
```

Trap macro	_SwapMMUMode
On entry	D0: mode (byte)
On exit	D0: mode (byte)

SwapMMUMode sets the address translation mode to that specified by the mode parameter. The mode in use prior to the call is returned in mode, and can be restored with another call to SwapMMUMode.

```
FUNCTION StripAddress (theAddress: LONGINT) : LONGINT;
```

Trap macro	_StripAddress
On entry	D0: theAddress (long word)
On exit	D0: function result (long word)

If the system is running in 24-bit addressing mode, StripAddress is identical in function to the global variable Lo3Bytes: it returns the value of the low-order three bytes of the address passed in theAddress. If the system is in 32-bit mode, however, StripAddress simply passes back the address unchanged.

33 OS Utilities

SUMMARY OF THE OPERATING SYSTEM UTILITIES

Constants

```
CONST { Addressing modes }

     false32b = 0;   {24-bit addressing mode}
     true32b  = 1;   {32-bit addressing mode}
```

Routines

```
PROCEDURE GetMMUMode   (VAR mode: Byte);
PROCEDURE SwapMMUMode  (VAR mode: Byte);
FUNCTION  StripAddress (theAddress: LONGINT) : LONGINT;
```

Assembly-Language Information

Routines

Trap macro	On entry	On exit
_SwapMMUMode	D0: mode (byte)	D0: mode (byte)
_StripAddress	D0: the Address (long)	D0: function result (long)

Constants

```
; Addressing modes

false32b  .EQU  0   ;24-bit addressing mode
true32b   .EQU  1   ;32-bit addressing mode
```

Variables

MMU32Bit   Current address mode (byte)

34 THE FLOATING-POINT ARITHMETIC AND TRANSCENDENTAL FUNCTIONS PACKAGES

The Floating-Point Arithmetic and Transcendental Functions packages have been extended to take advantage of the MC68881 coprocessor. Using the routines in these packages (described fully in the *Apple Numerics Manual*) will ensure compatibility on all past and future versions of the Macintosh; in addition, when the 68881 is present, floating-point performance will be improved, on average, by a factor of 7 or 8 over the Macintosh Plus.

While taking advantage of the speed of the 68881, the precision of the routines in both packages has been preserved.

> **Warning**: Certain highly-specialized applications will want to access the 68881 directly; be aware, however, that doing this virtually ensures that your application will not function on other, past and perhaps future, versions of the Macintosh. Moreover, the transcendental functions provided by the 68881 are actually less precise than the corresponding functions in the Transcendental Functions package.

To promote long word alignment of operands, the 68881 stores its extended type in a 96-bit format, putting 16 bits of filler between the 16-bit sign/exponent and the 64-bit significand. These 16 filler bits make the *mixing* of SANE calls and direct access of the 68881 a tricky business.

APPENDIX A: RESULT CODES

This appendix lists all the new result codes returned by the Macintosh system software. They're ordered by value, for convenience when debugging; the names you should actually use in your program are also listed.

The result codes are grouped roughly according to the lowest level at which the error may occur. This doesn't mean that only routines at that level may cause those errors; higher-level software may yield the same result codes. For example, an Operating System Utility routine that calls the Memory Manager may return one of the Memory Manager result codes. Where a different or more specific meaning is appropriate in a different context, that meaning is also listed.

Value	Name	Meaning

SCSI Manager Errors

Value	Name	Meaning
2	scCommErr	Communications error (operations timeout)
3	scArbNBErr	Arbitration failed during SCSIGet; bus busy
4	scBadparmsErr	Bad parameter or TIB opcode
5	scPhaseErr	SCSI bus not in correct phase for attempted operation
6	scCompareErr	SCSI Manager busy with another operation when SCSIGet was called
7	scMgrBusyErr	SCSI Manager busy with another operation when SCSIGet was called
8	scSequenceErr	Attempted operation is out of sequence; e.g., calling SCSISelect before doing SCSIGet
9	scBusTOErr	Bus timeout before data ready on SCSIRBlind and SCSIWBlind
10	scComplPhaseErr	SCSIComplete failed; bus not in Status phase

System Error Handler Errors

Value	Name	Meaning
31	dsNotThe1	Not the requested disk
33	negZcbFreeErr	ZcbFree is negative
84	menuPrgErr	Happens when a menu is purged

Sound Manager Errors

Value	Name	Meaning
−200	noHardware	No hardware support for the specified synthesizer
−201	notEnoughHardware	No more channels for the specified synthesizer
−203	queueFull	No room in the queue
−204	resProblem	Problem loading resource
−205	badChannel	Invalid channel queue length
−206	badFormat	Handle to 'snd ' resource was invalid

Slot Manager Errors (fatal)

Value	Name	Meaning
−300	smEmptySlot	No card in this slot

−301	smCRCFail	CRC check failed
−302	smFormatErr	The format of the declaration ROM is wrong
−303	smRevisionErr	The revision of the declaration ROM is wrong
−304	smNoDir	There is no directory
−305	smLWTstBad	The long word test failed
−306	smNosInfoArray	The SDM was unable to allocate memory for the sInfo array
−307	smResrvErr	A reserved field of the declaration ROM was used (fatal)
−308	smUnExBusErr	An unexpected Bus Error occurred
−309	smBLFieldBad	A valid ByteLanes field was not found
−310	smFHBlockRdErr	The F–Header block could not be read
−311	smFHBlkDispErr	The F–Header block could not be disposed of
−312	smDisposePErr	An error occured during execution of _DisposPointer
−313	smNoBoardsRsrc	There is no board sResource
−314	smGetPRErr	An error occured during execution of _sGetPRAMRec
−315	smNoBoardId	There is no board ID
−316	smInitStatVErr	The InitStatus_V field was negative after Primary Init
−317	smInitTblErr	An error occured while trying to initialize the Slot Resource Table
−318	smNoJmpTbl	Slot Manager jump table could not be created
−319	smBadBoardID	Board ID was wrong; reinit the PRAM record

Slot Manager Errors (non-fatal)

−330	smBadRefId	Reference ID was not found in the given list
−331	smBadsList	The IDs in the given sList are not in ascending order
−332	smReservedErr	A reserved field was not zero
−333	smCodeRevErr	The revision of the code to be executed by sExec was wrong
−334	smCPUErr	The CPU field of the code to be executed by sExec was wrong
−335	smsPointerNil	The sPointer is nil: no list is specified
−336	smNilsBlockErr	The physical block size (of an sBlock) was zero
−337	smSlotOOBErr	The given slot was out of bounds (or does not exist)
−338	smSelOOBErr	Selector is out of bounds
−339	smNewPErr	An error occured during execution of _NewPointer
−341	smCkStatusErr	Status of slot is bad (InitStatus_A,V)
−342	smGetDrvrNamErr	An error occured during execution of _sGetDrvrName
−344	smNoMoresRsrcs	No more sResources
−345	smGetDrvrErr	An error occured during execution of _sGetDrvr
−346	smBadsPtrErr	A bad sPointer was presented to a SDM call
−347	smByteLanesErr	Bad ByteLanes value was passed to an SDM call
−349	smNoGoodOpens	No opens were successful in the loop
−350	smSRTOvrFlErr	Slot Resource Table overflow
−351	smRecNotFnd	Record not found in the Slot Resource Table

Device Manager Error

−360	slotNumErr	Invalid slot number

AppleTalk Manager Errors

−1066	aspBadVersNum	Server cannot support this ASP version
−1067	aspBufTooSmall	Buffer too small

−1068	aspNoMoreSess	No more sessions on server
−1069	aspNoServers	No servers at that address
−1070	aspParamErr	Parameter error
−1071	aspServerBusy	Server cannot open another session
−1072	aspSessClosed	Session closed
−1073	aspSizeErr	Command block too big
−1074	aspTooMany	Too many clients
−1075	aspNoAck	No ACK on attention request

Returned by the Printing Manager when used with a LaserWriter

−4101		Printer not found, or closed
−4100		Connection just closed
−4099		Write request too big
−4098		Request already active
−4097		Bad connection reference number
−4096		No free Connect Control Blocks available

Returned by SysEnvirons call

−5500	envNotPresent	SysEnvirons trap not present (System file earlier than version 4.1); glue returns values for all fields except systemVersion
−5501	envBadVers	A nonpositive version number was passed—no information is returned
−5502	envVersTooBig	Requested version of SysEnvirons call was not available

APPENDIX B: ROUTINES THAT MAY MOVE OR PURGE MEMORY

This appendix lists all the new routines that may move or purge blocks in the heap. As described in chapter 1 of Volume II, calling these routines may cause problems if a handle has been dereferenced. None of these routines may be called from within an interrupt, such as in a completion routine or a VBL task.

Warning: Many more routines may disturb memory than did previously. In particular, the following generic classes of routines may move or purge memory:

- most new color QuickDraw routines
- all new Printing Manager routines
- all new TextEdit routines.

The specific routines you must be careful with are listed below.

Name	Name	Name
ActivatePalette	DisposCTable	FillRoundRect
ADBReInit	DisposePalette	FindWord
AddComp	DisposeRgn	Fix2SmallFract
AddSearch	DisposGDevice	FMSwapFont
AllocCrsr	DisposPixMap	Font2Script
BackColor	DisposPixPat	FontScript
BackPat	DrawChar	ForeColor
BackPixPat	DrawJust	FrameArc
Char2Pixel	DrawPicture	FrameOval
CharWidth	DrawString	FramePoly
ClipRect	DrawText	FrameRect
CloseCPort	EraseArc	FrameRgn
ClosePicture	EraseOval	FrameRoundRect
ClosePoly	ErasePalette	GetAuxCtl
ClosePort	ErasePoly	GetCCursor
CloseRgn	EraseRect	GetCIcon
CMY2RGB	EraseRgn	GetColor
Color2Index	EraseRoundRect	GetCTable
CopyBits	FillArc	GetFontInfo
CopyMask	FillCArc	GetGrayRgn
CopyPalette	FillCOval	GetMCInfo
CopyRgn	FillCPoly	GetNewCWindow
CTab2Palette	FillCRect	GetNewPalette
DelComp	FillCRgn	GetPixPat
DelMCEntries	FillCRoundRect	GetStylHandle
DelSearch	FillOval	GetStylScrap
DiffRgn	FillPoly	GetSubTable
DispMCInfo	FillRect	HiliteText

Name	Name	Name
DisposCIcon	FillRgn	HSL2RGB
HSV2RGB	PaintPoly	SetDeskCPat
InitCPort	PaintRect	SetEmptyRgn
InitGDevice	PaintRgn	SetMCEntries
InitGraf	PaintRoundRect	SetMCInfo
InitPalettes	Palette2CTab	SetRectRgn
InitPort	PenNormal	SetStylHandle
InitPRAMRecs	PenPat	SetWinColor
InitProcMenu	PenPixPat	sExec
InitSDeclMgr	Pixel2Char	sGetBlock
InitsRsrcTable	PlotCIcon	sGetcString
InsetRgn	PMBackColor	sGetDriver
IntlScript	PMForeColor	ShutDwnInstall
InvertArc	PopUpMenuSelect	ShutDwnRemove
InvertOval	PrClose	SmallFract2Fix
InvertPoly	PrCloseDoc	SndAddModifier
InvertRect	PrClosePage	SndDisposeChannel
InvertRgn	PrCtlCall	SndNewChannel
InvertRoundRect	PrDrvrClose	sPrimaryInit
KeyScript	PrDrvrDCE	StdArc
KillPicture	PrDrvrOpen	StdBits
KillPoly	PrDrvrVers	StdComment
Line	PrError	StdLine
LineTo	PrGeneral	StdOval
MakeITable	PrintDefault	StdPoly
MapRgn	PrJobDialog	StdPutPic
MeasureJust	PrJobMerge	StdRect
MeasureText	PrOpen	StdRgn
NewCDialog	PrOpenDoc	StdRRect
NewCWindow	PrOpenPage	StdText
NewGDevice	PrPicFile	StdTxMeas
NewPalette	PrSetError	StringWidth
NewPixMap	PrStlDialog	TEGetHeight
NewPixPat	PrValidate	TEGetOffset
NewPort	RealColor	TEGetPoint
NewRgn	RGB2CMY	TEGetStyle
OpenCPicture	RGB2HSL	TEReplaceStyle
OpenCPort	RGB2HSV	TESetStyle
OpenPicture	RGBBackColor	TEStylInsert
OpenPixMap	RGBForeColor	TEStylNew
OpenPoly	RGetResource	TEStylPaste
OpenPort	ScrollRect	TextWidth
OpenPort	SectRgn	Transliterate
OpenRgn	SetCCursor	UnionRgn
PaintArc	SetCPixel	XorRgn
PaintOval	SetCtlColor	

APPENDIX C: SYSTEM TRAPS

This appendix lists the trap macros for the new Toolbox and Operating System routines and their corresponding trap word values in hexadecimal. The trap macros are listed twice: first by name, then by value. The "Name" column gives the trap macro name (without its initial underscore character). In those cases where the name of the equivalent Pascal call is different, the Pascal name appears indented under the main entry. The routines in Macintosh packages are listed under the macros they invoke after pushing a routine selector onto the stack; the routine selector follows the Pascal routine name in parentheses.

Warning: Traps that aren't currently used by the system are reserved for future use.

Name	Trap word	Name	Trap word
ActivatePalette	AA94	FillCRoundRect	AA10
ADBOp	A07C	GetADBInfo	A079
ADBReInit	A07B	GetAuxCtl	AA44
AddComp	AA3B	GetAuxWin	AA42
AddSearch	AA3A	GetBackColor	AA1A
AllocCursor	AA1D	GetCCursor	AA1B
AnimateEntry	AA99	GetCIcon	AA1E
AnimatePalette	AA9A	GetCPixel	AA17
AttachVBL	A071	GetCTable	AA18
BackPixPat	AA0B	GetCTSeed	AA28
CalcCMask	AA4F	GetCVariant	A809
CharExtra	AA23	GetCWMgrPort	AA48
CloseCPort	A87D	GetDefaultStartup	A07D
Color2Index	AA33	GetDeviceList	AA29
CopyBits	A8EC	GetEntryColor	AA9B
CopyMask	A817	GetEntryUsage	AA9D
CopyPixMap	AA05	GetForeColor	AA19
CopyPixPat	AA09	GetGDevice	AA32
CountADBs	A077	GetIndADB	A078
CTab2Palette	AA9F	GetItemCmd	A84E
DelComp	AA4D	GetMainDevice	AA2A
DelMCEntries	AA60	GetMaxDevice	AA27
DelSearch	AA4C	GetMCEntry	AA64
DispMCInfo	AA63	GetMCInfo	AA61
DisposCCursor	AA26	GetNewCWindow	AA46
DisposCIcon	AA25	GetNewPalette	AA92
DisposCTable	AA24	GetNextDevice	AA2B
DisposePalette	AA93	GetOSDefault	A084
DisposGDevice	AA30	GetPalette	AA96
DisposPixMap	AA04	GetPixPat	AA0C
DisposPixPat	AA08	GetSubTable	AA37
DoVBLTask	A072	GetVideoDefault	A080
DTInstall	A082	GetWVariant	A80A
FillCArc	AA11	HiliteColor	AA22
FillCOval	AA0F	Index2Color	AA34
FillCPoly	AA13	InitCport	AA01
FillCRect	AA0E	InitGDevice	AA2E
FillCRgn	AA12	InitPalettes	AA90

Name		Trap word	Name		Trap word
InitProcMenu		A808	smSetEnvirons	(10)	
InternalWait		A07F	smGetScript	(12)	
SetTimeout	(0)		smSetScript	(14)	
GetTimeout	(1)		smCharByte	(16)	
InvertColor		AA35	smCharType	(18)	
KeyTrans		A9C3	smPixel2Char	(20)	
MakeITable		AA39	smChar2Pixel	(22)	
MakeRGBPat		AA0D	smTranslit	(24)	
MenuChoice		AA66	smFindWord	(26)	
NewCDialog		AA4B	smHiliteText	(28)	
NewCWindow		AA45	smDrawJust	(30)	
NewGDevice		AA2F	smMeasureJust	(32)	
NewPalette		AA91	SCSIDispatch		A815
NewPixMap		AA03	SCSISelAtn	(11)	
NewPixPat		AA07	SCSIMsgIn	(12)	
OpColor		AA21	SCSIMsgOut	(13)	
OpenCport		AA00	SeedCFill		AA50
OpenPicture		A8F3	SetADBInfo		A07A
Pack12		A82E	SetCCursor		AA1C
Fix2SmallFract	(1)		SetClientID		AA3C
SmallFract2Fix	(2)		SetCPixel		AA16
CMY2RGB	(3)		SetCPortPix		AA06
RGB2CMY	(4)		SetCtlColor		AA43
HSL2RGB	(5)		SetDefaultStartup		A07E
RGB2HSL	(6)		SetDeskCPat		AA47
HSV2RGB	(7)		SetDeviceAttribute		AA2D
RGB2HSV	(8)		SetEntries		AA3F
GetColor	(9)		SetEntryColor		AA9C
Palette2CTab		AAA0	SetEntryUsage		AA9E
PenPixPat		AA0A	SetGDevice		AA31
PlotCIcon		AA1F	SetItemCmd		A84F
PmBackColor		AA98	SetMCEntries		AA65
PmForeColor		AA97	SetMCInfo		AA62
PopUpMenuSelect		A80B	SetOSDefault		A083
PrGlue		A8FD	SetPalette		AA95
ProtectEntry		AA3D	SetStdCProcs		AA4E
QDError		AA40	SetVideoDefault		A081
RealColor		AA36	SetWinColor		AA41
ReserveEntry		AA3E	Shutdown		A895
RestoreEntries		AA4A	ShutDwnPower	(1)	
RGBBackColor		AA15	ShutDwnStart	(2)	
RGBForeColor		AA14	ShutDwnInstall	(3)	
RGetResource		A80C	ShutDwnRemove	(4)	
SaveEntries		AA49	SIntInstall		A075
ScriptUtil		A8B5	SIntRemove		A076
smFontScript	(0)		SlotManager		A06E
smIntlScript	(2)		sReadByte	(0)	
smKybdScript	(4)		sReadWord	(1)	
smFont2Script	(6)		sReadLong	(2)	
smGetEnvirons	(8)		sGetcString	(3)	

Appendices

Name	Trap word		Name	Trap word	
sGetBlock	(5)		sFindsRsrcPtr	(48)	
sFindStruct	(6)		sdeleteSRTRec	(49)	
sReadStruct	(7)		SlotVInstall	A06F	
sReadInfo	(16)		SlotVRemove	A070	
sReadPRAMRec	(17)		SndAddModifier	A802	
sPutPRAMRec	(18)		SndControl	A806	
sReadFHeader	(19)		SndDisposeChannel	A801	
sNextRsrc	(20)		SndDoCommand	A803	
sNextTypesRsrc	(21)		SndDoImmediate	A804	
sRsrcInfo	(22)		SndNewChannel	A807	
sDisposePtr	(23)		SndPlay	A805	
sCkCardStatus	(24)		StripAddress	A055	
sReadDrvrName	(25)		SwapMMUMode	A05D	
sFindDevBase	(27)		SysEnvirons	A090	
InitSDeclMgr	(32)		TEDispatch	A83D	
sPrimaryInit	(33)		TEStylePaste	(0)	
sCardChanged	(34)		TESetStyle	(1)	
sExec	(35)		TEReplaceStyle	(2)	
sOffsetData	(36)		TEGetStyle	(3)	
InitPRAMRecs	(37)		GetStyleHandle	(4)	
sReadPBSize	(38)		SetStyleHandle	(5)	
sCalcStep	(40)		GetStyleScrap	(6)	
InitsRsrcTable	(41)		TEStyleInsert	(7)	
sSearchSRT	(42)		TEGetPoint	(8)	
sUpdateSRT	(43)		TEGetHeight	(9)	
sCalcsPointer	(44)		TEGetOffset	A83C	
sGetDriver	(45)		TestDeviceAttribute	AA2C	
sPtrToSlot	(46)		TEStyleNew	A83E	
sFindsInfoRecPtr	(47)				

Trap word	Name		Trap word	Name	
A055	StripAddress		sDisposePtr	(23)	
A05D	SwapMMUMode		sCkCardStatus	(24)	
A06E	SlotManager		sReadDrvrName	(25)	
sReadByte	(0)		sFindDevBase	(27)	
sReadWord	(1)		InitSDeclMgr	(32)	
sReadLong	(2)		sPrimaryInit	(33)	
sGetcString	(3)		sCardChanged	(34)	
sGetBlock	(5)		sExec	(35)	
sFindStruct	(6)		sOffsetData	(36)	
sReadStruct	(7)		InitPRAMRecs	(37)	
sReadInfo	(16)		sReadPBSize	(38)	
sReadPRAMRec	(17)		sCalcStep	(40)	
sPutPRAMRec	(18)		InitsRsrcTable	(41)	
sReadFHeader	(19)		sSearchSRT	(42)	
sNextRsrc	(20)		sUpdateSRT	(43)	
sNextTypesRsrc	(21)		sCalcsPointer	(44)	
sRsrcInfo	(22)		sGetDriver	(45)	

Trap word	Name		Trap word	Name	
sPtrToSlot		(46)	RGB2HSL		(6)
sFindsInfoRecPtr		(47)	HSV2RGB		(7)
sFindsRsrcPtr		(48)	RGB2HSV		(8)
sdeleteSRTRec		(49)	GetColor		(9)
A06F	SlotVInstall		A83C	TEGetOffset	
A070	SlotVRemove		A83D	TEDispatch	
A071	AttachVBL		TEStylePaste		(0)
A072	DoVBLTask		TESetStyle		(1)
A075	DTInstall		TEReplaceStyle		(2)
A076	SIntRemove		TEGetStyle		(3)
A077	CountADBs		GetStyleHandle		(4)
A078	GetIndADB		SetStyleHandle		(5)
A079	GetADBInfo		GetStyleScrap		(6)
A07A	SetADBInfo		TEStyleInsert		(7)
A07B	ADBReInit		TEGetPoint		(8)
A07C	ADBOp		TEGetHeight		(9)
A07D	GetDefaultStartup		A83E	TEStyleNew	
A07E	SetDefaultStartup		A84E	GetItemCmd	
A07F	InternalWait		A84F	SetItemCmd	
SetTimeout		(0)	A87D	CloseCPort	
GetTimeout		(1)	A895	Shutdown	
A080	GetVideoDefault		ShutDwnPower		(1)
A081	SetVideoDefault		ShutDwnStart		(2)
A082	SIntInstall		ShutDwnInstall		(3)
A083	SetOSDefault		ShutDwnRemove		(4)
A084	GetOSDefault		A8B5	ScriptUtil	
A090	SysEnvirons		smFontScript		(0)
A801	SndDisposeChannel		smIntlScript		(2)
A802	SndAddModifier		smKybdScript		(4)
A803	SndDoCommand		smFont2Script		(6)
A804	SndDoImmediate		smGetEnvirons		(8)
A805	SndPlay		smSetEnvirons		(10)
A806	SndControl		smGetScript		(12)
A807	SndNewChannel		smSetScript		(14)
A808	InitProcMenu		smCharByte		(16)
A809	GetCVariant		smCharType		(18)
A80A	GetWVariant		smPixel2Char		(20)
A80B	PopUpMenuSelect		smChar2Pixel		(22)
A80C	RGetResource		smTranslit		(24)
A815	SCSIDispatch		smFindWord		(26)
SCSISelAtn		(11)	smHiliteText		(28)
SCSIMsgIn		(12)	smDrawJust		(30)
SCSIMsgOut		(13)	smMeasureJust		(32)
A817	CopyMask		A8EC	CopyBits	
A82E	Pack12		A8F3	OpenPicture	
Fix2SmallFract		(1)	A8FD	PrGlue	
SmallFract2Fix		(2)	A9C3	KeyTrans	
CMY2RGB		(3)	AA00	OpenCport	
RGB2CMY		(4)	AA01	InitCport	
HSL2RGB		(5)	AA03	NewPixMap	

Trap word	Name	Trap word	Name
AA04	DisposPixMap	AA37	GetSubTable
AA05	CopyPixMap	AA39	MakeITable
AA06	SetCPortPix	AA3A	AddSearch
AA07	NewPixPat	AA3B	AddComp
AA08	DisposPixPat	AA3C	SetClientID
AA09	CopyPixPat	AA3D	ProtectEntry
AA0A	PenPixPat	AA3E	ReserveEntry
AA0B	BackPixPat	AA3F	SetEntries
AA0C	GetPixPat	AA40	QDError
AA0D	MakeRGBPat	AA41	SetWinColor
AA0E	FillCRect	AA42	GetAuxWin
AA0F	FillCOval	AA43	SetCtlColor
AA10	FillCRoundRect	AA44	GetAuxCtl
AA11	FillCArc	AA45	NewCWindow
AA12	FillCRgn	AA46	GetNewCWindow
AA13	FillCPoly	AA47	SetDeskCPat
AA14	RGBForeColor	AA48	GetCWMgrPort
AA15	RGBBackColor	AA49	SaveEntries
AA16	SetCPixel	AA4A	RestoreEntries
AA17	GetCPixel	AA4B	NewCDialog
AA18	GetCTable	AA4C	DelSearch
AA19	GetForeColor	AA4D	DelComp
AA1A	GetBackColor	AA4E	SetStdCProcs
AA1B	GetCCursor	AA4F	CalcCMask
AA1C	SetCCursor	AA50	SeedCFill
AA1D	AllocCursor	AA60	DelMCEntries
AA1E	GetCIcon	AA61	GetMCInfo
AA1F	PlotCIcon	AA62	SetMCInfo
AA21	OpColor	AA63	DispMCInfo
AA22	HiliteColor	AA64	GetMCEntry
AA23	CharExtra	AA65	SetMCEntries
AA24	DisposCTable	AA66	MenuChoice
AA25	DisposCIcon	AA90	InitPalettes
AA26	DisposCCursor	AA91	NewPalette
AA27	GetMaxDevice	AA92	GetNewPalette
AA29	GetDeviceList	AA93	DisposePalette
AA28	GetCTSeed	AA94	ActivatePalette
AA2A	GetMainDevice	AA95	SetPalette
AA2B	GetNextDevice	AA96	GetPalette
AA2C	TestDeviceAttribute	AA97	PmForeColor
AA2D	SetDeviceAttribute	AA98	PmBackColor
AA2E	InitGDevice	AA99	AnimateEntry
AA2F	NewGDevice	AA9A	AnimatePalette
AA30	DisposGDevice	AA9B	GetEntryColor
AA31	SetGDevice	AA9C	SetEntryColor
AA32	GetGDevice	AA9D	GetEntryUsage
AA33	Color2Index	AA9E	SetEntryUsage
AA34	Index2Color	AA9F	CTab2Palette
AA35	InvertColor	AAA0	Palette2CTab
AA36	RealColor		

APPENDIX D: GLOBAL VARIABLES

This appendix gives an alphabetical list of all system global variables described in this volume, along with their locations in memory.

Name	Location	Contents
AtMenuBottom	$A0C	Flag for menu scrolling (word)
AuxWinHead	$CD0	Auxiliary window list header (long)
CPUFlag	$12F	Microprocessor in use (word)
DeviceList	$8A8	Handle to the first element in the device list
DTQueue	$D92	Deferred task queue header (10 bytes)
HiliteMode	$938	Set if highlighting is on
HiliteRGB	$DA0	Default highlight color for the system
JADBProc	06B8	Pointer to ADBReInit preprocessing/ postprocessing routine
JDTInstall	$D9C	Jump vector for DTInstall routine
JVBLTask	$D28	Jump vector for DoVBLTask routine
KbdLast	$218	ADB address of the keyboard last used (byte)
KbdType	$21E	Keyboard type of the keyboard last used (byte)
MainDevice	$8A4	Handle to the current main device
MBarHeight	$BAA	Height of menu bar (word)
MenuCInfo	$D50	Header for menu color information table
MenuDisable	$B54	Menu ID and item for selected disabled item
MMU32Bit	$CB2	Current address mode (byte)
QDColors	$8B0	Default QuickDraw colors
ROM85	$28E	Version number of ROM (word)
SynListHandle	$D32	Handle to synthetic font list
SysZone	$2A6	Address of system heap zone
TheGDevice	$CC8	Handle to current active device (long)
TimeDBRA	$D00	Number of times the DBRA instruction can be executed per millisecond (word)
TimeSCCDB	$D02	Number of times the SCC can be accessed per millisecond (word)
TimeSCSIDB	$DA6	Number of times the SCSI can be accessed per millisecond (word)
TopMenuItem	$A0A	Pixel value of top of scrollable menu

GLOSSARY

ADB device table: A structure in the system heap that lists all devices connected to the Apple DeskTop Bus.

auxiliary control record: A Control Manager data structure containing the information needed for drawing controls in color.

auxiliary window record: A Window Manager data structure that stores the color information needed for each color window.

background activity: A program or process that runs while the user is engaged with another application.

board sResource list: A standard Apple sResource list that must be present in every NuBus slot card that communicates with the Macintosh II.

break table: A list of templates that determine the general rules for making word divisions in a particular script.

byte lane: Any of the four bytes that make up the NuBus data width. NuBus slot cards may use any or all of the byte lanes to communicate with each other or with the Macintosh II.

cdev: A resource file containing device information, used by the Control Panel.

cGrafPort: The drawing environment in Color QuickDraw, including elements such as a pixel map, pixel patterns, transfer modes, and arithmetic drawing modes.

channel: A queue that's used by an application to send commands to the Sound Manager.

chunky: A pixel image in which all of a pixel's bits are stored consecutively in memory, all of a row's pixels are stored consecutively, and rowBytes indicates the offset from one row to the next.

Color Look-Up Table (CLUT): A data structure that maps color indices, specified using QuickDraw, into actual color values. Color Look-Up Tables are internal to certain types of video cards.

Color Look-Up Table (CLUT) device: This kind of video device contains hardware that converts an arbitrary pixel value stored in the frame buffer to some actual RGB video value, which is changeable.

Color Manager: The part of the Toolbox that supplies color-selection support for Color QuickDraw on the Macintosh II.

Color QuickDraw: The part of the Toolbox that performs color graphics operations on the Macintosh II.

color table: A set of colors is grouped into a QuickDraw data structure called a color table. Applications can pass a handle to this color table in order to use color entries.

color table animation: Color table animation involves changing the index entries in the video device's color table to achieve a change in color, as opposed to changing the pixel values themselves. All pixel values corresponding to the altered index entries suddenly appear on the display device in the new color.

complement: The numerical amount that must be added to a number to give the least number containing one more digit.

declaration ROM: A ROM on a NuBus slot card that contains information about the card and may also contain code or other data.

deny modes: File access modes that include both the access rights of that path and denial of access to others.

device address: A value in the range $00–$0F assigned to each device connected to the Apple DeskTop Bus.

device handler ID: A value that identifies the kind of device connected to the Apple DeskTop Bus.

DeviceList: A linked list containing the gDevice records for a system. One handle to a gDevice record is allocated and initialized for each video card found by the system.

direct device: A video device that has a direct correlation between the value placed in the video card and the color you see on the screen.

dithering: A technique for mixing existing colors together to create the illusion of a third color that may be unavailable on a particular device.

drag delay: A length of time that allows a user to drag diagonally across a main menu, moving from a submenu title into the submenu itself without the submenu disappearing.

Echo Protocol: An echoing service provided on static socket number 4 (the echoer socket) by which any correctly-formed packet will be echoed back to its sender.

fixed device: A video device that converts a pixel value to some actual RGB video value, but the hardware colors can't be changed.

font script: The script used by the font currently designated by thePort; hence the system that determines in what form text characters are displayed to the user.

format block: A structure in a declaration ROM that provides a standard entry point for other structures in the ROM.

gDevice: A QuickDraw data structure that allows an application to access a given device. A gDevice is a logical device, which the software treats the same whether it is a video card, a display device, or an offscreen pixel map.

graphics device: A video card, a printer, a display device, or an offscreen pixel map. Any of these device types may be used with Color QuickDraw.

GrayRgn: The global variable that in the multiple-screen desktop describes and defines the desktop, the area on which windows can be dragged.

hierarchical menu: A menu that includes, among its various menu choices, the ability to display a submenu. In most cases the submenu appears to the right of the menu item used to select it, and is marked with a filled triangle indicator.

invalidation: When a color table is modified, its inverse table must be rebuilt, and the screen should be redrawn to take advantage of this new information. Rather than being reconstructed when the color table is changed, the inverse table is marked invalid, and is automatically rebuilt when next accessed.

inverse table: A special Color Manager data structure arranged in such a manner that, given an arbitrary RGB color, the pixel value can be very rapidly looked up.

justification gap: The number of pixels that must be added to a line of text to make it exactly fill a given measure. Also called slop.

key script: The system that determines the keyboard layout and input method for the user interface. It may be different from the font script, which determines how text is displayed.

line-height table: A TextEdit data structure that holds vertical spacing information for an edit record's text.

localization: The process of adapting an application to different languages, including converting its user interface to a different script.

luminance: The intensity of light. Two colors with different luminances will be displayed at different intensities.

main screen: On a system with multiple display devices, the screen with the menu bar is called the main screen.

menu entry: An entry in a menu color table that defines color values for the menu's title, bar, and items.

MIDI synthesizer: This synthesizer interfaces with external synthesizers via a Musical Instrument Data Interface (MIDI) adaptor connected to the serial ports.

modifier: A program that interprets and processes Sound Manager commands as they pass through a channel.

note synthesizer: Functionally equivalent to the old square-wave synthesizer, the note sysntesizer lets you generate simple melodies and informative sounds such as error warnings.

null-style record: A TextEdit data structure used to store the style information for a null selection.

palette: A collection of colors provided and used by your application according to your needs.

Palette Manager: The part of the Toolbox that establishes and monitors the color environment of the Macintosh II. It gives preference to the color needs of the front window, making the assumption that the front window is of greatest interest to the user.

pixel: A dot on a display screen. Pixel is short for picture element.

pixel map: Color QuickDraw's extended data structure, containing the dimensions and content of a pixel image, plus information on the image's storage format, depth, resolution, and color usage.

pixel pattern: The pattern structure used by Color QuickDraw, one of three types: old-style pattern, full color pixel pattern, or RGB pattern.

pixel value: The bits in a pixel, taken together, form a number known as the pixel value. Color QuickDraw represents each pixel on the screen using one, two, four, or eight bits in memory.

pop-up menu: A menu not located in the menu bar, which appears when the user presses the mouse button in a particular place.

range locking: Locking a range of bytes in a file so that other users can't read from or write to that range, but allowing the rest of the file to be accessed.

raw key codes: Hardware-produced key codes on the Macintosh II and Apple Extended Keyboard, which are translated into **virtual key codes** by the 'KMAP' resource.

RGB space: How Color QuickDraw represents colors. Each color has a red, a green, and a blue component, hence the name RGB.

RGB value: Color QuickDraw represents color using the RGBColor record type, which specifies the red, green, and blue components of the color. The RGBColor record is used by an application to specify the colors it needs. The translation from the RGB value to the pixel value is performed at the time the color is drawn.

routine selector: A value pushed on the stack to select a particular routine from a group of routines called by a single trap macro.

sampled sound synthesizer: Functionally equivalent to the old free-form synthesizer, the sample sound synthesizer lets you play pre-recorded sounds or sounds generated by your application.

script: A writing system, such as Cyrillic or Arabic. This book is printed in Roman script.

script interface system: Special software that supports the display and manipulation of a particular script.

server: A node that manages access to a peripheral device.

service request enable: A bit set by a device connected to the Apple DeskTop Bus to tell the system that it needs servicing.

session: A session consists of a series of transactions between two sockets, characterized by the orderly sequencing of requests and responses.

slop: See **justification gap.**

slot exec parameter block: A data structure that provides communication with the Slot Manager routines sMacBoot and sPrimaryInit.

slot parameter block: A data structure that provides communication with all Slot Manager routines except sMacBoot and sPrimaryInit.

slot resource: A software structure in the declaration ROM of a slot card.

sResource: See **slot resource.**

sResource directory: The structure in a declaration ROM that provides access to its sResource lists.

sResource list: A list of offsets to sResources.

startup screen: When the system is started up, one of the display devices is selected as the startup screen, the screen on which the "happy Macintosh" icon appears.

style record: A TextEdit data structure that specifies the styles for the edit record's text.

style scrap: A new TextEdit scrap type, 'styl', is used for storing style information in the desk scrap along with the old 'TEXT' scrap.

style table: A TextEdit data structure that contains one entry for each distinct style used in an edit record's text.

submenu delay: The length of time before a submenu appears as a user drags through a hierarchical main menu; it prevents rapid flashing of submenus.

synthesizer: A program which, like a device driver, interprets Sound Manager commands and produces sound.

text styles: TextEdit records used for communicating style information between the application program and the TextEdit routines.

TheGDevice: When drawing is being performed on a device, a handle to that device is stored as a global variable **TheGDevice.**

type coercion: Many compilers feature type coercion (also known as typecasting), which allows a data structure of one type to be converted to another type. In many cases, this conversion is simply a relaxation of type-checking in the compiler, allowing the substitution of a differently-typed but equivalent data structure.

virtual key codes: The key codes that appear in keyboard events. See also **raw key codes.**

wave table synthesizer: Similar to the old four-tone synthesizer, the wave table synthesizer produces complex sounds and multipart music.

word-selection break table: A **break table** that is used to find word boundaries for word selection, spelling checking, and so on.

word-wrapping break table: A **break table** that is used to find word boundaries for screen wrapping of text.

workstation: A node through which a user can access a server or other nodes.

INDEX

Index

Index